Managing Sport Business

Contemporary sport is both a sophisticated and complex international business and a mass participatory practice run largely by volunteers and community organisations. This authoritative and comprehensive introduction to the theory and practice of sports management helps to explain the modern commercial environment that shapes sport at all levels and gives clear and sensible guidance on best practice in sports management, from elite sport to the local level.

The book is divided into three sections. The first examines the global context for contemporary sports management. The second explores the key functional areas of management, from organisation and strategy to finance and marketing, and explains how successful managerial techniques can be applied in a sporting context. The final section surveys a wide range of important issues in contemporary sports management, from corporate social responsibility to the use of information and communication technologies. Together, these sections provide a complete package of theory, applied practical skills and a state-of-the-art review of modern sport business.

With useful features included throughout, such as chapter summaries and definitions of key terms, and with each chapter supported with real-world data and examples, this book is essential reading for all students of sport management and sport business.

Linda Trenberth is Senior Lecturer in Management and Head of the Management Department in the School of Business at Birkbeck, University of London. She has edited several texts in this area. Her main research expertise is in the area of HRM and Performance and workplace stress and coping.

David Hassan is Senior Lecturer in Sport Studies at the University of Ulster. His research expertise concerns the relationship between sport and national identity, the politics of sport and sport governance. He is the Academic Editor of Sport in Society, an international, peer-reviewed journal published by Taylor and Francis Ltd. He is also a Series Editor of Foundations of Sport Management (with Dr Allan Edwards) published by Routledge.

Foundations of Sport Management

Series Editors:
David Hassan, University of Ulster at Jordanstown, UK
Allan Edwards, Griffith University, Australia

Foundations of Sport Management is a discipline-defining series of texts on core and cutting-edge topics in sport management. Featuring some of the best known and most influential sport management scholars from around the world, each volume represents an authoritative, engaging and self-contained introduction to a key functional area or issue within contemporary sport management. Packed with useful features to aid teaching and learning, the series aims to bridge the gap between management theory and practice and to encourage critical thinking and reflection among students, academics and practitioners.

Also available in this series:

Managing Sport Business
An introduction
Edited by Linda Trenberth and David Hassan

Managing Sport
Bu

An

Edi
Da

Routledge
Taylor & Francis Group

LONDON AND NEW YORK

First published 2012
by Routledge
2 Park Square, Milton Park, Abingdon, Oxon OX14 4RN

Simultaneously published in the USA and Canada
by Routledge
711 Third Avenue, New York, NY 10017

Routledge is an imprint of the Taylor & Francis Group, an informa business

British Library Cataloguing in Publication Data
A catalogue record for this book is available from the British Library

Library of Congress Cataloging in Publication Data
Managing sport business : an introduction / edited by Linda Trenberth and David Hassan.
p. cm. -- (Foundations of sport management)
1. Sports--Economic aspects. 2. Sports administration. I. Trenberth, Linda. II. Hassan, David.
GV716.M355 2011
338.43796--dc22
2011009211

ISBN: 978-0-415-57028-2 (hbk)
ISBN: 978-0-415-57029-9 (pbk)
ISBN: 978-0-203-85841-7 (ebk)

Typeset in Perpetua and Bell Gothic
by GreenGate Publishing Services, Tonbridge, Kent

Printed and bound in Great Britain by the MPG Books Group

Contents

List of figures

List of tables

List of case studies

List of contributors

Chris Auld is a Professor and Dean (International) with the Griffith Business School, Griffith University, Australia. He is a Member of the Editorial Board of the *Annals of Leisure Research* and has published extensively on sport management, especially relating to volunteers. He recently co-authored a research book entitled *Working with Volunteers in Sport: Theory and Practice* (Routledge, 2006). In 2010 he was elected as a Senior Fellow and Founding Member of the World Leisure Academy.

Raymond Boyle is Professor of Communications at the Centre for Cultural Policy Research at the University of Glasgow. He writes on media and sports issues and is the author of a number of books in this area including *Sports Journalism: Context and Issues* (2006) and co-author with Richard Haynes of *Power Play: Sport, the Media and Popular Culture* (2nd edition: 2009) and *Football in the New Media Age* (2004). He sits on the editorial board of *Media, Culture and Society* and his latest book *The Television Entrepreneurs* (with Lisa Kelly) will be published in 2011.

Cheri Bradish is an Associate Professor in her fourteenth year in the Department of Sport Management at Brock University, Canada. Her area of interest is with regard to sport marketing, sport sponsorship and corporate social responsibility in sport, with a special related focus on the management of the Olympic Games. Among a number of conference proceedings and publications, her research has appeared in the *Journal of Sport Management*, the *International Journal of Sport Management and Marketing*, the *Sport Management Review* and the *Sport Marketing Quarterly*. Cheri also has significant experience in the sport industry, including work with the Florida Sports Foundation, Nike Canada Inc., Florida State University Department of Athletics (NCAA), the Vancouver Grizzlies (NBA) and, most recently, as a Sponsorship and Sales Specialist with the Vancouver Organizing Committee for the 2010 Olympic and Paralympic Games (VANOC). Cheri completed her PhD at Florida State University. She is a proud and active supporter of the international humanitarian organisation Right To Play International.

Babatunde Buraimo is a Senior Lecturer in Sports Economics and Sports Management at the University of Central Lancashire. He was educated at the University of Sheffield and Lancaster University and has a doctoral degree in Economics. He has published extensively on the economics of professional team sports, economics of sports broadcasting, sports labour markets, and demand for both participant and spectator sports. Some of his work has featured in the *Journal of the Royal Statistical Society*, the *Journal of the Operational Research Society*, *Southern Economic Journal* and the *Journal of Sports Economics*. Babatunde is also a co-author of a text titled *Sport in the UK*. He is a member of the editorial boards of *Soccer* *and Society* and the *International Journal of Sport Finance*. As well as academic research, he engages in contract research for agencies in both the private and public sector.

Carlos Campos is a Professor of Sports Management in the Department of Business Administration at Universidad de Extremadura (Spain). Prior to this, he obtained a Bachelor in Business Administration at Universitat Autonoma de Barcelona and a PhD in Business Administration at Universidad de Cadiz in Spain. His current research interests include sports marketing, fitness management, sport sponsorship and turnaround strategies in professional sport. He is also Director of www.ManagingSport.com.

Laura Cousens is an Associate Professor in the Department of Sport Management at Brock University, Canada. Dr Cousens is a graduate of the University of Waterloo, the University of Ottawa and the University of Alberta. Her previous academic positions include lectureships at the University of British Columbia and Central Queensland University in Australia. Her research interests include inter-organisational relationships, local sport economies and sport for development. She has published articles in the *Journal of Sport Management*, *Sport Management Review*, *European Sport Marketing Quarterly*, the *International Journal of Sport Marketing and Sponsorship*, *Health Promotion International*, the *International Journal of Sport Management and Marketing* and the *Journal of Park and Recreation Administration*.

Graham Cuskelly is a Professor and Dean (Research) in the Griffith Business School, Griffith University, Australia. His research interests are predominantly in sport governance, organisation and development of community sport and volunteers in sport. He has published his research findings in a number of peer-reviewed journals including the *Journal of Sport Management*, *Sport Management Review*, *European Sport Management Quarterly*, *Event Management* and the *Journal of Sport Behavior*, and is currently editor of *Sport Management Review*. He has published two books, *Sport Governance* (Elsevier) with Russell Hoye and *Volunteers in Sport: Theory and Practice* (Routledge) with Russell Hoye and Chris Auld, research monographs and book chapters on sport organisations and volunteers. Graham serves as an International Reader for the Australian Research Council. In addition to working as a consultant and providing advice to federal, state and local governments, he is currently a member of the board of the Sport Management Association of Australia and New Zealand (SMAANZ).

Allan Edwards is a faculty member at Griffith University, Gold Coast, Australia. He has published widely in the major sport management journals and has a significant profile in the area of qualitative research methods in Sport Management. Allan is co-editor of the Routledge *Foundations of Sport Management* book series. Allan has served as the Oceania Regional Secretary General of the International Council of Health, Physical Education, Recreation, Sport and Dance (ICHPER). He has extensive international lecturing experience in Asia and Europe and has consulted with numerous national and international sport organisations as well as community sport associations.

Ron Garland is an Associate Professor of Marketing in the Waikato Management School, University of Waikato, New Zealand, where he teaches courses and conducts research in consumer behaviour, strategic marketing, market research and sport marketing. He has published several chapters on marketing issues in sport management texts as well as general marketing issues in a variety of journals, including the *European Journal of Marketing*, *Marketing Intelligence & Planning* and *European Sport Management Quarterly*, and he has been a best paper winner in the *International Journal of Retail & Distribution Management*.

Bill Gerrard is an economist at Leeds University Business School. He is an international authority on sports finance. He has published academic papers on the player transfer market, measuring player quality, coaching efficiency, sports sponsorship and the media ownership of teams. He is Acting Editor of the *European Sport Management Quarterly* and a member of the editorial boards of the *Journal of Sport Management* and the *Journal of Sports Economics*. He is a member of the North American Society of Sport Management and the European Association of Sport Management. He undertakes consultancy work in the sports industry, advising teams, governing bodies and financial institutions. Dr Gerrard has developed player transfer and wage valuation systems for use in the football industry. He has undertaken squad valuations for various football clubs, including Leeds United.

Chris Gratton is Professor of Sport Economics and Co-Director of the Sport Industry Research Centre (SIRC) at Sheffield Hallam University. He is a specialist in the economic analysis of the sport market. He is the co-author (with Peter Taylor) of six books specifically on the sport and leisure industry, and together they have published over 100 articles in academic and professional journals. Their first book, *Sport and Recreation: An Economic Analysis*, was generally regarded as one of the leading texts in the economics of sport. It has been completely rewritten and published as *The Economics of Sport and Recreation* in August 2000.

Steve Greenfield is a Senior Academic in the School of Law at the University of Westminster and a Director of the Centre for the Study of Law, Society and Popular Culture. He is a founding Editor of the *Entertainment and Sports Law Journal* and an Editor of the Routledge book series *Studies in Law, Society and Popular Culture*. Steve has published widely in the broad area of law and popular culture with books covering entertainment contracts (*Contract and Control in the Entertainment Industry*, Dartmouth, 1998), football (*Regulating Football*, Pluto Press, 2001) and film (*Film and the Law*, Hart Publishing, 2010). He teaches courses on Entertainment Law and Contract Law.

Sean Hamil is a Lecturer in Management at Birkbeck College, University of London, and a Director of Birkbeck Sport Business Centre – see www.sportbusinesscentre.com – one of Britain's leading academic centres for the study of the business of sport. Following an early career in economic forecasting and marketing consultancy with the Henley Centre for Forecasting, Sean went on to author and co-author two books on corporate social responsibility before focusing on his core interest – the corporate governance and regulation of sport – on which he has written and co-edited an extensive range of articles and books, including: *The Changing Face of the Football Business: Supporters Direct* (London: Frank Cass, 2001); *Football in the Digital Age: Whose Game Is It Anyway?* (Edinburgh: Mainstream, 2000); and *A Game of Two Halves? The Business of Football* (Edinburgh: Mainstream, 1999). Most recently he was the co-editor of *Managing Football: An International Perspective* (Oxford:

Butterworth Heinemann, 2009); and author and co-editor of *Who Owns Football? The Governance and Management of the Club Game Worldwide* (Oxford: Routledge, 2010).

Andrew Hanson is Strategic Lead at Sport England. He was Head of Policy at CCPR, the umbrella body for the national governing and representative bodies of sport and recreation in the UK. These organisations support a network of 151,000 local sports clubs, serving some 8 million members. Andrew has worked in the sport and recreation industry since 1993 and his career has encompassed operational, development and strategic roles within the public and voluntary sectors of sport. Andrew also has many years' experience as a volunteer youth leader, and his understanding of the daily pressures facing grass-roots organisations informs his policy work.

David Hassan (Co-Editor) is a Senior Lecturer within the Sport and Exercise Sciences Research Institute at the University of Ulster. He is Series Editor (with Dr Allan Edwards) of *Foundations of Sport Management*, the Routledge collection of which this is the opening text. He has held the post of Academic Editor of *Sport in Society*, the internationally respected and influential journal (Taylor and Francis), for the past six years. He is also the current Director of the Europe/Eurasia Research Collaborating Centre for Special Olympics International. In 2006 he was presented with a Distinguished Research Fellowship by the University of Ulster in recognition of his outstanding contribution to research. He is also an International Scholar with the International Football Institute and sits on the Advisory Board of the Irish Football Association's Football For All Strategy group.

Christopher Hautbois is an Associate Professor in Sport Management at the University of Paris-Sud, France. His research is mainly about sport marketing strategies of non-profit organisations (international or national sport federations, local governing bodies). He is also interested in mega-sporting events through the stakeholder approach.

Richard Haynes is a Senior Lecturer in Film, Media & Journalism and Director of Stirling Media Research Institute at the University of Stirling. He has published widely on the media, broadcasting and sport. He is the author of *The Football Imagination: The Rise of Football Fanzine Culture* (Avebury, 1995) and *Media Rights and Intellectual Property* (EUP, 2005) and with Raymond Boyle is co-author of *PowerPlay: Sport, the Media and Popular Culture* (2nd edition: EUP, 2009) and *Football in the New Media Age* (Routledge, 2004).

Paul Kitchin is a Lecturer in Sport Management at the University of Ulster. Paul is the co-editor of *Sport Public Relations and Communications* from Elsevier and currently an editorial board member of the *International Journal of Sport Management and Marketing*. Paul also works with community sporting organisations in London and Belfast providing a business planning, monitoring and evaluation and training service. A graduate of the University of Tasmania and Deakin University, he is currently completing his PhD at Loughborough University investigating qualitative perspectives on the management of disability cricket within England.

Themis Kokolakakis is a Senior Research Fellow within the Sport Industry Research Centre at Sheffield Hallam University, UK. His expertise lies in the comprehensive analysis of large-scale data sets and consequently the use of this for leisure forecasting. He has provided key note addresses at many leading sport and leisure conferences and has published widely around the economic importance of sport, examining work in the voluntary sphere in particular. A graduate of the University of Manchester (MA Econometrics) and Manchester Polytechnic (BA Economics) he is a regular commentator on sport economics in the UK media.

Cameron O'Beirne is a Lecturer in eBusiness at Edith Cowan University, Western Australia, and a consultant in eCommerce and sport management, specialising in aquatics. He was the project manager for the world's first artificial surfing reef at Cable, in Western Australia.

Danny O'Brien is a Senior Lecturer in the Department of Tourism, Leisure, Hotel and Sport Management at Griffith University's Gold Coast campus, Australia. His published work is in the areas of organisational theory and strategic change in sport, and, more recently, in sustainability issues related to sport events and adventure tourism management. Danny has published several book chapters, as well as articles in top-tier journals such as *Annals of Tourism Research*, the *European Journal of Marketing*, *Sport Management Review*, the *Journal of Sport Management*, *European Sport Management Quarterly*, the *Journal of Leisure Research*, the *International Journal of Culture, Tourism and Hospitality Research* and the *Journal of Hospitality and Tourism Research*.

Sean O'Connor has more than 30 years' experience in the global sports industry. He worked for 15 years as a manager with the Event Marketing Department of Philip Morris International covering sponsorships in Formula 1, rallying, Moto GP and sailing. In 2004 he was the co-founder of Ireland's successful bid to secure a round of the World Rally Championship (WRC). In 2007 Rally Ireland made its debut in the WRC, creating Ireland's largest sporting event with 250,000 spectators, 3,000 volunteers and a TV audience of 62 million viewers. He is currently a Director of the Automobile and Touring Club of the UAE supporting the delivery of the Abu Dhabi Formula 1 Grand Prix. He holds an MPhil from Dublin Institute of Technology (DIT) on the marketing of sport and an MA from Dublin City University in political communications, and is a PhD candidate at the University of Ulster.

Guy Osborn was the co-founder of the Centre for Law Society and Popular Culture at the University of Westminster along with his long-time collaborator Steve Greenfield. He is a Professor at the School of Law, and an Adjunct Professor at NTNU in Trondheim, Norway. He is an editor of the *Entertainment and Sports Law Journal* and of the Routledge book series *Studies in Law, Society and Popular Culture*. Current research projects include a second edition of the book *Film and the Law* and continued work on relational contract theory, building upon recent work published in the *Journal of Contract Law*. Along with Stephanie Roberts and Steve Greenfield from the Centre, he is also conducting research into the regulation of both ticket touting and mediums.

Juan Luis Paramio is a Senior Lecturer of Sports Management and Leisure Studies at Universidad Autónoma de Madrid, Spain. He obtained a PhD degree in sports management from the Institute of Sport and Leisure Policy at Loughborough University, UK. His recent research interests are focused on sports facilities and sports events, sport and urban regeneration in Western cities, commercial development and accessibility provision of stadia, and the economic impact of sports events. He has published widely in these areas.

Milena Parent is an Associate Professor in the School of Human Kinetics at the University of Ottawa, Ottawa, Canada. Her primary research area relates to organisation theory and strategic management of major sporting events. She is also interested in stakeholder and partnership governance issues. She is a Research Fellow of the North American Society for Sport Management. She has published articles in the *Journal of Sport Management*, the *Journal of Business Ethics*, *Corporate Reputation Review*, *European Sport Management Quarterly*, the *International Journal of Sport Management and Marketing*, the *International Journal of Sport Finance*, the *International Journal of Sport Policy* and *Event Management*. She has also published many book chapters, and is the co-author of *Understanding Sport Organizations: The Application of Organization Theory* (2nd edition) and co-editor of *International Perspectives on the Management of Sport*, both with Professor Trevor Slack.

Leigh Robinson is a Professor of Sport Management at the University of Stirling. As a result of her work experience as a facility manager, she developed an interest in quality management and received her PhD from Loughborough University in 1999, in the area of quality management and local authority leisure facilities. Dr Robinson moved to Loughborough University in January 2000 as a Lecturer in Sport and Leisure Management, having taught at the University of Sheffield. She works extensively with the Olympic Solidarity-funded MEMOS network.

Simon Shibli, of Sheffield Hallam University, is a Chartered Institute of Management Accountants (CIMA) qualified management accountant whose specialist areas of interest are the finance and economics of the sport and leisure industries. His recent work has been focused on five key areas: the evaluation of major sport and cultural events; athlete development systems and performance measurement in elite sport; participation data in sport and other cultural pursuits; the evaluation of community-based sport programmes; and monitoring the performance of local authority sport and leisure facilities via the Sport England National Benchmarking Service.

James Skinner is an Associate Professor and faculty member at Griffith University, Gold Coast Campus, Australia. His research has appeared in leading sport management journals such as the *Journal of Sport Management*, *European Sport Management Quarterly*, *Sport Management Review* and the *International Journal of Sport Management*. Dr Skinner has published extensively in the use of qualitative research methods and theoretical frameworks for sport management research. James' research focuses on culture as it relates to organisational change and sporting studies, drugs in sport, leadership in sport, and sport globalisation studies.

Trevor Slack is a Professor at the University of Alberta, Edmonton, Canada. In 2001 he was appointed as a Canada Research Chair. In 2002 he suffered an aneurysm that led to a stroke. Since that time he has published two books, *Understanding Sport Organizations*, the second edition of his text, and *International Perspectives on the Management of Sport*. He was a keynote speaker at the 2nd World Congress of Sport Management in Sparti, Greece, in 2007. In 2008 he was one of the convenors of the sport section of the EGOS (European Group on Organization Studies) conference in Amsterdam. His articles have appeared in all the major sport and leisure journals. He has also published in such management journals as *Organization Studies*, the *Journal of Management Studies*, the *Canadian Journal of Administrative Sciences*, *Human Relations*, the *Journal of Applied Behavioural Science*, the *European Journal of Marketing* and the *Academy of Management Journal*. He has received awards for his work on sport organisations from the North American Society of Sport Management, the European Association of Sport Management, the Canadian Administrative Sciences Association and the Academy of Management.

Richard Tacon is a third-year doctoral researcher at Birkbeck, University of London. In his PhD research, he is looking at how social capital develops in voluntary sports clubs and how realist evaluation can be used to assess the social impact of sport and inform sport and social policy. He is the co-author of *Good Governance in Sport: A Survey of UK National Governing Bodies of Sport* with Linda Trenberth and Geoff Walters and is currently undertaking research funded by UEFA on corporate social responsibility in European football. Previously, Richard worked as a researcher at the Central Council of Physical Recreation, the umbrella body for the national governing and representative bodies of sport and recreation in the UK, where he wrote a report on the contribution sport can make to the government's policy objectives.

Lucie Thibault is a Professor in the Department of Sport Management at Brock University, Canada. She served as editor of the *Journal of Sport Management* from 2006 to 2009. In 2008, she received the Dr Earle F. Zeigler Award from the North American Society for Sport Management (NASSM) and she was named Research Fellow (NASSM) in 2001. Lucie teaches in the area of sport policy, globalisation of sport, and organisational theory as it applies to sport and leisure organisations. She also investigates the role of the Canadian government in sport and athlete involvement in decision making in sport organisations. Lucie is co-editor of *Contemporary Sport Management* and she has published numerous book chapters in various edited books and articles in refereed journals.

Linda Trenberth (Co-Editor) is presently Head of the Management Department and Assistant Dean of Learning and Teaching at Birkbeck, University of London, after a long career in sport management. Her research interests include workplace bullying and stress, workplace stress and coping, human resource management and performance, and of course sport management. She was an Olympic gymnast and had a significant impact in setting up the very successful sport management programme at Massey University in New Zealand and then at Birkbeck in the UK. She has published four texts in sport management.

Wayne Usher, of Griffith University, Gold Coast, Australia, has research interests in school and community health and sport education. His past and current research examines twenty-first century pedagogical approaches that engage the teacher/interventionists and the student/audience in the co-construction of meaning, value and knowledge associated with school/community health education. He gives specific attention to modern communication technologies and how they are creating a paradigm shift surrounding traditional barriers of power and information dissemination. Other areas of research include medical education, general practitioners, the internet, WWW and social media applications and qualitative research methodologies. His current research includes online health information and the impacts of health websites on the general practitioner and e-health consumer relationship.

Geoff Walters is a Lecturer in Management at Birkbeck, University of London, and a Director of the Birkbeck Sport Business Centre. His PhD research involved the application of stakeholder theory to corporate governance in the football industry, and was funded by the Economic and Social Research Council. His main research interests are governance and regulation, corporate responsibility, and stakeholder theory in the sport industry.

Helen Whitrod-Brown is part of the Carnegie Faculty Leadership Team at Leeds Metropolitan University with responsibility for the strategic development and direction of enterprise activities and the relationship management of external partners. Their key sporting partnerships are with Leeds Rugby Ltd and Yorkshire County Cricket Club, who have joined with Leeds Met on a number of innovative and creative activities, including the renaming of the Headingley Stadium to the Headingley Carnegie Stadium.

Rob Wilson is a Principal Lecturer in Sport Business Managemnt at Sheffield Hallam University. His subject specialisms are financial reporting, management accounting and economic decision making in the sport industry, and his research interests are in the financing of professional team sport and the economics of major events. He is the co-author of *Finance for Sport and Leisure Managers: An Introduction* and a recognised expert in learning, teaching and assessment in higher education.

Chris Wolsey, of Leeds Metropolitan University, has a multidisciplinary background that has led to an eclectic mix of professional duties and publications in the broad area of leisure and sport management. In 2001, Chris jointly edited a Longman publication entitled *Understanding the Leisure and Sport Industry*, and is the co-author of a number of other books in the field of sport management.

Acknowledgements

We would like to thank all our contributors for their chapters. They co-operated fully with our demands and time scales, professionally, enthusiastically and at times humorously. Together they have contributed to the most relevant and up-to-date text in sport management there is currently available. It has been a privilege for us to work with them all and with our publishing colleagues at Routledge. Special thanks go to Professor Trevor Slack, an icon in the sport management academic community, who gave Linda the inspiration to begin this journey in the UK that has led to this new text and to which he has also contributed. Our thanks also go to our families and colleagues who as always act as sources of support without which this would not be possible.

Preface

There has been explosive growth in the sport industry in the last decade. The expansion of the health and fitness sector, the increasing professionalisation of national governing bodies and investment in the public sector by both local and commercial organisations have led to an increase in employment opportunities in the sport industry. Concomitant with that growth has been a demand for more qualified, better educated, professional sport business managers who both understand the special features of the sport market and who are able to apply a system of professional best practice management. There has been an increase in expectations of the level of qualification and training of those employed within the industry, and the number of students studying towards sport management qualifications has risen significantly. Over 1,000 higher education institutions in the UK have sport and/or leisure in the title. Presently, even with the proliferation of sport courses and sport books on the market, there is no one sport business management text that focuses on specific management functions essential for providing a service to fans, players, members and clients. This edited text seeks to redress that gap and provide a comprehensive and up-to-date introductory coverage of the principles and practice of management and their application to the business of sport in the UK and beyond.

This edited text takes into account that sport has become a significant global industry with enormous commercial potential. However, to ensure a successful outcome for all stakeholders, the sector has to become more professional at every level. Sport business managers must understand and engage in such functions as governance, strategy, financial management, marketing and sponsorship, facility and event management, human resource management and public relations management. The sport environment or context in which these functional areas are managed, which includes economic, political, technological, legal and social factors set in the context of the global marketplace, must also be taken into account when managing the relationship between sport and business.

The editors, Dr Linda Trenberth, a New Zealander, now a Reader at Birkbeck, University of London, who has already provided the New Zealand market with three such texts, and Dr David Hassan, Senior Lecturer within the Sport and Exercise Sciences Research Institute at the University of Ulster, have gathered together an impressive array of authors. The authors all have direct involvement in the academic delivery of management and sport management at academic institutions in the UK, Europe, Canada, USA, New Zealand and Australia and are also involved in a professional capacity consulting to national and international sport and business organisations.

The book is loosely structured into three parts. The first part of the book starts broadly, essentially representing the wider environmental context the sport industry operates in by looking at the economics of sport and the global marketplace, the social and cultural environment, the political environment and the development of policy, governance issues and issues that impact on managing sport in the non-profit sector. The book then moves on to consider the functions of management that represent the perspective of the classic management themes of planning, organising, leading and controlling, before covering the various business management functions that are deemed necessary for any successful sport business organisation such as marketing, sponsorship, media management and event and facility management. Because of time and financial constraints the book does not claim to be an exhaustive account of every area of sport business management and some areas are not covered as fully as we would have liked. However, it aims to give a theoretical and applied overview of the areas of sport business management regarded as particularly significant and relevant at this point in time. In all chapters an attempt has been made to link conceptual and theoretical works to practice and to specific relevant cases.

Chapter 1, by Linda Trenberth, introduces readers to the ways in which the business and management of sport has moved from being just about 'sport' to being about business, issues of governance, huge revenues, stadium construction and entertainment whilst not forgetting that sport relies on the passion of fans and the ability of sport managers to make sport accessible.

Chapter 2, by Chris Gratton – a leading commentator and researcher in the economic analysis of sport and leisure markets – and Themis Kokolakakis, provides a comprehensive account of the application of economics to the global sport market. The chapter defines the sport market and analyses consumer spending on sport and looks at changes in the sport market over the 1985–2010 period. Although data is only presented for one country in this chapter, these changes reflect what has been happening to sport in most Western developed countries over this period. Chris explores the transnational forces operating in the sport market that have led to increasing globalisation of this market.

Chapter 3, by David Hassan, reminds the reader that the management of sport is a multifaceted discipline, that sport managers must consciously delineate the highly professionalised and indeed commercial prerogative of some codes from the overwhelming nature of sport, which is organised for mass participation and garners widespread support through its fulfilment of a range of socially beneficial objectives. The chapter examines in depth the range of factors that impinge upon and shape modern sport.

Chapter 4, by Richard Tacon and Andrew Hanson, examines sport policy in the UK and the related issue of how sport is structured and managed there. Knowledge of these issues is essential for anyone studying or working in sport in the UK. The chapter reviews historical developments in sport policy as well as the current state of affairs. It also introduces a number of theoretical perspectives through which sport policy can be analysed, and the latter part of the chapter considers sport's multifaceted structures – the range of voluntary, public and private organisations and the roles each of these perform that are relevant for all Western developed countries.

Chapter 5, by Geoff Walters and Sean Hamil, addresses the peculiar economics of the sport industry by introducing the reader to the economics of the professional team sport industry and the implications for the regulation of league activity. The chapter compares professional sport leagues in the USA, which are characterised by profit maximisation and heavy regulation, with European sport and professional football in particular, in which utility maximisation takes precedence and where the leagues impose far less regulatory control than in the USA. Regulation in European sport has become a topical area for debate with a number of sports leagues and governing bodies in Europe implementing regulatory measures.

Chapter 6, by Chris Auld and Graham Cuskelly, outlines the nature and scope of the non-profit sector, highlights the range of external and internal influences impacting on the management of contemporary non-profit organisations and addresses the 'unique' attributes and requirements of management in the non-profit sport context. Management in the non-profit sport context is a highly complex task that requires flexibility and continual adaptation to changing (often unpredictable) circumstances and the frequently competing demands of a range of internal and external stakeholders.

Chapter 7, by Milena Parent, Danny O'Brien and Trevor Slack (the first to look at sport organisations through the lens of organisational theory and business management), looks at the relationship between organisational theory and the management of sport with an over-view of the organisational structure and design possibilities available to sport managers. The concepts of culture, power and decision making and their role in the organisational context are also examined. The chapter explores changes in structure and design and the way contextual factors are impacting change. A basic grounding in organisation theory helps the sport manager to recognise the symptoms of potential organisational problems *before* they actually arise, thereby keeping sport organisations 'on the road' and running efficiently.

Chapter 8, by Milena Parent, Danny O'Brien and Trevor Slack, focuses on how sport organisations can base their management on a planned approach. In this chapter strategy and planning, fundamental concepts and processes which can assist an organisation in surviving and thriving, are addressed. Sustainability issues and the type of organisation (for-profit, non-profit, public sector, entrepreneurial, electronic and enduring v. temporary) have an impact on sport managers' strategy and planning choices in today's globalised, electronic world.

Chapter 9, by Chris Wolsey and Helen Whitrod-Brown, looks at the key human resource considerations that need to be considered by sport organisations if they are to survive in a highly competitive and volatile marketplace. In both management theory and praxis, there is an increasing recognition of the need to engage in more sophisticated levels of people management. This chapter provides a holistic and applied review of the management of people within the UK sport sector. The evolving concept of human resource management (HRM) is viewed and applied to the twenty-first-century sport organisation, drawing on evidence from the public, commercial and voluntary sectors.

Chapter 10, by Leigh Robinson, addresses the need for performance management in the sport sector and its role in the delivery of services by primarily examining the situation within the UK. It considers issues relating to performance management and then discusses performance evaluation and measurement. Performance management is an essential requirement of managing the business of sport and should be an integral part of the operation of all sport organisations.

Chapter 11, by Simon Shibli – a qualified accountant who specialises in the finance and economics of the sport and leisure industry – and Rob Wilson, takes a lively and user-friendly approach to looking at the rationale behind funding and budgeting for sport, how they contribute to the overall management process, and the use and understanding of the financial information and the critical imperatives in that process. The chapter examines the importance and the process of budgeting as a management discipline in sport. Practical examples drawn from a variety of sports management scenarios are used to illustrate the theoretical points being made throughout the chapter.

Chapter 12, by Ron Garland and Christopher Hautbois, takes a transactional and relationship view of sport marketing to highlight the increasingly important role that marketing performs in sport businesses. They also discuss how marketing principles can be applied in sport to accommodate the distinctive aspects of the sport product/service by examining the role of marketing in sport and its specificities. The chapter's primary goal is to address sport marketers' information needs for the design, and execution, of their marketing strategies and it does this by analysing the services marketing mix (the 7 Ps) with a special focus on the role of sponsorship in the promotion of sport products and services.

Chapter 13, by Lucie Thibault, examines globalisation as an important phenomenon affecting sport. Economic, political, social, cultural and technological forces have all contributed to the increasing global nature of sport. Although globalisation has often been perceived as favourable for sport organisations and sport in general, some issues have emerged. This chapter identifies three factors: the exploitation of labour in developing countries by transnational corporations for the production of sporting goods (i.e. running shoes, sportswear, equipment); the migration of athletes who play on teams of different nations and represent their 'new' nations in international competitions; and the increasing concerns for the negative impact sport has on the environment. Clearly fascination with sport will likely continue to play an important role in the lives of many individuals across the planet, thus it is critical to continue to critically identify and examine the global issues that affect sport.

Chapter 14, by Graham Cuskelly and Chris Auld, looks at volunteers and the integral role they play in the development, management and operation of voluntary sport organisations (VSOs) and many sport events. This chapter defines volunteering, and explores the scope and roles of sport volunteering, place volunteering and VSOs within the wider sport system. It also considers the pressures faced by VSOs and volunteers and examines how a human resource management (HRM) approach can be applied to the management of sport volunteers.

Chapter 15, by Laura Cousens and Cheri Bradish, examines sponsorship issues for sport. Though sponsorship occurs in other areas of society, sport operates at the extreme with 80 per cent of sponsorship associated with sport. The chapter introduces the fundamental concepts and principles of sport sponsorship together with relevant issues that have emerged in the contemporary and global sport context.

Chapter 16, by Steve Greenfield and Guy Osborn, is designed to not only provide examples of where the law has been used in sport but also to indicate elements of the complicated relationship between sport and law. It is important for sport managers to have an understanding of not only the possible overt legal implications of everyday sporting practice, but also of the more subtle ramifications of law. In the context of sport the law is not just about injuries and contract disputes. The relationship is far more complicated and sophisticated and managers require an understanding of the nature of the relationship as well as the more obvious outcomes.

Chapter 17, by Bill Gerrard, an economist who has worked extensively with European football teams and also the Oakland Athletics of Major League Baseball, looks at high performance sport as an identifiably separate field of study in sport management. Focusing on professional team sports, a distinction is drawn between organisational effectiveness and organisational efficiency. Three case studies are provided to examine the different factors involved in achieving success in high performance team sports.

Chapter 18, by Raymond Boyle and Richard Haynes, both of whom have published widely on issues relating to sport and the media, focuses on the sport industry and its relationship with media industries. It highlights a number of issues around the engagement of the sports industry with the emerging digital media environment and the opportunities and challenges that digital platforms, such as the internet, offer media managers. It also focuses on issues for media managers relating to the developing relationship between digital media, journalism and public relations. Specifically the focus is on the theme of reputation management for sports stars and offers case studies around two high-profile cases that emerged in 2010 involving golfer Tiger Woods and England and Chelsea footballer John Terry.

Chapter 19, by Cameron O'Beirne, focuses on providing an understanding of the role of management information systems, information technology and the use of the internet by sport organisations. The role of information technology processes, convergence social network media and key components of information systems for the successful sport eBusiness are also discussed.

Chapter 20, by Paul Kitchin, provides an overview of how the planning and management of the stadium can impact on the customer experience. The increasing professionalisation of sport has seen stadium developments begin to reflect the requirements of the sport business. Modern stadia are more than just sporting facilities, and their services, sporting and non-sporting, now have to cater for more than one type of customer. This chapter reviews the key drivers of stadium developments and how stadia designs provide the link to allow operations to support memorable experience creation.

Chapter 21, by Juan Luis Paramio, Carlos Campos and Babatunde Buraimo, following on from the previous chapter, seeks to raise awareness about the need to promote universal accessibility at all venues for all people. The planning, design, management and operation of stadia should not be the concern of architects and engineers alone as it has been in the past and they should work closely with key stakeholders such as managers, professional experts like disability liaison officers (DLOs) at club level, groups of disabled fans and local officers from the outset. The main terms and concepts relating to disabled people and disabled fans and those that are central to understanding accessibility at large sports venues are explained and a brief historical overview of the transition of provisions for disabled fans across different generations of stadia is discussed. Further consideration is given to the legislation and minimum standards of access to stadia and arenas, and the types of policies promoted by different countries over the last half century.

Chapter 22, by Sean O'Connor, defines event management and outlines how the size and classifications of sport events have expanded within the public, commercial and voluntary sector, which has allowed event management to escalate in structure and stature as it adapts elements of project management and political science dimensions into its core. It is described as one of the most exciting and fastest-growing forms of leisure, business and tourism-related phenomena. The chapter explores the functions of planning, implementation and evaluation of a sports event which are normally referred to in the life cycle of an event.

Chapter 23, by Geoff Walters, introduces the concept of corporate social responsibility (CSR) and its implementation within the sport industry. It provides a background to the development of CSR and identifies five key managerial issues: communication; implementation; stakeholder engagement; measurement; and the business case. The chapter focuses on eight different ways in which CSR schemes are implemented in the sport industry, drawing on case study examples from the UK, Europe and the USA. These include athlete foundations; professional sport teams; professional sport leagues; sport governing bodies; sport events; sport venues; sport manufacturers; and commercial organisations.

Chapter 24, by Allan Edwards, James Skinner and Wayne Usher, discusses the importance of sport management research as well as the different research methods currently employed by sport management researchers. By looking at the current state of research in sport management, the chapter examines what the future of sport management research may look like – how new and innovative ways of conceptualising and investigating issues of importance to sport management researchers and practitioners can offer potential solutions to emerging problems in the world of sport management research.

Chapter 25, by David Hassan, draws some conclusions about the future of the sport industry and discusses some of the likely trends relevant to managing the business of sport in the twenty-first century.

Managing Sport Business makes extensive use of case studies, discussion questions, review questions and indicative further reading. It alludes extensively throughout to the football industry as a sector that is at the mature end of the sport business continuum. It is hoped that the text will be equally useful for students on sport business management courses, and for practitioners who are in the business of managing sport.

Part 1

The sport management context

Chapter 1

The sport business industry

Linda Trenberth, Birkbeck, University of London

TOPICS

Sport defined • Management • Sport business management • Sport organisation • The context of a sport organisation • Unique aspects of sport business • Sport and the media

---

OBJECTIVES

At the end of this chapter you should be able to:

■ Define sport, sport business management and the sport industry;
■ Describe the different aspects of the general environment that impact the business of sport;
■ Explain what distinguishes sport from most other businesses;
■ Consider the future issues for sport managers of sport organisations.

KEY TERMS

Competitive balance – nature of sports is such that competitors must be of approximately equal ability if any are to be financially successful.

General environment – includes those sectors which may not have a direct impact on the operations of a sport organisation but could influence the industry in general ways that might then have an impact on an organisation.

Intangibility – what each sport consumer sees in a sport is invariably intangible (vague) and subjective.

Perishability – products that are produced and consumed simultaneously.

Sport – regarded as physical activity that is competitive, requires skill and exertion and is governed by institutionalised rules.

Sport business management – a broad concept including all the people, activities, businesses and organisations involved in producing, facilitating, promoting or organising sports products and services.

Unpredictability – cannot predict the outcome of the sport experience because of the spontaneous and unpredictable nature of the activity.

OVERVIEW

Sport has become a significant global industry. As Westerbeek and Smith (2002) pointed out, and as discussed in Chapter 2, the sport market is a truly global market driven by the universal nature of sport competition. The worldwide appeal of sport and the age of television (Wolfe, Meenaghan and O'Sullivan, 2002) have created the basis for commercially exploiting the global market that sport represents and which has been expanded as television and retail global sports brands have been developed (see Chapters 2, 12 and 18). The emergence of the major commercial potential of sport has been in many respects, according to Meenaghan *et al.* (2002), a function of the parallel symbiotic relationships of sport and sponsorship (see Chapter 15) and sport and the media (see Chapter 18) (Boyle and Haynes, 2009). The attempted take-over of Manchester United by BSkyB in 1998 highlighted how sport and particularly football has become increasingly commercialised. Football easily wins the global supremacy in sport.

As we have moved into the twenty-first century there has been an increasing interest in the study of sport in its variety of forms and from a range of perspectives around the world. However, this book draws heavily on the research and experience of writers from Western Europe and North America. Authors from these parts of the world have written on such topics as sport in society (see Coakley and Hanning, 2002), sports development (see Hylton, Bramham, Jackson and Nesti, 2001), the leisure and sport industry (see Wolsey and Abrams, 2001), the economics of sport (see Gratton and Taylor, 2000), sport policy and politics (see Houlihan, 1997), sport marketing (see Shank, 2005), sport and the media (see Boyle and Haynes, 2003), the role of sport in the economic and social regeneration of the city (see Gratton and Henry, 2001), sport events (see Westerbeek *et al.*, 2005; Masterman, 2009) and sport market forecasting (see Gratton, Kokolakakis, Ping Kung and O'Keefe, 2001). It is not the intention of this book to duplicate any of this material but to try and draw together material that is particularly relevant for sport business managers and the business of managing sport in the hyper-competitive and commercialised world of sport today.

The idea that books and university courses should be given over to 'sport management' still raises eyebrows and comments about the necessity to do so. Some of the adherents to the belief that sport is a part of a generic business system have asked questions such as, 'What is unique about sport?' Questions have been posed as to what extent marketing management for services (of which sport is one) is different from the marketing management of goods. Assertions have been made that management is management and marketing is marketing and that sport should and can be managed and marketed like any other type of business, and so on. The belief from this camp, as Smith and Stewart (1999) stated, is to manage sport as one would any client-based service business, operating within a specific but not necessarily unique marketplace. But is sport just another business?

It is not just that there is a significant breadth of interest in sport that warrants sport business management being treated as a separate area of study. It is because there are unique features of the sport product or service and the sport market that make sport sufficiently different and difficult to manage and sufficiently unique in business terms to justify being treated as a special form of business and of study. Football, for example, is more than just a business: football clubs, and the same goes for other sport clubs, are cultural and community assets with associated sporting and community objectives. It is the dual mission of clubs – to promote sporting success and to increasingly operate as commercial businesses – that distinguishes them from standard business. Issues around this phenomenon are discussed below and in more detail in Chapters 7 and 8. It is not that management practices cannot be transferred from business to sport but rather how the idiosyncratic nature of the sport market can be managed within a commercial or some other framework. The unique features of sport have been addressed elsewhere (see Mullin *et al.*, 2007; Smith and Stewart, 1999; Leberman, Collins and Trenberth, 2006, for example). However, they will be briefly discussed again below along with definitions of sport, business management, the sport industry, organisations and the environment in order to set the context for the following chapters.

SPORT DEFINED

There will always be some debate about how any concept is defined, and sport is no different. At the outset it is important to note, as Trenberth and Collins (1999: 13) did, that there is no 'pure essence' or 'pure nature' of sport. Rather sport is a socially constructed phenomenon, situated within a social context and shaped by social processes creating that context, and comes to mean different things within different settings over time. Chapter 4 demonstrates this through its discussion of the changes of emphasis in government sport policies in Britain. If sport has no fixed or static state then sport business managers must be constantly monitoring change and be flexible enough to adapt structures and processes to suit (see also Chapters 5 and 6).

This book adopts the broad definition of sport as outlined in the Council of Europe's *European Sports Charter* (1992) where 'sport means all forms of physical activity which, through casual or organised participation, aims at improving physical fitness and mental well-being, forming social relationships, or obtaining results in competition at all levels' (see also Chapters 3 and 14). As Wolfe *et al.* (2002) stated, sport as an organised and codified activity is a late nineteenth and twentieth-century phenomenon and its current significance comes from a complex interplay of social, economic, technological, legal and cultural factors in industrial and post-industrial society. These factors are considered in more detail in Chapters 2, 3 and 16 and are introduced briefly below.

MANAGEMENT

Management also has been defined in innumerable ways. Traditionally management has been thought of as consisting of four main functions, planning, organising, leading and controlling, based on the work and definition of management by Henry Fayol (cited in Pugh and Hickson, 1997), the earliest-known proponent of a theoretical analysis of managerial activities. Mullins (2002: 28) wrote about management as a process, through which the efforts of members of organisations are co-ordinated, directed and guided towards the achievement of organisational goals. It is clear from this definition that the people aspect is crucial, as without people

5

there is no organisation and no meaningful activity. Carlson and Connerley (2003) also stated that, to function effectively in increasingly competitive environments, organisation decision makers need to better understand how the pieces of staffing systems work together to influence outcomes, and this is some of the focus of Chapter 9. This text is structured around these tasks to some extent with chapters focusing on strategy, organising, people management, and financial control. However, this text is not limited to a discussion of the traditional elements of management as noted previously. It is extended to incorporate other business functions such as governance, marketing, sponsorship and public relations that are all relevant and important to today's sport business manager, and hence the term 'sport business management' is used here rather than 'sport management'.

SPORT BUSINESS MANAGEMENT

Various authors (see Hood in Trenberth and Collins, 1999; and Smith and Stewart, 1999) have noted that the juxtaposition of the terms 'sport' and 'business' still makes some people uncomfortable with the connotations that 'business' and 'professionalism' brings of entrepreneurial and for-profit activities at the expense of the community and recreational focus of sport. Smith and Stewart (1999) noted the views of famous sport personnel such as Alan McGilvray, a well-known cricket commentator who lamented that the game was just not the same for him (p. viii). David Conn (1999) also stated that in his view football had lost its cultural and community roots to a new type of commercially driven football. However, whatever the nature of the sport organisation, grass-roots amateur or elite professional, Hood (cited in Trenberth and Collins, 1999: 16) argued that there was a definite convergence of sport and business, and that those who ignored the need for a business orientation with the appropriate managerial approach did so at their peril.

The business dimension of sport has become far more pronounced in recent years, evident through listings on the stock exchange, hostile take over bids, globalised markets for players/athletes and clubs as brands and even small sport clubs having to provide business plans for funding. It has been shown that all sports that are watchable have the potential for commercial exploitation. The commercial complexity of sport is well demonstrated by the scale of mega events such as the 2000 Olympic Games in Sydney with 10,651 participants, an operating cost in the region of $2 billion, nearly 50,000 volunteers and the presence of over 16,000 media (http://www.olympic.org). However, as this chapter will show below, the adoption of an appropriate business model and good, if not best, business practice still has a long way to go in various parts of the sport industry. This is most notable in sport clubs and associations where, for example, it is known that, within England, almost 50 football clubs went bankrupt between 1992 and 2009 (Hamil and Walters, 2010).

SPORT ORGANISATION

A large number of different types of organisations involved in the private, public and voluntary provision of sport services, goods and programmes make up the sport industry. Slack (1997) was the first to look at sport organisations through the lens of organisation theory and business management as noted in the preface, and he wrote an in-depth book about the structures and processes of sport organisations from an organisational theory perspective. Readers who would like to study organisation theory in more depth in relation to the sport industry are referred to this text which has been revised and updated with a second edition (see Slack and Parent, 2006, and also Chapter 7 in the present text). Slack and Parent (2006: 5) described organisations as 'social entities involved in the sport industry and as being goal directed, with a consciously structured activity system and a relatively identifiable boundary'. A large number of organisations are designed to make a profit for their owners, particularly in the context of US professional sports, while many sport organisations operate as voluntary or non-profit organisations. Other organisations, particularly those from the public sector, have as their primary function to aid and assist other organisations in the delivery of sport such as Sport England. This book focuses on business and management principles and issues that are relevant to all sectors, as it is essential to have highly trained staff at all levels of sport to ensure a successful outcome.

THE CONTEXT OF A SPORT ORGANISATION

Sport organisations do not operate in a vacuum. As noted in Leberman *et al.* (2006), sport organisations operate in an environment that is shaped by economic, social, political, legal and technological factors. Although they may not have a direct impact on the operations of a sport organisation, they can influence the industry in general ways that can ultimately have an impact on the organisation. It is the ability of sport organisations to understand and respond to changes that are shaping the social, political and economic environment it has to work in that determines whether they will be successful or not. The past few decades have seen major change in political, economic, social, cultural and organisational terms in the major industrialised societies (Henry and Theodoraki, 2000) and sport organisations cannot survive without acknowledging the dramatic changes that have taken place. The 1990s, for example, ushered in a new era for UK football with rising revenue streams, but the new opportunities for football clubs to become real business enterprises have not always been well managed. While the early chapters in this book cover some of the environmental sectors that impact on organisations, particularly the economic, political and legal sectors, this chapter will briefly consider a number of the interdependent processes shaping the environment of sport business.

The economic sector

Sport is now recognised as an important sector of economic activity (Gratton and Taylor, 2000). According to Gratton *et al.* (2001) sport accounted for close to 2 per cent of both GDP and employment and nearly 3 per cent of consumer expenditure in the UK and this remains largely the same today (see Chapter 2). The sport market consists of the sport goods sector and the sport services sector and it has seen some considerable changes since 1985. For example, in the 1980s, the public and voluntary sectors were the major providers of sporting opportunities and there was tremendous growth in public sector sport provision and strong growth in sport participation. However, following restrictions on local government spending, the new wave of investment came to an end and since 1990 sport participation has been static overall. Some activities have seen growth such as the health and fitness industry and sport has become more commercialised.

As Gratton *et al.* (2001) commented, many of the subsectors of the sport market depend on participation, just as clearly as the rest of the sport market relies on the strength and the spread of its customers, the fans. As noted below, the present government has acknowledged the problem of participation in its new sport strategy, *A Sporting Future for All*, and through its strategy and doubling of funding for sport should put sport participation back on a growth trend, according to Gratton *et al.*

Football dominates the spectator market in the UK and elsewhere, but there is real concern that, despite rising attendances since 1985 and more money in football than ever, fan equity is being eroded through the neglect of their base, as football accommodates business stakeholders at the fans' expense. As fans are the customers in sport business, sport business managers ignore them at their peril. Gratton elaborates on the economic impact of sport and its implications for sport business managers in Chapter 2. It is important to note here though, as Slack and Parent (2006) do, that the general economic conditions in which a sport organisation, fiscal policies and patterns of consumption operate, are all components of the economic sector of a sport organisation's general environment that can influence and impact sport organisations.

The political sector

The prevailing political situation, the extent to which political power is concentrated and the ideology of the party in power are all factors that impact on sport organisations. According to Henry and Theodoraki (2000) there has been a major shift in political terms from sport being an aspect of welfare policy reflecting consensus politics of social democracy toward the privatisation of many public leisure services and the marketisation of the services that remained in the public sector. This shift reflected the dominance of neoliberal thinking. Today sport plays a significant role for governments in the process of nation building and the reproduction of national identities.

Funding for sport in the UK and parts of Europe is provided not so much from the public purse today but from sources such as the national lotteries, football pools and other sport-related gambling income. The previous UK government announced expenditure on sport of £750 million, particularly targeted at young people. This was projected to have an influence on the sport market through increased participation by young people that would feed through to increases in adult sport participation and spending in the second half of the present decade (see Chapter 4).

One of the very interesting developments since the election of New Labour in 1997 was the establishment of the Football Task Force that is discussed in detail by Brown (1999). Whereas previous governments had legislated on football almost exclusively on a law and order or safety agenda (Brown, 1999), the Task Force had a remit to make recommendations to government on areas such as ticket prices and the role of public limited companies (see also Chapter 9). This represented a government interest in the national game of an unprecedented nature. Labour's increasing interest in football at the time, as an area for policy intervention, is an example of the extent to which the prevailing government of the time can impact on sport organisations and their management. The world economic crisis of 2008 and the change of UK government in 2010 reflect a significant shift in policy as drastic financial cuts are sought to reduce the UK's budget deficit. Business values and processes now dominate the political environment of the sport sector from grass roots to professional sport. Detailed in-depth consideration of the impact of the political environment on sport can be found in the chapter by Henry and Theodoraki (2000) in *The Handbook of Sport Studies*, Houlihan (1997), Holt and Mason (2000), and in Chapter 4 of the present book, which considers the role of government, policy and sport for sport business managers.

The legal environment

In 2006 Leberman *et al*. noted that the growing commercialisation of sport had led to the increased involvement of the legal system. This is particularly noticeable in issues relating to the legal status of participants in contracts as well as in contractual aspects relating to the organisation of sport events (see Chapter 22), sponsorships (see Chapter 15) and grant aid to sport organisations. The strong relationship between sport and the law is also evident in other areas such as legal liability of participants in tort and criminal law, the self-regulation of sporting bodies through tribunals, penalties and appeals, players' legal rights concerning moves between clubs and across borders, and the legal doctrine of 'vicarious responsibility', for example.

The type of legal system within the country in which sport operates, the jurisdictions overseen by various levels of government and the existence of laws covering such areas as taxation, unionisation and regulation of organisations all constitute the legal environment affecting a sport organisation. Take, for example, UEFA's proposals for football club licensing (Deloitte and Touche Sport, 2003). Effectively clubs have to demonstrate that they have a certain level of competence in a range of areas such as finance, personnel and administration, including having in place a marketing director, and infrastructure, before they can take part in UEFA competitions. While this licensing system is a way to force clubs to become more businesslike and financially viable, the question that has been asked is, how can compliance be measured in such a disparate market when participating countries have very different governance and legal structures? There are a number of ways now where legal conditions affect sport organisations as the above examples show, and Chapter 16 deals with some of these issues in more detail.

Technology

Westerbeek and Smith (2003) identified technology as one of the pillars essential for the success of the sport and business relationship. They stated that technology has the potential to shift the balance of power in sport away from the major media companies and towards the clubs and athletes. The proliferation of distribution channels for football broadcasting would provide a further source of revenue growth for clubs. But if clubs continue to operate on less than good business principles as many continue to do, they will not see the lasting benefits of the sort of money that has already gone into the football industry as a result of improved technology and media interest in sport. The rising revenue from the sale of television rights, which was supposed to represent a new era of commercialism, has failed to strengthen the financial performance of clubs. Between 1994/95 and 2001/02 the turnover of the Premier and Football Leagues increased by over 170 per cent. Despite this dramatic increase in revenue streams, operating profits declined over the same period by 332 per cent, with operating losses in the 2000/01 season (before the demise of the ITV Digital contract) totalling £58 million.

Technology will undoubtedly play a major role in the provision of services and the penetration of sport as discussed in Westerbeek and Smith (2003) and in Chapter 19 of this present text. However, how the nexus between sport and technology is managed, through the willingness of sport organisations to commit (and manage) resources to such activities as entrepreneurial Internet activities, will determine how effectively sport seizes the opportunities technology affords.

The Allen Consulting Group (cited in Westerbeek and Smith, 2003) concluded that the Internet specifically, and e-commerce in general, are the most powerful vehicles of the transformation and globalisation of services. Westerbeek and Smith (2003) claimed that the future will be customised, interactive, technologised sport, limited to a small bundle of globalised, core sport products which will generate enormous amounts of economic activity (p. 205). This kind of scenario requires sport business managers at all levels to be fully cognisant of global trends and be prepared to capitalise on new technologies in order to survive. The issue is not whether the technology will be available or whether it will be implemented but what the implications will be for the world of sport, as we know it, and how today's business managers meet the challenges in the fast moving and unpredictable environment. O'Beirne in Chapter 19 discusses some of the issues around the management of technology and media platforms for sport organisations.

UNIQUE ASPECTS OF SPORT BUSINESS

There is not room for a discussion on the evolution of sport here and it is covered fully elsewhere (see, for example, Westerbeek and Smith 2003); suffice to say that sport has evolved into an economic entity and has in its various parts become more professional and commercialised. Sport is clearly involved in complex business issues, and areas such as leadership, governance, organisational effectiveness and the need to allocate and manage scarce resources are all important. The sport industry has not been immune to the need for professionalism, that is, expert competence (Leberman *et al.*, 2006), as sport has become increasingly commercialised. The increasing emphasis on commerce, commodification, merchandising, sponsorship, contracting and entertainment has forced sport followers to agree that sport has developed into a business. But while it is clear that sport organisations, in order to remain viable, should to a greater extent be run along sound business principles and perform financially, the debate continues as to whether sport is a business like any other and should be treated as such. The answer is no, it isn't.

Unpredictability

One of the distinguishing features of sport is its unpredictability. While sport has moved toward pure entertainment and the packaging and merchandising may be indistinguishable, what is unique about sport is its essential unpredictability. The outcome of the game is never known (or barring fixing shouldn't be). The sport product is inconsistent and unpredictable. Consumer-product marketers market consistency whereas sport marketers market the excitement of unpredictability. Undoubtedly the goal for those in the business of baked bean production is not only to be the best baked bean producer but to be the only baked bean producer. The goal is to eliminate competition. Sport, however, requires competition for its economic survival. Those providing the sport experience cannot predict the outcome because of the spontaneous nature of the activity, the inconsistency of various events and the uncertainty surrounding the results.

There are of course, in marketing terms, product extensions. In sport, as the variability of the contest is almost a given, as much emphasis must be placed on the product extensions, such as a facility's amenities, concessions, food and merchandise, which do ensure some consistency and provide a baseline of satisfaction, as on the product (see Chapter 12). The evidence is clear that one of the factors that affect attendance and the success of the sport business as in no other business is the uncertainty of the result linked to the competitive balance of the game.

Competitive balance

As Westerbeek and Smith (2003: 65) noted, an examination of the Scottish Premier League showed that the games that were expected to be close, and that had a bearing on the championship, attracted the largest crowds. It can be argued on this basis that the economics of sport are quite unique. The core business of sport must remain raw competition guaranteed by a good competitive balance within a league. A warning sounded by Hamil (1999) stated that free-market forces that are shaping the direction of football are largely opposed to the concepts of competitive uncertainty and to 'fan equity'. Sport business managers must understand the importance of competitive uncertainty, that it is the uncertainty as well as the quality of football that creates the interest and the continued support of the fans so crucial to the success of the sport.

Intangibility

The sport product is also intangible and subjective. Mullin *et al.* (2007) noted that what each sport consumer sees in sport is quite personal and this makes it difficult to ensure a high probability of consumer satisfaction. No other product evokes such strong personal identification and such emotional attachment as sport and this can have both negative and positive effects. A backlash can occur when the fans' favourite players are moved or when, as Boyle (2003) noted, clubs move their grounds without their fans' support, as was the case with Wimbledon Football Club, which resulted in fans boycotting Wimbledon games. Organised sport, and football in particular, draws on the emotional investment by the fan described as 'fan equity' in a competitive environment which is highly unusual in the context of the typical consumer/producer interaction (Hamil, 1999). Fans are the customers in sport business. For fans, while winning is important, it is not always a condition for their support. The relationship between a team, for example, and its supporters is exceptional, and customer loyalty in the sport business is said to be at its highest possible level in a non-captive market. However, fan 'loyalty' cannot be taken for granted in the hyper-competitive world in which we live. The danger is that the increasing commercialisation of sport and football in particular will alienate fans.

While the importance of sport is reflected in the extent of its coverage in the media, it cannot be reduced to simply economics according to Boyle, Dinnan and Morrow (2002). As noted above, it is related to its wider social, political and historical significance. Boyle *et al.* stated that perhaps the key distinction between sport and football in particular and more conventional businesses is the inadequacy of the concept of the customer to describe sport supporters. They stated that the concept failed to consider the role played by the supporters in creating the product they are being asked to buy. It also failed to recognise that being a football supporter, for example, is fundamentally an issue of identity and attachment rather than one of economics.

However, other authors would say that elite professional sport is now big business and should be treated as such. It is suggested that clubs like Manchester United do have 'customers' in the true business sense all over the world while the clubs in the less elite groups have 'fans' as described above. It is suggested then that the different sectors within the sport industry should indeed have different management and marketing structures accordingly. This is clearly a matter for further debate and analysis.

Perishability

The sport product is also a perishable commodity, developed in anticipation of demand and consumed simultaneously, notwithstanding delayed broadcasts and videotaping. Unlike the producers of physical goods who manufacture their goods at a place of least cost and ship them to customers (via stores and shops) at points of greatest demands, sport managers/marketers have their customers travel to the sport venue. There the way service staff act and the way facilities at the venue perform all impinge on customer satisfaction with the sport event. Indeed all services experience this dual evaluation by consumers of the core product and its peripheral products because of simultaneous production and consumption.

Financial base

Financing sport organisations differs fundamentally from other businesses in a number of ways. Sport organisations earn significant income, not just from the sale of a service (e.g. a game or a marathon) but from sources extraneous to the sale of the service (e.g. sponsorship and television rights; see Chapters 15 and 18). Sport managers compete for the discretionary dollars of customers through the sale of items that may or may not be related to what might be thought of as the primary focus of the enterprise.

Most sport organisations are still run by five or six people in a back office and are on the whole unsophisticated organisations. In terms of finance, football clubs, for example, have a high fixed cost base which is difficult to change despite going up and down the league tables, with an income stream that is highly variable. As a result of such a unique financial base, sport managers require a different practice within their setting from that which occurs in other business, although obviously similar basic accounting and budgeting principles apply (see

Chapter 11). The so-called business model of many football clubs and indeed other sports consists of a limited company or member club with income from gate receipts and (maybe) TV monies, expenses on stadia, players' wages and general expenses, with some clubs' wage bills exceeding turnover. It is also one of the peculiarities of the sport industry that there are multiple layers of stakeholders who all make a contribution to the financial success (or not) of the organisation. If sport organisations, including football clubs, are to be successful, they need to, apart from having better business practices, build mutually beneficial relationships with a range of stakeholders including their fans (Boon, 1999).

Boyle (2003) made some useful distinctions between sport entities and other business entities. Boyle made the point that as football clubs for example are usually incorporated, mostly as Companies Limited by Shares operating within the Companies Acts, and exist as commercial entities with an operational need to maximise income, they should be returning profits. However, as Boyle pointed out, they rarely make a profit. Most clubs do not make a profit, so don't pay dividends, and those clubs quoted on the public exchanges have seen their shares fall below the initial offer price, so to use the word 'investment' in sport is some-what inaccurate. Other business shareholders would expect a dividend payment along with prudent investment in order to maintain the upward trend if they had increased their market share even if they were still behind the market leaders. Football clubs instead 'invest' in play-ers to strengthen the team to challenge for first place the following year. In fact football clubs have been known to sell off all their assets in order to invest in players, gambling on future results. This pressure, according to Boyle, comes from the supporters, a pressure that does not exist for other companies.

So there are unique aspects of the sport product and market that should at least be acknowledged when talking about the business of sport. However, once a sport is deemed an economic entity as is professional football and other sport, then it is subject to the full weight of Community Law. It doesn't matter whether sport organisations are big or small and make profits or not, they are still subject to a variety of legal and business imperatives, therefore making it vital that sport organisations adopt the most appropriate structures and strategies required for compliance and for survival (see Chapter 16).

SPORT AND THE MEDIA

Market forces being what they are, it is unlikely that sport would have grown into the massive business it is now without the assistance of the mass media. Newspapers, radio and later televi-sion have capitalised on the fact that they could make money by extensively covering sport. Murdoch, for example, revolutionised the sport marketplace by investing for long-term value rather than short-term profits and by building globally rather than nationally. Football, for example, would not be occupying its current status as the first and truly global game, capturing the interest of every continent, especially at the time of the World Cup, without television.

The growing interest in the business aspects of sport is evident across the media spec-trum. For example, as Boyle et al. (2002) pointed out, the *Financial Times* has published a weekly sport page specialising in the coverage of financial issues in sport since March 1997. According to Boyle et al., most sports are increasingly seeking to control their relationships with the media and Boyle and Haynes go into some detail into how to manage this aspect of the relationship between sport and the media in Chapter 18 in the present book. The appointment of Patrick Haverson in 2001, previously a journalist with the *Financial Times*, as Director of Communication for Manchester United, shows the growing recognition of the importance of communication with all clubs' stakeholders for sport business managers. It also shows the importance of having a financial background as interest in sport extends into the media and business pages of the media. Boyle and Haynes also address the implications of the 'new media' for sport organisations in Chapter 18.

SUMMARY

The debate continues as to whether the corporate governance model (see Chapter 5) is the correct model to pursue for sport organisations. Alternative forms of ownership and governance to that of the corporate model, however, have been proposed for sport organisations, as indicated by Boyle (2003). A sport organisation today can be thought of as an entertainment provider and run as a real business, with long-term strategic goals (see Chapter 8) for the development of its brand and the maximisation of its assets through the development of distribution channels available (stadium, television, merchandising, sponsorship, themed bars and restaurants, hotels, etc.). However, the core business of sport must remain raw competition guaranteed by a good competitive balance in order to sustain fan equity and long-term success. In the view of Boon (1999), future successes on the field in football will only be achieved by creating a strong customer-focused platform capable of capitalising on 'the good times' and insulating the club through the bad. Boon stated that clubs and governing bodies have the option of adopting a business structure and embracing market competition with attitudes and structures designed for a modern business age to get the best results for their organisations. On the other hand they can react to events and resist change and end up being swept along reluctantly or indeed swept away.

The factors discussed above contribute to our understanding of what differentiates sport from other types of business and should be taken into account when managing the business of any sport. Management is at the core of sport business but the distinctiveness of sport is also at the core. The following chapters, blending both theory and practice, look at the distinctive context of sport management within functional areas such as finance, marketing and human resource management and consider contemporary issues such as the media, the stadium experience, social responsibility and information communications technology. Through original case studies theory is applied to real examples.

REVIEW QUESTIONS

1   How would you define sport for the purpose of managing sport?
2   What is sport management?
3   Describe the sport industry.
4   How does sport contribute to the economy?

5 Identify the unique features of sport that make it important for sport managers to understand when managing sport.

6 Discuss how the environment impacts on the way sport is managed.

FURTHER READING

Slack, T. and Parent, M. (2006) *Understanding Sport Organizations: The Application of Organization Theory* (2nd edn), Champaign, IL: Human Kinetics.

Slack, T. and Parent, M. (2007) *International Perspectives on the Management of Sport*, Champaign, IL: Human Kinetics.

WEBSITES

Academic websites

European Association of Sport Management
http://www.easm.net
North American Association of Sport Management
http://www.nassm.org
Sport Management Association of New Zealand
http://www.smaanz.org

Government bodies

Sport England
http://www.sportengland.org
UK Sport
http://www.uksport.gov.uk

REFERENCES

Boon, G. (ed.) (1999) *Deloitte & Touche Annual Review of Football Finance*, Manchester: Deloitte & Touche Sport.

Boyle, D. (2003) *Submission to the London Assembly Inquiry on Football Stadia in London*, London: Supporters Direct.

Boyle, R. and Haynes, R. (2003) 'New Media Sport', in N. Blain and A. Bernstein (eds), *Sport in the Media Age*, London: Frank Cass.

Boyle, R. and Haynes, R. (2009) *Power Play: Sport, the Media and Popular Culture*, Edinburgh: Edinburgh University Press.

Boyle, R., Dinnan, W. and Morrow, S. (2002) 'Doing the Business? Newspaper Reporting of the Business of Football', *Journalism*, 3 (2): 161–181.

Brown, A. (1999) 'Thinking the Unthinkable or Playing the Game? The Football Taskforce, New Labour and the Reform of English Football', in S. Hamil, J. Michie and C. Oughton (eds), *A Game of Two Halves? The Business of Football*, London: Mainstream.

15

Carlson, K. and Connerley, M. (2003) 'The Staffing Cycles Framework: Viewing Staffing as a System of Decision Events', *Journal of Management*, 29 (1): 51–78.

Coakley, J. and Hanning, E. (2002) *Handbook of Sport Studies*, London: Sage.

Conn, D. (1999) 'The New Commercialism', in S. Hamil, J. Michie and C. Oughton (eds), *A Game of Two Halves? The Business of Football*, London: Mainstream.

Council of Europe (1992) *European Sports Charter*. Sports Council, http://www.coe.int/t/dg4/sport/sportineurope/charter_en.asp.

Deloitte and Touche Sport (2003) *Club Licensing for European Football*, http://www.deloitte.com.

Gratton, C. and Taylor, P. (2000) *Economics of Sport and Recreation*, London: Spon.

Gratton, C., Kokolakakis, T., Ping Kung, S. and O'Keefe, L. (2001) *Sport Market Forecasts 2001–2005*, Sheffield: Sport Industry Research Centre.

Hamil, S. (1999) 'A Whole New Ball Game? Why Football Needs a Regulator', in S. Hamil, J. Michie and C. Oughton (eds), *A Game of Two Halves? The Business of Football*, London: Mainstream.

Hamil, S. and Walters, G. (2010) 'Financial Performance in English Professional Football: "An Inconvenient Truth"', *Soccer & Society*, 11 (4): 354–372.

Henry, I. and Theodoraki, E. (2000) 'Management, Organizations and Theory in the Governance of Sport', in J. Coakley and E. Dunning (eds), *Handbook of Sport Studies*, London: Sage.

Holt, R. and Mason, T. (2000) *Sport in Britain 1945–2000*, Oxford: Blackwell.

Houlihan, B. (1997) *Sport, Policy and Politics*, London: Routledge.

Hylton, K., Bramham, P., Jackson, D and Nesti, M. (2001) *Sports Development: Policy, Process and Practice*, London: Routledge.

Leberman, S., Collins, C. and Trenberth, L. (2006) *Sport Business Management in Aotearoa/New Zealand*, Victoria, Australia: Thomson.

Masterman, G. (2009) *Strategic Sports Event Management: Olympic Edition*, London: Elsevier-Butterworth Heinemann.

Mullin, B., Hardy, S. and Sutton, W. (2007) *Sport Marketing* (3rd edn), Champaign, IL: Human Kinetics.

Mullins, L. (2002) *Management and Organizational Behaviour* (6th edn), Essex: Pearson Education.

Pugh, D. and Hickson, D. (1997) *Writers on Organizations*, London: Penguin.

Shank, M.D. (2005) *Sports Marketing: A Strategic Perspective* (4th edn), New Jersey: Prentice Hall.

Slack, T. (1997) *Understanding Sport Organizations: The Application of Organization Theory*, Champaign, IL: Human Kinetics.

Slack, T. and Parent, M. (2006) *Understanding Sport Organizations: The Application of Organizational Theory*, Champaign, IL: Human Kinetics.

Smith, A. and Stewart, B. (1999) *Sports Management*, Australia: Allen and Unwin.

Trenberth, L. and Collins, C. (1999) 'The Sport Business Industry', in L. Trenberth and C. Collins (eds), *Sport Business Management in New Zealand*, Palmerston North, New Zealand: Dunmore Press.

Westerbeek, H. and Smith, A. (2003) *Sport Business in the Global Marketplace*, London: Palgrave, Macmillan.

Westerbeek, H., Smith, A., Turner, P., Emery, P., Green, C. and Van Leeuwen, L. (2005) *Managing Sports Facilities and Major Events*, London: Routledge.

Wolfe, R., Meenaghan, T. and O'Sullivan, P. (2002) 'The Sports Network: Insights into the Shifting Balance of Power', *Journal of Business Research*, 55: 611–622.

Wolsey, C. and Abrams, J. (2001) *Understanding the Leisure and Sport Industry*, Essex: Pearson Education.

Chapter 2

Sport in the global marketplace

Chris Gratton and Themis Kokolakakis, Sport Industry Research Centre, Sheffield Hallam University

---

TOPICS

Definition of the sport market • The size of the sport market • Changes in the sport market 1985–2010 • Sport in the global marketplace

---

OBJECTIVES

At the end of this chapter you should be able to:

■ Define the sport industry and its component parts;

■ Recognise and comprehend the changing business environment in which the sport industry operates;

■ Review and critically evaluate the theories, concepts and principles underlying increasing globalisation in the sport market.

KEY TERMS

Globalisation – this refers to a range of developments that has led to the same products being made available throughout the world through the globalised marketing of brands as described in the Nike case study. National markets become less important as companies look to market their products on a global basis.

Outsourcing – this is part of the process of globalisation where products are designed in rich economies such as the United States but produced in low-wage economies, mainly in Asia.

OVERVIEW

This chapter analyses the increasing economic importance of sport and the emergence of what is now recognised as a sport industry. It begins by defining the sport market and analysing consumer spending on sport for one country, the United Kingdom. It then goes on to look at changes in the sport market over the 1985–2010 period. Although data will only be presented for one country, these changes reflect what has been happening to sport in most Western developed countries over this period. The argument put forward is that there are transnational forces operating in the sport market that have led to increasing globalisation of this market. The rest of the chapter concentrates on analysing these forces and illustrating them with two case studies, Nike and Everton Football Club.

CASE STUDY 1: NIKE

Nike is a classic case study of how the sport market has been affected by globalisation. Nike dominates the world sports shoe industry, an industry that has shown phenomenal growth over the last 20 years. Nike accounts for nearly a third of the total sales of sports shoes worldwide.

Nike started out as a company called Blue Ribbon Sports, based in Oregon, USA, and distributing running shoes produced by a Japanese company, Onitsuka Sports. By the early 1970s the company had severed ties with Onitsuka and was designing, marketing and distributing its own running shoes. In 1978 Blue Ribbon Sports changed its name to Nike. This company very quickly established itself in the lead in one of the fastest-growing leisure markets in the world. Although Nike produces other sportswear, sports shoes are its main area of activity and 75 per cent of the company's turnover comes from shoes.

There is some literature relating to the global production, distribution and marketing approach of Nike (Clifford, 1992; Willigan, 1992). What is perhaps surprising is that Nike is not a manufacturing company at all. All manufacturing is done by contractors, 99 per cent of them in Asia. Clifford (1992) described how Nike kept the cost of production down by constantly seeking out lowest-cost producers in the late 1980s and early 1990s:

> The company is forever on the lookout for cheap production sites. If costs in a particular country or factory move too far out of line, productivity will have to rise to compensate, or Nike will take its business elsewhere. The firm uses about 40 factories; 20 have closed in the past five years or so and another 35 have opened.
>
> (Clifford, 1992, p.59)

This tremendous dynamism and flexibility in the organisation of production is illustrated by Nike's response to soaring labour costs in South Korea in the late 1980s. In 1988, 68 per cent of Nike's shoes were produced in South Korea. By 1992, this percentage had fallen to 42 per cent (Clifford, 1992). Over this period Nike switched an increasing proportion of production to contractors in the cheaper labour cost countries of China, Indonesia and Thailand. In 1988, these countries accounted for less than 10 per cent of Nike's production. By 1992, this had increased to 44 per cent.

Not only was Nike able to move production rapidly in search of lower and lower costs, it was also able to alter its global distribution network in response to world events. Clifford (1992) reports that Nike was faced with a potentially dangerous commercial threat in September/October 1992. Having moved much of the production of sports shoes to China, the US government became involved in a dispute with China over demands to open up the Chinese markets to American goods. The USA threatened to impose punitive tariffs on Chinese goods unless agreement was reached by 10 October. In response to this threat Nike planned to switch most of the output from Chinese factories to Europe. It also made an agreement with its Chinese suppliers that any loss resulting from any remaining shoes entering the US market would be split equally between Nike and the Chinese suppliers. In the end the dispute was resolved and no action was needed.

Willigan (1992) emphasised how Nike developed its global marketing strategy in the late 1980s and early 1990s. One of Nike's major characteristics in marketing was the association of the product with the athlete: Michael Jordan with Air Jordan, the basketball shoe; John McEnroe, Andre Agassi and Pete Sampras with tennis shoes and clothing. This association was an ideal way of marketing to a global market. The global media coverage of major sports events allowed Nike to establish a global marketplace for its products, as this quote from Ian Hamilton, Nike's tennis marketing director, illustrates:

> When I started at Nike tennis, John McEnroe was the most visible player in the world, and he was already part of the Nike Family. He epitomised the type of player Nike wanted in its shoes – talented, dedicated, and loud. He broke racquets, drew fines, and, most of all, won matches. His success and behaviour drew attention on and off the court and put a lot of people in Nikes.
>
> (Willigan, 1992, p.95).

Similarly a further quote from Phil Knight stresses the importance of the association of the product with the athlete:

> The trick is to get athletes who not only can win but can stir up emotion. We want someone the public is going to love or hate, not just the leading scorer ... To create a lasting emotional tie with consumers, we use the athletes repeatedly throughout their careers and present them as whole people.
>
> (Willigan, 1992, p.98)

Thus as John McEnroe got older and Andre Agassi replaced him as the fiery newcomer, Agassi became the promoter of Challenge Court, the exciting and colourful tennis range, while John McEnroe launched a new, more subdued range, Supreme Court.

This policy of breaking down each individual sport into smaller and smaller sub-markets is another major characteristic of Nike's marketing approach. Thirty years ago there was only one type of basketball shoe on the market and very few specialist running shoes. A trainer was an all-purpose sports shoe catering to a wide variety of sporting activities. Now there are different shoes and equipment for every sport. The Air Jordan basketball shoe was a concerted effort by Nike to create a completely new market for basketball shoes. It succeeded, and later Nike further segmented the market with two other basketball shoe ranges, Flight and Force.

In the mid-1980s, Nike was losing out to Reebok, which was then the dominant force in the sport shoe market. In 1987, Reebok had a 30 per cent market share of the US sports footwear market compared to Nike's 18 per cent. Nike's aggressive global marketing alongside its massive expenditure on athletes' endorsement contracts projected Nike way ahead of Reebok. By 1996, Nike had a 43 per cent share of the US footwear market while Reebok's share had dropped to 16 per cent. In the 1997 financial year alone, Nike increased its global revenue by 42 per cent to $9.2 billion (see Figure 2.1). Only three years earlier in 1994, Nike's global revenues stood at only $3.8 billion.

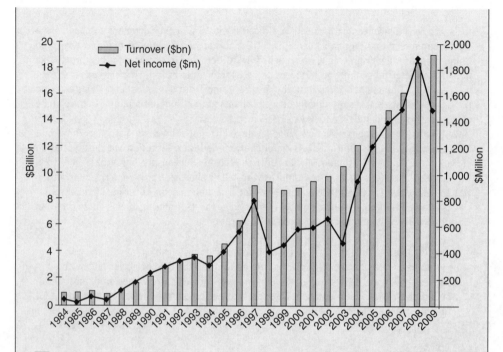

Figure 2.1 *Nike turnover and net income (Source: Nike Annual Reports, various years)*

At this point in time Nike was spending over $1 billion annually on marketing and athlete endorsement contracts compared with a spend of around $400 million by Reebok. In January 1998, Reebok announced that it would no longer attempt to compete head-on with Nike any more largely because it could not match this massive investment in marketing its brand. Although Nike won the 'trainer wars' battle with Reebok, while it was going on, Adidas expanded in 1997 to become the second largest sports company in the world with global sales of over $5 billion spread across sports shoes, clothing and equipment. Adidas had followed Nike in moving most of its manufacturing to Asia and aggressively marketing its brand with global advertising and athlete endorsement contracts.

However, things started to go wrong for Nike after its record-breaking 1996/7 financial results. As Naomi Klein, author of the book *No Logo*, reports:

Nike CEO Phil Knight has long been a hero of the business schools. Prestigious academic publications such as *The Harvard Business Review* have lauded his pioneering marketing techniques, his understanding of branding and his early use of outsourcing. Countless MBA candidates and other students of marketing and communications have studied the Nike formula of 'brands not products'. So when Phil Knight was invited to be a guest speaker at the Stanford University Business School – Knight's own alma mater – in May 1997, the visit was expected to be one in a long line of Nike love-ins. Instead, Knight was greeted by a crowd of picketing students, and when he approached the microphone he was taunted with chants of 'Hey Phil, off the stage. Pay your workers a living wage.' The Nike honeymoon had come to a grinding halt. No story illustrates the growing distrust of the culture of corporate branding more than the international anti-Nike movement – the most publicized and tenacious of the brand-based campaigns. Nike's sweatshop scandals have been the subject of over 1,500 news articles and opinion columns. Its Asian factories have been probed by cameras from nearly every major media organization, from CBS to Disney's sports station, ESPN.

(Klein, 2000, pp.365–6)

Nike's problem was also the source of its financial success, as Table 2.1 illustrates. The 1990s Nike Air Carnivore, retailing in the United States for $140, actually cost $4.40 in total labour cost. Chinese and Indonesian workers producing Nike's products were reported to earn $0.4 per hour. There were further allegations of use of child labour in Pakistan for sewing Nike footballs, and of sexual exploitation in factories producing Nike products.

Table 2.1 *The Nike Air Carnivore*

The Nike Air Carnivore		
Retail price		$140
Price at arrival in US		$38.10
	Shipping	$1.40
	Transport and warehousing in SE Asia	$7.20
Ex-factory		$29.50
	Raw materials	$17.70
	Labour cost	$4.40
	Other costs	$7.40

Source: Brookes and Madden (1995)

Nike's initial response that it did not own these factories satisfied nobody. As Figure 2.1 shows, the long rise in Nike's turnover and profitability was reversed and Nike could not afford to ignore the protests. As Holmes (2004) indicates: 'When Nike was getting pummelled on the subject in the 1990s, it typically had only two responses: anger and panic. Executives would issue denials, lash out at critics, and then rush someone to the offending supplier to put out the fire. But since 2002, Nike has built an elaborate program to deal with the charges of labour exploitation.' A new Vice-President for Corporate Responsibility was appointed and the first corporate responsibility report contained the admission that Nike knew far too little about what was happening in the factories and that its monitoring system was not working well enough.

By the end of the fiscal year ending May 2004, Nike was back on its growth trajectory. Its turnover shot up 15 per cent on the year before (see Figure 2.1), jumping from $10.7 billion to $12.3 billion. Its net income doubled from $474 million to $946 million. As Figure 2.1 indicates, this growth trajectory in turnover and net income then continued right through to the start of the global recession in 2008/9, with revenues peaking at $19.2 billion in 2009 and net income at $1.9 billion, both at almost double their 2004 values.

As Holmes (2004) indicates, this turnaround in financial performance was also associated with a turnaround in business approach: 'The New Nike ... No longer the brat of sports marketing, it has a higher level of discipline and performance.' Nike even became official US Olympic sponsor for Beijing 2008 and 'toned down its anti-Establishment attitude' (Holmes, 2004). The financial turnaround was not only brought about by greater emphasis on corporate responsibility, but also by greater concentration on global business performance.

Not everything has changed. Nike still invests up to 13 per cent of turnover in marketing. It still has 31 per cent of the global sports footwear market and this generates over half of its revenues. However, overseas sales are now larger and growing faster than US sales. Sales in China, for instance, increased by more than 50 per cent in 2009 alone, the year of the global recession.

DEFINITION OF THE SPORT MARKET

Sport is now recognised as an important sector of economic activity accounting for close to 2 per cent of both Gross Domestic Product and employment, and over 2.5 per cent of consumer expenditure. Although most recent attention has focused on the amount of money involved in sport at the elite level in terms of sponsorship, payments for broadcasting rights, transfer fees and players' salaries, in fact consumer expenditure on sport is not dominated by payments related to major professional sports. Instead, consumer expenditure in the sport market consists in the main of expenditure related to the consumer's own participation in sport rather than to sport spectating.

Figure 2.2 gives a diagrammatic breakdown of consumer expenditure on sport in the UK. Although these figures relate only to the UK sport market, the economic structure of the sport market and the various sub-sectors in it are similar across most developed economies, so that the UK can be regarded as typical, with the exception of the importance of sport-related gambling, which is not replicated in other similarly developed economies.

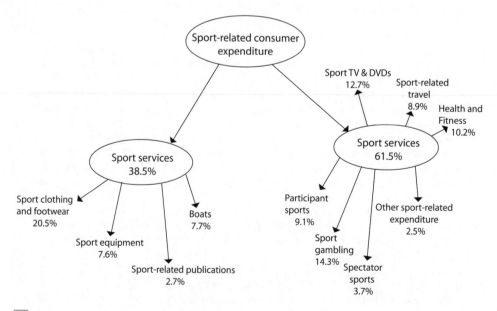

Figure 2.2 *Sport-related consumer expediture 2008*

The sports goods sector

The sport market consists of the sport goods sector and the sport services sector. The sport goods sector includes all products which are bought for use in sport: sport clothing and footwear, sport equipment, and sport and recreational boats. The latter is really part of the sport equipment market but it is such a large area of expenditure it is normally identified separately. The final part of the sport goods sector is sport-related publications (books, magazines and newspapers). Although it is possible to identify separately the sport magazines share of the total magazine market and the sport books share of the book market, sport is normally an integrated part of newspapers. Consequently we have attributed a specific share of total expenditure on newspapers to the sport market based on the average share of sport in the total content of newspapers.

The sport services sector

The sport services sector consists firstly of entrance charges and subscriptions related to sport. This divides into two sub-sectors, those related to participant sport and those related to spectator sport. The third sub-sector of sport services is sport-related TV and DVD expenditure, which includes sport-related subscriptions to satellite, digital and cable channels as well as the estimated sport component of the television licence fee. It also includes DVD rental/sales of sport DVDs. Sport gambling is the single largest sector of the sport services market, dominated by gambling on horse racing and football. Both sport participants and spectators spend money on travel directly as a result of taking part in, or watching, sport, and sport-related travel expenditure is another component of the sport services sector. The final element of consumer expenditure on sport in Figure 2.2 is 'other sport-related expenditure'. This item relates mainly to expenditure on food and drink, and accommodation, associated with both participation in sport and spectating at sport events.

THE SIZE OF THE SPORT MARKET

Total consumer expenditure on sport in the UK in 2008 was £21.4 billion. The comparative figure for 1990 was £8.9 billion, so the sport market has more than doubled in value terms since then.

The size of the sport goods market

The sport goods market accounts for 38.5 per cent of all sport-related consumer expenditure (see Table 2.2), with the most important item being expenditure on sport clothing and footwear, accounting for more than half of the total expenditure on sport goods. The sport clothing market is dominated by expenditure on outdoor clothing for walking and hiking, which has by far the largest participation rate for sport and recreation activities. The sport shoe market on the other hand is dominated by general sport trainers and running shoes. Expenditure on boats is 7.7 per cent of the total expenditure on sport, which is about the same as expenditure on sport equipment for all other sports. Expenditure on golf equipment dominates in this sector, followed by expenditure on fitness equipment.

23

Table 2.2 *Consumer expenditure in sport 2001*

	Consumer expenditure (£million)	% of total
Sport goods		
sport clothing & footwear	4,388	20.5
sport equipment	1,636	7.6
boats	1,642	7.7
sport-related publications	577	2.7
Subtotal	8,243	38.5
Sport services		
health & fitness	2,190	10.2
participant sports	1,958	9.1
spectator sports	788	3.7
sport gambling	3,065	14.3
sport TV & video	2,714	12.7
sport-related travel	1,904	8.9
other sport expenditure	543	2.5
Subtotal	13,162	61.5
Total	**21,405**	**100**

Source: Sport Market Forecasts 2009–2013, Sport Industry Research Centre (2009)

The size of the sport services market

Expenditure on sport services accounts for 61.5 per cent of total consumers' expenditure on sport. The largest sub-sector of the sport services market is sport gambling, accounting for 14.3 per cent of total consumer expenditure on sport. Gambling on horse racing dominates sport gambling, accounting for more than 70 per cent of all gambling on sport. Sport-related television and DVD expenditure, the second largest sector of sport services, accounts for a further 12.7 per cent of the total and this is also part of the total spectator market. This sector is dominated by sport-related subscriptions to satellite and cable television, an area that has grown rapidly over the last decade. The next largest sub-sector of expenditure on sport services is membership and subscriptions to health and fitness clubs, which are 10.2 per cent of total expenditure. Again this market has expanded rapidly since the early 1990s. Participant sports (excluding health and fitness) is the next largest sub-sector. This includes subscriptions to voluntary sport clubs and admission fees to public sector sport centres, swimming pools and other sport facilities. In total these account for 9.1 per cent of total consumer expenditure on sport. Admission fees for spectator sport, on the other hand, seem comparatively small at 3.7 per cent of total consumer expenditure on sport. Sport-related travel (8.9 per cent of total consumer expenditure on sport) and other sport-related expenditure (2.5 per cent) are the final two sub-sectors of the sport services market, both contributing to the increasingly important sport tourism market.

CHANGES IN THE SPORT MARKET 1985–2010

If we were to go back to 1985 the sport market would look radically different to today. For one thing, the public and voluntary sectors were the major providers of sporting opportunities through voluntary sector sport clubs and public sector indoor and outdoor sport facilities. From the early 1970s to the mid-1980s, there was tremendous growth in public sector sport provision mainly through massive investment in indoor sport centres and swimming pools. Many European countries experienced a similar expansion in public sector investment in sport during this period. Alongside this rapid expansion in sport facilities, the 1970s and 1980s saw strong growth in sport participation particularly in indoor sport and amongst women. There was 60 per cent growth in those taking part in indoor sport between 1977 and 1986, with women outnumbering men in these new participants.

Following restrictions on local government spending, this wave of new investment came to an end in the mid-1980s, as did the growth in participation. Since 1990 sport participation has been static overall, with some growth in older age categories matched by a worrying decline in younger age categories. This decline in the participation of younger people could have potentially serious implications for the sport market in the future. Within this overall picture of static sport participation in the 1990s, there has been growth in some activities (matched by decline in others). The strongest growth has been seen in health and fitness activities for indoor sport and cycling for outdoor sport (matched by declines in snooker, billiards, pool and squash). However, in the case of cycling, although the participation rate has risen, the average distance cycled has fallen.

Women's participation has continued to increase but has been matched by a similar fall in male participation. Although 64 per cent of the adult population take part in sport over a four-week period and over 80 per cent take part in sport at least once a year, only 18 per cent of the adult population take part at least twice a week. Within a static overall picture, however, we are seeing growth in this percentage as the message of the importance of regular exercise to health becomes more widely publicised.

One of the most significant developments within this area has been the growth in the number of commercial health and fitness clubs in the 1990s, catering to this increasing interest in a healthy lifestyle in which regular exercise plays such an important part.

Sport participation

Many of our sub-sectors of the overall sport market are dependent on the level of sport participation: sport clothing and footwear, sport equipment, boats, admission/membership fees, sport travel, and other sport-related expenditure. The more people that take part in sport, then the greater the expenditure in all these categories. However, despite the lack of overall growth in sport participation in the 1990s, all these markets have grown in real terms, quite substantially in some cases. As we have seen with the Nike case study, demand for sport clothing, equipment and footwear will be supplied by transnational companies such as Nike, with their production dominated by China and other Asian countries.

Sport participants now spend a lot more on sport clothing, equipment and footwear than they did 10 or 15 years ago. Similarly, overall entrance and membership fees have risen on average with the increasing importance of the relatively high-priced commercial health and fitness clubs. There has been some switching from relatively cheap sporting activities to relatively more expensive ones, which has allowed sport markets to rise in real terms in the 1990s. Whatever the activity, however, people taking part spend more money on clothing, shoes and equipment than they used to do. However, over the longer term the single most important variable that determines the economic health of the sport market is the level of sport participation.

International comparisons show that, although rates of sport participation in the UK are broadly comparable with the USA, the Netherlands and Ireland and are substantially higher than in Italy and Spain, the Nordic countries, notably Finland and Sweden, manage to achieve substantially higher rates of sport participation. Both Finland and Sweden show sport participation at higher levels than the UK in every age group and they even have participation increasing in the over-50s age group to a level higher than some of the younger age groups. Both countries also have much higher participation than the UK for young people and for women. The UK has some way to go to reach the levels of sport participation achieved by these countries.

Sport spectating

If a large part of the sport market is dependent on how many people take part in sport, the rest is largely dependent on how many people watch sport, either because they are interested in the sport or because they have a bet on the outcome. Many spectators are also participants, so there is a large overlap between the two parts of the market. The spectator market is dominated by football, which accounts for well over half of the number of people that watch sport either by going to sport events or watching them on television, and it is the fortunes of football that has dominated the spectator-related sport markets over the last 15 years.

In 1985, the football industry had reached its lowest point with the Heysel disaster in Belgium leading to the banning of English clubs from European competition. Following nearly 40 years of continually declining attendances, football seemed to be in terminal decline. However, 1985 proved to be the end of English football's long decline. Since then attendances have risen consistently as have revenues to the major clubs. By 2000, the industry seemed relatively healthy (though still in debt overall), with Premier League clubs negotiating a massive deal for TV rights. Manchester United alone has been valued at over £1 billion, whereas in the 1980s it could not get a buyer when it was put on the market for £10 million. In 1985, the income from television rights for football was £2.6 million. The change in the fortunes of football has had its most significant impact in the sport-related TV sector where consumer expenditure on subscriptions to sport channels grew from nothing to over £1 billion in the 1990s. People now pay substantial amounts of money for something they used to get at zero marginal cost. There is a lesson here for the sport market in general. Consumers of sport, whether spectator or participant, are now spending more on their sport consumption than ever before even though the numbers consuming has not risen substantially. This phenomenon alone suggests an optimistic future for the sport market. If the industry could also expand the number of its consumers, then the industry would be looking at a very healthy future.

SPORT IN THE GLOBAL MARKETPLACE

Increasingly it is more and more appropriate to talk about the global sport market. A small, but increasing, part of every country's sport market is international or global. There already exists sporting competitions that are of truly global dimensions: over two-thirds of the world's population (over 3.5 billion people) watch some part of the global television coverage of the summer Olympic Games. The cumulative global television audience for soccer's World Cup is over 40 billion. Companies such as Nike and Adidas target such sporting events for their marketing campaigns. Not only will they have advertising slots around the world when these events are being broadcast but such campaigns will themselves involve the top players or athletes taking part in these competitions and on contract to one of these major global companies. Changes in the relationship between sport and broadcasting have been important in accelerating the globalisation of the sport market. This is demonstrated by the story of BSkyB in the UK.

Sport and broadcasting

BSkyB was formed in 1990 from the merger of the two first British satellite television broadcasting companies. Sky Television started broadcasting in February 1989, British Satellite Broadcasting (BSB) about a year later. Both made massive losses, exacerbated by the competition between them. Within less than a year of BSB starting to broadcast, the two competitors merged to form BSkyB. By 1992, BSkyB was still not making a profit and the growth of new subscribers to the company had slowed and seemed to be levelling off at 1.5 million.

It was then that BSkyB made a huge gamble by bidding £191 million to secure live coverage of English Premier League soccer for the 1993–1997 period. By 1996, BSkyB had become Europe's most profitable broadcaster making profits at £8 per second. It spends close to one-half of its programme budget on sport. It was floated on the stock market in 1994 and within two years had a market capitalisation of over £10 billion, which made it the 188th largest company in the world, just behind Nike at 167th largest, in 1996. Analysts attributed 75 per cent of its market valuation as due to its ownership of broadcasting rights for sport. Subscriptions had risen to close to 10 million by 2010.

BSkyB acknowledged the importance of sport to its success when negotiations began on the next contract for televising the English Premier League. This time BSkyB bid £670 million, over twice the price of the previous deal, to cover the 1997–2001 period. In 1985, British football's income from television was £3 million per season. In 1997–8, the first year of the new deal, it was £170 million. When the deal for 2001–4 was negotiated the Premier League auctioned off a series of broadcast packages that together generated £1.6 billion or around £530 million a season for the 20 Premier League clubs. Total UK rights for the English Premier League over the 2007–10 period were £1.7 billion, with the overseas rights adding a further £625 million. When these overseas rights were sold for the 2010–13 period the price more than doubled to £1.4 billion. The Premier League is now broadcast live to over 600 million homes in 202 countries.

This escalation in the price of broadcasting rights for sport is the single largest factor affecting the global sports business. The broadcasting rights to the Olympic Games from 1996 to 2008 were sold to NBC for $4 billion.

The next most important global sports competition, the World Cup in soccer, saw the broadcasting rights for the 2002 and 2006 competitions sold to Kirch of Germany for $2.36 billion. The three competitions in 1990, 1994 and 1998 had previously been sold to a consortium of mainly public broadcasters for a total of $314 million. In early 1998, American broadcasters agreed to pay $18 billion for the rights of the National Football League for eight years. The previous deal, for 1995–8, was for $1.58 billion. This previous deal involved Fox for the first time, which is owned by Rupert Murdoch's News Corporation, also owners of BSkyB, and this deal projected Fox to be one of the big four broadcasters in the USA together with NBC, CBC and ABC.

The top eight television programmes in the United States are sports events. Around 130 million watch the Super Bowl on television. The result is that advertising rates are at a premium during the televising of such events, and it is the large sports companies such as Nike, Adidas and Reebok who will want to attach their advertising slots to this and other major televised sports competitions.

Coverage of the NFL by Fox in the United States and the English Premier League by BSkyB in England has been crucial to the economic success of these broadcasting companies. They have also been a major force in the globalisation of the sports market. Both NFL games and the Premier League are now broadcast live across many countries. The case study on Everton Football Club shows how 365 million people in China watched a Premier League soccer match between Everton and Manchester City because both teams had Chinese players. This global demand for major sporting competitions has not only raised the broadcasting rights fees for them but also has led to escalations in the price of sponsorship deals for both the events themselves and the athletes that take part in them. These sponsors are sometimes the major global sports companies, such as Nike, Adidas or Reebok, but more often they are non-sport companies (e.g. Coca-Cola, McDonald's) operating in the global marketplace and wanting to be associated with such globally significant events.

CASE STUDY 2: EVERTON FOOTBALL CLUB, CHINA AND THAILAND

The story of how Everton Football Club became the biggest football team in China in a few short months in 2002–3 is an interesting case study of sport in the global marketplace. Everton's first contacts with China were in early March 2002 when the football club announced plans to set up a youth academy in China to identify future footballing talent. The move followed a visit to four Chinese cities, Shanghai, Guangzhou, Nanning and Beijing, by an Everton delegation. Everton's community programme director, who was part of the delegation, said of the development:

Football is big in China but it still remains an untapped market as far as the Premiership is concerned. No other club has done anything like this in the Far East – we would be leading the way and, from the commercial aspect, China is untapped.

(Quoted in Latta, 2002)

Later in March 2002, an agreement was signed between the cities of Liverpool and Shanghai, as part of their twinning arrangement, to set up a series of sporting and cultural exchanges to benefit young sportsmen and women from both cities. The Liverpool/China relationship was further strengthened when Liverpool's John Moores University announced it was to fund several scholarships to celebrate the twinning of Liverpool and Shanghai. The university already had 75 Chinese students, in addition to several hundred more studying in the city at the University of Liverpool and Liverpool Hope College.

The crucial development, however, was in July 2002 when Everton became the first European football club to sign a sponsorship deal with a Chinese company. The deal with Kejian, China's top mobile phone manufacturer, was for two years. The deal was reported to be worth £1 million per season but Everton and Kejian saw wider benefits than simply sponsorship income. As part of the deal two Chinese internationals, Li Tie and Li Weifeng, would come to Everton on 12-month loans. Everton also planned to tour China, set up a Chinese-based club, and create a Mandarin page on its official website through which it could sell merchandise (e.g. replica shirts) to the massive Chinese market of 1.3 billion people. It also agreed to accept two Chinese players' youth-team players to its academy and send coaches to China.

Kejian saw the deal as a way of extending its brand into Europe. Also by televising Everton's games live in China it gave the company an opportunity to raise its profile in China, where it faced stiff competition from European and Japanese brands. By associating Li Tie with the Kejian brand and having journalists in Liverpool constantly providing stories about Li Tie to the Chinese television stations and sports websites, Kejian achieved more publicity in China from the Everton sponsorship than it had got previously from sponsoring a major Chinese team. All this publicity in China was also hugely beneficial to Everton.

By the time the 2002–3 season began in August 2002 Everton had overtaken Liverpool and Manchester United as China's favourite team. Liverpool was full of Chinese journalists plotting the progress of their national heroes. During the early part of the season one of the Chinese players, Li Tie, established a regular place in Everton's first team line-up, something many did not expect at the beginning of the season, and Everton enjoyed their best ever start to a Premiership season. On 1 January 2003, 365 million Chinese viewers watched Everton play Manchester City live on Chinese television. As well as Li Tie in the Everton line-up, Manchester City also had their Chinese star Sun Jihai playing. The result was a television audience in the Far East 200 times larger than the same game would have attracted in England. By February 2003, the Chinese version of Everton's website had received more than three million hits after it was set up in August 2002.

Although the Kejian sponsorship deal was not renewed after the two years, Everton continued its global policy by signing a sponsorship with Chang beer from Thailand. As Martin (2005) pointed out: 'obviously most pubs around Everton's stadium in Liverpool do not specialize in selling Chang beer, and the company is targeting the Asian audience, and Thai soccer fans in particular, by sponsoring a club based 6,000 miles away from Bangkok'.

In January 2008, Everton agreed a new three-year deal running from August 2008 for around £8 million, a 45 per cent increase on the previous deal. As part of the deal Everton launched the Chang Everton Football Academy, which is based at the ThaiBev Football Centre in Thailand.

Everton's new focus on Thailand, however, did not prevent it continuing to develop the China market. Plowright (2008) gives an example of how Everton in 2008 was still using Chinese television to target the Chinese market:

Everton partnered with Chinese regional TV station Hunan TV to produce a reality TV series, Soccer Prince, in which thousands of young Chinese football hopefuls from across the country battled it out to win a place at Everton's famous youth training academy, a centre that has produced talent such as England and Manchester United star Wayne Rooney. Everton's brand name was a prominent feature throughout the series, which attracted an estimated 130 million viewers, and the winner, 19-year-old Jin Hui, arrived on Merseyside in May to train with his new colleagues.

Everton were able to build on the success achieved during the Kejian sponsorship and the Li Tie association to use a completely novel marketing approach to build its brand further in China while at the same time broadening its Asian appeal to Thailand through the Chang sponsorship.

SUMMARY

Up until the 1960s sport was predominantly a local activity. People played sport locally and supported their local teams, both professional and amateur. People who played professionally received modest incomes and the only way to watch professional sport was to pay to attend the matches. The voluntary sector (i.e. sports clubs) was the leading sector and the size of the sports economy was insignificant. In the 1960s and 1970s, the increasing importance of international sporting competitions created the need for national policies and strategies for elite sport. At the same time, the *Sport for All* movement emphasised the health and social benefits of sport and created the need for national policies to enable mass participation sport. During this period many countries created national agencies for sport and the role of government in sport became increasingly important. Since the start of the 1980s, we have seen increasing globalisation of media coverage of major sports events, global recognition of top athletes taking part in such events, and association of these athletes with global sports brands. The main characteristics of this increasingly globalised sports market is the escalation in the price of broadcasting rights for major sports events, global marketing of major sports products using images (not words) recognisable worldwide, with global sports celebrities as the most important part of these images, and the escalation in the prices of sponsorship deals for both events and athletes by both sport and non-sport sponsors. Alongside these changes on the supply-side of the sports market we have seen rapid acceleration in the growth of consumer expenditure on sport, with expenditure on sectors such as health and fitness and sport-related broadcasting expenditure rising from virtually nothing in the 1980s to each take over 10 per cent of sport-related expenditure by 2001. The sports economy is no longer an insignificant part of a modern developed economy.

REVIEW QUESTIONS

1 Choose any sport and analyse how the globalising forces discussed in this chapter have changed the sport over the last 20 years.
2 How has increasing globalisation of the sports market changed the traditional role of the voluntary sector in sport?

3   What have been the main economic changes that have happened in English professional football over the last 20 years to create a global market for the sport and what factors have caused these changes?

FURTHER READING

Allison, L. (ed.) (2005) *The Global Politics of Sport,* London: Routledge.
Andreff, W. (2008) 'Globalization of the Sports Economy', *Rivista Di Diritto Ed Economia Dello Sport,* 4 (3): 13–32.
Giulanotti, R. and Robertson, R. (eds) (2007) *Globalization and Sport,* London: Blackwell Publishing.
Giulanotti, R. and Robertson, R. (2009) *Globalisation and Football,* London: Sage.
Gratton, C., Liu, D., Ramchandani, G. and Wilson, D. (2011) *The Global Economics of Sport,* London: Routledge.

WEBSITES

http://www.corporateinformation.com: A website providing individual company information with worldwide coverage

http://www.sportbusiness.com: A source of general sport business news

http://www.sports-city.org: The Sports Business Portal. 'Our Sports Business Platform gives you the ultimate guidance for opportunities across Sports Events worldwide by providing you with the latest sports business news, tenders, sports jobs and sports market reports.'

REFERENCES

Brookes, B. and Madden, P. (1995) *The Globe-Trotting Sports Shoe,* London: Christian Aid.
Clifford, M. (1992) 'Nike Roars', *Far Eastern Economic Review,* 155 (44): 58–59.
Holmes, S. (2004) 'The New Nike', *Business Week,* 20 September 2004.
Klein, N. (2000) *No Logo,* London: Flamingo.
Latta, I. (2002) 'Everton in China Deal', *Daily Post,* 4 March 2002, Liverpool Daily Post and Echo Ltd, Liverpool.
Martin, M. C. (2005) 'The Globalization of Soccer: A Look at the Growth of World's Game and Its Current Condition in the United States', paper presented at the Conference on Globalization and Sport in Historical Context, University of California, San Diego, March 2005.
Plowright, M. (2008) 'The Agony and the Ecstasy', *China International Business,* 9 July 2008.
Sport Industry Research Centre (2009) *Sport Market Forecasts 2009–2013.* Sheffield Hallam: Sport Industry Research Centre.
Willigan, G. (1992) 'High Performance Marketing: Nike', *Harvard Business Review,* 70 (4), July–August: 90–101.

Chapter 3

The social and cultural management of sport
Contemporary arguments concerning the case for specificity

David Hassan, University of Ulster

TOPICS

Introduction • The 'specificity' of sport • Governance models and the commercialisation of sport • Factors that distinguish sport from mainstream management practices

---

OBJECTIVES

At the end of this chapter you should be able to:

- Understand the arguments around sport's case for 'special significance' in its management and administration;
- Identify the factors that confirm sport as a multi-layered concept and in so doing refer to those issues that undermine sport's supposed case for specificity;
- Identify how certain governance models and sports contribute to the democratisation of sport management and how by disarming claims for aspects of modern sport to be afforded preferential treatment, including the arguments of already well-rewarded sports stars, the overarching ethos of sport can be achieved without its guiding principles being compromised.

KEY TERMS

European Commission White Paper on Sport – a paper published in 2007 by the European Commission which essentially had two key themes – first, recognition of the specificity of sport and its rules including the importance of preserving competitive balance throughout European sports leagues, and, second, further advancement of the so-called European Model of Sport.

European Model of Sport – in contrast to what is referred to as the 'American Sports Entertainment Model', this is a system that promotes a hierarchical, inter-dependent approach to the governance of sport which, crucially, favours the redistribution of revenue equitably throughout the entire sporting pyramid.

Gaelic Athletic Association (GAA) – a sporting body, which is primarily based in Ireland but with a presence in other parts of the world, that was formed in 1884 and oversees the indigenous Irish games of Gaelic football and hurling. Its players do not receive payment for their efforts, which is the primary reason why this not-for-profit, largely amateur organisation posted a net profit of €17 million in 2008.

Jean-Marc Bosman – the so-called 'Bosman rule' refers to the outcome of a court case lodged by a former Belgian professional footballer, Jean-Marc Bosman, against the Belgian Football Association in respect of what was perceived to be a restraint of trade. Prior to the European Court of Justice's decision, announced on 15 December 1995, players who had arrived at the end of their contracts were prevented from seeking employment elsewhere until their current club received satisfactory compensation. When the court found in favour of Bosman it effectively changed the dynamics of the professional transfer system overnight.

Utility maximisation – a term, which when deployed in the sporting realm, suggests that the prioritisation of sporting success ahead of all other considerations, including the financial well-being of a club or a sport, is its principal objective.

OVERVIEW

This chapter will provide analysis of the argument that those engaged in the management of sport should afford it special significance on account of its supposed social and cultural significance within society (Smith and Stewart, 2010). It will critically engage with the assertion that arguments around the 'specificity of sport' are conditional upon the particular type of sport one is referring to and indeed informed by the context in which certain sports exist. At its core this chapter reminds the reader that the management of sport is a multifaceted discipline and that sport managers must consciously delineate the highly professionalised and indeed commercial prerogative of some codes from the overwhelming nature of sport, which is organised for the purposes of mass participation and garners widespread support through its fulfilment of a range of socially beneficial objectives. Inevitably discussion around these issues, especially in the context of Europe, highlights a range of concerns relating to association football, and this analysis provides additional insights in this regard. Indeed, as this chapter examines in depth the range of factors that impinge upon and shape modern sport, initially a case study featuring the Gaelic Athletic Association (GAA), one of the largest amateur sporting bodies in Europe, serves to highlight the important role such a body can play in shaping multiple identities for its membership. This case also draws attention to a model of sport governance that is wholly democratic, which is conditional upon the desires of its membership and is not-for-profit (Hassan, 2010). It serves as a timely antidote to the increasingly commercialised nature of high-level sport in Europe, as well as elsewhere throughout the world, and provides an insight into a hugely successful and profitable governing body of sport.

CASE STUDY: THE GAELIC ATHLETIC ASSOCIATION – A DEMOCRATIC AND MEMBERS-OWNED SPORTS GOVERNING BODY

In 2009 the GAA celebrated its 125th anniversary having been founded on 1 November 1884 in Thurles, County Tipperary. It was formed as an important social and cultural adjunct to a rising sense of Irish nationalism, which when combined sought to eradicate the last remnants of British colonial rule in the country and thereby establish a sovereign and independent Ireland. Thus from the outset it had a clear set of ambitions concerning the promotion of Irish cultural nationalism and in order to command the support of the population at large it utilised the parish system, already established in light of the popular support for the Catholic Church that existed in Ireland at that time, as a method of organising a network of local clubs. Almost immediately GAA units, promoting the indigenous games of Gaelic football and hurling, emerged throughout Ireland as volunteer-led, membership-owned entities. Their well-being and success became a matter of parish or community pride and thus altruism, or 'sweat equity' to use a more contemporary euphemism, became (and for the most part continues to be) the defining feature of the GAA. In time the organisation grew out of relatively modest beginnings to take its place alongside the Irish state administration and the Roman Catholic Church as part of a dominant triumvirate in Ireland throughout the twentieth century.

Nowadays the GAA has evolved into a modern and highly successful sporting body, despite the fact that it remains true to its role as an important social and cultural agent within Irish society. It is social in the sense that it foregrounds the importance of community identity and attracts a cross-section of community support for its activities. It is cultural in the way it promotes Irish identity and other forms of national pride and associations, through the playing of indigenous games and the promotion of Irish music and dance, and by the importance it attaches to the Irish language and national identity generally. Ultimately, however, its continued success, and indeed the reason why the GAA attracts the attention of sport management scholars from throughout the world, is on account of its democratic system of governance, which prioritises the views of its membership and reflects the wishes of its constituency in its dealings with, for example, commercial agents intent on benefiting from the popularity of the association in Irish life. Crucially none of its players, including its elite performers, receive payment for their services – they are amateurs in the truest sense of the word – but it is this same body of athletes that serve as the principal method by which the association prospers financially. Thus the challenge for the GAA in the future is to retain its capacity to imbue a strong sense of volunteerism, born out of community pride, and indeed to promote the social value of the organisation within an increasingly commercialised sporting landscape.

INTRODUCTION

Those engaged in the academic study of sport management have established two broad positions regarding the supposed 'special status' afforded sport as an industry sector (Smith and Stewart, 2010). On the one hand is the argument that sport possesses unique cultural qualities that do not lend themselves readily to standardised management systems and indeed to deploy them in such settings would either distort the very nature of sport or give rise to unanticipated outcomes. On the other hand there are others who, upon witnessing the increasing commercialisation of elite sport, conclude that it is essentially comparable with any other enterprise and argue that it should be subject to the very same business practices that exist elsewhere (Petroczi, 2009). Of course this dichotomy, if indeed that is how the current position is best described, is distorted by evolving and different patterns of sport governance amongst a raft of other influencing factors, and the realisation that sport can be both highly professionalised at one end of its continuum and resolutely amateur at the other serves only to further complicate any such analysis.

Nevertheless most authors writing about the social and cultural significance of sport tend to begin by suggesting that there are 'special considerations' of which one must be mindful when differentiating sporting activity from what might be termed 'mainstream' business practices (Zeigler, 2007). It is difficult to argue with a substantial body of academic literature that advocates a special place for sport, except that on occasions it is by no means clear what type of sporting endeavour scholars have in mind when they arrive at such conclusions (Stewart and Smith, 1999). Indeed there is a danger in this analysis that sport becomes idealised and thus divorced from its reality. The fact is that in certain instances sport does deserve special consideration, but increasingly it is problematic to suggest that this should hold true in all situations and settings.

It might be argued that it is sport itself that has precipitated the development of the latter thesis and thus undermined its claim for any special treatment. Indeed those that have attempted to delineate professional sport from other forms of business have found it almost impossible to argue that the sports sector is anything other than highly commercialised in nature (Conn, 1998; Morrow, 1999). Moreover viewed against the perilous economic plight of a range of professional sports franchises, especially during the worldwide financial downturn of 2008 and beyond, it may be true that certain sporting ambitions and priorities were subdued in favour of mere survival. In fact as more and more sports clubs become dependent upon external commercial investment – in the form of media income or sponsorship – it appears the business models of many such entities engaged in high-level sport throughout the world will prioritise revenue generation over utility maximisation (Hassan and Hamil, 2010). In some cases this has simply to do with a lack of competitive balance evident within certain sports leagues, which means that clubs deploy a financial model that is relatively ambitious whilst advancing a set of sporting goals that fall some way short of what is considered necessary to challenge for sporting honours (Szymanski, 2009).

Ironically it is this sort of unbalanced sporting landscape that threatens the very future of professional sport in some countries around the world. Though by no means directly related to this issue it is appropriate to recognise that sport has also been the site of illegal and highly unethical business practices, including money laundering and tax evasion, and that this is likely to continue to be of concern as increasing levels of commercial transactions take place within the sports domain (Bower, 2003; Jennings, 2006). Finally, all of this reminds the reader of the important role of the professional (and in some cases amateur) athlete as the primary medium of revenue production. In this context the sportsperson is a key asset, but of less concern appears to be their potential to act as a significant liability and the considerable threat this can present for key stakeholders. If an athlete is in receipt of substantial levels of commercial sponsorship from global corporations and then presents difficulties in terms of violent activity on the field of play, substance abuse (including doping violations) or even soliciting what might be regarded as immoral relationships in their personal lives, the ramifications can be substantial both for the individual athlete and their supporters (Haynes, 2007).

THE 'SPECIFICITY' OF SPORT

In Europe the Nice Declaration on Sport, signed in 2000, sought to exercise a clear distinction around the place of sport in society by deploying the term 'specificity of sport' to describe what were perceived as the unique characteristics associated with sport. It engrained in law the cultural importance of sport and sought to elevate it from merely a peripheral set of pastimes to a key aspect of civil society throughout the continent. Although it has few specific sanctions to exercise in this field, the work of the European Commission did provoke a debate around the place of sport throughout the continent and led to the publication in 2007 of a White Paper on Sport (European Commission White Paper on Sport, 2007). Essentially this document had two key themes – first, recognition of the specificity of sport and its rules including the importance of preserving competitive balance throughout European sports leagues, and, second, further advancement of the so-called European Model of Sport. The latter is important because it presents a sporting model that exists in contrast to that considered typical within North America, which is 'top heavy' with private owners and a revenue distribution system that takes little account of 'grassroots' sport. The European Model of Sport, if it is possible to credibly deploy this term amid the apparent 'Americanisation' of many professional sports leagues throughout the continent, effectively constitutes a pyramid in which the various levels are interdependent, leading to a narrow, elite section at its pinnacle. It has a number of key distinguishing features (Nauright and Ramfjord, 2010).

First, the issue of revenue distribution is considerably more equitable under the European Model for Sport than is the case within the American system. Whilst the elite end of sport, notably in the game of association football, is the primary source of revenue generation, there is recognition that this is true largely as a result of the work undertaken by teams and individuals lower down the sporting 'food chain', many of whom discover young athletes, nurture them and make them available to professional clubs, who in turn then benefit disproportionately from their sports talent and labour.

Second, the question of promotion and relegation and, related to this, the issue of competitive balance are central to the European Model of Sport (See 'Platini plea for values', UEFA. com, accessed 24 January 2008). It is self-evident that, for sports leagues to prove attractive to supporters, broadcasters and sponsors there needs to be an overriding sense of competitive balance within them. If results prove lopsided or certain teams are uncompetitive then leagues quickly become distorted and with this their appeal to a wider viewing public may become adversely affected (Szymanski, 2006). At the elite end of sport in Europe it appears the biggest challenge facing national associations is to create an environment in which all participating teams feel inclined to remain competitive and thereby ensure the continued attraction of the league as a going concern.

Finally, the special place of sport in a Europe-wide context is underpinned by the regulations governing the free movement of sports labour as enshrined in the landmark case taken by Jean-Marc Bosman in 1995. Prior to this ruling by the European Court of Justice, professional athletes who had arrived at the end of their contracts with a sport franchise were prevented from leaving their former employers unless the club in question was in receipt of financial compensation (from any prospective new employer) that they considered satisfactory. It was patently a restriction of trade and the only remarkable thing was that it took so long for this antiquated ruling to be successfully challenged (Antonioni, 2000).

Bosman

That it did informs the reader about the cultural mores surrounding professional football in Europe. Historically it appears a level of exploitation may have existed amid the relationship between employers and their player rosters, a detrimental exchange in which players appeared complicit in, if seemingly incapable or unwilling to challenge, the established arrangements. That Bosman himself was construed in certain quarters to be something of a renegade perhaps lends weight to his image as the man that finally brought an end to the apparent inertia surrounding the trade in athletic talent within Europe. Countless players have benefited from Bosman's pioneering stance, including many that have profited in extremely handsome terms, but the benefit to the game itself has been perhaps overlooked (Haynes, 2007). It has led to a more equitable distribution of playing talent, has improved the terms and conditions of contracted players and provided them with a level of security that had been noticeably absent prior to the ruling. In effect professional footballers were now empowered in a manner which they had not been prior to the Bosman case. Of course it has also led to some players exploiting the situation for their own personal gain and arguably reaffirmed the suggestion that there is very little loyalty in elite sport, allowing players to move from one club to another simply to benefit from better contractual terms or 'signing on' fees.

What the Bosman ruling does underline, paradoxically, is the extent to which certain practices deemed conventional in a sporting sense actually run counter to wider European Union legislation. Some of these are fundamental to the successful staging of sporting events – it is not practical for every professional football team in Europe to compete for the UEFA Champions League title, for example – but restrictions in terms of which clubs may enter certain competitions, and, perhaps most obviously, the idea that professional footballers can only move between clubs during defined periods in any one season, are on the face of it further examples of restrictions of trade and thus in contravention to common employment law. There are of course other aspects of sport that are very closely aligned to common law, including the possibility of conflict of interests (e.g. one or more owners having a controlling influence in clubs competing in the same competition) and the use of performance-enhancing drugs, which remain a scourge at the elite end of sport and which threaten, in many cases, the very legitimacy of the sport itself, notably within professional cycling (Petroczi, 2009).

GOVERNANCE MODELS AND THE COMMERCIALISATION OF SPORT

As indicated at the outset, any analysis of the argument around the specificity of sport is complicated by the variation in governance models in existence throughout the world, trends in club ownership (where this is appropriate), geopolitical influences, the impact of international partnerships and wider issues surrounding the regulation of sport. Where membership-owned models are prevalent, including throughout Australasia, South Africa and parts of Asia, it is clear that certain forms of sports administration are in evidence (Stewart and Dickson, 2007). In Ireland, for example, the GAA promotes a series of indigenous games, including Gaelic football and hurling, but despite its huge popularity and success the association remains essentially amateur. In 2008 the GAA made an operating profit of €17 million, which for a not-for-profit organisation is a very healthy return indeed (GAA, 2009). That this remains the case is due in large part to the fact that the players – the primary revenue-producing agents – provide their services free of charge and thus the association is not burdened with the extortionate salaries typical of other professional sports organisations. More to the point the GAA is a membership-owned organisation, is essentially democratic in nature and exercises a protectionist stance around issues of free-to-air television rights for its leading games. It is considerably more conservative in its dealings with external stakeholders than many of its professional counterparts and thus places the integrity of its games at the centre of its operating model.

The GAA stands in contrast to other sports organisations throughout Europe, notably the football associations of Europe's so-called 'Big 5' leagues (England, Spain, Italy, France and Germany), where most clubs are privately owned and publically floated on the stock exchange and where shares can be bought and sold by those for whom little concern for the special case of sport is apparent (Hamil, 1999). It has meant that in the English Premier League, for example, where more than half the member clubs are owned by non-domiciles, significant foreign investment has profiled the league in a manner never previously considered possible. In turn it has attracted most of the leading professional footballers in the world game but the corollary of this has meant many 'locals', British-born players who would wish to play in their own domestic league, have been literally sidelined. This in turn has provoked a debate around the capacity of certain football clubs, which traditionally have been located within their local communities and offered a source of community pride and identity, to continue to do so in the modern era. Increasingly it is difficult to sustain an argument that these clubs are any more representative of their current locales than they are of other groups of people situated elsewhere and instead have become dislocated and distant from their traditional surroundings.

For some this has proved a source of disquiet, and certain supporters' groupings have reacted to the sale of 'their' clubs to foreign capitalists by establishing new, albeit more modest clubs, which are presented as 'genuine' and 'legitimate' and thereby contrasted with clubs where these qualities may appear to have declined in importance. It seems inevitable that amid the increasing commercialisation of professional sport in certain parts of the world, especially in those settings where these developments remain the source of continued resistance, issues of governance and ownership may continue to dominate discussions for some time to come. Of course in North America, where the 'Big 4' leagues (NBA, NFL, MLB and NHL) are already organised in an established system, where private ownership is widespread and where 'entertainment' is prioritised over most other concerns, many of these issues have been successfully overcome, albeit in a social and cultural environment considerably different to most other parts of the world (Nauright and Ramfjord, 2010).

Commercialisation

Thus the dominant theme arising from the study of sport in recent decades has been its widespread commercialisation (Thibault, 2009). In some cases it has simply been transformed into a mechanism by which successful businessmen and women have made large sums of money from the activities of others. The question is whether governing bodies of sport have been complicit in this process – a case of the 'absentee landlord' – or whether their resistance has been futile in the face of monumental amounts of money evident within sport. It has spawned a raft of academic work, from the considered to the extravagant, either documenting this phenomenon or inviting the reader to be outraged by the actions of those who in some cases were charged with protecting sport from being defaced by ruthless investors (Hargreaves, 2002; Sugden, 2002; Jennings, 2006). Combined, it has led even the most ardent sports fan to question the moral basis of some people's actions and, by implication, invited these same people to question whether all of it is still worth it. If sport is no longer about anything even remotely approaching the Victorian ideals of fair play and gentlemanly conduct then are we guilty of propping up a medium that serves only to provide a platform for some of society's worst excesses?

From cheating in all its forms, to the questionable issues surrounding sports labour migration and the exploitation of those at the lower end of the sporting pyramid generally, there is a lot about sport that should lead us to question its continuing integrity. Placed alongside the growing numbers of sporting mercenaries, benefiting as they are from the commercialisation of sport (or are they actually being exploited?), there are those who worry what all of this means for the very 'soul' of sport. If sport as we have known it to date spirals out of all control and ends up becoming something we would prefer to have little to do with then it threatens our future association with many of the pastimes we have until this point held dear (Humphreys and Howard, 2008).

At the core of the issue regarding sport's supposed 'specificity' in management terms therefore is whether there is sufficient evidence to qualitatively define this sector as different from other aspects of the cultural, or indeed of any other, sector (Slack, 1998). There are those who argue that whilst there is certainly something unique about sport there is no obvious need to manage it any differently. Instead the application of robust management principles evident elsewhere is as relevant to sport as it is in any other industry (Hoye and Cuskelly, 2007). This analysis is a little too simplistic because, as the discussion thus far has established, sport is not a monolith, something that is easy to define or instantly recognisable the world over. Instead, any examination of this field draws one's attention, perhaps too readily, to the elite end of sport, which is markedly different to sport at other levels of society.

Such analysis is then further complicated by national differences, the social significance afforded sport (including by governments who wish to use it for a raft of health benefits) and its cultural value within various nation states. It appears that to suggest that all sport should be managed differently or afforded special status is simply unsustainable (Smith and Stewart, 2010). Thus the question arises as to where the line should be drawn or at what point we should begin to treat sport as broadly similar to any other industry. Perhaps more pointedly, who has the right to decide the social and cultural value of sport? If there are considerable differences of opinion between those with a subjective investment in sport and those who recoil at the worst excesses of what might be termed 'headline' sport then where does the truth lie? Evidently there are a number of questions that are not easily answered simply by suggesting 'sport is different' and a number of objections that are cast aside in the face of commercialism and a businesslike approach to such matters. Instead it is appropriate to delve deeper into the perceived social and cultural significance of sport to see if its claims for differentiation stand up to critical interrogation.

FACTORS THAT DISTINGUISH SPORT FROM MAINSTREAM MANAGEMENT PRACTICES

In their impressive examination of this area Smith and Stewart (2010) argue that there are four interrelated dimensions of sport that separate it from more conventional forms of business. These include recognition that sport represents a 'heterogeneous and ephemeral experience mired in the irrational passions of fans, commanding high levels of product and brand loyalty, optimism and vicarious identification' (p.4). Thereafter the authors argue that sport favours on-field winning over profit making and that sport is variable in nature and quality. Put simply, not all athletes and not all teams are of commensurate quality, and thus the potential for inequality within leagues and the establishment of questionable practices designed to exploit this reality, including sporting cartels, betting syndicates and uncompetitive practices, are manifest. Finally, according to Smith and Stewart, sport has to manage a fixed supply schedule and moreover that there is only ever finite outcomes from any particular sporting contest. Each year the same competitions are staged and, whilst different teams or individual athletes, sportsmen or sportswomen may claim top prize, there is nevertheless a ceiling in terms of what any one entity can achieve by doing so.

It appears the overriding significance of sport has been its capacity to allow a passionate attachment to flourish, sometimes bordering on the irrational and obsessive, between performers and fans (Slack, 2003). Moreover few other mediums retain the ability to garner support and following from an otherwise latent population with little interest in its activities until the onset of international competition, including the Olympic Games and the World Cups of association football, rugby and cricket. Sport is thus a touchstone for a nation and is one of the primary sources of national identity (Bairner, 2001). It allows a disparate group of people from around the world to conjoin, often at the time of the playing of a national anthem, in a manner unmatched by any other medium. There are few other opportunities for people to celebrate their common bond and so there certainly appears to be some value, for this reason if for no other, to protect the sanctity of sport and the role it fulfils in society.

In other avenues of life, even those that give rise to intense pleasure or cathartic release, there is little to match sport's collectivism, its emotionality and its meaning. In their recent works Smith and Stewart (2007, 2010) invite the reader to question whether this is still indeed the case or whether the positive benefits accrued from sport are in fact available elsewhere, without the cheering or the controversy. They cite the example of retail shopping, suggesting that 'Shoppers who salivate over a $1000 Gucci handbag have much in common with sport consumers, since they too are prepared to pay good money to secure some vicarious identification and reflected status' (2010, p.4). However, to draw this conclusion is to adopt a very narrow, jaundiced view of sport. It automatically assumes that there has been an irreconcilable breakdown between the sports fan and their chosen teams or, more specifically, that the purchase of an inanimate object, regardless of how desirable it may prove to be, can somehow replace a sense of emotional belonging and reflective pride that individuals feel when engaged with thousands of likeminded others in support of 'their' team. Indeed many of these sporting contests take place in venues that themselves hold huge historical significance due to their heritage, the length of time they have been in continuous use or events that have unfolded there in the past. Objects do not in themselves create the types of identities that have the depth of meaning which a lifelong attachment to a team or a club allows.

Where Smith and Stewart's (2010) analysis does have some value is in its effective critique of certain types of sport, some sportsmen and women and individual clubs around the world. There is little doubt that sport harbours groups of athletes who have only a minimal interest in the emotional value of their employers to their supporters. Similarly there are individual sports people, golfers, cyclists and athletes to name but a few, who appear to have little concern for the sanctity of the sport and its importance to others and obsess instead over their capacity to garner ever more increasing amounts of money for themselves (Boyle and Haynes, 2004). Elite sport in some countries serves only to remind observers of the least desirable human qualities, spawn resentment and envy and does little to encourage everyday followers of certain teams to believe their investment is in any way valued or respected. Thus a continuum exists, which at one end is populated by those for whom sport is simply a means of making extortionate amounts of money, who have little regard for the emotional or cultural value of their sport or its social and cultural import and who may have created a cross section of sports fans for whom sport really is just another form of conspicuous consumption and comparable with a meal at an expensive restaurant, a top of the range motor car or a holiday at a desirable resort.

In contrast, at the polar opposite of this exist those who hold firm to the fundamental values of sport and who see a much wider role for it in society beyond merely offering a form of pleasurable consumption. It is instead a core part of who they are and of what they stand for. Of course there is a danger in over romanticising such individuals, imbuing them with qualities thought to make them more valuable than others where such attributes are absent and placing them on a moral sporting pedestal. Nevertheless they remain an inconvenient reminder to those who would wish to ride roughshod over decades of memories and emotional investment that sport wasn't designed for these purposes, and recognition of this view requires more than convenient rhetoric and the creation of a legacy industry, the latter often serving little purpose other than to lead to the further commercial exploitation of already overstretched supporters.

This analysis inevitably spills into the management of clubs and national associations because all aspects of sport, irrespective of what level it exists at, requires finance, and thus questions around the production of excess profit *vis-à-vis* utility maximisation dominate, especially in the arena of professional sport. All clubs demand a high degree of financial prudence to protect the future of these important social institutions, yet in many cases this remains noticeably absent (Morrow, 1999). On the one hand people with genuine ambitions to make a positive difference to local sports clubs become involved in the management and administration of such entities yet may lack the proper skills and necessary business acumen to execute their pecuniary responsibilities. Altogether more worrying are those who, in identifying the liquid nature of sport finance, see it as an opportunity to engage in practices that are either dubious or, more commonly, simply illegal. In between these two positions is a burgeoning mid-section that has witnessed the procurement of a controlling interest in sports clubs or outright ownership of the same as a desirable adjunct to other business interests on the part of an individual or a group of like-minded business people.

Crucially there exists a great disparity in the ambitions of these individuals – some (a minority) are genuine investors, keen to be portrayed as such and with little external motivation. Others see club ownership as a means of leveraging additional benefits either individually or for their non-sporting interests, and a third sub-group of people have only sinister intentions, including asset stripping, the sale of club grounds and financial malpractice (Bower, 2003). The most worrying aspect of this is that as more and more sports clubs, including those that were previously owned by individuals or families with their best intentions at heart, or indeed clubs that were mutually owned, fall into the hands of private owners or attract one or two investors who in turn have a controlling influence over their future direction, their management and the rationale for their ongoing importance within their established locales becomes less certain. It is entirely plausible that these owners, working in broad concert with one another, could remove any remaining veneer of cultural responsibility and simply homogenise their interests for further financial gain, court additional broadcasting revenue and further sideline the paying spectator. Yet for some sports it appears this is a most natural progression as the appetite of consumers for greater levels of innovation has led to a demand for 'guaranteed' entertainment, the demeaning of secondary competitions thought to be of lesser importance and a rationalisation of time and space in which sport adapts to modern expectations and lifestyles and not the other way around.

So it is this issue of the commercialisation of sport that appears to be the recurring theme in any analysis around the social and cultural place of sport in the modern age (Slack, 1998; Lewis, 2004). If sport goes too far in commercialising itself, by facilitating additional stakeholder investors who all want a degree of reciprocation and accommodation or by moving into new markets that may compromise the established integrity of the sport, then the meaning underpinning it is in turn diminished and, paradoxically, the reason why it was commercially attractive in the first instance becomes endangered. Conversely, as has been made clear, all sports at all levels need money, as in its absence clubs and sports become less attractive because they cannot secure the best available sporting capital and thus prove uncompetitive. It is clear a balance must be struck between financial stability, if such a thing is ever possible in the sports industry, and the need to remain competitive in the athletic arena. There is also little evidence that the 'live' fan has thus far grown disenchanted with the evolving commercialisation of sport; anecdotally there has perhaps been a slight downturn in spectator numbers in certain sports, but what is altogether more difficult to measure are possible levels of apathy towards sporting outcomes. If there is an overexposure of a given product then its desirability is diminished and therefore the challenge for sports managers is to retain the emotional attachment fans have to the sport in question, essentially through support of certain teams and athletes, whilst skilfully managing its commercial boundaries. It requires a very perceptive appreciation of the elasticity of certain groups of sports fans and followers of any given sport and their willingness to accept change, as to push these parameters too far is to risk the backlash of a sizeable and often influential constituency.

Sporting unpredictability

Aligned with this concern are the apparent attempts to secure some degree of predictability around the outcome of leading sports contests. This is clearly distinct from match fixing or the creation of circumstances where a certain individual or team becomes more, rather than less, likely to emerge victorious, but certain sports and governing bodies appear to derive benefit from ensuring the leading sides and athletes continue to dominate. Whilst many sports fans value the discipline on account of an apparent unpredictability of outcome, with increasing levels of investment in elite sport it is entirely possible that in future sport will have an evermore pronounced element of predictability and the role of the rank outsider confirmed as such. With many sports leagues, and some sporting contests, defined by significant levels of mutual investment on the part of those engaged in them, it is clear that something resembling a cartel is emerging in leagues where this was never previously the case and, despite the presence of regulations expressly prohibiting anti-competitive practices, there is nevertheless an appreciation of the benefits that may be garnered from ensuring an elite sector remains just that. Thus where certain athletes fall foul of non-sporting issues and decide to withdraw from their profession or clubs face extinction due to the deployment of an overly ambitious financial model then the implications of this extend beyond these immediate entities and onto their erstwhile opponents.

Modern sport is thus facing something of a paradox. On the one hand certain sports profit because fans and a range of other stakeholders consider them to be representative of a glorious unpredictability in the face of an otherwise entirely predictable social and professional landscape. On the other hand spectators appear to increasingly desire some guarantee that they are witnessing the 'best' that particular sport has to offer and are quite prepared to tolerate practices that permit this arrangement to continue and flourish. In the future, sport, especially that which takes place outside of North America, may be forced to grapple with the merits of these two increasingly divergent concepts.

SUMMARY

Almost a century after the establishment of a coherent form of international sport it is reasonable to assert that sport itself rests at something of a crossroads in terms of its future development and direction. At the heart of this dilemma lie two sets of considerations. On the one hand the degree to which sport should be read as one relatively homogenised whole, or, alternatively, when one refers to sport in management terms, the emphasis accorded to the dislocate between certain forms of sporting practice, which essentially presents its highly professionalised face on the one hand and the mass participation, broadly amateur format on the other. Whilst most people can readily draw a distinction between these two standpoints, whether they are prepared to accept the consequential outcome of doing so is less clear.

Arising from this is an implicit willingness to expose sport at its elite end to the same set of management practices evident in other industries and thus deny it any sense of social or cultural uniqueness. The appeals of leading sports administrators in Europe and elsewhere to preserve the specificity of sport are beginning to ring hollow in the minds of many, both inside and outside sport, who witness business practices that make a mockery of claims to preserve the sanctity of sport. Yet, in recognising the disproportionate fascination with the affairs of a small number of elite sportsmen and women, one is in danger of being equally blind to the overwhelmingly positive role sport performs at an individual, regional and national level. Sport deserves protection for the benefits it accrues in these spheres, and those involved in its management and administration should continue to accord it special consideration in light of this. What is ultimately required is a degree of healthy introspection on the part of sport itself and recognition that aspects of its current practice deserve, in fact require, exposure to the full rigours of established management practices. Whilst sport at the levels of mass participation also requires effective and professionalised administrative structures, the strategies evident at this level should also reflect the positive social and cultural benefits of sport and thus enjoy some degree of protection in the execution of these responsibilities.

REVIEW QUESTIONS

1   What are the key arguments advanced by those that claim that sport should be afforded specificity in its management and administration?
2   Sport is a term that covers a spectrum of activities from participation locally to elite competition at an international level. Detail how practices that are increasingly commonplace amongst sport's elite performers can undermine its case for specificity.
3   Summarise the concerns of those who fear that the fundamental principles of the European Model for Sport, as enshrined in the European Commission's White Paper, are being eroded by external forces exercising their influence within the continent.
4   Amid the apparent relentless commercialisation of sport throughout Europe, and the possible complicit nature of those charged with managing sport in this process, the governance structures in place within the GAA, Ireland's largest sporting organisation, are worth examining closely. What are the unique components of the GAA's management and governance approach that appear to set it apart from other large sporting bodies?
5   Specifically consider Smith and Stewart's (2010) arguments detailing why we should regard the management of sport as being quite separate from any other business practice. Critically assess these and consider if their arguments are valid in all settings.
6   In summary how do you see the future landscape for the management of sport in your country? Can we rely upon those charged with managing it currently to always act in the sport's best interests?

FURTHER READING

Bairner, A. (2001) *Sport Nationalism and Globalization* (New York: SUNY).
European Commission White Paper on Sport (2007) (Brussels: EU).
Jennings, A. (2006) *Foul!* (London: Harper Sport).
Petroczi, A. (2009) 'The Dark Side of Sport: Challenges for Managers in the Twenty-First Century', *European Sport Management Quarterly*, Vol. 9, No. 4, pp. 349–352.
Szymanski, S. (2009) *Playbooks and Checkbooks: An Introduction to the Economics of Modern Sports* (Princeton: Princeton University Press).
Thibault, L. (2009) 'Globalization of Sport: An Inconvenient Truth', *Journal of Sport Management*, Vol. 23, No. 1, pp. 1–20.

WEBSITES

Birkbeck Sport Business Centre
http://www.sportbusinesscentre.com
European Commission Sport
http://ec.europa.eu/sport/index_en.htm
Gaelic Athletic Association
http://www.gaa.ie

REFERENCES

Antonioni, P. (2000) 'The Bosman Ruling and the Emergence of a Single Market in Soccer Talent', *European Journal of Law and Economics*, Vol. 9, No. 2, p. 157.
Bairner, A. (2001) *Sport Nationalism and Globalization* (New York: SUNY).
Bower, T. (2003) *Broken Dreams: Vanity, Greed and the Souring of British Football* (London: Simon and Schuster).
Boyle, R. and R. Haynes (2004) *Football in the New Media Age* (London: Routledge).
Conn, D. (1998) *The Football Business: Fair Game in the 90s* (Edinburgh: Mainstream).
European Commission White Paper on Sport (2007) (Brussels: EU).
Gaelic Athletic Association (GAA) (2009) *Official Report 2009* (Dublin: GAA).
Hamil, S. (1999) 'A Whole New Ball Game: Why Football Needs a Regulator', in S. Hamil, J. Michie and C. Oughton (eds) *A Game of Two Halves: The Business of Football* (Edinburgh: Mainstream), pp. 29–32.
Hargreaves, J. (2002) 'Globalisation Theory, Global Sport, and Nations and Nationalism', in J. Sugden and A. Tomlinson (eds) *Power Games: A Critical Sociology of Sport* (London: Routledge), pp. 25–43.
Hassan, D. (2010) 'Governance and the GAA: Time to Move beyond the Amateur Ideal?', in D. Hassan and S. Hamil (eds) *Who 'Owns' the Game?* (London: Routledge), pp. 72–85.
Hassan, D. and S. Hamil (2010) 'Introduction: Models of Football Governance and Management in International Sport', in D. Hassan and S. Hamil (eds) *Who 'Owns' the Game?* (London: Routledge), pp. 1–11.
Haynes, R. (2007) 'Footballers' Image Rights in the New Media Age', *European Sport Management Quarterly*, Vol. 7, No. 4, pp. 361–374.

45

Hoye, R. and G. Cuskelly (2007) *Sport Governance* (Oxford: Elsevier).

Humphreys, B. and D. Howard (2008) *The Business of Sport* (Westport: Praeger Perspectives Series).

Jennings, A. (2006) *Foul!* (London: Harper Sport).

Lewis, M. (2004) *Moneyball: The Art of Winning an Unfair Game* (New York: Norton and Norton).

Morrow, S. (1999) *The New Business of Football: Accountability and Finance in Football* (London: Macmillan).

Nauright, J. and J. Ramfjord (2010) 'Who Owns England's Game? American Professional Sporting Influences and Foreign Ownership in the Premier League', in D. Hassan and S. Hamil (eds) *Who 'Owns' the Game?* (London: Routledge), pp. 86–99.

Petroczi, A. (2009) 'The Dark Side of Sport: Challenges for Managers in the Twenty-First Century', *European Sport Management Quarterly*, Vol. 9, No. 4, pp. 349–352.

'Platini plea for values', UEFA.com, accessed 24 January 2008.

Slack, T. (1998) 'Is There Anything Unique about Sport?', *Journal for Sport Management*, Vol. 5, pp. 21–29.

Slack, T. (2003) 'Sport in the Global Society: Shaping the domain of Sports Studies', *International Journal of the History of Sport*, Vol. 20, No. 4, pp. 118–129.

Smith, A. and B. Stewart (2007) 'The Travelling Fan: Understanding the Mechanisms of Sport and Consumpton in a Sport Tourism Setting', *Journal of Sport Tourism*, Vol. 12, Nos 3 and 4, pp. 155–181.

Smith, A. and B. Stewart (2010) 'The Special Features of Sport: A Critical Revisit', *Sport Management Review*, Vol. 13, No. 1, pp. 1–13.

Stewart, B. and G. Dickson (2007) 'Crystal-Ball Gazing: The Future of Football', in B. Stewart (ed.) *The Games Are Not the Same: The Political Economy of Football in Australia* (Carlton: Melbourne University Press), pp. 71–113.

Stewart, B. and A. Smith (1999) 'The Special Features of Sport', *Annals of Leisure Research*, Vol. 2, pp. 87–99.

Sugden, J. (2002) 'Network Football', in J. Sugden and A. Tomlinson (eds) *Power Games: A Critical Sociology of Sport* (London: Routledge), pp. 61–80.

Szymanski, S. (2006) 'Competitive Balance in Sports Leagues and the Paradox of Power', *International Association of Sports Economists*, Working Paper Number 0618, pp. 1–12.

Szymanski, S. (2009) *Playbooks and Checkbooks: An Introduction to the Economics of Modern Sports* (Princeton: Princeton University Press).

Thibault, L. (2009) 'Globalization of Sport: An Inconvenient Truth', *Journal of Sport Management*, Vol. 23, No. 1, pp. 1–20.

Zeigler, E. (2007) 'Sport Management Must Show Social Concern as It Develops Tenable Theory', *Journal of Sport Management*, Vol. 21, pp. 297–318.

Chapter 4

Sport policy and the structure of sport in the UK

Richard Tacon, Birkbeck, University of London
Andrew Hanson, Sport England

TOPICS

Sport policy in the UK from the nineteenth century to the present day • Theoretical frameworks for analysing sport policy • The current structure of sport in the UK

OBJECTIVES

At the end of this chapter you should be able to:

■ Understand how sport policy has developed historically;
■ Identify how developments in sport policy have affected the UK's sporting structures;
■ Understand how broader social policy developments have impacted on sport;
■ Understand the roles of various sporting organisations and the relationships between them.

KEY TERMS

National governing body – the organisation that governs a particular sport.
Political ideology – a set of basic beliefs about the political affairs held by the majority of people within a society.
Social policy – policy related to the welfare state, and the range of responses to social need.
Sport policy – sport can be used to help deliver a range of policy aspirations, such as health improvement and local economic viability.

OVERVIEW

This chapter examines sport policy in the UK and the related issue of how sport is structured and managed. Knowledge of these issues is essential for anyone studying or working in sport in the UK. The chapter reviews historical developments in sport policy as well as the current state of affairs. It also introduces a number of theoretical perspectives through which sport policy can be analysed. The latter part of the chapter considers sport's multi-faceted structures – the range of voluntary, public and private organisations and the roles each of these perform. These organisations are described each in turn, and the way in which they interact to support and deliver sport is considered. Throughout the chapter, case studies are used to highlight developments in sport policy and to illustrate the structure of particular sporting organisations and the relationships between them.

CASE STUDY 1: SOCIAL POLICY IMPACTING ON SPORT

Whilst government sports policy has an important impact on sports organisations and their funding in particular, policy in other areas can have an equally significant, if often unintended, impact. Two examples of recent government legislation provide good illustrations of the consequences of social policy for sport.

Safeguarding

During the 1990s, a structured approach to protecting children from abuse evolved in the UK, including suitability checks on adults wishing to work with children. Whilst this work emerged initially within social care and education settings, the need for similar practices in sport was soon recognised. As a result Sport England now co-funds a Child Protection in Sport Unit based at the National Society for the Prevention of Cruelty to Children. This unit has developed standards for national governing bodies to meet with regard to child protection. Furthermore, many national governing bodies of sport now employ welfare officers, and a lot of clubs also have a designated voluntary welfare officer. These individuals are responsible for ensuring good practice within the sport, extending to the use of Criminal Records Bureau disclosures and the implementation of the requirements of the independent Safeguarding Authority, which now extends to the protection of vulnerable adults.

Immigration

At first glance it is hard to discern what relationship sport has with immigration policy. However, when the UK Government began developing its points-based system for inward migration in 2007, it soon became clear that the initial proposals could have a significant detrimental impact for sport. This included the possibility of:

■ Overseas professional sports people being unable to join UK-based teams or play in UK tournaments;

■ Overseas amateur sports people being treated as 'migrants' when wishing to visit the UK for sporting purposes; and

■ National governing bodies of sport losing regulatory control of overseas sports persons within their sport.

The Government was clear in its intention of managing migration for the benefit of both the UK economy and society, by enabling only those who had the skills necessary to benefit the UK economy entry into the country. However, the Home Office officials charged with developing this system understandably were not aware of the potential adverse impacts on sport. As the Government consulted on its proposals, the Department for Culture, Media and Sport, and sporting interest groups including the Central Council of Physical Recreation and its members, registered their concerns. As a result sports bodies were invited to work with the Home Office and the UK Borders Agency to devise a system that was consistent with the Government's overall objectives, but also ensured that national governing bodies remained integral to the system, and that professional and amateur sports people were not unnecessarily excluded from the UK.

SPORT POLICY IN THE UK FROM THE NINETEENTH CENTURY TO THE PRESENT DAY

The early years

For the greater part of its history, sport policy in the UK has been poorly considered and reactive in nature, rather than systematic and strategic. Moreover, until the late 1950s, government involvement in sport was extremely rare. Instead, the field was dominated by the emerging national governing bodies of sport (NGBs). During the nineteenth century, the UK led the way in codifying sports and establishing management structures – NGBs – to oversee their rules and regulations. Many of today's NGBs, from the Football Association and the Rugby Football Union to the Amateur Swimming Association and the British Mountaineering Council, were formed in the late nineteenth and early twentieth centuries.

Although this was not a period of direct government involvement in sport, it is still possible to discern some general areas of government interest. Houlihan (1997) identifies three broad themes that characterise this movement.

- First, paternalism towards the 'lower classes'. As Holt (1989) points out, nineteenth-century philanthropy helped shape education and housing policy and likewise influenced policy directed at sport.
- Second, a concern to defend privilege. This was manifested in various disputes over access to the countryside, pitting wealthy landowners against a growing urban population eager to use the countryside for sport and recreation (Shoard 1987).
- Third, a belief that too much undisciplined leisure for the poor could pose a danger to social stability. As such, rational recreation was promoted, while the street sports deemed more riotous were increasingly prohibited.

Perhaps the clearest demonstration of government interest in sport during this period was related to the issue of public health. A concern with hygiene and disease within increasingly overcrowded industrial cities led to the planning and provision of bath houses, swimming pools, public parks and playing fields. This reflected both the first and third themes of government interest described above, namely paternalism and the encouragement of rational

49

recreation. As Jackson and Nesti (2001) point out, it also exemplified the functional and utilitarian view of sport – i.e. that sport can have a series of wider social and economic benefits – that has characterised sport policy for much of its history.

This period also saw the establishment, in 1935, of the Central Council of Recreative and Physical Training, which later became the Central Council of Physical Recreation (CCPR) and has recently changed its name to the Sport and Recreation Alliance. Initially concerned with providing recreation for people in communities, CCPR soon became an umbrella body, representing a large number of NGBs and other sports bodies. Given the lack, during this period, of a strategic approach to sport from government, CCPR played a key role in shaping policy, particularly in the area of youth sport and recreation (Houlihan and White 2002).

A change of gear

The second half of the twentieth century saw a step-change in government involvement and investment in sport. Indeed, as Coalter (2007: 9) states, 'systematic central government interest in sport dates largely from the 1960s'. A significant landmark in this regard was the publication, in 1960, of *Sport and the Community*, the report of the Wolfenden Committee. The latter, set up by CCPR to examine sport and recreation in the UK, made 57 recommendations in areas such as coaching, facility provision and post-school participation. Its key proposal was that a Sports Development Council ought to be created, which would distribute public funding, but prove only indirectly accountable to government. In this way, the Committee sought to protect the voluntary sector's central position within sport.

The report, as Houlihan and White (2002: 20) declare, 'had a substantial and long-term impact on the shape of British sport'. An Advisory Sports Council was established by the Labour Government in 1965 and, in 1972, under a Conservative administration, this was replaced by the Sports Council, which had executive, rather than solely advisory, powers. The establishment of the Sports Council effectively marked the Government's intention to become formally and strategically involved in sport.

The longer term impact of the Wolfenden Committee report was manifested in the increased provision of facilities for sport and recreation in the UK. This was highlighted in the report as a necessary step and was given impetus through the work of the Sports Council. Between 1972 and 1976, the Sports Council provided £4.7 million for a range of voluntary sector facilities (Houlihan 1997). This period also saw local authorities (the sub-national level of government in the UK) become key players in sport policy and the structure of sport in the UK. In the 1970s, it was local authorities that invested in the new facilities, supported by Sports Council grants. It was a period of massive expansion. For example, local authority provision of sport and leisure centres increased from four in 1970 to more than one thousand by the end of the decade (Jackson and Nesti 2001).

This acceptance of sport as a legitimate responsibility of government was reinforced by the publication, in 1975, of a White Paper on Sport and Recreation (Department of the Environment 1975). This acknowledged the importance of sport for the general welfare of the community and emphasised the necessity of national and local government involvement alongside the existing contribution of the voluntary sector.

The free market in sport

From 1979, the policies of successive Conservative governments had a major impact on sport. Whilst there was little clear sport policy *per se*, the Government's broader objectives – minimising the role of the State at national and local level and introducing market forces in public services – were highly influential. The most significant policy development was the introduction of compulsory competitive tendering (CCT), which required local authorities to open up a range of services, including the management of sport and leisure facilities, to free competition in the marketplace. This paved the way for private sector contractors to operate facilities and, later, for charitable trusts to do the same. The impact of CCT also highlights the fact that sport is often a 'policy taker', rather than a 'policy maker' (Dery 1999; King 2009). That is to say, sport is regularly affected by policies designed and implemented in other policy areas, such as health and education.

Jackson and Nesti (2001) argue that the rigidity of CCT led to an over-emphasis on financial efficiency at the expense of quality. Moreover, local authority investment in sport and recreation facilities slowed, effectively halting the massive expansion that defined the previous decade. Indeed, Houlihan (1997) suggests that this period witnessed a decline in local government's key role in fostering wider participation – partly due to financial pressures and partly because CCT resulted in homogenised provision and a reduced incentive for local authorities to take risks. While CCT has long been superseded by other performance management regimes, including Best Value (introduced by the New Labour Government in 1998), private contractors and charitable trusts are now key features of the sports management landscape.

In the 1990s, the status of sport within government improved. The British Sports Council was replaced by a UK Sports Council and an English Sports Council – now known as UK Sport and Sport England. The creation of the National Lottery in 1994 was yet another significant staging post for sports management in the UK, leading to the creation of state-of-the-art facilities within local authorities, and an upgrade of the facility stock in many sports clubs. It also saw the introduction of funding for elite athletes, precipitating a modernisation process in many governing bodies, which until this date had not received significant amounts of public money, and now needed to adapt to their new responsibilities. In 1995, the Department of National Heritage (DNH), where sport policy was then co-ordinated, published *Sport: Raising the Game* (DNH 1995), a wide-ranging document that reinforced several sport policy themes. It emphasised elite sport, traditional competitive sport in schools and accountability among national governing bodies.

The current state of play

The election of the New Labour Government in 1997 resulted in another noticeable shift in sport policy. The main focus, during the next decade, was sport's presumed benefits – both economic and social. As Coalter (2007) points out, the increased emphasis on sport can be explained by key aspects of New Labour's agenda. Sport, it was argued, could contribute to a stronger civil society, address social exclusion, encourage active citizenship and help to develop social capital. Moreover, these presumed externalities were stated more precisely

51

than ever before. The report of *Policy Action Team 10* (Department for Culture, Media and Sport 1999: 23) stated that 'sport can contribute to neighbourhood renewal by improving communities' performance on four key indicators – health, crime, employment and education'. Yet, as Coalter (2007) and others point out, the evidence base around sport's social and economic outcomes is in fact weak and patchy and the report itself acknowledged this assertion. Nevertheless, politicians and policy makers seized on the *potential* benefits of sport highlighted in the report and the latter has remained highly influential, underpinning much sport policy thinking since its publication.

Another important aspect of New Labour's broader agenda was its concern with 'joined-up' government, that is, the notion that key policy themes should be cross-cutting, not strictly demarcated. Here again, sport gained policy prominence precisely because of the assumption that its benefits were wide-ranging and its appeal transcended demographic boundaries. Houlihan and White (2002) describe this broader process as a shift from developing sport *in* the community to developing communities *through* sport. And such developments were also evident outside the UK. In Australia and Canada, certainly, there has been a similar emphasis on sport's socio-economic benefits (Australian Sports Commission 2006; Bloom *et al*. 2005).

In 2007, however, this policy emphasis on the instrumental value of sport was reversed somewhat. James Purnell, the then Secretary of State for Culture, Media and Sport, stated: 'Sport matters in itself … too often sport is justified on the basis of its spill-over benefits' (Purnell 2007). This policy shift has resulted in a firmer focus on sport for sport's sake – perhaps a shift back towards developing sport *in* the community. It has also led to the restructuring of Sport England and a new three-year strategy (Sport England 2008), focused on increasing and maintaining participation, ensuring the quality of people's sporting experience and improving talent development – traditional sports development goals. The broader government focus on sport's presumed social and economic benefits has not been abandoned, but the Department for Culture, Media and Sport now aims to spread responsibility for funding to achieve these outcomes across a wider range of government departments (Tacon 2009).

This latest development also highlights the impact of sport policy on the structure of sport in the UK. A shift in policy emphasis at national government level has led to the restructuring of Sport England, one of the key organisations in the sport landscape. Often the effects of sport policy are less pronounced than this and indeed often effects can run the other way – the structure of sport influencing the way in which policy is conceived and implemented. This was highlighted earlier in relation to CCPR's policy influence in the mid-twentieth century. Despite all the changes and policy shifts, however, enduring themes of policy remain evident today, such as a concern with sport's intrinsic value and its instrumental benefits, the tension between mass participation and elite success and the notion of sport and recreation as welfare. The next section takes a step back from specific sport policy developments to look at some of the theoretical frameworks through which policy, in general, and sport policy, in particular, can be analysed.

THEORETICAL FRAMEWORKS FOR ANALYSING SPORT POLICY

The role of the State

One way to analyse sport policy and the structure of sport is to examine the broad role of the State. In so doing, it is traditional to distinguish between the State, the market and civil society, although these 'social orders' are often interdependent. Hoye *et al.* (2006) define them as follows. The State refers to the structures that govern and rule societies. The market refers broadly to business activity, the home of the private sector. Civil society comprises a web of informal, non-market relationships based around households and communities. Hoye *et al.* show how the intersections of these three social orders create four different sectors: the public sector; the commercial sector; the informal sector; and the voluntary sector. These are illustrated in Figure 4.1.

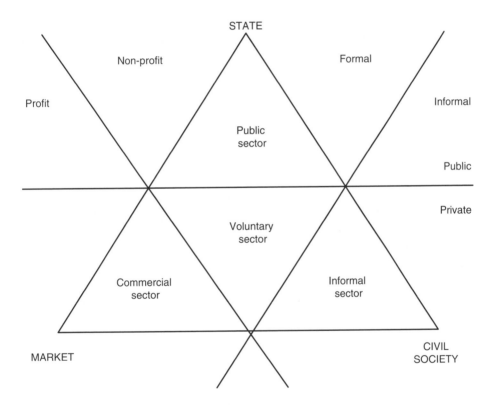

Figure 4.1 *A sector model of society. Adapted from Hoye et al. (2006) and Ibsen and Jorgensen (2002)*

This model provides a framework through which to examine sport policy and the structure of sport. Looking back at the developments within sport policy in the UK outlined in the first section of the chapter, historically sport took place mainly in the informal and voluntary sectors. Indeed, Houlihan (1997) considers that one of the defining features of British sport is the extensive network of national governing bodies and their influential role, certainly in the nineteenth century and the first half of the twentieth century. From the 1960s onwards, when government became more directly involved in sport, through investment via local authorities and the Sports Councils, the public sector became increasingly influential. Likewise, in the last 30 years or so, the commercial sector has become increasingly important. Of course, there have long been professional sports organisations, but the increasing commercialisation of sport, fuelled by pay television, has amplified their role. Also, after the introduction of compulsory competitive tendering in the 1980s, private contractors began to manage sports facilities previously managed within the public sector. Moreover, many large commercial organisations have become increasingly involved in sport through sponsorship of professional sports teams and major sporting events.

Within this framework, several authors have identified key reasons for the State to intervene in how sport is managed. Hoye *et al.* (2006), for example, suggest the following rationale. First, to correct market failure. As discussed, sport is presumed to have a range of social benefits. However, private organisations managing and delivering sport may be unwilling to invest in such social benefits due to a lack of profit incentive. Consequently, the State may opt to intervene in order to fund the gaps in market provision, for example through facility building. Second, because sport, or certain of its aspects, is sometimes seen as a public good, that is, something that once produced can be consumed by additional consumers at no extra cost (Samuelson 1954). Private investors often underproduce such goods, again because of the lack of profit incentive, so again the State may step in. Third, to ensure equity. Where sport is considered widely beneficial, perhaps by improving people's physical health, and where access to it is inequitable, for example because of low income or lack of facilities, the State may interject to address these issues. Finally, the State may intervene in order to regulate or control certain sports or associated activities. For example, following the Hillsborough Stadium disaster, which claimed the lives of 96 Liverpool supporters attending a FA Cup Semi-Final at the home ground of Sheffield Wednesday in 1989, the Government acted to ensure safety in stadia through the Football Spectators Act 1989, which created the Football Licensing Authority and, in turn, established stadium seating requirements.

Other authors have also addressed the question of why governments become involved in sport. Through a comparative analysis of sport policy in the United Kingdom, Australia, Canada, Ireland and the United States, Houlihan (1997) identifies seven main themes that characterise government involvement, some of which overlap with those described above. They are: the control of sports and pastimes of the community; the health benefits of sport and recreation; the use of sport for social integration; sport's role in military preparedness; sport and international prestige; sport as a diplomatic resource; and sport's use in economic development. It is appropriate to highlight one of those themes – the presumed health benefits of sport and recreation, as it appears common to all of the cases. In the nineteenth century, the presumed health benefits of sport and recreation provided the rationale for constructing swimming pools and parks in the UK, identified in the first section of the chapter as one of the first examples of sport-related national government policy. In February 2009, more than 150 years later, the Department of Health published *Be Active, Be Healthy*, a strategy for getting more people involved in physical activity in order to 'benefit individuals and communities, as well as delivering overall cost savings' (Department of Health 2009: 5). The strategy also set out how the Government will support the Physical Activity Alliance, a sector-led umbrella body comprised of leading physical activity-promoting organisations from the voluntary and private sectors.

This illustrates two important issues. First, there are broad continuities in some of the rationales for government involvement in sport. Second, sport policy and the organisations that manage and deliver sport are now situated across a range of interconnected sectors. Looking back at Figure 4.1, it can be seen that this national-level strategy, *Be Active, Be Healthy*, involves the State, the market and civil society. It will be delivered through the public sector, the commercial sector, the voluntary sector and the informal sector. When analysing sport policy and the role of the State, therefore, it is necessary to consider how each of these different areas – and the motivations driving the organisations within them – relate to one another.

Ideologies

Another means of analysing sport policy is to look at the political ideologies that underpin different government approaches to sport. Bramham (2001: 9) describes political ideologies as 'reflections of the world and reflections on the world. They offer a prescription of how the world ought to be and subsequently a guide or mandate for political parties and action.' He then goes on to discuss three broadly defined ideologies: conservatism; liberalism; and social reformism. Conservatism is based on key values of tradition, allegiance and authority, along with an affinity for pragmatism (Scruton 1980). Liberalism stresses a clear divide between public and private spheres and emphasises the efficiency of market forces and consumer choice. Social reformism is underpinned by a belief that substantial government intervention is necessary to address market failure and the inequality and other negative externalities it produces. Linked to this is the key value of altruism (Titmuss 1963). Hoye *et al.* (2006) develop their analysis along similar lines, including socialism as a fourth, separate ideology, which stresses the strong role of the State and centrally controlled resource allocation.

Inevitably, seeking to describe such broad political ideologies involves a great deal of simplification. Nevertheless, examining the implications of these differing ideologies for sport policy can be a useful exercise, one that has been undertaken by a number of authors, including Bramham and Henry (1991), Henry (1993) and Hoye *et al.* (2006). For example, Hoye *et al.* (2006) argue that social reformists tend to see sport as a tool for social development and aim to make sport accessible to the whole community. It is possible to discern elements of this in the sport policy of the UK Labour Government in the 1970s, which sought to promote sporting opportunities as part of the expanding welfare state. More penetrating analyses in this vein can illuminate key aspects of government ideology and how they underpin the direction of sport policy.

Policy analytic frameworks

The theoretical perspectives examined so far are broad and provide a generalised means of looking at developments in sport policy. However, in order to examine sport policy closely, it is necessary to incorporate more detailed theoretical concepts and frameworks developed within the policy analysis literature. Moreover, in order to understand the fine detail of policy decision-making, implementation and so on, it is important to employ theoretical frameworks at the meso-level, that is, the level of national organisations, rather than at the macro, societal level. In a seminal contribution, Houlihan (2005) assesses the value of four such theoretical frameworks – the stages model, institutional analysis, multiple streams and the advocacy coalition framework – and discusses their implications for analysing sport policy.

Several important criteria have been identified against which any theoretical framework for policy analysis needs to be judged (Houlihan 2005: 167–8). First, it should be able to explain both policy stability and change. Second, it should have the capacity to illuminate a range of aspects of the policy process, rather than concentrating on discrete aspects, such as agenda setting or policy impact. Third, it should apply across a range of policy areas. Finally, it should facilitate a medium-term historical analysis of policy – at least five years – to avoid a snapshot approach.

The stages model, previously dominant in policy analysis, divides the policy process into a series of discrete stages. For example, Hogwood and Gunn (1984) identify a nine-stage process, running from 'agenda setting' through to 'policy maintenance, succession or termination'. Many critics, however, have pointed out the weaknesses of such a model. Considering the criteria outlined above, the stages model struggles to explain policy change, due to its assumptions of linearity and rationality, and while it can illuminate many aspects of the policy process, it assumes neat, sequential relationships between discrete stages. It has been applied across a range of policy areas, yet, as Houlihan (2005) points out, it is subject to the same strong criticisms in each. Finally, the model tends to capture particular moments in the policy process, rather than allow examination of dynamic patterns of influence and outcomes over a sustained period (Houlihan 2005).

Institutional analysis can refer both to the role of particular institutions – agencies, departments, etc. – and to shared values and beliefs. Such a perspective can be particularly useful for sport policy analysis as a number of authors (e.g. Green 2004; Henry 1993; Houlihan and White 2002) discuss the importance of a range of institutions in shaping sport policy in the UK. However, as Houlihan (2005: 170) points out, institutionalism is more of an 'analytic orientation' than a specified theoretical framework. Besides, it is weak in explaining change and illuminating a range of aspects of the policy process, as it tends to focus somewhat statically on structures. The multiple streams framework is primarily concerned with agenda setting and disputes the sequential, rationalistic assumptions of previous theoretical frameworks, such as the stages model. Kingdon (1984) identifies three streams – problem, policy and political – which may combine together, through a contingent, even contradictory, process, to enable an issue to get onto the policy agenda. Houlihan (2005) argues that such a framework offers only a partial analysis of stability and change and, also, fails to illuminate a range of policy areas, restricting its focus largely to agenda setting.

The advocacy coalition framework focuses on policy sub-systems, the various coalitions within them and the beliefs that permeate these coalitions. It also incorporates the concept of a 'policy broker', who often mediates between coalitions. Houlihan (2005) argues that this framework broadly meets the criteria outlined above, although its explanation of change is somewhat weak and it perhaps does not take sufficient account of power. He proposes for the analysis of sport policy a modified version of the advocacy coalition framework, which is sensitive to beliefs and values and recognises a number of levels, where each level is partially autonomous, but embedded within a deeper level. For example, it is possible to examine the level of administrative arrangements in relation to sport policy. As described in the first section of the chapter, initially sport in the UK was managed and delivered by national governing bodies, then local authorities became increasingly involved through the management of sports facilities. More recently, the sports councils have played an increasingly important role, as have private organisations, so this level has become increasingly complex. Houlihan describes how the modified advocacy coalition framework allows an analyst to examine the effect of this level on sport policy through the tendency of such administrative units to develop relatively stable preferences for policy tools, perceptions of problems and modes of working.

THE CURRENT STRUCTURE OF SPORT IN THE UK

Government interest and investment in sport has resulted in many upheavals in sports management structures over recent years. Whilst the bodies ultimately responsible for funding and delivering sport have not changed substantially, those under government control have seen their strategic direction and the ways in which they operate change frequently. The devolution of sports policy responsibility to Wales, Scotland and Northern Ireland is just one example of such change. Houlihan and Green (2009) also provide a detailed description of the way in which New Labour's modernisation agenda has affected the structures and priorities of Sport England, UK Sport and national governing bodies. Other non-governmental bodies have some protection from such changes, but are frequently dependent on funding tied to government objectives.

Since late 2007, the structure for funding and delivering sport has been fairly stable. Table 4.1 sets out the key organisations that together constitute the structure of sport in the UK.

Table 4.1 *Key organisations in the structure of sport in the UK*

Organisation	Responsibility	Status	Scope
Government	The Department for Culture, Media and Sport sets sports policy for England, and the devolved administrations set policy for sport in each of their countries. Other departments, such as (in England) the Department for Communities and Local Government and the Department for Environment, Food and Rural Affairs, set the broader policy context within which sport takes place (e.g. by determining the funding received by local authorities, setting the parameters around access to land and water).	Governmental	Home nation
UK Sport	Manages the Government's investment into Olympic and Paralympic sport, with a target of achieving fourth in the Olympic medal table and second in the Paralympic. It distributes funding to national governing bodies of sport to implement their Olympic and Paralympic plans.	Non-departmental public body	UK

Continued

57

Table 4.1 Continued

Organisation	Responsibility	Status	Scope
Home country sports council	Each of the UK's four nations has its own sports council charged with delivering its government sports policy outside of elite sport (and in the case of England, outside school sport). These are: Sport England Sport Northern Ireland sportscotland Sports Council for Wales These bodies also distribute government and lottery funding to sport, supporting capital build and development programmes.	Non-departmental public body	Home nation
Youth Sport Trust	The Youth Sport Trust was established to improve young people's sporting opportunities. It is now charged with managing the Government's investment in school sport in England.	Charity	UK
National governing bodies of sport	Responsible for setting the rules and competition frameworks for individual sports. Most require clubs or individuals to affiliate in order to compete. Many have programmes to grow participation and improve performance in their sport, and receive funding from the sports councils to do so.	Various legal forms	Varying geographical coverage, e.g. home country, Great Britain or UK
Sport and Recreation Alliance (formerly CCPR)	The representative body for the national governing bodies of sport and recreation. It has no direct delivery responsibilities, but ensures the voice of sport is heard in government, and assists its members to meet their responsibilities.	Independent not-for-profit organisation	UK
British Olympic Association & British Paralympic Association	These independent organisations are responsible for preparing Britain's Olympic and Paralympic teams respectively. This includes event logistics and relations with the International Olympic and Paralympic Committees. The 'Commonwealth Games Council' in each home country prepares teams for each Commonwealth Games.	Independent not-for-profit organisation	Great Britain
Local authorities	Local authorities are responsible for key services in their geographical area. As such they are a significant investor in sport and recreation. Local authority expenditure on sport is estimated at £1.7 billion per annum in England.	Local government	Borough, district, county

Organisation	Responsibility	Status	Scope
Management contractors	The majority of local authority sports facilities are now managed by specialist management organisations. These include large-scale private companies which operate facilities throughout the country, and also charitable trusts, established by individual authorities to manage their facilities.	Independent firms and trusts	Varied
County sports partnerships	These partnerships are responsible for bringing together local authorities and sports bodies in local areas to drive up sporting participation. They receive core funding from Sport England.	Range of legal forms	English county
Professional bodies	A number of professional bodies support the individuals working in sport and recreation. These include the Institute of Sport, Parks and Leisure and the Institute of Sport and Recreation Management. The standards for sporting qualifications are set by SkillsActive.	Range of legal forms	UK

Getting ready for 2012

The successful bid to host the 2012 Olympic and Paralympic Games in London required the addition of some further organisations to deliver a successful games. These are set out in Table 4.2.

Table 4.2 *Key organisations responsible for the 2012 Olympic and Paralympic Games*

Organisation	Responsibility	Status
London Organising Committee for the Olympic and Paralympic Games	LOCOG is responsible for preparing and staging the Games. This includes agreeing the event venues with the International Olympic Committee, managing the venues during games time, ensuring effective athlete and official transportation and accommodation, etc.	Independent limited company. Activities largely financed through commercial partners
Olympic Delivery Authority	The ODA is charged with developing and building the new venues and infrastructure required to deliver the Games.	Public body
Olympic Park Legacy Company	The OPLC will take charge of those areas of the Olympic Park which fall outside the Lee Valley Regional Park Authority. It will be responsible for ensuring viable post-games usage for key venues such as the main Olympic stadium and the aquatics centre. A key aim of the OPLC is to ensure sporting usage of such venues.	Company established by the Government and Mayor of London

CASE STUDY 2: BRITISH CYCLING – MEETING THE NEEDS OF MEMBERS WHILST ACHIEVING GOVERNMENT TARGETS

This case study will illustrate how an independent national governing body of sport has interacted with government across a range of agendas.

The British Cycling Federation was formed in 1959, bringing together the cycling bodies interested in road and track racing. Now known simply as British Cycling, the organisation is recognised as the national governing body for cycle-sport by the Union Cycliste Internationale, and is responsible for competition across the majority of cycling disciplines. Whilst best known for its success at track cycling in recent Olympics, British Cycling is also significantly involved in efforts to increase recreational participation in cycling.

As with many NGBs, British Cycling must meet the needs of a wide range of stakeholders to secure its success. This begins with its membership of 29,000 individuals, who in return for their subscription fee require information, racing licences and insurance plus participation and competition opportunities, and coaching and development pathways. Some of these services are delivered direct to members, whilst others are delivered via British Cycling's network of 1,400 affiliated clubs.

British Cycling operates a number of schemes to increase cycling across all age groups. These include its 'Go-Ride' scheme, offering 90,000 opportunities for children in 2008–9, and the 'Everyday Cycling' and more recent 'Skyrides' targeting adults and families. This work is supported both by Sport England funding, as part of its strategy to increase adult participation in sport, and also by commercial sponsorship from British Sky Broadcasting. The high performance element of British Cycling's work is substantially supported by UK Sport, with clear targets for Olympic and Paralympic performances, in line with UK Sport's own objectives of securing fourth place at the 2012 Olympics and second place at the Paralympics.

The potential for cycling to contribute to wider policy agendas such as increasing levels of active travel also enables British Cycling to partner other government departments. For instance, British Cycling is represented within Cycling England which allocates Department for Transport funding to promote cycling.

Government policy, rules and regulations can of course also impact adversely on a sport, and cycling in particular is affected by restrictions in its ability to stage races on roads. In recent years many road races have been cancelled due to increases in policing costs. This is a clear example of an unrelated element of government policy inadvertently undermining successful sports policy. Notwithstanding this, the recent history of British Cycling demonstrates how an independent sporting body can be an effective delivery partner for government policy.

Ian Drake, Chief Executive Officer of British Cycling, commented:

British Cycling is 83 per cent funded through national and local government and this support has transformed the organisation over the past decade and seen our world ranking grow from seventeenth to the number one cycling nation in the world with 14 Olympic and 20 Paralympic Medals won by the GB cycling team in the Beijing 2008 Olympic and Paralympic Games.

We have successfully worked with the Department for Culture, Media and Sport, UK Sport and Sport England to implement a robust and transparent strategy to deliver both international success and, more recently, a significant increase in participation in cycling. This increase has been recorded across all areas of cycling – as a sport, recreational activity and a form of sustainable transport supported by our work with the Department for Transport.

By bringing together government support and commercial funding, through our principal partner British Sky Broadcasting, as well as our volunteer network, we have a winning formula which has the potential to deliver the single biggest legacy of London 2012 in terms of more people playing sport and more people being active.

SUMMARY

This chapter has outlined how the current sporting landscape in the UK has evolved through the combined efforts of independent, sport-focused associations and the interest and investment of government, sometimes for the sake of sport itself, but more often in pursuit of specific social outcomes. Furthermore, sport has also been shaped by broader political agendas, such as the desire to introduce competition in public services. This pattern will no doubt continue in years to come, but there does now seem to be a growing understanding of the respective roles and responsibilities of the funding, development and delivery agents of sports, and an emerging consensus of the value of sport in its own right, alongside its potential to contribute to wider social agendas.

REVIEW QUESTIONS

1   How would you characterise government sport policy until 1960?
2   Describe various theoretical frameworks that can be used to analyse sport policy.
3   Explain the importance of the sports councils in the UK.
4   Outline the various stakeholder groups whose needs national governing bodies of sport may seek to meet.

FURTHER READING

Bergsgard, N., Houlihan, B., Mangset, P., Nodland, S.I. and Rommetvedt, H. (2007) *Sport policy: A comparative analysis of stability and change*, Oxford: Butterworth-Heinemann.

Houlihan, B. (1997) *Sport, policy and politics: A comparative analysis*, London: Routledge.

Houlihan, B. and White, A. (2002) *The politics of sports development: Development of sport or development through sport?*, London: Routledge.

Hylton, K., Bramham, P., Jackson, D. and Nesti, M. (2008) *Sports development: Policy, process and practice*, 2nd ed., London: Routledge.

King, N. (2009) *Sport policy and governance: Local perspectives*, Oxford: Butterworth-Heinemann.

For specific policy-related documents, see the report of the Wolfenden Committee (1960) *Sport and the community*. Also, more recently, the PAT 10 report – Department for Culture, Media and Sport (1999) *Policy Action Team 10: Report to the Social Exclusion Unit – Arts and Sport* – and the joint Department for Culture, Media and Sport/Strategy Unit (2002) *Game Plan* are both important.

WEBSITES

Sport England
    www.sportengland.org
UK Sport
    www.uksport.gov.uk
Youth Sport Trust
    www.youthsporttrust.org

For up-to-date knowledge on policy developments affecting sport, visit the Sport and Recreation Alliance website (www.sportandrecreation.org.uk). This also has links to the websites of over 300 governing and representative bodies of sport and recreation that are members of the Sport and Recreation Alliance.

REFERENCES

Australian Sports Commission (2006) *The case for sport in Australia,* Canberra: Australian Sports Commission.

Bloom, M., Grant, M. and Watt, D. (2005) *Strengthening Canada: The socio-economic benefits of sport participation in Canada,* Ottawa: Conference Board of Canada.

Bramham, P. (2001) 'Sports policy', in K. Hylton, P. Bramham, D. Jackson and M. Nesti (eds) *Sports development: Policy, process and practice,* London: Routledge.

Bramham, P. and Henry, I. (1991) 'Explanations of the organisation of sport in British society', *International Review for the Sociology of Sport* 26: 139–50.

Coalter, F. (2007) *A wider social role for sport: Who's keeping the score?,* London: Routledge.

Department for Culture, Media and Sport (1999) *Policy Action Team 10: Report to the Social Exclusion Unit – Arts and Sport,* London: Her Majesty's Stationery Office.

Department of the Environment (1975) *Sport and recreation,* Cmnd. 6200, London: Her Majesty's Stationery Office.

Department of Health (2009) *Be active, be healthy: A plan for getting the nation moving,* London: Her Majesty's Stationery Office.

Department of National Heritage (1995) *Sport: Raising the game,* London: Department of National Heritage.

Dery, D. (1999) 'Policy by the way: When policy is incidental to making other policies', *Journal of Public Policy* 18, 2: 163–76.

Green, M. (2004) 'Changing policy priorities for sport in England: The emergence of elite sport development as a key policy concern', *Leisure Studies* 23, 4: 365–85.

Henry, I. (1993) *The politics of leisure policy,* London: Macmillan.

Hogwood, B. and Gunn, L. (1984) *Policy analysis for the real world,* London: Oxford University Press.

Holt, R. (1989) *Sport and the British: A modern history,* Oxford: Oxford University Press.

Houlihan, B. (1997) *Sport, policy and politics: A comparative analysis,* London: Routledge.

—— (2005) 'Public sector sport policy: Developing a framework for analysis', *International Review for the Sociology of Sport* 40, 2: 163–85.

Houlihan, B. and Green, M. (2009) *Modernisation and sport: The reform of Sport England and UK Sport,* Loughborough: Political Studies Association.

Houlihan, B. and White, A. (2002) *The politics of sports development: Development of sport or development through sport?,* London: Routledge.

Hoye, R., Smith, A., Westerbeek, H., Stewart, B. and Nicholson, M. (2006) *Sport management: Principles and applications,* London: Elsevier.

Ibsen, B. and Jorgensen, P. (2002) 'Denmark: The cultural and voluntary development of sport for all', in L. DaCosta and A. Miragaya (eds) *Worldwide experiences and trends in sport for all,* Oxford: Meyer and Meyer.

Jackson, D. and Nesti, M. (2001) 'Sports practice', in K. Hylton, P. Bramham, D. Jackson and M. Nesti (eds) *Sports development: Policy, process and practice,* London: Routledge.

King, N. (2009) *Sport policy and governance: Local perspectives,* Oxford: Butterworth-Heinemann.

Kingdon, J. (1984) *Agendas, alternatives and public policy*, Boston, MA: Little, Brown.

Purnell, J. (2007) *World Class Community Sport – Speech by Rt. Hon. James Purnell*, Secretary of State for Culture, Media and Sport, London: Department for Culture, Media and Sport.

Samuelson, P. (1954) 'The pure theory of public expenditure', *Review of Economics and Statistics* 36: 387–9.

Scruton, R. (1980) *The meaning of conservatism*, Harmondsworth: Penguin.

Shoard, M. (1987) *This land is our land: The struggle for Britain's countryside*, London: Paladin.

Sport England (2008) *Sport England strategy 2008–2011*, London: Sport England.

Tacon, R. (2009) *Getting the ball rolling: Sport's contribution to the 2008–2011 public service agreements*, London: Central Council of Physical Recreation.

Titmuss, R. (1963) *Essays on 'The welfare state'*, 2nd ed., London: Unwin University Books.

Chapter 5

Corporate governance and the regulation of sport

Geoff Walters and Sean Hamil, Birkbeck, University of London

TOPICS

The peculiar economics of the sport industry • Regulation in US sports • Regulation in European sport

OBJECTIVES

At the end of reading this chapter you should be able to:

- Understand the 'peculiar' economics of the professional sport industry;
- Discuss the differences between the US model of sport and the European model of sport;
- Identify different ways in which US Major Leagues regulate professional sport;
- Understand why there is a growing recognition of the need for regulation in European sport.

KEY TERMS

Competitive balance – long-term outcome uncertainty of a sports league is synonymous with maintaining a degree of competitive balance in sporting competition.
Joint production and interdependence – in sport, there is a need for competition in order to produce a sporting contest, hence the need for a degree of interdependence and cooperation between teams.
Outcome uncertainty – to maintain high levels of interest there is a need for sporting teams to be relatively evenly matched to create uncertainty.
Regulation – the coordination of sport teams' activities through regulation in order to create competitive balance and sporting uncertainty, and to help to provide financial stability.

OVERVIEW

The aim of this chapter is to introduce the reader to the economics of the professional team sport industry and the implications for the regulation of league activity. The peculiar economics of the sport industry have long been recognized since the seminal articles by Rottenburg (1956) and Neale (1964). This chapter begins by providing a background to three key characteristics of professional sports leagues: joint production and interdependence; outcome uncertainty; and competitive balance. These features demonstrate the peculiar economics of sport and illustrate that there is a need for the coordination of sport teams' activities through regulatory controls at the league level in order to ensure that no one team achieves dominance/market power in a league, to create competitive balance and sporting uncertainty, and to help to provide financial stability. The chapter then focuses on professional sport leagues in the US, which are characterized by profit maximization, and are heavily regulated. Three types of regulatory controls are discussed. The US leagues are then contrasted with European sport and professional football in particular, in which utility maximization takes precedence and where the leagues impose far less regulatory control than in the US. The financial implications of a lighter regulatory environment are considered, before discussing how regulation in European sport has become a topical area for debate with a number of sports leagues and governing bodies in Europe implementing regulatory measures. The chapter concludes by considering how increasing regulatory controls in European sports are precipitating the move towards a more coordinated and overarching licensing system.

CASE STUDY: FINANCIAL INSTABILITY IN ENGLISH FOOTBALL

Since the formation of the Premier League in English football in 1992, the 92 clubs in the Premier League and Football League have, on aggregate, consistently failed to achieve pre-tax profits. There has not been a single year during this period in which the 20 member clubs in the Premier League have made a collective pre-tax profit. This is also the case for the three leagues within the Football League. For example, in the three seasons between 2005–06 and 2007–08, the 92 football clubs in the Premier League and Football League collectively lost £972 million (Deloitte, 2008, 2009). Chronic unprofitability has two implications: increasing debt levels and bankruptcy. Aggregate debt for the clubs in the Premier League in 2007–08 reached £3.1 billion (Deloitte, 2009: 59). This has led to the situation where unless a football club is able to trade their way out of debt, which for the vast majority of clubs given the long history of loss-making in the Premier League and Football League is unlikely, the only way they will ultimately be able to address their debt issues is either by debt write-off through new investment from existing or new investors, or through entering the financial administration process. Between 1992 and 2009, the period when English football entered an unprecedented period of financial revenue expansion through lucrative television broadcasting deals, increased attendances and very beneficial sponsorship deals, paradoxically there have been financial problems at a significant number of Football League clubs, resulting in 52 incidences of administration (well over half of the 72 clubs in the Football League have been bankrupt between 1992 and 2009) (Deloitte, 2009, Appendices, page 13). Does the poor financial performance of clubs within English football demonstrate a need for a stronger regulatory framework?

THE PECULIAR ECONOMICS OF THE SPORT INDUSTRY

Over the last 30 years the professional sport industry has undergone rapid commercialization and overseen large increases in revenues, particularly from broadcasting. This has led to an increasing focus on the business of professional sports. However, there are particular features of the professional sport industry that distinguish it from conventional business. In particular, the seminal work of Neale (1964) outlined the peculiar economic characteristics of professional sports leagues and teams, demonstrating that the analysis of professional sports is distinct from conventional industry analysis. Neale identified three distinct features that distinguish the way that sports operate; these features have implications for the way that sport leagues are regulated.

Joint production and interdependence

Conventional economic analysis assumes that a position of monopoly power in an industry is desirable. In this market, a firm has significant control over price, the demand curve is relatively inelastic and a firm is able to make supernormal profits. However, in professional team sports, it is impossible for a position of monopoly power to exist. In order for professional sport to function, a sports team or individual athlete requires a competitor to produce the sporting product – a match and/or the league competition. Professional sports are therefore reliant upon a degree of interdependence and cooperation between teams. For example, in the English football industry, the 20 competitors within the structure of the Premier League are reliant upon each other in order to function as individual football teams, and therefore they have no desire to eliminate their competition. As such, the product of a Premier League team is an 'inverted joint product' (Neale, 1964: 2) in the sense that what is produced is not entirely the product of an individual team, illustrating the interdependence that exists within sporting competition.

Neale (1964) argued that the league occupies a position of monopoly power and therefore acts as a firm (within a conventional economic framework). For instance, there are a fixed number of league members; the league determines the games played; entry to a league is restricted; and often there are no other leagues that are in direct competition. However, this perspective assumes that an individual sports team has no control over output (Downward et al., 2009). In contrast, Sloane (1971) argued that the teams that compete within a league had certain decision-making powers and therefore leagues operate more like a cartel of firms in an oligopoly market rather than a monopoly. In the context of the UK, this analysis is particularly insightful given the creation of the Premier League; in effect this was a breakaway of the top clubs from the previous cartel model of the Football League. While the cartel model is considered a more appropriate model to understand sports leagues (Downward et al., 2009), both the monopoly model and cartel model demonstrate that professional sports leagues are made up of competing interdependent teams, which highlights the peculiarity of the structure and the functioning of sporting competition in contrast to conventional business industry.

Outcome uncertainty

A second feature of the professional sports industry is that the sporting product is not only reliant upon collaboration and interdependence but it is also affected by the degree of outcome uncertainty. It is held that demand for the sports product is positively related to uncertainty of outcome (Gratton and Taylor, 2000) and that to maintain high levels of supporter interest there is a need for sporting teams to be relatively evenly matched to create uncertainty. Outcome uncertainty is a key feature underpinning the economics of professional sports leagues and was first recognized in the seminal articles by Rottenburg (1956) and Neale (1964). However, outcome uncertainty can take three forms (Cairns *et al.*, 1986). Short-run uncertainty relates to the outcome of an individual match. Medium-term uncertainty relates to within-season uncertainty (who will win the league) or seasonal uncertainty that is team specific. Finally long-term uncertainty refers to the level of uncertainty within a league over a number of years. The promotion of long-term uncertainty requires that leagues are not dominated by a small number of teams and that they are competitively balanced.

Competitive balance

Long-term outcome uncertainty of a sports league is synonymous with maintaining a degree of competitive balance in sporting competition and underpins the redistributive mechanisms in US sports (see next section). Competitive imbalance is seen as a negative aspect that arises from the dominance of large-market clubs with higher turnovers, larger budgets and the ability to pay greater salaries and attract the most talented players. It has been argued that competitive balance is important for three reasons. First, it can lead to the creation of large income gaps within and between leagues (Michie and Oughton, 2004: 1). This creates an incentive to gamble on playing success which, second, can lead to the threat of bankruptcy. Third, competitive imbalance can result in the threat of rival league formation (such as a European Super-League). While Kesenne (2004) argued that competitive imbalance could actually be good for a sport in the case of a small-market club dominating, in a win-maximizing league – as in the case of English football – this type of imbalance is unlikely to occur. Indeed, throughout the course of the 1990s, it has been argued that competitive balance in the Premier League has decreased (Michie and Oughton, 2004).

CASE STUDY: COMPETITIVE BALANCE IN MAJOR LEAGUE BASEBALL – THE BLUE RIBBON REPORT

In 2000 a report produced by the Independent Members of the Commissioner's Blue Ribbon Panel on Baseball Economics was published setting out the concerns about competitive balance in Major League Baseball. The report argued that growing disparities in revenue and payroll between teams in Major League Baseball was causing problems of competitive imbalance. It looked at the period 1995–99 and concluded that the changes introduced as part of the 1996 Collective Bargaining Agreement with the Major League Baseball Players Association, including limited revenue sharing and payroll tax, had not enabled low-revenue teams to gain sufficient revenues in order to compete, with the resultant effect being that success was more related to market size (the larger teams) and there was a decrease in competitive balance. It argued that it had led to many clubs increasing ticket prices to remain competitive, thereby potentially damaging the position of baseball as the affordable family spectator sport.

The Blue Ribbon Report claimed that major changes were needed in order to improve the competitive balance of baseball. Six key recommendations were suggested, including greater revenue sharing; a competitive balance tax; increasing central fund distributions through the creation of a 'Commissioner's Pool'; a competitive balance draft; a rule 4 draft; and franchise locations (Levin et al., 2000: 8–10). Despite these recommendations, it was argued that the calls for change were based on an incorrect diagnosis of the problem within Major League Baseball as the National League had seen an increase in competitive balance and there was little evidence to show a positive relationship between market size and winning (Eckard, 2001). Whilst the economic evidence does not point to a relationship between market size and competitive balance in Major League Baseball, what this case study demonstrates is that maintaining competitive balance and sporting competition is a key regulatory concern of league organizers in US sports.

The preceding three key features of the professional sport industry demonstrate that the peculiar economics of professional sport requires regulation over and above what is expected within conventional industries. It can be argued that regulatory controls at the league level are necessary in order to prevent one team achieving dominance and market power in a league, to create competitive balance and sporting uncertainty, and to help to provide financial stability. The following section considers the issue of regulation in US sports before contrasting the US model of sport with the European model of sport.

REGULATION IN US SPORTS

In the five main professional team sports in the US (National Football League (NFL); Major League Baseball (MLB); National Basketball Association (NBA); National Hockey League (NHL); and Major League Soccer (MLS)) the leagues operate as closed leagues and there is no promotion or relegation at the end of the season. The leagues also have the authority to impose strong regulatory controls in the product and labour markets that limit the ability for one team to dominate league competition. These controls involve cross-subsidies or redistributive mechanisms, the purpose of which are to ensure a high level of competitive balance and uncertainty of outcome (El Hodiri and Quirk, 1971; Fort and Quirk, 1992). The owners of the Major League franchises accept these restraints on individual business autonomy in order to create competitive balance and to enhance the attractiveness of the sport product to spectators and TV viewers. However, critically, they also create an environment where all owners of sport franchises can make profits and the league is financially stable. Indeed, the professional sports model in the US is fundamentally driven by the desire for clubs and leagues to maximise profit. This has long been accepted and understood as the objective of US sports (Fort and Quirk, 1995; Neale, 1964). Although such regulatory controls would normally be prohibited under US legislation, professional sports leagues have been granted exemption from antitrust legislation. The following regulatory controls are common within the major leagues in the US. The first two – the player draft system and salary caps – are targeted at player labour markets while revenue sharing focuses on the redistribution of income.

The player draft system

The draft system in US sports involves professional sports teams in the major leagues picking players for the following season, predominantly from the US college system. The draft system was first introduced in the NFL in 1936, followed by the Basketball Association of America in 1947 (the precursor to the NBA), the NHL in 1963 and the MLB in 1965. The draft system is considered a way to reallocate talent between teams in order to maintain competitive balance. This is particularly the case in the NFL which operates a reverse order of finish draft in which the teams finishing at the bottom of the league get first pick, allowing them to select the most promising college players. In the other Major Leagues the draft system is based on a lottery, although the lottery is skewed in favour of the teams finishing lower down the leagues from the previous season.

Salary caps

In US sports one of the key regulatory mechanisms is the salary cap. Salary caps have been justified on the basis that it will help to maintain competitive balance by ensuring that teams from smaller cities in the US with smaller revenues are able to compete with large city teams. Salary caps can focus on individual wages and set a maximum (and minimum) limit on player earnings. This is the case in the NBA where both maximum and minimum salary levels are dependent upon the number of years of service in the league (see case study). Alternatively salary caps can be applied at the aggregate level and a maximum and minimum limit set on the total that a team can spend on their players. Often this limit is determined by the league in association with the players association through a collective bargaining agreement (CBA). In the NFL, for instance, the league negotiated the CBA with the National Football League Players Association. For 2009 the maximum salary cap was $123m per team and the minimum cap was $107.748m (www.nfllabor.com). However, for season 2010–11, the NFL have scrapped the salary cap after the team owners opted out of the final year of the CBA, arguing that players were paid too much.

The aggregate salary cap can also be a hard cap or a soft cap. In the NFL the cap has always been a hard cap; this means that teams are not allowed, under any circumstances, to exceed the cap and face a variety of penalties for doing so, including fines and losing their pick in the NFL draft. A soft cap allows teams to exceed the cap level for certain reasons. This is the case in the NBA (see case study) and in the MLB where a luxury tax exists for teams where aggregate salaries exceed the cap. In the MLS there is a designated player rule that, from 2010, allows the salaries of two players in the squads to be exempt from the salary cap (www. mlssoccer.com). This has been a way for teams in the MLS to attract international players and to improve the brand of the MLS (for example, David Beckham at LA Galaxy and Freddie Ljungberg at Seattle Sounders). However, a soft cap does not necessarily have an impact on competitive balance. For example, although Fort and Quirk (1995) argued that a salary cap could impact on competitive balance, in a study of the NBA they found that the soft cap had no significant effect.

CASE STUDY: THE NBA SALARY CAP

In the NBA the salary cap is determined by the Collective Bargaining Agreement between the National Basketball Players Association and the league (the NBA). The league calculates the salary cap based on the projected Basketball Related Income (BRI) for the forthcoming season and an agreed percentage of the BRI is reserved for player salaries. In 2005 a six-year CBA was agreed between the league and the Players Association. The deal runs until the 2010–11 season with an option to extend it for a further season. In the CBA it was agreed that the percentage of BRI that can be spent on player salaries was 49 per cent in 2005–06, rising to 51 per cent for seasons 2006–07 through to 2010–11. The league then divides this figure by 30 (the number of teams in the NBA). For the 2009–10 season this produced an overall salary cap per team of $57.7m. The CBA also states that NBA teams must pay a minimum aggregate salary that is no less than 75 per cent of the salary cap ($43.275m). However, the NBA salary cap is a soft cap as there are certain exceptions and teams are able to pay aggregate salaries that exceed the cap. For example, NBA teams are allowed to exceed the cap to re-sign their own players and they are allowed to have one player in the squad outside of the salary cap. Moreover, those teams that go over a set level (61 per cent of BRI) face a tax of $1 for every $1 over this level. In 2008–09 the New York Knicks paid a tax of $23.7m. This tax goes back to the league, which then redistributes it amongst teams under the tax level. The CBA also states the maximum and minimum salaries of individual players in the NBA dependent upon years of service in the NBA. The maximum salary for a player of between 0 and 6 years' service is 25 per cent of the salary cap; between 7 and 9 years it is 30 per cent; and for 10 years or more it is 35 per cent of the salary cap.

Source: www.nba.com

Revenue sharing

Revenue sharing exists as a way to redistribute income amongst sports teams within a league to ensure a level of parity between those teams that generate smaller revenues and those with much larger revenues. There are two main types of revenue sharing. The first relates to broadcasting income. In 1961 the US Congress passed the Sports Broadcasting Act which meant that US sports leagues were exempt from antitrust legislation and were therefore able to negotiate collective deals and redistribute the income between their member teams. This was a result of the NFL appealing to Congress after they had been prohibited from signing collective broadcasting contracts (Szymanski, 2009). Television contracts negotiated and sold by the Major Leagues to the national broadcasters are redistributed between member teams whilst local television contracts are not shared (Downward *et al.*, 2009). The second main type of revenue sharing is from gate receipts. The rationale underpinning this is that teams with large support that generate large revenues on a match day would subsidize those with much smaller revenues from gate receipts. While the NFL redistributes 40 per cent of revenues from gate receipts to the away team, over time this has become less common. Both the NBA and NHL do not share gate revenues. In the case of the NBA, attempts to introduce sharing of gate revenue in 1980 were blocked by the teams with the largest attendances (Downward *et al.*, 2009).

REGULATION IN EUROPEAN SPORT

The model of professional sport in Europe is different to that of the US, so much so that the 'European model of sport' has been recognized and debated within the European Union. Two key characteristics of the European model that differentiate it from US sports are that sports are structured around a pyramid system. The pyramid structure recognises that there is interdependence between all levels of a sport, from the governing body at the top of the pyramid to the grassroots at the bottom; this is in stark contrast to US sports where few links exist between professional leagues and grassroots sport (Gardiner *et al.*, 2006). Second, whereas the US leagues are closed leagues, in Europe sports leagues are based on promotion and relegation. This means that teams are able to move between leagues within a particular sport, which again is very different to the US closed league system.

There are further features that distinguish European sport from the US model. For example, added complexity exists because there is competition not just at the national level but at a European level. In professional football, the most successful clubs from the 53 European nations affiliated to UEFA compete in the two main UEFA club competitions – the Champions League and the Europa League. In Rugby Union teams from a number of European countries compete in the Heineken Cup. An additional feature of European sports is the focus on sporting success. Whereas teams from the major leagues in the US are focused on profit maximization, in Europe it can be argued that sporting success takes priority and that sports teams are utility maximizers. This was first recognized by Sloane (1971), who declared that the objective of a football club was to maximize utility (defined as playing success, average attendance, league health, recorded profit and after-tax profit) whilst remaining financially solvent. More recently, it has been suggested that the objective of a football club is to maximize win percentage (Szymanski and Smith, 1997).

These features demonstrate that sports leagues in Europe are more complex than in the US. The complexity of the structure and organization of sport in Europe has implications for the way that leagues are regulated. For example, the open league system negates the need for pure competitive balance in that there is uncertainty of outcome at different levels of the league/pyramid; therefore it can be argued that there is not the same requirement for regulatory intervention in order to maximize uncertainty of outcome and competitive balance. Where sporting success prevails over profit maximization, there is less incentive to implement regulation to ensure that collectively teams are able to make a financial profit. The European dimension of professional sports leagues also adds complexity to the issue of regulation as the regulatory framework that governs many sports needs to have both supranational and national specificity (Gardiner *et al.*, 2006). In this sense there is less incentive for a national governing body to implement strong regulatory controls if this puts teams from within its jurisdiction at a sporting disadvantage compared to other teams in Europe.

These features of professional sports leagues in Europe have meant that, over the course of the 1990s and the growing commercialism of professional sport, there has been a laissez-faire approach to regulation. This approach has three key implications. First, it has created a situation where those teams with lower revenues are unable to accumulate playing talent. While in the US there are labour market regulations that act as redistributive measures to ensure that no one team, or a small number of teams, can accumulate the best players and that there is a relatively equal distribution of playing talent across all teams in the league, such labour market regulations are not in place to the same extent in many European sports. Second, where teams with lower revenues are unable to accumulate playing talent, this has resulted in a small number of rich clubs (usually those clubs within large cities) that are able to build more competitive teams, particularly given that the source of competitive advantage on the field of play is the best players. Third, evidence has shown that there is a strong relationship between league position (sporting success) and wage levels (Szymanski and Kuypers, 1999); within a utility-maximizing league where there is a free, unrestrained market for player contracts and player salaries then there are clear incentives for all clubs, not just those seeking to win the league title, but those seeking to compete to qualify for European competition or to avoid relegation, to engage in the bidding to hire and retain the best playing talent. The impact of a lack of regulation is that clubs drive a highly inflationary spiral in player wages and transfer fees, which then leads to many spending beyond their means to achieve their immediate sporting objectives.

This is best illustrated by the situation in English football where there has been a huge increase in player wages during the past 20 years and many clubs have suffered financially as a result of overspending. For example, since 1992 there have been 54 instances of administration. While it has been argued that football clubs are not in danger of going out of business due to poor financial management (Kuper and Szymanski, 2009), it can be argued that the large number of clubs entering into administration has damaged the integrity of professional football due to the large number of unprotected creditors that have to accept a proportion of the total debt that they are owed. The example of Portsmouth Football Club is indicative of this trend (see case study). Moreover the UK tax authorities have also lost out so that a large part of the cost of failing English football clubs has been carried by the public purse; in effect a public sector subsidy to a failing private business sector. Therefore, while the US leagues justify regulation in order to prevent competitive imbalance, create sporting uncertainty and help to provide financial stability, it can be argued that the overriding argument for regulation within the European model of sport is to protect the financial stability of member clubs.

CASE STUDY: PORTSMOUTH FOOTBALL CLUB

Following a season of turbulence off the pitch, in which the club had four different owners, in February 2010 Portsmouth Football Club attained the dubious honour of becoming the first team from the Premier League to enter into administration. The level of financial mismanagement was contained within the creditors report, published in April 2010. The accounts show that increasing player wages led to losses of almost £54m between 2007 and 2009, with wages accounting for 109 per cent of turnover in 2009. This led to increasing debts which totalled £119m. (See Table 5.1.)

Table 5.1 *Portsmouth Football Club: Financial performance, 2006–09*

	2006	2007	2008	2009
Turnover (£000s)	36,068,331	40,245,150	70,476,266	59,920,362
Staff wages (£000s)	24,801,707	36,857,581	54,679,563	65,187,128
Wage–turnover ratio	68.76	91.58	77.59	108.79
Pre-tax loss (£000s)	–912,397	–23,452,246	–16,882,334	–13,473,320

Source: Portsmouth City Football Club (Ltd), Creditors Report: 31

This situation was clearly unsustainable and led to administration. However, what the creditors report lays bare is that when a football club enters into administration the tax authorities and other unprotected creditors lose out. In total Portsmouth Football Club owes £17.1m in unpaid tax and VAT. Many other small creditors are owed significant sums including the City Council (£29,000); South Central Ambulance Service (£19,535); and the St John's Ambulance (£2,701). For Portsmouth to exit administration, 75 per cent of the creditors will have to accept a proportion of the total debt owed; this could have implications for many of the small businesses. However, the Football Creditors Rule ensures that players and other clubs are protected and are given secured creditor status, thereby guaranteeing that they will continue to receive wages or monies owed to them. While this football industry-specific rule is designed to protect football clubs from the reckless financial behaviour of those peer clubs which fall into bankruptcy and financial administration, the morality of this ruling is firmly tested when a player earning many thousands of pounds per week is guaranteed his money yet many other creditors have to accept a proportion of the money owed. This situation damages the integrity of the football industry and, in May 2010, the HMRC issued a writ against the Premier League and the Football League challenging the legality of the Football Creditors Rule.

In light of the financial implications arising from the lack of regulatory controls within the European model of sport it can be argued that proper and appropriate regulation is an issue that governing bodies and leagues in Europe have to address. Although historically there has been a lack of regulation, over the past decade there has been a gradual increase in regulatory assertiveness. This is particularly true in English football, where set against the context of a very high level of financial instability and bankruptcy in the Football League, and over-indebtedness and over-dependence on altruistic owners in the Premier League, there has been an evolution in the regulatory role of the governing bodies from an essentially laissez-faire approach with regulatory intervention seen as a last resort, to one where the Football Association, the Premier League and the Football League have increasingly found it necessary to undertake direct regulatory intervention in order to address a series of challenges emanating from the inability of member clubs to operate in a financially sustainable manner. In other sports within Europe, similar regulatory controls exist. Four types of regulation that are aimed at improving financial performance are discussed below.

Salary caps

Salary caps have been introduced in a number of sports within Europe. For example, they have been in place in League Two of the Football League since 2003 (the Salary Cost Management Protocol), limiting the amount that a club can spend on player wages to 60 per cent of turnover, while total spending on wages must not exceed 75 per cent. Despite the best efforts of the Football League, the chairmen of the clubs in League One and the Championship have never voted to implement the salary cap on a mandatory basis as this is seen as excessive regulation. This demonstrates the difficulties in implementing a salary cap within an open league system – clubs do not want to face restrictions on what they pay players in the pursuit of promotion or to avoid relegation. A salary cap has also never been a realistic consideration in the Premier League given that clubs compete in Europe and do not want to be at a disadvantage. This is currently a concern in rugby union. In the Guinness Premiership in England, clubs face a maximum salary cap of £4m, which has had two implications: a number of English players have left to play in France where the cap is set at £6m, and the top English sides are expressing concern that they will not be able to compete in European competition (the Heineken Cup). What is also interesting, however, is that, even with the salary cap, a number of clubs in rugby union and rugby league (where a cap of £1.6m was in place in 2010) have faced financial difficulties. This suggests that a salary cap does not necessarily guarantee financial stability.

Sporting sanctions

In 2004 the Football League introduced a sporting sanction whereby member clubs receive a ten-point penalty for entering into administration. The objective of the sporting sanction rule is to act as a deterrent to administration following poor governance and financial management. It is also designed to ensure that clubs do not gain a competitive advantage by writing off debt and to make directors more accountable for the way they run the club. However, given that there have been a large number of clubs that have entered into administration since 2004, the extent to which this ruling acts as a deterrent is unclear. Portsmouth (see case study) were the first club in the Premier League to enter into administration and faced a nine-point deduction.

Fit and proper test

Within a number of sports there are moves towards increasing transparency and accountability through the application of a fit and proper test. For example, in football, the Football League first introduced a fit and proper person test for club directors in 2004, with the Premier League and the Football Association (who apply their test to clubs in the Football Conference) also doing so shortly after. The three versions of the test are similar and currently forbid an individual from owning or being a director at a football club if they are subject to a number of criteria such as having an unspent conviction relating to fraud or dishonesty or are disqualified from acting as a director of a UK-registered company. Since the introduction of the fit and proper person test, all three of the football authorities have made a number of additions. For example, in the Premier League, club shareholders who own a controlling stake in a club, defined as owning more than 30 per cent of the shares, also have to pass the fit and proper person test. In 2010 the British Horseracing Authority is also introducing new regulations that will apply to race horse owners in order to promote honesty and integrity within the sport.

HMRC monitoring

The Portsmouth case study demonstrated that when a football club goes into administration the tax authorities are often one of the major creditors to lose out. With Her Majesty's Revenue and Customs (HMRC) a major creditor at many football clubs, the situation arises where they could potentially act as a barrier in the negotiation of a Company Voluntary Arrangement, the mechanism that allows a football club to exit administration. To counteract this, the football authorities in England have introduced a monitoring system to ensure that clubs keep up to date with their tax payments to HMRC. In 2008 the FA introduced this mechanism for clubs in the Football Conference. A similar mechanism was passed by club chairmen at the Football League's AGM in June 2009 and ensured that all clubs have to report to the Football League on a monthly basis whether they have paid their PAYE and National Insurance on time. The ruling also ensures that clubs must keep up payments on historic debt. If clubs fail to report to the Football League, the League has the authority to obtain the information from HMRC. If a club fails to report to the League that it has failed to pay HMRC on time, they are charged with misconduct and an immediate transfer embargo is placed on the club. This is a highly significant development as it represents a very serious attempt to address the impact of spiralling debt at clubs.

CASE STUDY: THE UEFA LICENCE AND FINANCIAL FAIR PLAY

Although club governance and regulation has not been part of the historic role of UEFA, in recent years UEFA has sought to have an increasing regulatory influence on clubs and improve standards of governance through the development of the UEFA Club Licensing System. The UEFA Licence represents a move to regulate football clubs that take part in European club competitions – the Champions League and the Europa League – and improve transparency and standards of club governance with the requirement that clubs must meet certain standards relating to sporting, legal, infrastructure, administrative and financial criteria. With respect to financial criteria, clubs are required to be more transparent with their finances and ensure that they prepare annual financial statements containing a balance sheet; a profit and loss account; a cash flow statement; a summary of significant accounting policies; and a financial review by management (UEFA, 2005: 66). The objectives of the financial criteria are to improve the economic and financial capability of the clubs; increase clubs' transparency and credibility; place the necessary importance on the protection of creditors; safeguard the continuity of international competitions for one season; and monitor financial fair play in UEFA competitions (UEFA, 2005: 58).

For season 2012–13 UEFA are introducing more stringent financial criteria for clubs that compete in the Champions League and the Europa League. The UEFA Club Licensing and Financial Fair Play Regulations will be phased in over the three preceding seasons and by 2012–13 will require that clubs do not spend more than they generate over a period of time; that there will be no overdue payments to other clubs, employees and/or social/tax authorities;

and that they provide future financial information to ensure clubs can meet their future obligations (www.uefa.com). The UEFA Club Licensing and Financial Fair Play Regulations system is one way in which UEFA can monitor financial fair play in a bid to avoid 'financial doping', a situation in which the owners of a club are willing to sustain an unusually high level of debt, as a result of which the club gains a sporting advantage. This debt may often be underwritten by a private businessman, by a state authority in some countries, or not at all in some cases where reckless lending decisions have been made, leaving creditors exposed in the event that a club becomes bankrupt and unable to meet interest payments.

SUMMARY

This chapter has provided an introduction to the issue of league regulation in the professional sport industry. The regulatory implications arising from the peculiar economics of the professional sport industry were demonstrated through the discussion of the US model of sport, which is characterized by closed leagues with no promotion or relegation, a strong central governing body, and a clear focus on profit maximization; these allow for strong regulatory controls in order to protect competitive balance and outcome uncertainty, and to deliver financial results. In contrast, the European model of sport has open leagues, promotion and relegation, and a more laissez-faire approach to regulation. This has resulted in many instances of financial failure, particularly in European football, and increasing calls for more regulation.

Over the past decade there has been a move towards a more regulated league system, with a number of measures implemented in European football and other sports. However, despite the implementation of various regulatory measures, financial instability within European football remains a key issue going forward. It could perhaps be argued that a fundamental weakness of the regulatory reforms adopted in England so far is that they have been uncoordinated in their application, and this has undermined their effectiveness. To overcome this there is a need to integrate the various measures into an over-arching system of regulation, a licensing system, which addresses aspects of financial regulation at all levels of league competition. This is necessary as the football industry is structured as an eco-system, where a problem occurring in any one part of the system inevitably impacts elsewhere.

There are a number of sports that are moving away from the implementation of individual regulatory controls towards a more complete licensing system. For example, in 2008 rugby league in England introduced a licence system requiring clubs to meet criteria relating to stadium facilities, financial performance, commercial and marketing, and playing strength in order to be granted a licence for three years. Whilst it is beyond the scope of this chapter to outline exactly what form a licence might take, the existing UEFA Club Licensing and Financial Fair Play Regulations (see case study), which the majority of Premier League clubs apply for and receive each year as a requirement for entry into UEFA competitions should they qualify, serves as a useful starting point to begin the process of devising such an operating licence. However, there is an argument to be made that a comprehensive licensing system incorporating the fundamental aspects of the UEFA Licence needs to be applied to leagues that fall outside of European qualification. In the Football League in England there are many examples of clubs that demonstrate poor financial management, and the implementation of a licence system is also necessary in order to protect the financial stability of the clubs within these leagues.

REVIEW QUESTIONS

1   What are the peculiar economics of professional sport leagues?
2   What are the differences between the US model of sport and the European model of sport?
3   Why is there strong regulation within US sport?
4   Is there a need for more financial regulation within European football?

FURTHER READING

Neale, W. (1964) The Peculiar Economics of Professional Sport, *Quarterly Journal of Economics*, 93: 385–410
Sloane, P. (1971) The Economics of Professional Football: The Football Club as a Utility Maximiser, *Scottish Journal of Political Economy*, June: 121–146

WEBSITES

Official website of Major League Soccer
    www.mlssoccer.com
Official website of the National Basketball Association
    www.nba.com
Official website of the National Football League
    www.nfl.com
Official website of NFL Labor news
    www.nfllabor.com
Official website of UEFA
    www.uefa.com

REFERENCES

Cairns, J.A., Jennet, N. and Sloane, P.J. (1986) The Economics of Professional Team Sports: A Survey of Theory and Evidence, *Journal of Economic Studies*, 13: 1–80
Deloitte (2008) *Annual Review of Football Finance*, Deloitte: Manchester
Deloitte (2009) *Annual Review of Football Finance*, Deloitte: Manchester
Downward, P., Dawson, A. and Dejonghe, T. (2009) *Sport Economics: Theory, Evidence and Policy*, London: Butterworth-Heinemann

Eckard, E.W. (2001) Baseball's Blue Ribbon Economic Report, *Journal of Sports Economics*, 2 (3): 213–227

El Hodiri, M. and Quirk, J. (1971) An Economic Model of a Professional Sports League, *Journal of Political Economy*, 79: 1302–1319

Fort, R. and Quirk, J. (1992) *Pay Dirt: The Business of Professional Sports Teams*, Princeton: Princeton University Press

Fort, R. and Quirk, J. (1995) Cross-Subsidization, Incentives and Outcomes in Professional Team Sports Leagues, *Journal of Economic Literature*, 33: 1265–1299

Gardiner, S., James, M., O'Leary, J. and Welch, R. (2006) *Sport Law* (3rd edn), Abingdon: Routledge-Cavendish

Gratton, C. and Taylor, P. (2000) *Economics of Sport and Recreation*, London: Spon Press

Keśenne, S. (2004) Competitive Balance and Revenue Sharing: When Rich Clubs Have Poor Teams, *Journal of Sports Economics*, 5 (2): 206–212

Kuper, S. and Szymanski, S. (2009) *Why England Lose: And Other Curious Phenomena Explained*, London: Harper Sport

Levin, R.C., Mitchell, G.J., Volcker, P.A. and Will, G.F. (2000) The Report of the Independent Members of the Commissioner's Blue Ribbon Panel on Baseball Economics

Michie, J. and Oughton, C. (2004) *Competitive Balance in Football: Trends and Effects*, FGRC Research Paper, No. 2, Birkbeck, University of London

Neale, W. (1964) The Peculiar Economics of Professional Sport, *Quarterly Journal of Economics*, 93: 385–410

Portsmouth City Football Club Ltd (In Administration): Report to Creditors pursuant to Paragraph 49 B1 of the Insolvency Act 1986

Rottenburg, S. (1956) The Baseball Player's Labor Market, *Journal of Political Economy*, 64: 242–258

Sloane, P. (1971) The Economics of Professional Football: The Football Club as a Utility Maximiser, *Scottish Journal of Political Economy*, June: 121–146

Szymanski, S. (2009) *Playbooks and Checkbooks: An introduction to the Economics of Modern Sports*, Princeton: Princeton University Press

Szymanski, S. and Kuypers, T. (1999) *Winners and Losers: The Business Strategy of Football*, London: Penguin Books

Szymanski, S. and Smith, R. (1997) The English Football Industry: Profit, Performance and Industrial Structure, *International Review of Applied Economics*, 11: 135–153

UEFA (2005) *UEFA Club Licensing System: Version 2.0*, Nyon: UEFA

Chapter 6

Managing sport in the nonprofit sector

Chris Auld and Graham Cuskelly, Griffith University, Australia

---

TOPICS

Defining the nonprofit sector • The scope of the nonprofit sector • Characteristics of nonprofit sport organisations • Factors influencing nonprofit sport organisations • Managing nonprofit sport organisations

---

OBJECTIVES

At the end of this chapter you should be able to:

- Understand the nature and scope of the nonprofit sector and how nonprofit organisations are different to those in other sectors;
- Articulate the current and emerging trends impacting on the nonprofit sector and in particular on sporting organisations operating in this context;
- Appreciate the significance of how the attributes of nonprofit sporting organisations influence management behaviour.

KEY TERMS

Board–staff relations – the nature and quality of the working relationship and overall interactions between the unpaid members of an NFP management committee and the paid staff in the organisation – especially the Executive Director.

For-profit sector – 'a distinct part of the social organisation of a society' comprised of business enterprises (often termed 'firms') 'whose principal goal is to make a profit' (adapted from Horton-Smith, Stebbins and Dover, 2006, p.205, p.89).

Governance – the rules and processes by which organisations are operated and controlled, 'usually mainly the province of the board of directors, and to a lesser extent, between board meetings, the executive director or president plus committees' (adapted from Horton-Smith, Stebbins and Dover, 2006, p.156).

Member-serving organisations – nonprofit groups 'whose principal goal is to benefit and serve its members rather than non-member outsiders' (Horton-Smith, Stebbins and Dover, 2006, p.142).

Nonprofit (NFP) sector – 'the nonprofit sector encompasses all aspects of all nonprofit groups in a society, in addition to all individual action found there' (Horton-Smith, Stebbins and Dover, 2006, p.159).

Public sector – 'a distinct part of the social organisation of a society' comprised of organisations funded by public money that are concerned with the provision of goods and services to citizens (adapted from Horton-Smith, Stebbins and Dover, 2006).

Sport delivery system – the combination of public, private and third sector organisations that collectively provide the range of sport participation opportunities available across the 'sport pyramid' from the local to the international level.

Volunteer management – 'the process of managing volunteers in volunteer programs' and also 'nonprofit groups, usually associations and organizations' (Horton-Smith, Stebbins and Dover, 2006, p.240, p.158).

Volunteering – formal volunteering is 'an activity which takes place through not for profit organizations or projects and is undertaken: to be of benefit to the community and the volunteer; of the volunteer's own free will and without coercion; for no financial payment; and in designated volunteer positions only' (Volunteering Australia, 2009).

OVERVIEW

In many international jurisdictions, sport is typically delivered through volunteer-managed nonprofit (NFP) organisations (albeit often in cooperation with paid staff) that can vary quite markedly in size, scope and complexity. Nonprofit sport delivery systems have long histories and generally have satisfactorily served their immediate constituents, as well as a broader array of stakeholders, in terms of both community level and elite sport outcomes. But the NFP operating environment has become much more complex in recent decades and the overall NFP sector (of which sport is a component) has come under the influence of a range of emerging external and internal pressures. Amongst the most important are: the increasing frequency of government interventions related to rising expectations of positive benefits accruing to communities from the provision of programmes by nonprofit and voluntary organisations; heavier compliance burdens related to accountability of the organisations delivering such programmes; and the movement towards professionalisation and financial independence. As well as these more direct influences, the NFP sector is also facing a raft of broader societal shifts such as those related to perceptions of time pressures and work–life balance that seem to be impacting on the availability and willingness of people to volunteer.

The nonprofit sport sub-sector has not been exempt from such trends and the potential impacts on the managers of nonprofit sport organisations may be even more acute due to the inherent tensions between traditional, democratic and less formal approaches to organisational governance and the growing focus on managerialism. Consequently, the management of NFP sport organisations has become more challenging as the sport industry in general responds to an increasingly turbulent and dynamic environment. This viewpoint suggests that management in the nonprofit sport context is a highly complex task that requires flexibility and continual adaptation to changing (often unpredictable) circumstances and the frequently competing demands of a range of internal and external stakeholders. As suggested by Auld and Cuskelly (2006, p.126), just because

> a structure or process worked in the past is no guarantee that it will continue to function effectively in the future. Even more disquieting is that in an era of discontinuity, history and past trends may provide little guidance in determining what may occur in the future. Some of these changes may involve commercial impacts, increasing professionalization, changing interests of members, participants and spectators and, in general, a world that is increasingly influenced by technology in ways that will affect the manner in which sport organizations deliver their services.

This chapter outlines the nature and scope of the nonprofit sector, highlights the range of external and internal influences impacting on the management of contemporary nonprofit organisations and, lastly, addresses the 'unique' attributes and requirements of management in the nonprofit sport context.

CASE STUDY: SHIFTING THE POWER – WHO SHOULD HAVE THE POWER?

In the car park after a meeting of the club management committee, a group of volunteer board members of a large local sport club are discussing the committee meeting that had just concluded. 'I'm getting really worried – the Executive Director and the President are taking over and all we seem to do is talk about sponsorship and dollars all the time,' said James, one of the long-term members.

'I'm sick of it,' agreed Patrick. 'And what gets me even more, I think all the decisions are made before the meetings even start – I'll bet they get together beforehand with the new sponsor and make sure they get what they want.'

'Even if they didn't,' added Catherine, 'I'm not sure we even receive all the information we need to know so we can be more involved in decision-making.'

'Hang on!' interjected Lauren, one of the new board members. 'Didn't we employ Allie because of her knowledge and experience and elect the President to provide leadership and get things done? We were in real trouble financially a couple of years ago and things have improved a lot recently – shouldn't they be working together? And let's be honest about it, some of us don't exactly have the best attendance records or always read everything before the meetings anyway!'

James quickly responded. 'Maybe... but a number of people have spoken to me about their concerns and I think they are really angry. They feel that they are not being kept informed and also that a lot of the decisions, especially about sponsorships and some of the new commercial partners we are signing up with, are not in the best interests of the club. There are also some rumours going around that we may be relocated to another ground because of the requirements of the new league – if that happens then we will have a membership revolt on our hands.'

'Too late, it's already happening,' said Patrick. 'My son told me that there is already a petition going around seeking an extraordinary AGM and a spill of all committee positions – apparently there is a group forming who want to get voted in as a bloc. A lot of people have signed it. They want to back out of the big sponsorship and get more membership control over the sponsors and other partners.'

DEFINING THE NONPROFIT SECTOR

Most market economies typically comprise three main elements generally described as being the private (for profit), public (government) and third (nonprofit) sectors. The three sectors interact to varying degrees to produce and deliver a wide range of goods and services. According to the Australian Government Productivity Commission (2010, p.xxv), the nonprofit sector, also often termed the 'voluntary sector' or the 'social economy', includes a range of different types of organisation, a distinguishing feature of which is that 'the NFP sector is what it is not – households, government or for-profit businesses'. The Productivity Commission report further suggests that NFP organisations are usually 'established for a community purpose, whether altruistic or mutual in nature' (2010, p.xxv), and, as such, offer members and participants opportunities for self-development, to exercise influence as well as to build self-worth and social connections. This is a key point of differentiation between the NFP and the for-profit and public sectors, as NFP organisations, in contrast to those in the other sectors, generally have a strong 'member-serving' or 'member-benefit' focus. Member-serving organisations are those established by people with a common interest who tend to be the main recipients of the services of the organisation.

CHARACTERISTICS OF ORGANISATIONS IN THE NONPROFIT SECTOR

Organised: some degree of institutionalisation and internal organisational structure; relative persistence of goals, structure and activities; meaningful organisational boundaries; as well as a legal charter of incorporation;

Private: institutionally separate from government. While nonprofit organisations may receive significant government support and government officials may sit on their boards, they must be structurally separate from government, and not exercise governmental authority;

Nonprofit-distributing: not returning profits generated to their owners or directors. Nonprofit organisations may accumulate a surplus, but the profits must be used to further the basic mission of the agency;

Self-governing: control their activities. Some organisations may be so closely aligned with government or private businesses that they essentially function as parts of these despite structural separation. NFP organisations must have significant control over their activities and autonomous internal governance procedures; and

Voluntary: involving some meaningful degree of voluntary participation. This includes the use of volunteers in both operations and management, with the participation by volunteers reflecting 'non-compulsory' engagement. Organisations in which membership is required (e.g. some professional associations) are therefore excluded.

Helmig, Bärlocher and von Schnurbein (2009, pp.2–5)

However, according to Steinberg (2006), although many nonprofit organisations share the traits outlined above, they may also differ on governance structures and management processes as well as on a number of other 'economic' characteristics. For example, while some nonprofits deliver services directly to clients, others provide grants only. Similarly, some rely almost exclusively on grants and donations as revenue sources while others depend on membership dues and some tend to focus on commercial activities. Boris and Steuerle (2006, p.66) argued that a 'common misperception ... is that the nonprofit sector is mainly concerned with charity and depends on donations and volunteers for most of its resources. In fact, many parts of this varied sector are not engaged in serving the poor, depend little or not at all on contributions and pay wages, sometimes substantial, to individuals.' Other features distinguishing nonprofit organisations from those in the business sector are summarised in Table 6.1.

Table 6.1 *Major differences between the business and social sector*

Issue	Business sector	Social sector
Accountability	Primarily responsible to stakeholders	Primarily responsible to constituents
Defining and measuring success	Widely agreed-upon financial metrics of performance Money is both an input (means to success) and an output (measure of success)	Fewer widely agreed-upon metrics of performance Money is only an input, not an output Performance relative to mission, not financial returns, is the primary measure of success
Focus	Doing things right (efficiency) Competition to deliver the best products	Doing the right things (effectiveness) Collaboration to deliver the best outcomes
Leadership/ governance	Governance structure and hierarchy relatively clear and straightforward Concentrated and clear executive power often substituted for leadership	Governance structures often have more components and inherent ambiguity More diffuse and less clear executive power with leadership more prevalent
Talent	Often have substantial resources to attract and retain talent Can more easily get the wrong people 'off the bus' for poor performance	Often lack the resources to acquire and retain talent Tenure systems and volunteer dynamics can complicate getting the wrong people 'off the bus'
Access to capital	Efficient capital markets that connect to the profit mechanism Results attract capital resources which in turn fuel greater results	No efficient capital markets to channel resources systematically to those who deliver the best results

Source: Productivity Commission (2010, p.7)

THE SCOPE OF THE NONPROFIT SECTOR

There is little doubt that the NFP sector plays a significant role in terms of both its social and economic contributions to society. As a result, day-to-day life in many communities around the world would be very different if it was not for NFP organisations and the volunteers that deliver their services.

Cuskelly, Hoye and Auld (2006) reported that the economic value of the voluntary sector is typically estimated at between 7 and 14 per cent of gross domestic product in a number of international jurisdictions. For example, the Productivity Commission (2010) reported that the NFP sector in Australia comprises approximately 600,000 organisations. Of these, the Commission identified 59,000 economically significant NFPs, contributing AUD$43 billion to Australia's GDP and around 8 per cent (890,000 persons) of employment in 2006/07. Reinforcing the important role played by volunteers in the NFP sector, the Productivity Commission also reported that around 4.6 million volunteers work with NFPs, with an annual wage equivalent value of AUD$15 billion.

In the USA, the Urban Institute (2008) reported that in 2005 there were 1.4 million nonprofit organisations (a 25 per cent increase since 1995), with US$1.6 trillion in revenues and assets of US$3.6 trillion. Furthermore, in 2006, 26.7 per cent of adults in the USA volunteered through an organisation, contributing a total of 12.9 billion hours, the equivalent of 7.6 million full-time employees and worth around US$215.6 billion. Similarly in the UK, the National Council for Voluntary Organisations (2009) reported that in 2006/07 there were 870,000 civil society organisations with a total income of £116 billion and assets of £210 billion. The sector's paid workforce experienced a 24 per cent cumulative increase over a ten-year period to a total of 634,000 employees in 2006. Approximately 73 per cent of adults were involved in some form of volunteering in the UK in 2007/08.

When the data for the specific NFP sport sector are examined they also reveal a large and significant level of activity with a great deal of potential to contribute to community life. For example, of the 59,000 economically significant NFPs in Australia identified by the Productivity Commission (2010), around 11,500 were in the Culture and Recreation Category (i.e. including sport). These organisations employed 103,000 paid staff (11.5 per cent of total paid staff) but utilised approximately 44.9 per cent (2.1m) of all volunteers, highlighting the substantial level of volunteer involvement in NFP sport organisations in Australia. Furthermore, data reported by Cuskelly, Hoye and Auld (2006) suggested that the combined total of sport clubs in England, Australia and Canada was probably more than 150,000. These clubs depended on approximately 8.3 million volunteers, who contributed around 1.5 billion hours of their time to mainly community-level sport.

These data not only reinforce the significant scope and scale as well as the contributions made by the overall NFP sector, but also the large proportion of overall sector activity and level of volunteer engagement accounted for by voluntary sport organisations.

CHARACTERISTICS OF NONPROFIT SPORT ORGANISATIONS

One of the important distinctions between non-sport and sport organisations (whether voluntary or commercial) is the operating environment peculiar to sport. Sport tends to encourage strong passions and irrational emotive responses in people that are not usually observed in relation to consumer relationships with other types of goods and services. Furthermore, sport is also often linked to feelings of local and national pride and identity (generally associated with a combination of spatial and social loyalty). As discussed earlier in the chapter, sport goods and services are delivered by the three sectors of the economy whose activities are interdependent and frequently overlap (see Figure 6.1).

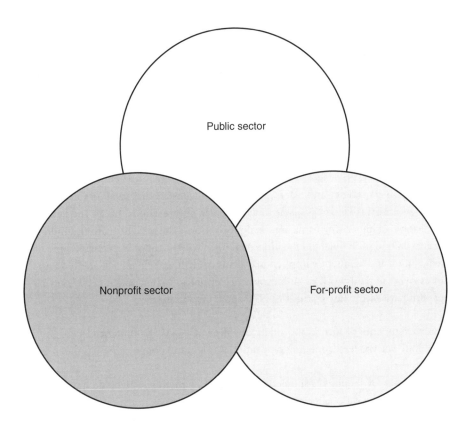

Figure 6.1 *Sport delivery sectors. Adapted from Hoye et al. (2006)*

While many sport service delivery organisations operate either as government agencies or as commercial profit-seeking entities, the majority of sport organisations throughout the world are categorised as nonprofit in nature. Thus rather than undertaking activities to meet the needs of shareholders or the broader public, such organisations 'are more concerned with servicing their members, developing the sport, and improving their on-field performances' (Stewart, 2007, p.80). However, this does not mean that NFP sport organisations are not interested in generating financial surpluses but 'are indeed interested in money' and 'may well be business-like in their operating methods' (Roberts, 2004, p.23). When a surplus is generated, the funds are typically reinvested in the organisation in such areas as facilities and member services.

Furthermore, a key feature of NFP sport organisations with important implications for their management is the long tradition of and heavy dependence on volunteering. 'Voluntary organizations are potentially different from work organizations given that there may be little or no economic necessity to join or remain a member' (Byers, Henry and Slack, 2007, p.270). Thus managers in the NFP sport context are faced with a different set of HRM and decision-making parameters and organisational dynamics than their counterparts in the for-profit and public sectors.

These features, coupled with a long tradition of strong democratic values and the irrational/emotive context of sport, have profound implications for the managers of these organisations. For example, O'Brien and Slack (2004) argued that the membership was the key constituency of, and was able to exert considerable influence in, a rugby club undergoing a transition to a more commercialised operating context. They found that the membership utilised resistance and non-compliance strategies to counteract decisions made at the board level that were shifting the power balance in the club away from volunteer control and influence over decision making towards more management control. The findings of O'Brien and Slack were later reinforced by Byers, Henry and Slack (2007), who suggested that small organisations do not emphasise administrative protocols as much as work organisations due to the constraints on their decision making arising from personal motivations, the social situation, emotions, cognitive capacity and individual personalities. In other words, there is a considerable degree of informal, subtle and frequently implicit protocols evident in NFP management decision making not as overt in paid work organisations. Friederici and Heinemann (2007, pp.289–291) further summarised the key features of NFP sport organisations:

- The 'curious' mix of formal and relatively informal social groupings;
- Behaviour derives less from aims and rational rules, and cooperation has more expressive characteristics;
- Are identified by feelings of subjective belonging by members, who do not calculate their involvement on a rational cost/usage basis;
- Have less reliance on division of labour and thus require minimal coordination;
- Influence and effectiveness are more dependent on personality and persuasive skills of office bearers as in 'communities of interest'. Cooperation and fulfilment of tasks are largely determined by face-to-face relationships and emotions; and
- Most members interpret sports clubs as 'mutually supportive societies' in which people gain feelings of belonging and solidarity.

Despite the well-documented increasing levels of professionalisation evident in the sport sector, it is also apparent that the 'market penetration' of professionalisation is somewhat patchy, especially at the community club level. Therefore, NFP sport organisations can be loosely categorised into either the traditional 'kitchen table' (more likely at the local level) or the emerging 'executive office' category (more likely at the national or international level) (Kikulis, 2000; Taylor, 2004).

Types of sport organisations

Kitchen table

- An absence of a central office, paid staff and strategic plans
- Heavy reliance on volunteers who often hold multiple roles
- Flat organisational structure with few formal rules and little specialisation of roles
- Centralised decision making amongst a few volunteers
- Strong collective identities
- Consider professionalism and assistance from government as a threat

Executive office

- Systematic organisational design defined by structures and systems
- Business-like approach with a number of professional staff with specialised roles
- Defined and specialised roles for volunteers
- Comprehensive plans, policies and strategies
- Decision making decentralised to paid staff with reduced volunteer involvement
- Open to external assistance

(Kikulis, 2000; Taylor, 2004)

FACTORS INFLUENCING NONPROFIT SPORT ORGANISATIONS

As indicated earlier in the chapter, there have been a number of NFP sector level trends, as well as other factors more relevant to the specific sport context, that have caused a number of changes in NFP organisations with consequent implications for managers in this sector.

At the broader policy level, the recognition by governments that they are not always the best agency to deliver social and welfare-related services is not a new phenomenon (Cuskelly *et al.*, 2006). The Productivity Commission (2010) suggested that many of the activities of the NFP sector would not be undertaken by the for-profit or government sectors because of the lack of financial return, the high risk of some activities (including political risk), or because they lack the necessary trust or client relationships for effective service delivery. As a result, many governments now rely increasingly on nonprofit organisations to provide a wide range of services to the community – policies frequently termed as the 'third way' or 'social coalition' approaches to service delivery. The overarching aims of such services and programmes can, in the main, be characterised as attempts to build and maintain community cohesion, mutual trust and social solidarity (Hodgkinson, 2003). Consequently expectations regarding the nature and scope of outcomes arising from the activities of the NFP sector have been substantially raised.

One outcome of third way and social coalition policies for managers of NFP sport organisations is a shift in the nature of the relationship with government (typically the most important source of finance for community sport) from one that could have been previously described as 'grant recipient' to one that is increasingly likely to be perceived as a 'contract signatory'. This shift is also likely to be associated with an increasing focus on accountability, compliance and reporting requirements as well as increasing competition for resources. For example,

Statistics Canada (2000) found in a study of provincial NFP organisations that a substantial majority indicated they now spend much more time reporting to funding agencies.

Additional issues and trends affecting the NFP sector include the following (Productivity Commission, 2010):

- Current reporting protocols required for funding and evaluation purposes are poorly designed and burdensome;
- The regulatory framework for the sector is complex, lacks coherence and transparency, and is expensive;
- Organisations delivering community services face increasing workforce pressures that require long-term planning to overcome;
- The challenges in retaining staff threaten the sustainability and quality of services; and
- Volunteers play a critical role in delivering services but rising compliance costs associated with volunteer recruitment and management (e.g. background checks; workplace health and safety) constrain the viability of their engagement.

While the issues outlined above affect the entire NFP sector, there are a number of other factors specific to the sport context that are particularly relevant here. These tend to centre on rising expectations that sport can deliver policy outcomes related to positive externalities resulting from both increased levels of community sport participation as well as enhanced performance by teams and individuals at the elite level. This is not a new development and has continued relatively unabated for a number of decades, albeit with more interest recently. Houlihan (1997, p.109) argued that the 'trend over the past thirty years has clearly been for central governments to become more closely involved in sport and to seek to exploit sports in pursuit of a broad range of domestic and international policy objectives', and this view was more recently reaffirmed by Hoye, Nicholson and Houlihan (2010). The array of potential outcomes includes such diverse areas as improved social (e.g. increasing social capital) and health (e.g. decreasing obesity) benefits as well as broader goals related to national pride, elements of foreign policy and, increasingly, economic development and urban regeneration.

The increasing policy-driven demands on sport have also coincided with broader societal trends, many of which have constrained the capacity of NFP organisations to recruit and retain volunteers – just at the time NFP organisations have needed to rely even more on volunteers in order to deliver on these raised expectations (Auld, 2008; Lockstone, Jago and Deery, 2002; Seippel, 2004; Statistics Canada, 2000). As summarised by Cuskelly, Hoye and Auld (2006, pp.11–12), the intersecting pressures impacting on NFP sport organisations

> include … an ageing population, increasing social inequalities, disruption of marriage and family ties, reduction in religious attachment, suburbanization, and the fragmentation of traditional community life and interaction patterns due to residential mobility. Factors related to time use and work also appear to influence volunteering including changes in workforce participation and composition (especially as more women have moved into the workforce), perceived time squeeze and increased television viewing, the pressures on dual-income families, and the focus on consumerism and materialism and the concomitant need to increase paid employment time to afford a consumer lifestyle.

Furthermore, the necessary adjustments made by NFP sport organisations in order to respond to increased levels of professionalisation and commercialisation have tended to shift the culture of these organisations from one of friendship, social interaction and informality to something that more resembles a highly structured and professionalised paid workplace. It appears that the changing nature of the NFP sport organisations is likely to result in more volunteer burnout and adverse impacts on volunteer recruitment and retention. The potential impacts of these developments can also be exacerbated by the increasingly important role of paid staff, who, although theoretically still under the control of a volunteer board, can, by virtue of their 'central' positions, exert high levels of influence over the organisation. This process is typically associated with acceleration towards a more business-like approach to the delivery of sport programmes. Consequently, as paid staff assume more responsibility and exert more control over the direction and activities of the organisation, volunteers may feel that they are no longer needed or indeed that they do not have the necessary skills to cope with the new environment of professionalised management, compliance and accountability expectations. Therefore, volunteers often report feelings of marginalisation (Auld, 1997; Auld and Godbey, 1998) at a time when their continued engagement with the organisation is crucial to the effective functioning and long-term viability of such organisations.

In summary, as indicated by Cuskelly, Hoye and Auld (2006), the emphasis on a social coalition approach to service delivery, together with more rigorous compliance and accountability protocols, have occurred during a period in which NFP sport organisations are experiencing difficulties in attracting and retaining volunteers. Subsequently many will struggle to cope with increased service delivery expectations. The key challenge for managers of NFP sport organisations is to simultaneously shift the organisation to adapt to external societal-level factors that are beyond their control (e.g. work–life balance; changing demographics) by focusing on the factors over which they do have some degree of influence (e.g. member relations, contemporary models of service delivery and volunteer management).

MANAGING NONPROFIT SPORT ORGANISATIONS

While NFP sport organisations may vary in their nature, size and complexity, many of the issues faced by their managers are similar. This is not unexpected given that their operating environment can for the most part be contextualised in the generic sport delivery system structure. The 'sport pyramid' that incorporates NFP organisations from the local (club) level through to the national and international levels frequently represents this structure. While such organisations are likely to differ in degrees of sophistication and commercialisation, in most cases they are all nonprofit in nature. As indicated previously, the NFP sport sector is continually evolving towards a more professionalised management model, and these broad changes are summarised in Table 6.2.

Table 6.2 *Changing management of volunteer sport systems*

Levels of involvement	Traditional sport structure	Contemporary sport structure
Club	Volunteer committees and boards	Volunteer committees and boards. Some clubs may have a paid administrator
Regions/state/ provincial	Volunteer councils and boards	Volunteer board that oversees function and determines policy. Professional management and paid staff with defined roles and duties
National	Volunteer councils and boards determine key decisions. May have a paid administrator	Volunteer board that oversees function and determines policy. Professional management and paid staff with defined roles and duties

Source: O'Beirne (2004, p.202)

The preceding sections suggest that one of the most important roles for managers in the NFP sport sector is to blend the demands of a rapidly changing external environment with the traditional volunteer ethos to develop and sustain a culture that not only delivers performance and accountability but also still feels friendly, social and informal to its key constituents. Downward, Dawson and Dejonghe (2009) succinctly captured this tension when they described 'hybrid' organisations struggling to cope with the responsibility for delivering broad social policies such as sport for all, while at the same time increasingly trying to operate on a more commercial basis.

The Productivity Commission (2010) noted that the NFP sector has different motivations and constraints to those faced by the public and business sectors. For member-serving non-profit organisations, member satisfaction is crucial. Given the organisational culture, history and tradition as well as emotive context associated with much of the sport sector, this is a particularly important consideration for NFP sport managers. This is especially the case as the Productivity Commission further emphasised that many of the participatory (and sometimes inefficient) processes found in such organisations are important because they deliver 'value to the volunteers and members' and their central role in 'maintaining trusting relationships that form the basis for effective service delivery' (2010, p.13). Trust is essential to effectively functioning NFP sport organisations, and the Commission further argued that such 'messy', loosely defined and informal processes appear to be crucial in facilitating continuing volunteer engagement and retention – a central concern for NFP sport managers. As suggested by Schulz, Nichols and Auld (2010), an important implication for sport managers is that because rational management techniques often deal with volunteers simply as a means to achieve organisational goals, without due recognition of their commitment and loyalty, then this can have serious impacts on volunteer retention. Furthermore, Roberts (2004, p.36) argued that neither 'state agencies nor commerce can arouse or sustain comparable enthusiasm, dedication, and the corresponding satisfactions, to those that are found in the voluntary sector'.

NFP organisational characteristics relevant to NFP sport managers

■ *NFPs are established for a community purpose* but member control over how the NFP achieves this purpose can also be very important and even a reason for the existence of the NFP.

■ *Many NFPs add value to the community through how their activities are undertaken.* The way in which NFPs are organised, engage people, make decisions and deliver services is often itself of value even though such participatory and inclusive processes can be time consuming and costly.

■ *NFP activities may generate benefits* such as social inclusion that go beyond the recipients of services and the direct impacts of their outcomes such as generating community connections and strengthening civil society.

Productivity Commission (2010)

The combination of the characteristics of NFP sport organisations and their operating context makes for a challenging (yet potentially very rewarding) management environment but it is unclear how well equipped NFP sport managers are to function effectively in this specific setting.

According to Schulz, Nichols and Auld (2010), many volunteers with management responsibilities in the NFP sport context (including board members) are likely to have minimal training or experience and rely on management ideas found in the popular press or experienced in their paid workplace. The underlying assumption is that management principles applied to for-profit organisations apply equally to the NFP sector. Schulz *et al.* also argued that NFP sport organisations are frequently influenced by government agencies and other private sector stakeholders who may tend to perceive the NFP sector through their own generally more formal management perspectives. If this is the case, then many NFPs may utilise management processes typically comprising classical management theory and rational systems perspectives more suited to the for-profit context, without sufficient thought given to the differences between the two sectors (e.g. organisational mission, character and culture). However, such approaches to sport sector management have been encouraged in some academic circles. For example, Auld and Cuskelly (2006) suggested an understanding of organisational and management theory (based largely on research conducted in the for-profit context) assists sport managers in making informed decisions about the most appropriate organisational adaptations to an increasingly uncertain environment.

Despite this view, Schulz, Nichols and Auld (2010) argued that there was little evidence supporting the adoption of such approaches to management in the NFP sport context and, furthermore, that such approaches are generally unsuitable because of the following:

■ It is difficult for NFPs to identify clear aims and objectives due to the value-laden nature of their activities and conflict based on differing interpretations of these values (see also Hoye *et al.*, 2006);

■ The interactions between different NFP internal constituencies (e.g. players, coaches, officials, paid staff and board members) and external constituencies (e.g. government, sponsors) are complex;

91

- The convergence of policy development and implementation is often confounded by the overlaps and conflicts between organisational roles. For example, members may be involved on the board as well as in programme delivery. The situation is made even more complicated because many are also simultaneously programme participants. In addition, there is frequent input by paid staff into policy development and volunteers into operational matters;

- If paid staff assume more control, such a process can jeopardise the democratic nature of NFPs and reduce the legitimacy of the organisation in the eyes of stakeholders (Cuskelly, Hoye and Auld, 2006; O'Brien and Slack, 2004); and

- At the local club level, many costs are internalised by the members and volunteers and, as such, the financial viability of many NFPs is dependent on the availability and generosity of volunteers and members rather than revenue generated through 'external' means.

While these barriers to the adoption of formal management processes are now becoming more widely acknowledged, Schulz, Nichols and Auld (2010, p.435) argued that there were 'few alternative models or ideas. Despite recent attempts to break down the "one size fits all" ... rational management approaches appear to dominate the thinking about management' of NFPs. Byers, Henry and Slack (2007) indicated that, despite the size of the sector and contribution made by the more than 100,000 sport clubs in England, there has been little research undertaken about how they operate.

Hoye *et al.* (2006) argued that sport managers should utilise 'generic' management techniques derived from other sectors and outlined seven key areas of management that differentiated sport management from that in other sectors:

1 Strategic management – sport managers have been slow to embrace strategic management concepts due to the inherently turbulent and uncertain nature of their 'business'. However, this must be a priority if NFP sport organisations are to effectively adapt to the future;

2 Organisational structure – a challenge for sport managers due to the need to ensure formalisation and control without stifling the social and member-serving nature of NFP sport organisations;

3 Human resource management – the mix of volunteers and paid staff with differing motivations and perceptions of organisational purpose also make this a volatile issue for NFP sport managers;

4 Leadership – sport organisations require leaders who are able to collaborate externally, nurture and influence internal constituencies, and empower people to work towards a common goal;

5 Organisational culture – NFP sport managers must be cognisant of the 'peculiar' nature of culture within sport organisations both as a driver and inhibitor of organisational performance;

6 Performance management – different stakeholders will have varying perceptions about the performance of sport organisations. Aspects of performance may range from social needs being met to on-field performance or financial sustainability; and

7   Governance – a crucial issue for NFP sport managers given the central importance of volunteer boards and the need for balance between strategic policy setting and operational management.

This last point is a key priority for NFP sport managers. Effective management of the relationship between volunteers (especially board members) and paid staff has profound implications for effective organisational governance. As indicated by the Productivity Commission (2010), control can be a major motivating factor for the managers of NFPs. While generally motivated by altruism, NFP managers can also benefit personally from their role when it confers status or power builds their skills and contacts, and where it improves the environment for their other activities. This may be especially the case for volunteer management, and suggests that problems may arise as paid staff and volunteer office bearers seek to exert influence in the organisation.

Potential for conflict between volunteers and paid staff as well as role ambiguity develops as organisations evolve and introduce new management and governance structures. O'Beirne (2004, p.204) argued that this issue is an important concern for NFP sport organisations and that potential conflicts between volunteer and paid staff arose as paid staff assumed some of the roles and made decisions about matters that were previously the preserve of volunteers. He suggested that tensions were more likely in the sport setting due to 'rich traditions and deeply-embedded values prevalent in most sport organisations' that made it difficult for 'volunteer board members to let go of governance and decision-making'. Board–staff relations are important for managers given the overriding consensus regarding the fundamental role played by the board in NFP organisational decision making and governance.

SUMMARY

This chapter has outlined the scope and scale of the broader NFP sector as well as that of the specific NFP sport subsector. The data clearly demonstrate the significance of the social and economic impacts of nonprofit organisations and the crucial role they can play in community life. This context implies that management of NFP organisations may face a different set of challenges to that of managers in either the government or for-profit sectors especially given the range of current and emerging issues affecting the NFP sector, particularly in sport. However, the member-serving nature of NFP sport organisations, the important role played by volunteers and the impact of NFP sport organisations on community life means that, despite the challenges confronting managers, their role can also be especially rewarding. Managers of NFP sport organisations need to consider the setting in which they work and be aware of the nuances related to the emotive and often irrational passions generated by sport, coupled with the rich history and traditions of democratic decision making and volunteer engagement. Importantly, managers must balance these considerations with the trend towards further formalisation and professionalisation in the sport sector. It is also apparent that much more work is required to assist NFP sport managers in the development of management techniques appropriate to their 'unique' context.

REVIEW QUESTIONS

1 How does the member-serving nature of the NFP sector impact on sport managers?
2 Describe the five characteristics of organisations in the NFP sector.
3 In what ways can sport managers respond to the environmental factors influencing NFP sport organisations?
4 What aspects of NFP sport organisations and their role in community life can be especially rewarding for the people that manage them?
5 Why are board–staff relations crucial to the future of NFP organisations?
6 How does the operating environment peculiar to sport differentiate the sport product from that of other goods and services?
7 Why don't classical management theory and rational systems approaches to management always suit the NFP sport context?
8 What are seven key areas of management that are especially important to sport managers?

FURTHER READING

Cuskelly, G., Hoye, R. and Auld, C. J. (2006) *Working with Sport Volunteers: Theory and Practice*, London: Routledge.
Schulz, J., Nichols, G. and Auld, C. J. (2010) 'Issues in the management of voluntary sport organisations and volunteers', in B. Houlihan and M. Green (eds), *The Routledge Handbook of Sports Development*, London: Routledge.

WEBSITES

Productivity Commission (2010) *Contribution of the Not-for-Profit Sector: Research Report*, Canberra
   http://www.pc.gov.au/projects/study/not-for-profit/report
Running Sports (England)
   http://www.runningsports.org

REFERENCES

Auld, C. J. (1997) 'Professionalisation of Australian sport administration: the effects on organisational decision making', *The European Journal for Sport Management*, 4, 2: 17–39.
Auld, C. J. (2008) 'Voluntary sport clubs: the potential for the development of social capital', in R. Hoye and M. Nicholson (eds), *Sport and Social Capital*, Oxford: Elsevier.
Auld, C. J. and Cuskelly, G. (2006) 'Organisational theory and sport management', in S. Leberman, C. Collins and L. Trenberth (eds) *Sport Business Management in Aotearoa/New Zealand*, (2nd ed.), South Melbourne: Thomson Dunmore Press.

Auld, C. J. and Godbey, G. (1998) 'Influence in Canadian national sport organizations: perceptions of professionals and volunteers', *Journal of Sport Management*, 12, 1: 20–38.

Boris, E. T. and Steuerle, C. E. (2006) 'Scope and dimensions of the nonprofit sector', in W. W. Powell and R. Steinberg (eds), *The Nonprofit Sector: A Research Handbook*. (2nd ed), Yale University. Online. Available at http://books.google.com.au/books?id=7n8dPi2ew9YC&pg=PA118&lpg=PA118&dq=non+profit+sector+definitions&source=bl&ots=1ynTnmjVUN&sig=EQbmXC4ZTkG3QIZlx8s6vV4XLcs&hl=en&ei=0YpvS4_VLsqHkAW27YHUBw&sa=X&oi=book_result&ct=result&resnum=10&ved=0CCwQ6AEwCQ#v=onepage&q=non%20profit%20sector%20definitions&f=false (accessed 3 February 2010).

Byers, T., Henry, I. and Slack, T. (2007) 'Understanding control in voluntary sport organizations', in M. M. Parent and T. Slack (eds), *International Perspectives on the Management of Sport*, Oxford: Elsevier.

Cuskelly, G., Hoye, R. and Auld, C. J. (2006) *Working with Sport Volunteers: Theory and Practice*, London: Routledge.

Downward, P., Dawson, A. and Dejonghe, T. (2009) *Sports Economics: Theory, Evidence and Policy*, Oxford: Elsevier.

Friederici, M. R. and Heinemann, K. (2007) 'Sport clubs – computer usage – emotions', in M. M. Parent and T. Slack (eds), *International Perspectives on the Management of Sport*, Oxford: Elsevier.

Helmig, B., Bärlocher, C. and von Schnurbein, G. (2009) *Defining the Nonprofit Sector: Switzerland*. Working Papers of the Johns Hopkins Comparative Nonprofit Sector Project, No. 46. Baltimore: The Johns Hopkins Center for Civil Society Studies. Online. Available at http://www.ccss.jhu.edu/pdfs/CNP_Working_Papers/CNP_WP46_Switzerland_2009.pdf (accessed 3 February 2010).

Hodgkinson, V. A. (2003) 'Volunteering in global perspective', in P. Dekker and P. Halman (eds), *The Values of Volunteering: Cross Cultural Perspectives*, New York: Kluwer Academic.

Horton-Smith, D., Stebbins, R. A. and Dover, M. A. (2006) *A Dictionary of Nonprofit Terms and Concepts*, Bloomington: University of Indiana Press.

Houlihan, B. (1997) *Sport, Policy and Politics: A Comparative Analysis*, London: Routledge.

Hoye, R., Nicholson, M. and Houlihan, B. (2010) *Sport and Policy: Issues and Analysis*, Oxford: Elsevier.

Hoye, R., Smith, A., Westerbeek, H., Stewart, B. and Nicholson, M. (2006) *Sport Management: Principles and Applications*, Oxford: Elsevier.

Kikulis, L. (2000) 'Continuity and change in governance and decision making in national sport organisations: institutional explanations', *Journal of Sport Management*, 14, 4: 293–320.

Lockstone, L., Jago, L. and Deery, M. (2002) 'The propensity to volunteer: the development of a conceptual model', *Journal of Hospitality and Tourism Management*, 9, 2: 121–133.

National Council for Voluntary Organisations (2009) *The UK Civil Society Almanac 2009*. Online. Available at http://www.ncvo-vol.org.uk (accessed 25 February 2010).

O'Beirne, C. (2004) 'Managing small and not-for-profit sport organisations', in J. Beech and S. Chadwick (eds), *The Business of Sport Management*, Essex: Prentice Hall.

O'Brien, D. and Slack, T. (2004) 'Strategic responses to institutional pressures for commercialisation: a case study of an English rugby union club', in T. Slack (ed.) *The Commercialisation of Sport*, London: Routledge.

Productivity Commission (2010) *Contribution of the Not-for-Profit Sector: Research Report*, Canberra. Online. Available at http://www.pc.gov.au/projects/study/not-for-profit/report (accessed 25 February 2010).

Roberts, K. (2004) *The Leisure Industries*, Houndmills: Palgrave Macmillan.

Schulz, J., Nichols, G. and Auld, C. J. (2010) 'Issues in the management of voluntary sport organisations and volunteers', in B. Houlihan and M. Green (eds), *The Routledge Handbook of Sports Development*, London: Routledge.

Seippel, O. (2004) 'The world according to voluntary sport organizations: Voluntarism, economy and facilities', *International Review for the Sociology of Sport*, 39, 2: 223–232.

Statistics Canada (2000) *Voluntary Organizations in Ontario in the 1990s*, Ottawa, Canada: Author.

Steinberg, R. (2006) 'Economic theories of nonprofit organizations', in W. W. Powell and R. Steinberg (eds), *The Nonprofit Sector: A Research Handbook*. (2nd ed), Yale University. Online. Available at http://books.google.com.au/books?id=7n8dPi2ew9YC&pg=PA118&lpg=PA118 &dq=non+profit+sector+definitions&source=bl&ots=1ynTnmjVUN&sig=EQbmXC4ZTkG 3QlZlx8s6vV4XLcs&hl=en&ei=0YpvS4_VLsqHkAW27YHUBw&sa=X&oi=book_result&c t=result&resnum=10&ved=0CCwQ6AEwCQ#v=onepage&q=non%20profit%20sector%20 definitions&f=false (accessed 3 February 2010).

Stewart, B. (2007) *Sport Funding and Finance*, Oxford: Elsevier.

Taylor, P. (2004) 'Driving up participation: sport and volunteering', in *Driving Up Participation: The Challenges for Sport*, London: Sport England.

The Urban Institute (2008) *The Nonprofit Sector in Brief: Facts and Figures from the Nonprofit Almanac 2008. Public Charities, Giving, and Volunteering*. Online. Available at http://www. urban.org (accessed 25 February 2010).

Volunteering Australia (2009) *Definitions and Principles of Volunteering*. Volunteering Australia. Online. Available at http://www.volunteeringaustralia.org/files/Z9PTZ1AKD2/Def_and_Princ_ English.pdf (accessed 15 June 2011).

Part 2

The application of business management to sport

Chapter 7

Organisation theory and sport management

Milena Parent, University of Ottawa, Ottawa, Canada
Danny O'Brien, Griffith University, Gold Coast, Australia
Trevor Slack, University of Alberta, Edmonton, Canada

TOPICS

Basic tenets of organisation theory • Organisational characteristics • Contextual dimensions • Organisational processes

OBJECTIVES

At the end of this chapter you should be able to:

- Understand the basic tenets of organisation theory;
- Explain the various factors that influence the structure of a sport organisation;
- Describe five fundamental organisational design configurations;
- Relate how contextual factors can impact upon the structural and design features of sport organisations;
- Recognise the relationship between change management and ongoing competitive advantage in sport organisations;
- Grasp some basic approaches to understanding the notion of organisational leadership.

KEY TERMS

Organisation theory – organisation theory is the scientific study of organisational structure, processes, and design. Topics of interest include leadership, change, culture, conflict, performance, technology, and the impact of contextual factors.

Organisational change – organisational change is an alteration or modification in the organisation's technology, structure and systems, people, and/or products and services (cf. McCann, 1991; Slack and Parent, 2006).

Organisational design – organisational design is the coming together of structural (e.g. formalisation, centralisation, complexity) and contextual (e.g. size, technology, environment) dimensions into a given configuration to garner efficiency and effectiveness (Daft, 2009; Slack and Parent, 2006).

Organisational structure – organisational structure pertains to how an organisation's tasks 'are broken down and allocated to employees or volunteers, the reporting relationship among these role holders, and the coordinating and controlling mechanisms used within the sport organisation' (Slack and Parent, 2006, p. 6).

Sport organisation – a sport organisation is a social entity involved in the sport industry that is focused on attaining goals, and has a consciously structured activity system with identifiable boundaries (Slack and Parent, 2006).

OVERVIEW

Why would you want to know about organisation theory? Well, look around you. We live in a world that is full of organisations of different sizes, types, and goals. Sport organisations, of course, are no exception. Most of you will likely work in some type of organisation(s) now or in the future, notwithstanding the fact that the university or college you now attend is also a type of organisation. But why should a sport manager be concerned with organisation theory? The analogy of a car is useful here. Many of us know how to drive a car, but relatively few of us know what to do when it breaks down! So what do we do? We lift the hood and look at the motor. Again, relatively few of us know what we're looking at. We might take a stab at a quick fix, but are never really sure if we've sorted out the problem. Sometimes we might even ignore the problem, hoping it will go away. More often than not, this leads to a worsening of the situation. Eventually, the car breaks down altogether and is rendered useless and in need of costly servicing or, worse, total destruction. Now think of a sport organisation. What is the manager's role when something goes wrong? Of course, s/he is expected to know how to solve organisational problems as and when they arise. But how many sport managers know exactly what to do when they 'lift the hood' on their organisation? A basic grounding in organisation theory arms the sport manager with this knowledge, and helps us to recognise the symptoms of potential organisational problems before they actually arise, thereby keeping our sport organisations 'on the road' and running efficiently.

CASE STUDY: CHANGE IN AUSTRALIA'S NATIONAL RUGBY LEAGUE

In 1995, the introduction of pay-TV in Australia sparked a long and divisive battle between media companies for the broadcast rights of Australian professional rugby league. By 1998, the conflicting parties reached agreement and the National Rugby League (NRL) was formed as a joint venture between the media conglomerate News Limited and the Australian Rugby League (ARL), the code's national governing body in Australia. Presently, the NRL is one of

Australia's most popular professional sport leagues, and is comprised of 16 franchises from across the eastern states of Australia, plus one from Auckland, New Zealand.

The governance of the NRL joint venture consists of News Limited and the ARL each holding a 50 per cent stake and each appointing three delegates to a partnership committee and board, where most of the major decisions in the code are made. After almost a decade of operating under this joint venture arrangement, the NRL clubs became dissatisfied with the ongoing financial and governance issues that plagued the league. Finally, on 18 January 2010, the chief executives, coaches, captains, and chairs of the 16 NRL clubs attended a meeting in Sydney to discuss ways to restructure the NRL's governance. The Chief Executive of the NRL was not invited to the meeting, nor were other officials from the NRL, ARL, or News Limited; this was the first time the clubs had ever met en masse independently of the NRL. The meeting resulted in a united demand from the clubs for an independent commission to take over the running of the game from News Limited and the ARL, with the clubs electing the eight independent commissioners (Walter, 2010).

The clubs also demanded that change be swift, proposing the new commission be up and running before the March commencement of the 2010 season, and well before negotiations for a new television deal which are due to begin in early 2011. The clubs feared that, if News Limited and the ARL delay in relinquishing their 50 per cent stakes in the NRL, the full financial benefits of an independent commission may not flow through to the clubs and players until the next television deal in 2017. The response from News Limited and the ARL to the proposed changes was lukewarm, at best. Walter and Proszenko (2010) suggest the main stumbling blocks to an agreement are:

- The ARL want to appoint up to half of the eight independent commissioners to protect its control of the lucrative State of Origin series and grassroots development;
- News Limited want an exit fee of up to AUD$30 million to cover the financially troubled Melbourne Storm's losses for six years; and
- Safeguards to prevent the clubs changing the constitution to get a bigger share of profits.

BASIC TENETS OF ORGANISATION THEORY

Organisation theory is the scientific study of organisational structure, processes, and design. Early in the twentieth century, sociologists began to see organisations as miniature replicas of society. By studying the different patterns in organisational structure and design, these early scholars sought a better understanding of society itself (Daft, 2007). However, the theory of organisations soon emerged as a field of study in itself. While it may be a discipline within the larger field of management studies, scholars work closely with practitioners in order to help them better manage and understand their organisations.

ORGANISATIONAL CHARACTERISTICS

In order to better understand how sport organisations work, three key concepts – complexity, formalisation, and centralisation – help to describe the various structural characteristics of organisations that must be managed. Moreover, these structural elements work within a number of organisational design configurations. We will now explore these factors.

Structural dimensions

Organisational structure can be described in various ways. The three most fundamental structural dimensions are complexity, formalisation, and centralisation (Pugh and Hickson, 1976). Complexity refers to how differentiated an organisation is. For example, a Premier League football club may have a football section that includes playing, coaching, physiotherapy, and medical staff, as well as departments responsible for football development, management, legal issues, finance, marketing, multi-media, community-based activities, and public relations. On the other hand, a local lower division football club will typically have a comparatively tiny coaching and playing staff, a volunteer board, a small administrative staff, and some local volunteer support. Obviously, a Premier League football club is more complex organisationally than the local lower division football club. The concepts of horizontal, vertical, and spatial differentiation help explain these differences in complexity.

Horizontal differentiation can be separated into two interrelated aspects: specialisation and departmentalisation. Specialisation is seen in organisations where people are separated according to their most simple and repetitive tasks (functional or task specialisation); or through the separation of specialists according to their specific skills or training (social specialisation). Departmentalisation is seen in organisations that separate units according to the products or services they produce; their particular function, such as marketing or human resource management; or by their geographical location. Clearly, a Premier League football club has more specialists and is more departmentalised than a local football club, and can be described, therefore, as more complex.

Vertical differentiation refers to the number of hierarchical levels of management found in an organisation. For example, a local football club would have a flatter structure than a Premier League Club since there are fewer levels of management. However, should the club move up through the divisions, it would have to add departments and grow in size. Therefore, more levels of management would be needed to maintain control over the new employees in the organisation. These additional levels of management increase the organisation's level of vertical differentiation and, hence, its complexity.

Spatial differentiation simply refers to how geographically dispersed an organisation is. The initial local football club is very low in spatial differentiation as it is located in only one geographic location. However, if the club were to move up through the divisions and grow in size by adding, for example, development programmes in neighbouring cities, its spatial differentiation would be increasing. Typically, when spatial differentiation increases, more layers of management are needed, and thus the sport organisation becomes more complex. Figure 7.1 illustrates the different elements of complexity.

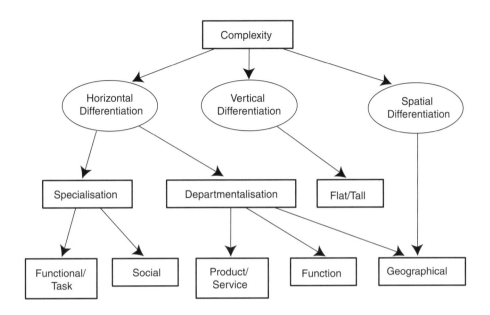

Figure 7.1 *Elements of the structural dimension of complexity*

The second structural dimension is formalisation. This refers to documentation such as the rules, regulations, policies, procedures, job descriptions, etc., that dictate the workings of a sport organisation. For example, the opening case for this chapter mentions that one of the obstacles to implementing change in Australia's National Rugby League (NRL) is the governing body's insistence on safeguards being instituted to prevent changes to the NRL's constitution. These proposed safeguards, and the constitution itself, are examples of formalisation. At the other end of the scale, the policies and procedures that govern the roles and responsibilities of a volunteer-run amateur netball club's management committee is another example of formalisation. Alternatively, many of you will be familiar with the conspicuously displayed signs in public swimming facilities that inform patrons of safe and unsafe practices within the facility; this is also an example of formalisation. The more prevalent these documented rules, policies, and procedures in a sport organisation, the higher the level of its formalisation. With high formalisation, organisational members have less discretion. However, the need for formalisation will be different from one sport organisation to the next; and in larger organisations, it can even be different among different subunits. For example, in a stadium construction firm, the work of the tradespeople doing the actual construction will be highly formalised. Conversely, the research and design department will have very little formalisation to enable its highly trained architects and other professionals to exercise their creativity. Thus, professional training, in this case a relevant degree and experience in architecture, can act as a surrogate for formalisation. The architects do not need to be told how to do their job, while at the same time it is crucial for the construction crew to work to very exacting plans.

The third structural dimension is centralisation. This simply refers to the level in the sport organisation's hierarchy where decisions are made. If ultimate decision-making authority is vested in the hands of the chief executive officer (CEO), or very few senior associates, then the organisation is centralised. However, in large organisations, this is less likely to be the case. For example, the CEO of International Management Group (IMG) is unlikely to seek direct input into the contract negotiations for one of the company's athlete clients. Rather, managers with the appropriate training and experience make these more specialised decisions. Similarly, the type of ink used in the printers in the Union of European Football Associations' (UEFA) marketing department is unlikely to be decided by its General Secretary. These minor operational decisions are more appropriately made at lower levels of management. Therefore, typically, the more specialists working in a sport organisation, and the higher the level of complexity, the more decentralised its decision making. This leaves upper management, such as CEOs, to deal with larger, more strategic decisions and issues, rather than ones that are more specialist or operational in nature.

Organisational design differences

Although all sport organisations are fundamentally different, many do, nonetheless, display a number of common characteristics in how their structural dimensions are patterned. This patterning of structural dimensions is referred to as organisational design. In his seminal work on organisational design types, Henry Mintzberg (1979) posited five different configurations that differ in their structural dimensions and strategic focus: the simple structure, the machine bureaucracy, the professional bureaucracy, the divisional form, and the adhocracy. Importantly, these configurations are meant as ideal types. Therefore, it is highly unlikely that a focal sport organisation would fit exactly into *one* of these design types. More likely, sport organisations will display aspects of two or more of these configurations.

An organisation featuring a simple structure is small in size with only one or a few members, and is typically young in age. There is little complexity or formalisation, but it features strong centralisation as the owner makes most decisions as rapid responses to environmental conditions and opportunities. These characteristics make the simple structure particularly appropriate in dynamic, fast-moving environments, where the main strategies and goals are basically growth and survival. As Berrett, Burton, and Slack (1993) showed, this type of organisational configuration is particularly prevalent among entrepreneurs in the sport and leisure industries.

The machine bureaucracy features extensive vertical differentiation, is highly formalised, and decision making is centralised. Typically, this design configuration is favoured by particularly large organisations. As modern economies have become more service oriented, however, machine bureaucracies have become much less prevalent due largely to their high level of complexity and difficulty in responding to environmental change. Nonetheless, elements of machine bureaucracies remain, particularly in organisations using stable technologies and operating in relatively certain environmental conditions. For example, organisations that mass-produce sport equipment such as Slazenger and Helly Hanson are likely to operate with many elements of the machine bureaucracy. Strategically, machine bureaucracies aim at defending their market position and focus on efficiency and cost reduction in their operational practices.

The professional bureaucracy is characterised by the presence of people with professional training. For example, a department in a university is composed of academics trained to do research and teach in specialised areas. While professional bureaucracies may be relatively formalised and complex, the professionals within them are usually quite autonomous in what they produce and how they perform their jobs. Such organisations usually offer a wide range of products and services and considerable variation among departments. For example, the accounting department at Manchester United might be quite stable and bureaucratic in nature, while the need for creativity and innovation in the marketing department may make it much more dynamic and freewheeling. Strategically, the professional bureaucracy typically tries to minimise risks while maximising profit opportunities, and simultaneously strives for effectiveness and quality. National sport organisations in Canada have notably been found to act as professional bureaucracies (see Slack and Hinings, 1992, 1994).

The fourth design configuration is the divisionalised form. As Daft (2007) pointed out, the distinctive feature of the divisionalised form is that groupings are based on organisational outputs. This output-orientation makes the divisionalised form incredibly complex since it is usually subdivided according to products, services, or major projects, programmes, divisions, or businesses. A good example of the divisionalised configuration is the giant surfwear corporation, Billabong, which operates in over 100 countries and owns 11 subsidiary companies. Billabong International Limited's core business is in marketing, distributing, wholesaling, and retailing of apparel, accessories, eyewear, wetsuits, and hardgoods in the boardsports sector ('Billabong Biz: Behind the Brand', 2010). In this design type, each subdivision is quite autonomous since they often operate in somewhat different markets. Each subdivision will also be quite formalised and geared toward profit maximisation. This diversity of products or service offerings refers to a portfolio strategy, and follows the logic of decreasing uncertainty by spreading risk and not putting all of the organisation's 'eggs in one basket'.

The final organisation design type is the adhocracy. The adhocracy, sometimes referred to as the matrix or lattice design type, is usually found in highly complex and information-intensive environments where technology, innovation, and flexibility are critical to organisational success. Sporting events are a good example of a sporting context where adhocracies are common. Adhocracies are characterised by the presence of professionals and exhibit low formalisation and decentralised decision making. For example, the outdoor equipment company Patagonia prides itself on the research, development, and manufacture of innovative, though environmentally conscious, sport equipment and apparel. Patagonia maintains its innovative edge by employing a team-based approach where cross-functional groups work towards problem solving through mutual adjustment ('Patagonia's History: A Company Created by Climber Yvon Chouinard', 2010). The process of management in this type of structure is, therefore, more one of facilitation and coordination rather than direct supervision. Typically, managers operating in adhocracies strive for innovation and are always on the lookout for new markets.

So far, we have examined the structural aspects of organisations, which can be described according to complexity (vertical, horizontal, and spatial differentiation), formalisation, and centralisation. These aspects can then be combined into organisational designs, such as the five ideal configurations proposed by Henry Mintzberg (1979): the simple structure, the machine bureaucracy, the professional bureaucracy, the divisional form, and the adhocracy.

CONTEXTUAL DIMENSIONS

The structural and design characteristics discussed above provide markers for comparing and measuring the internal characteristics of sport organisations. However, these internal characteristics are a reflection of the sport organisation's context. The contextual dimensions of a sport organisation include strategy, size, environment, and technology. We will now examine each of these dimensions in turn.

Strategy

Like all organisations, sport organisations are subject to constant changes in their contextual situation. To successfully adapt, sport managers need to formulate and implement strategies for their organisation. This process of strategic management is a critical, though under researched, area of sport management. Basically, the strategic management process involves examining the opportunities and threats in the sport organisation's external environment, while also identifying any internal organisational strengths and weaknesses. Based on this analysis, sport managers then formulate, select, and implement strategies to successfully take advantage of environmental opportunities, while also undertaking strategies to nullify environmental threats. Critical to this process is the implementation of appropriate organisational structures and processes that effectively support and monitor the strategies employed. Decisions regarding strategy implementation are usually founded upon the sport organisation's pursuit of a competitive advantage, that is, to outperform competitive rivals in its industry (Harrison and St John, 2008). Even better, a *sustainable* competitive advantage is achieved when the sport organisation maintains this high rate of performance over a number of years. Finally, the last and often overlooked piece of the strategic management process involves evaluating strategic initiatives and feeding any lessons learnt back into the strategic management loop so that future strategic initiatives benefit from past experience. You can find more information on strategic management in Chapter 8 of this book.

Size

The size of a sport organisation profoundly impacts its processes. For example, a small start-up firm providing athlete representation services will have very different management practices to a large firm like IMG. But what is organisational size? Does it simply mean the number of employees? Is it the profit ratio or market share? Is it something else? In a classic work on this subject, Kimberly (1976) posited that there are four aspects to consider when describing size: the *physical capacity* of the organisation (e.g. the amount of floor space available to a fitness facility); the *personnel* available to the organisation (e.g. the number of full-time, part-time, and occasional workers in a tennis camp); the *volume* of the organisation's inputs (or outputs, depending on the nature of the business); and the *discretionary resources* available to the organisation (e.g. the wealth and net assets of Nike).

But does size influence structure? As for complexity, an increase in size is also usually related to an increase in formalisation. There are two main reasons for this. The first reason is that, as organisations grow, there is an increase in the need for product control and service quality, so *standardisation* of processes takes place (Parsley, 1987; Slack and Parent, 2006). The second reason is that, as organisations get larger, there is a greater need for *control of personnel and processes*. So instead of costly direct supervision, management will instead turn to formalisation. However, the nature of the organisation itself may impact the size–formalisation relationship. For example, if an organisation is a professional bureaucracy composed of trained professionals, as opposed to a machine bureaucracy geared to mass production with a high number of unskilled workers, it is less likely to feature excessive formalisation (Slack, 1997).

In terms of the relationship between size and centralisation, research is less clear on the exact nature of the connection. Some researchers such as Blau and Schoenherr (1971) argued that, as the organisation gets larger, more pressure is placed on top management, thereby increasing the likelihood of centralisation. However, the general trend in research follows Child (1973) in that, as the organisation grows, decisions are increasingly delegated to lower management to decrease pressure on senior-level managers. The exception to this may be in times of extraordinary organisational crisis when fast, decisive action is required from top management.

However, the results of the little research conducted on the size–structure relationship in the context of sport organisations tell a somewhat different story to that of the general management literature. Using a group of voluntary sport organisations (VSOs) in Canada as their research site, Amis and Slack (1996) explored the relationship between increasing organisational size and structure. Their findings, particularly those pursuant to the centralisation of decision making as organisations grow in size, diverged from previous research findings in non-sport settings. They observed that, even in VSOs that had undergone substantial growth, 'decisions are made relatively informally, and for the most part, have not been decentralized to the level of professional staff' (Amis and Slack, 1996, p. 84). Essentially, Amis and Slack found that the central role of decision making as a means of control created reluctance among volunteer board members to forfeit the authority necessary for meaningful decision making to professional staff. Thus, the relationship between volunteer and professional staff in VSOs was seen as one of inherent conflict where, despite growth in the size of organisations, control remained with volunteer boards.

Environment

A sport organisation's environment is typically separated into two components: the task and the general environment. The task environment is composed of those aspects that are external to the organisation, but nonetheless *directly* impact its day-to-day structure and operation. Thus, depending on the type of sport organisation being examined, its task environment will include suppliers, regulatory agencies, athletes' groups, competitors, and consumers such as clients, members, and fans. Alternatively, the general environment has a more *indirect* influence on the sport organisation's operations, and is composed of political, demographic, economic, socio-cultural, legal, ecological, and technological aspects (Slack and Parent, 2006).

But how does the environment affect the structural dimensions of a sport organisation? Well, organisational environments can be discussed as sitting somewhere on a continuum between stable and dynamic. A stable environment is characterised by low levels of uncertainty and predictable and secure access to resources, and is usually associated with more mechanistic management systems such as the machine bureaucracy. Conversely, a dynamic environment features high levels of uncertainty and turbulence, which makes organic structures such as the adhocracy more appropriate for responding to rapid and constant change.

In attempting to control environmental uncertainty, Child (1984) explained that decision makers sometimes increase inter-organisational linkages in order to obtain and evaluate more information, thus increasing complexity. O'Brien and Slack (2003, 2004) provided empirical support for this dynamic in their examination of the professionalisation of English rugby union. After more than a century of amateur operation, the governing body of the sport in England, the Rugby Football Union (RFU), and its member rugby union clubs were suddenly faced with unprecedented uncertainty as they grappled with the challenges posed by professionalism. Despite widespread conflict and intense competitive and financial pressures, the clubs constituting the top levels of English rugby eventually formed coalitions to exchange vital strategic information. The increased resource flows among key actors decreased environmental uncertainty and led to somewhat of a consolidation of the game's infrastructure and future development in England.

Technology

It has been five decades since Woodward (1958) and Burns and Stalker (1961) proposed that technology determines the nature of the organisation's design. More recently, Scott (2000) posited that technology refers generically to the work performed by an organisation. From this perspective, the sport organisation is a location where inputs are transformed into outputs through the application of technology and energy. Some sport organisations process material inputs into tangible outputs such as football boots or hockey sticks. Others, such as amateur sport clubs, ski schools, and health retreats, provide services where they 'process' people, transforming them into more skilful, knowledgeable, fit, or stronger individuals. Meanwhile, other sport organisations process knowledge-based resources into less tangible outputs such as strategic advice from a sport sponsorship brokerage to a client. Clearly, the technology of a sport organisation is dependent upon the nature of its inputs and desired outputs, and, as Scott (2000, p. 21) contended, is 'often embedded in part in machines and mechanical equipment but also comprises the technical knowledge and skills of participants'.

As we have seen, organisational structure and design are affected by various contextual dimensions. We have focused on strategy, size, environment, and technology.

ORGANISATIONAL PROCESSES

Rather than the structural and design elements we have addressed in the previous sections, we will now explore some of those aspects of managing sport organisations that are more processual in nature. Specifically, we will now turn to the management of organisational change; decision making; and power, politics, and conflict, and will then conclude the section with a brief discussion of leadership in sport organisations.

Organisational change

In this last section, we touch upon the notion of Bedeian and Zammuto (1991), who suggested that the most unchanging aspect of organisational life is the existence of change itself; and for sport organisations, this seems particularly true. Therefore, it is appropriate that there is a growing literature in sport management that explores this very topic (cf. Amis and Slack, 1996; Cousens, 1997; Cousens and Barnes, 2009; Cousens and Slack, 1996, 2005; Heffernan and O'Brien, 2010; Kikulis, Slack, and Hinings, 1995; Malcolm and Sheard, 2002; O'Brien and Slack, 1999, 2002, 2003, 2004; Shaw and Allen, 2006; Skinner, Stewart, and Edwards, 1999; Slack and Hinings, 1994).

To be effective, sport managers need to know how to strategically respond to shifting organisational environments, and require the skills and vision necessary to guide their organisations through such periods. Typically, successful sport organisations avoid unnecessary uncertainty by sticking to what works well. As Tushman, Newman, and Romanelli (1986, p. 92) contended, 'a snug fit of external opportunity, company strategy, and internal structure is a hallmark of successful companies'. However, such stability is not always possible as organisations pass through long periods of convergence that are punctuated by short, turbulent periods of frame breaking, radical, organisational change.

During periods of convergent organisational change, there is an effective dovetailing between environmental conditions and the sport organisation's strategy, structure, people, and processes. Minor changes are made as and when necessary, but these are just fine tuning or incremental adjustments that are only made in order to reinforce the status quo. For those organisations whose strategies fit environmental conditions, convergence continually improves effectiveness. Over time, patterns of behaviour, norms, and values are reinforced and become taken-for-granted, or *institutionalised*. This institutionalisation of structure, strategy, and process contributes to increased organisational momentum. Eventually, this momentum leads to the sense of organisational history, tradition, and pride that is so pervasive in many sport organisations. However, it can also lead to complacency. And, when environmental conditions change, and organisational strategy and structure must change in sync, the momentum of convergence can create inertia and restrict the organisation's ability to adapt and remain competitive (see also Miller, 1990). Kondra and Hinings (1998) referred to this phenomenon as *paradigm stasis*, where patterns of organisational behaviour become so entrenched that, by the time managers recognise the need for change, they lack the will and/ or skill with which to implement it. Thus, convergent change can be seen as a double-edged sword. The social and technical consistencies that were the very sources of past success and tradition can also be the seeds of failure once conditions change.

Conversely, frame-breaking organisational change occurs in response to, or preferably in anticipation of, major environmental changes – those changes that require more than just fine tuning or incremental adjustments. What leads to frame-breaking change? Frame breaking, radical organisational change can result from a number of sources. For example, *industry discontinuities* from sweeping changes in legal, political, or technological conditions may shift the basis of competition. Major changes in the *regulatory environment* of a sport organisation may also do this. For example, the opening and concluding case studies for this chapter describe frame-breaking change phenomena that have emanated from the regulatory environments of the focal professional sport leagues. Alternatively, there may be fundamental shifts in *internal organisational dynamics*. For example, the sheer size of a rapidly growing sport organisation may necessitate a management reconfiguration. Alternatively, key people may leave, or new people may join a sport organisation with new ideas that force stakeholders to reassess what was once taken for granted. Access to essential resource flows may also be gained or denied due to the coming or going of these key people. Finally, frame-breaking organisational change can also be prompted through *product lifecycle shifts*. Over the course of a product lifecycle, different strategies, structures, and technologies will be appropriate. As a product emerges, competition is based on innovation and performance; whereas, when products mature and eventually go into decline, emphasis shifts to cost, volume, and efficiency (Tushman *et al.*, 1986).

Essentially, frame-breaking organisational changes involve revolutionary changes *of*, rather than incremental changes *in*, the system (Tushman *et al.*, 1986). This usually involves reformed missions and core values; altered power and status for particular groups and individuals; reorganisation of structures and roles that deliberately break 'business-as-usual' behaviour; and revised patterns of interaction as new procedures, workflows, communication networks, and decision-making apparatus are established. Finally, new leadership will typically be recruited from outside the sport organisation to lead the change process. New leadership will usually bring commitment to a new mission, energy to overcome lingering inertia, and freedom from prior allegiances (Tushman *et al.*, 1986). Crucially, to most effectively overcome inertial tendencies, these things usually happen *all at once*.

Decision making

Decision making is one of the most fundamental jobs that sport managers perform. Some would describe it is a manager's most important role. Decision topics in sport organisations vary widely – from minor operational decisions through to major strategic decisions that have the potential to either bankrupt or bankroll the sport organisation.

Most decisions are made under one of three conditions: certainty – where we know *all* of the alternatives and ramifications for a given decision; risk – where we know *some* of the alternatives and their ramifications; or uncertainty – where we know *little or nothing* about potential decision alternatives and their ramifications. As human beings, even the most gifted and intelligent of managers cannot know *everything* there is to know about a given topic. Therefore, in his classic work on managerial work, Simon (1945) proposed the notion of bounded rationality – that managers are bounded rationally in their decision making by their emotions, limited cognitive ability, and constraints such as time, money, and access to information. Relating this to sport organisations, it is safe to say that most decisions are made under conditions of risk and uncertainty.

Regarding the actual *process* of decision making, Yukl (2002) usefully outlined four distinct procedures based on Vroom and Yetton's (1973) model. The first is autocratic decision making. This refers to a manager taking sole responsibility for decision making, without seeking opinions, advice, or influence from colleagues, and without any other individual or group having input into the decision. The second procedure, consultation, is where a manager still makes the final decision but, nonetheless, seeks the extensive counsel of colleagues. The third procedure is joint decision making and refers to managers meeting with others to discuss the issue in question before jointly making the final decision. Delegation, the final procedure suggested by Yukl, is where senior management decentralises decision-making authority to an individual or group. In this case, managers will often provide guidelines or limits within which the final decision must fall, but will not seek final approval of the ultimate decision.

Decisions made in sport organisations are more likely to fall into consultation, joint, or delegation processes that involve more than one or a few managers. Usefully, Chalip (2001) provided a synopsis of group decision-making procedures for sport organisations, and suggested that, although time consuming, group decision-making is beneficial in four basic ways. The first is that, where there is a lack of ideas on a given topic, increasing the number of people involved in the decision process increases the number of *novel ideas* and approaches to solving the focal problem. Second, group decisions increase the *amount of available information*. This decreases the problems of bounded rationality and simultaneously increases the potential data upon which to base a more informed decision. Third, a group approach facilitates access to *alternative perspectives* not otherwise available. For example, in preparing its bid for the right to host the 2010 Olympic Winter Games, the Vancouver bid committee consulted – and actually included as an official partner, a first in Olympic history – the four First Nations on whose territory the Games would take place (the Vancouver–Whistler corridor). This ensured that the Four Host First Nations would obtain benefits/legacies post-Games should the bid be successful. Ultimately, this inclusion was one reason Vancouver was successful in obtaining the right to host the Games. The final advantage of group decision-making is that the status and identity of the individuals that constitute the group can enhance the *fairness and legitimacy* of the focal decision. A number of national sport federations in Europe, North America, and Australia have successfully adopted this form of decision making where representatives from the countries' different geographic regions, different officials' and/or administrators' groups, and athletes' representatives are involved in making important decisions (Chalip, 2001). Though such a participative approach can be time consuming and raises the potential for conflict, it is seen as very productive because decisions and any related actions come with the input and ultimate 'ownership' of all interested parties.

Power, politics, and conflict

The sources of power in a sport organisation are varied, and include individual and organisational bases. The most fundamental sources of power include legitimate, reward, coercive, referent, and expert power (French and Raven, 1959). *Legitimate power* is identical to authority, and is acquired by virtue of the individual's hierarchical position within the organisation. For example, the chair of a board of directors in a VSO can expect some level of compliance from subordinates. *Reward power* comes from an individual's or subunit's control of rewards or remuneration in a sport organisation. For example, a coach may reward players who train or play well with extra game time. Conversely, *coercive power* stems from the ability to punish (or withhold rewards from) organisational members. Thus, extending the previous example, when players fail to attend training sessions or transgress team rules, their head coach or manager may cut their playing time, impose substantial fines, or, in extreme cases, cut them from the team. *Referent power* refers to the power generated through an individual's charisma. For example, Muhammad Ali enjoys a substantial degree of power and respect throughout the world due largely to his social and sporting achievements, but also as a result of his extremely charismatic personality. Similarly, leading sport coaches such as Sir Alex Ferguson at Manchester United, and athletes like the Association of Tennis Professionals' Roger Federer, enjoy a certain degree of referent power. *Expert power* comes from the possession of special knowledge or experience. Scouts in sports such as baseball become extremely powerful due to their specialised knowledge of their chosen sport, but also from their proven judgement and intimate knowledge of the abilities and weaknesses of a large number of players.

Inevitably, the exercise of power involves political activity, as individuals and groups seek to protect or increase their current power bases (Pfeffer, 1981). The most common political process aimed at achieving this involves *coalition formation*. This takes place when a group of individuals, subunits, or organisations ally together in support or opposition to a common cause (Stevenson, Pearce, and Porter, 1985). For example, the opening NRL case study describes coalition formation by clubs hoping to use their combined coercive power to force changes in the NRL's governance. Alternatively, the European Club Forum was formed between the governing body of European football, UEFA, and over 100 clubs from its 51 member associations. The Forum held its inaugural meeting in Monaco in August 2002, and aimed to improve the level of dialogue and communication between UEFA and European clubs on issues such as the future structure of the UEFA Cup.

As has been well documented, political activity such as that described above invariably entails, at the very least, the *potential* for considerable conflict. Thomas and Schmidt (1976) found that, on average, managers spent 20 per cent of their time dealing with conflict. Indeed, Amis, Slack, and Berrett (1995) suggested that conflict is endemic to all organisations, and that certain aspects of the structure of sport organisations can predispose them to ongoing conflict. One useful way of examining conflict is to consider its structural antecedents. More precisely, *vertical conflict* is conflict among different hierarchical levels of a sport organisation, while *horizontal conflict* refers to conflict among different subunits (Slack, 1997). Further, *differentiation* can be a source of latent or actual conflict due to incompatibility among the goals of different organisational subunits. Alternatively, high levels of *interdependence* can easily transform latent tension among subunits into outright actual conflict. A *lack of formalisation* in the rules, regulations, policies, and operating procedures of a sport organisation can also lead to ambiguity, frustration, and, ultimately, conflict (Slack and Parent, 2006).

While conflict often has a negative connotation, this ignores the fact that conflict can also be beneficial to sport organisations. Indeed, Robbins (1990), talking about organisations in general, explained that effectiveness is greatest when there are optimal levels of conflict. He argued that conflict allows the organisation to be self-critical, viable, and innovative. Ultimately, therefore, the maintenance of a sport organisation's competitive position is a function of how well conflict is managed or, if necessary, stimulated. Too much conflict will be time consuming and disruptive for staff, while too little conflict may lead to apathy, decreased organisational effectiveness, and the risk of obsolescence. Obviously, organisational leadership, to which we now turn, plays a key role here.

Leadership

Before the 1960s, most approaches to leadership were *trait based*. This approach worked on the assumption that leaders were 'born, not made'. By the early 1960s, however, the *behaviour-based* approach had emerged, which viewed leadership as more task oriented and focused on interpersonal relationships. During the late 1960s, the *contingency or situational theory* proposed that leadership was neither solely trait nor behaviour based, but depended upon unique situations and the psychological maturity of a specific leader's subordinates.

Effective leaders are often described as being charismatic. However, it was not until the late 1970s that organisational theorists really began to study what makes a person a *charismatic leader*. There are various theories of charisma that have been developed; we will briefly outline two of these theories. The first theory is the *attribution theory of charisma*, which explains that followers' acknowledgement of a leader's charismatic qualities is determined by a combination of the leader's behaviour, skill, and organisational context (Conger, 1989; Yukl, 2002). The *self-concept theory of charismatic leadership* includes a set of testable propositions related to observable processes about the charismatic leader's 'profound and unusual effects on followers' (Yukl, 2002, p. 244). This theory uses followers' personal identification with the leader, their social identification to the group or organisation, their internalisation of the leader's vision, and certain facilitating conditions, such as congruency between the leader's vision and the followers' values and beliefs, to explain charisma.

The charismatic approach to leadership has led to the notion of *transformational leadership* (Bass, 1985). Transformational leaders inspire followers through idealised influence, individualised consideration, and intellectual motivation (Bass, 1996). Indeed, Macintosh and Whitson (1990) explained how transformational leaders are important during change processes within national-level sports organisations, not only to arouse strong emotions from followers, but also to empower and to elevate them to increase commitment to the organisation's objectives.

As long ago as 1974, Stogdill noted that a review of the literature on leadership failed to provide a definitive conceptualisation of the term. This statement still holds true today. One of the problems, as contended by both Yukl (2002) and Slack and Parent (2006), is the lack of consistency and conclusive results in the findings. There has been a tendency to portray the good leader in almost mythical terms as a 'knight in shining armour riding a white horse'. As such, men have been the prime focus of research, while women have rarely been used as subjects (Slack and Parent, 2006).

Meanwhile, Kellett (1999) raised serious questions regarding how we perceive the notion of leadership in sport organisations. She used data from professional head coaches in the Australian Football League (AFL) to argue that 'our emerging understandings of coaches as leaders can and should inform the literature about leadership in general' (Kellett, 1999, p. 151). Interestingly, Kellett proposed that our current understandings of coaches as leaders, and what leaders actually *do*, are fundamentally flawed. While the AFL coaches in her study readily described certain players as leaders, they were reluctant to describe themselves as leaders, but instead saw their roles more as facilitators of players' development. As a result, the coaches heavily emphasised social skills such as communication, counselling, empowerment of others, and group facilitation – skills traditionally associated with women, and in no way consistent with the 'knight in shining armour' view discussed above. Thus, Kellett questioned the oft-quoted argument by management scholars that sport coaches provide a legitimate analogue of business leaders, and concluded that our fundamental conceptions of what it actually means 'to lead', and in particular how we train our coaches and leaders, may be in substantial need of revision.

Earlier in the chapter, we examined how an organisation may look (its structure, design) and what contingencies or contextual dimensions may impact upon it. In this section, we have addressed the inner workings of a sport organisation, specifically related to four aspects: organisational change; managerial decision-making; power, politics, and conflict; and leadership.

CASE STUDY: CHANGES IN UEFA'S CLUB LICENSING SYSTEM

The popularity of football in Europe and the vast amounts of money it generates are well known. We are amazed on an almost daily basis by the figures quoted for players' and coaches' contracts, transfer fees, sponsorship deals, endorsements, and so on. For European clubs, the international stage provided by the Champions League, administered by Europe's football governing body, UEFA, can be incredibly lucrative. Clearly, European clubs have plenty of incentive to gain entry to UEFA club competitions. However, performance on the playing field is not the only rationale that qualifies clubs for European competition.

Recently, UEFA launched its new Club Licensing Manual to its 51 member associations. Under the UEFA club licensing system, clubs hopeful of gaining entry to UEFA competitions must satisfy specific criteria. The aim of the licensing system and its associated accreditation process is 'to improve overall standards within the European game' (Rawnsley, 2002, p. 21). Thus, clubs must ensure investment in youth development, improved stadia facilities, health and safety, administrative and management procedures, and, of course, the overall quality and transparency of financial operations. The licensing criteria comprise five key areas of club operations: (i) sporting; (ii) infrastructure; (iii) personnel and administrative; (iv) legal; and (v) financial.

Interestingly, UEFA made each of its 51 member national associations the licensors in each of their respective territories for the implementation and governance of the system. By the end of 2002, these national associations were required to have developed their respective licensing documentation in compliance with the minimum requirements mandated by UEFA. The respective licensors in each country – the national associations or, in some countries, affiliated leagues – will then issue licences that entitle holders to enter UEFA club competitions. Although UEFA only requires those clubs that qualify for UEFA club competitions to gain a licence, it has encouraged national associations to persuade all clubs in their respective top divisions to meet the licensing criteria.

For some of the more efficiently run clubs and associations, the first phase of implementation of the Club Licensing Manual in the 2004/05 season was nothing more than business-as-usual. However, for many, the implementation of UEFA's licensing system posed significant challenges. In particular, the last set of financial criteria comprises around 50 per cent of the manual! Nonetheless, the procedure for the initial 2004/05 implementation phase was relatively straightforward. Clubs simply presented audited annual financial statements, unaudited interim accounts, and proof that there were no residual payables due from agreements with employees and transfer activities. However, in the second phase, from 2006/07 onwards, in addition to the initial requirements, clubs were required to submit budgeted monthly liquidity plan/cashflow statements to demonstrate adequate cash resources for the season, as well as examined Financial Licensing Documentation (FLD). The FLD mandated clubs to supply detailed historic balance sheets; profit, loss, and cashflow data; as well as additional information relating to general financial operations. The third phase for implementation included additional requirements for audited interim accounts and scope for clubs to prove that their balance sheets are not 'in the red'. However, when a 2010 report commissioned by UEFA revealed that half of Europe's leading clubs are still losing money, and 20 per cent are facing huge deficits, it set in motion the institution of yet another set of new rules regarding European club licensing regulations. This will mean that, unless they undertake still more organisational reforms in line with the new regulations, from the 2013/14 season clubs will face exclusion from the Champions and Europa Leagues (Cutler, 2010).

SUMMARY

This chapter was obviously a very brief summary of organisation theory. Nevertheless, we have seen that organisation theory has its roots in sociology and is concerned with the study of organisational structure, design, processes, and context. An organisation's structural dimensions include:

- Complexity: the degree of horizontal, vertical, and spatial differentiation of an organisation;
- Formalisation: the documentation of rules, regulations, policies, procedures, job descriptions, etc., that dictate the workings of a sport organisation; and
- Centralisation: the degree to which decision-making power is vested in the hands of one or a few senior managers of a sport organisation.

The patterning of these structural dimensions in a sport organisation is referred to as organisational design. This patterning can resemble a simple design, a machine bureaucracy, a professional bureaucracy, a divisionalised form, or an adhocracy. These organisational design configurations are ideal types, and most sport organisations will exhibit characteristics of two or more of each of the design types. Nonetheless, these structural and design characteristics provide markers for comparing and measuring the internal characteristics of a sport organisation, which are themselves a reflection of the sport organisation's contextual dimensions. Contextual dimensions include the strategic, size, environmental, and technological characteristics of a sport organisation.

Throughout the lifecycle of a sport organisation, it will move through long periods of convergent, gradual change that will be punctuated by short periods of frame breaking, radical organisational change. The organisation's structural, design, decision making, and leadership characteristics must be adjusted to fit with shifting contextual conditions in order to effectively manage and survive periods of change. Most decisions made by sport managers will be made under conditions of risk or uncertainty. This is related to the fact that managers are rationally bounded in their decision making and, not knowing *all* of the possible decision alternatives, must make decisions based on limited information and intellectual resources. In actually making a decision, sport managers have a number of different options. Decisions may be made autocratically by one senior manager or, more likely, by means of consultation, joint decision-making processes, or delegation to a particular group.

Power, politics, and organisational conflict are aspects that are inherent to all sport organisations, and therefore take up much of a sport manager's time and energy. Power has many forms, and may be legitimate, reward, coercive, referent, and/or expert in nature. Political activity takes place in the pursuit of power as individuals or groups form coalitions to arrive at desired outcomes. This political activity raises the potential for organisational conflict. While conflict typically has a negative connotation, it can also be beneficial for an organisation in that it can foster new ideas and provide the organisation with a self-critical approach that makes it receptive to innovation and change.

Finally, leadership plays a key role in the success of any sport organisation. Approaches to understanding leadership have been trait based, where leaders are perceived as 'born, not made', and behaviour based, where leadership is perceived as a task-oriented behaviour that can be taught to anyone; while some have argued that leadership is a function of the different contingencies and unique situations faced by a leader. Charisma is often used to describe a good leader and has, more recently, led to the notion of transformational leadership. It was argued that there is still much work to be done before a more complete understanding of leadership, particularly in sport organisations, can be generated.

REVIEW QUESTIONS

1 Explain how a basic knowledge of organisation theory can help individual managers more effectively manage their sport organisations.
2 Think of a sport organisation with which you are familiar. Describe the structural elements of that organisation.
3 Using the same sport organisation described above, how would you describe its organisational design?
4 Identify one voluntary sport organisation, one professional sport organisation, and one sport governing body. How do the contextual dimensions of each sport organisation differ?
5 Identify a major decision recently taken in a sport organisation with which you are familiar – either as a participant in the decision-making process or as an observer. Using the relevant concepts outlined in this chapter, describe the decision-making process and explain how the ultimate decision choice was reached.

6 Think of a leader figure in a sport organisation with which you are familiar. Using the leadership concepts outlined in this chapter, explain why you think this leader is effective or ineffective.

FURTHER READING

Baum, J.A.C. and Rowley, T.J. (2001) *Companion to Organisations*. Oxford, UK: Blackwell.

Child, J. (1972) 'Organisational Structure, Environment and Performance: The Role of Strategic Choice', *Sociology*, 6: 1–22.

Clegg, S.R., Hardy, C., Lawrence, T.B., and Nord, W.R. (2007) *The SAGE Handbook of Organization Studies* (2nd ed.). Thousand Oaks, CA: SAGE Publications Inc.

D'Aunno, T., Succi, M., and Alexander, J.A. (2000) 'The Role of Institutional and Market Forces in Divergent Organisational Change', *Administrative Science Quarterly*, 45: 679–703.

Greenwood, R. and Hinings, C.R. (1996) 'Understanding Radical Organisational Change: Bringing Together the Old and the New Institutionalism', *Academy of Management Review*, 21: 1022–1054.

Greenwood, R., Suddaby, R., and Hinings, C.R. (2002) 'Theorizing Change: The Role of Professional Associations in the Transformation of Institutionalized Fields', *Academy of Management Journal*, 45: 58–80.

Ocasio, W. (1994) 'Political Dynamics and the Circulation of Power: CEO Succession in US Industrial Corporations', *Administrative Science Quarterly*, 39: 285–312.

Pugh, D.S., Hickson, D.J., Hinings, C.R., and Turner, C. (1968) 'Dimensions of Organisational Structure', *Administrative Science Quarterly*, 13: 65–105.

Shaw, S. and Allen, J.B. (2006) '"It Basically Is a Fairly Loose Arrangement ... And That Works Out Fine Really." Analysing the Dynamics of an Interorganisational Partnership', *Sport Management Review*, 9: 203–228.

WEBSITES

Academy of Management
http://www.aomonline.org

European Group of Organisational Studies
http://www.egosnet.org/jart/prj3/egosnet/main.jart

The National Rugby League
http://www.nrl.com

The Union of European Football Associations
http://www.uefa.com

REFERENCES

Amis, J. and Slack, T. (1996) 'The Size–Structure Relationship in Voluntary Sport Organizations', *Journal of Sport Management*, 10: 76–86.

Amis, J., Slack, T., and Berrett, T. (1995) 'The Structural Antecedents of Conflict in Voluntary Sport Organizations', *Leisure Studies*, 14: 1–16.

Bass, B.M. (1985) *Leadership and Performance Beyond Expectations*. New York, NY: Free Press.

Bass, B.M. (1996) *A New Paradigm of Leadership: An Inquiry into Transformational Leadership*. Alexandria, VA: U.S. Army Research Institute for the Behavioral and Social Sciences.

Bedeian, A.G. and Zammuto, R.F. (1991) *Organizations: Theory and Design*. Chicago, IL: Dryden Press.

Berrett, T., Burton, T.L., and Slack, T. (1993) 'Quality Products, Quality Service: Factors Leading to Entrepreneurial Success in the Sport and Leisure Industry', *Leisure Studies*, 12: 93–106.

'Billabong Biz: Behind the Brand' (2010) http://www.billabongbiz.com/phoenix.zhtml?c=154279 &p=irol-homeProfile. Retrieved from the World Wide Web on 27 January 2010.

Blau, P.M. and Schoenherr, R.A. (1971) *The Structure of Organisations*. New York, NY: Basic Books.

Burns, T. and Stalker, G.M. (1961) *The Management of Innovation*. London, UK: Tavistock.

Chalip, L. (2001) 'Group Decision Making and Problem Solving', in B.L. Parkhouse, *The Management of Sport: Its Foundation and Application* (3rd ed.). New York, NY: McGraw-Hill.

Child, J. (1973) 'Parkinson's Progress: Accounting for the Number of Specialists in Organisations', *Administrative Science Quarterly*, 18: 328–348.

Child, J. (1984) *Organisation: A Guide to Problems and Practice* (2nd ed.). London, UK: Chapman.

Conger, J.A. (1989) *The Charismatic Leader: Behind the Mystique of Exceptional Leadership*. San Francisco, CA: Jossey-Bass.

Cousens, L. (1997) 'From Diamonds to Dollars: The Dynamics of Change in AAA Caseball Franchises', *Journal of Sport Management*, 11: 316–334.

Cousens, L. and Barnes, M.L. (2009) 'Sport Delivery in a Highly Socialized Environment: A Case Study of Embeddedness', *Journal of Sport Management*, 23: 574–590.

Cousens, L. and Slack, T. (1996) 'Emerging Patterns of Inter-Organizational Relations: A Network Perspective of North American Professional Sport Leagues', *European Journal for Sport Management*, 3: 48–69.

Cousens, L. and Slack, T. (2005) 'Field-Level Change: The Case of North American Major League Professional Sport', *Journal of Sport Management*, 19: 13–42.

Cutler, M. (2010) 'UEFA: More Than Half of Clubs Losing Money' (http://www.sportbusiness.com/news/171652/uefa-more-than-half-of-clubs-losing-money). Retrieved from the World Wide Web on 28 January 2010.

Daft, R.L. (2007) *Organization Theory and Design* (9th ed.). Mason, OH: Thomson/South-Western.

Daft, R.L. (2009) *Organization Theory and Design* (10th ed.). Mason, OH: South-Western Cenpage Learning.

French, J. and Raven, B. (1959) 'Bases of Social Power', in D. Cartwright (ed.), *Studies in Social Power*. Ann Arbor: University of Michigan.

Harrison, J.S. and St John, C.H. (2008) *Foundations in Strategic Management* (4th ed.). Mason, OH: Thomson/South-Western.

Heffernan, J. and O'Brien, D. (2010) 'Stakeholder Influence Strategies in Bidding for a Professional Sport Franchise License', *Sport Management Review*, doi:10.1016/j.smr.2010.01.007.

Kellett, P. (1999) 'Organisational Leadership: Lessons from the Professional Coaches', *Sport Management Review*, 2: 150–171.

Kikulis, L.M., Slack, T. and Hinings, C.R. (1995) 'Toward an Understanding of the Role of Agency and Choice in the Changing Structure of Canada's National Sport Organizations', *Journal of Sport Management*, 9: 135–152.

Kimberly, J.R. (1976) 'Organisational Size and the Structuralist Perspective: A Review Critique, and Proposal', *Administrative Science Quarterly*, 21: 571–597.

Kondra, A.Z. and Hinings, C.R. (1998) 'Organizational Diversity and Change in Institutional Theory', *Organization Studies*, 19: 743–767.

Macintosh, D. and Whitson, D.J. (1990) *The Game Planners: Transforming Canada's Sport System*. Montreal and Kinston: McGill-Queen's University Press.

Malcolm, D. and Sheard, K. (2002) '"Pain in the Assets": The Effects of Commercialization and Professionalization on the Management of Injury in English Rugby Union', *Sociology of Sport Journal*, 19: 149–169.

McCann, J.E. (1991) 'Design Principles for an Innovating Company', *Academy of Management Executive*, 5: 76–93.

Miller, D. (1990) *The Icarus Paradox: How Exceptional Companies Bring About Their Own Downfall*. New York, NY: Harper Business.

Mintzberg, H. (1979) *The Structuring of Organisations: A Synthesis of the Research*. Englewood Cliffs, NJ: Prentice Hall.

O'Brien, D. and Slack, T. (1999) 'Deinstitutionalizing the Amateur Ethic: An Empirical Investigation of Change in a Rugby Union Football Club', *Sport Management Review*, 2: 24–42.

O'Brien, D. and Slack, T. (2002) 'Strategic Responses to Institutional Pressures for Commercialisation: Case Study of a Senior English Rugby Union Club', in T. Slack (ed.), *The Commercialisation of Sport*. London, UK: Frank Cass.

O'Brien, D. and Slack, T. (2003) 'An Analysis of Change in an Organizational Field: The Professionalization of English Rugby Union', *Journal of Sport Management*, 17: 417–448.

O'Brien, D. and Slack, T. (2004) 'The Emergence of a Professional Logic in English Rugby Union: The Role of Isomorphic and Diffusion Processes', *Journal of Sport Management*, 18: 13–39.

Parsley, J.D. (1987) 'Solving the Facility Scheduling Puzzle', *Athletic Business*, 11: 72–75.

'Patagonia's History: A Company Created by Climber Yvon Chouinard' (2010) http://www.patagonia.com/web/us/patagonia.go?slc=en_US&sct=US&assetid=3351. Retrieved from the World Wide Web on 20 March 2010.

Pfeffer, J. (1981) *Power in Organisations*. Marshfield, MA: Pittman.

Pugh, D.S. and Hickson, D.J. (1976) *Organisation Structure in its Context: The Aston Programme I*. Farnborough, Hants, UK: Saxon House.

Rawnsley, P. (2002) 'Club Licensing for European Football', *Football Business International*, October: 21.

Robbins, S.P. (1990) *Organisation Theory: Structure, Design and Applications* (3rd ed.). Englewood Cliffs, NJ: Prentice Hall.

Scott, W.R. (2000) *Organisations: Rational, Natural and Open Systems* (5th ed.). Englewood Cliffs, NJ: Prentice Hall.

Shaw, S. and Allen, J.B. (2006) '"It Basically is a Fairly Loose Arrangement ... And That Works Out Fine Really": Analysing the Dynamics of an Interorganisational Partnership', *Sport Management Review*, 9: 203–228.

Simon, H.A. (1945) *Administrative Behavior*. New York: Macmillan.

Skinner, J., Stewart, B., and Edwards, A. (1999) 'Amateurism to Professionalism: Modelling Organisational Change in Sporting Organisations', *Sport Management Review*, 2: 173–192.

Slack, T. (1997) *Understanding Sport Organisations: The Application of Organisation Theory*. Champaign, IL: Human Kinetics.

Slack, T. and Hinings, C.R. (1992) 'Understanding Change in National Sport Organizations: An Integration of Theoretical Perspectives', *Journal of Sport Management*, 6: 114–132.

Slack, T. and Hinings, C.R. (1994) 'Institutional Pressures and Isomorphic Change: An Empirical Test', *Organization Studies*, 15: 803–827.

Slack, T. and Parent, M.M. (2006) *Understanding Sport Organisations: The Application of Organisation Theory* (2nd ed.). Champaign, IL: Human Kinetics.

Stevenson, W.B., Pearce, J.L., and Porter, L.W. (1985) 'The Concept of Coalition in Organisation Theory and Research', *Academy of Management Review*, 10: 256–268.

Stogdill, R.M. (1974) *Handbook of Leadership: A Survey of Theory and Research*. New York, NY: Free Press.

Thomas, K.W., and Schmidt, W.H. (1976) 'A Survey of Managerial Interests with Respect to Conflict', *Academy of Management Journal*, 19: 315–318.

119

Tushman, M.L., Newman, W.H., and Romanelli, E. (1986) 'Convergence and Upheaval: Managing the Unsteady Pace of Organizational Evolution', in H. Mintzberg and J.B. Quinn (eds.) (1998), *Readings in the Strategy Process* (3rd ed.). Englewood Cliffs, NJ: Prentice Hall.

Vroom, V.H. and Yetton, P.W. (1973) *Leadership and Decision Making*. Pittsburgh, PA: University of Pittsburgh Press.

Walter, B. (2010) 'NRL Clubs Start Push for Independent Commission' (http://www.brisbanetimes.com.au/rugby-league/league-news/nrl-clubs-start-push-for-independent-commission-20100118-mf49.html). Retrieved from the World Wide Web on 16 February 2010.

Walter, B. and Proszenko, A. (2010) 'D-Day: Clubs and Players Set to Demand a Declaration of Independence' (http://www.brisbanetimes.com.au/rugby-league/league-news/dday-clubs-and-players-set-to-demand-a-declaration-of-independence-20100117-meew.html). Retrieved from the World Wide Web on 16 February 2010.

Woodward, J. (1958) *Industrial Organisation: Theory and Practice*. Oxford, UK: Oxford University Press.

Yukl, G. (2002) *Leadership in Organisations* (5th ed.). Upper Saddle River, NJ: Prentice Hall.

Chapter 8

Strategy and planning in the context of sport

Milena Parent, University of Ottawa, Ottawa, Canada
Danny O'Brien, Griffith University, Gold Coast, Australia
Trevor Slack, University of Alberta, Edmonton, Canada

TOPICS

The nature of strategy • The strategic management process • Strategic sport management in the twenty-first century

---

OBJECTIVES

At the end of this chapter you should be able to:

■ Explain the concepts of strategy and the strategic management process;

■ Understand the different approaches that can be used in strategic planning, formulation, implementation, control, and evaluation;

■ Recognise the different strategic contexts that influence strategic management in sport organisations;

■ Explore the growing influence of sustainability issues on strategic management in sport.

KEY TERMS

Competitive advantage – we say that a sport organisation has competitive advantage when its profit rate (or however success is broadly defined in that organisation's particular sector) is higher than average among competitors (cf. Hill and Jones, 2001).

Strategic management – strategic management is the process of planning, implementing, controlling, and evaluating many *different* strategies that are all aimed at fulfilling the vision of the sport organisation.

Strategic planning – strategic planning is a process involving external and internal environment analyses and visioning (identifying/revising the vision, mission, and core purpose) (Slack and Parent, 2006).

Strategy – strategy is a plan, ploy, pattern, position, or perspective, where all sets of organisational activities are integrated in a coherent manner (fit) so that the organisation may meet its goals (Mintzberg, 1987; Poister and Streib, 1999; Porter, 1996).

Sustainability – sustainability in business pertains to organisations fostering not only economic value but also healthy ecosystems and strong communities (see The Network for Business Sustainability, 2010).

OVERVIEW

As the former Major League Baseball player and manager Yogi Berra once said, 'If you don't know where you are going, you might wind up someplace else' (Brainy Quote, 2010). Thus, it is important, especially for organisations – which include two or more people whose work must be coordinated towards a common goal – to have a strategy. Moreover, organisations must compete for a variety of resources in order to survive, and hopefully thrive. In this chapter, you will learn about strategy and planning, fundamental concepts, and processes which can assist an organisation in surviving and thriving. Nike understood the importance of these concepts and processes when it appointed a vice-president of global strategic planning in 2005.

CASE STUDY: SHENZHEN 2011 SUMMER UNIVERSIADE

In recent years, public sector strategic planners have increasingly focused attention on differentiating their respective cities and regions from their competitors (Chalip, 2001, 2002; Kotler *et al.*, 1993). In so doing, civic planners often focus on the strategic development of regional competencies by fostering the growth and promotion of particular industries or sectors (Bramwell, 1998; Judd, 1995; Tyler, 1998). Thus, to market a city or region as an attractive place to live and work, or as a business or tourism destination, regional planners often develop and implement strategic plans that make the most of regional points of differentiation. Interestingly, the sport sector, particularly the hosting of sport events, has emerged as a primary means by which to enhance the awareness and image of a particular region (Chalip, 2001; De Knop, 1998; Gibson, 1998; Van den Berg *et al.*, 2000) and to engender certain economic, social, and environmental (triple bottom line) outcomes for host communities (O'Brien and Chalip, 2008).

The world's largest university-based sport event is the Universiade. The word 'Universiade' is a combination of 'University' and 'Olympiad', and is an international sporting and cultural festival that, within the Olympic Movement, is considered second in size after the Olympic Games. Both the 2007 and 2009 Summer Universiades, hosted by Bangkok, Thailand, and Belgrade, Serbia, respectively, each attracted over 10,000 participants. The Universiade is open to all university student athletes aged between 17 and 28 years. Every two years,

Summer and Winter Universiades are held in cities under the supervision of Fédération Internationale du Sport Universitaire (FISU). On 16 January 2007, FISU announced that the host of the 2011 Summer Universiade would be Shenzhen in Southern China. With five candidates, it was the most competitive race ever for hosting a Universiade.

Shenzhen has a population of 10 million people, about 32 times what it was when it was designated as China's first special economic zone (SEZ) in 1981. There are only five SEZs in China, and being designated an SEZ means Shenzhen benefits from preferential government development policies. Since becoming an SEZ, the Shenzhen economy has grown 1,800 times bigger, with gross domestic product (GDP) reaching US$60 billion in 2005 (Universiade 2011 Shenzhen, 2007). Shenzhen has a reputation as one of the most open cities in China with rapid economic growth, a dynamic market system, and easy rail access to the international hub of Hong Kong. However, fast urbanisation has caused Shenzhen many social and environmental problems, raising questions about the sustainability of further development. Rapid industrialisation and the transfer of a formerly rural population to a large city have also caused social problems such as increased gambling and suicide rates. Thus, creating a new look for urbanised rural communities is a key aspect in any further development in Shenzhen. The Chinese leader, Premier Wen, announced strategic objectives for Shenzhen's future development as being to create innovation; lead the way in new business opportunities; establish new development; and achieve special marketable characteristics.

Meanwhile, in June 2007, the Administration of Sports of China, a Chinese Federal Government agency, announced that Shenzhen will become a regional sport centre integrating research, manufacturing, and marketing of high-end sports products and services, and named the city as the nation's first pilot in developing the sports industry. Federal financial support includes subsidies and advance payments to the 2011 Universiade organising committee, investment in sports facilities, and generous tax exemptions. At the local level, Shenzhen city authorities are building a 'Universiade City' to accommodate the 54 sports venues and 12,000 participants that are anticipated for the 2011 Universiade. This development is all part of Shenzhen's 16 billion Yuan (US$2.05 billion) strategic plan to become a regional sports centre by 2010. This expenditure accounts for 1.8 per cent of Shenzhen's GDP. By 2020, the added value of the city's sports industry is targeted to reach 50 billion Yuan, accounting for 2.5 per cent of its GDP (Universiade 2011 Shenzhen, 2007). Despite being a young city with a short history and youthful population, Shenzhen has a lot of experience in hosting large-scale domestic and international events, and wide exposure to world cultures due to its proximity to the international metropolis of Hong Kong. With reference to the role that the 2011 Summer Universiade plays in Shenzhen's plans, Vice Mayor Liang Daoxing commented: 'It will be a milestone for the city's progress toward becoming an international city to host this influential world sports event ... The event [Universiade] will be good to the young generation yearning for more integration with their world peers and to be more influential in Asia and the world' (Universiade 2011 Shenzhen, 2007, ¶ 2).

THE NATURE OF STRATEGY

Strategy is a difficult concept to define. Indeed, many authors avoid actually defining the concept, and simply assume that the reader understands what is meant by the term. Nonetheless, one useful definition comes from Poister and Streib (1999), who suggested that strategy refers to 'the integration of all other management processes to provide a coherent approach to establishing, attaining, monitoring, evaluating and updating an organisation's strategic agenda' (p. 308). Alternatively, Michael Porter, one the most prolific researchers on organisational strategy, provides a three-part explanation in his 1996 article 'What is Strategy?'. He suggested that 'strategy is the creation of a unique and valuable position, involving different sets of activities' (p. 68). He also pointed out that 'the essence of strategy is choosing what not to do' (p. 70) and, further, that strategy is 'creating fit among a company's activities' (p. 75). While these observations on strategy may seem quite different, by weaving them together we can start to generate an understanding of the formulation, implementation, and evaluation aspects of strategy.

However, this is not the only way to conceptualise strategy. Henry Mintzberg (1987) recognised that researchers and practitioners understand the term differently and, even within their respective groups, there may be different conceptualisations of what is meant when referring to strategy. As a result, he provided an explanation which he refers to as the *five Ps of strategy*: strategy as plan (a premeditated course of action); as ploy (an action intended to beat a competitor); as pattern (a series of actions); as position (a 'location' within an environment or market); and as perspective (a way to look at and perceive the organisational environment).

Strategy versus strategic management and planning

Is there a difference between strategy and strategic management? Many people use the two terms interchangeably. However, this is not entirely accurate. Think of a sport organisation that you are familiar with; does the organisation pursue only *one* strategy? The short answer to this question is probably not! Typically, sport managers are simultaneously responsible for the management of numerous strategies related to the different activities their organisation is involved in. It is not unheard of to have a manager in a small national sport organisation, for example, simultaneously be the event manager, the marketing and communications manager, and the office administrator. Thus, in order to do this successfully, he or she must manage many strategic agendas related to financial management, sponsorship, marketing/promotion, media, volunteers, athlete and officials' development, and infrastructure. Therefore, strategic management is the process of planning, implementing, controlling, and evaluating many different strategies that are all aimed at fulfilling the *vision* of the sport organisation. The vision of the sport organisation refers to its highest aspirations, its broadest and most desirable goals. This vision is articulated in more concrete terms in the sport organisation's mission statement, which defines its central purpose, what business/es it is involved in, the skills and competencies it intends to foster in order to succeed, and its principal customers, users, and clients (Pitts and Lei, 2003). As such, the mission statement serves as a foundation for the organisation's strategic planning process by prescribing a direction for the future. We will deal with this in more detail later in the chapter.

Strategic management, strictly speaking, is therefore broader than planning. What is important to remember is that planning is only the first part of the strategic management process, which also includes implementation and control of the plans and the evaluation of the outcomes to establish key learnings for the next strategic management process an organisation will undertake. However, you will find that some readings and professionals use strategic management, strategic planning, and planning interchangeably.

Why is strategic management important?

Strategic management involves understanding the relationship between your sport organisation and its environment. This understanding provides the sport manager with a foundation on which to base his or her decisions and thus to effectively create or sustain a competitive advantage in the marketplace. We say that a corporation has a competitive advantage when its profit rate is higher than average for its industry (cf. Hill and Jones, 2001). In the context of sport organisations, competition may also be defined by participation rates or number of medals won (locally, nationally, or internationally), for example. Clearly, sustaining a competitive advantage is the central purpose of strategic management because it allows the sport organisation to maintain an edge over its rivals (Pitts and Lei, 2003).

As can be seen from the above, there are differences between the concepts of strategy, strategic management, and planning. However, all these concepts are important for sport managers to understand in order to help their organisations gain and sustain a competitive advantage (whatever the organisation's definition of competitive advantage may be).

THE STRATEGIC MANAGEMENT PROCESS

As Chappelet (2005) highlighted, the strategic management process is cyclical in nature, especially for organisations which already exist, and the process can take a long time. For example, Nike's brand realignment and overall restructuring strategy is a more than two-year process (see Nike, 2009).

Nevertheless, any new strategic management process begins with the formulation (or review) of a vision. This vision is then articulated more specifically in a mission statement and/or a statement of the sport organisation's core purpose. Then an assessment of the threats and opportunities present in the organisation's external competitive environment should be carried out. Following this, an internal assessment of the sport organisation should reveal its strengths and weaknesses. These analyses will underpin the selection of appropriate organisational strategies, and their supporting structures and processes. Once selected, these strategies, structures, and processes should be implemented to build on organisational strengths, while simultaneously correcting potential or actual weaknesses. This selection and implementation phase is integral to seizing external opportunities and appropriately responding to environmental threats. Once implemented, strategic activity needs to be controlled and evaluated in light of the sport organisation's desired goals. Each individual aspect of this process will now be examined independently.

Strategic planning

Strategic planning starts with an identification of the overriding aims of the organisation, that is, its vision, mission, and core purpose. As outlined earlier, the vision of a sport organisation is its 'dream state' and describes the organisation's long-term aspirations (Hubbard, 2000). A vision should be succinct, often no longer than one sentence, and should be future oriented and inspiring to organisational members. For example, the Commonwealth Games Federation's vision is 'To promote a unique, friendly, world class Commonwealth Games and to develop sport for the benefit of the people, the nations and the territories of the Commonwealth, and thereby strengthen the Commonwealth' (Commonwealth Games Federation, 2007, p. 4). The mission statement then operationalises the vision by articulating what the organisation is currently doing that, over the longer term, will lead to the fulfilment of its vision. Here, the organisation defines the scope of its products and/or services and provides general organisational objectives. For example, the FIVB's (*Fédération Internationale de Volleyball*) mission is:

> The FIVB governs, manages and communicates all forms of Volleyball and Beach Volleyball worldwide. It aims to develop Volleyball as a major world media and entertainment sport through world-class planning and organisation of competitions, marketing and promotional activities. The FIVB is part of the Olympic Movement, contributing to the success of the Olympic Games.
>
> (FIVB, n.d., ¶ 1)

Finally, many sport organisations now also articulate a core purpose. A core purpose incorporates the values of the organisation and answers the question 'Why are we here?' The Union of European Football Associations' (UEFA) core purpose is 'To create the right conditions for the game in Europe to prosper and develop' (UEFA, 2009, ¶ 5). The core purpose, along with the sport organisation's vision and mission, provides the foundation upon which sport managers begin their strategic planning. Once this fundamental understanding of the sport organisation's current and desired directions has been generated, an external analysis of the organisational environment needs to be undertaken.

External environment analysis

Many researchers describe the organisational environment according to two levels: the task environment is the immediate environment that surrounds the organisation; while the general environment is more removed and influences the organisation less directly. In turn, both of these aspects of environment are multifaceted.

The task environment, sometimes referred to as the specific, proximal, or competitive environment, comprises those groups or individuals that are closest to the organisation and have a daily impact on its operation. Earle Zeigler (1985) used sport and physical education departments within universities to illustrate the various facets of the task environment. He identified six components of a sport organisation's task environment: (1) *clients* are the customers, members, or fans of the sport organisation (e.g. the students and faculty of a physical education department); (2) *suppliers* are individuals/organisations that are associated with or provide some form of resource support to the organisation (e.g. the university administration's funding support for a department); (3) *advisers* provide some form of counsel to the organisation (e.g. the university's top administrators or visiting experts); (4) *controllers* are often legislative agencies, government departments, funding agencies, or governing bodies; (5) *adversaries* are the organisation's competitors (e.g. similar departments in other universities who compete for the same students and faculty members, or even other departments in the same university since they compete for the same funding); and (6) *publics with opinions* can be community stakeholders with a vested interest in the organisation (e.g. community members who make use of the department's facilities).

In turn, the general environment, sometimes referred to as the distal environment, is usually described using seven subcomponents: economic, political, legal, socio-cultural, demographic, ecological, and technological (Slack and Parent, 2006). The *economic environment* is fairly easy to understand: organisational activities may be different during a recession as opposed to during an economic boom. Similarly, the *political environment* may moderate managers' actions, whether through political instability or the spending whims of a government leading into an election period, for instance. Of course, any laws in place must be followed; therefore, the *legal environment* will profoundly influence any important strategic decisions. The *socio-cultural environment* refers to the social system and cultural mores of a particular society and may dictate, for example, the attitudes and tastes of potential clients/customers. In the same way, *demographics*, which refer to societal characteristics such as age and gender distributions, occupations and income, ethnicity, etc., will influence the appropriateness of strategy selection for a particular target market. Next, the *ecological environment* is an important factor, as all organisations, to some extent, impact upon nature. For instance, most sport event owners such as the IOC now have formalised protocols in place to measure not only their events' economic and social impacts, but also how their events impact on the environment. Finally, in this information age, the *technological environment* is crucial as managers constantly scan for innovative, state-of-the-art technology that may give their organisation an edge on competitors. For instance, in February 2010, the Association of Surfing Professionals, the world governing body for professional surfing's elite World Championship Tour (WCT), announced its launch of a mobile phone application that enables fans to download live scores, heat results, photos, and live video feeds from WCT events around the world. In addition, many European football clubs now utilise the services of player-scouting database companies that provide access to player, team, and match profiles via both web-based and desktop applications. In scanning the environment for innovations, the major implication is that a competitive advantage is usually reserved for those who adopt the innovation first, rather than those who follow later in an effort to 'catch up' with early adopters (O'Brien and Slack, 2004).

Another way of conceptualising a sport organisation's environment is through stakeholder analysis. A stakeholder is 'any group or individual who can affect or is affected by the achievement of the firm's objectives' (Freeman, 1984, p. 25). For example, Figure 8.1 demonstrates the various types of stakeholders for a sport mega-event. An identification of stakeholders, and an analysis of their respective needs, demands, and centrality to the operation of the sport organisation, should provide managers with a greater sense of their environment. Further, stakeholder analysis can reveal the expectations that key stakeholders have of the sport organisation (Merrilees *et al.*, 2005; Parent and Deephouse, 2007). Meanwhile, Heffernan and O'Brien (2010) note the importance to a focal sport organisation's survival of understanding the strategic behaviours employed by key stakeholders. As such, stakeholder analysis can be a catalyst for management to formulate strategic actions to effectively address environmental demands and pressures (Mitchell *et al.*, 1997; O'Brien and Slack, 2005; Wolfe and Putler, 2002).

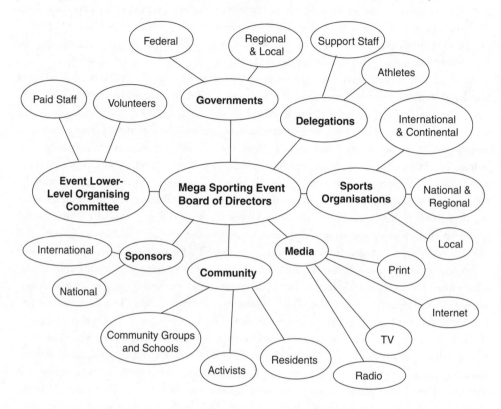

Figure 8.1 *A generic stakeholder map for a mega sporting event*

Thus, careful environmental scanning can bestow certain advantages on sport organisations, while simultaneously alerting managers to any actual or potential threats. In order to effectively respond to these environmental contingencies, sport managers must regularly conduct internal organisational audits, both of organisational strengths and weaknesses.

Internal organisational analysis

One useful way of conducting an internal organisational analysis is to examine the sport organisation's core competencies. Prahalad and Hamel (1990) explained that core competencies are the peculiar knowledge and skill reserves present within an organisation. Essentially, a core competence should comprise three characteristics: (1) it should provide the organisation with access to multiple markets; (2) it should make a significant contribution to an end product's perceived benefits; and (3) competitors should not be able to easily imitate it (Prahalad and Hamel, 1990). Thus, core competencies are those aspects of the organisation in which it particularly excels. Depending upon what type of business activity the sport organisation is involved in, core competencies may be aspects such as research and development, human resource management, or, perhaps, junior sport development. This approach is an effective way of understanding the strengths of an organisation and, when done exhaustively, should simultaneously alert sport managers to where their organisation is lacking. That is, in order to respond appropriately to environmental threats and opportunities, while seeking to identify and foster organisational core competencies, sport managers must also identify any particular weaknesses.

Typically, one aspect of organisational operation that often presents problems for management is the availability and ease of access to resources. Besides skills, an organisation will have different resources that help it achieve its core purpose and mission. Tangible resources may be material, for example high-tech communication equipment, state-of-the-art production facilities, or, simply, the raw materials that go into particular products. Obviously, access to adequate financial resources is also critical to the survival of most sport organisations. Conversely, intangible resources refer to aspects such as skills, general knowledge, culture, brand recognition, know-how, and the reputation of an organisation. Amis *et al.* (1997) contended that it is these intangible resources that are more likely to bestow a sustainable competitive advantage on a sport organisation. These researchers empirically demonstrated that sound access to intangible resources, in this case sport sponsorship, is integral to a sport organisation's ability to sustain a competitive advantage. Clearly, weaknesses in this area of intangible resource availability could be catastrophic to the ongoing viability of a sport organisation.

SWOT analysis

Having scanned the external environment and internal operations of the sport organisation, the next step in strategic planning is to generate a series of strategic alternatives. This can be done by what is referred to as a SWOT analysis. A SWOT analysis consists of listing the strengths and weaknesses of the sport organisation, and also its opportunities and threats, hence the acronym SWOT. Strengths and weaknesses may be present in terms of personnel, products, services, resources, skills, structure, or knowledge; while opportunities and threats may be present in the form of concept or product development, impending legal changes, new technologies, or new openings in a market, all of which may impact upon the sport organisation's competitive advantage. Obviously, these are but a few examples of strengths, weaknesses, opportunities, and threats, the exact nature of which will be dependent upon the actual business or activity the sport organisation is involved in. The information generated by thorough scanning of the organisation's external environment and internal operations, and the subsequent SWOT analysis, underpins the next task of strategy formulation, to which we now turn. See http://www.businessballs.com/swotanalysisfreetemplate.htm for further information and free templates on the SWOT analysis method.

Strategy formulation

The next task in strategic management is that of strategic choice – the process of deciding among the strategic imperatives generated from the SWOT analysis. These strategic alternatives will typically include strategies at the business level, and strategies at the corporate level. We will now briefly discuss the types of strategies found at each level.

The business level of strategy

The business level of strategy includes the overall theme that a sport organisation chooses to emphasise, the way in which it positions itself in the marketplace to gain a competitive advantage, and the various strategies it uses to position itself in its chosen industry setting(s). Michael Porter (1980) described three generic business-level strategies. The first is overall cost leadership. This strategy involves the sport organisation stressing a low-cost position in its marketplace. Thus, it attempts to generate superior market share and yield above-average returns by controlling costs and offering a comparatively cheaper product or service in relation to competitors. A key advantage of this strategy is that it allows a firm to capitalise on the spending of competitors on expensive research and development. The low-cost leader will closely monitor the market and simply replicate new products or services as soon as they hit the market. For example, in the outdoor sport equipment market, Helly Hanson does relatively little research and development as compared to a key competitor such as Patagonia. Instead, it carefully monitors the market for innovative new products and materials and, once identified, sets about replicating them at a cut rate, passing any saving onto its customers by offering similar equipment at a cheaper price. However, this strategy still requires significant capital investment (e.g. for the latest production equipment), aggressive pricing, sound market intelligence, and continuous controls on cost.

The second business-level strategy, differentiation, refers to the creation of a product, service, brand image, technology, or level of customer service that is unique in the industry. In turn, this *uniqueness* allows the business to charge premium prices for its offerings. The key advantage of this strategy is the building of loyalty among its customers or clients. However, the endurance of this sense of uniqueness, and therefore customer loyalty, depends on a number of factors, in particular the amount of competition present in the industry and the ease with which competitors can imitate the unique element. A sport organisation that chooses a differentiation strategy must have strong communication and coordination among its research and development, product development, and marketing departments; and must also be capable of attracting experts or 'innovators' to the organisation. This presents a disadvantage in that such experts are usually highly trained in their chosen fields, and thus demand large salaries, expensive support networks and equipment, and significant resource investments to effectively perform their jobs. In the example of outdoor equipment providers Helly Hanson and Patagonia discussed previously, Patagonia employs experts such as chemists to research new technologies applicable to the development of superior and more environmentally friendly outdoor sport equipment. Obviously, this requires significant investments of organisational resources. However, it allows Patagonia to maintain an image of being environmentally friendly and 'cutting edge', which in turn legitimises the premium price consumers are willing to pay for their products.

The third type of strategy, focus, targets a particular market segment. This could be a specific demographic group, or perhaps a market in a particular geographic area. Strategists develop the product or service with the particular segment in mind. This allows them to offer a superior product or service to that segment in comparison to competitors' offerings. The primary advantage of this strategy is that the sport organisation can develop a close relationship with its customers/clients, which can, of course, be conducive to generating loyalty in notoriously fickle markets. However, a focus strategy may also involve smaller profit margins due to generally smaller production and sales volumes. There is also the very real risk that the focus niche market could disappear. Many smaller sport and leisure-based organisations pursue focus strategies, servicing small though potentially fickle customer bases. For example, activities such as skateboarding regularly move in and out of fashion in youth markets. An organisation that pursues a focus strategy and invests heavily in the latest trend to hit their particular market runs the risk of being left with oversupplies of stock, and therefore irretrievable sunk costs, should the trend prove to be short-lived, or an alternative product or 'craze' arrives unexpectedly on the market.

While the three preceding strategies can be viable approaches to maintaining competitiveness, as the example above suggests, not all organisations read their environment correctly, and as a result may pursue inappropriate strategies. Or alternatively, they may pursue the right strategies but lack the necessary organisational characteristics, resources, or, simply, the required amount of resolve to achieve competitive advantage. This poor strategic situation is what Porter (1980) referred to as being 'stuck in the middle'.

The corporate level of strategy

When a sport organisation is large and diversified, and competes in a number of different industries, it requires corporate-level strategies that are followed by the organisation as a whole. Hodge and Anthony (1991) identified four different types of corporate-level strategies: growth, stability, defensive, and combination strategies.

Growth strategies entail diversification and/or integration. *Diversification* is when a sport organisation redistributes resources to move into new products or markets. These may be related or unrelated to the organisation's existing operations. For example, when the giant surfwear corporation Billabong purchased both Von Zipper (sunglasses and ski goggles) and Element (skate wear) in 2001, Nixon (watches and accessories) in 2006, Xcel (specialist wetsuits) and Tigerlily (girls' swimwear) in 2007, and Sector 9 (skateboards) and DaKine (boardsport accessories) in 2008 (Billabong, n.d.), it was pursuing *related diversification*. Alternatively, *integration* can occur both horizontally and vertically. *Horizontal integration* is when a sport organisation buys another organisation, usually a competitor in the same business. The instance of adidas-Salomon AG (adidas group) buying Reebok in 2006 (adidas group, 2009) would be an example of horizontal integration. Meanwhile, *vertical integration* occurs when a supplier is purchased (backward vertical integration), or when a distributor is acquired (forward vertical integration). Patagonia's purchase of cotton farms in the early 1990s to increase the reliability of its supply of organic fabric for its clothing lines was an example of backward vertical integration.

When there is a decreased demand for a sport organisation's products or services, defensive strategies can be employed and involve turnaround, divestiture, or liquidation. *Turnaround* strategies involve cutting costs, laying off staff, or changing the markets in which the company operates. *Divestiture*, a more radical measure, involves selling part(s) of the business that are seen as inefficient. *Liquidation*, the most drastic measure of all, involves the shutdown and sale of all or part of a company to obtain capital.

When the management of a sport organisation does not seek growth but simply hopes to maintain current market share and optimal levels of activity, it may pursue a stability strategy. That is, it will simply seek to provide the same level of service and operation as it has traditionally done. Finally, many sport organisations, indeed most, employ some combination of all of the strategies outlined. This is referred to as a combination strategy, and according to Hodge and Anthony (1991), next to growth, is probably the most common of all the strategies addressed here. For example, while refocusing its brands, Nike bought Umbro (growth strategy) but also set out to cut 5 per cent of its workforce (defensive strategy) in order to be more competitive (see http://www.nikebiz.com/company_overview for more information). The precise nature of the strategic combination will be dependent upon management's assessment of their portfolio of business activities, and the strategic direction they propose the organisation should move in. One useful means of charting the sport organisation's strategic trajectory is by means of portfolio analysis.

Portfolio analysis

Larger sport organisations that pursue combination strategies regularly conduct portfolio analyses in order to determine the relative merits and profitability of their various strategic business units (SBUs), that is, the products and services they offer. The Boston Consulting Group (BCG; see http://www.bcg.com) developed one of the more popular techniques for assessing and comparing SBUs. The model proposed by BCG consists of a four-cell matrix, called the BCG matrix. On the BCG matrix, each SBU is analysed using two dimensions: relative market share, and growth rate. Relative market share is determined using the ratio of the SBU's market share over that of its nearest competitor. If the ratio is above 1, then relative market share is high and the SBU is a market leader. A relative market share below 1 is considered low. For example, if an SBU's market share is 15 per cent while its main rival has a market share of 30 per cent, then the SBU's relative market share is ½ (.50), which is considered low. Growth rate is determined by assessing whether the SBU's industry is growing faster than the overall economy. BCG contends that high-growth industries offer a better competitive environment and more favourable long-term prospects than low-growth industries (Hill and Jones, 2001).

On the BCG matrix, high growth rate and high market share describe the SBUs referred to as *stars*. Once established, these SBUs become self-sufficient and provide long-term profit even when the growth rate falls below average. When this happens, they become *cash cows*, which require relatively little ongoing investment but still produce consistently high profit margins that can then be 'milked' to fund further strategic initiatives. For example, with sufficient capital investment, an SBU in a high-growth industry that has only low market share, known as a *question mark*, may eventually become a profitable *star*. However, should the question mark's relative market share remain low and its growth rate declines, according to

BCG, this is indicative of a *dog*. With low growth rate and low market share, management may cease investment in the SBU, and eventually divest it from the organisation.

Strategy implementation, control, and evaluation

Once the choice of strategy has been made, it has to be implemented. Many new strategic initiatives involve various degrees of organisational change and can, therefore, lead to some resistance. It is imperative, therefore, to appropriately manage and control the process of strategy implementation. According to Cummings and Worley (1993), there are five basic steps in managing and controlling the implementation of new strategic initiatives: (1) motivating change; (2) creating and communicating a vision for change; (3) mobilising political support for change; (4) managing the transition; and (5) sustaining the momentum of the strategic initiative. We will now, in turn, address each of these steps.

In order to implement a new strategy, the sport manager must first *motivate change* by creating an environment where the need for change is accepted and members are physically and psychologically committed to any transitions. Openly addressing any reservations that organisational members or key stakeholders may have regarding the new strategic direction is essential here, and can help overcome any resistance to the proposed change process. The second step is to *create a vision* of the organisation's desired future state by relating the new strategy to the sport organisation's mission and core purpose. Then, clearly articulating the strategy's outcome goals and intermediary goals can serve as a benchmark for assessing progress. Next, the manager must *develop the political support* for the change at all levels. This involves mobilising support for the strategic initiative from the sport organisation's more powerful actors and key stakeholders, and, indeed, all organisational members. The legitimacy and access to resources this support provides will then help create the foundation for the fourth step, the actual *management of the transition*. This step refers to the implementation of management structures and processes that will operationalise the strategy. Once the strategy has been initiated, managers need to *sustain the momentum*. This last step includes providing the necessary resources for change, building support systems, facilitating the development of new skills and competencies, and reinforcing new behaviours by linking them to the formal reward system of the sport organisation.

Strategy and structure

Obviously, the choice of strategy by a sport organisation profoundly influences its structure. For example, a sport organisation that employs a defensive strategy will most likely adopt a more bureaucratic, mechanistic structure; while those that seek diversification into new markets will need flexibility, making less rigid, more organic structures appropriate. Logically, therefore, there must be a 'fit' between strategy and structure. However, does strategy necessarily determine structure, or does structure determine strategy? Early work by Chandler (1962), and much of the work by other researchers that has followed, has posited that structure unequivocally follows strategy. However, Mintzberg (1990) provided an alternative view of the strategy–structure relationship. Using the analogy of walking,

133

Mintzberg suggested that just as the right foot follows the left and the left foot follows the right in the action of walking, so too does structure follow strategy and strategy follow structure throughout the lifecycle of an organisation. This presents a more complete picture of the strategy–structure relationship, and recognises the temporal dimension of strategy, rather than a simple snapshot of organisational activity. This approach also takes into account the fact that strategy and structure are inextricably linked; both support each other and neither takes precedence as one always precedes the other and then follows it (Mintzberg, 1990).

Strategic control and evaluation

Once strategies have been implemented, strategic control and evaluation must be instituted. Strategic control and evaluation refers to the 'overall evaluation of the strategic plan, organisational activities, and results that provide information for future action' (Daft, 1995, p. 311). This typically involves gathering feedback on strategic initiatives, and then processing this information to inform future strategic activity. The evaluative process entails assessing both the emergent results and final outputs of the focal strategy(ies), and comparing these with the outcomes articulated in the original strategic plan. Importantly, the fact that *emergent* results are included emphasises the fact that this process should be *ongoing* so that adjustments to organisational processes and structures can be made as and where required. Thus, combined with the use of schedules and budgets to keep track of organisational performance, information is 'fed forward' to assist with organisational forecasting (Robbins and Stuart-Kotze, 1990). This control, evaluation, and recycling of strategic information allows sport managers to proactively meet environmental contingencies, and ultimately fulfil the organisation's strategic objectives.

In this section, we have learned about the strategic management process. This includes:

- Strategic planning: vision, mission, core purpose, and internal and external analyses (SWOT analysis);
- Strategy formulation: business- and corporate-level strategies and portfolio analysis; and
- Strategy implementation, control, and evaluation: managing change, strategy–structure fit, and ongoing strategic control and evaluation.

STRATEGIC SPORT MANAGEMENT IN THE TWENTY-FIRST CENTURY

So far, we have looked at the concepts of strategy and strategic management, and the processes involved in strategic planning, choice, implementation, control, and evaluation. This is known as the *classical approach* to strategy and can be a suitable starting point in considering strategic management. In this section, we address some current issues that are influencing how sport organisations approach strategic management in the twenty-first century. We live in an electronic and globalised world; globalisation may be essentially economic in nature, but it is also political, cultural, and social (St-Germain and Harvey, 2000). International sport competitions, the global and instantaneous broadcasting of sport events in multiple formats (e.g. TV, internet, mobile phones), and the sourcing of global manufacturing locations for the production of sporting goods are but a few of the common occurrences seen in the sport industry today (cf. St-Germain and Harvey, 2000). Sport managers must contend with these parameters, as well as those presented below. Hopefully, you will get the impression that strategic management involves more than developing a 'shopping list', and you will come to appreciate that, for most sport organisations, strategic management is an incredibly complex, but nonetheless essential, task.

Sport, strategy, and sustainability

Over recent years, *the* key issue that has dominated discussions of strategy has been that of sustainability. In the sport event context, early work by May (1995) and Lenskyj (1998) has led to further promising leads by Ritchie (2000), Kearins and Pavlovich (2002), Valera and Guàrdia (2002), Waitt (2003), O'Brien and Gardiner (2006), Schmidt (2006), Collins *et al.* (2007), and O'Brien and Chalip (2008). Related work on corporate social responsibility (CSR) and sport by Smith and Westerbeek (2007) and by Walker and colleagues (Walker and Kent, 2009, 2010; Walker *et al.*, 2010), and a special issue of the *Journal of Sport Management* devoted to CSR and sport (Volume 23, Issue 6, November 2009), illustrate the increasing influence that sustainability-related issues are having on strategic thinking in sport. A useful tool for understanding the issues germane to sustainability and how sport organisations might approach these issues was offered in a *Harvard Business Review* article by Nidumolu *et al.* (2009).

Nidumolu *et al.* (2009) conducted a longitudinal study on the sustainability initiatives of 30 large corporations, arguing that, 'In the future, only companies that make sustainability a goal will achieve competitive advantage … [and t]he quest for sustainability is already starting to transform the competitive landscape' (pp. 3–4). They note that most senior managers wrongly believe that minimising their organisation's harmful social and environmental impacts will negatively impact upon their economic bottom line. From their research, Nidumolu and his colleagues derived a five-stage change process by which successful organisations not only confront sustainability, but turn their pursuit of sustainability into the foundation for innovation and competitive advantage. Innovation comes from the development of new capabilities that are developed to confront fresh challenges at each respective stage of the change process. Nidumolu *et al.* conclude that, in order for their organisations to survive, executives must recognise 'a simple truth: Sustainability = Innovation' (p. 10). Although Nidomolu *et al.*'s work is not specifically in a sport context, their findings are extremely applicable for sport managers. The basis of their five-stage change process is presented in Table 8.1.

Table 8.1 *Sustainability challenges and opportunities (adapted from Nidumolu et al., 2009, pp. 6–7)*

	STAGE 1 View compliance as opportunity	STAGE 2 Make value chains sustainable	STAGE 3 Design sustainable products and services	STAGE 4 Develop new business models	STAGE 5 Create next-practice platforms
Central challenge	To ensure that compliance with norms becomes an opportunity for innovation.	To increase efficiencies throughout the value chain.	To develop sustainable offerings or redesign existing ones to become eco-friendly.	To find novel ways of delivering and capturing value that will change the basis of competition.	To question through the sustainability lens the dominant logic behind business today.
Innovation opportunity	Use compliance to induce the organisation and its partners to experiment with sustainable technologies, materials, and processes.	Develop sustainable sources of raw materials and components. Increase the use of clean energy sources. Find innovative uses for returned products.	Apply techniques such as biomimicry in product development. Develop compact and eco-friendly packaging.	Develop new delivery technologies that significantly change value-chain relationships. Devise business models that combine digital and physical infrastructures.	Build business platforms that enable customers and suppliers to manage energy in radically different ways. Design technologies that will allow industries to use the energy produced as a by-product.

The diverse strategic contexts of sport organisations

While most research in management has focused on private, enduring, for-profit firms, the sport industry is composed of many other types of strategic contexts. First, in many countries, local sport clubs operate on a non-profit basis. For example, a local figure skating club may not be in business to derive profits, but will be more intent on maintaining an adequate membership base to stay in operation. Haberberg and Rieple (2001) maintained that non-profits are usually service-oriented and often receive tax relief or government grants in order to provide services that the government may not be able to provide. They vary in structure from kitchen table formats through to international organisations. They also vary in terms of their involvement and associations from pure sport involvement, to education, religious, and work groups, or purely social outlets. Based on these fundamental 'reasons for being', non-profit sport organisations also vary in their funding sources. Some receive funding from local, state/provincial, or national governments; others rely on sponsorship, donations, or membership for their financial resources. Most operate using some combination of these funding sources. Most non-profits are volunteer based, while others may have volunteer boards that employ professional managers for the actual day-to-day management of the organisation. While non-profits' effectiveness is not usually judged by profit-oriented goals, there is an increase in the commercialisation of these organisations. For instance, Thibault *et al.* (2004) explore the complexities of partnerships for sport and leisure delivery between public sector actors, that are concerned with achieving social missions, with organisations in the commercial sector that have an obviously more commercial mindset. Therefore, in the non-profit context, the development and implementation of efficient mechanisms for financial planning and reporting are every bit as critical as they are in the commercial context (Haberberg and Rieple, 2001).

Next, many countries also have government departments that deal specifically with sport. These organisations, therefore, operate in a public sector context and have characteristics of their own. A public sector sport organisation is subject to the vagaries of continuously changing political groups and ideologies. As such, the planning timeframe is usually fairly short (one to five years). The programmes and structure of public sector sport organisations are typically large, complex, and varied, and are concerned with inputs through (sometimes excessive) planning, budgeting, evaluation, and review processes. However, the trend in public sector sport organisations in most countries has been toward maximising outputs through more business-oriented strategies. As such, some of the strategies public sector sport organisations employ today have been aimed at public–private partnerships, increasing transparency and accountability, increasing resources, and monitoring trends and changes in the environment (Haberberg and Rieple, 2001; Poister and Streib, 1999).

Third, the entrepreneurial context usually includes small or new firms and/or firms that rely on innovation to compete in dynamic, fast-changing environments. As Mintzberg and Quinn (1996, p. 616) contended, 'Entrepreneurial firms are often young and aggressive, continually searching for the risky markets that scare off the bigger bureaucracies. But they are also careful to avoid the complex markets, preferring to remain in niches that their leaders can comprehend'. Being small in nature, the entrepreneurial firm needs strong leadership, vision, and purpose in order to survive. A single leader, often the owner, will take charge of this simple yet dynamic organisation, and strategic management may be totally informal, existing only in the senior manager's head (Berrett *et al.*, 1993). While the entrepreneurial firm is typically created for profit purposes, this need not be the case. An entrepreneurial sport organisation may, for example, be a local volunteer-based football club started by an ex-player to create participation opportunities for local children.

A fourth context has emerged within the last decade, the electronic context. The development of the World Wide Web has created a unique electronic business (e-business) environment where traditional notions of time and physical place have been irreversibly changed. Sport organisations operating in this electronic context may have little in the way of tangible resources; therefore, intangible resources such as reputation and quality of service rise in salience for gaining competitive advantage (Haberberg and Rieple, 2001). Clearly, e-businesses must, therefore, be acutely aware of the technological environment for potential opportunities and threats.

Most management literature focuses on traditional notions of long-term, enduring organisations. However, within sport, there is another context of great significance, the temporary context. The temporary context refers to sport organisations such as event organising committees, for example the London Organising Committee of the Olympic and Paralympic Games (LOCOG; see http://www.london2012.com). Temporary organisations such as the LOCOG face many of the same contingencies as enduring organisations, but their timeline is accelerated, and their lifecycle condensed. Parent (2008) found that major sporting event organising committees went through three operational modes: planning (bid phase, business plan, operational plans), implementation (venue plans, games time), and wrap-up (report writing and legacy management). Managerial processes and activities which may take years for an enduring organisation to undertake must be done in usually less than seven years. For example, organisational culture is an aspect of organisational life that normally evolves over a significant time period. However, McDonald (1991) provided an excellent insight into the strategies employed by the Los Angeles Olympic Organizing Committee, in its efforts to develop an organisational culture 'in the short run'. Another feature of sport organisations operating in this context is that they are generally volunteer based; and they have a predetermined beginning and end. They are also usually very much dependent upon community support and the backing of other key stakeholders such as governments, sponsors, and broadcasters in order to be successful. Therefore, for temporary sport organisations, given the condensed scope of their lifecycle, the environment and the resources extracted from it are even more critical to organisational success. Strategies used by such organisations will, therefore, be a reflection of all contexts. For example, they must be able to recruit, train, and manage volunteers like non-profits, while simultaneously initiating and managing public–private partnerships, being entrepreneurial, and using the e-environment effectively to reach national and international customers and stakeholders.

In sum, this section argues that there are different contexts to consider. Sustainability issues and the type of organisation (for-profit, non-profit, public sector, entrepreneurial, electronic, and enduring v. temporary) have an impact on sport managers' strategy and planning choices in today's globalised, electronic world.

CASE STUDY: A STRATEGIC PLAN FOR SUSTAINABLE SURFING IN PAPUA NEW GUINEA

Since its ancient Polynesian origins, the sport of surfboard riding has been synonymous with travel. Indeed, the willingness of surfers to go to extraordinary lengths to surf in new and exotic locations is a longstanding part of the sport's subculture (Dolnicar and Fluker, 2003). Surf tourism, Buckley (2002) suggests, is core to an annual US$10 billion global surf industry. However, Ponting et al. (2005) caution that surfers' predilection for venturing into geographically and culturally isolated regions in pursuit of uncrowded waves means that surf tourism has sometimes 'nudged unprepared destinations down the slippery slope to large scale industrialised tourism and its related issues' (Ponting et al., 2005, p. 152).

In more established surf tourism destinations such as Indonesia, the Maldives, and Fiji, surf tourism has often brought more problems to its indigenous host communities than benefits. The 'typical' surf tourism business model consists of an overseas-owned operation that pursues unfettered growth and channels profits back to offshore owners, often leaving host communities with social and environmental degradation and little or no economic benefits. In this model, development of the sport of surfing in the host community is frowned upon because it would increase the number of surfers in the water, thus making it more crowded and potentially damaging to the surf tourism product.

One emerging and 'off the beaten track' surf tourism destination is Papua New Guinea (PNG). The Surfing Association of Papua New Guinea (SAPNG) is the national governing body of the sport and has been headed by its President, Andy Abel, since its establishment in 1989. In a world first for surfing, and mindful of the problems surf tourism has brought to other developing nations, the SAPNG has formulated plans with sustainability as the key objective.

The centrepiece of the SAPNG's sustainability initiative is its formal recognition of indigenous ownership of the country's surfing resources – the reefs, beaches, and marine environments where surfing takes place. Each surfing area in the country has its own regional 'Surf Management Plan' (SMP). The SMPs ensure that the owners of surfing resources – local communities – are consulted as to whether they wish to become involved in the sport of surfing. If so, in concert with the SAPNG, community leaders then establish the number of surf tourists per day they will allow to use their resources, and the type of commercial operation they wish to establish for surf tourists. The maximum number of surf tourists permitted per day in most areas is 20, and in the majority of cases the commercial operations are owned and managed by PNG nationals. Incorporated into each surf tourist's accommodation costs is a daily levy that supports the development of surfing at the village level by the SAPNG, its regional associations, and local clubs. Funds are also directed towards community development projects such as aid posts, educational facilities, and water sanitation projects.

This approach has steadily grown surfing in PNG. As a surf destination, it now attracts around 1,500 surf tourists annually from core markets in Australia, New Zealand, and Japan. And, since the first surfing club established at Lido Beach in Vanimo in 1987, there are now 10 clubs spread throughout the country in Sandaun, Madang, and New Ireland Provinces, each varying between 20 and 50 members, and each with its own SMP. In January 2007, the SAPNG held its first national titles, and selected a team to compete in the South Pacific Games in Samoa that year. At the opening of the national titles, the Prime Minister and Grand Chief of PNG, Sir Michael Somare, opened the event and unveiled the SAPNG's first strategic plan. Significantly, the plan was developed in collaboration with the World Bank and formalised the SAPNG's sustainability initiatives. The second PNG National Surfing Titles took place in March 2011 at the recently opened Tupira Surf Club in Madang Province. Wary of the future, SAPNG President Andy Abel suggests the next important step for the sustainability of PNG surfing will be when the SAPNG propose a bill to the PNG legislative assembly to have the SMPs enshrined into law (Abel, personal communication, 2 February 2010).

In their work on Indonesian surf tourism, Ponting et al. (2005, p. 150) argue that 'Unregulated free-market approaches to development ... place local people as just one relatively powerless stakeholder group amongst many others. As a result, local people are usually the last to benefit from economic development based upon the exploitation of their resources, yet shoulder the bulk of deleterious impacts.' Ponting and his colleagues propose that, for more sustainable, equitable surf tourism, three main inter-related prerequisites must be met: (a) a move away from Western business models and economically neo-liberal approaches to development; (b) the need for formal long-term coordinated planning that recognises limits to growth; and (c) a systematic attempt to foster cross-cultural understanding. With this in mind, it seems that, in PNG at least, sustainability may actually be a possibility.

SUMMARY

We have only skimmed the surface of strategy, strategic management, and planning with basic concepts and approaches. We saw that strategic management is the process of planning, implementing, controlling, and evaluating the various strategies of an organisation. These strategies are expected to help the organisation achieve its vision. The classical approach to the strategic management process involves the following:

1 Strategic planning: This includes developing the organisation's vision, mission statement, and core purpose; analysing the organisation's external environment (either the task and general environment or the stakeholders); doing an internal organisational analysis using the core competencies approach and tangible/intangible resources; and combining these analyses into a SWOT analysis.
2 Strategy formulation: An organisation has various strategy alternatives both at the business level (overall cost leadership, differentiation, and focus) and at the corporate level (growth, stability, defensive, and combination strategies). Larger, diversified organisations may conduct portfolio analyses.
3 Strategy implementation: In order to correctly implement strategy, the process must be managed by (a) motivating an acceptance of change; (b) creating and communicating the chosen vision; (c) mobilising political support; (d) managing the transition period; and (e) sustaining the momentum.
4 Strategy control and evaluation: This whole process must be controlled and evaluated using not only final results, but also ongoing, emergent results and organisational feedback.

For enduring success, the chosen strategy(ies) must be sustainable, and fit neatly with the organisation's structure, environment, and strategic context. This context may be for-profit, non-profit, public sector, entrepreneurial, electronic, or temporary. Moreover, sport managers must be cognisant of the pressures contributing to and emanating from globalisation.

Hopefully, this chapter has contributed to the development of a basic understanding of the interrelationships between a sport organisation and its environment, and how the strategic management of these interrelationships can contribute to the creation and sustainability of competitive advantage in the context of sport.

REVIEW QUESTIONS

1 Strategic management involves far more than simply setting goals and objectives. What else does it involve?
2 If you were formulating a strategy for a volunteer rugby club, what factors might you need to consider in your external analysis?
3 How might the age of a sport organisation affect the choice of strategy?
4 Think of a small sport organisation with which you are familiar; what business-level strategies does it pursue? Justify your answer with examples.

5   Think of a large, diversified sport organisation; what corporate-level strategies does it pursue? Justify your answer with examples.

6   How would strategic planning differ for each of the following types of organisations in comparison to a large, enduring, for-profit multi-national: an e-business, an entrepreneurial business, a non-profit, and a temporary organisation?

7   Discuss the benefits and the challenges of incorporating sustainability principles in a sport organisation.

FURTHER READING

Anderson, C.R. and Zeithaml, C.P. (1984) 'Stage of the Product Life Cycle, Business Strategy, and Business Performance', *Academy of Management Journal*, 27: 5–24.

Harvey, J., Rail, G., and Thibault, L. (1996) 'Globalization and Sport: Sketching a Theoretical Model for Empirical Analyses', *Journal of Sport and Social Issues*, 20: 258–277.

Haspeslagh, P. (1982) 'Portfolio Planning: Uses and Limits', *Harvard Business Review*, 60: 58–73.

Miles, R.E. and Snow, C.C. (1978) *Organizational Strategy, Structure, and Process*. New York: McGraw-Hill.

Mintzberg, H. (1973) 'Strategy-Making in Three Modes', *California Management Review*, 16: 44–53.

Mintzberg, H., Ahlstrand, B., and Lampel, J. (2005) *Strategy Bites Back*. Glasgow, Great Britain: Prentice Hall.

Nelson, R.R. and Winter, S.G. (1982) *An Evolutionary Theory of Economic Change*. Cambridge, MA: Belknap.

Schumpeter, J. (1950) *Capitalism, Socialism, and Democracy*. New York: Harper and Row.

Smith, K.G., Mitchell, T.R., and Summer, C.E. (1985) 'Top Level Management Priorities in Different Stages of the Organizational Life Cycle', *Academy of Management Journal*, 28: 799–820.

Thietart, R.A. and Vivas, R. (1984) 'An Empirical Investigation of Success Strategies for Businesses along the Product Life Cycle', *Management Science*, 30: 1405–1423.

WEBSITES

Academy of Management
   http://www.aomonline.org
Network for Business Sustainability
   http://www.nbs.net
The Quick MBA
   http://www.quickmba.com/strategy
Shenzhen 2011 Summer Universiade
   http://www.sz2011.org/eng/index.htm
Strategic Management Society
   http://strategicmanagement.net
Surfing Association of Papua New Guinea
   http://www.surfingpapuanewguinea.org.pg

REFERENCES

adidas group (2009) '"At a Glance": The Story of the adidas group'. Retrieved 7 July 2009 from http://www.adidas-group.com/en/ourgroup/history/history.aspx.

Amis, J., Pant, N., and Slack, T. (1997) 'Achieving a Sustainable Competitive Advantage: A Resource-Based View of Sport Sponsorship', *Journal of Sport Management*, 11: 80–96.

Billabong (n.d.) 'Company History.' Retrieved on 7 July 2009 from http://www.billabongbiz.com/phoenix.zhtml?c=154279&p=irol-history.

Berrett, T., Burton, T.L., and Slack, T. (1993) 'Quality Products, Quality Service: Factors Leading to Entrepreneurial Success in the Sport and Leisure Industry', *Leisure Studies*, 12: 93–106.

Brainy Quote (2010) http://www.brainyquote.com/quotes/authors/y/yogi_berra_2.html

Bramwell, B. (1998) 'User Satisfaction and Product Development in Urban Tourism', *Tourism Management*, 19: 35–47.

Buckley, R. (2002) 'Surf Tourism and Sustainable Development in Indo-Pacific Islands: I. The Industry and the Islands', *Journal of Sustainable Tourism*, 10: 405–424.

Chalip, L. (2001) 'Sport and Tourism: Capitalising on the Linkage', in D. Kluka and G. Schilling (eds), *Perspectives, 2001, Volume 3: The Business of Sport*. Oxford, UK: Meyer and Meyer.

Chalip, L. (2002) 'Beyond Impact: A General Model for Host Community Event Leverage', in B.W. Ritchie and D. Adair (eds), *Sport Tourism: Interrelationships, Impacts and Issues*. Clevedon, UK: Channel View Publications.

Chappelet, J.-L. (2005) 'The Process of Strategic Management and its Practical Tools', in J.-L. Chappelet and E. Bayle (eds), *Strategic and Performance Management of Olympic Sport Organizations*. Champaign, IL: Human Kinetics.

Chandler, A.D. (1962) *Strategy and Structure*. Cambridge, MA: MIT Press.

Collins, A., Flynn, A., Munday, M., and Roberts, A. (2007) 'Assessing the Environmental Consequences of Major Sporting Events: The 2003/04 FA Cup Final', *Urban Studies*, 44: 1–20.

Commonwealth Games Federation (2007, November) 'Constitution, Regulations, Codes of Conduct.' Retrieved 7 July 2009 from http://www.thecgf.com/about/constitution.pdf.

Cummings, T.G. and Worley, C.G. (1993) *Organization Development and Change*. St Paul, MN: West Publishing Company.

Daft, R.L. (1995) *Organization Theory and Design* (5th ed.) St Paul, MN: West Publishing Company.

De Knop, P. (1998) 'Sport Tourism: A State of the Art', *European Journal of Sport Management*, 5: 5–19.

Dolnicar, S. and Fluker, M. (2003) 'Behavioural Market Segments Among Surf Tourists – Investigating Past Destination Choice', *Journal of Sport Tourism*, 8: 333–344.

FIVB (n.d.) 'FIVB Mission.' Retrieved 7 July 2009 from http://fivb.com/EN/FIVB/Cp_fivbMission.htm.

Freeman, R.E. (1984) *Strategic Management: A Stakeholder Approach*. Boston: Pitman.

Gibson, H.J. (1998) 'Sport Tourism: A Critical Analysis of Research', *Sport Management Review*, 1: 45–76.

Haberberg, A. and Rieple, A. (2001) *The Strategic Management of Organisations*. Harlow: Prentice Hall.

Heffernan, J. and O'Brien, D. (2010) 'Stakeholder Influence Strategies in Bidding for a Professional Sport Franchise License', *Sport Management Review*, doi:10.1016/j.smr.2010.01.007.

Hill, C.R. and Jones, G.R. (2001) *Strategic Management: An Integrated Approach* (5th ed.). Boston: Houghton Mifflin.

Hodge, B.J. and Anthony, W.P. (1991) *Organization Theory: A Strategic Approach*. Boston: Allyn and Bacon.

Hubbard, G. (2000) *Strategic Management: Thinking, Analysis and Action*. Frenchs Forest, NSW, Australia: Prentice Hall.

Judd, D.R. (1995) 'Promoting Tourism in US Cities', *Tourism Management*, 16: 175–187.

Kearins, K. and Pavlovich, K. (2002) 'The Role of Stakeholders in Sydney's Green Games', *Corporate Social Responsibility and Environmental Management*, 9: 157–169.

Kotler, P., Haider, D.H., and Rein, I. (1993) *Marketing Places: Attracting Investment, Industry, and Tourism to Cities, States, and Nations*. New York: The Free Press.

Lenskyj, H.J. (1998) 'Sport and Corporate Environmentalism', *International Review for the Sociology of Sport*, 33: 341–354.

McDonald, P. (1991) 'The Los Angeles Olympic Organizing Committee: Developing Organizational Culture in the Short Run', in P.J. Frost, L.F. Moore, M.L. Reis, C.C. Lundberg, and J. Martin (eds), *Reframing Organizational Culture*. Newbury Park, CA: Sage.

May, V. (1995) 'Environmental Implications of the 1992 Winter Olympic Games', *Tourism Management*, 16: 269–275.

Merrilees, B., Getz, D., and O'Brien, D. (2005) 'Marketing Stakeholder Analysis: Branding the Brisbane Goodwill Games', *European Journal of Marketing*, 39: 1060–1077.

Mintzberg, H. (1987) 'The Strategy Concept I: Five Ps for Strategy', *California Management Review*, 30: 11–24.

Mintzberg, H. (1990) 'The Design School: Reconsidering the Basic Premises of Strategic Management', *Strategic Management Journal*, 11: 171–195.

Mintzberg, H. and Quinn, J.B. (1996) *The Strategy Process: Concepts, Contexts, Cases* (3rd ed.). Upper Saddle River, NJ: Prentice Hall.

Mitchell, R.K., Agle, B.R., and Wood, D.J. (1997) 'Toward a Theory of Stakeholder Identification and Salience: Defining the Principle of Who and What Really Counts', *Academy of Management Review*, 22: 853–886.

Nidumolu, R., Prahalad, C.K., and Rangaswami, M.R. (2009) 'Why Sustainability is Now the Key Driver of Innovation', *Harvard Business Review*, September: 1–10.

Nike (2009, 10 February) 'NIKE, Inc. Announces Restructuring and Cost Reductions to Enhance Consumer Focus and Drive Innovation More Quickly to Market – Restructuring May Include Up to Four Percent in Workforce Reductions.' Retrieved 7 July 2009 from http://www.nikebiz.com/media/pr/2009/02/10_Nike.html.

O'Brien, D. and Chalip, L. (2008) 'Sport Events and Strategic Leveraging: Pushing Towards the Triple Bottom Line', in A. Woodside and D. Martin (eds), *Advancing Tourism Management*. Cambridge, MA: CABI Publishing.

O'Brien, D. and Gardiner, S. (2006) 'Creating Sustainable Mega-Event Impacts: Networking and Relationship Development Through Pre-Event Training', *Sport Management Review*, 9: 25–48.

O'Brien, D. and Slack, T. (2004) 'The Emergence of a Professional Logic in English Rugby Union: The Role of Isomorphic and Diffusion Processes', *Journal of Sport Management*, 18: 13–39.

O'Brien, D. and Slack, T. (2005) 'Strategic Responses to Institutional Pressures for Commercialisation: Case Study of a Senior English Rugby Union Club', in T. Slack (ed.), *The Commercialisation of Sport*. London, UK: Frank Cass.

Parent, M.M. (2008) 'Evolution and Issue Patterns for Major-Sport-Event Organizing Committees and Stakeholders', *Journal of Sport Management*, 22: 135–164.

Parent, M.M. and Deephouse, D.L. (2007) 'A Case Study of Stakeholder Identification and Prioritization by Managers', *Journal of Business Ethics*, 75: 1–23.

Pitts, R.A. and Lei, D. (2003) *Strategic Management: Building and Sustaining Competitive Advantage* (3rd ed.). Mason, OH: South-Western.

Poister, T. and Streib, G. (1999) 'Performance measurement in municipal government: Assessing the state of the practice', *Public Administration Review*, 59: 325–339.

Ponting, J., McDonald, M., and Wearing, S. (2005) 'De-constructing Wonderland: Surfing Tourism in the Mentawai Islands, Indonesia', *Society and Leisure*, 28: 141–162.

Porter, M. (1980) *Competitive Strategy*. New York: Free Press.

Porter, M. (1996) 'What is Strategy?', *Harvard Business Review*, 74: 61–78.

Prahalad, C.K. and Hamel, G. (1990) 'The Core Competence of the Corporation', *Harvard Business Review*, 68: 79–91.

Ritchie, J.R.B. (2000) 'Turning 16 Days into 16 Years through Event Legacies', *Event Management*, 6: 155–165.

Robbins, S.P. and Stuart-Kotze, R. (1990) *Management* (Canadian 2nd ed.). Scarborough, ON: Prentice Hall.

Schmidt, C.W. (2006) 'Putting the Earth in Play: Environmental Awareness and Sports', *Environmental Health Perspectives*, 114: A286–A295.

Slack, T. and Parent, M.M. (2006) *Understanding Sport Organisations: The Application of Organization Theory* (2nd ed.). Champaign, IL: Human Kinetics.

Smith, A. and Westerbeek, H. (2007) 'Sport as a Vehicle for Deploying Corporate Social Responsibility', *Journal of Corporate Citizenship*, 7: 43–54.

St-Germain, M. and Harvey, J. (2000, March) 'Commodification, Globalization and the Canadian Sports Industry.' Article on the internationalization of the Canadian Sport Industry, consulted on 17 February 2001.

The Network for Business Sustainability (2010) 'Business Sustainability.' Retrieved 22 January 2011 from http://www.nbs.net/knowledge/business-sustainability.

Thibault, L., Frisby, W. and Kikulis, L. (2004) 'Partnerships Between Local Government Sport and Leisure Departments and the Commercial Sector: Changes, Complexities, and Consequences,' in T. Slack (ed.), *The Commercialisation of Sport*. London: Frank Cass, 119–140.

Tyler, D. (1998) 'Getting Tourism on the Agenda: Policy Development in the London Borough of Southwark', in D. Tyler, Y. Guerrier, and M. Robertson (eds), *Managing Tourism in Cities: Policy, Process and Practice*. West Sussex: John Wiley and Sons.

UEFA.com (2009) *Information*. Retrieved 7 July 2009 from https://www.facebook.com/uefacom?sk=info.

Universiade 2011 Shenzhen (2007) 'City is Able to Host a Successful Universiade.' Retrieved 18 February 2010 from http://www.sz2011.org/eng/competition/content/2007-07/08/content_13 16504.htm.

Valera, S., and Guàrdia, J. (2002) 'Social Identity and Sustainability: Barcelona's Olympic Village', *Environment and Behavior*, 34: 54–66.

Van den Berg, L., Braun, E., and Otgaar, A.H.J. (2000) *Sports and City Marketing in European Cities*. Rotterdam: Euricur.

Waitt, G. (2003) 'Social Impacts of the Sydney Olympics', *Annals of Tourism Research*, 30: 194–215.

Walker, M.B. and Kent, A. (2009) 'Do Fans Care? Assessing the Influence of Corporate Social Responsibility on Consumer Attitudes in the Sport Industry', *Journal of Sport Management*, 23: 749–769.

Walker, M.B. and Kent, A. (2010) 'CSR on Tour: Attitudes towards Corporate Social Responsibility among Golf Fans', *International Journal of Sport Management*, 11: 179–206.

Walker, M.B., Heere, B., Parent, M.M., and Drane, D. (2010) 'Social Responsibility and the Olympic Games: The Mediating Role of Consumer Attributions', *Journal of Business Ethics*, 95(4): 659–680.

Wolfe, R.A. and Putler, D.S. (2002) 'How Tight Are the Ties That Bind Stakeholder Groups?', *Organization Science*, 13: 64–80.

Zeigler, E.F. (1985) 'Understanding the Immediate Managerial Environment in Sport and Physical Education', *Quest*, 37: 166–175.

Chapter 9

Human resource management and the business of sport

Chris Wolsey and Helen Whitrod-Brown,
Leeds Metropolitan University

TOPICS

The management of people • The structure of sport in the UK • The importance of the third sector • Organisational culture • The management of people in sport • The changing face of HRM • Towards a model of HRM for sport organisations

---

OBJECTIVES

At the end of this chapter you should be able to:

- Understand the differences between personnel and human resource issues;
- Understand the emerging thinking with respect to human resource management;
- Apply contemporary and related 'people management' literature to the sport sector;
- Suggest areas for further development in HRM theory and praxis, as applied to the sport sector.

KEY TERMS

Human resource management – HRM is essentially a business-oriented philosophy designed to obtain value from employees, which increases competitive advantage in the marketplace.

Leadership – part of a behavioural process in which interpersonal skills are utilised in order to facilitate the motivation of both employees and volunteers towards organisational goals.

Organisational change – designates a fundamental and radical reorientation in the way the organisation operates.

Organisational culture – a specific collection of values and norms that are shared by people and groups in an organisation and that influence the way they interact with each other and with stakeholders outside the organisation.

Professionalisation – the process whereby people come to engage in an activity for pay or as a means of livelihood.

Stakeholders – a person, group or organisation that has a direct or indirect stake in an organisation because it can affect or be affected by the organisation's actions, objectives and policies.

The three lens approach to HRM – a comparative analysis of three different paradigms for examining HRM issues using a camera lens analogy (normal, zoom and wide angle).

OVERVIEW

In both management theory and praxis, there is an increasing recognition of the need to engage in more sophisticated levels of people management. The traditional need for 'manpower planning' and the functions offered by 'personnel' departments are being overtaken by a more progressive view of the key role played by people within organisations. Against this backdrop, this chapter will provide a holistic and applied review of the management of people within the UK sport sector. The evolving concept of human resource management (HRM) will be reviewed and applied to the twenty-first-century sport organisation, drawing on evidence from the public, commercial and voluntary sectors.

CASE STUDY: THE FALL AND RISE OF UK ATHLETICS AND TEAM GB

After many years in the wilderness, athletics in the UK is experiencing a resurgence. There can be little doubt that a greater government interest and funding has made an important contribution in preparation for the 2012 London Olympics. However, sporting success is rarely about money alone. In the UK, the Lawn Tennis Association has so far been unable to produce sustained performance improvements despite high levels of both capital and human resources being invested in the game. Resources have to be used wisely in order to produce the correct environment to nurture sporting talent in a way that makes it competitive on the world stage. In 2010 the British Athletics team won nine medals at the World Junior Championships in Canada – their best haul in 20 years. Better still, the senior squad had their best European Championships ever, with an unprecedented 19 medals, finishing third in the medals table overall. Charles Van Commenee, the Head Coach of UK Athletics, has been the architect of both structural and cultural changes during this period. He seems to work by demanding more and more of his athletes and instilling a winning belief in his charges. Success breeds success, which can then snowball and act as a catalyst throughout the team. Kessel (2010) argues that, whilst he is an authoritarian by nature, he makes decisions on the basis of individual differences and has an eye for spotting latent talent and unfulfilled potential. This means that, whilst control and consistency is enhanced, this is not to minimise the need to be flexible as circumstances dictate. The mark of many good managers! According to Sebastian Coe, the former double Olympic Champion and Chairman of the London Organising Committee for the Olympic Games (LOCOG):

> He refocused on coaching rather than the more nebulous concept of general performance management. He began working with 30 per cent of the athletes and their coaches to find a 10 per cent improvement, in his words, to move them from good to outstanding. At our two key centres of excellence, Loughborough and Lee Valley, coaches rather than venue managers now hold sway.
>
> (Coe, 2010)

Although related specifically to sports coaching, this represents a wider recognition that managers need to better target their efforts and be more responsive to individual differences by nurturing employees in ways that are positively related to the goals of the organisation.

THE MANAGEMENT OF PEOPLE

Fundamentally, sport is about people and, for many, is one of the most important and emotive issues to impact upon their daily lives. Similarly, sport organisations represent people-oriented operations (Sawyer and Owen, 1999) where 'human resources' should be the single most important managerial consideration (Chelladurai, 1999; Gratton, 2001). However, service delivery, staff recruitment, retention, motivation and absenteeism have all been identified as problems within the sport industry which continues to face 'a shortage of skilled, motivated staff, who are discouraged by the rates of pay, working conditions and perceived lack of career opportunities' (Salmon, 1998:7).

During the 1980s and 1990s, an over-reliance on 'personnel management', with its narrow, functional and inward-organisation focus, has been gradually eroded and usurped by a more holistic and strategic approach to human resource management (HRM). Although Slack (1997:233) draws no distinction between personnel management and HRM, Frisby and Kikulis (1996:104) argue:

> The shift in terminology to HRM reflects a more strategic approach whereby people are viewed as the most important resources for accomplishing organisational goals. HRM is essentially a business-oriented philosophy designed to obtain value from employees, which increases competitive advantage in the market place. Instead of seeing employees as cost factors that must be controlled by management, newer approaches to HRM view human resources as assets worthy of investment. In turn, HRM investments are designed to release the creative talents of people to accomplish the strategic plans of the organization.

Whilst there are several generic models of HRM, all are predicated on people management measures designed to extract the maximum value from employees. This has to be viewed in the context of prevailing organisational objectives and the variable impact of the external environment.

Sport attracts a plethora of interested stakeholders from financial institutions to government departments; governing bodies to volunteers; participants to parents; spectators and supporters, to a plethora of media organisations. By recognising the interrelationships between stakeholders and situational (external) factors, the 'Harvard' model of HRM provides a clear framework in which to explore and understand many of the people issues prevalent in sport (see Van Looy and Van Dierdonck, 2003). However, it assumes that this occurs in a relatively prescriptive and top-down way at the stage of policy implementation. This may not always be appropriate as increasingly, particularly for sports organisations, it is the ability to adapt to the fluidity of the external environment that dictates the effectiveness of any HRM strategy. This requires organisations to recognise, integrate and embrace the changing dynamics of the internal and external business environment. The importance of both context and process is recognised by the 'Warwick' model (see Van Looy and Van Dierdonck, 2003), which allows for the possibility that the external environment may drive HRM strategy. It is important, therefore, to provide a review of the external environment in order to better understand the antecedents of HRM in the sport industry.

> The structure of the government of sport is a complex jigsaw, in which international, UK, home country, regional and local associations and their member clubs interlock in a manner which is not always harmonious. The wide range of organizations, their motivations and their frustrations provides a dynamic framework in which the various players compete for their interpretation of success.
>
> (Welch, 2001:50)

The London 2012 Olympics has provided a catalyst for a more active governmental interest in sport and its potential for providing a positive sporting, social and economic impact in the United Kingdom (UK). This is reflected in the role of the Parliamentary Secretary of State for Culture, Olympics, Media and Sport who reports directly to the cabinet at the very heart of the UK government. Similarly, this is also reflected in the role of the Minister of Sport and the Olympics who, as a Parliamentary Under Secretary of State, sits on the Olympics cabinet sub-committee and reports directly to the Secretary of State. However, successive governments have different priorities which have the potential to have a dramatic impact upon both the Olympic Games preparation and subsequent legacy. Hugh Robertson is the first non-Labour Minister of Sport to hold the post after a 13-year UK Labour government (1997–2010). Robertson reflects the changing priorities of a new coalition Conservative/Liberal Democrat government by refocusing the work of Sport England to concentrate exclusively on the legacy of the 2012 Olympics. He argues:

> We're coming at this from a standing start. It was not the last government's policy to get Sport England to do this, it is ours. They have come up with plans that we are now market testing and integrating those plans with what LOCOG and the BOA are doing. What I don't want is lots and lots of tiny legacy plans going off all over the landscape. I want a very clear direction of travel from government that all the delivery partners can buy into.
>
> (Gibson, 2010)

149

Given the central importance of strategic objectives as drivers of HRM and the multiplicity of competing priorities, this adds to the complexity of managing people in sport. The world economic crisis of 2008 and the change of UK government in 2010 reflect a significant shift in policy as drastic financial cuts are sought to reduce the UK's budget deficit. For the public and voluntary sectors, including Olympic preparation, the substantial reduction in public spending is likely to have a significant impact upon managers, staff, athletes and customers in this area. A preoccupation with cost and efficiency considerations is likely to put further pressure upon both capital resources (facilities) and human capital (rationalisation, reorganisation and redundancies), as increasing levels of financial stringency militates against investment and development in both areas. This has implications for the preparation of Olympic athletes as the financial and specialist support available will be under increasing scrutiny – both in the short term and with respect to the longer term ambitions of both individual athletes and their associated sports governing bodies/associated agencies. This also includes local authorities who will have to increasingly prioritise mandatory services over areas such as sport and leisure provision. The consequence is that all sports bodies will have to engage in more imaginative forms of provision, partnership and, thus, policy development and HRM practice.

Changes in the public sector have occurred against a backdrop of increasing levels of disposable income and an increasingly discerning consumer. As Wolsey and Whitrod-Brown (2001:65) argue, 'there is increasing evidence to suggest the emergence of a "money rich, time poor" consumer … . This has important consequences for both leisure consumers and producers.' Unsurprisingly, changing consumer behaviour and the concurrent decline of public sector 'leisure' provision has been exploited by the commercial leisure sector, which continues to expand. In many areas, commercial provision now represents a direct challenge to the historical dominance of public sport and leisure facilities. Previously unassailable public sector monopolies, such as swimming pool provision, are now threatened by an influx of commercial operators, appealing directly to those willing to pay for a more exclusive level of service through the commercial expansion of the health and fitness sector. The Sports Industry Research Centre (SIRC) (2007:22) reports:

> Sport-related consumer expenditure has increased from £3.5bn in 1985 to £16.5bn in 2005. As a percentage of total consumer expenditure the sport sector has increased from 2% to 2.6% correspondingly. Particularly strong was the effect from the sport-related satellite television and the growth in the private Health and Fitness market. The participation subscription and fees market for Health and Fitness clubs and Leisure Centres increased from £0.5bn in 1985 to almost £3.5bn in 2005.

The previous Labour government's intention to promote a more inclusive and joined-up approach to sport, physical activity and health, through its strategy document *Game Plan* (DCMS/Strategy Unit Report, 2002), provided a demarcation point between public and commercial providers by promoting the potential of sport to positively impact issues of social exclusion through extended and, often, publicly subsidised participation opportunities. However, this changed in 2008 with the publication of a new strategy entitled *Playing to Win: A New Era for Sport* (DCMS, 2008). Although still pursuing the goal of extending sports participation, the lens through which this would now be viewed would be one of sporting excellence. This represents a refocusing of priorities in the run up to the London 2012 Olympics – something that the incumbent coalition government are looking to extend by emphasising competition through, amongst other things, new Olympic-style schools sports competitions. To some extent this move is mirrored by structural changes in UK government as UK Sport is merged with Sport England in order to jointly promote both participation and excellence. However, the extent to which a declining direct government subsidy can be adequately offset by efficiency gains and a greater reliance on lottery funding will be mitigated by the ability of related sports agencies to successfully adapt and respond positively to such a changing economic and policy landscape.

The increasing commodification of leisure and sport provision has also resulted in professional sport clubs being run on more commercial criteria and the fan base being drawn from a wider, more discerning and, thus, fickle segment of the entertainment industry. More importantly, perhaps, is that changes in the external environment have fundamentally affected the structural balance between the voluntary, public and commercial sectors. The demise of the public sector leisure and sport provision and expansion of the commercial sector has left the voluntary sector exposed as a key target for both local and national policy in this area.

THE STRUCTURE OF SPORT IN THE UK

There is no simple definition of what constitutes the UK sport sector. In terms of its structure, the industry is both complex and unique. The public sector combines local authority sport provision with that of pre- and post-sixteen educational provisions. The private sector includes voluntary/professional sport clubs and commercial provision through works facilities and those provided by dedicated operators such as David Lloyd Health and Fitness Clubs.

Skills Active, the Sector Skills Council for Active Leisure, Learning and Well-being (formerly SPRITO), has produced a number of Workforce Development Plans (WDPs). The WDP for the Sport and Recreation Sector provides one of the most comprehensive assessments of the sector's workforce and occupations to date. Whilst acknowledging the difficulties of using the government's Standard Industrial Classifications, the report provides a classification based on sport core sub-sectors, as below:

- Sport facilities management
- Sport development
- Coaching
- Stadia management
- Professional sport.

Chelladurai (1999) categorised sport employees into:

- Paid professionals
- Volunteers
- Clients and customers.

The paid employee is salaried, bound by a contractual agreement and generally hired for a specific job role which is bound by strict organisational codes of conduct and which contributes to the organisation's mission. The employee will follow a set procedure to appointment that is bound by legislation; this will include recruitment and selection, induction and training, job description, welfare, appraisal and reward. It is a formalised process within strict legal and operational boundaries. They can be full or part time, temporary, seasonal, contractual or self-employed.

The volunteer gives time, skills and/or knowledge to others for which they generally do not receive financial reimbursement. There is clear evidence that the role of the volunteer is becoming more 'professionalised' and that the phenomenon of the 'professional volunteer' is an increasing feature of sport organisations, particularly in the public and voluntary sectors (Chelladurai, 2006; Sports Council, 1996).

The clients or customers are the consumers of the services or products. They are particularly important to the sport service industry as the way they interrelate to employees and other consumers can influence both the consumption experience and the environment – for themselves, other consumers and employees. Often the service experience requires active participation by the consumers – a process that should be recognised and managed as part of an organisation's HRM strategy (Chelladurai, 1999). Other complexities peculiar to professional sport arise when volunteers, or paid employees, are also clients; for example, the volunteer football steward. Managing their expectations and emotional drivers is important, as the majority of (if not all) football volunteers are also clients (fans) who view themselves as stakeholders in the club. Their volunteer performance can affect the whole football experience of others and their interaction with other clients is powerful because of perceived status by association as an 'employee' of the club and therefore an 'insider' or 'expert'. Importantly their value system may be very different from the value system of the club but no less influential (and damaging) externally.

There are a variety of statistics offering differing interpretations of the economic and employment position of sport within the UK (see Labour Market Trends, Mintel Leisure Intelligence, General Household Survey, Family Expenditure Survey, Leisure Forecasts, Skills Active). Building on previous evidence of the UK sports economy (SIRC, 2007), it is interesting to note that, despite the ongoing consequences of the world financial crisis of 2008, Skills Active (2009) report that several related areas, such as health and fitness and the outdoors, continue to experience growth. According to SIRC (2007), sports employment in the UK accounts for approximately 2 per cent of all employment, a rise of 43 per cent during the 20-year period to 2005. Sports-related employment is dominated by the commercial sector (76 per cent), whilst the public and voluntary sectors account for circa 12 per cent of all sports jobs in 2005.

The professionalisation of sport is reflected by an increased tendency to refer to the 'third sector', which consists of all non-profit organisations that sit between the public and business commercial sectors (Lyons, 2001). This represents a unique mix of both paid (managers, administrators and development officers) and non-paid workers (volunteers) in sport.

THE IMPORTANCE OF THE THIRD SECTOR

Despite the increasing significance of the third sector, it continues to be marginalised by the national bodies/agencies that operate in this area. In response to SPRITO's (2003:14) draft WDP, one consultee argued that 'the work of SPRITO (now Skills Active) continues to be biased toward the private and public sectors'. This may be the result of several factors that conspire against a greater understanding of this area, as below:

- The move towards increased professionalism and accountability in sport places real pressures on the resources, abilities and motivations of those working in the voluntary sector.
- The voluntary sector is, by its very nature, heterogeneous and consists of thousands of loosely associated clubs.
- Its unique and highly disparate structure makes it difficult to research, understand, communicate and, ultimately, engage with.
- It does not conform to traditional models of people management, which are predicated on the exchange of labour for money.
- It does not come under the direct control of national agencies charged with the administration and leadership of sport in the UK.
- The primary aim of many voluntary sector sport organisations is to serve its members at the local level. It is not to conform to national policy agendas relating to either participation and/or excellence; at best, these are seen as secondary considerations.

The nature and importance of the voluntary sector poses unique challenges for the future strategic direction of sport in the UK. As a consequence of the above, and in line with the previously discussed 'Warwick' model of HRM, policy development and implementation is often constrained by the reaction and co-operation of the voluntary sector and those that work within it. This leads to inevitable tensions, as the desire to adopt a more professional approach may be undermined and, effectively, alienate those individuals who are asked to do more at the grass-roots level. This is further compounded by the fact that:

> Social pressures and changes in the sporting world have affected the number of people willing to volunteer and the number of volunteers opting for other pastimes. It is more important than ever for sporting organizations to plan a volunteer management strategy to ensure they have the volunteers necessary to survive and grow.
>
> (Sport England, 1999:6)

The ability of government and governing bodies to work with the voluntary sector continues to be a central issue in the management of sport.

ORGANISATIONAL CULTURE

Whilst the on-going growth of positions within the third sector is to be applauded, there can be little doubt that the need to facilitate partnerships, through inter-sector co-operation, will be an important arbiter of the future development of sport in the UK. This has direct consequences for the work of sport managers, administrators and development officers in all sectors, who need to work collectively towards agreed common goals (DCMS/Strategy Unit Report, 2002:12). The key to this will be its people – whether they are paid or unpaid, full or part time, seasonal or self-employed (SPRITO, 2003). The way they engage at work will be strongly influenced by the way they are managed, and an holistic approach to HRM will be a critical success factor. As Frisby and Kikulis (1996:115) noted:

> HRM is important to sport because *proper* [our italics] human resource management gives an organization a competitive advantage; provides employees with the information they need to keep productive in their market; will allow an organization to retain and reward valued employees or volunteers; provides an important link between meeting employee needs which in turn affects customer satisfaction and ensures that the organization is meeting its legal obligations to its employees.

However, the *proper* management of people, as previously stated, is greatly influenced by the culture of the environment within which they are managed. Creating this culture depends on a number of conspiring influences – internal, external and personal. The significance of these influences on the internal environment is sector, organisation, occupational and employee determined, the balance of which is in a constant state of flux. An holistic approach to HRM is, therefore, a necessity for any manager, as it allows for the recognition of such influences on human performance and potential.

Buchholz (2001) argues that all effective managers are successful because they learn from the past, live in the present and plan for the future. They become expert at scanning their environment for clues about the future and refining and improving their organisations to remain competitive in their industry. Hughes (2010) argues that Fabio Capello, the England football manager, has always proven to be both pragmatic and adaptable throughout his career. After a very successful qualifying campaign for the 2010 World Cup in South Africa, England performed poorly in the actual tournament, failing to progress beyond the last 16 teams. In many ways Capello appears to share many leadership traits with Charles Van Commenee. Furthermore, he has expressed a recognition that mistakes were made during the 2010 World Cup. Whereas Van Commenee insists on the professionalism of his athletes, he also likes them to have fun and enjoy the experience of major championships. Capello recognises that the decision to locate the England squad in relative isolation did lead to difficulties in this regard, no doubt influenced by the idiosyncratic way in which sporting decisions are often taken and thus influenced by the pervasive effects of media intrusion. Particularly with regard to high-profile sporting events, very few managers outside sport have to contend with such considerations. No doubt Capello will seek to better address and balance such issues at the next major championship.

For sports governing bodies in general, relative success will be measured in terms of their ability to facilitate intra/inter-sector partnerships and be critical advocates for sport within a much wider and dynamic policy arena. As Houlihan (2001:8) argued, 'cultural services are at the forefront of "joined up thinking" and are expected to contribute to the achievement of policy objectives in areas as diverse as life-long learning, social inclusion, healthier lifestyles, and urban and rural regeneration'.

Sport has been slow to respond to the implications of the above, particularly in relation to the management of its key resource, i.e. its people. It now must also recognise the changing political and economic landscape that redefines performance objectives. However, whilst advocating changes to the HRM practices of this area, one must also recognise the difficulties of facilitating changing attitudes as a prelude to changing organisational structures and, thus, behaviours.

This is particularly true of sport organisations that are often characterised by tradition and an unwillingness to bend to the pressures of the external environment. Initially, Charles Van Commenee met with strong opposition to his plans for UK Athletics. However, he had the personal presence and power of position to positively influence events in his favour. This is not always the case in sport, which is often characterised by a multiplicity of stakeholders. Ian Watmore, for example, resigned from his position of Chief Executive at the Football Association after his frustrations at failing to make a positive impact in several areas where he deemed progress needed to be made. He lasted only nine months in the role and, despite some successes, found that structural issues limited his ability to positively influence issues. Kay (2010) reports that, according to a source:

> Ian is disappointed with the way this has worked out. It boiled down to the realisation that the job wasn't what he thought it was going to be. He took a position as chief executive which, ultimately, he found wasn't chief and wasn't executive.

Clearly, there are both opportunities and barriers to change within governing bodies of sport in the UK. There will always be some degree of conflict between the two, but it is the way that these are proactively balanced that will make a significant contribution to future sporting successes at the individual, local, regional, national and international level.

THE MANAGEMENT OF PEOPLE IN SPORT

The importance of an holistic approach to HRM, for optimum business performance, has been widely reported; however, its implications for sport have been rarely explored. Given the inherent socio-economic and cultural significance of this highly visible consumer sector, it is surprising that there has been very little academic treatment of the 'people management' aspects of the sport industry. Existing literature tends to provide a generic treatment of the functional aspects of people management in sport (Critten, 1994; Grainger-Jones, 1999; Whitrod-Brown and Green, 2001) and is often written from a US perspective (Chelladurai, 1999; Flannery and Swank, 1999; MacLean, 2001; Parkhouse, 1991; Parks and Zanger, 1990; Slack, 1997). Latterly, Hoye et al. (2006) and Taylor, Doherty and McGraw (2008) have a made a positive contribution to this area, although Adcroft (2009) maintains that there is still a paucity of bespoke management research related to the specific context of sport organisations.

One exception to this is the research conducted by Gilson et al. (2000) who provided a review of ten 'world class' professional sport organisations, in an attempt to uncover how they have sustained 'peak performance' over the longer term. They present a model of 'peak performing organisations' (PPOs) founded on three basic principles:

1 Peak purpose. This provides meaning and direction and has three components:
   ■ Greatest imaginable challenge: Gives purpose, direction and opportunities for per-
     sonal/organisational advancement in a mutually reinforcing way.
   ■ Inspirational dream: In strategy parlance this relates to an effective mission statement
     which has the power to motivate workers.
   ■ Focus: This provides the foundation of peak flow by identifying the specific actions to
     be undertaken and utilises appropriate intrinsic and extrinsic rewards to sustain the
     dream.

2 Peak practices. This is the organisational context that supports peak performance and has
   three components:
   ■ Sharing the dream: With key stakeholders who have an intense personal and shared
     belief in being the best.
   ■ Creating the future: through physical and financial infrastructures. Mentoring future
     inspirational players is regarded as being important here.
   ■ Fostering community: Creating a culture of hard work but with confidence, trust and
     informality simultaneously.

3 Peak flow. The people processes that ensure teamwork and continuity and which has
   three components:
   ■ Exceeding personal best: Through hard work, commitment and discipline.
   ■ Imagining game-breaking ideas: Enthusiasm for risk taking which improves perform-
     ance and gains credit; people not vilified for failure.
   ■ Catching the last detail: Through a combination of personal judgement and attention
     to detail.

This has been one of the most publicised pieces of empirical research to emerge in the
history of sport management and, as such, is worthy of further attention. The study has an
undeniable resonance when applied to sport organisations, and helps to explain its popularity
with many sport administrators. It provides a highly readable blend of a number of interrelated management areas. The idea is for all three principles and nine sub-components to
exist harmoniously together through time. Presumably, any variations in the above are only
temporary aberrations for PPOs, which are always moving forwards in order to achieve a
position of equilibrium in relation to the above principles.

Factors such as 'exceeding personal best' and 'catching the last detail' help to explain the
difficulties experienced between Roy Keane and Mick McCarthy, the Republic of Ireland
team manager, prior to the 2002 FIFA World Cup in Japan and South Korea. At Manchester
United, Roy Keane had become accustomed to a more professional approach. Over a number
of years, he had grown disillusioned by the inability of the FAI to deliver comparable standards and was sent home ahead of the 2002 World Cup after vociferously airing such views
in public. Similar problems have also emerged in the world of rugby union, where well-
resourced professional club players have spoken out against the organisation and quality of
training facilities available to some home country sides. Likewise, during the 2010 soccer

World Cup in South Africa, the French team boycotted training in support of a fellow player who was sent home after allegedly insulting the French coach after their defeat by Mexico. There are many similar examples that further illustrate the idiosyncrasies of attempting to manage millionaire sports stars in the glare of the world's media.

However, despite its intuitive appeal, it could be argued that the PPO study merely provides a reworking of generic tried and tested approaches to management and, as such, fails to add anything significantly different from that which has gone before, particularly in the context of the idiosyncrasies of professional sport (see Hoye *et al.*, 2006; Wolsey, Minten and Abrams, 2011). In many ways, PPO represents an applied version of the 1982 Peters and Waterman classic *In Search of Excellence*, and presents a model of business practice characterised by many of the basic principles espoused by the original book. It is, also, very reminiscent of the literature and thus critiques surrounding total quality management. Gilson *et al.* (2000:xv) justified a largely atheoretical approach to this area by declaring that 'we have observed passing trends in organizational theory and attempted to apply them. And we have found them wanting.'

Organisations are complex and constantly evolving. Organisational theory is often guilty of either over-simplification or presenting highly specialised analysis that fails to fully recognise the wider picture. It is not surprising, therefore, that the recent history of some of the PPO case studies does not inspire confidence. This mirrors the fate of the original Peters and Waterman (1982) study. For example, from a position of continued dominance amongst Europe's football elite, Bayern Munich have struggled to recapture similar consistency, notwithstanding their appearance in the 2010 UEFA Champions League Final, whilst despite their previous successes, the 'Williams' Formula One team have been unable to deliver a competitive car and driver package for many seasons.

The PPO study serves to illustrate the difficulty of responding to increasing levels of competition, whilst attempting to balance many competing pressures in the real world. Moreover, it recognises that the essence of sporting competition requires both fierce competition whilst simultaneously co-operating within a more inclusive structure – the collective bargaining for television rights in football being a case in point. The appeal of the PPO model relates to its broad coverage of a number of interrelated management areas that have been linked to performance; for example, organisational culture, leadership, motivation, teamwork, performance appraisal, etc. These issues are not mutually exclusive and, therefore, should be dealt with in a more holistic and integrative way, as implied by the PPO model. However, these issues sometimes appear irreconcilable, inconsistent and contradictory when attempting to find compromises between best practice and the dynamic forces at play in the real world. This is compounded by sport organisations, which frequently adopt an *ad hoc* and unsophisticated approach to HR issues. Paradoxically, the vast majority of sporting bodies, particularly in the voluntary sector, are simply too small to justify a HR specialism within their structure!

THE CHANGING FACE OF HRM

The 100 best companies to work for provide a tremendous example but also a great challenge to the rest of the UK industry. They are the living proof that highly motivated and happy workforces go hand-in-glove with delighted customers and superior business performance.

(The Sunday Times, 2003)

These are the findings of research undertaken by <i>The Sunday Times</i>, sponsored by the Department of Trade and Industry, to identify what makes excellent companies. Their research captured the detailed opinions of 47,000 employees across a range of occupational sectors evaluating policies, processes and services that influence work environments. It is the most comprehensive study of its kind undertaken in the UK and indicates that putting staff before profits is a sound business strategy. Given the rapidly changing nature of the public sector, it is not surprising that Oswald (2003) reported that job satisfaction, in this area, had collapsed during the 1990s, influenced by the need to do more with less and the strong drivers towards increasing levels of accountability. Furthermore, Oswald suggested that 'a key factor is who controls the pace of work ... Satisfaction is low in places where the boss controls the pace of work and is high where customers or colleagues control how fast the work is done.'

Taken together, the two studies suggested that strict adherence to a top-down, functionally driven approach to people management, based on sometimes spurious measures of accountability, may not be the best way forward. <i>The Sunday Times</i> research suggested a revised model of HRM, which suffuses the internal and external environments to create an empathetic and productive organisational culture founded on high levels of employee satisfaction. This places the employee at the heart of the consumer-driven markets of the twenty-first century. However, although this concurs with other longitudinal research, there is a need to adopt a more critical view when attempting to apply such good intentions to sport organisations. As Wolsey (2001:84) argues:

> The importance of nurturing employees to produce appropriate outcomes is now fundamental to business success. Pemberton (1998:17) reported on research conducted by The University of Sheffield and The London School of Economics that concluded from a 10-year study of 42 U.K. companies 'that overall job satisfaction was a better predictor of the company's economic performance than competitive strategy, market share, or spend on research and development'. Slack (1997:233) argued that the 'central purpose of the human resources management function is to provide a sport organization with an effective and satisfied work force'. However, for typically staff intensive sport and leisure organizations, there are often very real differences between organizational rhetoric and reality (Legge 1995, Gratton 1997, Barney & Wright 1998).

There are many related examples of this within sport organisations, although one of the most obvious relates to the difficulties experienced by Leeds United Football Club and its chairman, Peter Ridsdale, during the 2002/03 football season. One of the key components of effective people management relates to the quality of communication and trust between management and key stakeholders. Argyris and Schon (1978) developed the idea of 'espoused theory' (what managers say) and 'theory in use' (what managers do). Often these two ideas are conflicted, as words and actions fail to match up. In this context, Abrams (2001:176) argues:

From a leisure and sport manager's perspective this is an important point which is often not fully considered during a period of transformational change. In order to address this issue leisure and sport managers need to consider the impact of their change management process on key stakeholders.

Furthermore, Argyris and Schon (1978) argued that managers are frequently unaware of this mismatch.

TOWARDS A MODEL OF HRM FOR SPORT ORGANISATIONS

It has been argued that the management of people, in sport, represents a number of unique challenges for the industry. Whilst traditional industrial relationships are governed by employment contracts and the exchange of personal time and effort for monetary gain, this does not apply to many volunteers working across the industry. As a consequence, it is the psychological contract that is fundamental to understanding the perceptions, behaviours and success of many volunteers in this area. Individuals are driven by a complex and unique set of human emotions, making it difficult and, indeed, dangerous to categorise human nature into neatly defined functional boxes. The means by which human beings are most effectively managed is through a management process which recognises the complexities of the industry, the interdependency between the working environment and its workforce, and the impact of internal, external and personal factors on procuring the optimum balance for superior business performance. This is equally true of the public, commercial or voluntary sectors. As Frisby and Kikulis (1996:115) argued, 'The future success of sport organizations rests on the capacity of sport managers to deal with human resource issues from multiple points of view.'

They go on to provide a comparative analysis of three different paradigms for examining HRM issues using a camera lens analogy (normal, zoom and wide angle). The 'normal' model of people management is most closely aligned to personnel management and is concerned with the functional or 'hardware' elements such as recruitment and selection, training, appraisal, etc. According to Frisby and Kikulis (1996), this myopic and restrictive view does little to reflect the complexities of people management and is more likely to be found in contemporary sport organisations. In this context, Harding is damning of the leadership shown by sport organisations:

> In ten or 20 years' time I hope sport will have lost the shackles of the blazer brigade and be populated by forward thinking, creative and commercial leaders with integrity for their shareholders, the sports and the fans ... It's all about recognition of the need to change and unfortunately people who are typically in key decision-making positions right now are very set in their ways, people who are against change anyway.
>
> (Quoted in Wallace, 2003:50)

For some, the historical context and prevailing hegemonies within many UK sport organisations has held back the sector in recent years. According to Will Lloyd, Head of the UK-based Sports Recruitment Company, many people involved in the organisation of sport have a desire to give something back to the sport that they once actively participated in. However:

159

> ... that attitude is very passion-focussed rather than professional-focussed and has stalled the progression of the sector ... passion is great but it's no longer the sole contributor to the people that work in sport. The wheel is slowly turning towards people that are professionals and then passionate. There should be a balance but it should be professional-led.
>
> (Lloyd quoted in Wallace, 2003:50)

According to Frisby and Kikulis (1996), a 'zoom lens' is needed to provide an 'interpretative' insight into the myriad of micro issues that provide barriers to change and, thus, conspire against organisational development. Broadly speaking it is concerned with creating an organisational culture which appreciates and facilitates diversity in individuals and groups, empowering them to be creative, participate in decision making and contribute to the overall effectiveness of the organisation. This will be an increasingly critical factor for HR managers if, like America, our workforce becomes more diverse. In America increasing numbers of immigrants, asylum seekers, the elderly and disabled are redefining work cultures. Traditional assumptions and values are being challenged, cultural diversity is more apparent and legal requirements more demanding as organisations recognise that the most effective way to increase participation in physical activity amongst 'non-traditional' groups is by recruiting from these groups. In some ways, this is mitigated by the 2008 government decision to change focus towards sports participation and excellence. However, this does not have to be at the expense of previous policy initiatives designed to positively impact upon issues of social exclusion. That said, it is likely that future initiatives in this area will only be targeted around inclusive participation strategies to the extent that they make a contribution to the development of sporting excellence in the longer term.

If, as Chelladurai (1999:51) suggests, individual differences can be classified broadly into abilities, personality, needs and values and motivation, the adoption of an interpretative paradigm will help to uncover, understand and extract value from such diversity. Wherever there is change, there is a risk of upsetting the status quo, of threatening the 'comfort zone' and disturbing the organisation's traditional norms and values. This is the 'dark side' of HRM, which can only be exposed by looking through the third 'wide-angle lens':

> The critical paradigm encourages us to stand back and examine how existing power relationships benefit some groups and get reproduced over time, which, in turn, alienate other individuals and groups. It is only then that issues such as employee exploitation, workplace safety, corruption and discrimination get raised.
>
> (Frisby and Kikulis, 1996:103)

They concluded that there is no one 'fixed and rigid standpoint' but that the use of different lenses provides alternative ways of viewing the 'people side' of organisations resulting in 'creative solutions to increasingly complex and unusual problems' (Frisby and Kikulis, 1996:104, 115).

The 'three lens approach' provides sport organisations with a more sophisticated and holistic approach to HRM. This is needed in order to:

- Meet the needs of an increasingly diverse workforce
- Create organisational cultures which empower individuals and groups
- Provide an inward and outward focus
- Enhance an organisation's citizenship through appropriate representation within the workforce
- Recognise the negative influences of power
- Protect and intervene in employees' and participants' welfare.

A central theme of this chapter has been the importance of creating an empathetic working culture and the role people play in this. In order for the sport industry to move forward and respond pro-actively to external pressures, there is a need to better understand the drivers of a positive, productive and pro-active work culture. These include leadership, motivation, empowerment and citizenship, which were seen as significant determinants of employee satisfaction in *The Sunday Times* Survey. Both motivation and leadership practice will be influenced, to a greater or lesser extent, by the size, type and nature of the organisation and the service or product it delivers. However, in people-oriented organisations, it is the workforce that is the critical determinant of successful outcomes. As Stacey (2003:66–67) contended:

> An organization succeeds when its people, as individuals, are emotionally engaged in some way, when they believe in what their group and their organization are doing, and when the contribution they make to this organizational activity brings psychological satisfaction of some kind, something more than simple rewards.

Generally lip service is paid to related theory when employee motivation and reward systems are considered (see Chelladurai, 1999; Slack, 1997). However, when faced with a dynamic internal and external environment, a tendency to go with 'tried and tested systems' may no longer be sufficient. As the workforce becomes increasingly diverse, a fresh approach is required which recognises individuality – ability, values, personality and external influences. Systems need to be flexible, open and equitable, clearly linking reward to performance. In today's work environment, flexibility is one of the key motivators. Discussions relating to reward and motivation (Chelladurai, 1999; Critten, 1994) advocated a 'cafeteria style' benefits approach that facilitates employee negotiation, choice and ownership.

Making sure all employees are (and feel that they are) treated with equivalence is critical to creating a conducive working environment and productive working relations. Sport England, in their publication *Volunteer Management Good Practice Guide*, had this to say:

> All organizations have to work hard at making volunteers feel valued. Making sure they are properly inducted, trained and rewarded is extremely important. Volunteers should be treated exactly the same as paid employees and must be offered lots of support and encouragement.
>
> (Sport England, 1999:10)

That paid employees and volunteers can be rewarded in similar ways may be a reflection of their converging motives for working or volunteering. The reasons for volunteering indicate a clear parallel to many paid work motives:

161

- Earning rewards and recognition
- Learning new skills
- Meeting people
- Helping others (family, friends)
- Enhanced status
- Thrills and excitement – FUN
- Work up to a paid position (promotion)
- Need for power
- Self-fulfilment
- Requirement – i.e. community service order, student work placement.

(List compiled from a range of sources: Chelladurai, 1999;
Green in Kluka and Schilling, 2001; Sports Council, 1996)

These parallels become even more pronounced when looking at employment within professional sport organisations. Volunteers for professional sport organisations tend to be clients (i.e. fans) who place a unique spin on their motives. Much research has been undertaken into the 'behaviour' of sport fans and participants, which could helpfully inform motivation and reward strategy. Three main reasons emerge, including social opportunity, attachment to the game and identification with the team.

Consequently, participation in sport events and therefore the sport's subculture is a powerful motivator for many volunteers (Green cited in Kluka and Schilling, 2001:96). It could logically follow that the employees of professional sport clubs are similarly motivated. The motivation levels of such employees will be variably affected by the outcome of work-related events such as sport matches and competitions, player transfers, manager and coach appointments and so on. Team success on the field could be the most influential motivator and a reward in itself due to 'glory by association'. The complexity of managing human resources within such an emotional and unpredictable environment is self-evident. However, the quality of leadership, throughout the organisation, can act as a powerful influence on this.

Leadership is closely aligned to motivation. Poor and inappropriate leadership can adversely affect the working environment, de-motivate the work force and alienate customers, particularly where employees have an emotional stake in their work – a recurring feature of sport organisations. Given previous discussions it is no surprise that Chelladurai (1999:160) argued that 'a critical purpose of leadership is to enhance members' productivity and satisfaction'. Furthermore, leadership is seen as being part of a behavioural process in which interpersonal skills are utilised in order to facilitate the motivation of both employees and volunteers towards organisational goals. There is not always agreement about the most appropriate leadership style for sport organisations. According to Gilson et al. (2000:242):

We use the term 'inspirational players' to denote agents within a PPO who are instrumental in actioning the PPO principles – they provide the integrating link between PPO principles and concepts. We avoid the traditional terminology of 'leadership' because of the multiplicity of theoretical perspectives about what constitutes effective leadership, and because 'leadership' necessarily implies 'followship'.

This has some similarities with concepts of 'charismatic leadership', but only works if placed within the context of the wider organisation. Kent and Chelladurai (2001) presented evidence to suggest that transformational leadership, particularly charismatic leadership, leads to high levels of commitment. Furthermore, they suggest that the quality of line management relationships, governed through communication and trust, is positively associated with positive behavioural and attitudinal factors 'such as job performance, satisfaction, commitment, role clarity and innovation' (p.137). Workers need to be inspired, but also have the opportunity to grow through involvement and empowerment in the development of both themselves and the organisation. In this sense, leadership needs to be both transactional (doing things right) and transformational (doing the right things).

We have seen a similar approach adopted by Charles Van Commenee, the Head Coach of UK Athletics. Interestingly, businesses are now growing to appreciate the potential benefits of understanding sports coaching techniques and applying these to related management and business issues. Business coaching is not the same as sports coaching but does share many commonalities. Coaching, in a business context, is about promoting positive future actions by allowing the coaches the time and help to explore the issues they face in their daily working and personal lives. The coach acts as a critical friend, who is able to prompt and cajole better personal insight without offering direct advice. This is different from sports coaching or business mentoring, which can be more directive and instructional in nature. Wolsey, Minten and Abrams (2011) argue the case for the integration of such practices within sports organisations:

> ... this is not just about well-resourced talent development programmes and the executive coaching of senior managers. It must also have a much greater reach in order to get the very best out of all staff; particularly as they are much more likely to understand the needs of the customer. This relates as much to part-time, casual and voluntary staff as it does to full-time employees; arguably more so dependent upon the sector under consideration.

In this way, such concepts have the ability to integrate the three lens approach, both top-down and bottom-up, into the HRM architecture and performance-oriented culture of the sports organisation.

SUMMARY

> Many sports are still run in an amateurish way and there is a huge need for modernisation in British sport ... Unless this happens, this country will never have any meaningful success.
> (David Moffet, former Chief Executive of Sport England;
> cited in Chaudhary, 2002:11)

This chapter has provided an applied and critical overview of the developing empirical and theoretical literature in the area of people management. If people are now viewed as the main source of competitive advantage, it follows that the importance of the human dimension applies equally to both longer-term strategic development and operational considerations/performance in the shorter term. Both issues are symbiotic and mutually reinforcing in nature, presenting unique challenges for the UK sport sector.

There is a fundamental need to reconcile the competing priorities of a plethora of stake-holders in order to move forward. This requires a level of maturity, at both the individual and organisational level, that facilitates positive discussions about the bigger picture. This is equally applicable to changing government ambitions regarding social inclusion and sports participation as it is for professional sport teams negotiating over the future of the game.

The ability to realise overarching sporting ambitions is complicated by the perception and use of power for both individual and organisational gain, which is not, necessarily, the same thing. This is further compounded by the sometimes ineffectual leadership exhibited at the national and, therefore, strategic level.

Money makes the world go around and this is clearly applicable to the world of sport. Sport is about competition, about the thrill of the win, the anguish of defeat. However, in order to move sport forward, there is a need to develop a more inclusive and professional approach to the game, whilst still retaining the fundamental purity of emotional involvement. This involves a more empathetic and relationship-oriented approach to the organisation and development of sport in the UK. Individual differences must be identified and respected in order to find more inventive ways towards win–win strategic developments that minimise difference and build on commonality. For professional sport, this could entail a fundamental re-evaluation of world-wide sporting calendars. This has the potential to minimise areas of conflict and, as such, is in the broad interests of players, clubs and national/international governing bodies. For the public and voluntary sectors there is a need to agree a reasonable division of labour. As the sports sector is predicted to expand, this may create even more pressure on the third sector to justify their existence. This is particularly important where public funding is involved and related bodies need to be adaptive to the dynamics of the external environment and its impact upon the national and international policy agendas in sport. Clarification, with respect to role demarcation, is important in order to promote a more symbiotic relationship between governing bodies, development officers and volunteers. This does not, however, mean the marginalisation of the important work of volunteers. On the contrary, sport administrators/developers must work hard to identify, develop and reward key/willing stakeholders, at the local level, in line with a more holistic and empathetic approach to HRM.

It is clear, therefore, that organisations cannot operate in a vacuum; there are a host of internal, external and personal factors that have to be considered within the human resources conundrum. If these factors are internal to the organisation the impact could be organisation wide (new director of coaching), department wide (change of facilities) or individual (promotion). Conversely, the influencing factors could be external but still affect the organization (world financial crisis), department (specific legislation, e.g. working with children) or individual (family crisis). The balance of these influencing factors will fluctuate and change according to each individual and affect a myriad of work-related issues.

Based on discussions within this chapter, the key principles that should be adopted by HR managers in sport organisations are:

- Adopt an holistic approach to HRM
- Recognise and value diversity
- Acknowledge the power of employees (paid, volunteers, clients)

- Understand the motives for working or volunteering in sport
- Reconcile reward with individual motive
- Identify and nurture the 'value added' within each individual in order to gain competitive advantage
- Adopt a coaching framework that helps to facilitate all of the above issues.

It would be wrong to minimise the difficulties of what is being suggested. It would be equally wrong to reject the above, out of hand, as being unworkable. PPO represents a road map that charts the broad requirements of effective professional sport organisations, whilst a coaching philosophy and culture provides a framework in which the interrelationships and three lens framework can be better explored. As the sector adopts an increasingly professional approach, it is important to develop a deeper and more integrative understanding of such issues, as a prelude to moving forward. Although it is beyond the scope of this chapter, the application of critical systems thinking to this area would be a useful way to progress (see Wolsey, Minten and Abrams, 2011). This recognises the importance of an holistic approach to sport by both recognising and respecting the importance of internal and external processes, relationships and interactions. It is only through a proactive approach to diversity and individual differences that the sector, and those that work within it, can hope to progress.

REVIEW QUESTIONS

1 Using a SWOT approach, provide an analysis of personnel and HRM approaches to people management.
2 What are the unique characteristics of managing people in sport?
3 What are the main issues in the external environment likely to impact upon managing people in sport?
4 What are the main considerations when applying HRM to the 'third sector'?
5 To what extent can all sport employees share similar needs, aspirations and motives? What implications does your answer have for managing people in sport?
6 Consider a topical issue relating to managing people in sport (this can be taken from the news, newspapers, related magazines, etc.). Outline the main issues as reported.
7 Outline in what ways the 'three lens approach' advocated by Frisby and Kikulis (1996) provide further insight into the issue.
8 In what ways can the PPO model advocated by Gilson et al. (2000) provide further insight into the issue?
9 In what ways can the concept of business coaching provide a possible source of coherence for many of the above issues?

FURTHER READING

Macleod, D. and Clarke, N. (2009) *Engaging for Success: Enhancing Performance through Employee Engagement*, Department for Business, Innovation and Skills, July 2009.

Wolsey, C. and Abrams, J. (2010) 'Managing People in the Leisure and Sport Sector: A HR Perspective', in P. Taylor (ed.) *Torkildsen's Sport and Leisure Management*, London: Routledge.

Wolsey, C., Minten, S. and Abrams, J. (2011) *Human Resource Management in the Sport and Leisure Industry*, London: Routledge.

WEBSITES

http://www.businessweek.com

http://www.cbi.org.uk

http://www.cipd.co.uk

http://www.hbr.org

http://www.imd.org

http://ispal.org.uk

http://www.managers.org.uk

http://www.sportbusiness.com

http://www.sportindustry.biz

http://uksport.gov.uk

REFERENCES

Adcroft, A. (2009) 'Taking Sport Seriously', *Management Decisions*, no. 47, pp.5–13.

Argyris, C. and Schon, D. (1978) *Environments of Organizations: A Theory of Action Perspective*, Boston, MA: Addison Wesley.

Buchholz, K. (2001) 'Issues Concerning Volunteerism and Paid Professionals', *The Business of Sport*, no. 3, March.

Chaudhary, V. (2002) 'Moffet Fires Parting Shots', *The Guardian, Sports Section*, 11.10.2002, p.11.

Chelladurai, P. (1999) *Human Resource Management in Sport and Recreation*, Champaign, IL: Human Kinetics.

Chelladurai, P. (2006) *Human Resource Management in Sport and Recreation,* 2nd edn, Leeds: Human Kinetics.

Coe, S. (2010) 'Sebastian Coe: Charles van Commenee Has Breathed New Life into British Athletics', http://www.telegraph.co.uk/sport/othersports/athletics/7921255/Sebastian-Coe-Charles-van-Commenee-has-breathed-new-life-into-British-athletics.html (accessed 2.8.2010).

Critten, P. (1994) *Human Resource Management in the Leisure Industry*, Harlow: Longman.

DCMS (2008) *Playing to Win: A New Era for Sport*, London: DCMS.

DCMS/Strategy Unit Report (2002) *Game Plan: A Strategy for Delivering Government's Sport and Physical Activity Objectives*, London: Strategy Unit.

Flannery, T. and Swank, M. (1999) *Personnel Management for Sport Directors*, Champaign, IL: Human Kinetics.

Frisby, W. and Kikulis, L. (1996) 'Human Resource Development in Sport', in B. Parkhouse (ed.), *The Management of Sport*, 2nd edn, Chicago: Mosby, pp.102–116.

Gibson, O. (2010) 'Olympic Legacy Will Not Be Derailed by Cuts, Says Sports Minister', http://www.guardian.co.uk/sport/2010/jul/27/london-2012-two-years-to-go-olympics2012 (accessed 27.7.2010).

Gilson, C., Pratt, M., Roberts, K. and Weymes, E. (2000) *Peak Performance: Business Lessons from the World's Top Sports Organizations*, London: HarperCollins Business.

Grainger-Jones, B. (1999) *Managing Leisure: Oxford Institute of Leisure & Amenity Management*, London: Butterworth-Heinemann.

Gratton, L. (2001) 'Building Companies Founded on People', in J. Pickford (ed.), *Financial Time: Mastering Management 2*, Harlow: Pearson Education.

Houlihan, B. (2001) 'Citizenship, Civil Society and the Sport and Recreation Professions', *Managing Leisure*, no. 6, pp.1–14.

Hoye, R., Smith, A., Westerbeek, H., Stewart, B. and Nicolson, M. (2006) *Sport Management Principles and Applications*, London: Elsevier and Butterworth-Heinemann.

Hughes, M. (2010) 'England Keep the Faith with Capello', *The Times Newspaper, 'The Game' Supplement*, 3.7.2010, pp.2–3.

Kay, O. (2010) 'Ian Watmore Resigns as FA Chief Executive', http://www.timesonline.co.uk/tol/sport/football/article7071558.ece (accessed 15.6.2010).

Kent, A. and Chelladurai, P. (2001) 'Perceived Transformational Leadership, Organizational Commitment, and Citizenship Behaviour: A Case Study in Intercollegiate Athletics', *Journal of Sport Management*, no. 15, pp.135–159.

Kessel, A. (2010) 'Charles van Commenee Shows Fabio Capello How to Succeed with Tough Love', http://www.guardian.co.uk/sport/blog/2010/jul/31/charles-van-commenee-european-athletics-championships (accessed 1.8.2010).

Kluka, D. and Schilling, G. (2001) 'The Business of Sport', *Perspectives: The Multidisciplinary Series of Physical Education and Sport Science*, no. 3. pp.143–164.

Lyons, M. (2001) *Third Sector: The Contribution of Non-Profit and Co-Operative Enterprises in Australia*, Australia: Allen Unwin.

MacLean, J. (2001) *Performance Appraisal for Sport and Recreation Managers*, Champaign, IL: Human Kinetics.

Oswald, A. (2003) 'The Quest for Job Satisfaction', *The Sunday Times*, 2.2.2003, section 7, p.9.

Parkhouse, B. (1991) *The Management of Sport: Its Foundation and Application*, St Louis: Mosby-Year Book Inc.

Parks, J. and Zanger, B. (1990) *Sport and Fitness Management: Career Strategies and Professional Content*, Champaign, IL: Human Kinetics.

Peters, T. and Waterman, R. (1982) *In Search of Excellence*, London: Harper and Row.

Salmon, J. (1998) 'Rich Get Richer and Managers Stay Much the Same', *Leisure Opportunities*, 20 July–2 August, no. 213, p.7.

Sawyer, T. and Owen, S. (1999) *The Management of Clubs, Recreation and Sport Concepts and Applications*, Champaign, IL: Sagamore Publishing.

Skills Active (2009) *Rising to the Challenge: Active Insight*, Summer, pp.10–11.

Slack, T. (1997) *Understanding Sport Organizations: The Application of Organization Theory*, Champaign, IL: Human Kinetics.

Sport England (1999) *Volunteer Management Good Practice Guide*, London: Sport England.

Sports Council (1996) *Valuing Volunteers in UK Sport*, London: Sports Council.

Sports Industry Research Centre (2007) *The Economic Importance of Sport in England 1985–2005*, London: Sport England.

SPRITO (2003) *Workforce Development Plan for the Sport and Recreation Sector* (Fifth Draft), London: SPRITO.

Stacey, R. (2003) *Strategic Management and Organizational Dynamics: The Challenge of Complexity*, London: Pearson Education.

Taylor, T., Doherty, A. and McGraw, P. (2008) *Managing People in Sport Organizations: A Strategic Human Resource Management Perspective*, London: Elsevier.

The Sunday Times (2003) '100 Best Companies to Work For', *Special Supplement*, 2.3.2003.

Van Looy, B. and Van Dierdonck, R. (2003) *Services Management: An Integrated Approach,* 2nd edn, Harlow: Pearson Education.

Wallace, T. (2003) 'Bringing in the Outsiders', *Sportsbusiness International*, March, pp.50–51.

Welch, M. (2001) 'The UK and International Sports Organizations', in C. Wolsey and J. Abrams (eds), *Understanding the Leisure and Sport Industry*, Harlow: Pearson Education.

Whitrod-Brown, H. and Green, A. (2001) 'Human Resource Management in the Leisure Industry', in C. Wolsey and J. Abrams (eds), *Understanding the Leisure and Sport Industry*, Harlow: Pearson Education.

Wolsey, C. (2001) 'Strategy, Competition and the Commercial Leisure Markets', in C. Wolsey and J. Abrams (eds), *Understanding the Leisure and Sport Industry*, Harlow: Pearson Education.

Wolsey, C. and Whitrod-Brown, H. (2001) 'Consumerism and the Leisure Markets', in C. Wolsey and J. Abrams (eds), *Understanding the Leisure and Sport Industry*, Harlow: Pearson Education.

Wolsey, C., Minten, S. and Abrams, J. (2011) *Human Resource Management in the Sport and Leisure Industry*, London: Routledge.

Chapter 10

The management and measurement of organisational performance

Leigh Robinson, University of Stirling

TOPICS

The performance management process • The benefits of performance management for sport organisations • Performance management frameworks • Performance evaluation • Comparison and benchmarking • Barriers to the performance management process

---

OBJECTIVES

At the end of this chapter you should be able to:

- Understand why performance management is important;
- Know how performance management can help organisations;
- Understand the role of performance evaluation in the management of sport organisations;
- Create good performance indicators;
- Identify appropriate benchmarking partners for a particular sport organisation.

KEY TERMS

Comparison – the process of comparing current performance data with another set of data.
Performance evaluation – assessment of how the organisation is performing.
Performance indicators – a piece of empirical data representing performance that can be compared over time or with similar organisations.

Performance management – the process of ensuring objectives are met by implementing and evaluating appropriate plans.

Performance management framework – a structure set of performance dimensions that encourages a focus on a number of aspects of the organisation.

OVERVIEW

Performance management can be defined as 'actively monitoring the organisation's performance levels to continuously improve' (Andersen, Henriksen and Aarseth, 2006: 63). It is a process that makes use of the systems and procedures that an organisation has, in order to meet the requirements of stakeholders. Performance management operationalises organisational strategy in that strategy and planning activities set the objectives and establish the plans that the performance management process must deliver. Thus, performance management is an essential requirement of managing the business of sport and should be an integral part of the operation of all sport organisations.

This chapter addresses the need for performance management in the sport sector and its role in the delivery of services by primarily examining the situation within the United Kingdom (UK). It considers issues relating to performance management and then discusses performance evaluation and measurement. It concludes with a case study of the performance framework within which UK national governing bodies work.

CASE STUDY: TOWARDS AN EXCELLENT SERVICE (TAES)

The TAES performance framework, which has been implemented in UK public and voluntary sport organisations, seeks to manage performance by evaluating 'how' the organisation is functioning and provides the organisation with an assessment of strengths and areas for improvement. The intention is that areas for improvement can then be incorporated into overall business planning and subsequent performance management processes. TAES focuses on eight themes or areas of performance management, which are:

- *Leadership*: The key decision makers in the organisation demonstrate leadership, a sense of ambition, direction and support for delivering and improving their sport.
- *Policy and strategy*: A clear sense of direction and priorities based on effective consultation translated into measurable objectives, targets and outcomes.
- *Community engagement*: The active involvement of communities in the process of planning, delivering and improving sport through communication, consultation and engagement.
- *Partnership working*: Working effectively with other organisations to improve the delivery of sport.
- *Use of resources*: The efficient and effective use of resources to achieve the delivery of sport.
- *People management*: The effective management and development of people (paid staff and volunteers) throughout the organisation to support the delivery of their sport.
- *Standards of service*: The development and maintenance of high standards of service in consultation with stakeholders in order to improve delivery.

■ *Performance measurement and learning*: The monitoring, review and evaluation of performance to facilitate learning and continuous improvement.

Within each area, performance criteria have been developed which define the key aspects of a quality service, with 'equality' and 'service access' being effectively integrated into every area. The organisation then has to provide evidence of performance against each criterion. The end result is that the organisation can plot the performance of the organisation as being one of four standards:

■ *Poor*: A poor organisation is one where there is little, or no, evidence of the specific criteria, or no awareness or commitment to create or develop the criteria.
■ *Fair*: A fair organisation is one where there is evidence that the processes of planning and developing the criteria has commenced and is progressing.
■ *Good*: A good organisation is one where there is evidence that demonstrates the key criteria are in place.
■ *Excellent*: An excellent organisation can evidence all the aspects of a good organisation but will also be able to demonstrate that the key criteria have been in place long enough for it to evidence the impact of what it has achieved in terms of real outcomes.

The organisation is then subject to external scrutiny and review and from this an improvement plan is created which forms the basis of the performance management framework for the organisation's next few years.

THE PERFORMANCE MANAGEMENT PROCESS

The performance management (PM) process is somewhat simplistic and, as set out in Figure 10.1, is made up of four stages. The process starts with the *objectives*, which will have been set by the strategic planning process. This will have to have been refined from the strategic level to a more applied level, for example, for the service, athlete or team. Performance objectives are a statement of what is to be achieved and as such should be directly linked to what the organisation as a whole is going to achieve. These should be expressed in terms known by the acronym 'SMART':

Significant: they should be important to the organisation and contribute to its strategic objectives
Measurable: it must be possible to evaluate whether they have been achieved
Action oriented: they should enable plans to be developed
Realistic: the VSO should be able to achieve the objective
Time-bound: the objective must be achieved within a certain time period.

For example, a health and fitness facility may wish to increase its levels of membership. An objective to help achieve this could be expressed as follows: *To increase family membership by 10 per cent by June 2012.* This will make a significant contribution to the objective of increasing membership, it sets out what plans need to be developed, that the target is realistic and has to be achieved within a certain time period. Finally, it can be easily measured.

171

Once the objectives are established, detailed plans to achieve these objectives need to be developed. These set out the activities that are to be delivered, how they are to be delivered and the resources required, such as advertising, extra staff and equipment. These plans are then put into operation, which is what is actually done to meet the stated objective. This process needs to be managed carefully to make sure that resources are appropriate, well planned, in the right place and delivered in the correct manner. Finally, the outcomes of plans and operations need evaluation against the objectives they were intended to achieve. This is the role of performance evaluation, which will be discussed later in this chapter. This evaluation may lead to changes in the plan or operations or, as a last resort, a review of the objectives. This evaluation phase needs to be carried out at regular intervals in order to make sure that the final goal is achieved. For example, in Figure 10.1, which shows a performance management process for increasing family membership, the evaluation of plans would need to be done on a regular basis, for example monthly, in order to assess whether the 10 per cent target will be achieved.

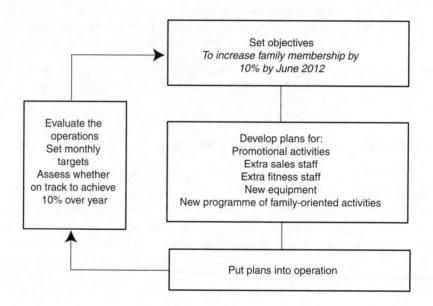

Figure 10.1 *The performance management process*

This process is ongoing in that it will continue until the objective has been achieved.

THE BENEFITS OF PERFORMANCE MANAGEMENT FOR SPORT ORGANISATIONS

Performance management assists in the following ways. First, and somewhat obviously, performance management assists with planning as it operationalises strategies. It provides a structure for controlling the implementation of plans to meet objectives, provides information on how the organisation is performing against stated targets and generates information that can be fed into future planning. Indeed, without performance management, planning is a pointless process. Second, organisations that manage performance are less likely to rely simply on subjective management judgement as managers are being continuously provided with up-to-date information on how well their operation is doing. Third, performance management assists with meeting stakeholder expectations. If the performance objectives and indicators that are set are agreed by stakeholders, the organisation can be managed to meet these targets. Fourth, performance management will also allow managers to evaluate and communicate successes in achieving strategies and in implementing policy. As a consequence, performance management makes sport organisations more transparent and accountable because stakeholders can see how the organisation is performing. Finally, performance management allows managers to focus on what is important to the organisation as the information produced from performance management allows managers to evaluate how they are doing against objectives set in targeted areas.

PERFORMANCE MANAGEMENT FRAMEWORKS

Performance management frameworks are sets of processes and procedures that lead managers to take a holistic view of the performance of their organisation. They have been developed in response to a historical tendency to over-emphasise financial performance to the detriment of other aspects of operations. There are many frameworks available to sport managers, such as those described below.

Quest

Quest is a sport and leisure-specific performance management framework which aims to set industry standards for customer-focused management, by encouraging managers to consider their operations from the point of view of their stakeholders. Supported by the national sport councils throughout the UK, there is a Quest scheme for Facility Management and for Sport Development. The Quest scheme for Facility Management identifies 22 critical management issues that are grouped under the areas of *facilities operation*, *customer relations*, *staffing* and *service development and review*. The Quest scheme for Sport Development identifies 11 critical management issues that are grouped into *strategy*, *people* and *delivery*. A key strength of Quest is that it requires managers to address all aspects of their operations including customer satisfaction.

The box below shows how sport and leisure organisations with Quest accreditation have managed the customer relations performance dimension.

CASE STUDIES: MANAGING CUSTOMER FEEDBACK

Ferndale Leisure Centre: Managed by Fusion Lifestyle, London, UK
The Duty Managers at Ferndale Leisure Centre are tasked with seeking feedback from customers using the Fusion 'What do you think?' leaflet. The target is to obtain one completed questionnaire per shift. The information from these surveys is reviewed on a quarterly basis.

173

Shaftesbury Sports Centre: Managed by Derby City Council, East Midlands, UK

All customers who have block bookings at the Centre were written to by one of the Assistant Managers to ask for feedback on the Centre and inviting them to the Centre to discuss any issues they may have. Several customers took up the invitation and attended a meeting to discuss payment problems.

Swan Pool: Managed by Serco Leisure, Buckinghamshire, UK

An example of good practice was noted in the party feedback forms and in the 'H$_2$O Swim Life Feedback Diary' which is available for both coaches and parents to pass on to the H$_2$O Co-ordinator.

Tenbury Swimming Pool: Managed by SLM, Worcestershire, UK

In the case of this centre the Opinionmeter is deployed to assess the views of its users, which is an electronic survey device offering a simple, yet flexible, method for the on-site collection and analysis of customer feedback. The Opinionmeter instantly tabulates responses and provides immediate access to survey results. There was good evidence that information from the Opinionmeter was being acted upon by centre management.

(Source: http://www.questnbs.org, accessed 23/03/10)

The assessment process for Quest includes three main stages:

1   Managers are required to carry out a self-assessment phase when they compare the operations of their organisation against the assessment criteria for the Quest award. This indicates areas of strength and areas for improvement. For many managers, this process itself is enough to improve the performance of the service.

2   The next stage is an objective external assessment, undertaken by trained assessors from the industry. The assessment reviews progress against industry standards and provides a percentage score. Quest scores are classified into the following categories:

- Approved – above 60%
- Commended – 68% to 74%
- Highly Commended – 75% to 83%
- Excellent – 84% and above.

3   Finally, as Quest Approval status lasts for two years, it is supplemented by an additional Maintenance Visit. This ensures that quality of service delivery is maintained and/or continuously improved in line with the Quest standards. After every two years the process needs to be repeated.

The main benefit of Quest is its potential for reviewing procedures and getting feedback on these. As a result, the self-assessment aspect of this performance framework is considered to be vitally important. In addition, Quest is felt to be a useful tool for benchmarking the industry as it is the only industry-specific quality framework.

The Balanced Scorecard

One other popular framework is the *Balanced Scorecard* developed by Kaplan and Norton (1996). This performance management approach is based on a number of performance measures with associated targets, which are used to assess whether performance meets expectations. The Balanced Scorecard has four main components:

- A destination statement which sets out what the organisation will look like at a defined point in the future assuming that the current strategy has been successful.
- The strategic plan segmented into activities and outcomes.
- A set of definitions for each of the strategic objectives.
- A set of definitions for each of the *measures* selected to monitor each of the strategic objectives, including *targets*.

The Balanced Scorecard encourages managers to focus on four areas of their organisation's operations.

- The customer: managers need to ask what existing and new users value from the service they are provided with. In addition, they need to identify potential users and find out why they are not using the service. This allows targets that matter to users to be developed and incorporated into the performance management system.
- Internal: the purpose of this is to improve internal processes and decision making by looking at the operations of the organisation in order to identify what has to be done to meet objectives.
- Innovation and learning: this requires managers to identify areas of improvement and to learn from past performance.
- Financial: managers are required to consider the financing of the organisation in the context of creating value for stakeholders, which requires the choice of financial performance measures to be determined in consultation with key stakeholders.

The scorecard is balanced as managers should think in terms of all four areas of performance and to measure their performance in these areas. A key feature of this approach is that it considers both the internal and external aspects of the organisation, focusing in particular upon customers. In addition, it should be related to the organisation's strategy as it considers operations in the light of organisational objectives.

Like all management techniques, problems can arise in the implementation of the Balanced Scorecard. First, there may be a problem with conflicting measures. Some measures such as increases in gold medals and cost reduction naturally conflict. Second, performance measurement is only useful if it initiates appropriate management action. There is little point in developing a set of measures for the four aspects of the scorecard if managers are not going to do anything with, or about, the information. Finally, managers need to have the skills to be able to interpret the information that the Balanced Scorecard generates.

There are many other performance management frameworks that can be adopted but, notwithstanding this, there are two specific factors that are important in making these as effective as possible in respect of performance management. First, the organisation has to have a culture that supports a performance management approach. An effective performance management framework is more than just a system of controlling the operations of an organisation; it must also encourage staff to consider performance management as a fundamental way of doing business.

Second, in order to be effective, performance management systems must involve effective performance measurement and target setting. This is perhaps the key to making performance management work, because if measures of performance are not established, then managers are not in a position to assess how they are doing, or to be able to take corrective action if required. In addition, it is important to set levels of performance, or targets that are to be achieved, as this aids comparison with other organisations and with previous performance.

In reviewing the use of performance management frameworks in the public sector, the Audit Commission (2002:14) noted that many providers needed to improve their performance management systems. In their inspection of these services, inspectors found a number of common weaknesses, which are set out below. It is worth noting that these represent potential weaknesses around performance management frameworks in all sport organisations. The weaknesses were:

- An absence of a robust performance framework or a system that was in its infancy and not yet well understood or applied.
- Too many or too few performance indicators (PIs) that failed to measure key outcomes or did not enable the whole service to be appraised. For example, the use of financial indicators only, or facility PIs only.
- No use of wider PIs to measure personal leisure activity such as cycling, yoga or jogging.
- A series of inconsistent, imprecise or ambiguous definitions concerning what data actually meant. For example, an inability to distinguish the number of users from the number of visitors or relate financial performance to the achievement of outcomes such as increased participation levels.
- A lack of robust baseline data and/or no trend analysis, which meant little or no capacity to measure or analyse performance over time. There was also a lack of overall analysis of performance information across the whole service to identify areas of good and poor performance across all service areas, as well as specific aspects of the service.
- A limited monitoring of whether service objectives were being achieved, often due to a lack of targets or inappropriate and immeasurable performance measures being selected.
- Little or no analysis of existing customers and management information to match provision to the needs of different communities.
- A limited use of PIs to measure the performance of contracted organisations or other partners who may be delivering key services on behalf of the authority.
- A lack of comparison around performance, either across services or with other authorities or partners.

Performance management frameworks have an important role to play in performance management by encouraging a more holistic consideration of the performance of the organisation.

It is important that managers identify a framework that fits the operations and objectives of the organisation and that they consider the above limitations when implementing and using their chosen framework.

PERFORMANCE EVALUATION

Evaluation considers how well plans have been implemented and assesses whether the work done will have the impact it is intended to have. In order to evaluate performance it needs to be measured, and all possible aspects of operations should be evaluated in order to inform management practice. Performance measurement is usually carried out through the use of PIs which can be defined as 'a piece of empirical data representing performance that can be compared over time or with similar organisations' (Taylor *et al.*, 2000:4). For example, the number of members, cost of marketing activities and the number of athletes who qualify for championships. In order to make PIs more useful for management, they are usually associated with a target, or level, that managers need to obtain.

Performance indicators are essential to evaluation because they:

- Clarify the organisation's objectives;
- Evaluate the final outcome resulting from the organisation's activities;
- Enable citizens to be informed about performance;
- Enable citizens to make informed choices about their services;
- Indicate the contribution of the service towards the organisation's objectives;
- Act as a trigger for the further investigation of (and possible action to improve) the quality of inputs and outputs;
- Assist with managerial decision making when allocating resources;
- Provide staff with feedback to enable them to develop and improve operations.

(Holloway, 1999)

Six factors are necessary for performance indicators to be valuable for evaluation. These are:

- *Purpose*: Managers must know who will be using the information and for what purpose. For example, members will want to know how their membership fee is being spent, while managers will want to monitor efficiency and effectiveness. These differing purposes are likely to require different PIs and will certainly require different presentations of the data.
- *Linked to objectives*: Performance indicators are meaningless unless they are evaluated in comparison with objectives. For example, member numbers may increase but may have done so by offering discounted membership prices to potential clientele. In this case, a manager may have been effective from a membership perspective, but ineffective financially. Actual evaluation of performance has to be done in the context of what is to be achieved.
- *Balance*: Sets of performance indicators used should give a balanced picture of the organisation's performance. The PIs chosen should reflect the main aspects of the organisation, including outcomes and the perspectives of users.

- *Reliability*: The data used to form PIs must be collected from the same sources and in the same manner. This will ensure that the performance is being evaluated accurately and allows for comparisons to be formed.
- *Accuracy*: PIs must measure what they are considered to measure – otherwise they may lead to mistakes in decision making. For example, counting the number of members of a national governing body is not a true indication of the number of participants in the sport. Membership numbers do not include non-members who participate outside the club system and often include people who are no longer active.
- *Interpretation*: PIs should only be used as a guide for management, as they do not provide an explanation for performance. For example, a PI will show that expenditure in equipment increased, but not explain why. The management of the organisation will need to interpret the indicator and explain performance.

Measuring the performance of national governing bodies

Chappelet and Bayle (2005) have proposed six dimensions for measuring the performance of a sport organisation, notably at the national level. These are set out below:

Performance dimensions of voluntary sport organisations

Dimensions	Aims	Measurement
Sport	Obtaining the best sport results and increasing the number of members	Results and membership *Quantitative and qualitative*
Internal/social	Improving the social climate and the involvement of internal stakeholders	Satisfaction of stakeholders *Qualitative and quantitative*
Societal	Contributing to society and increasing social capital	Legitimacy and impact *Qualitative*
Financial	Obtaining the resources necessary to achieve the objectives Managing financial independence from main funders	Financial resources or value in kind *Quantitative*
Promotional	Improving the awareness of the sport among all stakeholders and the public	Reputation and image *Quantitative and qualitative*
Organisational	Well-organised, clearly defined policies and procedures	Internal processes and assurance mechanisms *Qualitative*

From this it is clear that performance should be evaluated across a range of dimensions, including internal dimension and contributions to society. Chappelet and Bayle have also set out a range of PIs which can be measured both qualitatively and quantitatively. This emphasis on qualitative measurement is important as most managers will focus on what produces 'numbers', rather than seeking the richer detail available from qualitative measures.

Comparison and benchmarking

The main purpose of performance measurement is comparison; that is, comparison with existing targets, with previous performance or with external organisations. The use of performance indicators to compare with previous performance has long been established within sport organisations. However, in recent years external comparison and benchmarking have become increasingly important.

In the public sector, external comparison of performance was promoted by the introduction of the Best Value legislation instigated in 1997. This originally set out a requirement for a national level of comparison using the set of the Audit Commission Performance Indicators for Cultural Services (outlined in Table 10.1). This comparison with other local authorities was statutory and managers had to collect data to allow these indicators to be established. This process of national comparison was, however, heavily criticised as the national performance indicators took no account of location, service priorities or catchment population. As a result, the national indicators did not present an explanatory picture of performance and have subsequently been replaced with broader, more generic evaluation indicators.

Table 10.1 *National performance indicators for cultural and leisure services*

Dimensions of performance	Performance indicator
Strategic objective	Number of pupils visiting museums and galleries in organised school groups Does the local authority have a local cultural strategy?
Cost/efficiency	The cost per visit to public libraries Spend per head of population on cultural and recreational facilities
Service delivery outcome	The number of visits per head of population to public libraries
Quality	The percentage of library users who found the book(s) they wanted and/or the information they needed
Fair access	Percentage of residents by targeted group satisfied with the authority's cultural and recreational activities

Source: Robinson, 2004

Managers of sport organisations often make use of 'local' indicators that are specific to their local context, allowing them to take account of relevant geographical, policy or catchment area characteristics. In addition, they compare themselves with services that are similar, in a 'like with like' comparison. For example, a small sports hall may compare itself with other small sports halls, and urban parks can be compared with other urban parks. This type of comparison makes more sense than any national comparison because the comparator is more appropriate.

Another method of comparison is known as *process benchmarking*. This occurs when managers compare organisational operations in order to learn from others. This type of comparison

179

or benchmarking has been particularly prevalent within the management of elite sport systems where benchmarking has been considered as a good method of identifying the factors that lead to international sporting success. Underpinning the benchmarking approach is the concept of *learning from best practice*, and this method of comparison seeks to improve practice as a consequence of a detailed analysis of the practices used in successful organisations. These are then introduced into an organisation wishing to improve success. Managers of elite sport systems have studied the operations of successful sport systems in other parts of the world and then attempted to introduce the performance practices that are perceived to lead to success. This has led to a convergence of the makeup of elite sport systems which now have a similar construction throughout the world.

BARRIERS TO THE PERFORMANCE MANAGEMENT PROCESS

There are a number of barriers to the effectiveness of the performance management process:

- Managers must accept the need for performance management and use it appropriately.
- There needs to be a performance management structure in place in the organisation, which incorporates the setting of objectives, the procedures for the collection and analysis of information and for comparison with targets.
- Performance management requires certain skills to be effective and, without a clear understanding of the process involved and what the components mean, there is a danger that mistakes may occur in decision making.
- Significant misuse of data or utilisation of incorrect performance measures can cause organisations of all sizes to experience difficulty in implementing performance management.

There is also some debate about whether it is actually possible for sport organisations to fully manage their performance. Sanderson (1998) presented several concerns regarding the use of performance indicators in public services and these concerns are applicable to all sport organisations. First, he is unconvinced that performance indicators can deal with environmental complexity, which is a characteristic of the operating context within which sport organisations work. For example, not only does a judo club deliver services directly to its members, it may also be working in partnership with other agencies such as British Judo – the sport's governing body – and schools to increase participation in the sport. To try and identify the contribution the club makes to the partnership, and to measure how effective it is, is considered by Sanderson to be too complex.

Second, performance management is based on the assumption of *controllability*, which is that all aspects of the organisation are under the control of managers. Sanderson argues that this assumption is also flawed, as managers have no control over a number of features of their environment such as changes in customer tastes, new competition, changed political priorities concerning sport or even the performance of athletes.

Third, and perhaps most importantly, Sanderson argues that performance management and measurement is based upon a fundamental assumption of *measurability*. The underlying premise of performance management is that all aspects of management can be measured. This assumption is clearly flawed, in that, although it is possible to measure many aspects of a sport organisation, there are some factors that simply cannot be evaluated. Performance indicators have existed for some time in areas such as customer satisfaction, member numbers and finance. However, they are yet to be fully developed to measure the contribution of sport in combating obesity or social exclusion or in contributing to 'human capital'. Sanderson feels that this will lead managers to focus on those aspects of the organisation that can be easily measured. For example, measuring the number of children in a swimming class, but not how well they swim, would clearly be to miss the point of the exercise.

It is difficult to present a direct argument against these concerns; however, these can be addressed in the way that PIs are interpreted and presented to stakeholders for their review. As long as a balanced set of PIs are collected and are interpreted in a sensible manner, then performance management is a valuable tool for the management of sport organisations.

SUMMARY

This chapter has considered the role of performance management in the management of sport organisations. Performance management is a four-stage process that begins with objectives which are then delivered by plans. These then need to be evaluated. There are a number of benefits to the systematic management of performance utilising a holistic performance management framework. These benefits are better planning and strategy delivery, a structured approach to the implementation and monitoring of plans and an improvement in the subjectivity of management decision making. Performance management also helps with the management of stakeholders and helps managers to focus on organisational priorities. The use of performance management frameworks is important as they encourage a structured, holistic approach to managing performance.

Evaluation is fundamental to the performance management process and is reliant on good and appropriately developed performance indicators. Performance indicators must have a purpose and be clearly linked to the organisation's objectives, and organisations should have a balanced set of PIs. They also need to be reliable, and accurate. Finally, it is important to realise that PIs need to be interpreted and this is the role of the manager.

There have also been concerns expressed about the viability of performance management due to the complexity of the operating environment and because managers cannot measure and control all aspects of their organisation's performance. The main solution to these concerns is in the interpretation of the performance indicators collected, and managers must use such indicators to explain performance, which highlights the need for a holistic programme of evaluation.

CASE STUDY: THE PERFORMANCE FRAMEWORK FOR UK NATIONAL GOVERNING BODIES (NGBs)

This case study sets out the performance framework within which the national governing bodies of the UK must operate. This framework, developed as a result of perceived inefficiencies in the management of NGBs, focuses on key aspects of the organisation in an attempt to improve the effectiveness of these organisations. In this framework, NGBs are categorised on the basis of size, using a series of criteria including turnover, membership numbers and participation levels. Five different categories of NGB were identified, from the very smallest with a turnover of less than £35,000 per annum, no paid staff and fewer than 50 members or clubs, through to the largest mass participation sports. This categorisation was perceived to be necessary in order to reflect the resources and capacity of the NGB. For example, it is unrealistic to expect a small NGB with few members and limited resources to achieve the same level as a large NGB with professional athletes and significant commercial income. This assists with like-with-like comparison. This model also acknowledges that small NGBs can be just as efficient and effective as a very large NGB when judged against criteria which are appropriate for that individual NGB.

This framework sets out specifically, and in detail, what an NGB in each category should aim to achieve across a range of 12 criteria, or performance areas, which are:

- *Effective corporate governance*: the system by which organisations are directed and controlled.
- *Sport and business administration*: the system by which organisations are managed based on a management audit.
- *Financial management*: requiring effective financial procedures and competencies.
- *Exploitation of commercial opportunities*: this requires NGBs to identify ways to generate more income from 'commercial opportunities'.
- *Performance management*: NGBs need to develop a range of performance measures which are linked to more than just elite performance (see below).
- *Talent ID/development and elite performance*: each sport should aim to develop a cohesive system to guide the long-term development and support of its talented athletes/players.
- *Coach education and development system*: it is essential that NGBs have an effective coaching structure in place.
- *Services to members*: it is vital that the services provided should be sufficiently compelling to ensure those who actively participate in the sport want to take up NGB membership.
- *Volunteer management*: it is essential that NGBs take an active role in securing, motivating and retaining volunteers.
- *Event management*: NGBs must organise competition and seek to host major events.
- *Partnerships with local authorities, education and the commercial sector*: it is essential that NGBs have a strong relationship with the other main delivery agents of the sport.
- *Structure of sport*: there needs to be adequate co-ordination between home country and UK/GB NGBs.

Each performance area is associated with a set of performance indicators which are used to evaluate the performance of the NGB. This creates a performance management framework which structures the operations of NGBs.

From this it is clear that NGBs have a structured performance environment which is intended to improve the management of their organisations. The above framework certainly encourages NGBs to consider all aspects of the organisation and is valuable in that it takes into account factors which impact on performance such as size and income. However, this does not seem to be a feature of the PIs associated with the framework as all NGBs have the same PIs. In addition, these PIs are all numeric, which means that, although they are relatively easy to collect if data collections procedures are in place, they do not provide any detail to explain performance. Thus, NGBs will need to supplement these PIs with more qualitative indicators and managers will need to interpret their performance for stakeholders.

REVIEW QUESTIONS

1   Why would a sport organisation embark on a performance management process?
2   Is performance management the same as planning?
3   What does an organisation need to manage performance effectively?
4   What are the characteristics of a good performance indicator?
5   What is the difference between like-with-like comparison and benchmarking?

FURTHER READING

Chappelet, J. and Bayle, E. (2005) *Strategic and Performance Management*. Champaign, IL: Human Kinetics.
Slack, T. and Parent, M. (2006) 'Organisational goals and effectiveness,' in *Understanding Sport Organisations*. (2nd ed.). Champaign, IL: Human Kinetics.
Wiscombe, C. (2009) 'Planning, monitoring, controlling and evaluating sports organisations', in K. Bill (ed.) *Sport Management*. Exeter: Learning Matters.

WEBSITES

Balanced Scorecard
     http://www.balancedscorecard.org
Improvement and Development Agency
     http://www.idea.gov.uk
NBS and Quest
     http://www.questnbs.org

REFERENCES

Andersen, B., Henriksen, B. and Aarseth, W. (2006) 'Holistic performance management: An integrated framework', *International Journal of Productivity and Performance Management*, 55(1), 61–78.
Audit Commission (2002) *Sport and Recreation: Learning from Audit Inspection and Research*. London: Audit Commission
Chappelet, J. and Bayle, E. (2005) *Strategic and Performance Management*. Champaign, IL: Human Kinetics.

183

Holloway, J. (1999) 'Managing performance', in A. Rose and A. Lawton (1999) *Public Services Management*. Harlow: Pearson Education.

Kaplan, R. and Norton, D. (1996) *The Balanced Scorecard*. Boston: Harvard Business Press.

Robinson, L. (2004) *Managing Public Sport and Leisure Services*. London: Routledge.

Sanderson, I. (1998) *Achieving Best Value through Performance Review*. Warwick/DETR Best Value series, Paper No. 5. Coventry: Warwick University.

Taylor, P., Robinson, L.A., Bovaird, A., Gratton, C. and Kung, S. (2000) *Performance Measurement for Local Authority Sports Halls and Swimming Pools*. London: Sport England.

Chapter 11

Budgeting and budgetary control in sport

Simon Shibli and Rob Wilson, Sheffield Hallam University

TOPICS

The meaning of budgeting • Budgeting as a logically sequenced planning process • Common methods of budgeting • Types of budget using worked examples • Actual performance compared with budgeted performance

---

OBJECTIVES

At the end of this chapter you should be able to:

■ Describe the meaning of budgeting in operational, tactical and strategic contexts;

■ Express budget compilation in terms of a logically progressive sequence of stages;

■ Differentiate between continuation and zero-based budgeting and their relative appropriateness in given situations;

■ Apply recognised budgeting techniques to the construction of budget statements;

■ Analyse a budget and actual performance using recognised evaluation techniques.

KEY TERMS

Balance sheet – a list of an organisation's assets and liabilities, which when netted off (i.e. assets minus creditors) gives a valuation of the organisation's net worth (also known as capital).

Budget – the business or overall plan of an organisation expressed in financial terms.

Cash budget – an analysis of how the cash available to an organisation is expected to change over a given period of time.

Continuation budgeting – budgets compiled on the basis of no change in policies or priorities, i.e. business as usual.

Financial performance – the profit or loss made by an organisation over a given period of time (see income statement).

Financial position – a snapshot of the net worth of an organisation at a given point in time (see balance sheet).

Income statement (or profit and loss account) – an analysis of how the resources available to an organisation have changed over a given period of time.

Loss – a decrease in the resources (capital) available to an organisation as a result of trading.

Profit – an increase in the resources (capital) available to an organisation as a result of trading.

Variance – the difference between actual performance and planned performance.

Zero-based budgeting – a method of budgeting which starts with the priorities of an organisation and allocates resources to the priorities according to their rank order of importance.

OVERVIEW

This chapter examines the importance and process of budgeting as a management discipline in sport. From an 'importance' perspective, budgeting is an integral part of an organisation's operational, tactical and strategic planning. Consequently it is vital that those of you looking to build a career in the sport industry should have an appropriate level of knowledge and skill in budgeting. This important skill will help you to contribute meaningfully to your organisation's business objectives. Whilst it would be unreasonable to expect a single chapter of a book to be a one-stop shop for all you need to know about budgeting, it is possible for it to provide a sound overview of the subject.

Practical examples drawn from a variety of sports management scenarios are used to illustrate the theoretical points being made throughout the chapter. We start by using some case study material drawn from events in 2009/10 to illustrate what can happen if budgeting is ineffective.

CASE STUDY: FIRST PRINCIPLES AND PORTSMOUTH FOOTBALL CLUB'S FINANCIAL CRISIS

Regardless of the sector of sport in which a business operates, whether it is a small voluntary sector club, a local authority swimming pool or a stock market listed company, it is vital that an organisation's management underpin their activities by using the techniques of budgeting. There are two key questions to which all businesses should be able to respond positively.

First, 'Is the selling price higher than the cost?' That is, is the organisation making a profit? For non-profit-making organisations such as members' sports clubs and local authority facilities, we can modify the first question to: 'Is the organisation operating within the resources allocated to it?' We understand in the context of our own lives that if we live beyond our means, that is, do not operate within our resources, then varying degrees of problems will follow. Initially, we may experience a cash flow problem; next we might become burdened with interest payments we are unable to meet; and finally we end up being declared 'bankrupt'. The same analysis is applicable to businesses that do not operate within their resources. If we cast our minds back to the events of 2008/9, a significant number of Football League clubs were experiencing acute financial difficulties following the collapse of the Setanta Sports contract for television rights to Premier League and Football League matches. From Setanta's perspective, liquidation happened because significantly fewer people subscribed to the service than the company had originally forecast. Less revenue than expected resulted in an inability to pay the clubs what they had been promised and led to Setanta being 'liquidated' (i.e. its assets were sold in order to release cash to pay its creditors). From the perspective of the football clubs, the Setanta deal offered a higher level of guaranteed income for a number of years. Many clubs entered into expensive financial commitments based on this guaranteed income such as players' wages and stadium improvements. When the 'guaranteed' income failed to materialise as Setanta went into administration, a number of clubs were unable to meet their own commitments and themselves became candidates for financial failure. Setanta's demise was triggered by its failure to meet a £3m payment to the Scottish Premier League and a £10m payment to the Premier League in England. Conditions in the contracts between the Premier League and Setanta led to an auction whereby the rights that Setanta held were sold off to the highest bidder. Sir Robin Miller, the chairman of Setanta, was quoted as saying:

> This is a sad day for all concerned. Since its inspired inception a number of years ago, Setanta and its financial backers have invested hundreds of millions of pounds buying up UK and international sports rights. With the hard work and dedication of its staff, a pay-TV broadcaster was created which entertained people in three million homes with top-class sport. Unfortunately, in a difficult and highly competitive market, and despite strenuous efforts by the board and management, it has not been possible to find sufficient additional funds in the time available to ensure its survival.

Rarely has there been such a high-profile example to illustrate the point that the selling price must be higher than the cost. In the case of Setanta, the revenue generated from their three million household subscriptions was not sufficient to pay their 200 employees and the property rights holders such as the SPL and EPL. When costs exceed revenue such that a business is no longer viable, an inevitable spiral of decline follows.

The second question all businesses must answer is: 'Is the business well set to continue trading?' In practical terms the second question is a reference to a firm's ability to pay its creditors as they fall due and having the autonomy to pursue policies of its own unfettered by external influences. Many business failures are not because there is limited demand for the product. One of the principal causes of business failure is that, despite decent demand for a product, the organisation runs out of cash and is unable to meet its obligations. In some cases, despite being profitable, a business may be 'highly geared'; that is, it has a high level of borrowing. A situation can arise whereby the providers of loans have more control over a business than the shareholders. A classic example is the way in which football clubs borrow against the value of their stadium or playing squad in order to help meet day-to-day operational costs. When the providers of loans become nervous about their debtors' ability to pay, they may call in a loan or force the business to make a decision that is not in its best long-term interest. Portsmouth Football Club incurred debts of over £60m building up a squad of players thought good enough to compete in the Premier League in England. After winning the FA Cup in 2008, the club then went on to have a promising campaign in the UEFA cup narrowly missing out on qualification for the last 32 after a 2–2 draw with AC Milan. Everything seemed to be going to plan for the unfashionable south coast team and yet 15 months after playing AC Milan, the club was placed into administration, incurring a nine-point penalty, which almost certainly ensured relegation. The financial warning signs had been on the wall for some time and are a classic example of what happens when businesses get into difficulty. Players and other club staff were not paid their wages on time and some of the best and highest-earning players were sold off during transfer windows; money that should have come to the club from the Premier League was paid to clubs owed money by Portsmouth. In the meantime the club had changed hands four times during the 2009/10 season and the manager Paul Hart was sacked after a run of poor performances that left the club bottom of the Premier League. The final indignity came in February 2010 when Her Majesty's Revenue and Customs, to whom millions of pounds was owed in tax payments, filed a winding-up petition against the club in the courts, which in turn led to the club being placed into administration. In short, Portsmouth Football Club could not be described as being well placed to carry on trading and this situation has been caused directly by the club living beyond its financial means.

Successful organisations need to operate within their resources, pay their bills as they fall due, and have effective control over their business activities. The case study above illustrates what can happen when these conditions are not met. The remainder of the chapter illustrates how the use of budgeting and budgetary control techniques can help businesses to answer these two questions positively.

THE MEANING OF BUDGETING

Budgeting is a subject area which takes its roots from the field of management accounting. In essence, management accounting is about the collection, collation, analysis and reporting of financial information for planning, decision making and control purposes. Budgeting can be shown to be part of the overall planning process for a business by defining it as 'the overall plan of a business expressed in financial terms'. These plans might involve trying to achieve a predetermined level of financial performance such as a profit of £x over the year, or having sufficient cash resources to be able to replace the equipment in a gym. Organisational business planning can be summarised as an analysis of four key questions:

1 Where are we now?
2 How did we get here?
3 Where are we going?
4 How are we going to get there?

To illustrate the link between general business planning and budgeting, the question 'Where are we now?' can be modified to 'Where are we now in financial terms?'. Similarly the question 'Where are we going?' can be modified to 'Where are we going in financial terms?'. To diagnose where a business *is* in financial terms requires the ability to be able to 'read' an income statement (profit and loss account), a balance sheet and a cash flow statement. To predict where a business is going is difficult (as is any attempt to predict the future), but techniques such as compiling an expected income statement, balance sheet and cash flow can help to focus attention on the business essentials. Furthermore, the very process of planning ahead using budgets can help to test whether what you wish to achieve and the accompanying financial consequences are compatible or 'internally consistent'. The concept of internal consistency will be covered in the next section, but let's complete this section by being clear that the meaning of budgeting is 'the overall plan of a business expressed in financial terms'.

BUDGETING AS A LOGICALLY SEQUENCED PLANNING PROCESS

A key point about budgeting is that it is an ongoing process rather than a time-limited one-off event. The actual mechanics of drawing up the numbers involved in a budget are but a small part of the overall budgeting process. By bearing in mind that budgeting is designed to help an organisation with planning, decision making and control, it is possible to appreciate that budgeting is a continuous part of business life. This point can be reinforced by viewing budgeting as steps in a logically sequenced planning process, as shown in Figure 11.1.

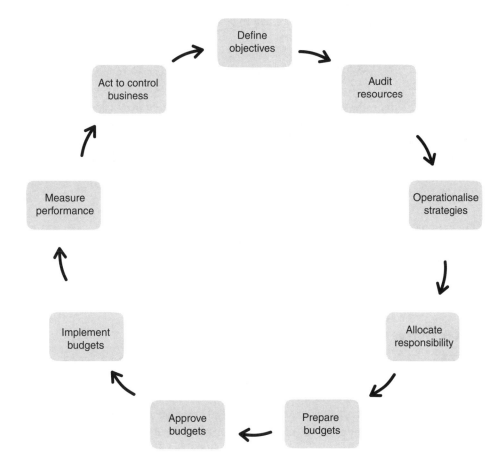

Figure 11.1 *The budgeting process*

Figure 11.1 can be reinforced by a commentary on each of the nine stages of budgeting.

Define your business objectives

The first question to ask when involved with any financial business planning is 'In monetary terms, what are we trying to achieve?'. This question should provide a clue that most sane business people would not answer by saying 'making a loss'. Losses are made in business but it is inconceivable to imagine that managers set out deliberately to make losses. Losses normally occur when there is a mismatch between what was planned and what happened in reality. Organisational objectives will vary according to the nature of the business. A community sports club which exists for the benefit of the members may desire nothing more than to break even or to make a small surplus to maintain its existing facilities. A more complex organisation such as a professional football team needs to balance the requirements of producing a successful team on the pitch (utility maximisation) with the requirements of being a commercial franchise (profit maximisation). Whatever the objectives of an organisation, they need to have certain qualities that enable them to be measured. These qualities are contained within the mnemonic 'MASTER'.

Measurable	For example, a profit of £3m in the financial year, or simply to break even;
Achievable	The organisation must have the capability to attain its objectives; capability means staff, other resources and competitive advantage;
Specific	Objectives must be specific, e.g. £3m profit, not 'to do well this year';
Time limited	Objectives must have a stated date for being achieved;
Ends related	Objectives must relate to achieving outputs (ends) rather than describing means (how);
Ranked	Ideally objectives should be ranked in priority order.

An example of an objective meeting the MASTER mnemonic might be:

Our first priority is to achieve a net profit of £3m in the financial year 1 April 2009 to 31 March 2010. This target is considered to be attainable as the organisation has increased its capacity and the market is expanding.

Audit resources

The audit of resources is a 'reality check' on the objectives. Its purpose is to ensure that the objectives and the resources required to achieve them are internally consistent. As an example, Sheffield United need around 15,000 spectators per home match to break even. With a stadium capacity of nearly 31,000, it is clear that 15,000 people can be accommodated at a home match so long as they can be attracted to the match in the first place.

Where there is a discrepancy between the objectives and the resources available to achieve them, two courses of action are possible. First, the objectives can be changed so that they are compatible with the resources. Second, the gap between the resources available and the resources required can form the basis for prioritising capital investment such as increasing the

190

capacity of a stadium, or identifying training and development needs to ensure that staff have the skills to deliver what is required of them.

Operationalise strategies

Having defined what you want to achieve and confirmed that you have the resources to deliver the objectives, the budgeting process evolves to consider the day-to-day tactics to be used to meet the objectives. In a private health and fitness club these might include the marketing plans, pricing policies, customer care protocols and opening hours. If organisational objectives can be regarded as 'what' we wish to achieve, then operational strategies can be regarded as 'how' we plan to achieve the objectives. Thus a football club aiming for average match day turnover of £300,000 might set out to achieve it via operational strategies for spectators, corporate hospitality customers, programme sales, half-time draw tickets, catering and beverage sales, merchandising sales and car parking.

Allocate responsibility

Successful achievement of objectives does not happen by chance, nor as a result of a mechanical exercise. Sport is primarily a service industry and the most important people in determining the extent to which objectives are met are an organisation's staff. In order for people to see where their contributions fit into an organisation's overall plan, they need to have agreed responsibility for particular areas of work. Agreed responsibility is particularly important in situations where staff can be rewarded, or indeed punished, on the basis of their performance. For example, basic performance for a sales adviser in a health club might be 20 new peak-time members per month, with incentives available if the basic target is exceeded. By contrast, a private sector company managing a leisure facility on behalf of a local authority might be punished by deductions from its management fee for not meeting the terms of its agreement, for example cleanliness standards. If it is known and clearly stated 'Who is going to do what and by when?', then there is the basis for a meaningful comparison of actual performance compared with planned or expected performance.

Preparation of budgets

It is worth noting that the actual preparation of budgets does not occur until the mid-point of the budgeting process. This is important because it makes the point that budgeting is not an isolated process and is integral to overall business planning. When preparing a budget there are two important considerations, namely 'how much' income or expenditure, and 'when' will the income or expenditure occur? To illustrate the point, if an average swimming pool is expecting 52,000 admissions per year at an average price of £4, then the answer to 'How much income will be generated?' is £208,000. However, it is unlikely that a pool will average 1,000 admissions per week for 52 weeks. There will be peak times such as during school holidays and half-terms and off-peak times such as during the winter when it is cold and there are shortened hours of daylight. Thus in order to make sure that the appropriate level of resources (for example, staff) are in the right place and at the right time, it will be necessary to plan the predicted level of activity on a week-by-week or month-by-month basis.

Doing such an exercise will enable managers to plan ahead for situations where expenditure is greater than income and there is insufficient cash to meet the shortfall. Having identified situations requiring management attention, strategies can be put in place to deal with them such as negotiating an overdraft facility at the bank, rescheduling expenditure on capital items, or simply not paying creditors on time. The important point of note is that the process of budgeting identifies potential problems in advance of them happening so that pre-emptive action can be taken.

It is unlikely that at the first time of asking the figures produced in the preparation of budgets will deliver the outcomes required. Therefore managers may be asked to revise their budgets in such a way that the desired outcome is achieved. In practice there are five ways in which a budget can be revised.

1 Increase revenue *and* keep costs constant. This could be achieved by increasing prices, increasing throughput, or a combination of the two methods. The key assumption here is that any increase in price will not be offset by a reduction in demand.
2 Decrease expenditure and keep income constant. This could be achieved by making savings on non-essential expenditure or reducing the quality of the service on offer (for example, fewer staff on duty).
3 Increase income *and* decrease costs, as 1 and 2 above are not necessarily mutually exclusive.
4 Alter the financial outcome required. It may be the case that it is not possible to bring the required outcomes and the budget into line by using 1, 2 and 3 above. Therefore, rather than alter income and expenditure, management may decide to alter the financial outcome required. This approach can work both positively and negatively. If staff provide managers with a budget that exceeds the required bottom line and the assumptions underpinning the budget are correct, then it would make sense to increase the overall budget target accordingly. A much more likely scenario is that the targeted outcome cannot be met by revisions to income and expenditure and management agree to settle for a reduced financial outcome, for example an annual profit of £2.9m rather than £3.0m.
5 Change the overall business objectives. It may well be the case that it is impossible to arrive at an acceptable solution to a budget using steps 1–4 above. Under these conditions it may be that the required outcomes and the organisation's capabilities are not compatible. The only remaining alternative is to change the organisation's objectives. As an example, it is often the case that private contractors managing local authority sport facilities are required to meet social as well as financial objectives. On occasion, pursuit of these differing aims may be mutually incompatible in the sense that programming activities for priority groups at certain times prevents revenue maximisation. Every use of resources has an opportunity cost; that is, the price of the best alternative foregone. Thus in order to make the budget balance, it may be that some priorities which are no doubt desirable and equitable have to be sacrificed to the cause of wider business interests. For this reason, it is important that where possible objectives are ranked (see 'R' in the MASTER mnemonic above).

The significance of preparing a budget, comparing it with business objectives and taking corrective action where appropriate indicates the importance of achieving internal consistency. Using the budgeting model described thus far ensures that what an organisation wishes to achieve in overall terms and the financial consequences of doing so are consistent. If potential problems can be identified at the planning (input) stage, pre-emptive action can be taken by drawing up plans to deal with adverse circumstances. Clearly this approach has a greater chance of success and is more desirable than trying to deal with situations reactively as they materialise without prior warning. The process of modelling the financial consequences of various scenarios until an acceptable outcome is achieved is known as an 'iterative' approach or, in less scientific terms, 'trial and error'.

Approval of budgets

Once an acceptable match has been achieved between an organisation's business objectives and the financial consequences of those objectives, then a line needs to be drawn under the 'preparation of budgets' stage. The point at which this line is drawn is at the 'approval of budgets' stage, which effectively puts an end to the various iterations of the budget and leads to the formal adoption of the budget the organisation wishes to pursue. It is recognised good practice for the approval of a budget to be formalised in the minutes of a board or committee meeting. Furthermore, budgets should be approved in advance of the financial period to which they relate. The wider significance of a budget being approved formally is that those who have compiled it, and those whose performance will in part be judged by it, know exactly what their responsibilities are. This in turn has two benefits. First, if you know what is expected of you, then evaluation of performance can be objective rather than subjective. Second, expectation generates accountability, which in turn gives managers the focus to concentrate on those things which are important in terms of meeting the organisation's objectives.

Implementation of budgets

As a logical consequence of a budget being approved, it can be implemented with effect from the date to which it applies. For example, if an organisation's financial year operates from 1 April to 31 March, then it would be a reasonable expectation for the budget to be approved by the committee or board at least a month before the new financial year started. A less than ideal situation would be an organisation entering a financial period without an approved budget, which would be the managerial equivalent of a boat trying to operate without a rudder.

Measurement of performance

To reinforce the notion of budgeting being integral to overall business planning, it is vital to realise that the budgeting process does not end once the preparation and implementation phases are over. Once the budget is operational, it is essential that, periodically (say at least monthly), a check is made between how the organisation is actually performing compared with how it planned to perform. One of the greatest motivators in life is feedback and the same is true in budgeting. Management accountants use the mnemonic CARROT as a way of categorising the features of good quality information for feedback purposes. Each component of CARROT is explained below.

Concise   Information fed back to managers needs to be to the point;

Accurate   Feedback is used for planning, decision making and control purposes, therefore it follows that feedback should be error free;

Reliable   Similar to 'accurate', the same results of an actual versus budget comparison should be obtained if different people carried out the analysis, i.e. the source information is robust;

Relevant   Different levels of management require different levels of information; therefore feedback should be presented in terms that are relevant to the intended recipient;

Objective   Feedback should be concerned with verifiable factual evidence and not with individual interpretation of findings;

Timely   There is a trade-off between timeliness and accuracy; nonetheless feedback should be received in sufficient time for it to be of value in terms of planning, decision making and control purposes.

Measurement of performance is not an end in itself and is only valuable as an exercise if it is used to add value to the process of management in an organisation.

Taking action to control the business

If we accept that rational decisions require information that meets the requirements of the CARROT mnemonic, the final stage of the budgeting process is to use the information to inform the direction of the organisation. It is highly unlikely that there will be a perfect match between budget and actual comparisons, so the first decision to make is whether or not overall variance is within a tolerable range. If variances are tolerable, then significant changes in policy will be unlikely. By contrast, if variances are considered to be so significant that the organisation is 'out of control' (in financial terms), then proactive management action may be needed. On a positive note, if performance is considerably ahead of target, it may be prudent to revise targets upwards. If, however, actual versus budget comparisons reveal a significant shortfall in performance, then corrective action may be needed. Such action might include extra marketing to increase sales, reducing price to stimulate sales, improving the quality of sales to boost repeat business or, more predictably, cutting costs to try and maintain profit margins.

In concluding this section it is worth making three points relating to the assertion that budgeting is a logically sequenced planning process.

1   Budgeting is a process designed to help managers make sensible decisions about running their organisations. It helps to inform decisions, but clearly budgeting is not in itself a decision-making process.

2 Compiling a budget is an iterative process. It is unlikely that the first draft of a budget will produce an acceptable result. Various scenarios will be modelled and differing assumptions will be tested until an acceptable solution is found. Figure 11.1 is a simple model of an ideal process; in practice the numerous iterations will result in a more complicated picture. However, the basic point is that each step of the model is a reality check on the previous step, which is designed to ensure that an organisation's overall plans and the financial consequences of those plans are internally consistent.

3 Although Figure 11.1 implies a step-by-step approach to compiling a budget, in reality some steps are seamless. For example, defining your objectives (step 1), conducting an audit of resources (step 2) and devising operational strategies (step 3) are likely to be interrelated and to occur simultaneously.

COMMON METHODS OF BUDGETING

In this section, 'methods of budgeting' refers to types of budgeting processes and behavioural aspects of budgeting. In terms of budgeting processes there are two common ways in which budgets tend to be compiled. The most frequently used budgeting process is 'continuation' budgeting (or business as usual) and the other, somewhat rarer, process is 'zero-based budgeting' (ZBB). Continuation budgeting refers to situations whereby the business objectives of an organisation do not change significantly from one financial period to the next. Under these circumstances, it makes perfect sense to continue with essentially the same business objectives and hence the same approach to budgeting. An example of a continuation budget might be a voluntary sector sports club whose main aim is to break-even and to provide a service to the membership. If the club's basic operations lead to a situation whereby the selling price is higher than the cost, then apart from increasing membership subscriptions and bar prices to keep up with inflation, there is no point wasting time and resources on a more complicated approach to the club's finances. Continuation budgeting is also referred to as 'incremental' or 'decremental' budgeting. Incremental budgeting refers to a situation whereby an organisation increases its income and expenditure, usually by the rate of inflation, in order to pursue its existing policies. Decremental budgeting refers to a situation whereby an organisation agrees either a standstill level of funding (a cut in real terms) or an absolute decrease in funding. When faced with a decremental budget, managers are faced with the problem of deciding whether to pursue existing policies with less resources; to reduce funding to all policies by the same relative amount ('the equal misery' approach); or to cut funding to some activities in order to preserve the more highly ranked priorities (see 'R' in the MASTER mnemonic). An example of a simple continuation budget for a small professional football club is shown in Table 11.1.

Table 11.1 *Football club continuation budget*

	This year	Inflation	Next year
INCOME			
Season ticket sales	540,000	3%	556,200
Other ticket sales	125,000	3%	128,750
Television revenue	450,000	3%	463,500
Sponsorship	80,000	3%	82,400
Catering	110,000	3%	113,300
Merchandising	65,000	3%	66,950
Total income	1,370,000	3%	1,411,100
EXPENDITURE			
Players' wages	850,000	3%	875,500
Ground expenditure	109,000	3%	112,270
Marketing activities	68,000	3%	70,040
Administration	171,000	3%	176,130
Other expenses	151,000	3%	155,530
Total expenditure	1,349,000	3%	1,389,470
PROFIT/(LOSS)	21,000	3%	21,630

The basic assumptions in Table 11.1 are that the club will pursue the same policies from one year to the next and will increase income and expenditure by the rate of inflation (in this case 3 per cent). Thus all that has happened to the numbers in the budget is that they have increased by 3 per cent. There are some advantages and disadvantages of using continuation budgeting, and these are highlighted below.

Advantages of continuation budgeting

■ Continuation budgeting is intuitively simple and easy to understand.
■ It is an effective use of resources if business objectives, infrastructure and strategies have remained unchanged.
■ It is quick and easy to update figures and budget templates that are readily to hand.
■ It requires less staff resources and therefore costs less than zero-based budgeting.

Disadvantages of continuation budgeting

■ The overall rate of inflation within a country does not necessarily equal the rate of inflation within a particular industry and therefore the use of the headline inflation figure to increase budgets is somewhat crude.

- Continuation budgeting does not encourage growth in real terms; in Table 11.1 the net position is that the business stands still. Businesses need to grow in real terms to remain competitive and to have the resources to maintain their operating infrastructure.

- Changes may be occurring within the marketplace which require change such as the application of internet technology and e-marketing. By not taking advantage of business opportunities as they present themselves, standing still may actually be going backwards relative to your competitors.

- There is the danger that if income and expenditure budgets are not challenged occasionally then targets are 'soft' rather than a fair test of an organisation's capabilities. Managers can build 'slack' (unnecessary expenditure) into budgets, which can be 'rewarded' when budgets for the next year are confirmed without detailed scrutiny.

Despite the fact that continuation budgeting is by far the most commonly used budgeting technique, if an organisation is facing a fundamental change to its operating circumstances, a more analytical approach may be needed. Rather than starting with last year's budget and updating it, the zero-based budget starts with a blank piece of paper and challenges every item of income and expenditure. An example of zero-based budgeting questions might be:

1   What is the purpose of this expenditure?
2   On what exactly will this expenditure be made?
3   What are the quantifiable benefits of this expenditure?
4   What are the alternatives to this proposed expenditure?
5   What would be the outcome of cutting this expenditure completely?

In order for funds to be allocated to a given item of expenditure, a robust defence would have to be made for the expenditure through the five questions listed above. If some expenditure was not defendable, then it might be cut and reallocated to more deserving areas of an organisation's activities. As an example, consider the case of a large professional football club that runs its own laundry to wash and iron players' kit. The laundry will make use of staff, space, equipment, energy and consumables – all of which cost money. Furthermore, in the long run, equipment will need to be replaced and service contracts will have to be in place in case machinery breaks down. If commercial laundry facilities were available locally, which could match the quality of service provided in-house at a cheaper price, then not only would the club save money, it could also use the staff, space and other resources released on more important business objectives. Clearly, using the zero-based approach would be a more rigorous way of questioning existing business practices than simply accepting that the club has always provided an in-house laundry and will continue to do so.

The purpose of zero-based budgeting is the allocation of resources in a systematic manner which is consistent with an organisation's wider business objectives. It makes an implicit assumption that people within an organisation act rationally and prioritise business objectives rather than personal agendas – sometimes this can be a very ambitious assumption. Compared with continuation budgeting, zero-based budgeting is resource intensive and therefore can be wasteful if there has been no significant change in business objectives and operating procedures. It is therefore unsafe to make sweeping generalisations about one budgeting process being better than another. As in many instances of using applied management techniques, the best methods to use are the ones most appropriate to the circumstances faced by an organisation. Therefore, if a business is stable with no major changes on the horizon, continuation budgeting might be the best method to use. By contrast, if a business requires a major strategic overhaul, then zero-based budgeting might be the best method to use. Like many things in life, compromise can help to keep most of the people happy for most of the time. So, too, a business could use continuation budgeting most of the time, but once every three or five years a zero-based approach could be used to challenge the status quo and reallocate resources to where they are most needed.

In addition to being familiar with methods of budgeting such as continuation or zero-based approaches, it is also important to realise the human dimension of budgeting. Sport is a people business, and ultimately the extent to which business objectives are realised depends on the extent of staff motivation towards meeting targets. One of the great demotivators in life is having targets imposed on you from above (top-down) without consultation. Equally, for management, there is nothing more depressing than letting staff set their own budgets and finding out that the so-called 'bottom-up' budgets do not deliver the organisation's overall business objectives. The compromise approach is for a participatory budgeting style whereby all staff whose performance will in part be judged by meeting the budget have some influence in the compilation of the figures by which they will be judged. There are no hard and fast rules about when to use 'top-down', 'bottom-up' or 'participatory' methods. Good managers need to have a broad range of skills and techniques in their managerial toolboxes. Furthermore, these skills and techniques should be used in a context-sensitive manner, contingent upon the particular circumstances of the business and its operating environment.

TYPES OF BUDGET USING WORKED EXAMPLES

Business organisations report a summary of their financial transactions in three standard formats:

■ the income statement (previously called the profit and loss account [or income and expenditure statement in the case of non-profit organisations]);
■ the balance sheet; and
■ the cash flow statement.

The income statement is a measure of an organisation's financial performance; the balance sheet is a measure of financial position; and the cash flow statement illustrates how the cash available to an organisation has changed over a given period of time. In financial terms, the answers to the questions 'Where are we now?' and 'Where are we going?' can be seen by constructing an income statement, balance sheet and cash flow statement to show the change between the starting point and the ending point. In this section, examples of each financial statement are modelled and issues relating to them are discussed. Perhaps most importantly the linkages and non-linkages between the statements are also illustrated.

Table 11.2 is the first two columns from Table 11.1 above and shows how a small football club might produce a summary of its income statement. The key message emerging from Table 11.2 is that the club is planning to make a profit of £21,000 during the financial year.

Table 11.2 *An income statement (or profit and loss account)*

	This year
INCOME	
Season ticket sales	540,000
Other ticket sales	125,000
Television revenue	450,000
Sponsorship	80,000
Catering	110,000
Merchandising	65,000
Total income	1,370,000
EXPENDITURE	
Players' wages	850,000
Ground expenditure	109,000
Marketing activities	68,000
Administration	171,000
Other expenses	151,000
Total expenditure	1,349,000
PROFIT/(LOSS)	21,000

The problem with Table 11.2 is that a year is a long time and it is unlikely that income and expenditure will occur at the same rate throughout the year, that is, the budget does not tell you when profits or losses will occur. Many businesses are seasonal and will have peaks and troughs in terms of their level of activity. This in turn has implications for other areas of management such as staff scheduling, the purchase of fixed assets and cash flow management. If the data in Table 11.2 were to be allocated over 12 months on the basis of when such income and expenditure were predicted to occur, the monthly budget would appear like the example shown in Table 11.3.

Table 11.3 Football club annual budget sub-analysed by month

	Aug	Sept	Oct	Nov	Dec	Jan	Feb	March	April	May	June	July	Total
INCOME													
Season ticket sales	270,000	270,000	0	0	0	0	0	0	0	0	0	0	540,000
Other ticket sales	15,000	12,000	11,000	16,000	20,000	18,000	15,000	9,000	9,000	0	0	0	125,000
Television revenue	0	0	200,000	0	0	50,000	0	0	0	0	200,000	0	450,000
Sponsorship	40,000	0	0	0	0	0	20,000	0	0	0	0	20,000	80,000
Catering	9,000	11,000	10,000	12,000	14,000	13,000	10,000	7,000	8,000	6,000	5,000	5,000	110,000
Merchandising	6,000	5,000	6,000	8,000	16,000	3,000	2,000	3,000	2,000	5,000	5,000	4,000	65,000
Total income	340,000	298,000	227,000	36,000	50,000	84,000	47,000	19,000	19,000	11,000	210,000	29,000	1,370,000
EXPENDITURE													
Players' wages	75,000	75,000	75,000	75,000	75,000	75,000	75,000	75,000	79,000	57,000	57,000	57,000	850,000
Ground expenditure	50,000	4,000	6,000	5,000	10,000	4,000	2,000	2,000	6,000	15,000	2,000	3,000	109,000
Marketing activities	4,000	0	0	12,000	12,000	0	0	0	0	0	20,000	20,000	68,000
Administration	17,000	14,000	14,000	14,000	14,000	14,000	14,000	14,000	14,000	14,000	14,000	14,000	171,000
Other expenses	12,000	12,000	12,000	12,000	12,000	12,000	12,000	12,000	12,000	12,000	12,000	19,000	151,000
Total expenditure	158,000	105,000	107,000	118,000	123,000	105,000	103,000	103,000	111,000	98,000	105,000	113,000	1,349,000
PROFIT/LOSS	182,000	193,000	120,000	−82,000	−73,000	−21,000	−56,000	−84,000	−92,000	−87,000	105,000	−84,000	21,000
Cumulative	182,000	375,000	495,000	413,000	340,000	319,000	263,000	179,000	87,000	0	105,000	21,000	

Two important points emerge from Table 11.3. First, simply by looking at the profit or loss per month, it is clear that seasonality is a factor in the club's financial fortunes. Large amounts of income are received during the first three months of the financial year in the form of season ticket sales and television revenues, and as the year progresses, expenditure exceeds income from November until May. Second, a simple table of figures is not particularly helpful to somebody reading the budget. It would be much more helpful if the numbers were explained by a series of notes such as the examples below.

Income: Season ticket sales will occur in August and September and we expect 2,160 fans to purchase a season ticket at an average price of £250 (£540,000). (Last year 2,000 sales @ £240 = £480,000.)

Expenditure: Players' wages are based on core costs of £57,000 per month, plus an average of £18,000 per month in bonus payments during the playing season. There is an additional one-off payment of £4,000 budgeted for April in the event of the playing squad avoiding relegation.

In practice, it would be expected that all items of income and expenditure would be qualified by a written explanation. By providing a brief written commentary to the key figures and assumptions that underpin the budget, it is possible for those people who look at it to have a much clearer idea of the organisation's plans. If the club planned to make a profit of £21,000 (financial performance), then it follows that the club's overall financial position would increase by £21,000. This can be verified by examining the club's opening and closing balance sheets as shown in Table 11.4.

Table 11.4 *Opening balance sheet, change, and closing balance sheet*

	This year	Change	Next year
FIXED ASSETS			
Intangible assets	75,000	−25,000	50,000
Tangible assets	395,000	−50,000	345,000
CURRENT ASSETS			
Stock	6,000	−3,000	3,000
Debtors	30,000	6,000	36,000
Cash	45,000	92,000	137,000
CREDITORS < 1 YEAR	56,000	1,000	57,000
Net current assets	25,000	96,000	121,000
NET ASSETS	495,000	21,000	516,000
CAPITAL & RESERVES			
Share capital	100,000	0	100,000
Profit & loss a/c	395,000	21,000	416,000
TOTAL CAPITAL	495,000	21,000	516,000

The income statement in Table 11.3 showed the club making a profit of £21,000 and the balance sheet in Table 11.4 shows the club's net worth increasing by £21,000. This is not a coincidence. The income statement (financial performance) 'explains' the change in an organisation's financial position (balance sheet). Although an analysis of the income statement should be carried out monthly, it would be unusual to analyse the balance sheet with the same frequency.

Having established that the income statement and the balance sheet are linked, it is worth demonstrating that profit and cash are not linked. Simply because an organisation has made a profit of £21,000 does not mean that the organisation has an extra £21,000 in cash to spend. This can be demonstrated easily using the data in Tables 11.4 and 11.5. The profit made during the year was £21,000, yet cash has changed by +£92,000 (opening cash £45,000, closing cash £137,000). Why is this the case? There are three reasons why cash (liquidity) and profitability are not directly linked.

1 Expenditure is recognised on a income statement when it is incurred rather than when it is paid. Thus, immediately an invoice is received, it is logged as being an expense, even though it might not actually be paid until 30 or even 90 days later. The same is true for income, whereby a business will recognise a sale as income on receipt of an order, not when the client actually pays for the good or services supplied. This is known as the accruals or matching principle. Thus, in Table 11.3, the budget figures are referring to when income and expenditure are incurred and not actual movements in cash.

2 Income statements do not include the purchase or sale of fixed assets (capital expenditure). Thus a football club might make a profit of £21,000 and actually decrease the cash available to it as a result of investing in new players or stadium improvements. By the same logic, it would be possible to make a loss and to increase cash, for example by selling a member of the playing squad.

3 Income statements contain non-cash transactions such as depreciation, which is the way of spreading the cost of an asset over its useful life. If a top professional footballer is purchased on a four-year contract for £10m, this is equivalent to an annual cost of £2.5m. The way of recording this transaction would be to reduce cash by £10m and to increase fixed assets by £10m. This makes no difference to the net worth of the business as one asset, cash, has been exchanged for another asset, a player. At the end of each year of the player's registration, fixed assets would be reduced by £2.5m until the cost of the player was written off. However, the 'writing off' of the value of a player is a paper transaction in the sense that no cash is involved. The actual movement of cash was recorded when the player was bought for £10m.

As a result of profitability and liquidity not being identical, and of the importance of cash to businesses, it is common practice to produce a cash budget that documents the actual movements of cash during a financial year. The cash budget provides a link between the opening cash balance, the income statement, the balance sheet and the closing cash balance. In the interests of simplicity, if we assume that the income statement in Table 11.3 has been compiled on a cash basis and there is no need to account for depreciation, a basic cash budget for the club might look like the example shown in Table 11.5.

Table 11.5 *Abbreviated cash budget*

	Aug	Sept	Oct	Nov	Dec	Jan	Feb	March	April	May	June	July	Total	Data source
Opening cash for month	45,000	231,000	401,000	574,500	490,000	417,500	378,500	367,000	282,000	213,000	120,000	217,000	137,000	Balance sheet
Profit/ loss for month	182,000	193,000	120,000	-82,000	-73,000	-21,000	-56,000	-84,000	-92,000	-87,000	105,000	-84,000	21,000	Profit & loss a/c
Change in stock	2,000	-1,000	500	500	-2,000	3,000	-500	-500	-1,000	1,000	-2,000	3,000	3,000	Balance sheet
Change in debtors	2,000	-3,000	5,000	-4,000	500	-1,000	3,000	500	2,000	-3,000	-3,000	-5,000	-6,000	Balance sheet
Change in creditors < 1 year	0	1,000	-2,000	1,000	2,000	-5,000	2,000	-1,000	2,000	-4,000	-3,000	6,000	-1,000	Balance sheet
Purchase of fixed assets	0	-20,000	0	0	0	-15,000	0	0	0	0	0	0	-35,000	Balance sheet
Sale of fixed assets	0	0	50,000	0	0	0	40,000	0	20,000	0	0	0	110,000	Balance sheet
Change in cash	186,000	170,000	173,500	-84,500	-72,500	-39,000	-11,500	-85,000	-69,000	-93,000	97,000	-80,000	92,000	Cash budget
Closing balance for month	231,000	401,000	574,500	490,000	417,500	378,500	367,000	282,000	213,000	120,000	217,000	137,000		Balance sheet

The important point of note in Table 11.5 is that it documents how the opening cash of £45,000 increased during the year by £92,000 to result in a closing cash balance of £137,000. The main reason why cash increased considerably in excess of profit (£21,000) was because of the sale of fixed assets (£110,000). The final column in Table 11.5 shows where the data for the cash budget was obtained and confirms that the cash budget is a link between the opening balance sheet, the income statement for the financial period under review, and the closing balance sheet. The sale of fixed assets (usually playing staff) is a classic method used by football clubs to balance their books and to ease cash flow problems. From a management perspective, the information in Table 11.5 indicates that at no point will the club run out of cash and furthermore there will be a regular cash surplus. This cash surplus could be invested in an interest-earning current account in order to generate further income for the club – a good example of success (sensible cash management) breeding success (extra income derived from interest on cash investments).

For most sport managers, budgeting tends to start and end with a budgeted income state-ment, sub-analysed on a monthly basis (Table 11.3). This is a perfectly acceptable level of skill for most managers. However, for those with ambitions to have full responsibility for all aspects of an organisation's financial performance, skills are also needed to be able to produce and act upon budgeted balance sheets and cash flow statements.

In the final section of this chapter, the review of budgeting is concluded with an example of measuring actual performance against budget.

ACTUAL PERFORMANCE COMPARED WITH BUDGETED PERFORMANCE

The ultimate purpose of budgeting is to assist managers in the planning, decision making and control of a business. To achieve this aim, periodic comparison of actual performance com-pared with planned or budgeted performance is required. Table 11.6 is an example of how such a comparison might be presented to the managers of an organisation.

The layout of Table 11.6 has a deliberate structure to it and each component is explained in turn below:

1 'Actual' income and expenditure refers to entries made to an organisation's accounting system which are supportable by documentary evidence such as invoices, receipts, staff time sheets, etc. 'Actual' figures are drawn from the financial accounting systems and can be supported by an audit trail of evidence.

2 'Incurred' (or 'committed') expenditure refers to expenditure which relates to the finan-cial period in question that we know has been made, but as yet has not been billed for. This sort of data can be picked up from documentation such as purchase order forms. In order to produce timely budget reports, it is sometimes not possible to wait until all of the paperwork relating to expenditure in a period has been received. Thus in order to reflect a more realistic picture of events, the 'Incurred' column is used to log known expenditure that is not formally in the books of account. The 'Incurred' column tends to be used for expenditure only – it would be unusual to have incurred income.

Table 11.6 *Actual versus budget comparison*

	Actual	Incurred	Total	Budget	Variance	Direction	Note
INCOME							
Season ticket sales	272,000		272,000	270,000	2,000	F	1
Other ticket sales	14,000		14,000	15,000	−1,000	U	1
Television revenue	0		0	0	0		
Sponsorship	43,000		43,000	40,000	3,000	F	2
Catering	9,500		9,500	9,000	500	F	
Merchandising	7,000		7,000	6,000	1,000	F	
Total	345,500	0	345,500	340,000	5,500	F	3
EXPENDITURE							
Players' wages	77,000		77,000	75,000	2,000	U	4
Ground expenditure	48,500	750	49,250	50,000	−750	F	
Marketing activities	5,000		5,000	4,000	1,000	U	5
Administration	16,000	1,250	17,250	17,000	250	U	5
Other expenses	13,000		13,000	12,000	1,000	U	5
Total	159,500	2,000	161,500	158,000	3,500	U	
PROFIT/(LOSS)	186,000	−2,000	184,000	182,000	2,000	F	6

3 The 'Total' column is simply the sum of the 'Actual' and the 'Incurred' columns.
4 'Budget' refers to the approved budget for a given financial period; in this case it is for the first month (August) of the budget shown in Table 11.3.
5 'Variance' is the difference between the 'Total' column and the 'Budget' column.
6 'Direction' is a reference to whether the variance on any given line of the budget is favourable (F) or unfavourable (U). One characteristic of good information is that it is relevant to the intended recipient. For non-finance specialists, spelling out whether a variance is favourable or unfavourable is a helpful aid to understanding the underlying meaning of the figures.
7 'Note' is a cross-reference to a written qualitative explanation of a variance. Numbers in isolation do not explain a variance and therefore it is sometimes useful for a written explanation to accompany some of the more significant variances.

To illustrate how qualitative explanations can help to explain the meaning of variances, presented below are the notes that might have accompanied the actual versus budget comparison in Table 11.6. Note how it is written in the form of a report and can easily be cross-referenced to Table 11.6.

Report

To: Club Directors
From: Management Accountant
Date: 10 September 20XY
Re: Actual v. Budget Notes for Month of August

Note 1: Season ticket sales/other ticket sales
Season ticket sales (1,088 at £250) are 8 ahead of target (1,080 at £250) and it seems that the overall target of 2,160 will be exceeded. More season ticket sales have been achieved by persuading people who previously attended the club on an *ad hoc* basis. Therefore there has been a direct trade-off between season ticket sales and other ticket sales. We expect overall ticket sales for the season to be £8,000 ahead of budget.

Note 2: Sponsorship
Following the club's promising start to the season, a new sponsor has been found for the club's kit which will be worth £3,000 per year. Overall sponsorship revenues are expected to exceed budget by this £3,000.

Note 3: Total income
Total income is £5,500 ahead of target in the period. As explained in Notes 1 and 2, these are considered to be genuine performance over budget. However, it is not all net gain (see Note 6 below).

Note 4: Players' wages
The successful start to the season has led to bonus of payments of £2,000 over and above the expected level. So long as the club continues to be successful, extra ticket sales and match day activity should more than compensate for bonus payments to players.

Note 5: Marketing activities/administration/other expenses
The increase in the club's activity at the start of the season has led to overspends on marketing, administration and other expenses. However, extra expenditure has been made in order to obtain extra revenue.

Note 6: The bottom line
The club is £2,000 ahead of budget for the period as a result of increased profitable activity. This is primarily as a result of generating extra revenue (£5,500). Should this promising start to the year continue, then it is likely that the club will exceed its overall profitability target of £21,000.

Signed
Management Accountant

Any director reading the above report would be able to grasp the basic point that the club was performing ahead of budget and had made a promising start to the year. At this stage the actual versus budget comparison would be noted and no action would need to be taken, other than to congratulate and encourage those responsible for delivering the better-than-planned for performance.

SUMMARY

The purpose of this chapter was to provide an overview of budgeting as a management discipline and to examine the role of budgeting in the context of overall business planning. The five key points emerging from the chapter are as listed below.

1 The first principles of business are that organisations need to operate within the resources allocated to them and to be in a position whereby the business is well set to continue trading. Budgeting can help in this process by expressing in financial terms where a business hopes to be at some time in the future.
2 Budgeting is a management accounting discipline and helps to provide information for planning, decision making and control purposes. Budgeting is a logically sequenced planning process starting with the definition of 'MASTER' objectives and finishing with a feedback or control loop.
3 There are two commonly used methods of budgeting, namely continuation budgeting and zero-based budgeting. They have different objectives and their use is dependent upon the circumstances faced by a business.
4 Businesses report a summary of their financial transactions in the standard formats of income statement, balance sheet and cash flow statement. It is good practice to produce budgets (or plans) for all of these financial statements so that managers can have a comprehensive overview of a business's financial affairs.
5 To reinforce the point that budgeting is a continuous process, regular (monthly) checks should be made between how an organisation actually performed compared with how it planned to perform. Where significant variances are found, these should be highlighted and explained so that non-finance specialists can grasp their underlying meaning.

It is not possible for a single chapter in a book to be a one-stop shop for all there is to know about budgeting. However, readers should have seen sufficient thus far to realise that budgeting is an integral part of the sport manager's toolbox of skills. The best way to acquire the necessary skills is via a solid grounding in the theory, complemented by real-life experience of budgeting.

REVIEW QUESTIONS

1 To what extent is any budgeting experience you have had consistent with the approach discussed in this chapter? If there are any differences, why do you think this is the case?
2 If you were in charge of a business, what financial information would you like to have presented to you? How frequently would you like it to be presented and in what format?

3   Compare and contrast continuation budgeting and zero-based budgeting. You should pay particular attention to what each method is trying to achieve and the processes used.
4   What are the qualities of good objectives and good information?
5   How could the use of computer spreadsheets help in the compilation and monitoring of budgets?

FURTHER READING

Beech, J. and Chadwick, S. (eds) (2004) *The Business of Sport Management*, Pearson Education, Harlow, England.
Owen, G. (1994) *Accounting for Hospitality, Tourism and Leisure*, Pitman Publishing, London.
Naylor, D. (2001) *Managing Your Leisure Service Budgets*, Ravenswood Publications, London.
Robinson, L. (2004) *Managing Public Sport and Leisure Services*, Routledge, London.
Russell, D., Wilkinson-Riddle, G.J. and Patel, A. (2001) *Cost Accounting: A Concise Guide*, FT Prentice Hall, London.
Schwarz, E., Hall, S. and Shibli, S. (2010) *Sport Facility Operations Management: A Global Perspective*, Butterworth-Heinemann, Oxford, England.
Shibli, S. (1994) *Leisure Manager's Guide to Budgeting and Budgetary Control*, ILAM/Longman, Essex.
Trenberth, L. (ed.) (2003) *Managing the Business of Sport*, Dunmore Press, New Zealand.
Wilson, R. (2010). *Managing Sport Finance*, Routledge, Oxon.
Wilson, R. and Joyce, J. (2008) *Finance for Sport and Leisure Managers: An Introduction*, Routledge, Oxon.

WEBSITES

For free annual reports from organisations in the sport and leisure industry, visit:
    http://www.precisionir.com/investors/ars.aspx
For a critical insight into academic papers concerning sport finance, visit:
    http://www.fitinfotech.com/IJSF/IJSF.tpl
Sport and leisure finance is often discussed in both the business and sport sections of daily publications. Consider:
    http://news.bbc.co.uk/sport/default.stm
    http://www.ft.com/arts-leisure
    http://www.timesonline.co.uk/tol/sport/ (note that this is now a subscription website)
For some excellent advice on budgeting and access to a simple Microsoft Excel budgeting spreadsheet for your personal finance, visit:
    http://www.understandingmoney.gov.au/content/consumer/financialliteracy/budgeting
For a whole variety of business budget spreadsheets in Microsoft Excel for purposes such as revenue forecasting, balance sheet budgeting and break-even analysis, visit:
    http://www.affiliatetips.com/affiliate-spreadsheets.html

Chapter 12

Sport marketing management and communication

Ron Garland, University of Waikato, New Zealand
Christopher Hautbois, University of Paris-Sud, France

TOPICS

Introduction • Marketing of sport • The role of marketing • The services marketing mix: the 7 Ps • Marketing strategy

OBJECTIVES

At the end of this chapter you should be able to:

- Appreciate that sport marketing follows basic marketing principles but with a change of emphasis to suit particular sporting contexts;
- Recount how marketing's role can be applied to sport and sport organizations with special emphasis on service marketing's '7 Ps';
- Evaluate the application of marketing strategies and tactics to chosen sport codes;
- Identify the management information needs of sport marketers;
- Describe the purpose of sport market research and identify different groups of sport fans;
- Understand how sponsorship strategies represent suitable options for marketing communication plans in sport.

KEY TERMS

Brand – the identity of a specific product, individual, service or business which can take many forms, including a name, sign, symbol, colour combination or image.

Market research – is any organized research to gather information about markets or customers.

Marketing information system (MIS) – a repository where marketing information is formally gathered, stored, analysed and distributed.

Marketing mix – the '7 Ps': product, price, promotion, place, physical evidence, people, process.

Marketing plan – a business document usually part of a business strategy written for the purpose of describing the current market position of a business and its marketing strategy for a period covered by the marketing plan.

Public relations – the main goal of public relations is to enhance a company's or an individual's reputation.

Relationship marketing – involves using methods and tactics to develop long-term relationships with customers in order to retain them.

Sponsorship – is a cash and/or in-kind fee paid to athletes, teams or sporting events.

OVERVIEW

Sport marketing addresses the satisfaction of sport consumer needs with sport products and services. In this chapter, we examine the role of marketing in sport and its specificities. A sport marketing plan contains a variety of marketing mix elements. The chapter's primary goal is to address sport marketers' information needs for the design, and execution, of their marketing strategies. As a result, the chapter analyses the services marketing mix (the 7 Ps), with a special focus on the role of sponsorship in the promotion of sport products and services.

CASE STUDY: KEEPING THE PARTY GOING – THE RISE AND RISE OF BEACH VOLLEYBALL AT SUCCESSIVE SUMMER OLYMPIADS, BY JAN CHARBONNEAU, MASSEY UNIVERSITY, NEW ZEALAND

You've already got sun, sand, bronzed athletes, and a crowd in party mode. How do you improve beach volleyball ... and why would you want to? If you're the competition manager for beach volleyball for London 2012 the answer is simple ... it's your job. And beach volleyball's survival as an Olympic sport depends on it!

To understand the challenge facing the competition manager, you have to appreciate that competition at the Olympics is not limited to the track, pool or court. The Olympics are, by any measure, the largest and most successful sporting event in the world. Millions of spectators watch athletes compete live, with many more watching the Games from the comfort of their homes. Consider that, for Beijing 2008, 6.5 million tickets were sold for live events, 4.3 billion viewers in 220 countries watched over 61,700 hours of television coverage, the Games' internet channel on YouTube generated over 21 million video views, and Beijing2008.cn, the Games' official website, had over 100 million hits in August 2008 alone (IOC 2002, 2004, 2008a).

The Olympics is also big business, with broadcasting, corporate sponsorships, tickets and licensing generating $US 3 billion for Sydney 2000. For Athens 2004, broadcasting rights alone generated almost US$ 1.5 billion (IOC 2004); for Beijing 2008 this rose to over US$ 1.7 billion. Global corporate sponsors – including Coke, McDonald's and Visa – paid US$ 866 million to sponsor Turin 2006 (winter Olympics) and Beijing 2008 (IOC 2008a). And for this kind of money, broadcasters, sponsors, ticket holders and licensees expect value!

The International Olympic Committee (IOC) finds itself in the enviable position that 'more sports want to participate in the Olympic Games, more athletes want to compete in the Olympic Games, more people want to attend the Olympic Games, and more media want to cover the Olympic Games' (IOC 2002). Adding new sports adds audience, allowing this tradition-steeped organization to maintain a modern image. For example, introducing table tennis increased television audiences in Asia, handball increased Scandinavian television revenues, and snowboarding and beach volleyball have drawn in a younger demographic.

However, each new sport or discipline not only adds audience but increases the size, time, complexity and resources required to stage the Games. Each new sport brings athletes, coaches and officials that need to be housed, fed and transported, and competitions that need venues and other infrastructure requirements. The IOC realizes that future growth must be limited to ensure that the Olympics' unique features of atmosphere, athlete experience, universality and brand value are not lost. Resisting the temptation to extend competition over multiple host cities, the IOC has officially limited the duration of competition to 16 days, capped the number of sports at 28 and competitors at 10,500, and committed to a single host city (IOC 2000, 2003, 2008b).

To keep within these parameters, the IOC carefully evaluates new sports seeking Olympic status (IOC 2002). For Beijing 2008, the IOC received 18 applications for inclusion of new sports. For Rio 2016, seven applications were received, with rugby sevens and golf making the cut, assuring themselves a place at both the 2016 and 2020 Games. The continued inclusion of existing Olympic sports is also evaluated on a per-Games basis (IOC 2002).

Six main criteria are used in these evaluations:

- History and tradition – e.g. competitive history
- Universality – e.g. number of affiliated federations and continental participation
- Popularity of sport – e.g. spectator attendance and media interest
- Image and environment – e.g. gender equity and anti-doping policies
- Development of the international federation – e.g. financial viability
- Costs – e.g. competition costs and complexity of television production.

Olympic sports now find themselves in the unenviable position of having to compete to stay within the Olympic family.

Beach volleyball as an Olympic sport

As a sport, beach volleyball has a long history, staging its first competitive tournament in California in 1930, and is now played in more than 150 countries on five continents. Beach volleyball was officially recognized as an Olympic sport in 1994, debuting at Atlanta 1996. The FIVB (Fédération Internationale de Volleyball), beach volleyball's international federation, had modest objectives for Atlanta – make a good first showing. By Sydney 2000, according to Blair Harrison, competition manager for beach volleyball, SOCOG (Sydney Olympic Organising Committee), the objective was 'to ensure its long-term future as an Olympic sport'.

In regular competition, beach volleyball has a tradition of combining sport and entertainment, creating a beach party atmosphere with entertainment enhancers such as music, announcers and dancers. Athletes train specifically for the 'party atmosphere' so music and dancers do not present a distraction for players. The FIVB incorporates this sports/entertainment theme into their slogan, billing itself in corporate communications as 'The Leader in World Sports Entertainment'. At all times, the overriding objective of the FIVB is not to disappoint their fans, whether at local competitions, World Championships or at the Olympics. At Sydney 2000, extensive use was made of music and scripted match entertainment including lifesaver-themed characters and mock beach rescues to 'push the entertainment envelope'. The end result was a vibrant party atmosphere that generated positive spectator and media reactions.

For Athens 2004, according to Nikos Sofianos, competition manager for beach volleyball, ATHOC (Athens Olympic Organising Committee), the FIVB had three objectives:

- Add value to spectator and television viewer experiences
- Maintain or increase attendance and media coverage
- Ensure beach volleyball's position in the top five overall sports.

The IOC criteria 'Popularity of Sport' offered the most potential for beach volleyball to differentiate itself from other Olympic sports. According to Andrew Hercus, FIVB Control Committee, beach volleyball sought to carve out a niche for itself in the Olympic family, combining the sport's athleticism and robust competition with its existing regular competition 'entertainment culture'.

Athens 2004 – Adding spectator value

A typical spectator spends five hours at a beach volleyball session. The FIVB did not want its Olympic spectators to be passive viewers but to take an active role in creating the party atmosphere. Downtime was minimized within and between matches by expediting side switches and limiting timeouts. During these times, music was provided and announcers actively encouraged spectators to cheer and sing to songs like Men at Work's 'Land Down Under' and the Village People's 'YMCA'. The FIVB employed DJs instead of the usual audio operators, providing them with scripts to hype up the crowd. As one announcer said, 'You'll never hear us say "quiet please" at beach volleyball' (Charles 2004). The players also got into the act, encouraging spectators to cheer, sing and dance. And dance they did – especially when the bikini-clad dance troupe Personal Plus took to the sand. This troupe of female dancers entertained with choreographed routines in timeouts and between matches, keeping crowd energy high. The aim, according to Chronis Chichlakis, beach volleyball's venue coordinator for sports presentation, ATHOC, was to 'provide enough entertainment to keep audiences occupied, without compromising athlete performance'.

Two mock Olympic match courts were constructed, providing both spectators and volunteers with their own Olympic competition venue. Olympic competitors were contracted by the FIVB to play spectators on these courts. SWATCH, the FIVB's World Tour sponsor, provided speed servicing guns, allowing spectators to compare their speed of service with the athletes.

To reinforce their commitment to maximizing the entertainment value for spectators and television viewers, one member of the FIVB's Control Committee was assigned the task of monitoring all entertainment features, feeding back to both the FIVB and ATHOC on a daily basis.

Athens 2004 – Adding television value

For many sports, the duration of an individual match is not easily defined, presenting particular challenges for television broadcasters. Recognizing this, the FIVB changed its scoring system to ensure that each match would last under an hour (80 per cent certainty) – ideal for both television and Olympic scheduling. Under the new scoring system, a point was scored on each serve, adding excitement as the score quickly advanced, providing lots of opportunities for crowd cheers.

To accommodate the demands of television broadcasting, the FIVB made several rule changes for Athens 2004. Defining the time between rallies as 12 seconds reduced delays (no playing action) while being sufficient for television broadcasters to insert a replay and on-site announcers to play a short music clip or engage the crowd.

Referees were connected directly by earpiece to TV producers, allowing producers to advise referees on a continuing basis of their requirements. TV producers utilized three calls: 'Hold', indicating the need for a replay; 'Go', indicating play could recommence; and 'Stop', indicating a significant stoppage such as equipment failure. A new hand signal was developed to indicate a call of 'Hold'. If the arm was held vertically outwards from the referee, players knew that TV producers had requested a delay in commencement of play. Approximately 6–8 of these occurred per match, with announcers and dancers entertaining spectators during these 'television breaks'.

Twenty-two cameras, including super slow motion, net cam and aerial shots, were employed at Athens 2004, up from nine at Sydney 2000. Ball and line colours were changed to maximize contrast and microphones embedded in nets and under sand to provide referee/player audio. Media and stadium announcers were provided with extensive guides including biographies and match histories of all competitors for adding flavour to commentaries. The FIVB consulted official host broadcasters concerning match scheduling to ensure that home country matches would air in their home country prime viewing times.

Athens 2004 – Maintaining attendance and media coverage

The beach volleyball venue at Athens 2004 held approximately 10,000 spectators. Some 2,200 seats were reserved for Olympic sponsors, media, guests and other dignitaries, leaving 7,800 for the FIVB and ATHOC to fill. Selling out finals and evening games (especially when Greece played) at the top ticket price was not a problem. However, filling seats for morning and afternoon games in the Athens heat presented the FIVB with a real challenge. To fill the venue, ATHOC agreed to price tickets for these sessions in the lowest price category.

According to Nikos Sofianos, competition manager for beach volleyball, ATHOC, 'sponsor seats were heavily utilized', with attendance for publicly available seats averaging between 3,000 and 6,000 for morning sessions and 4,000 and 6,000 for afternoon sessions. While down from the 98 per cent capacity reached at Sydney 2000, beach volleyball outperformed most other Olympic sports at Athens 2004. On a daily basis, beach volleyball was in the top five sports in terms of percentage fill of capacity. Even the Olympic mascots, Athená and Phévos, whose attendance was dictated by spectator attendance and appreciation, were regular spectators.

How did beach volleyball score at Athens 2004?

The *Washington Post* referred to beach volleyball at Athens 2004 as a 'sell-out, foot-stomp-ing success', calling it 'one of the most popular spectator sports at the Olympics' since its debut in Atlanta (Charles 2004). Beach volleyball's appeal extends from spectators at live competitions to television viewers. At Sydney 2000, beach volleyball attracted the fifth-larg-est television audience of the 28 sports (Charles 2004). For Athens 2004, beach volleyball was judged the most popular sport in terms of TV viewer hours (IOC 2005).

213

Did the FIVB achieve its objectives for Athens 2004? Attendance and television viewership figures, especially when compared to some sports, would suggest that spectators', television viewers' and broadcasters' expectations were satisfied. Not only was beach volleyball going to Beijing 2008, its place was confirmed for London 2012 and Rio de Janeiro 2016!

Beijing 2008 – Did the FIVB top Athens 2004?

The bar was set high for Beijing. The objective, according to FIVB president Dr Acosta, was simple – ensure beach volleyball was the most successful sport at the Games (Jingyu 2008). While 6.5 million tickets were sold, organizers grappled with low actual attendance, eventually employing yellow t-shirted state-trained 'cheer squads' to fill empty seats. Beach volleyball tickets sold out within three days and fared better than many sports in terms of actual attendance, filling most of its 12,000 seats. The 'girls of Athens' were back on the sand, again often sharing their dances with the official mascots, the Fuwa. This time, however, the proviso was that half of the dancers had to be Chinese and routines had to include traditional Chinese dances featuring red fans and nunchuks. Not that this mattered to the crowds or media. Also back were the professional DJs, many of whom were Chinese, spinning out well-known tunes and cranking up the crowds to shout 'jia you!' to encourage the athletes. Even then US President George W. Bush attended and joined in the beach party. According to MSNBC.com, 'Beach volleyball + 10,000 fans + beach girls = formula for fun', referring to beach volleyball as 'one of the best produced events of the Olympics' (Wu 2008). Beach volleyball was able to 'keep the party going' for Beijing 2008, meeting attendance and media coverage targets.

But the lessons learned from beach volleyball at Athens 2004 were not lost on other sports or BOCOG (Beijing Organizing Committee for the Olympic Games). 'Entertainment enhancers' were not just employed by other sports but BOCOG itself, eroding beach volleyball's competitive advantage. A pep squad of 200,000 volunteers trained in simple dance routines and 28 elite squads of 400 cheerleaders trained by the New England Patriot football team's professional cheerleaders were employed by BOCOG to 'stir up spirit for any national team that needs it' (Huang 2008). At Beijing 2008, the 'party' was not just on the beach but spread to all venues.

All of this begs the question – what will beach volleyball do for London 2012 and beyond? Will its competitive advantage of using a party atmosphere to add value to spectators and media be further eroded? Will the 'party atmosphere' become the Olympic standard? Or will beach volleyball remain as it is – the perfect combination of sport, music and sex' (Tom Blauemauer, stadium announcer at beach volleyball, Athens 2004, *USA Today*).

Interviews

Chronis Chichlakis, venue coordinator for sports presentation, ATHOC.
Blair Harrison, competition manager for beach volleyball, SOCOG.
Andrew Hercus, Control Committee, FIVB, Atlanta, Sydney, Athens and Asian Games.
Nikos Sofianos, competition manager for beach volleyball, ATHOC.

Case sources

Anon (2004) 'Fans party at beach volleyball', *USA Today*, 15 September.
Charles, D. (2004) 'Capacity crowds at beach volleyball rock the joint', *Washington Post. com*, 17 August.
Duncan, C. (2004), 'Dance team stirs up beach volleyball venue', *Washington Post.com*, 17 August.

Huang, C. (2008) 'China trains 200,000 cheerleaders – for other Olympic teams', *CSMonitor.com*, 8 July.

IOC (2000) *Coordination Commission for the Sydney 2000 Olympic Games Final Report.*

IOC (2002) *Olympic Games Study Commission.*

IOC (2003) *Olympic Games Study Commission.*

IOC (2004) *Athens 2004 Marketing Report.*

IOC (2005) *Global Sport Report.*

IOC (2008a) *Marketing Report Beijing 2008.*

IOC (2008b) *Olympic Marketing Fact File.*

Jingyu, W. (2008) 'FIVB President expects volleyball to peak in Olympics', *News.Xinhuanet.com*, 16 August.

Shipley, A. and Fan, M. (2008) 'Beijing all dressed up, but no one is going', *Washington Post.com*, 13 August.

Wu, S. (2008) 'Nightlife: Eye candy at beach volleyball leads to fun times', *MSNBC.com*, 18 August.

Based on

Charbonneau, J. and Hercus, A. (2007) '"The perfect combination of sport, music and sex": beach volleyball's efforts to attract Olympic spectators and media', in P. Quester, R.L. McGuiggan, W.D. Perreault and E.J. McCarthy (eds) *Marketing*, 5th edn, McGraw-Hill, Sydney.

INTRODUCTION

Increasingly, marketing has assumed a prominent role in sport organizations. Despite sport marketing being in its infancy as an academic field of study, marketing principles have been applied to sport organizations worldwide for several decades. Earlier definitions of sport marketing such as 'the process of designing and implementing activities for the production, pricing, promotion and distribution of a sport product' (Pitts and Stotlar 1996: 80) have now been supplemented by recognition of service relationships and by societal goals (in addition to managerial goals), 'Sport marketing is a social and managerial process by which the sport manager seeks to obtain what sporting organizations need and want through creating and exchanging products and value with others' (Shilbury *et al*. 2009: 15).

It is well to remind the reader that a financial perspective should always be present; meeting an organization's financial objectives (for example, 'breaking even and staying in business') is obvious but sometimes overlooked.

Sport marketing, and its operational underpinning of marketing management, were probably first enunciated in 1978 in the United States in *Advertising Age* (Shilbury *et al*. 2009; Fullerton 2010). Over the next three decades the term 'sport marketing' has become synonymous with two different, although converging, marketing genres: marketing 'of' sport, and marketing 'through' sport.

MARKETING OF SPORT

Shilbury *et al.* (2009) and Fullerton (2010) agree that marketing 'of' sport covers the deliberate, planned efforts by sport organizations to influence consumer demand (from participants and spectators) for a variety of sport products and services.

> Ultimately, the goal is to ensure the ongoing survival of the sport in rapidly changing environmental circumstances. This aspect of marketing has only recently developed in sporting organizations. Survival depends largely on the principal purpose of the sporting organization. National sporting organizations predominantly associated with elite-level professional sporting competitions will be striving to develop their marketing mix [the 7 Ps of services marketing: see below] to ensure that the sport product is attractive as a form of live entertainment and live broadcast through television, the internet and other mobile outlets. Sports-governing bodies will also be responsible for ensuring that participation in their sport remains healthy. Participants are the lifeblood of sport, as they become the next generation of champions and spectators.
>
> (Shilbury *et al.* 2009: 15)

Notice that the sport marketer's emphasis is upon influencing spectatorship and participation. While marketing a sport is a business function (and is usually overseen by someone with 'marketing' in their business title), the marketing of any product or service, sport included, should be a total corporate or organizational effort. Every employee or volunteer has the responsibility to cater for customer needs. In effect, then, every employee is a 'part-time marketer' (Gronroos 2007).

Yet there is another layer to sport marketing: that of the sporting goods and services domain, with sports equipment, apparel, footwear and the processes (services) that are put in place (for example, ticketing, e-commerce, media processes) to assist the distribution and selling of these goods and services. Now the other genre of sport marketing emerges – marketing 'through' sport (almost always involving some form of sponsorship) – which is the way organizations (usually large corporations)

> use sport as a vehicle to promote and advertise their products, usually to specifically identifiable demographic markets known to follow a particular sport. Sports with significant television time are very attractive to firms seeking to promote their products through an association with sport. Developing licensing programs [paying for the right to use a sport logo to place on products to stimulate sales] is another example of marketing through sport.
>
> (Shilbury *et al.* 2009: 15)

Despite our best attempts at defining sport marketing, there is still debate and contention about definitions. Yet sport marketing need not be made difficult; marketing practice has a unity irrespective of the product or service being sold. The challenge comes in the choice of those concepts, tools and tactics that are appropriate in each context. In sport contexts, marketing is not just the 'contest on the field'. Of equal importance are issues of pricing, promotion and distribution of that contest to different groups of customers in either real time or recorded time.

THE ROLE OF MARKETING

With today's intense competition for consumer discretionary dollars, successful sport organizations have adopted marketing into their business function to:

- segment the markets of a sport organization and select the target markets for today and the months after
- guide this organization in its design and selection of the 'sport product' (which includes more than the 'contest on the field') and its *target* customers
- identify and monitor the activities of business competitors
- develop and implement suitable pricing strategies in regard to the position of the organisation in the competition context (do the prices have to be lower, higher or equal to those of competitors?)
- develop and implement suitable promotional strategies (what is the most relevant commercial endorsement for a brand? What are the values and messages that the sport organization should use to promote its products?)
- develop and implement distribution strategies (that is, getting the sport product to the customers or vice versa) and distribution processes
- develop and implement (preferably in conjunction with the human resources manager) human resource strategies to deliver sport products and processes
- coordinate the research and information needed to carry out the marketing functions (above), audit their performance and help ensure their repeated success.

Therefore, marketing is a process that needs to be managed like any other process. It is much wider than merely promoting an event or activity and its lifeblood is information. Herein lies the necessity for the sport marketer to have a sound grasp of market research – if not the nuances of data analysis, then at least a sound working knowledge of the market research process. That becomes important for briefing and working alongside market research consultants. While gaining and gathering information is part of the marketing function, storage and retrieval of that information is also required. Often this is managed using a *marketing information system* (MIS) (Shilbury *et al.* 2009: 56), which can be anything from a few index cards in a shoebox to an advanced computer system.

Sport marketers require knowledge of their external environment (the so-called PEST analysis – political, economic, social and technological domains), of their customers and of their business competitors, both current and potential, for informed decision-making about their sport's direction. Identifying particular types of consumers for a sporting code is in essence a method of selecting the *target* market. Stanton *et al.* (1995) suggest that market segmentation is the process of dividing the total heterogeneous market for a product or service into several segments, each of which tends to be homogeneous in all similar aspects. According to Harris and Elliott (2007: 128),[1] this can be done according to demographic characteristics (e.g. gender, age, presence or absence of children), psychographic characteristics (personality, lifestyle, psychological), behavioural characteristics or geographical characteristics, but also location, attitudes to and involvement in the sport, prior participation, level of spectator patronage, etc. Irrespective of how they are selected, target markets become the basis of marketing strategy because they identify who the sport product is aimed at. Marketing mix decisions involving pricing, promotion, distribution and facility and event planning are subsequently made with these prospective customers in mind. Herein lies another challenge for a sport marketer – an appreciation of their customers', and potential customers', behaviour. At the very least, an appreciation of sport fan segmentation – focusing on the different behaviours and requisite different marketing mixes – for *aficionados* (or hard-core fans), *fair-weather fans* and *theatre goers* is required.

Market segmentation in sport industry – Character merchandising in football

Character merchandising refers to a marketing technique by which products are associated with well-known characters, since such association effectively enhances the commercial value of the products. In Europe, football clubs seek to develop strategies in the commercial exploitation of the names and images of their team and their players. In these strategies, the fan base of the club is the primary market for this commercial activity. But in order to develop and to improve this business, marketers have to segment this fan base into suitable target markets. Thus, not all the fans behave the same. The role of marketing is to identify the specific demand of each target market in order for the club to sell each of the appropriate products. For example, in this market segmentation, 13 criteria or values have been used by Octagon, a consulting firm specializing in the sport area, ranging from devotion to the team to TV preference for football matches. Depending on the importance of each indicator, Octagon identified four target markets: the 'big fan' (8 per cent of the global market); the 'stadium supporter' (25 per cent); the 'TV supporter' (31 per cent); and the 'occasional fan' (36 per cent). For a football club, the core target is the 'big fan', captive consumers interested in all the products related to their club. In contrast, the 'occasional fan' cannot be considered a viable target.

Market segmentation in sporting events – 'The Parisienne' running race

Running races are popular sporting events all around the world. Typically, each of the famous marathons (Chicago, Boston, Berlin, New York, London) cater for about 35,000 runners from any country, gender or age. These races can be seen as global events. But other running events use market segmentation. For example, in France, a famous running race created in 1997, called 'The Parisienne' (Parisian girl), caters only for female runners (about 18,000). The organizers of this event used the gender criterion to segment and design the race. As a result, the entire business model for this event (especially in terms of sponsors) is female gender based.

Implementing the overall marketing strategy for a sport will involve the 7 Ps of services marketing. These are the mechanisms used by sport marketers to try and influence potential customers to patronise their sport, that is, to buy their 'product'. The knowledge for informed decision-making about the 7 Ps is gained through marketing research, and the central role of the sport organization's marketer(s) is to combine the first four (product, pricing, promotion and place) of the 7 Ps in such a way as to meet the sport organization's objectives.

THE SERVICES MARKETING MIX: THE 7 Ps

Product

Sport as a 'product' differs somewhat from other competitive leisure and recreational activities. The unpredictability of the product (the event), inconsistency of product quality, strong emotional attachment and identification (with a team, nation or individual) and the subjectivity of judgement of the consumers with respect to the product typifies sport (Garland and Ferkins 2006). Now, also, the quality of venues, the 'entertainment' experience that surrounds any major event, the types of promotion used to garner interest, the accessibility of the venue, etc. all impinge on the customer experience. The 'main event' in a sport product is intangible and, as Veeck and Linn (1965: 20) state, 'the customer comes out of the park with nothing except a memory'. Thus, sport marketers need to have their minds firmly focused on their participants, spectators and supporters. Sport managers are often lovers of the game they are marketing – there is nothing wrong with this, provided that management is not blind to such fundamentals as insufficient demand for their 'product' or living the sport through their own eyes rather than through those of their potential customers. This phenomenon is sometimes referred to as 'marketing myopia'. A number of failures in the marketing of sport have come from assuming that consumers will want the sport 'product' merely because it is available. If it was this simple, there would be no need for marketing or marketers.

Seeking to satisfy consumer wants (i.e. demand) by offering sport products and services, which may be tangible or intangible, is at the centre of the sport business. The way these products and services are priced, promoted and 'placed' (i.e. offered to the market) becomes crucial in their sale. The 'contest on the field' is, of course, the core service product, yet that is only the tip of the iceberg. The stadium, arena or ground in which the contest is held, the team website, the variety of merchandise (apparel, banners, gifts, etc.) available, the entertainment provided before, during and after the game, the role of sponsors and the amount of community involvement are examples of the 'peripherals' or wider view of a sport service product. Many of these 'peripherals' are services. Any sporting event is simultaneously staged and viewed or participated in. It cannot be stored (or at least the live action cannot be stored), meaning unsold seats become lost sales (although the size of media right contracts and sponsorships in some modern professional sporting leagues makes empty stadiums – lost sales – less problematic than in the past). Service intangibility (not being able to sample the experience before engaging in the experience) forces the sport consumer into a reliance on the reputation of the event, the event manager and the 'peripherals' (service product extensions) such as venue, facilities, entertainment, atmosphere created, etc. Sport marketers use a variety of ways to 'tangibilize the intangible', as discussed below under 'Physical evidence'.

Branding a sport product or service is about differentiation from competitors, that is, making a service product sufficiently different and distinct from rival offerings. The core service product, the 'contest on the field', can be difficult to differentiate. Thus the branding of sport and sport organizations tends to focus on the peripheral elements. Not every team in a competition can win all the time or have the best players. As a result, sport marketers help sport organizations to find their points of difference and then help them to emphasize these as elements of their brand in order to stand apart from their rivals. Despite inherent difficulties in differentiating core product, some sports have been successful in doing just that. For example, different forms of rugby (7-a-side, 15-a-side) and cricket (indoor cricket, twenty-20, 1-day limited over cricket, 3-day, 4-day and 5-day domestic or international 'test' cricket) show that product differentiation by time duration, player numbers, rule changes, etc. is possible. Obviously these points of difference or brand elements need to be important to the consumer. In the world of international rugby, the power and relevance of the All Black brand with its connotations of strength, history, tradition, winning and striving for perfection is plain to see. Nonetheless, the financial value of the All Blacks brand was not fully appreciated until the professional rugby era from 1995 onwards. As an example, New Zealand Rugby Union receives substantial revenue from brand licensing arrangements with corporate partners such as Adidas and the Lion Corporation (Australasia's leading brewer) for its All Blacks brand.

Price

What price should be charged for a sport event? Buying any sport product will be affected by its perceived value, comparisons with competitive products and feedback from friends, relatives and significant others, whether it is unique or a copy. Like any business, a sport 'product' has its own costs of production which are usually reflected in the entry price (for participants) or seat price (for spectators). As all spectators know, different viewing positions (in a stadium) can be charged out at different prices.

> Increasingly sport organizations are charging different consumers different prices for the same product at different times or different 'locations'. Amid growing concerns that premium pricing (price skimming – charging high prices over the short-term without special regard to long-term, repeat purchase customers) can be damaging, especially to family-based sport attendance, some sport organizations are exploring more 'repeat-attendance' strategies, based on the philosophies of relationship marketing.
>
> (Garland and Ferkins 2006: 217)

Therefore, pricing strategies involving price discrimination will often apply unless a sport event is so popular that demand for entry always exceeds supply (such as the SuperBowl, Wimbledon finals and Summer Olympics opening and closing ceremonies).

Promotion

Sport marketers have to be careful to not confuse promotion – the 'exciting part of the marketing mix' – with marketing *per se*. The sheer visibility of promotion, particularly advertising, creates misconceptions. Sport marketers, like any marketer, can use a myriad of methods (known as the promotional mix) to promote their product:

- advertising (print, television, radio, internet, mobile telephony)
- sponsorship (naming rights, media rights, cause-related sponsorship), direct mail, special deals, special packages involving other goods and services

- pre-match entertainment, corporate 'boxes', merchandising paraphernalia (caps, key rings, collectibles, posters, etc.) and clothing (tee shirts, casual wear, dress clothing, replica team wear, etc.)
- signs and signage, games programmes, 'Old Timers' days, 'Meet the Players' days, exhibition games to promote the sporting code, coaching clinics for young fans, autograph sessions and autographed photos and sporting equipment, free-to-enter competitions, internet gaming and gambling, etc.

Any or all of these are promotion. The sport organization's promotional aims are to inform its targeted customers about the sport product and to encourage purchase of that 'product'. Marketers have to decide if their promotional mix methods can be used separately or together. Advertising refers to a classical way of promoting products and services. Except for its timing (usually immediately before a sporting event), advertising does not often present important specificities in the promotion of sport products or services. These are attended to in pre-match entertainment, signs, games programmes, etc. which are part of what marketers call 'experiential marketing' – a 'global' method allowing the fan to not only be a spectator of the show but a part of it too. 'Experiential marketing' is used to enhance the link between the fan and the team, the event or the players. It is a relevant way to promote the brand and to develop emotion, passion and enthusiasm. Allied to experiential marketing is sponsorship, the promotional mix method so fundamentally important to sport. Certainly other domains – culture, media, etc. – are dependent upon sponsorship, yet Slack and Amis (2004: 270) estimate 'that two-thirds of all global investment in sponsorship is devoted to sport'. Sponsorship is mainly used in 'marketing through sport' strategies to promote products or services. Sport sponsorship strategies can be designed depending on, first, the objective that marketers want to reach (awareness, image, turnover, teambuilding) and, second, the choice of the commercial endorsement to support a player, a team, an event or an organization.

Increases in awareness, image, turnover and teambuilding are the four typical aims for sport sponsorship. First, many sponsors who support players, teams or events seek to enhance their awareness either on the global market or in specific target markets. Sport sponsorship offers good opportunities for promoting brands when companies have just been created, when companies launch new products or services and when there is a corporate name change or a change in product or service positioning. During or after a commercial endorsement, companies can evaluate their awareness (or compare their awareness to the previous situation before the sponsorship strategies). Typically, this is a quantitative evaluation which can distinguish 'top of mind awareness' (the percentage of respondents who, without prompting, name a specific brand or product *first*), 'spontaneous awareness' (the percentage of respondents who, without prompting, name a specific brand or product) and 'prompted awareness' (the percentage of respondents who, with prompting, name a specific brand or product).

Example 1: Atos Origin (information technology services company) supports the IOC and the Summer and Winter Olympics
Example 2: Banco Itau (bank) supports the Brazilian Football Federation

Second, image-oriented sponsorship strategies deal more with a qualitative approach rather than a quantitative one. In this situation, companies are already well known by target markets but wish to gain a part of the positive image associated with sport in general and athletes, teams or sporting events in particular. In these strategies, marketers want sport values such as modernity, dynamism, competitiveness, aesthetic appeal, friendship, youth, valour, health, integrity, etc. to be associated with the brand or product.

Example 1: BP (energy company) supports the 2012 London Olympics
Example 2: Areva (nuclear company) supports the French Athletic Federation

Third, sport sponsorship strategies aim to boost the turnover of companies which support sport activities. This goal is central for managers, but it is notoriously difficult to measure the direct link between sport sponsorship and turnover due to all the other revenue-boosting activities undertaken by companies. Comparing turnover before and during the commercial endorsement is too simplistic.

Example 1: Budweiser (beer) supports the NHL
Example 2: BT (telecommunications) supports the 2012 London Olympics

And fourth, one of the major goals for sponsorship is corporate teambuilding, ensuring that people who work in the sponsoring company feel part of the sporting event endorsed and take pride in their company's support for a team, player or event. In this situation, sponsorship strategies should create excitement and allegiance for the company, and its network, by internal competitions, signage, meeting with players, invitations for the event, etc.

Example 1: UBS (bank) supports Alinghi Challenge for the America's Cup (yachting)
Example 2: Visa (financial services company) supports the FIFA World Cup

After deciding on goals their company has set through a sponsorship strategy, marketers need to choose which 'vehicle' related to the sport area will be supported: team, individual athlete, and event or sport organization. There are various advantages and disadvantages attached to each vehicle, as summarized in Table 12.1.

Table 12.1 *Strengths and weaknesses of different vehicles supported in sport sponsorship*

	Strengths	Weaknesses
To support a team[1]	• The sponsor takes advantage of the number of players in the team. The bigger the number of players in the team, the more visible the brand. • The visibility of the brand does not depend on the results or the performance of just one athlete. • The team can have its own identity. As a result, fans can identify with the team and develop a positive relationship to the brand. • Managers look for values associated with team sports (friendship, team spirit, solidarity, etc.)	• Efficiency of the strategy depends on the results of the team. • Fans cannot identify with the team as much as with an individual athlete.
To support an athlete	• When a brand supports an athlete, fans can easily identify with that athlete. • Market segmentation becomes easier for the sponsoring brand. For example, for Nike, Rafael Nadal is very appropriate for youth, Roger Federer for people 20–39 years old and Tiger Woods for the over-40s. • When the athlete is successful in a competition, the brand takes a huge advantage in terms of image and awareness.	• Efficiency of the strategy depends on the results of the athlete. • Conflicts between team sponsors and individual athletes' sponsors can occur where a company is supporting an athlete. • The sponsor can get into trouble if the image of the athlete declines due to injury, lower performance on the field or troubles in personal life (loose morals, drug consumption, etc.). • Supporting only one athlete can be risky, whereas supporting several athletes spreads the risk. • Supporting one athlete who has their own brand power runs the risk of the 'vampire effect' – the sponsor's name is relegated to second place behind the athlete.
To support an event	• Brand visibility does not depend on the performance of the athletes. • The brand has event-long exposure.	• The brand has no visibility before and after the event: short 'within-event' exposure. • Supporting an event sometimes suffers from lack of association or allegiance between fans and sponsor brand.

1 See Wakefield (2007: 152).

Place

Where and *how* customers buy the sport product comes under the auspices of 'place'. Any sort of active participation or spectatorship by customers means travelling to a sport venue, whereas consumption of the sport product through mediated elements – television, internet, mobile telephony – is more passive participation or spectatorship. The sport service product's simultaneity of production and consumption (and hence its perishability) means 'nothing is "manufactured" until the contest begins, and as a spectator, if the live action is missed, the first opportunity (and its inherent excitement and tension) is missed' (Garland and Ferkins 2006: 220).

Distribution (place) also covers ticketing. From where and how do potential patrons buy tickets for sports events? Sport marketers can choose to mount their own ticketing operations or subcontract them to intermediaries (wholesalers, agents, etc.). Yet it is the liaison with the sport event's venue and facilities in respect of staging events that offers a considerable challenge for a sport marketer. Couple that with the array of communication possibilities (discussed above) one might have with fans and stakeholders (Shilbury *et al.* 2009) and one can appreciate the complexity of 'distribution' issues.

> Fans and participants expect up-to-date information about draws, results, players, coaches, teams, tactics, the club, etc. from sport organization web sites along with opportunities to buy tickets, special offers, merchandise, sponsors' products and services, etc. Archived match coverage can be made available for 'history buff fans', chat rooms with the players for younger fans, online gaming and online gambling for older fans and virtual stores for online shoppers. Depending upon contractual arrangements with television networks, there can be possibilities for netcasting some home games.
>
> (Garland and Ferkins 2006: 220)

The marketing mix with its emphasis upon integrating each of the 7 Ps is an integral part of the marketing process. Yet carried out in isolation from one another (such as an emphasis on promotion alone or in an absence of a focus on relationship building) usually courts disaster as the sport service product is bought repeatedly by the same customers. Therefore, sport marketing needs to incorporate a relationship focus into its processes, emphasizing the building of long-term relationships with stakeholders. Nowhere is this more obvious than in event planning when not only are product, price and promotion brought together at a venue (or venues), but also the operations (people and processes) to make the event happen. Services marketers call these aspects 'physical evidence', 'process' and 'people'.

Physical evidence

We have seen already that much of the sport service product – the 'contest on the field' – is intangible. It is advantageous for the sport marketer to try and 'tangibilize' the sport service product for customers to assist participation and spectatorship (demand). Sport marketers try to enhance the sport service product with physical evidence – thus the emphasis is upon product extensions rather than the core service product. The venue – often a stadium – is an obvious example, and many stadia in their own right have become attractive to spectators, even to the extent of the stadium (for example, the Allianz Arena in Munich, Germany, the Emirates Stadium in Arsenal, England, the National Stadium or 'bird's nest' in Beijing, China, the Melbourne Cricket Ground in Melbourne, Australia, Stade Roland Garros in Paris, France, Old Trafford in Manchester, England, or various 'domes' in the USA like the new Yankee Stadium, NYC) becoming the draw card as much as the event for some spectators. One not only expects all the facilities associated with a modern stadium, but additional features such as the most up-to-date technology for in-depth viewing, museums, exhibitions, etc. to encourage demand and help produce a memorable experience for spectator and participant alike. The types of promotion used to promote an upcoming event help too, along with event organizers' reputations (based on past events), the types and range of sponsors, the reputation of the athlete endorsers used to endorse the event, etc. – they all help to provide 'physical evidence' to consolidate an event's reputation.

Process

For any event the venue is the point of convergence for the marketing and operational functions. Gronroos (2007) highlights the roles played by marketers, and others, in service delivery. Delivering service to customers is not exclusive to those people with 'marketing' or 'customer service' in their job title; everyone in a sport organization is a 'part-time marketer' with responsibilities for delivering an enjoyable, worthy customer experience. The 'process' part of the marketing mix is the 'how' of service delivery: how the sport service product in its entirety is planned, produced and delivered to sports fans and participants. For a moment just let your mind dwell on all the service provider encounters spectators of a major sporting event might have from the time they decide to attend that event, to the time they return home after attendance – a considerable amount of 'process'.

People

All those sport service providers encountered in the consumption of the major sporting event alluded to above are the 'people' component of the marketing mix.

> The selection and training of human resources for service delivery in sport are tasks in which the sport marketer should have strong involvement. The level of training, skills and abilities of potential employees of the sporting organization become 'people variables' that will make the difference between mediocre and excellent service provision.
>
> (Shilbury *et al.* 2009: 135)

MARKETING STRATEGY

Sport managers must try and identify those issues beyond their control, such as environmental factors, social conditions, economic conditions, legal changes, technology challenges and, of course, business competition. Like any other business management process, the sport marketing process should be strategically and systematically planned. Well-managed marketing is essential in the development of a successful sport. Yet even with the best intentions, well-managed marketing will never offset an organization's fundamental problems (for example, environmental and financial problems). Sport marketing strategies and tactics can be applied to a whole sport (a large task) as well as to the somewhat smaller tasks at club or regional levels. Irrespective of the level, the decisions that face a sport marketer have been illustrated at the beginning of this chapter in the 'Keeping the party going' case study on beach volleyball's entry to the Olympic Games.

SUMMARY

Marketing sport today is akin to the marketing of many services. Most sport codes and sport organizations

> recognize that marketing and promotion of their sport or activity is essential for its survival. The advance of professional and demanding sponsors, sophisticated media outlets, professional playing teams and increased communications has meant sport organizations are recognizing and reacting to the need for marketing.
>
> (Garland and Ferkins 2006: 232)

Sport marketing will continue to develop to satisfy consumer needs and in the process has an exciting future with increased opportunities and entertainment. In summary, the major factors influencing sport marketing will include:

- increasing competition from all forms of leisure activity
- increasing cultural awareness
- continued growth of sport in general, and Xtreme sports in particular
- expansion and improvement of electronic media and communications, with emphasis on internet communication
- increasing use of electronic aids
- high standards of performance
- increasing reliance on revenue from sponsorship and media rights
- increasing importance of role models
- substantial improvement to venues and facilities
- innovative product extensions and promotional gimmicks
- increasing leisure time
- increasing wealth.

Sport organizations need to project their plans out to a longer-term horizon: three to five years and beyond. While visualizing the market, social conditions and sport's place in society several years ahead is difficult, that exercise should involve the sport marketing manager in conjunction with the sport organization's governing body (Board, Executive Committee, etc.). The beach volleyball case study exemplified the use of planning and implementation of marketing strategies. Considerable market research and analysis was backed by an integrated process of marketing: production, pricing, promotion and 'placing' (distribution) of the sport service product as entertainment for targeted customers.

NOTE

1　See also Mullin *et al.* (2007: 129).

REVIEW QUESTIONS

1   Review the role of market research in any of the examples attached to this chapter and then try and adapt their lessons to a sport organization of your choice.
2   Show how sport's selling points (or consumer benefits) are affected by economic, social and cultural factors.
3   Demonstrate how sport marketing can help match the varying needs from sport with those that both players and spectators have.
4   Review the role of sport sponsorship in a marketing communication plan (for promotion of both products and services), then outline the key factors to make your sponsorship strategy successful.
5   A sport event is both a product and a service. List the product and service features of such an event and review the differences between products and services.
6   Outline your argument for convincing a friend to attend your favourite sport event rather than visiting a fast-food restaurant to spend his or her leisure dollar.
7   You have been hired as a marketing consultant to market your favourite sporting code at the national level from next year. Using any of the examples in this chapter, what marketing actions would you recommend to help your code's success in the next five years?

FURTHER READING

Beech, J. and Chadwick, S. (2007) *The Marketing of Sport*, Pearson Education, Harlow, Essex.
Fullerton, S. (2010) *Sports Marketing*, 2nd edn, McGraw-Hill Irwin, New York.
Leberman, S., Collins, C. and Trenberth, L. (2006) *Sport Business Management in Aotearoa/New Zealand*, 2nd edn, Thomson Dunmore Press, Melbourne.
Shank, M.D. (2005) *Sports Marketing: A Strategic Perspective*, 3rd edn, Pearson/Prentice Hall, Upper Saddle River, New Jersey.
Shilbury, D., Westerbeek, H., Quick, S. and Funk, D. (2009) *Strategic Sport Marketing*, 3rd edn, Allen & Unwin, Sydney.

WEBSITES

www.allsports.com
www.espn.go.com/sportsbusiness/index.html
www.fifa.com
http://formula1zone.com
http://golf.com
www.sponsorship.com
www.sportbusiness.com
www.sportscareers.com

REFERENCES

Fullerton, S. (2010) *Sports Marketing*, 2nd edn, McGraw-Hill Irwin, New York.

Garland, R. and Ferkins, L. (2006) 'Sport Marketing', in S. Leberman, C. Collins and L. Trenberth (eds) *Sport Business Management in Aotearoa/New Zealand*, 2nd edn, Thomson Dunmore Press, Melbourne.

Gronroos, C. (2007) *Service Management and Marketing: Customer Management in Service Competition Approach*, Wiley, Chichester, West Sussex, England.

Harris, K. and Elliott, D. (2007) 'Segmentation, targeting and positioning in sport', in J. Beech, and S. Chadwick (eds) *The Marketing of Sport*, Prentice Hall, Harlow, England.

Mullin, B., Hardy, S. and Sutton, W. (2007) *Sport Marketing*, 3rd edn, Human Kinetics: Champaign, IL.

Pitts, B. and Stotlar, D. (1996) *Fundamentals of Sport Marketing*, Fitness Information Technology, Morgantown, WV.

Shilbury, D., Westerbeek, H., Quick, S. and Funk, D. (2009) *Strategic Sport Marketing*, 3rd edn, Allen & Unwin, Sydney.

Slack, T. and Amis, J. (2004) 'Money for nothing and your cheques for free?', in T. Slack (ed.) *The Commercialisation of Sport*, Routledge, NYC, USA.

Stanton, W.J., Miller, K.E. and Layton, R. (1995) *Fundamentals of Marketing*, 3rd edn, McGraw-Hill, Sydney.

Veeck, W. and Linn, E. (1965) *The Hustler Handbook*, Pitman, New York.

Wakefield, K. (2007) *Team Sports Marketing*, Elsevier Butterworth-Heinemann, Amsterdam.

Part 3
Facets of sport business

Chapter 13

Delivering sport in the global context

Lucie Thibault, Brock University, Canada

TOPICS

Developing sport in the global context • Sport labour in developing countries • Athlete migration • Environmental impact of global sport

OBJECTIVES

At the end of this chapter you should be able to:

- Understand the concept of globalisation in general and the economic, political, social, cultural, and technological forces at play in the globalisation of sport;
- Understand issues related to the globalisation of sport; more specifically,
    - understand the use of labour from developing countries in the production of sport products;
    - understand the impact that athletes migrating to other countries have on sport systems and donor countries; and
    - understand the impact sport events and sport organisations have on the environment;
- Understand the role sport managers and leaders can play in addressing these issues and as such minimise the negative impact globalisation can have for individuals, groups, countries' sport systems, and the environment.

KEY TERMS

Athlete migration – refers to the movement of athletes from one nation to another in order to pursue their athletic careers.

Carbon footprint – 'a measure of the greenhouse gases that are produced by activities of a person, a family, a school or a business that involve burning fossil fuels' (United States Environmental Protection Agency 2009: ¶ 10).

Developing country labour force – a country where income level is low relative to other countries. Citizens face low standard of living as a result of low levels of economic and social development.

Environmental impact – the positive and negative consequences that activities have on the natural environment.

Globalisation – defined as 'a process through which space and time are compressed by technology, information flows, and trade and power relations, allowing distant actions to have increased significance at the local level' (Miller, Lawrence, McKay, and Rowe 2001: 131).

Transnational corporations – corporations that have entities in more than one country. Their head office is typically located in a developed country and production factories may be located in developing countries.

OVERVIEW

Globalisation is an important phenomenon affecting sport. Economic, political, social, cultural, and technological forces have all contributed to the increasing global nature of sport. Although globalisation has often been perceived as favourable for sport organisations and sport in general, some issues have emerged. In this chapter, three issues related to the globalisation of sport are addressed. These consist of: the exploitation of labour in developing countries by transnational corporations for the production of sporting goods (i.e. running shoes, sportswear, equipment); the migration of athletes who play on teams of different nations and represent their 'new' nations in international competitions; and the increasing concerns for the negative impact sports have on the environment.

DELIVERING SPORT IN THE GLOBAL CONTEXT

The United Nations (UN) identified 2005 as the International Year of Sport and Physical Education. In celebration of this year, Kofi Annan, Secretary-General of the UN at the time, exclaimed that 'sport is a universal language that can bring people together, no matter what their origin, background, religious beliefs or economic status' (United Nations 2005: ¶ 5). Sport is clearly an international phenomenon. Its global appeal is evident when one considers the viewership of recent sport events. For example, the 2008 Beijing Olympic Games were watched by 4.7 billion people (The Nielsen Company 2008). According to the Nielsen Company (2008: ¶ 1), this level of viewership represented 'the largest global TV audience ever'. Another example of the trend toward globalisation is the recent introduction of 'new' countries (typically non-winter sport countries) and their athletes in the Olympic Winter Games. Specifically, in 2006, in Torino, Italy, athletes from Albania, Madagascar, and Ethiopia participated for the first time in the Winter Olympics while in 2010, in Vancouver,

Canada, athletes from the Cayman Islands, Colombia, Ghana, Montenegro, Pakistan, and Peru participated for the first time (International Olympic Committee 2009b, 2009d).

Furthermore, on the global trend of sport, the prominence of the International Olympic Committee (IOC) and the Fédération Internationale de Football Association (FIFA) has often been compared to the UN. Based on the number of member countries, the IOC and FIFA are larger than the UN (cf. Tomlinson and Young 2006; Wertheim 2004). As of March 2010, the IOC's membership was 205 National Olympic Committees each representing one country whilst FIFA's membership was 208 countries (Fédération Internationale de Football Association 2010; International Olympic Committee 2009a). At the same time, the UN reported a membership of 192 countries (United Nations 2010). As such, sport is an excellent medium to unite people from different cultures, race, socio-economic status, gender, language, and religions. It is a 'shared form of communication' among the world's population (Amara 2008: 73).

The increasing global nature of sport has generally been perceived as beneficial for sport organisations. Extending programmes and services to the world has often meant a greater pool of athletes from which to recruit, increased markets and clients to which tickets can be sold, higher rights charged to media in order to broadcast sport events because of larger audiences, and greater financial resources generated from corporations and sponsors. As such, the global expansion of sport has generally led to more profits for sport organisations. The IOC and its premier property, the Olympic Games, is an appropriate case in point. As well, professional teams in the English Premier League or in the UEFA Champions League, the National Rugby League, or the National Basketball Association are a few examples of professional sport leagues and franchises that have financially benefited from the increasing global nature of sport.

Globalisation is defined as 'a process through which space and time are compressed by technology, information flows, and trade and power relations, allowing distant actions to have increased significance at the local level' (Miller, Lawrence, McKay, and Rowe 2001: 131). To further clarify the concept of globalisation, Maguire, Jarvie, Mansfield, and Bradley (2002: 7) explained that

> globalisation leads not only to greater degree of interdependence but also to an increased awareness of the world as a whole. People become more attuned to the notion that their lives and places of living are part of a single social space – the globe.

Several forces have been attributed to this increasing globalisation. Specifically, economic, political, social, cultural, and technological forces have been instrumental in the globalisation of several domains (e.g. politics and international governance, economics, business, media, education, health, development, environment, and culture). These forces have also been applied to discussions about the globalisation of sport (Andrews and Grainger 2007; Giulianotti and Robertson 2007a, 2007b; Harvey, Rail, and Thibault 1996; Thibault 2009). In the following paragraphs, these forces are briefly explained and their connection to the globalisation of sport outlined.

Economic forces refer to the important financial investments professional and amateur sports represent in the world. Sport infrastructures, hosting of major sport events, and ongoing competitions in various sports ensure that financial resources are invested in jobs, in people, and in different regions of the world. As Forster (2006: 72) explained, 'sport is an important part of global culture and an industry worth hundreds of billions of dollars'. In addition to the economic power of international sport organisations, non-sport organisations are also extensively involved in the business and finances of sport. For example, corporations and media conglomerates are eager to financially invest in sport properties in order to enhance the visibility of their products and services and their profits. Issues arising from the economic forces deal with the questionable fate of certain sports that do not, for various reasons (e.g. popularity, visibility), generate monies, profits, and/or benefits for other organisations (e.g. media, corporations). Their ability to truly become global sports may be limited.

Political forces refer to the governance of sport and the agencies that have power over its delivery in the world. At the international level, sport is governed by a complex network of organisations including multi-sport and single-sport organisations. The IOC, FIFA, the International Association of Athletics Federations, and the World Anti-Doping Agency have been considered to be some of the most prominent and powerful organisations governing sport internationally (Forster 2006; Houlihan 1994; Katwala 2000). Their reach in different countries, their leadership, and their ability to generate revenues for their organisations through various sources (e.g. various countries' governments, corporate partnerships, media rights) have been unparalleled in international sport. Considerations arising from these political forces include which organisation(s) should have power and how this power is used to enhance sports' access for all. As well, another issue includes which organisation(s), if any, should have the responsibility for the global governance of sport. One could argue that the IOC is positioned and resourced to assume this leadership.

Social forces refer to the power of sport to address social inequities in various domains such as international development, gender, and race relations. Sport has served as a medium to assist in the development of disadvantaged regions of the world. Sport has also contributed to redress gender inequities in some societies. Through sport-related activities, organisations such as the UN, Football 4 Peace International, Boxgirls International, and Right to Play have used sport to enhance the health, education, child and youth development, and/or wellbeing of individuals living in various regions of the world. The International Platform on Sport and Development (IPSD) lists more than 250 initiatives, programmes, and organisations that are 'interested in the potential of sport as a tool to reach personal, community, national and international development objectives … and a tool for addressing some of the challenges that arise from humanitarian crises and in conflict and post-conflict settings' (International Platform on Sport and Development 2010: ¶ 1–2). Issues arising from social forces deal mainly with sport's ability to truly solve major issues in the world. Sport may help in addressing some social issues but may not be enough to solve major global crises such as poverty, systemic inequities and injustices, war and conflict, and disease.

Cultural forces consider the existence of a global culture and the role sport plays in transcending borders, culture, language, gender, race, religion, and socio-economic status

234

leading to a common bond shared by all. Not all sports are practised to the same extent across the world. Certain sports strive globally while other sports never shine on the international stage. Media coverage may play an important role in ensuring that sports become visible and perhaps popular in different parts of the world, but not all sports benefit from media exposure. Female sports, for example, are generally not covered extensively by the media. As well, certain sports that are culturally specific have not propagated throughout the world, for example sumo (Japan), kabaddi (Bangladesh), buzkashi (Afghanistan), capoeira (Brazil), pelote basque (France and Spain), and lacrosse (Canada), while sports such as football, rugby, basketball, and baseball have reached greater levels of popularity globally. Issues arising from cultural forces relate to the extent to which the diffusion of sports in general and specific sports can occur on a global scale and the extent to which sports are part of a global culture phenomenon.

Technological forces refer to new communication and media technologies that have been developed and have considerably enhanced the flow of information available to the general population. These technologies have made sport events and competitions more accessible to the world. For example, during the 2010 Vancouver Olympic Winter Games, sport results and news features were instantaneously available through traditional television and radio coverage as well as new media technologies such as the Internet, web applications, and social networking (e.g. *Twitter*, *Facebook*, *YouTube*, blogs). Issues arising from technological forces relate to the costs (i.e. financial and infrastructure) of these new forms of communication. As such, not all individuals and countries have access to this technology. Sports that become globalised are often the ones that are perpetuated through technology because of their visibility and the financial support (i.e. media rights and corporate sponsorships) they receive.

Collectively, these five forces, economic, political, social, cultural, and technological, all play an important role in the diffusion of sport on the global stage. Even though globalisation may contribute to the financial prosperity of sport, it is important to note that globalisation is also a source of unintended and unfavourable consequences for certain individuals and organisations involved with sport. It is critical for current and future sport leaders and managers to understand what the 'other side' of globalisation may represent for individuals and organisations in relation to sport. Given the discussion thus far throughout this chapter on the power of sport to unite people, it is important to acknowledge that sport can unfortunately also prove divisive. In the following sections, some aspects of unfavourable outcomes of the globalisation of sport are addressed. Specifically, the following global issues in sport will be outlined:

1 the exploitation of the labour force in developing countries by transnational corporations for the production of sporting goods (i.e. running shoes, sportswear, equipment);
2 the migration of athletes who serve on the teams of different nations and represent their 'new' nations in international competitions; and
3 the increasing concerns for the negative impact sports have on the environment.

235

SPORT LABOUR IN DEVELOPING COUNTRIES

It is common knowledge that most transnational corporations (TNCs) involved in the production of sporting goods rely almost exclusively on the labour force of developing countries. TNCs are corporations that have entities in more than one country. Their head office is typically located in a developed country and production factories may be located in developing countries. For sport-related TNCs, individuals from developing countries are an extremely important resource in the manufacturing of products.

From the perspective of individuals from developed nations, it might be reasonable to conclude that manufacturing in developing countries is positive for their economies and for providing much-needed jobs to the population of these countries. Whilst there may be the creation of new jobs for some individuals in the developing country, it is important to remember that there is a level of exploitation of the developing country's labour force that occurs – where production decisions made by executives of TNCs are largely based on ensuring cheap labour costs and where labour standards (legislation) and work conditions are lower (or non-existent) than the country/ies where the TNCs have their head offices. Executives at TNCs such as Nike, adidas, Puma, Fila, Mizuno, and Umbro choose to set up production facilities in developing countries, often in Asia (e.g. China, Vietnam, Bangladesh, Indonesia, India, Thailand), in order to maximise their profits.

The Maquila Solidarity Network (2008) published a report focusing on strategies to avoid the systemic exploitation of workers in developing countries by TNCs. In this report, researchers argued that,

> despite more than 15 years of codes of conduct adopted by major sportswear brands such as adidas, Nike, New Balance, Puma and Reebok, workers making their products still face extreme pressure to meet production quotas, excessive undocumented and unpaid overtime, verbal abuse, threats to health and safety related to the high quotas and exposure to toxic chemicals, and a failure to provide legally required health and other insurance programs.
>
> (The Maquila Solidarity Network 2008: 6)

Earlier reports from Oxfam International (2006), Clean Clothes Campaign (2007), and Play Fair at the Olympics (2004) presented similar scenarios regarding the exploitation of the labour force in developing countries. Researchers for Oxfam International (2006) compared and contrasted the multi-million dollar sponsorship deals afforded to high-profile teams and athletes with the wages of workers responsible for the production of sport shoes and sportswear. They noted that TNCs pay millions of dollars to individual athletes and teams in endorsements while the Asian workers are paid approximately 60 cents per hour or $4.75 for a standard working day (Oxfam International 2006). The exploitation of workers is not isolated to the Asian population. Similar reports have been identified in Central American countries (cf. Grassi 2006; The Maquila Solidarity Network 2008). Grassi (2006) explained that Costa Rican workers responsible for the manufacturing of Major League Baseball products must complete one baseball every 15 minutes (i.e. performing 108 stitches by hand in cowhide leather). 'They are required to reach a minimum

236

quota of 156 balls a week in a factory without air conditioning, in temperatures exceeding 90°, requiring permission to use bathrooms, and denying speaking between workers on the factory floor' (Grassi 2006: ¶ 7). The average hourly wages of these workers is $1.15 and they can receive a weekly bonus if they produce 180 baseballs in a week (Grassi 2006). In addition to the extremely low wages, employees do not have the freedom to bargain collectively as a group for better working conditions and wages. They also have no job security, and employees who choose to question or complain about the abysmal work conditions are often fired from their job.

The major issue related to TNCs' prosperity in global markets is that it occurs on the backs of workers in developing countries – workers (often women and children) who cannot afford the products they are responsible for manufacturing whilst record profits are being achieved by sport-related TNCs. In any given business model, the object is to make a profit, and it is a truism that TNCs such as Nike, New Balance, adidas, FILA, and Umbro record a profit at the end of the financial year. However, it is reasonable to ask whether it is feasible for these TNCs to increase wages for workers in developing countries and truly enhance the quality of work conditions in factories while generating a little less profit for owners and shareholders and investing less sponsorship dollars for high-profile athletes and teams in developed countries. Sharing the wealth of TNCs with the workers most responsible for generating this wealth seems to be a logical and viable option.

One of the strategies discussed is the establishment of a living wage (The Maquila Solidarity Network 2008; Oxfam International 2006; Play Fair at the Olympics 2004). A living wage is defined as a wage that is 'sufficient to meet basic needs of workers and their families and provide some discretionary income' (The Maquila Solidarity Network 2008: 32–33). The issue with this definition relates to the interpretation of what constitutes basic needs. In essence, the level of wages and the cost of living in the country are critical questions to answer in determining basic needs and thus in establishing what is an appropriate living wage. In addition to the living wage, conditions in the workplace need to be changed. Employees regularly face 'excessive long hours of forced and underpaid overtime, exploitative terms of employment, bullying, sexual harassment, and physical and verbal abuse' in their workplace (The Maquila Solidarity Network 2008: 11).

Even though progress has been made to the work environment for employees in developing countries in the past 20 years, more changes are needed. Organisations such as Oxfam International, Clean Clothes Campaign, and The Maquila Solidarity Network acknowledge the progress made in factories but they also challenge leaders of sport-related TNCs to go further with improving work conditions and adopting fair living wages for their valuable workforce.

ATHLETE MIGRATION

In this section, another topic dealing with labour, sport, and globalisation is addressed. Increasingly athlete migration is gaining exposure in the pantheon of international sport. Athlete migration refers to the movement of athletes from one nation to another in order to pursue their athletic careers. Weston (2006: 831) defined athlete migration as 'player movement in international athletics [and] is, essentially, sports' version of free trade'. In most cases, migration occurs because of increased opportunities and access to resources (e.g. financial, coaching expertise, training facilities and equipments, support services, increased quality of competition), the existence of a climate more appropriate for the sport in question, and athletes' quest to reach their goal of participating in the Olympic Games or achieving a career in professional sports (Bale and Maguire 1994; Lafranchi and Taylor 2001; Maguire 2004).

Although migration may benefit the athletes with respect to greater access to resources and opportunities, it can be detrimental for some countries and their sport system. In some cases, athlete migration drains certain countries' sport systems from their star athletes and their resources. A number of concerns have been raised about the 'deskilling of "donor" countries' (Maguire and Bale 1994: 282) where certain countries' sport systems often lose their best athletes to other countries. These countries' sport systems lose more than simply their best athletes – they lose valuable resources as they have invested time, training, coaching expertise, facilities, and other resources in their athletes' development. This issue is particularly relevant to developing countries as the limited resources of their sport systems may actually contribute to other countries' sport success. Maguire and Bale (1994: 282) argued that

> less developed countries have invested in nurturing athletic talent. Once this talent reaches maturity, more economically developed leagues, such as Major League Baseball, cream off the best. Native audiences are thus denied direct access to native talent nurtured and developed in their countries.

Maguire and Bale (1994) and others have explained how athlete migration has contributed to undermining the sport systems of donor countries (Bale and Sang 1996; Bretón 2000; Wertheim 2004). Indeed, incidences of active recruitment by developed countries of athletes in developing countries have been addressed in the media. Carlson (2004) discussed how the Persian Gulf countries of Qatar and Bahrain recruited runners from Kenya with financial incentives so that they could compete for their new country. Latin and Central American countries have been major contributors to high-profile leagues in sports such as football and baseball in Europe and the United States (Bretón 2000; Magee and Sugden 2002; Maguire and Bale 1994). In yet another example, in their quest to participate in the Olympic Winter Games, the countries of Madagascar and the Republic of Macedonia recruited downhill skiers from Canada with the right heritage to represent their country (Kingston 2005).

Carlson (2004: D01) explained that 'this country-jumping is possible because Olympic rules permit each nation to decide who is eligible for its team ... Needless to say, the sluggish bureaucracy of citizenship is frequently streamlined for Olympians.' In recent years, sport leaders have actively recruited athletes from other countries to compete for their country. For example, American baseball and softball players with Greek descent were recruited to compete for their new country, Greece, in time for the Athens 2004 Olympic Games (cf. Carlson 2004; The San Diego Union-Tribune 2004; Softball West Magazine 2004).

In addition to the ongoing recruitment that occurs by professional teams, franchises, leagues, and/or by countries' sport systems at the expense of other countries' sport systems, there are several issues associated with athlete migration. For example, concessions are often made to accommodate 'new' athletes with respect to immigration laws and other policies (e.g. mandatory military service and years of residency waived for the new athletes). As well, some 'local' athletes are often excluded because better athletes have been recruited from other countries (e.g. Greek baseball and softball players overlooked for their national team in favour of more skilled American athletes with Greek heritage). This issue can generate resentment from some 'local' athletes and can subsequently affect team dynamics. In addition, 'new' athletes may have to undergo a number of adjustments and may need to assimilate to a new culture, language, and traditions (e.g. Yao Ming's introduction into American basketball; Ronaldo Luis Nazário de Lima's introduction into European football). These life adjustments in the 'new' country can be challenging for the athletes and their families.

Related to the topic of athlete migration, recent discussions about the migration of coaches and foreign ownership of professional sport franchises have also been raised (cf. Thibault 2009; Vecsey 2007; Weiner 2008). Enhancing the quality of athletes and teams in international competitions has led several sport leaders to recruit coaching expertise outside of their countries. Bose (2008) captured well the notion of foreign coaching in football during the 2004 European Championships. He explained that 'Greece's unknown footballers unexpectedly won the [2004] European Championship coached by the German Otto Rehhagel, beating a Portuguese team coached by a Brazilian, Felipe Scolari, in the final, which had previously beaten an England team coached by a Swede' (Bose 2008: ¶ 5).

Foreign ownership of professional sport franchises has also been debated in the media (Vecsey 2007; Weiner 2008). Vecsey (2007: D4) explained the controversy of foreign ownership in the English Premier League when he noted:

> When the Glazer family from the United States took control of Manchester United in 2005, many loyal fans rushed the city walls with pitchforks and pots of boiling oil in a vain attempt to save the purity of British soccer. Yet the foreign hordes of investors keep arriving, bringing dollars or rubles or even Thai baht or Icelandic krona to the flourishing Premier League, by far the best soccer league in the world.

As with the case of Manchester United and other teams in the English Premier League, most past incidents of foreign ownership of teams have generated concerns from the general public because they have been perceived as undermining nationality, as well as cultural and social identity (Thibault 2009; Vecsey 2007; Weiner 2008).

ENVIRONMENTAL IMPACT OF GLOBAL SPORT

In this section, issues of sport on the environment are discussed. Increasingly, sport management researchers and leaders are concerned with the impact that athletes, sport franchises, sport venues, and sport events have on the environment. The use of pesticides and herbicides and water to maintain golf courses, the development of alpine skiing, snowboarding, and mountain biking trails, and the increasing consumption of energy for large indoor sport venues (including indoor downhill ski venues, surf wave pools) are examples of the consider-able environmental impact of our participation in sport.

Several researchers have studied the negative environmental outcomes sport has in soci-ety (Babiak and Trendafilova 2011; cf. Centre for Business Relationships, Accountability, Sustainability and Society 2007; Collins, Flynn, Munday, and Roberts 2007). Economic impacts are often undertaken to emphasise the importance of hosting sport events in cities, regions, and countries; however, as Collins *et al.* (2007: 458) pointed out, there is increasing 'recognition of broader impacts [on sports] in terms of … a series of more "hidden" envi-ronmental and social costs that are becoming more difficult to ignore in the context of local duties towards sustainable development'. Large-scale sport events are extremely impactful on the environment. Travel of athletes, coaches, support personnel, media, and fans, to name a few, has serious implications for the environment and the carbon footprint. Carbon footprint is defined as 'a measure of the greenhouse gases that are produced by activities of a person, a family, a school or a business that involve burning fossil fuels' (United States Environmental Protection Agency 2009: ¶ 10). Fossil fuel is 'a general term for a fuel that is formed in the Earth from plant, animal remains, including coal, oil, natural gas, oil shales, and tar sands' (United States Environmental Protection Agency 2009: ¶ 25).

After much criticism of the environmental damages caused by the hosting of the 1992 Albertville Olympic Winter Games, Lillehammer's Organising Committee for the 1994 Olympic Winter Games came to the rescue with what Cantelon and Letters (2000: 303) called 'the collective consciousness of the sanctity of the Norwegian environment'. In fact, Lillehammer's concern for the environment led to the 'creation of a mature environmental policy and specific regulations for the organization of future Games' for the IOC (Cantelon and Letters 2000: 305). Then, in 1995, the IOC created the Sport and Environment Commission in order to promote sustainable development within the Olympic Games. As a focus of the commission and the IOC, it is important to organise 'Green Games' – where emphasising 'environmental protection and, more importantly, sustainability, are prime ele-ments of Games planning and operations' (International Olympic Committee 2009c: ¶ 1). The environmental policy of the IOC covers the Summer and Winter Olympic Games, and countries wishing to host the Games must closely follow guidelines including an assessment of the environmental impact of hosting the Olympic Games in the city and region prior to hosting the Games (e.g. venue construction), during the Games (e.g. transportation, waste management), and after the Games (e.g. environmental legacies, operations and maintenance of venues) (International Olympic Committee 2009c).

The Olympic Games is not the only sport event where environmental concerns have been expressed. Collins *et al.* (2007) and scholars from the Centre for Business Relationships, Accountability, Sustainability and Society (CBRASS) (2007) have examined the carbon foot-print of major sport events. Researchers from Cardiff University's CBRASS examined the carbon footprint of the Wales versus Scotland game during the 2006 Rugby Six Nations tour-nament. The environmental assessment of the sport event covered four areas: 1) travel to the event, 2) food and drink consumption, 3) infrastructure of the event venue, and 4) waste. The event was attended by more than 85,000 spectators and results showed that food and drink consumption by spectators had the most significant environmental impact. According to the researchers, spectators drank approximately 626,000 pints of beer/lager and 393,000 other alcoholic beverages. They ate nearly 41,000 burgers, pies, and pasties and 21,000 orders of chips (Centre for Business Relationships, Accountability, Sustainability and Society 2007). More than 66 tonnes of waste were produced and less than 1 per cent of this waste was recycled. Travel to attend the game (and return after the game) was calculated at an average distance of 284 kilometres per spectator. Since most spectators used their cars to drive to the stadium, the carbon footprint of spectators was significant. The researchers also considered the carbon footprint of the stadium where the game was played (e.g. resources required for its construction and operation). Collins *et al.* (2007) found similar results in their evaluation of the 2004 Football Association Cup Final between Manchester United Football Club and Millwall Football Club.

Another line of research on the environmental impact of sport has focused on the strategies professional teams, franchises, and leagues have initiated to address the carbon footprint of their organisations and events (Babiak and Trendafilova 2011; Babiak and Wolfe 2006). Babiak and Trendafilova found that leaders of professional sport franchises from five North American leagues had several motives for undertaking 'green' initiatives for their operations. The most popular motives were: to be good corporate citizens; to be leaders in environmental practices (relative to other sport organisations and within their community); to be aligned with the norms, values, and expectations of society; to mimic what is being done in other franchises and leagues; to develop relationships with community partners; to save money; and/or to enhance their organisation's image. Examples of 'green' practices by professional sports included: planting 1,500 trees in Detroit to offset the carbon footprint which occurred during the 2006 Super Bowl XL event (National Football League); building sport venues that comply with the Leadership in Energy and Environmental Design certification and/or that have environment-friendly designs (e.g. Minnesota Twins Target Field, US; Princes Park, UK; Stade de Suisse, CH); developing strategies to reach venue operational efficiency (i.e. decrease water and electricity consumption, and other resources); instituting recycling programmes at the venues; and purchasing carbon credits to offset the carbon footprint involved with team travel throughout the sport season (Babiak and Trendafilova 2011; Babiak and Wolfe 2006; Wroth 2009).

The environmental impact of sport is a global issue. With hosting major events like the Olympic Games and FIFA World Cup, with the construction of large venues, and with the required extensive travel by athletes, coaches, officials, media personnel, and spectators to attend sport events, our carbon footprint should be carefully considered and managed. The work of leaders in sport management is particularly important in decreasing the carbon footprint related to sport.

SUMMARY

Although sport can be a great vehicle for social, cultural, economic, and political development, it is important to remember that not all are favoured by the phenomenon of globalised sport. As future leaders of sport organisations and as participants in various roles (e.g. participants/athletes, coaches, officials, volunteers, fans), it is important to be aware of global issues that affect sport. In this chapter, three of these global issues have been examined: the exploitation of the labour force in developing countries by TNCs for the production of sporting goods; the migration of athletes who serve on the teams of different nations and represent their 'new' nations in international competitions; and the increasing concerns for the negative impact sports have on the environment.

When one purchases sporting goods, should one consider the TNCs behind their manufacturing and the labour force who may have been exploited for the fabrication of these products? Should one consider as well the implications that the recruitment of athletes from other countries has on these countries' sport systems and on the new countries' sport systems? What about the impact that our participation in sport has on the environment? We may be easily charmed by the promises of globalised sport. While we can all acknowledge the valuable outcomes of globalisation for sport on the economic, political, social, cultural, and technological spheres, we need to remember that the globalisation of sport has contributed to the exploitation of certain resources, including athletes, workers in developing countries, and the environment, to name a few.

There are other global issues that affect sport that need our consideration – for example, issues such as media conglomerates increasingly acquiring and controlling sport properties (e.g. sport venues, franchises, leagues, events) to increase their revenues; the use of performance-enhancing drugs in sports; the democratisation of sport organisations at the international level (i.e. athletes and other stakeholders' involvement in the decision- and policy-making process of organisations); the increasing role of sport in international development and relations; and the role of nationality, national identity, and nationalism in the globalisation of sport.

In conclusion, there is no indication that the global interest in sport and its power will fade. This fascination with sport will likely continue to play an important role in the lives of many individuals across the planet; it is therefore critical to persevere in our examination of sport and its issues. To this end, this quotation from Wertheim (2004: 79) is an appropriate place to draw this chapter to a close:

> For all its virtues, globalization [is] not without its drawbacks: widening chasms between rich and poor societies, plummeting environmental standards and increasing dependence on outsourcing. Peril [is] riding tandem with so much promise. Which is to say, globalization is like sports: For all the winners there are, necessarily, losers as well.

REVIEW QUESTIONS

1 Check the labels on your running shoes, your sportswear, and your sport equipments. Where (i.e. countries) were these products manufactured? How many of these were produced in developing nations?

2 Review the following three websites: http://www.cleanclothes.org/home; http://www.clearingthehurdles.org; and http://www.fairolympics.org/index.html. Discuss the

strategies these organisations are proposing to address the poor labour conditions for developing countries' workers producing sport shoes, sportswear, and/or sport equipments.

3   What can we do as individuals to limit the negative effects the globalisation of sport may have on some groups?

4   Consider a case of athlete migration. Identify all the individuals/groups/organisations that benefited from this athlete's migration to their new country. Identify the individuals/groups/organisations that lost from this athlete's migration.

5   What can sport organisations do to minimise the impact their events have on the environment? What can we do as individuals?

6   Review the elements of the International Olympic Committee's Sport and Environment Commission (see http://www.olympic.org/en/content/The-IOC/Commissions/Sport-and-Environment-/?Tab=4). Is the IOC effective in their quest to make their events (i.e. Summer and Winter Olympic Games) 'green'?

7   Identify who benefits and who is disadvantaged from the globalisation of sport.

FURTHER READING

Andrews, D. L. (2008) Nike nation. *The Brown Journal of World Affairs, 14*(2), 41–53.

Darnell, S. (2010) Power, politics and 'Sport for Development and Peace': Investigating the utility of sport for international development. *Sociology of Sport Journal, 27*(1), 54–75.

Harvey, J., Horne, J., and Safai, P. (2009) Alterglobalization, global social movements, and the possibility of political transformation through sport. *Sociology of Sport Journal, 26*(3), 383–403.

Westerbeek, H. and Smith, A. (2003) *Sport business in the global marketplace.* Hampshire, UK: Palgrave Macmillan.

WEBSITES

http://www.cleanclothes.org/home

http://www.clearingthehurdles.org

http://www.fairolympics.org/index.html

http://www.fifa.com/aboutfifa

http://www.olympic.org

http://www.sportanddev.org

http://www.un.org/sport2005

REFERENCES

Amara, M. (2008) The Muslim world in the global sporting arena. *The Brown Journal of World Affairs, 14*(2), 67–75.

Andrews, D. L. and Grainger, A. D. (2007) Sport and globalization. In G. Ritzer (ed.), *The Blackwell companion to globalization* (pp. 478–497). Malden, MA: Blackwell Publishing.

Babiak, K. and Trendafilova, S. (2011) CSR and environmental responsibility: Motives and pressures to adopt green management practices. *Corporate Social Responsibility and Environmental Management, 18*(1), 11–24.

Babiak, K. and Wolfe, R. (2006) More than just a game? Corporate social responsibility and Super Bowl XL. *Sport Marketing Quarterly, 15*(4), 214–222.

Bale, J. and Maguire, J. (1994) *The global sports arena: Athletic talent migration in an interdependent world.* London: Frank Cass.

Bale, J. and Sang, J. (1996) *Kenyan running: Movement culture, geography and global change.* London: Frank Cass.

Bose, M. (2008, 23 January) *Foreign coaches are a home-grown problem.* BBC, Sport Editors' Blog. Online. Available HTTP: http://www.bbc.co.uk/blogs/thereporters/mihirbose/2008/01/post_7.html (accessed 5 March 2010).

Bretón, M. (2000) Fields of broken dreams: Latinos and baseball. *ColorLines, 3*(1), 13–17.

Cantelon, H. and Letters, M. (2000) The making of the IOC environmental policy as the third dimension of the Olympic Movement. *International Review for the Sociology of Sport, 35*(3), 294–308.

Carlson, P. (2004, 8 August) Flag relay. For Olympians in training, flexibility is everything: Especially when it comes to citizenship. *Washington Post*, p. D01. Online. Available HTTP: http://www.washingtonpost.com/wp-dyn/articles/A48948-2004Aug7.html (accessed 2 November 2004).

Centre for Business Relationships, Accountability, Sustainability and Society (2007, 9 February) *Rugby internationals leave large environmental footprint.* Cardiff University. Online. Available HTTP: http://www.cardiff.ac.uk/news/mediacentre/mediareleases/feb07/rugby-internationals-leave-large-environmental-footprint.html (accessed 5 March 2010).

Clean Clothes Campaign (2007) *Making a difference for workers.* Clean Clothes Campaign Solidarity Action. Online. Available HTTP: http://www.cleanclothes.org/resources/ccc/urgent-appeals-system/clean-clothes-campaign-solidatiry-action (accessed 5 March 2010).

Collins, A., Flynn, A., Munday, M., and Roberts, A. (2007) Assessing the environmental consequences of major sporting events: The 2003/04 FA Cup Final. *Urban Studies, 44*, 457–476.

Fédération Internationale de Football Association (2010) *About FIFA: Associations.* Online. Available HTTP: http://www.fifa.com/aboutfifa/federation/associations.html (accessed 5 March 2010).

Forster, J. (2006) The global sports organisations and their governance. *Corporate Governance, 6*(1), 72–83.

Giulianotti, R. and Robertson, R. (eds) (2007a) *Globalization and sport.* Malden, MA: Blackwell.

Giulianotti, R. and Robertson, R. (2007b) Sport and globalization: Transnational dimensions. *Global Networks, 7*, 107–112.

Grassi, D. M. (2006, 26 July) Baseball and Rawlings bring new meaning to free trade. *American Chronicle.* Online. Available HTTP: http://www.americanchronicle.com/articles/view/11870 (accessed 5 March 2010).

Harvey, J., Rail, G., and Thibault, L. (1996) Globalization and sport: Sketching a theoretical model for empirical analyses. *Journal of Sport and Social Issues, 20*(3), 258–277.

Houlihan, B. (1994) *Sport and international politics.* Hertfordshire, UK: Harvester Wheatsheaf.

International Olympic Committee (2009a) *205 National Olympic Committees.* Online. Available HTTP: http://www.olympic.org/en/content/National-Olympic-Committees (accessed 5 March 2010).

International Olympic Committee (2009b) *Media: February 13, 2010. Record participation in Vancouver.* Online. Available HTTP: http://www.olympic.org/en/content/Media/?articleNewsGroup=-1&articleId=76977 (accessed 5 March 2010).

International Olympic Committee (2009c) *The Sport and Environment Commission.* Online. Available HTTP: http://www.olympic.org/en/content/The-IOC/Commissions/Sport-and-Environment-/?Tab=4 (accessed 5 March 2010).

International Olympic Committee (2009d) *Turin 2006.* Online. Available HTTP: http://www.olympic. org/en/content/Olympic-Games/All-Past-Olympic-Games/Winter/Turin-2006 (accessed 5 March 2010).

International Platform on Sport and Development (2010) *What is sport and development?* Online. Available HTTP: http://www.sportanddev.org/learnmore/what_is_sport_and_development (accessed 5 March 2010).

Katwala, S. (2000) *Democratising global sport.* London: The Foreign Policy Centre.

Kingston, G. (2005, 10 February) 'Poacher' countries take aim at Canadian athletes. *The Vancouver Sun,* p. E1.

Lafranchi, P. and Taylor, M. (2001) *Moving the ball: The migration of professional footballers.* Oxford, UK: Berg.

Magee, J. and Sugden, J. (2002) 'The world at their feet': Professional football and international labor migration. *Journal of Sport and Social Issues, 26*(4), 421–437.

Maguire, J. (2004) Sport labor migration research revisited. *Journal of Sport and Social Issues, 28*(4), 477–482.

Maguire, J. and Bale, J. (1994) Postscript: An agenda for research on sports labour migration. In J. Bale and J. Maguire (eds), *The global sports arena: Athletic talent migration in an interdependent world* (pp. 281–284). London: Frank Cass.

Maguire, J., Jarvie, G., Mansfield, L., and Bradley, J. (2002) *Sport worlds: A sociological perspective.* Champaign, IL: Human Kinetics.

Maquila Solidarity Network (The) (2008) *Clearing the hurdles: Steps to improving wages and working conditions in the global sportswear industry.* Toronto, ON: Play Fair 2008 Campaign.

Miller, T., Lawrence, G., McKay, J., and Rowe, D. (2001) *Globalization and sport: Playing the world.* London: Sage.

Nielsen Company (The) (2008, 5 September) *The final tally – 4.7 billion tunes in to Beijing 2008 – More than two in three people worldwide: Nielsen.* The Nielsen Company. Online. Available HTTP: http://blog.nielsen.com/nielsenwire/wp-content/uploads/2008/09/press_release3.pdf (accessed 5 March 2010).

Oxfam International (2006) *Offside! Labour rights and sportswear production in Asia.* Online. Available HTTP: http://www.oxfam.org.au/resources/filestore/originals/Aus-OffsideLabourRightsAsia-1206.pdf (accessed 12 January 2006).

Play Fair at the Olympics (2004) *Play fair at the Olympics: Respect workers' rights in the sportswear industry.* Oxford, UK: Oxfam GB. Online. Available HTTP: http://www.fairolympics.org/background/olympicreporteng.pdf (accessed 12 January 2006).

San Diego Union-Tribune (The) (2004, 10 August) Greek Olympic baseball team *The San Diego Union-Tribune.* Online. Available HTTP: http://www.signonsandiego.com/uniontrib/20040810/news_1s10greekbox.html (accessed 6 May 2008).

Softball West Magazine (2004, August) The Greek Olympic team has a U.S. flavor. *Softball West Magazine.* Online. Available HTTP: http://softballwest.com/articles/51 (accessed 6 May 2008).

Thibault, L. (2009) Globalization of sport: An inconvenient truth. *Journal of Sport Management, 23*(1), 1–20.

Tomlinson, A. and Young, C. (2006) Culture, politics, and spectacle in the global sports events: An introduction. In A. Tomlinson and C. Young (eds), *National identity and global sports events* (pp. 1–14). Albany, NY: State University of New York Press.

United Nations. (2005) *International Year of Sport and Physical Education.* Available HTTP: http://www.un.org/sport2005 (accessed 5 March 2010).

United Nations (2010) *UN at a glance: Quick facts.* Online. Available HTTP: http://www.un.org/en/aboutun/index.shtml (accessed 5 March 2010).

United States Environmental Protection Agency (2009) *Create a new climate for action: Glossary of climate change terms.* Online. Available HTTP: http://www.epa.gov/climate4action/learn/glossary.htm (accessed 5 March 2010).

Vecsey, G. (2007, 26 October) N.F.L. tries to turn globalization into a team sport. *The New York Times*, p. D4. Online. Available HTTP: http://www.nytimes.com/2007/10/26/sports/football/26vecsey.html (accessed 5 March 2010).

Weiner, E. (2008, 7 March) Sports: American sports may soon face a foreign invasion. *The New York Sun*. Online. Available HTTP: http://www.nysun.com/article/72504?page_no=2 (accessed 6 May 2008).

Wertheim, L. J. (2004, 14 June) The whole world is watching. *Sports Illustrated, 100*(24), 72–86.

Weston, M. (2006) Internationalization in college sports: Issues in recruiting, amateurism, and scope. *Willamette Law Review, 42*, 829–860.

Wroth, K. (2009, 8 April) Life's a pitch: 15 green sports venues. *Grist*. Available HTTP: http://www.grist.org/article/2009-04-07-15-green-sports-venues/PALL (accessed 5 March 2010).

Chapter 14

Managing sport volunteers

Graham Cuskelly and Chris Auld, Griffith University, Australia

---

TOPICS

Defining sport volunteering • The scope of sport volunteering • Roles of sport volunteers • Volunteering and voluntary sport organisations (VSOs) within the wider sport system • Human resource management and sport volunteers

---

OBJECTIVES

At the end of this chapter you should be able to:

■ Understand the roles and scope of volunteers within the context of the sport system;

■ Articulate the processes of managing sport volunteers from an HRM perspective;

■ Have an appreciation of the complexity and some of the limitations of applying an HRM approach to the management of sport volunteers.

KEY TERMS

Human resource management (HRM) – a rational process which takes a strategic planning approach in which the needs and expectations of volunteers are matched with the labour requirements of VSOs.

Management roles – typical management positions in a traditionally structured VSO include president or chairperson, secretary, treasurer and registrar. Volunteers in management roles are members of the management committee or board with responsibility for the governance of the organisation and its assets.

Operational roles – usually encompass coaching coordinators, coaches, team managers, equipment coordinators, ground marshals and general helpers amongst a number of other positions.

> **Performance management** – a process whereby organisations 'try to achieve strategic goals consistently through better formal and informal motivation, monitoring, evaluating and rewarding performance' (Pinnington and Lafferty, 2003: 158).
>
> **Psychological contract** – characterises the perceptions of agreements beyond what was formally agreed between employees and employers when a new staff member joined an organisation.
>
> **Volunteer** – volunteers contribute their time through both formal and informal organisational settings and may volunteer for more than one organisation and in more than one role at varying levels of frequency, from as little as once per year (e.g. an annual sport event) to several times per week (e.g. coaching a local football team).

OVERVIEW

It is widely accepted in most sport systems that volunteers are integral to the development, management and operation of voluntary sport organisations (VSOs) and many sport events. The importance of volunteers across a broad array of community organisations and services from international aid organisations to local community welfare programmes was recognised by the United Nations when it designated 2001 as the International Year of the Volunteer. Within the context of sport, it is through volunteers that a large proportion of programmes, activities, services and events are delivered to athletes, spectators, club members and the wider community. Sport national governing boards (NGBs) play an important strategic and visioning role for sport. They are often well versed in developing structures, strategies and plans and communicating these to their constituent clubs and associations. However, it is through VSOs and the many hundreds of thousands of volunteers that the grass-roots development of sport is achieved.

In its simplest form, managing sport volunteers has been described as a process of gain–train–retain. While capturing the essence of volunteer management, the gain–train–retain approach understates the complexities of working effectively with volunteers within VSOs and the wider sport service delivery system. The purpose of this chapter is, therefore, to define volunteering, understand the scope and roles of sport volunteering, place volunteering and VSOs within the wider sport system and consider the pressures faced by VSOs and volunteers. The chapter then examines how a human resource management (HRM) approach can be applied to the management of sport volunteers. The focus of this chapter is sport volunteers who participate in structured voluntary activities in an organisational setting – what has been described by Sport England (2002) as formal volunteering.

DEFINING SPORT VOLUNTEERING

A statement originally developed by Volunteering Australia in 1996 captures the essence of volunteering by defining formal volunteering as 'an activity which takes place through not for

CASE STUDY: COACHING COORDINATOR FOR THE LOCAL NETBALL ASSOCIATION

Bernadette Wilson has held the voluntary position of coaching coordinator for her local netball association for six years. The netball association has a total of 920 players aged from under 7 to adults (of which about half are under 18 years of age) and 62 registered and accredited coaches. When Bernadette first started as the coaching coordinator she was well liked and respected by the players and coaches in the association and in the wider netball community largely because of the profile she had developed as a player of ten years' standing in the successful national team and as an A-grade coach within the association. As coaching coordinator she reviewed the coaching recruitment and development programme and implemented a vastly improved skill development programme. At least once each year she observed every association coach's performance and has been generous with her feedback, advice and support. Since Bernadette took over the position of coaching coordinator, turnover has been reduced from 40 to 10 per cent per year, the proportion of accredited coaches has increased from 60 to 100 per cent and last year more than 50 players were selected to play in representative age group teams – up from 12 players three years ago. The increasing standards in player development have largely been attributed to Bernadette's skills and commitment as coaching coordinator and the coaching programme she has demanded that all coaches of junior teams follow.

Over the past year there has been an increasing chorus of reports from coaches, players and parents. Several coaches have resigned from the association citing major problems working with Bernadette. Unconfirmed reports suggest that Bernadette's attendance at the association has dropped off. When she has observed coaches and provided feedback she has been highly critical and negative and has, at times, verbally abused a number of coaches, in the presence of their teams, for not following her coaching programme. Other players, parents and coaches believe that those who have been complaining are overreacting. They have been openly as strong in their support of Bernadette to continue as the coaching coordinator as the critics who want her removed from the role.

The management committee is meeting this evening to review applicants for the position of coaching coordinator. There are two applicants. Bernadette has reapplied for a further two-year term as allowed under association by-laws and has made it clear that she expects to be reappointed. The other applicant is the father of a 12-year-old player. He is an accredited netball coach but has had limited coaching experience having been an assistant coach to his daughter's team for the past year. He is popular and well liked by the small number of parents, players and coaches who know him and they like his approach to coaching.

A chairperson of the management committee, how are you going to handle this matter? Is it time for a change or should Bernadette be offered another two years as coaching coordinator? If Bernadette was reappointed, what actions should the management committee take to address concerns about her performance? If Bernadette is not reappointed, who is going to inform her and how? How might she react to not being reappointed? How might association members (players, parents and coaches) feel about the appointment of the other candidate given his lack of coaching experience? What alternative courses of action might be available to the management committee?

profit organisations or projects and is undertaken: to be of benefit to the community and the volunteer; of the volunteer's own free will and without coercion; for no financial payment; and in designated volunteer positions only' (Volunteering Australia, 2009). In a frequently cited journal article, Cnaan, Handy and Wadsworth (1996) delineate several dimensions of volunteering which seek to extend our understanding of what defines volunteering. Their dimensions of volunteering enable what to many is simply unpaid work to be examined in more depth by situating volunteering along continuums across four dimensions. These are:

- Free choice, which ranges from free will to relatively uncoerced to obligation to volunteer.
- Remuneration, which ranges from none at all to none expected to reimbursement of expenses to stipend or low pay.
- Structure, which extends from formal to informal organisational settings.
- Intended beneficiaries, which extend from benefiting strangers to benefiting friends or relatives to benefiting oneself.

It is important to understand some of the complexities of volunteering if one is to fully grasp the processes involved in managing volunteers. In a VSO setting one volunteer might feel obligated to volunteer, perhaps because their children play on a team, but would prefer to volunteer informally by not accepting a designated role such as that of team manager. Another volunteer may freely choose to take on the role of coach but, because formal qualifications are required, might expect that the club will reimburse her expenses or provide a stipend. Volunteer motives and the relationship between volunteers and VSOs are discussed later in this chapter.

THE SCOPE OF SPORT VOLUNTEERING

The level of participation in sport volunteering depends to some extent on how volunteering is defined, measured and reported. Volunteers contribute their time through both formal and informal organisational settings and may volunteer for more than one organisation and in more than one role at varying levels of frequency, from as little as once per year (e.g. an annual sport event) to several times per week (e.g. coaching a local football team). With these limitations in mind, statistics provided by agencies in England (Sport England, 2002) and Australia (Australian Bureau of Statistics, 2006a) provide a snapshot of the scope of volunteering in sport (see Table 14.1). The sport sector represents the single largest contribution to total volunteering and involves more than one-tenth of the adult population in both England and Australia.

Table 14.1 *Sport volunteering statistics*

Statistic	England	Australia
Number of volunteers	5,821,400 sports volunteers, representing nearly 15% of the adult population.	1,712,800 volunteers in formally organised sport and physical recreation or about 11.2% of the adult population.
Hours contributed	Sport volunteers contribute 1.2 billion hours each year to sport or the equivalent of 720,000 full-time paid workers.	136 average hours per volunteer per year (all sectors, not disaggregated for sport and physical recreation).
Value of time	The value of the time contributed by sports volunteers is estimated at over £14 billion.	N/A
Clubs and members supported	The volunteers help to sustain over 106,400 affiliated clubs, serving over 8 million members.	N/A
Sport sector relative to other volunteer sectors	The sporting sector makes the single biggest contribution to total volunteering with 26% of all volunteers citing 'sport' as their main area of interest.	Sport and physical recreation accounts for the single biggest contribution to total volunteering with 33% of all volunteer involvement.

ROLES OF SPORT VOLUNTEERS

The management and delivery of sport programmes, activities and events requires volunteers to fill an array of roles with varying time demands and skill levels. Volunteers contribute their time and labour across management and operational roles in sport, often concurrently. Management-level responsibilities include planning, policymaking and coordinating the efforts of others. At the operational level, volunteer roles are more hands-on and involve direct service delivery (see Table 14.2).

Table 14.2 *Volunteer roles at management and operational levels within VSOs*

Organisational level	Examples of volunteer roles
Management	President/chairperson, board or committee member, vice-president, secretary, treasurer, registrar, volunteer coordinator.
Operational	Coaching coordinator, coach, team manager, assistant coach, referee or umpire, sports trainer, first-aid officer, equipment coordinators, ground marshals, competition/results secretary, social organiser, fund-raising coordinator, newsletter/communications/website coordinator, general helper (e.g. transport, food and beverages, uniforms).

Typical management positions in a traditionally structured VSO include president or chairperson, secretary, treasurer and registrar. Volunteers in management roles are members of the management committee or board with responsibility for the governance of the organisation and its assets. Their functions and responsibilities are often defined and specified in the organisation's constitution. At an operational level the activities of volunteers are more numerous. The number and types of roles are developed to suit the overall size (e.g. number of members or teams) and specific requirements of a particular VSO. Such roles usually encompass coaching coordinators, coaches, team managers, equipment coordinators, ground marshals and general helpers amongst a number of other positions. Large VSOs with sufficient financial resources sometimes buy out volunteer labour by hiring paid staff or contractors to carry out some of the more complex or demanding responsibilities. The appointment of paid staff to formerly volunteer roles comes with the risk of alienating some volunteers who may reduce their involvement in a VSO and expect that paid staff will pick up the slack.

Dividing volunteer roles into managerial and operational levels provides some clarity about how VSOs might go about managing their volunteers and emphasises the point that at least some volunteers often have direct managerial responsibility for other volunteers. Reflecting on the seminal work of Pearce (1993) on the organisational behaviour of unpaid workers, it is often the case that sport volunteers are simultaneously owners and managers of VSOs as well as workers and clients of the organisation. Members of VSOs are concurrently the 'owners' and clients (players and parents of junior players) of their organisation in that it is established and continues as a going concern by virtue of its members. Some members take on management roles by running for office and in so doing take on responsibility for managing the work of other members in operational roles. Importantly, each of these 'organizational roles comes with its own set of behavioral expectations' (Pearce, 1993: 151) which must be taken into account in the management of sport volunteers.

VOLUNTEERING AND VSOS WITHIN THE WIDER SPORT SYSTEM

VSOs are at the core of sport systems within most Western democracies. Sport England (2005) defined community amateur sport clubs as properly constituted as a not-for-profit organisation, with no provision for payment to members during the life of the club or upon dissolution. It can be either unincorporated (i.e. an association of members with unlimited liability) or incorporated as a company limited by guarantee (not shares). The club must operate an open membership policy that allows anyone, within reason, to join and use its facilities.

There are more than 100,000 VSOs in England (see Table 14.1). In Canada, more than 33,000 sport and recreation organisations comprise 21 per cent of all voluntary not-for-profit organisations in 71 per cent of VSOs serving local communities (Doherty, 2005). It is important to note that while VSOs are a dominant feature of sport at a local community level they are also part of a wider sport system at a regional, provincial/state, national and international level. The International Olympic Committee and many international sport federations are not-for-profit organisations which involve volunteers at management and operational levels. The summer games of the past three Olympiads, for example, have been staged with the assistance of at least 40,000 volunteers.

Government agencies with responsibility for sport development, sport NGBs and major sport event managers have long recognised the importance of volunteers to and as a consequence of the need for effective volunteer management practices. Over the past decade sport club development and management programmes have incorporated resources on volunteer management. Programmes and resource kits targeted at managing volunteers and VSOs include Sport and Recreation New Zealand's 'Club Kit: Tools to Run Your Club', Sport England's 'Running Sport', and the Australian Sports Commission's 'Volunteer Management Program'. Provision of these resources has emerged to a certain extent as a response to the increasing pressures being faced by volunteers and VSOs in recruiting and managing volunteers within the club-based sport system (see box: Pressures faced by VSOs).

Pressures faced by VSOs (Sport England, 2002)

- Recruiting volunteers remains difficult for many sports, with many people not knowing what might be required of them as volunteers;
- Retaining volunteers is increasingly difficult, and currently there is one 'lapsed' volunteer for every two active volunteers;
- Pressures from other commitments are squeezing the time available for volunteering at the same time as the workload is growing;
- New rules and regulations are bringing more pressures, especially linked to child protection and health and safety obligations;
- Core volunteer roles are becoming more demanding and officials are being given less and less respect;
- Changing expectations from sporting institutions, players and parents also translate into a need for a greater 'professionalism' that matches other providers of sport;
- Older volunteers dominate key roles, which may constrain opportunities for younger volunteers.

Sport England (2002: 17) summarised the three main challenges identified by NGBs and sports club volunteers as 'shortages of volunteers; a problem in recruiting new volunteers; and consequently the loading of the required voluntary tasks on to fewer people'. Such pressures have the potential to limit the capacity of VSOs and volunteers to deliver sport services, programmes and events. VSO administration and development resources recommend the appointment of a volunteer coordinator and advocate the use of an HRM approach to work with volunteers. Because of the importance of sport volunteers, 'it is no longer a question of whether volunteers ought to be managed but how should they be managed in a way that does not impinge upon a fundamental condition of volunteering – to freely choose when, where and how to volunteer in sport' (Cuskelly, Hoye and Auld, 2006: 80).

HUMAN RESOURCE MANAGEMENT AND SPORT VOLUNTEERS

The purpose of this section is to examine the application of an HRM approach to volunteer management in VSOs. The concept of HRM is discussed in much greater detail in Chapter 9. It is recognised that there are a range of HRM paradigms and that the approach discussed here is regarded as classic or traditional. From this perspective traditional HRM is a rational process which takes a strategic planning approach in which the needs and expectations of volunteers are matched with the labour requirements of VSOs. A drawback of the HRM approach is the possible tension between volunteer management and volunteer motives, which was captured by LIRC (2003: 80) when it stated:

> ... the importance of shared enthusiasm and social benefits from volunteering militates against a managerialist approach to volunteers, whilst motivations concerned with helping a club improve and succeed, and 'giving something back', are more compatible with formal approaches to volunteer management.

The HRM approach to managing sport volunteers in this chapter is closely aligned with what Meijs and Karr (2004) describe as programme management of volunteers which they contrast with membership management. In a goal-oriented programme management approach, VSOs identify the operational tasks to be undertaken by the organisation and then assign volunteers to specific tasks. A membership management approach is more socially oriented and volunteer focused. It takes into account the needs and expectations of volunteers and endeavours to design tasks to fit individual volunteers. HRM is not the only approach to volunteer management; however, research by Cuskelly, Taylor, Hoye and Darcy (2006) used an HRM model to test the efficacy of volunteer management practices on the retention of community rugby club volunteers and found that clubs which reported more extensive use of HRM practices reported fewer problems in the retention of volunteers.

HRM involves the recruitment, selection, induction, training, performance management, recognition and rewarding, and retention or replacement of sport volunteers. It is a cyclical process in which new volunteers are recruited to replace volunteers who leave a VSO to ensure that organisational capacity, from a human resource viewpoint, is maintained or developed to meet the demands of an expanding participant base. Consistent with the gain–train–retain method, in its broadest sense the key functions of HRM are acquiring, developing and retaining volunteers. The role of HRM is to attract volunteers to the organisation, develop a sense of commitment to the organisation and to their job, provide training and offer support, as well as to recognise and reward performance. The longer term objective is to retain those who contribute positively to furthering VSO goals. The following subsections outline and critically examine these processes from the viewpoints of three significant phases in HRM: acquiring, developing and retaining volunteers.

> The professional sports development sector must make the most of the volunteer ethos in English sport without at the same time stifling its contribution and alienating its volunteers, young and old. Volunteers need to be better supported to enable them to continue to contribute time and effort.
>
> (Sport England, 2002)

Acquiring volunteers

The first major phase of HRM is the acquisition of volunteers and involves planning, recruitment, screening and selection. HRM begins with planning, wherein the current and future need for volunteer labour to service current planned programmes, services and events is forecast. In VSOs this process, whether formal or informal, would take place at least annually and several months in advance of a new sport season. HRM planning may coincide with the organisation's annual general meeting at which the major office bearers (e.g. president, secretary and treasurer) are elected and then get on with the task of planning the season ahead. An important aspect of HRM planning is matching the skills and qualifications of volunteers with task demands to ensure that volunteers fit with the culture, values and goals of the organisation (Chelladurai, 1999).

The volunteer coordinator or a small committee appointed by the VSO should develop an inventory of the skills, qualifications (e.g. coaching accreditation) and experience for current volunteers. VSOs with sufficient financial resources might consider the appointment of a paid staff member to fill the important role of managing volunteers. The goal of HRM planning is to identify projected needs for volunteers and for which particular roles. If little has changed within an organisation since the previous sport season then HRM planning is largely about identifying which volunteer positions are not already filled for the coming seasons. If a need for a new position is identified then a job analysis is used to develop a position description (PD). VSOs have the advantage of readily available PD templates available from government agencies. For example, Running Sports (2010a) provides readily adaptable role outlines for more than a dozen volunteer positions. A PD usually specifies the title of the role (e.g. team manager), main duties, skills and, where appropriate, qualifications required (e.g. first-aid certification), to whom the person is responsible, an estimate of the hours and times the volunteer is required and the term of office (start and end dates) for the position. Any particular requirements of the position (e.g. access to own personal computer and internet) are also specified in the PD. An accurate PD is necessary for a new volunteer to get a realistic preview of what the role entails and a feel for whether their needs and interests might fit the job.

255

In many VSOs the acquisition phase is much less formal than the planned approach outlined here. In reality, responsibility filling an existing volunteer position, particularly at the operational level, often rests with the incumbent volunteer if they foreshadow their intention to leave either their current role or they decide to leave the VSO altogether. A limitation of HRM planning is that it is modelled on government and commercial sector organisations where paid staff are recruited and financially compensated for providing their time and particular skill set. In contrast, some volunteer positions, particularly at a management level, are filled through an election process, by virtue of a VSO's constitution. Elections do not always attract nominees with the necessary qualifications, skills and experience to be effective in the role to which they are elected. Other volunteer positions are often filled on an *ad hoc* basis when a VSO realises that it needs an extra 'pair of hands' to get a job done. These types of situations are not always an outcome of poor planning, but they can be difficult to manage and are often exacerbated by chronic shortages of volunteers.

The goal of the recruitment stage of acquiring volunteers is to attract a pool of good quality applicants to vacant positions. Central to a successful recruitment campaign is a clear and concise PD, an understanding of the values and motives of volunteers and a communication plan. Amongst the most frequently cited reasons for sport volunteering (Australian Bureau of Statistics, 2006b) are: help others/community, personal/family involvement, personal satisfaction, and to do something worthwhile. Messages designed to attract volunteers, whether spread through asking individuals directly, advertising or by some other means of communication, should emphasise these values. Importantly, communication materials designed to attract potential volunteers need to promote the benefits of volunteering such as getting to know other community members, learning new skills or building a better club.

Volunteer motivation

It is beyond the scope of this chapter to discuss the application of the extensive literature on motivation theory as it applies to sport volunteers. Suffice to recognise the work of Knoke and Prensky (1984) has been influential in understanding volunteer motivation. Knoke and Prensky identified three motives for volunteering that they described as incentives which they labelled utilitarian, affective and normative. Utilitarian motives are the personal benefits gained from volunteering. Unlike paid employees, volunteers are not financially compensated for their efforts, so motives such as facilitating their children's participation in sport, gaining work experience or accessing local community networks to further business interests may be important drivers of volunteer behaviour. Affective motives are the benefits derived from social interaction through volunteering. Interpersonal relationships initiated through sport volunteering can engender a sense of group identification and status and develop into friendships that extend beyond sport. Normative motives are different to the personal benefits of volunteering and appeal to volunteers with a genuine and unselfish concern for others. Essentially volunteering is motivated by both altruism and self-interest (Stebbins, 1996) and it is important to understand that these motives coexist amongst sport volunteers. While altruism may motivate a volunteer in one situation, self-interest might be the over-riding motive in another situation within the same VSO. Because volunteer motives are dynamic they also tend to change over time. A volunteer may be strongly motivated by altruism early in their involvement with a VSO, whereas motives more associated with self-interest may assume greater importance over time. Equally, a volunteer may become involved in sport through self-interest and altruistic motives emerge as they spend more time in the organisation.

The screening and selection processes follow soon after the recruitment stage has been finalised. Assuming the number of volunteers recruited exceeds the positions available, selection and screening involve exercising judgement in relation to who best meets the PD and would be suited to a particular role. Selection processes for volunteers normally include an interview and, depending upon the level of responsibility associated with the position (e.g. controlling assets such as equipment and money), reference checks. Interviews might be anything from an informal chat about a position to a formal process with a selection committee and a set of predetermined interview questions. At the conclusion of the screening and selection stage, volunteers are appointed to a position. Potential volunteers who are not offered a position should also be contacted about the outcome and possibly encouraged to take up another position within a VSO. It should be noted, however, that having more than one potential volunteer available for a position is likely to be an infrequent occurrence in the majority of VSOs.

Child protection legislation

As discussed previously, volunteer positions that are elected rather than appointed are not subject to the usual selection processes. However, in many jurisdictions child protection and safety legislation mandates that all sport volunteers who may have contact with children are required to undergo a formal police or criminal record check. This legal requirement is designed to minimise the risk of volunteers with a record of particular offences or convictions (e.g. child abuse or accessing child pornography material) gaining access to children through a VSO and applies equally to elected and appointed volunteers. Many VSOs require police and criminal checks to be completed in advance of being considered for a volunteer position to deter individuals deemed inappropriate for contact with children from considering volunteering.

Developing volunteers

The start of the second major phase of HRM is marked by the transition that a volunteer makes by moving from being an outsider to an insider of the formal organisation. Called an induction process, this is a critical time for both a volunteer and the VSO. At this juncture volunteers consider whether the volunteer job was really what they wanted and whether their expectations are likely to be met. The purpose of an induction process is to manage and support new volunteers to help them learn about the organisation, their position within it and with whom they will be working. Some VSOs prepare a welcome pack (see box: Retaining volunteers) and a formal induction meeting. A well-designed induction session reduces stress, makes volunteers feel welcome and may reduce the likelihood of turnover (Cuskelly, 1995).

Training is generally more job specific than induction and is designed to ensure that volunteers gain the skills necessary to be effective in their position. Chelladurai (1999: 147) refers to training as 'the process of cultivating job-related skills, interpersonal skills, and organizational values ... and [to] learn the culture of the organization'. Training and development programmes and delivery modes available to VSOs and their volunteers offer an array of choices. Some of the websites at the end of this chapter provide links to sport volunteer training and development programmes. The selection of a training programme is largely determined by the needs and policies of the organisation (e.g. appointment of accredited coaches to all teams) and whether particular volunteers have the requisite qualifications and skills for their position. However, training is not only for commencing volunteers. From time to time, continuing volunteers need to update their skills and may need to complete refresher courses to maintain the currency of their accreditation particularly in positions with high levels of technical skills (e.g. sports trainers, first-aid officers and coaches). Other considerations are training costs, timing, specificity and relevance, flexibility, mode of delivery and prerequisite knowledge. There is an increasing range of delivery modes and formats to suit the wide-ranging needs and interests of sport volunteers and VSOs. Training programmes can be either generalised (e.g. health and safety) or specific (e.g. coach accreditation for a particular sport), or formal (e.g. class based or e-learning) or informal (e.g. through a mentoring approach), and undertaken either on or off the job. The internet is an important resource for the flexible delivery of sport volunteer e-learning programmes, particularly for people with busy work or family schedules and/or those who are in rural or regional areas which may limit their availability for face-to-face training sessions. VSOs need to make decisions about whether training is optional or compulsory and who pays for the direct (e.g. course registration) and indirect costs (e.g. food, accommodation and transport allowances) associated with attendance at training and development courses. Clear policies in the areas of training and development provide commencing volunteers with some assurance that they will be adequately supported to fulfil their role.

Retaining volunteers

Having volunteers recruited to positions, inducted and trained to do their job is necessary but not sufficient to ensure that VSOs deliver the programmes, services or events expected by club members and the wider community. The final phase of HRM is largely focused on managing the ongoing relationship between volunteers and VSOs (see box: Retaining volunteers). The concept of psychological contract is an emerging area of research which explains the relationship between volunteers and VSOs (see box: Psychological contract). The HRM processes which contribute to retaining sport volunteers are performance management, and recognising and rewarding performance.

Retaining volunteers (adapted from Running Sports, 2010b)

Have a welcome pack and induction which should include information on the following:

- Club structure
- Contact details
- The volunteers role outline

- A welcome and introductions
- How to claim expenses
- Buddy/mentoring arrangements
- Advice on equipment/specialist clothing

Communicate with your volunteers:

- Clear, regular communication is vital
- Hold regular volunteer briefings
- Use text or email for quick communication
- Have a volunteer page or section in your Club newsletter

Make sure they are enjoying the challenge:

- Variety and challenge is important
- Give recognition and reward (say Thank You!)
- Make the volunteer feel wanted and valued
- Give your volunteers increased confidence
- Use team work where appropriate

Give your volunteers skills and training:

- Identify, with the volunteer, what, if any, training is needed
- Understand that training will give confidence
- Internal – training given by your own team or volunteer mentor
- External – many organisations provide skills and training courses.

Performance management

The performance of volunteers is founded on their ability to do their job, the commitment and effort they are prepared to put into their job and the support provided by the VSO. Performance management is a process whereby organisations 'try to achieve strategic goals consistently through better formal and informal motivation, monitoring, evaluating and rewarding performance' (Pinnington and Lafferty, 2003: 158). In a paid work setting performance management determines job expectations, supports, reviews and appraises achievements and manages performance standards. Performance management is often closely tied to reward systems. Volunteer performance management is both necessary for VSOs to be effective but problematic to the extent that the 'rewards that seem to be most important … [to volunteers] … are not under the control of the organization' (Pearce, 1993: 181). Pearce argues that volunteer performance can be managed either through informal, social and normative controls or through more bureaucratic systems, but 'no organization can be effective with neither' (Pearce, 1993: 179). Whichever approach is adopted, it is likely that volunteers who believe their efforts are being noticed and supported are more likely to feel appreciated and inclined to continue to work towards the goals of a VSO.

Psychological contract

An emerging body of research that helps to explain the volunteer–organisation relationship is psychological contract. The concept of psychological contract is based on social exchange theory and was originally developed by Argyris (1960) to characterise the perceptions of agreements beyond what was formally agreed between employees and employers when a new staff member joined an organisation. The psychological contract relies on the exchange of benefits and rewards which are categorised as either transactional or relational. In a study designed to explore the set of expectations and obligations that community sport club volunteers regard as part of their volunteering experience, Taylor, Darcy, Hoye and Cuskelly (2006) found that club administrators and volunteers place different emphases on different aspects of the psychological contract. Club administrators had substantial expectations of volunteers in relation to adherence to professional, legal and regulatory standards, whereas volunteers were concerned primarily with rewarding work in a pleasant social environment that was able to fit within their time constraints.

Recognising and rewarding volunteers for the time and effort they put into a VSO is an important component of HRM which is closely linked to volunteer motivation and ultimately to volunteer retention. From a VSO perspective, it is important that volunteers are motivated to direct effort towards organisational goals. However, volunteers are not only motivated by the achievement of organisational goals. Such motives can be secondary to the fulfilment of personal rewards. As discussed earlier in this chapter, volunteers are motivated by some combination of altruism and self-interest. To a large extent, volunteering is motivated by enjoyment of the activity, the social interaction which surrounds it and the satisfaction which comes from contributing to a larger social good such as building a stronger club, all of which are beyond the control of VSOs. It is vital that VSOs recognise that rewards and recognition that are not linked to performance or distributed unequally between volunteers may not be valued and may negatively impact on volunteer performance and retention. Rewards and recognition in the form of certificates, plaques or gifts are extrinsic rewards which, while important in managing volunteers and their retention in a VSO, may not be as highly valued as intrinsic rewards which are not controlled by the organisation.

The retention of volunteers provides a sense of continuity within VSOs for club members and the volunteers themselves. Higher volunteer retention rates mean that less VSO resources, which are largely the time and effort of current volunteers, are required to recruit, screen, select, induct and train new volunteers. A certain level of volunteer turnover is to be expected and is also necessary to facilitate organisational renewal. As current volunteers feel the need to move on and new volunteers are recruited, VSOs continue to evolve, develop and adapt in response to the changing expectations of their members as well as maintaining relevance to the external environment. Volunteer turnover, particularly at the management level, provides opportunities to introduce new points of view and refocus the strategic direction of a VSO. However, high levels of volunteer turnover in a short time period can be indicative of deep-rooted problems in a VSO and may threaten its continued existence. A challenge for HRM is to balance the need for new volunteers with that for continuity, growth and development of the organisation.

SUMMARY

Volunteers are critical to the effective operation and management of VSOs in the delivery of programmes, services and events. Sport volunteers are an essential and integral resource in the sport systems of many countries around the world. As critical as volunteers are to sport, if they are not managed appropriately, sport participation opportunities at a local community level can be put at risk. This chapter examined the scope of sport volunteering and the roles of volunteers in the management and operation of VSOs. An HRM approach discussed the acquisition, training and retention of sport volunteers. While HRM provides a useful framework for conceptualising the management of sport volunteers, it is important to balance the needs of VSOs to deliver programmes, services and events with the principle that volunteering is a free-choice activity.

REVIEW QUESTIONS

1   Why should HRM be considered a critical management function in VSOs and why do sport volunteers need to be managed?
2   In order for a volunteer to effectively perform their job, what is the relative importance of an individual's ability, commitment, effort and the support provided by the organisation?
3   Should a PD for a coaching coordinator in a district hockey club with 12 volunteer coaches be identical to a club with 40 volunteer coaches? Why or why not? What information should be included in such a PD?
4   What are the advantages and disadvantages of dividing a complex or labour-intensive role within a VSO between two volunteers? What might the impact be on current volunteers if a decision is made to hire a paid staff member to take over a complex or labour-intensive role?
5   How might volunteer roles be adapted to fit with the work and family schedules of busy individuals?
6   What information would you need to develop an individualised training and development programme for a recently appointed volunteer?
7   Why might performance management be considered controversial when working with volunteers in sport? Can a volunteer be fired? Why or why not?

FURTHER READING

Chelladurai, P. (1999) *Human Resource Management in Sport and Recreation*. Champaign, IL: Human Kinetics.
Cuskelly, G., Hoye, R. and Auld, C. (2006) *Working with Volunteers in Sport: Theory and Practice*. London: Routledge.
Sport England (2002) *Sports Volunteering in England in 2002*. London: Author.

WEBSITES

Running Sports (England)
   http://www.runningsports.org
Sport and Recreation New Zealand
   http://www.sparc.org.nz/en-nz/communities-and-clubs/Toolkit-for-Clubs
Volunteering Australia
   http://www.volunteeringaustralia.org
Volunteering England
   http://www.volunteering.org.uk

REFERENCES

Argyris, C. (1960) *Understanding Organizational Behavior.* Homewood, IL: Dorsey.
Australian Bureau of Statistics (2006a) *Voluntary Work, Australia,* Cat. No. 4441.0. Canberra: Commonwealth of Australia.
Australian Bureau of Statistics (2006b) *Volunteers in Sport,* Cat. No. 4440.0.55.001. Canberra: Commonwealth of Australia.
Chelladurai, P. (1999) *Human Resource Management in Sport and Recreation.* Champaign, IL: Human Kinetics.
Cnaan, R.A., Handy, F. and Wadsworth, M. (1996) 'Defining who is a volunteer: conceptual and empirical considerations', *Nonprofit and Voluntary Sector Quarterly,* 25(3): 364–383.
Cuskelly, G. (1995) 'The influence of committee functioning on the organisational commitment of volunteer administrators in sport', *Journal of Sport Behavior,* 18(4): 254–269.
Cuskelly, G., Hoye, R. and Auld, C. (2006) *Working with Volunteers in Sport: Theory and Practice.* London: Routledge.
Cuskelly, G., Taylor, T., Hoye, R. and Darcy, S. (2006) 'Volunteer management practices and volunteer retention: a human resource management approach' (Special Issue: Volunteerism in Sport). *Sport Management Review,* 9(2): 141–163.
Doherty, A. (2005) *A Profile of Community Sport Volunteers.* Ontario: Parks and Recreation Ontario and Sport Alliance of Ontario.
Knoke, D. and Prensky, D. (1984) 'What relevance do organization theories have for voluntary associations?', *Social Science Quarterly,* 65(1): 3–20.
LIRC (2003) *Sports Volunteering in England 2002.* London: Sport England.
Meijs, L.C.P.M. and Karr, L.B. (2004) 'Managing volunteers in different settings: membership and programme management', in R. Stebbins and M. Graham (eds), *Volunteering as Leisure/Leisure as Volunteering.* Wallingford, Oxfordshire: CABI Publishers.
Pearce, J.L. (1993) *Volunteers: The Organizational Behavior of Unpaid Workers.* London: Routledge.
Pinnington, A. and Lafferty, G. (2003) *Human Resource Management in Australia.* Victoria, Australia: Oxford University Press.
Running Sports (2010a) *Running Sport: Role Outlines.* London: Sport England. Online: http://www.runningsports.org (accessed 2 February 2010).
Running Sports (2010b) *Running Sports: Retaining Volunteers.* London: Sport England. Online: http://www.runningsports.org/club_support/all_resources/top_tips/Retaining+Volunteers.htm (accessed 2 February 2010).

Sport England (2002) *Sports Volunteering in England in 2002*. London: Author.

Sport England (2005) *Tax Breaks for Community Amateur Sports Clubs*. London: Sport England. Online: www.sportengland.org/index/news_and_media/news_gs/news_tb.htm. Cited in G. Cuskelly, R. Hoye and C. Auld (2006) *Working with Volunteers in Sport: Theory and Practice*. London: Routledge.

Stebbins, R.A. (1996) 'Volunteering: a serious leisure perspective', *Nonprofit and Voluntary Sector Quarterly*, 25(2): 211–224.

Taylor, T., Darcy, S., Hoye, R. and Cuskelly, G. (2006) 'Using psychological contract theory to explore issues in effective volunteer management', *European Sport Management Quarterly*, 6(2): 123–147.

Volunteering Australia (2009) *Fact Sheet: Definitions and Principles of Volunteering*. Melbourne, Victoria: Volunteering Australia.

Chapter 15

Sport and sponsorship

Laura Cousens and Cheri Bradish, Brock University, Canada

TOPICS

The special nature of sport sponsorship • Trends in sport sponsorship • Sponsorship measurement and evaluation • Sponsorship relationships • Cause-related sport sponsorship • Ambush marketing, brand protection and sport sponsorship

---

OBJECTIVES

At the end of this chapter you should be able to:

■ Understand the nature of sponsorship and partnerships;
■ Recognize trends within and beyond the context of sport that affect sponsorship;
■ Realize the need for, and approaches to, sponsorship research and evaluation;
■ Understand relational views of sponsorship that consider various forms of linkages including partnerships, alliances and networks;
■ Comprehend the relationship between sponsorship and cause-related marketing and corporate social responsibility;
■ Appreciate the need to protect corporate brands against ambush marketing.

KEY TERMS

Ambush marketing (also referred to as guerrilla marketing) – describes an attempt by a competing company to associate its brand with a sponsorship activity without securing the formal rights or paying the official sponsorship fee to do so.

Brand protection – efforts to protect the value of sport brands and properties, primarily focused on countering the ambush marketing practices.

Cause-related marketing – a marketing partnership that brings a 'for-profit' and 'not-for-profit' organization together for mutual benefit, often incorporating fundraising objectives (such as a percentage of sales from an identified product to a charitable effort).

Hybrid partnerships – describes linkages that align philanthropic giving with the donor's marketing, advertising and promotional efforts.

Inter-organizational network – a social structure that connects a collection of groups, organizations or agencies. It is also viewed as a strategic mechanism to improve a firm's competitive advantage through cost minimization while maintaining flexibility.

Issues-based sponsorship – describes when sport properties link to key societal issues such as the environment, education, health and community, which are viewed as being as important to sponsor and their customers.

Joint ventures – when two or more 'parent' organizations create a *third entity* that encompasses the distinctive competencies of each and enables both companies to pursue an opportunity that meets the capabilities. A primary rationale for joint ventures is to augment the market power of the involved organizations.

Partnerships – a form of inter-organizational linkage connotes higher levels of continuity, loyalty and mutual understanding between organizations.

Relational views of sponsorship – sponsorship relationships are seen as embedded within broader webs of interacting organizational linkages.

Sponsorship – a cash or in-kind investment in an activity in return for access to the exploitable commercial potential associated with that activity.

Sponsorship measurement and evaluation – research that demonstrates the overall 'return on investment' (ROI) of a sponsorship programme.

Strategic alliances – forms of relationship that provide further opportunities for integration that are warranted by the strategic value of each partner to the other. An alliance is necessitated when the distinctive or unique competencies of two organizations create the rationale for a joint competitive advantage.

OVERVIEW

The purpose of this chapter is to introduce the fundamental concepts and principles of sport sponsorship together with relevant issues that have emerged in the contemporary and global sport context. In the opening section, we introduce sport sponsorship and review the sponsorship objectives. The chapter then continues with a discussion of some recent trends in sponsorship research followed by an overview of key guidelines for sponsorship measurement and evaluation. We then transition to discuss sponsorship relationships and why firms should view sponsorship as a strategic investment. This is followed by a review of cause-related sponsorship and the related important concept of corporate social responsibility relative to sport. Our final section of the chapter examines ambush marketing relative to sport and sponsorship and includes an analysis of the current brand protection movement to counter this growing and threatening marketing practice. We conclude with suggestions for future research and practice for both the sport sponsorship industry and its study. This chapter also includes leading cases to supplement these sections, with the intent to encourage further examination of the related theories and practice of sport sponsorship. While our focus is on the UK and Europe, given the global nature of the sponsorship industry and the significant volume of related theory and insights, inevitably our chapter will reflect on some developments in North America. Ultimately, the goal of this chapter is to convey the unique capacity of sport sponsorship, while also highlighting some of the current opportunities and challenges related to this most powerful and popular marketing tool.

CASE STUDY ONE: THE OLYMPIC TOP PROGRAMME

Sport sponsorship partnerships and relationships have become quite sophisticated and elaborate, but perhaps no case best represents this than the complex and powerful International Olympic Committee's (IOC) The Olympic Partner (TOP) programme. This partnership programme contributes significantly to Olympic marketing revenue, which is generated from five important sources: broadcast rights, ticketing, licensing, and two streams of sponsorship including a) domestic partnerships and b) the internationally recognized TOP programme.

Specifically, the TOP programme was created in 1985 to develop a diversified revenue base for the Olympic Games and to establish long-term corporate partners that would benefit the Olympic Movement as a whole (in particular, enabling sustained revenue to all member NOCs for the first time; creating sustained support for global sport development, especially to those from less fortunate countries). The programme generates over $850 (US) in revenue for each Games period, 90 per cent of which is in turn redistributed to other National Organizing Committees (NOCs), International Federations (IFs) and Games Organizing Committees (OCOGs), with the remaining funds supporting over 30 per cent of other IOC programmes.

While corporations have been supporting the modern Olympic Games through advertising since 1896, the diversity and number of sponsors and suppliers in Games history has escalated over time, and as a result the TOP programme was created based on the 1984 Los Angeles Games model, which first promoted Olympic partnerships according to product exclusivity. Thus, the TOP programme was designed to provide a strategic clarity to Games partnerships, with the intent to alleviate an over-commercialization of the Games marketing platform by controlling the overall number of global Olympic partners.

The TOP programme has resulted in a very sophisticated and complex agreement between sponsors and the IOC, where a corporation assumes the Worldwide Olympic Partner status, and is granted the global marketing rights to specific Olympic intellectual property and receives Olympic marketing opportunities, in exchange for financial support and goods and services contributions within a specific product or service category. It is estimated that, according to the nature of these agreements, TOP partners pay between $50 and $100 million for the rights to at least one Olympic Winter and Summer Games. The management and protection of these unique and exclusive partnerships is highly valued and serviced by the IOC.

For the 2005–2008 IOC Quadrennial (Torino/Beijing), the programme was supported by 12 partners. As of 2010, there numbered nine TOP VII Partners (representing the Vancouver 2010 and London 2012 Games), which include (with category exclusivity): Coca-Cola (non-alcoholic beverages), Acer (computing technology equipment), Atos Origin (information technology), GE (select products and services), McDonald's (retail food services), Omega (timing, scoring and venue results services), Panasonic (audio/television/video equipment), Samsung (wireless communication equipment) and VISA (consumer payment systems). The

IOC TOP programme is regarded as the 'gold standard' of sponsorship partnership development and, as such, we encourage readers to further examine the many related documents and discussions of this programme which are widely available.

Sources: Giannoulakis, Stotlar and Chatziefstathiou (2008); IOC (2009)

THE SPECIAL NATURE OF SPORT SPONSORSHIP

Why sport managers need to understand sponsorship

The monetary and strategic value of sponsorship involving sport organizations and corporate or community partners has increased dramatically over the last two decades. According to the International Events Group (IEG), worldwide sponsorship reached $44 billion in 2009. North American companies spent $16.51 billion, with other global institutions spending $27.5 billion during the same year (IEG, 2010). Sport remains the largest segment of sponsorship, with 69 per cent of all such spending. Notably, this figure declined in 2009 from 2008, in part due to the overall poor marketplace conditions associated with the economic downfall of 2008 (IEG, 2010). Notwithstanding the vulnerability of sponsorship spending in turbulent economic times, corporate sponsors continue to recognize the capacity of sport to achieve a return on their investment, and to accomplish their strategic goals.

Theoretical perspectives employed by academics and practitioners to enhance our understanding of this aspect of sport management have evolved accordingly over the last 30 years. By way of example, the focus on consumer-linked marketing (Cornwell, Weeks and Roy, 2005), the value of sport as an element of a firm's demonstration of corporate social responsibility (Babiak and Wolfe, 2006) and the value of sport sponsorship to build and enhance corporate branding to extend traditional conceptions of sponsorship amid a global environment saturated by advertising clutter (Hein, 2002) have provided insight into our understanding of sport sponsorship. Furthermore, ambush marketing has emerged as an area worthy of attention as resourceful corporations seek to circumvent traditional buyer–supplier relationships through the unauthorized associations with sport properties. These and other contemporary issues relevant to sport sponsorship highlight some of the distinctive areas that have emerged within this discipline. Understanding various facets of sport sponsorship is crucial for managers seeking to navigate their sport organization through the turbulent and highly competitive landscape that characterizes the global sport industry.

What is sport sponsorship?

Relationships between sport organizations and corporations are frequent topics for discussion in the popular press. For example, Barclay's sponsorship of the Premier League and Sony's support of the UEFA Champions League exemplify the types of sponsor–sport relationships dissected by the media. Yet, what aspects of a business-to-business relationship characterize it as sponsorship? Certainly the exchange of financial resources delimits the scope and contribution of these relationships to sport organizations and corporate partners alike. The definition of sponsorship used in this chapter is that provided by Meenaghan (1991, p. 36), who states that sponsorship is 'an investment, in cash or kind, in an activity in return for access to the exploitable commercial potential associated with that activity'. There are four key elements in this definition that require further explanation:

- *Investment*. Corporations have moved beyond philanthropic motives for providing resources, financial or otherwise, to sport organizations. Organizations are seeking a return on their investment, be it increased market share, a financial return on their investment or image enhancement, through their relationship with a sport organization.
- *In cash or kind*. The exchange of resources between sport organizations and corporate sponsors extends beyond the narrow confines of financial transfers between actors to include as desired goods in-kind (such as products or facilities) as well as human resources, or access to them through a firm's network of inter-organizational contacts.
- *In an activity*. Sponsorship may involve one or more of the various properties, or platforms, involved in sport, including the athlete, the event, the sport and the team (Brooks, 1990).
- *Exploitable commercial potential associated with that activity*. Sponsors of sport properties are seeking the rights to various categories made available by the sport entity. According to Brooks (1990), sponsors' access is dependent upon the level of exclusivity desired by and/or offered by the sport entity. Agreed-upon elements may include, for example, use of logos, access to signage, television advertising, athlete appearances and/or executive social or networking opportunities. Exploitable benefits available to corporations through sport may include increased visibility of their brand(s) in selected target markets, image enhancement, revenue generation through sales promotions or opportunities to entertain clients on-site.

Sponsorship objectives

The identification of sponsorship objectives is clearly a vital part of the process in determining what or who to sponsor. Burton, Quester and Farrelly's (1998) comparative investigation of sponsorship decision-making among 200 North American and 200 Australian executives responsible for sport sponsorships revealed that a corporation's communication and strategic objectives were primary considerations when assessing a linkage with sport organizations (Burton *et al.*, 1998). Other considerations included the integration of the sponsorship into the firm's broader marketing mix, the sport organization's past sponsorship performance, and the sponsorship's potential contribution to the corporate brand or image. Interestingly, these researchers did uncover defensive motives for investing in particular sponsorship underpinned by the notion 'if we don't [sponsor this event], the competition will' (Burton *et al.*, 1998, p. 30).

Slack and Amis (2001) reviewed the sponsorship literature to reveal ten major objectives of sponsors. They suggested that increasing public awareness of a firm or brand and altering the firm/brand image were the two most cited reasons for entering into a sponsorship agreement. An early example of the former involved Cornhill, a British insurance agency. Keen to increase public awareness of the brand, the firm invested £2 million in a five-year sponsorship of English Test Cricket. As a consequence, public recognition of Cornhill rose from 2 to 21 per cent, something that it was estimated would have cost approximately £50 million through conventional advertising; Cornhill's sales increased by between £15 million and £20 million (Witcher, Craigen, Culligan and Harvey, 1991). Lucozade provides an excellent example of a firm seeking to alter its image through sport sponsorship. Traditionally regarded in the UK as a drink given to sick children, it rebranded as Lucozade Sport in 1990 and has entered into sponsorship agreements with high-profile sporting institutions such as the Premier League, the English Rugby Football Union and the London Marathon to transform its image and become the leader in the UK energy/sport drink sector (MarketingWeek, 2001).

Other objectives cited by Slack and Amis (2001) included overcoming cultural or linguistic barriers, gaining direct media access, building links with politicians and other business leaders, entertaining corporate clients, improving employee morale, testing products under intensified conditions, targeting a specific segment of the population, and satisfying the personal interests of a senior executive. As the cost of securing sponsorship rights has increased in recent years, sponsors have demanded more for their money and are utilizing sponsorship agreements in increasingly sophisticated ways. Howard and Burton (2002) suggested that a declining economy has further affected the amounts that sponsors are willing to invest, and what they expect in return.

Linking sport organizations and corporations is facilitated by a range of decision-making approaches and mechanisms. For example, websites such as the UK Sponsorship Database (http://www.uksponsorship.com/spt2.htm) serve as information bulletin boards for corporations seeking sponsorship opportunities. Organizations such as IEG provide consulting services to corporations seeking to sponsor sports, the arts or so-called 'good causes'. This firm also links sponsors to sport properties through a website service entitled SponsorDirect (http://www.conxeo.com) that enables corporations to evaluate the merits of numerous sport organizations. Alternatively, organizations like Coke, Kodak, Gillette and Nike hire full-time senior executives to direct and maximize global partnership investments (Burton et al., 1998).

TRENDS IN SPORT SPONSORSHIP

The landscape of sport sponsorship has changed dramatically over the last decade. New media, a growing social consciousness among consumers and emergent sport properties have each contributed to profound changes in the context of sport sponsorship. These have resulted in increased uncertainty among corporate buyers, in challenges among sport organizations to attract corporate buyers, and in opportunities for emergent sport or nonprofit sport organizations to capitalize upon shifting consumer values.

The impact of new media on sponsorship

The evolution of new media including high-definition television and direct streaming of sport events via high-speed Internet have altered the way sport is consumed and the platforms available to sponsors seeking to achieve their strategic objectives through sport. Shifts in the ways new technologies are used to capture sport are underpinned in part, according to Brunt (2010), by the need to attract the next generation of sport consumers. Attracting this younger target market is challenging because of 'a different, diminished attention span, accustomed to having the whole world laid out for them every minute of the day, literally, at their fingertips' (p. 59).

Shifting societal expectations of sponsors

Shifting societal expectations of corporations have also influenced the types of sponsorship properties that are valued by companies. According to Angus Reid Public Opinion, a leading public opinion and polling organization, consumer willingness to purchase a company's products is largely influenced by the perceived corporate reputation of the firm (see Figure 15.1). Accordingly, issues-based sponsorship by corporations means that properties linked to key societal issues, such as the environment, education, health and community, are as important to sponsor as are the Olympic Games or professional sport organizations (Angus Reid Public Opinion, 2009).

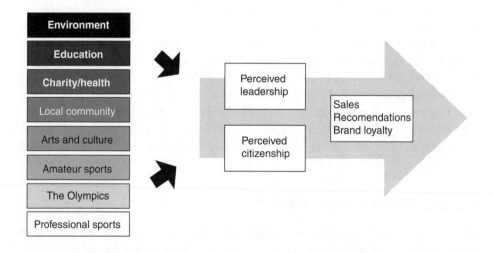

Figure 15.1 *Consumer awareness of sponsorship. Source: Angus Reid Public Opinion (2009)*

Sport sponsorship continues to be a central mechanism used to enhance corporate reputation and increase sales; however, there are numerous examples in the sponsorship landscape where the preferred type of sport targeted for sponsorship includes cause-related sport programmes that encompass issues of concern to consumers. According to Du, Hou and Huang (2008), more companies are sponsoring social causes as a marketing tool to reflect changing consumer perceptions. Accordingly, marketing campaigns and promotions with a social dimension have become more visible (Drumwright, 1996) and important to the practice and theory of sport sponsorship (see the 'Cause-related sport sponsorship' section below).

Emergent sports

The emergence of new sports and sponsorship properties competing with more traditional sport organizations is also evident. The Ultimate Fighting Championship (UFC) exemplifies one sport that has evolved from relatively unstructured two-man contests in its inception in 1993 to a codified mixed martial arts brand that seeks to challenge existing professional sports to capture mainstream markets. Today, the UFC is broadcast in over 130 countries reaching 450 million homes worldwide (Al Bawaba, 2010). Companies such as Anheuser-Busch Inc. have sponsored the sport organization as, according to Tony Ponturo, UFC Vice President of Global Media and Sports Marketing, the 'UFC has developed a huge following in recent years and is wildly popular with the 21–34 year old fans we want to reach. The number of people attending live events, buying the pay-per-views and talking about UFC around the water cooler continues to grow. It's just a great place for us to be' (Asian Business Newsweekly, 2008, n.p.).

The UFC is but one example of emergent sports that are attracting the attention of corporate sponsors. According to Paula Lehman (2010) of *Newsweek*, 'novel athletic endeavors in the U.S. are expanding fast, boosted by the mainstreaming of "action sports" such as snowboarding and skateboarding'. The expanding fan base of these sports is attracting global corporations such as Toyota, Dell and Hewlett-Packard. Recognizing emergent sports in the marketplace is vital according to Day (2006) because 'brands are increasingly investing a large part of their marketing budgets to integrate more fully into the lives of their consumers'. As traditional forms of marketing become less effective, building an association between your brand and today's generation is strategically important.

Navigating the contemporary context of sport sponsorship necessitates creativity among sports and sponsors alike. Sport organizations' efforts to explore new media to reach new target audiences, and to demonstrate corporate social responsibility (Godfrey, 2009; Sheth and Babiak, 2010) in response to shifting societal and corporate expectations, are evidence of adaptation to their changing environment. Corporate sponsors have also adapted to the evolving context by considering emergent sports as a means to attract consumers, by sponsoring nonprofit sport organizations (Du *et al.*, 2008), and by strategically sponsoring sport to demonstrate corporate social responsibility to key stakeholders (Walters, 2009).

SPONSORSHIP MEASUREMENT AND EVALUATION

The growth in sponsorship measurement and evaluation – specifically, to demonstrate the overall 'return on investment' (ROI) of the sponsorship programme – has been fuelled primarily by the heightened demands for greater accountability by sport partners, given sharp increases in their sponsorship-related expenditures, and the need to reconcile these investments with the overall corporate bottom line (Clancy and Krieg, 2006; Meenaghan, 1999). Also interpreted as key event 'measurables', a sound sport sponsorship platform must integrate a broad sponsorship measurement and evaluation plan to examine both short- and long-term metrics into their overall operational plan to be successful. This includes broadly assessing spectator perceptions and consumption patterns, property performance indicators and evaluative measures to assess the overall contribution of sponsorship to strategic corporate objectives (Meenaghan, 1999). While it should be noted that no one model of sponsorship measurement and evaluation is widely accepted, this area of sponsorship management has increasingly become more strategic and complex (see ESPN case study below) and several related contributions and perspectives are worthy of mention.

The evaluation of any agreement should be inextricably linked to the objectives of the sponsorship (see section above). According to Aaker and Myers (1987, p. 86), a 'function of an objective is to evaluate results. Thus [a] test of [an operational objective] is whether it can be used to evaluate a campaign at its conclusion.' Yet, practitioners and theorists alike have discussed the difficulty of measuring stated sponsorship objectives (Pope and Voges, 1994). Despite these challenges, however, demands by sponsors for evaluative techniques with respect to sponsorship remain. Accordingly, several research techniques hold promise for further use and exploration. For example, McAuley and Gladden (2002) suggested that a number of sponsors have developed revenue models that encompass media-based measurement tools to indicate whether or not a sponsorship has met its return-on-investment objectives. However, these proprietary models are rarely shared across companies as the specific needs of the organization tend to dictate and specialize the methodology (McAuley and Gladden, 2002). Further, a general weakness of these evaluative measures is their failure to assess the longer-term objectives and broader reach and scope of sponsorship.

Of interest then are models of measurement and evaluation that speak broadly to capturing the complexity of the sponsorship platform. As Clancy and Krieg (2006) suggest, a sound sponsorship measurement and evaluation plan includes pre- and post-event measures, understood as *inputs* that influence performance, and *outputs* that gauge performance (see Figure 15.2). In implementing a broader measurement and evaluation programme, such as they prescribe, a sponsorship manager will best incorporate the complex myriad of 'effectiveness' factors of their property, and ultimately speak more accurately to an overall assessment of their organization.

Perhaps most important here is to also speak to the current 'industry standard' areas of sponsorship and evaluation. Specifically, within the sport sponsorship industry, it is considered that there are four primary areas of measurement and evaluation used when assessing the value of sponsorship partnerships. The first area of measurement is documenting event and programme activity; thus, this is primarily linked to sales. This can be accomplished through measuring on-site components, such as attendance and other measures of spectator consumption. This also includes recording media impressions and other extensions of the property. The second area of sponsorship measurement encompasses determining a property's impact using attitudinal measures. This can be accomplished in three ways: measurement of sponsorship fit (with key audiences and partners), tracking (to target audiences) and overall assessments of property image. Third, sport sponsorship managers must consistently measure themselves against their competitors by benchmarking their sport property with similar organizations. This can often be a revealing measure, highlighting best practices

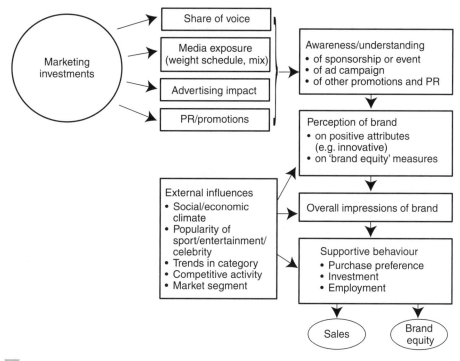

Figure 15.2 *Sponsorship property inputs and outputs*

and characteristics of the most highly effective sponsorship (Clancy and Krieg, 2006). Finally, it is imperative that sport sponsorship managers develop research measures to establish the efficiencies of their sponsorship portfolios. This includes documenting measurables which address key programme objectives and other important cost ratios.

In short, it should be understood that sponsorship measurement and evaluation is a key component to a successful sport sponsorship plan. Sport managers need to incorporate a variety of measurement tools to assist in assessing and improving their organization performance as well as to demonstrate the overall ROI for their stakeholders. Evolving industry perspectives and related academic study continue to reveal important contributions in this area – including calls for broader and more comprehensive analysis. Ultimately, there will always be the need for further work here, with the ongoing goal to identify the most sophisticated and revealing measurement model of sponsorship investment, described by Meenaghan (1999) as the 'Holy Grail' of sponsorship management.

CASE STUDY TWO: EYEBALLS, ESPN AND THE 2010 FIFA WORLD CUP

Assessing the accurate value of a sponsorship platform is essential for sport managers to consistently and clearly articulate their property 'measurables', which translates to attaining and maintaining partnership relationships as well as documenting overall sustained organization success. Specifically, measurement for sport properties must include the evaluation of all relevant stakeholders, including consumers (both participants on-site and spectators off-site), as well as an increasing focus on measured media value or 'share of voice' (such as total number of impressions).

An example of this is ESPN's research initiative during the 2010 FIFA World Cup, which is noted as 'the most ambitious effort yet' to scientifically measure consumer consumption around a sole sporting event. Utilizing four research companies and an additional scholarly media research centre, they intend to vigorously examine consumption of the 2010 World Cup through systematic 'cross-platform' (live, time-shifted, out-of-home) measurement. For example, ESPN will link to iPhone technology which will serve as 'media diaries' for 'mobile research panels' participating in the study, which will measure 'changes in the volume and tone' as well as 'electronic word of mouth' related to ESPN World Cup sponsor brands. Other facets of the research initiative include the collection and analysis of ESPN's internet and mobile server data, as well as a component to analyse digital consumption of the event. Eventually, the conglomerate would like to amass a groundbreaking broad-based study to assess a myriad of consumer 'eyeball' indicators, which will have important and significant implications for all sport sponsorship research.

Source: Neff (2010)

SPONSORSHIP RELATIONSHIPS

Conceptions of interactions between sport organizations and corporate sponsors as partnerships emerged in the 1980s as sport organizations sought to establish more enduring ties with key buyers and suppliers (Cousens and Slack, 2005). Cousens and Slack highlight the constellation of factors, including an emerging awareness among sport organizations of the value of corporations and broadcasting companies, and the advantages of enduring relationships. Similarly, sport was increasingly recognized by corporations as a means to achieve their strategic objectives, to develop stronger relationships with consumers, and to enhance their image. Today, the term 'partnerships' is part of our contemporary lexicon when considering collaborative, integrated linkages involving sport organizations and those that would link with them.

Enduring ties between sport organizations and corporations may take an assortment of forms including partnerships, alliances or joint ventures, with each type of relationship varying in its duration, level of integration and value of resource sharing. For example, the partnership that links Manchester United to risk adviser and human capital consultant Aon Corporation highlights the benefits of collaboration. In this linkage, Aon Corporation's logo on the Manchester United jersey exposes this company's brand to over 330 million fans, while the Premier League club will receive an estimated £80 million over four years (MarketingWeek, 2009). According to Philip Clement, Aon Corporation's chief marketing officer, this linkage builds brand recognition globally and fosters growth in emerging insurance markets in regions such as Asia (Marketing Week, 2009). Stronger links such as strategic alliances also enable organizations in the sport industry to realize their strategic objectives.

The Sport Network (TSN), North America's premier sports wire service, extended its global reach through its alliance with Contec Innovations, the mobile media network that provides live news, sports, finance and entertainment. TSN and Contec are jointly developing mobile sports services for mobile operators and media properties in emerging markets in China and Southeast Asia. The alliance was forged to produce real-time mobile value-added services for properties including the English Premier League to the NBA, MLB, NFL and NHL (Entertainment Newsweekly, 2008).

Thus, views of sponsorships as inter-organizational relationships emerged among concomitant discussions in the broader realm of sport management. Described as the relational view of sponsorship, Olkkonen (2001) suggests that exploring the inter-organizational relationships between and among sport organizations holds promise to address the gaps in existing sponsorship literature. Relational views extend our understanding by exploring how relationships between sponsors and those sponsored evolve and are managed, and of the theoretical and managerial implications of these relationships. In this view, sponsorship relationships are seen as embedded within broader webs of interacting organizations. Linkages between firms enable them to reduce uncertainty, to gain access to resources and to gain legitimacy or power (Cousens, Babiak and Bradish, 2006).

Scholars exploring links between sport organizations and sponsors have also looked beyond dyadic (two firms) linkages to explore the contextual factors that may affect these ties. Hence, the network perspective holds promise to situate these dyadic ties within a broader collection of linkages. According to Babiak and Thibault (2008), sport managers would benefit by conceiving of partnerships as a web of alliances rather than several discrete relationships. Similarly, Olkkonen (2001, p. 311) posits that the sponsorship discourse should be 'broadened by adopting theoretical perspectives from the network approach, an approach that clearly demonstrated its ability to generate rich and detailed "thick descriptions" and analysis of inter-organizational relationships'. Scholars Wolfe, Meenaghan and O'Sullivan (1998) also advocate network approaches to exploring links between sponsors, the media and sport organizations given the capacity of this lens to explore change, power and dependence, and evolving relationship patterns among these actors. Drawing attention to the 'sport–media nexus' that recognizes the media's interest in sport programmes which then draws the attention of corporate sponsors, these authors adopt a network approach to exploring the intersecting relationships between sport, broadcasters and corporate sponsors (Wolfe et al., 1998). The resulting network of ties has the potential to influence sport bodies to become more professional in their marketing operations.

Thus, relational views of sponsorship may extend the level of analysis beyond the dyadic tie that links sports and sponsors, to network views that recognize the web of relationships in which these ties are encompassed. Furthermore, relational views call attention to the dynamic interaction between the sponsor and the sponsored wherein linkages are initiated, managed, evaluated and renegotiated on a continual basis (Cousens et al., 2006). Sponsorship-focused interactions between organizations extend beyond one-off exchanges of services for money to include varying strategic objectives, strengths of relationships, contextual factors and internal resources. Capturing the dynamic interaction between sports and sponsors necessitates a view of these linkages as on-going relationships that are influenced by, and influence, other organizations.

275

CAUSE-RELATED SPORT SPONSORSHIP

Nonprofit organizations are also seeking a larger share of the sport sponsorship pie. According to IEG, sponsorship spending on causes totalled $1.55 billion in North America alone in 2009 (IEG, 2009). The increase in sponsorship revenues among nonprofit and charitable organizations is due, at least in part, to what Tracy Goldberg, senior project director of IEG, calls 'hybrid partnerships' (Goldberg, 2009). Hybrid partnerships align philanthropic donations with the donor's marketing, advertising and promotional efforts. According to IEG's 2009 Annual Nonprofit Survey, 93 per cent of all nonprofit organizations use hybrid partnerships to join corporate giving with corporate marketing objectives. Sponsorship among nonprofit organizations may be in the form of title sponsorship of a particular programme, event tickets and hospitality, or the right to promote the partnership on marketing materials.

The growth in sponsorship of nonprofit organizations may be attributed, at least in part, to changing consumer attitudes about the companies they patronize. As a result, firms are using corporate social responsibility and social causes as a marketing tool to enhance their brand (Du et al., 2008). Nonprofit organizations are central to corporate efforts to combine their product brand with sales promotions that link consumer spending with charitable giving. By way of example, companies such as American Express enabled purchasers to donate to specific causes, in this case the Statue of Liberty renovation, when purchasing products or services (Du et al., 2008).

The growth in England's community sports trusts also demonstrates the fit between nonprofit or charitable organizations and commercial organizations (Walters, 2009). According to Walters (2009), nonprofit and charitable organizations offer unique opportunities for corporations to demonstrate their commitment to the community. Walters draws upon the cases of the Charlton Athletic Community Trust and the Brentwood Football Club Community Sports Trust to highlight the unique features available to corporations through sport. These unique features include the popularity and reach of sport, sport's youth appeal, its ability to deliver positive health programmes, group participation, sport's capacity to improve cultural understanding and environmental awareness, and the immediate gratification benefits of sport participation (Smith and Westerbeek, 2007).

Notwithstanding the unique features available through the sponsorship of nonprofit sport organizations, challenges for nonprofits remain. According to Doherty and Murray (2007), a need exists for these organizations to develop more sophisticated sponsorship packages and proposals. Furthermore, these organizations need to differentiate themselves from other sport organizations in the marketplace. In their case study, Doherty and Murray identified challenges for nonprofit organizations seeking to secure sponsorships that included the difficulty of identifying potential sponsors that appropriately complement a sport property, potential partners' lack of knowledge about the benefits of sport sponsorship, and the challenge of catering to the needs of major and minor sponsors simultaneously.

Corporate social responsibility

As noted previously, there is an increasing trend within sponsorship to develop and incorporate partnership programmes with a cause overlay. No more is this evident or more successful than within the sport arena. In fact, over the past ten years, a tremendous number of sports-related giving entities have been successfully established and which serve as beacons of excellence for the entire giving industry. For example, Right to Play (formerly Olympic Aid) originated through the Olympic movement, and serves as an international humanitarian organization with the goal of using sport and play programmes for the development of the world's most disadvantaged communities and children, under the important global banner of 'Sport for Development and Peace'. Other sport-related events and organizations have also successfully incorporated giving into their corporate initiatives, including the National Basketball Association's (NBA) 'NBA Cares' programme, which encourages global outreach for key social issues. Of particular note here is the Fédération Internationale de Football Association (FIFA), which is credited for taking a most definitive lead in sport with regard to a strategic commitment to social development and in being one of the first sport organizations to establish a 'corporate social responsibility' unit within the organization (and which gives a considerable percentage of their revenues to corresponding programmes, including 'Football for Hope'.

The notion of 'giving' in sport is clearly well established, and is based on the philosophy of corporate social responsibility (CSR). CSR has seen a renewed focus and importance in the past 20 years in both social development and corporate initiatives. Historically over 100 years old, this philosophy of action originated as 'corporate philanthropy', with the onset of industrialization (and big business and changing social structures) creating a recognized corporate concern and care for giving back to the local citizenry as a necessary resource. Also interpreted and understood as corporate citizenship, the notion of corporate philanthropy became more strategic and aligned with business interests – much like the principles inherent to successful sport sponsorship partnerships – and is now positioned within a contemporary framework as 'corporate social responsibility'. While a number of definitions and interpretations have been offered here (Carroll, 1979, 1999), CSR is best understood as 'the responsibility of organizations to be ethical and accountable to the needs of their society as well as their stakeholders' (Bradish and Cronin, 2009) and, as such, strategically aligns both social and economic mandates (Varadarajan and Menon, 1988). The principles of CSR can be articulated in a number of different initiatives, including cause-related marketing and cause-related sport sponsorship.

Cause-related marketing within the sport sponsorship context is typically understood as a marketing partnership which brings a 'for-profit' and 'not-for-profit' organization together for mutual benefit, often incorporating fundraising objectives (such as a percentage of sales from an identified product to a charitable effort). Cause-related marketing is the most examined area of CSR within the sport management academy, with regard to both consumer and organization concerns, and has offered important findings and contributions in this area. Of importance here, Lachowetz and Gladden (2003) established that cause-related sponsorship can enhance company image, differentiate a firm or brand from its competitors, induce more favourable attitudes among consumers, and increase positive publicity about a firm.

There are three main ways in which sport organizations can become involved in cause-related sponsorship. The first is through a direct involvement in which the sport organization affiliates with a 'good cause' to achieve particular objectives, such as an enhancement of public image or reputation, such as Manchester United's agreement to raise over £1 million for UNICEF to end child exploitation (Perry, 2001). The second (and more important in the context of sport sponsorship) use of sport is when a sponsor supports a particular event that raises money for a charity. The Professional Golf Association tour in the USA mandates that each one of their events must have a charity as a beneficiary. Thus, the FedEx St. Jude Golf Classic in Memphis provides not only increased awareness for Memphis-based FedEx and a substantial donation for St. Jude Children's Research Hospital located in downtown Memphis, it also allows FedEx to benefit from an affiliation with St. Jude's nationally, internationally and perhaps most importantly in Memphis itself (Lachowetz and Irwin, 2002). The London City Marathon is also an excellent example of this practice (see case study to follow). The third area of cause-related sponsorship involves direct support of a sport organization or event that is seen in and of itself as a good cause. For example, Avon has long been regarded as supporting several health programmes through the creation of a series of road races for women, the Avon Running Circuit, while at the same time aligning themselves with the principles of CSR and establishing their company as a true corporate citizen.

CASE STUDY THREE: RUNNING WITH THE LONDON CITY MARATHON

While there are a number of important and impressive sport-related charities, events and fundraising initiatives in operation today, the London City Marathon is well regarded as the world's premier philanthropic sporting event, and in fact holds the title of 'Raising the Most Money for Charity in Sport' by the Guinness Company of World Records (Guinness, 2003) as well as noted as being the 'Largest Single Annual Fundraising Event in the World' (Guinness, 2007, 2008). Started by two British track athletes, John Disley and Chris Brasher, the race was first run in London in 1981 with the intent to create a road marathon to bring together racers from across the world to generate a spirit of friendship, and is now one of the major marathons on the world circuit. As part of this, a spirit of giving has been engrained in the race, with more than 500 million pounds being raised for more than 750 national and international charities, including Well Child, Help the Hospice, Spinal Cord Research, Breast Cancer Care, Water Aid and Multiple Sclerosis Society.

Attracting more than 35,000 runners annually, participants are encouraged and supported to tie their participation to good causes and charities each year through individual and private fundraising and sponsorship initiatives (featuring a process that has increasingly become more sophisticated and formalized, and now includes electronic giving websites, such as Justgiving.com). As of 2010, the 30th anniversary of the race, more than three-quarters of the participants competed for a specific charity; over 15,000 entries were reserved for charitable organizations to further assist their organizational fundraising by providing guaranteed 'pledge' spaces to athletes who had not previously qualified for the race. In addition, each year the race also now selects an official charity of choice. Finally, London Marathon Limited also represents its own trust – the London Marathon Charitable Trust – which has distributed funds to assist in supporting and developing more than 700 community sport facilities and recreational projects around London. Clearly, this event is a stellar example of the importance of partnerships, giving and 'good works' in sport.

Sources: Camara Ropeta (2010); Hill (2010); Virgin London Marathon (2010)

AMBUSH MARKETING, BRAND PROTECTION AND SPORT SPONSORSHIP

At its core, the value of a sport property to a corporate sponsor rests in the exclusive benefits a sponsor receives through its association with an affiliated athlete, team or event. Efforts by competitor organizations to circumvent traditional avenues to be associated with sport properties have been attributed to increasing sponsorship rights fees and accompanying activation costs, as well as due to the unique and strict 'exclusivity' clauses for official corporate partners. As a result, a number of factors – including intense external pressures from partners, increasing internal awareness from the sport property to protect these valuable partnerships, and even firm directives from other related sport stakeholders and rights holders – have resulted in a clear and present focus on ambush marketing and brand protection within the sponsorship arena.

Ambush marketing (also referred to as guerrilla marketing) is used to describe an attempt by a competing company to associate its brand with a sponsorship activity without securing the formal rights or paying the official sponsorship fee to due so. As such, ambush marketing serves as a serious threat to the sponsorship of the sport property, as the questionable practices and marketing activities associated often results in the weakened impact of an official partner's platform (most often through confusing consumers by creating clutter in the marketplace) and causes extreme stress on the strength of the sport property which must also earnestly protect and police these occurrences through their sponsorship and marketing units (while at the same time strategically addressing the impact of these concerns on the overall image of the sport property). In addition, as it would reason, it is important to note that sport's most elite and top tier properties (such as the Olympic Games, the FIFA World Cup and the NFL Super Bowl) are the most susceptible to ambush marketing.

Brand protection

As a result of the intense pressure to protect the value and integrity of the sponsorship programme, sport properties have turned to proactively incorporating sophisticated 'brand protection' strategies and programmes by enforcing the legal rights of their sponsorship agreements. As interpreted by the Vancouver 2010 Organizing Committee (VANOC) as 'commercial rights management', this function and responsibility has become increasingly paramount to the sound operation of a leading sport sponsorship programme. In fact, VANOC is credited for piloting a very successful 'brand protection' strategy and procedure during the 2010 Games which was most aggressive and forward thinking in its strategy, evaluating concerns by content and relevance, and effectively addressing a number of varying ambush concerns during the Games (see Lululemon case study below).

The sponsorship industry is also aggressively examining this concern, with a leading marketing (Farrell, 2010) initiative, 'Doing Away With Foul Play in Sports Marketing', tasked to study brand, licensing and trademark infringements surrounding the world's largest sporting events, including ambush marketing (as well as ticket, merchandise and online violations). Of concern here is that the efforts of these illegal infractors to the world's largest sport properties have become a big and damaging business. For example, it is estimated that the value of the world's ten largest sport brands (FIFA World Cup, Olympic Games, NFL Super Bowl) ranges from $67 million to $420 million dollars (Schwartz, 2010). By means of contrast, the competing 'brand violation' market sector (including ambush marketing-related activities) is expected to record approximately $141 billion in revenues by 2012 (Farrell, 2010). Therefore, there is ample evidence that sport properties are prime targets for ambush marketing and related brand violations – especially those sport events and organizations with a global reach and international franchise presence, where sponsorship rights and legal systems are more difficult to interpret, control and enforce. Additionally, just as sport is perceived as an excellent vehicle to reach key consumers, competitors unfortunately also see sport properties as prime outlets for ambush marketing activities to also capture those important demographics, ultimately greatly affecting the objectives of corporations to be an exclusive partner with a sport property. In short, this area of sponsorship must be of utmost concern for sponsorship management.

CASE STUDY FOUR: AMBUSH MARKETING AND THE VANCOUVER 2010 GAMES – 'A COOL SPORTING EVENT THAT TAKES PLACE IN BRITISH COLUMBIA BETWEEN 2009 AND 2011'

Broadly consumed with worldwide attention, the Olympic Games often provides the most interesting cases regarding sponsorship. Here, we will discuss current brand management, licensing infractions and trademark concerns, and will highlight the importance of strategic 'commercial rights management'. One such 'ambush' marketing case that demonstrates the need for enhanced brand protection is that regarding the Canadian clothing company Lululemon Athletica, which launched a clever Olympic-themed promotion in January 2010 to coincide with the Vancouver Olympics, ultimately in the hope of capitalizing on the commercial success associated with the Games. This was significant as it received considerable attention for being regarded by the Vancouver 2010 Organizing Committee (VANOC) as practising acts akin to 'ambush marketing', effectively introducing the marketing concern and VANOC process to the public.

Specifically, Lululemon promoted a line of clothing closely linked to the registered 'Vancouver 2010' brand marks, entitled 'Cool sporting event that takes place in British Columbia between 2009 and 2011' (see Figure 15.3). While this collection was very successful in the marketplace, it was perceived by VANOC as a violation of the Vancouver 2010 brand and sponsors, specifically those in the same product category. Ultimately, it was determined that the apparel company's actions fell within a legal boundary for non-sponsors, but it was an important case in testing and revealing VANOC's brand protection model.

Source: Shaw (2010)

Figure 15.3 *Lululemon Athletica*

SUMMARY

Our intent with this chapter has been to introduce a number of sport sponsorship topics with which managers of modern organizations must be aware. The landscape within which sport sponsorship thrives has changed dramatically over the past two decades, as changing marketplace conditions, consumer demographics and corporate objectives have all contributed to increased opportunities and challenges for those involved with sport sponsorship. Accordingly, this chapter presents an overview of the key considerations and concerns for contemporary sport sponsorship, including an overview of current measurement and evaluation tools, as well as a discussion of the importance of understanding and incorporating a cause-related marketing overlay in the sponsorship portfolio. We have also presented considerable evidence of how the sport sponsorship industry is embracing the increasing challenges and complexity of sport sponsorship, encouraging further growth and development in this important marketing strategy for sport.

Similarly, we suggest that sport sponsorship will continue to be an important research area of study in the sport management discourse, with a number of interesting research questions emerging. First, there is a need to explore sponsorship in the context of corporate citizenship. Consumers' patronage of companies that demonstrate corporate social responsibility and act as good corporate citizens has shifted the landscape of sponsorship away from sport. Second, we suggest a need for more work that uses relational perspectives to understand interactions between sport organizations and corporate partners. In keeping with the work of Olkkonen (2001), exploring sponsorship using the network level of analysis offers insight into the web of corporations that influence, and are influenced by, sponsorship relationships. Adopting a network lens through which to view sponsorship would offer insight into the broader set of interactions among interdependent firms that share information, financial resources and social capital. Third, we encourage further work into the complex needs of the sponsorship measurement and evaluation tools given the increasingly complex organizations and dynamics involved.

To conclude, we hope that this chapter has provided a sound theoretical underpinning regarding the important frameworks related to sport sponsorship, as well as offering a clear understanding of the opportunities and challenges of the sport sponsorship industry. Sport management students and practitioners should embrace this dynamic marketing function, as should sport-related organizations. As such, we are confident that the future of sport sponsorship in both study and practice will continue to be a vibrant and important component of the sport industry.

REVIEW QUESTIONS

1   Discuss the concept of sport sponsorship, and the value of strategic sport partnerships.
2   What are some of the leading and emerging trends with regard to sport sponsorship?
3   Why is research and evaluation key to successful sport sponsorships?
4   Consider the importance of sponsorship linkages, and discuss some leading sport partnerships, alliances and/or networks.

5   Why is it important for sponsorship managers and rights holders to incorporate a cause overlay into their sponsorship platform?
6   How has the increased need for a brand protection strategy changed the landscape of sponsorship management?

FURTHER READING

Lagae, W. (2005) *Sport Sponsorship and Marketing Communications: A European Perspective.* Essex, England: Pearson Education.
Ferrand, A., Torrigiani, L. and Camps I Povill, A. (2006) *Routledge Handbook of Sport Sponsorship.* Abingdon, Oxon: Routledge.

WEBSITES

http://www.imrpublications.com/imr/journal-landing.aspx?volno=L&no=L&page=About
http://www.olympic.org/sponsorship
http://www.performanceresearch.com
http://www.sponsorship.com
http://www.sportsbrandprotect.org/board.php
http://www.virginlondonmarathon.com

REFERENCES

Aaker, D. and Myers, J. (1987) *Advertising Management* (3rd ed.). Englewood Cliffs, NJ: Prentice Hall.
Al Bawaba (2010, 13 January) Flash Entertainment purchases minority interest in Ultimate Fighting Championship. Al Bawaba. http://proquest.umi.com.proxy.library.brocku.ca/pqdweb?did=1938112181&sid=1&Fmt=3&clientId=17280&RQT=309&VName=PQD
Angus Reid Public Opinion (2009, June) *Consumer Awareness of Sponsorship.* Vancouver, BC: Angus Reid Public Opinion.
Asian Business Newsweekly (2008, 3 March) Anheuser-Busch: Bud Light enters the Octagon as exclusive beer sponsors of the Ultimate Fighting Championship. *Asian Business Newsweekly,* 323.
Babiak, K. and Thibault, L. (2008) Challenges of multiple cross-sector partnerships. *Non-Profit and Voluntary Sector Quarterly, 8*(1), 117–143.
Babiak, K. and Wolfe, R. (2006). More than just a game? Corporate social responsibility and Super Bowl XL. *Sport Marketing Quarterly, 15*(4), 214–224.
Bradish, C. and Cronin, J.J. (2009) Corporate social responsibility in sport: An introduction to the Special Issue. *Journal of Sport Management, 23*(6), 691–697.
Brooks, C. (1990, December) Sponsorship by design. *Athletic Business,* 59–62.
Brunt, S. (2010, 9 January) Sport consumption will undergo revolution in the decade ahead. *The Globe & Mail,* S1, S9.
Burton, R., Quester, P. G. and Farrelly, F. J. (1998) Organizational power games. *Marketing Management, 7*(1), 27–36.

Camara Ropeta, P. (2010, 27 April) London Marathon celebrates 30th anniversary. *ABS–CBN News*, 4.

Carroll, A. (1979) A three dimensional conceptual model of corporate social performance. *Academy of Management Review*, 4(4), 497–505.

Carroll, A. (1999) Corporate social responsibility: Evolution of a definitional construct. *Business and Society*, 38(3), 268–295.

Clancy, K. and Krieg, P. (2006, May/June) Go beyond faith when making decision about sponsorships and events. *Marketing Management*, n.p.

Cornwell, T. B., Weeks, C. S. and Roy, D. P. (2005) Sponsorship-linked marketing: Opening the black box. *Journal of Advertising*, 34(2), 21–42.

Cousens, L. and Slack, T. (2005) Field-level change: The case of North American major league professional sport. *Journal of Sport Management*, 19, 13–42.

Cousens, L., Babiak, K. and Bradish, B. (2006) Beyond sponsorship: Re-framing business-to-business relationships in the context of sport. Special Issue of the *International Journal of Sport Marketing and Sponsorship* or *Sport Marketing Quarterly*, 9(1), 1–23.

Day, C. (2006, January) Five emerging sports. *Promotions & Incentives*, S18.

Doherty, A. and Murray, M. (2007) The strategic sponsorship process in a non-profit sport organization. *Sport Marketing Quarterly*, 16, 49–59.

Drumwright, M. (1996) Company advertising with a social dimension: The role of noneconomic criteria. *Journal of Marketing*, 60, 71–87.

Du, L., Hou, J. and Huang, Y. (2008). Mechanisms of power and action for cause related marketing: Perspectives of enterprise and non-profit organizations. *Baltic Journal of Management*, 3(1), 92–104.

Entertainment Newsweekly (2008, 11 August) The Sports Network extends global reach in alliance with Contec Innovations. *Entertainment Newsweekly*, 18.

Farrell, M. (2010, 13 April) *Brand and Trademark Infringement in Global Sports Draw Red Card from CMO Council*. Palo Alto, CA: CMO Council.

Giannoulakis, C., Stotlar, D. and Chatziefstathiou, D. (2008, July) Olympic sponsorship: Evolution, challenges and impact on the Olympic Movement. *International Journal of Sports Marketing and Sponsorship*, 9(4), 256–270.

Godfrey, P. C. (2009) Corporate social responsibility in sport: An overview and key issues. *Journal of Sport Management*, 23(6), 698.

Goldberg, S. (2009) Beyond corporate donations: Putting the 'strategy' into strategic philanthropy. Presentation to the 47th Association of Fundraising Professionals International Conference on Fundraising. 13 April.

Guiness Book of Records (2003). London: Guiness World Records Ltd.

Guiness Book of Records (2007). London: Guiness World Records Ltd.

Guiness Book of Records (2008). London: Guiness World Records Ltd.

Hein, K. (2002, 16 December) Snapple forms marketing unit to build brand. *Brandweek*, 43(46), 6.

Hill, A. (2010, 18 April) Sponsorship: An etiquette minefield. *The Guardian*, 22.

Howard, D. and Burton, R. (2002) Sports marketing in a recession: It's a brand new game. *International Journal of Sport Marketing and Sponsorship*, March/April, 23–40.

IEG (2009, 27 March) Sponsorship spending on causes to total $1.55 billion this year. *IEG Sponsorship Report*, 1.

IEG (2010) Worldwide sponsorship spending. http://www.wpp.com/wpp/press/press/default.htm?Guid=%7B43DC6EF8-73C5-4B5A-82BE-64A59EE25AA8%7D

International Olympic Committee (IOC) (2009) *Olympic Marketing Fact File*. Lausanne, Switzerland: IOC.

Lachowetz, T. and Gladden, J. (2003) A framework for understanding cause-related sport marketing programs. *International Journal of Sports Marketing and Sponsorship*, 4(4), 313–333.

Lachowetz, T. and Irwin, R. (2002) FedEx and the St. Jude Classic: An application of a cause-related marketing program (CRMP). *Sport Marketing Quarterly*, *11*(2), 114–118.

Lehman, P. (2010) The wild world of emerging sports. *Newsweek*. http://images.businessweek.com/ss/07/08/0823_emerging_sports/index_01.htm

MarketingWeek (2001, 22 November) Coca-Cola muscles in on the sports sector. *MarketingWeek*. http://www.marketingweek.co.uk/previous-issues/22-november-2001/3094.issue

MarketingWeek (2009, 18 June) Sponsorship: Marketers split over Aon's Man United deal. *MarketingWeek*, 9.

McAuley, J. and Gladden, J. (2002) An interview with Alycen McAuley, Director of Corporate Sponsorships, Charles Schwab. *International Journal of Sport Marketing and Sponsorship*, June/July, 99–108.

Meenaghan, J. A. (1991) The role of sponsorship in the marketing communications mix. *International Journal of Advertising*, *10*, 35–47.

Meenaghan, J. A. (1999) Commercial sponsorship – The development of understanding. *International Journal of Sport Marketing and Sponsorship*, *1*(1), 19–31.

Neff, J. (2010, 22 March) ESPN plans massive cross-platform research on World Cup. *Advertising Age*, 2.

Olkkonen, R. (2001) Case study: The network approach to international sponsorship arrangement. *Journal of Business and Industrial Marketing*, *16*(4), 309–329.

Perry, B. (2001) Playing fair? Vision, values and ethics: A study of the co-existence of big business and football. In P. Murphy (ed.) *Singer and Friedlander Review 2000–2001 Season*. London: Singer and Friedlander.

Pope, N. K. and Voges, K. E. (1994) Sponsorship evaluation: Does it match the motive and the mechanism? *Sport Marketing Quarterly*, *3*(4), 37–45.

Schwartz, P. J. (2010, 3 February) The world's top sports brands. *Fortune*, 10.

Shaw, H. (2010, 6 February) Olympic ambush: Interlopers sideswipe makers of sanctioned Games apparel. *Financial Post*, B1.

Sheth, H. and Babiak, K. M. (2010) Beyond the game: Perceptions and practices of corporate social responsibility in the professional sport industry. *Journal of Business Ethics*, *91*, 433–450.

Slack, T. and Amis, J. (2001) Sport sponsorship. In D. Pickton and A. Broderick (eds) *Integrated Marketing Communications*. London: Financial Times/Prentice Hall.

Smith, A. and Westerbeek, H. (2007) Sport as a vehicle for deploying corporate social responsibility. *Journal of Corporate Citizenship*, *25*, 43–54.

Varadarajan, P.R. and Menon, A. (1988) Cause-related marketing: A coalignment of marketing strategy and corporate philanthropy. *Journal of Marketing*, *52*(3), 58–74.

Virgin London Marathon (2010, April) *History of the London Marathon*. London, England: Virgin London Marathon.

Walters, G. (2009) Corporate social responsibility through sport: The community sport trust model as a CSR delivery model. *Journal of Corporate Citizenship*, *35*, 81–94.

Witcher, B., Craigen, J. G., Culligan, D. and Harvey, A. (1991) The link between objectives and function in organizational sponsorship. *International Journal of Advertising*, *10*, 13–33.

Wolfe, R., Meenaghan, T. and O'Sullivan, P. (1998) Sport, media and sponsor – Shifting balance of power in the sports network. *Irish Marketing Review*, *10*(2), 53–66.

Chapter 16

Sport and the law

Considerations for sport managers

Steve Greenfield and Guy Osborn, University of Westminster

TOPICS

Introduction • Governing sport • Managing participation • Managing spectators • The commercial dimension

---

OBJECTIVES

At the end of this chapter you should be able to:

■ Understand the increasing role that law plays within sport;

■ Appreciate the effects of both civil and criminal law;

■ Appreciate the role of sports governing bodies in regulating sport;

■ Evaluate the distinction and impact between different levels of juridification.

KEY TERMS

Civil law – the body of laws of a nation regulating everyday private matters, as distinct from laws regulating criminal, political or military matters.

Criminal law – the body of law dealing with the constitution of offences and the punishment of offenders, which typically carries with it custodial sentencing.

Events management – is the application of established management techniques, including project management, to the creation and development of carnivals, events and conferences.

Law – the principles, procedures and regulations established in a state by a given authority and applicable to its subjects, whether in the form of legislation or of custom and policies recognized and enforced by judicial decision.

> **Legislation** – the act of making or enacting laws which is usually undertaken by democratically elected parliamentarians, albeit not exclusively so.

OVERVIEW

Sport is subject to a variety of regulatory forms. At the most basic level, competitors are bound by the rules of the sport at which they compete, whether amateur or professional, and tellingly these are often termed 'Laws of the Game'. Beyond that there may be a swathe of administrative regulations that detail who is entitled to play and on what terms. In some sports such as boxing and horse racing, competitors will have to be licensed, whilst in others, even at the amateur and junior level, players will need to be registered with a team, club and/or league in order to be eligible to play. There are also international bodies such as the World Anti-Doping Agency (WADA) that have introduced requirements for drug testing that binds competitors. There is also a specific court for sport-based disputes: the Court of Arbitration for Sport (CAS; see http://www.tas-cas.org).

In contemporary society, law has an ever-increasing role, and this can be easily identified as a trend within sport (Foster and Osborn, 2010). It is not just the more traditional areas, such as contract, where the law's influence can be seen, but across a broader spectrum encompassing aspects of both the civil and criminal law. European law has also been influential through cases such as *Bosman*. The increasingly developed and sophisticated legal and quasi-legal structure for the arbitration of sporting disputes begs the question whether the apparatus has emerged to deal with existing disputes because the previous structure was inadequate or whether new disputes have emerged because of the construction of new methods of hearing claims. One obvious development has been disputes over commercial aspects such as intellectual property rights, sponsorship, broadcasting rights and even the transfer of ownership of clubs. These represent attempts to exploit or protect valuable commercial interests. One of the most controversial of these has been attempts by international bodies such as the IOC and FIFA to restrict ambush marketing in order to protect the interests of official sponsors.

In addition to clear disputes, the ways in which the law impacts upon sport is often more subtle and less obvious. For example, some of the ways in which sports are organized and administered have clearly been affected by the law and the potential of legal intervention. The conduct of the Harlequins case, noted below, indicates quasi-legal processes and the influence of human rights considerations such as the right to a 'fair hearing'. Management in the context of sport covers a wide range of areas from personal management through the administration of commercial rights and events to the governance of sport itself. Law impacts upon all of these areas and may inform and affect practices. Interestingly, though, there are examples of practices remaining largely unaffected by legal decisions. The post-boxing litigation paperwork demonstrates a continuation of existing management agreements with little alteration, despite the fact that the court determined the standard form contract to be unenforceable on the grounds of restraint of trade (Greenfield and Osborn, 1995).

Management must encompass not just knowledge of the potential for legal intervention but also the range and application of cultural and social factors that overlap and interact with law. In an increasingly risk-averse society, law is sought as a means to provide a remedy. So for sports managers it is important to have an understanding of not only the possible overt legal implications of everyday sporting practice, but also of the more subtle ramifications of law. So in the context of sport the law is not just about injuries and contract disputes; the relationship is far more complicated and sophisticated, and managers require an understanding of the nature of the relationship as well as the more obvious outcomes. This chapter is designed to not only provide examples of where the law has been used but also to indicate elements of the complicated relationship between sport and law.

CASE STUDY: THE FAKE 'BLOOD INJURY': HARLEQUINS V. LEINSTER

During a Heineken Cup Quarter Final on 12 April 2009 between Leinster and Harlequins, winger Tom Williams left the field with a few minutes remaining with an apparently cut mouth. This allowed the fly half, Nick Evans, who had previously been substituted because of a thigh injury, to return to the field. The game was tight at 6–5 to Leinster and Evans missed a drop goal attempt with only two minutes remaining that would have put Harlequins in a winning position. Speculation quickly arose as to the authenticity of the 'injury' and European Rugby Cup officials announced an inquiry.

An independent Disciplinary Committee sat and heard evidence; the initial outcome was that Williams was found guilty of having faked his injury using a blood capsule and suspended for 12 months and the club fined €250,000, of which 50 per cent was suspended. However, charges against the Director of Rugby (Dean Richards), the Club Doctor (Wendy Chapman) and the physiotherapist (Steph Brennan) were dismissed. This seemed somewhat perverse. It suggested that the incident was instigated by Williams himself, without any direction from either the coaching or medical staff. There was also the unresolved question concerning the extent to which those responsible for the management and administration of the club itself were aware of the events.

The Disciplinary Officer of the European Rugby Cup, Roger O'Connor, instituted an appeal against the decision of the Disciplinary Committee for not upholding the misconduct claims against Richards, Brennan and Chapman and the sanction imposed on the club given that it was fined but not banned from the competition. Williams also appealed against the ban on the grounds that it was severe given the punishment handed out to players found guilty of serious offences such as gouging, and provided new evidence which ultimately led to the findings against Richards and Brennan who had admitted purchasing the fake blood capsules from a joke shop. At the appeal hearing Williams' ban was reduced to four months, taking account of the important evidence he had provided which led to the decisions against the others. The Appeal Committee noted that had he not provided new evidence the truth would not have been uncovered. Consequently Richards was banned for three years and Steph Brennan for two years. The sanction against the club was also increased to a fine of €300,000, none of which was suspended.

The case raises a number of interesting issues around the administration and organization of competitions and the disciplinary sanctions that may be imposed by governing bodies. A large part of the appeal hearing was occupied with the question of whether the Disciplinary Committee had jurisdiction to consider the Appeal. It also demonstrates that sanctions can be severe and the type of processes that are used. For example, at the original hearing, Williams didn't have independent legal advice but was represented by the club's lawyers and later sought advice from the Professional Rugby Players' Association. In terms of regulation this case demonstrates that internal processes are just as important for sport as the wider role of the law.

This one relatively small incident (a seemingly innocuous blood substitution) produced severe consequences for a number of individuals beyond Williams which seriously affected their careers. The club doctor Wendy Chapman faced a misconduct hearing at the General Medical Council in August 2010 whilst Steph Brennan was the subject of disciplinary hearing by the Health Professions Council. Chapman admitted cutting Williams' lip in the aftermath of him leaving the field. She was given a warning as her actions were not considered in her patient's best interest but she was not struck off. Brennan, however, having admitted to using fake blood capsules four occasions previously, was struck off as his misconduct had 'impaired his fitness to practise'.

INTRODUCTION

The area of sport and law is a fast-developing one, although its exact definition and parameters are less easy to gauge with any certainty (James, 2010). What can be established is that the law is increasingly involved within some areas of sport particularly at the professional level. Foster (2003) identified two groups of sport law sources. First, domestic and global sports law created by sporting governing bodies and federations through sport-specific tribunals and adjudicative mechanisms, such as the Court of Arbitration for Sport (CAS). Second, instances of sports law that indicate the increasing application of both national and international law upon the sporting field. The sport-specific bodies have become more 'legal' in their approaches, something that has been analysed previously under the umbrella of the 'juridification of sport' (Foster, 2006; Greenfield and Osborn, 2010). This chapter deals with a number of these manifestations of the increasing incursion of law into sport. It focuses particularly upon the governance of sport and consequent liability for, and control of, a) participants, and b) spectators. In addition, it touches upon issues relating to commercial activities that are becoming more prominent and are also of concern for sport managers.

GOVERNING SPORT

The daily organization, administration and control of sport are carried out by the authorized governing body. Administration will often be carried out at a local level, but there may be links to both a national and international organization. Football, for example, is a pyramid with the Football Association at the top. The FA splits its responsibilities into two parts – governance and development – and has ultimate responsibility for all aspects of the game of football, whether the national team, the highly paid professional version or the Sunday morning amateur alternative that takes place across the country. Authority is delegated downwards and football is organized geographically through County Associations who are affiliated to the national Football Association and represented on its Governing Council. For example, the Hertfordshire Football Association was formed in 1885 and has over 2,500 clubs affiliated. Beyond the national level there are also six Confederations (Asia; Africa; North, Central America and Caribbean; South America; Oceania; and Europe) that govern competitions at a regional level. UEFA, the largest of the Confederations, has 53 members and represents a broader organization than solely the European Union. UEFA organizes competitions between clubs from different countries within its jurisdiction such as the Champions League and the European Championship, which is open to countries that are members. UEFA in turn is affiliated to FIFA, which is the controlling body of world football. Football is however more complicated as authority may be devolved to run specific competitions such as the Premier League and the Football League. In smaller sports, national authority may be exerted more easily with fewer tiers of governance.

Different levels of governance and control can create tensions and this has emerged in the 'club versus country' conflict. Availability of players for the national representative team has caused problems in football, rugby union and cricket when the employers, in this instance club or county, are reluctant to release players as the interests seem to conflict. In football this has expressed itself over 'injured' players not being released for national duty. In rugby union there has been concern expressed at a national level about players moving abroad, notably to France, for economic reasons to play club rugby. What these examples do indicate is that at the highest elite level financial issues are impacting on national representation. The response of governing bodies such as FIFA has been to protect national sides through regulations requiring participation. One solution that has been adopted in cricket with some success is to issue central contracts that give the management of the national team a much greater degree of control over player selection by altering the contractual nexus. Interestingly in 2009 Andrew Flintoff opted out of Test Cricket and his central contract left him with greater flexibility to exploit his marketability in the international Twenty20 arena.

Governing bodies themselves may be subject to a review of their procedures particularly if they control admission into the field. However, judicial review has generally not been applied to such actions largely on the basis that the relationship between a governing body is a private one, and largely contractual in nature, and therefore the rights that accrue for an aggrieved party will largely be based on this and judicial review is not appropriate (Anderson, 2006). However, the anti-discrimination legislation has been applied notably by Jane Couch to rectify the failure of the British Boxing Board of Control to permit the licensing of women boxers (*Couch* v. *British Boxing Board of Control*, unreported, EAT, 31 March 1998).

MANAGING PARTICIPATION

In physical contact sports, actions that go beyond the rules of the game could involve a breach of the statutory criminal law relating to offences against the person. These are contained within the Offences Against the Person Act 1861. This carries with it the threat of prosecution as well as potentially a civil action for damages for any injuries caused. Such sports occupy an uneasy relationship with the criminal law as it appears that in some cases the touchline offers some type of immunity from the criminal law. Actions that in a different environment would be the subject to criminal action are left to the sports themselves to police. The most obvious example is boxing, which occupies an anomalous position given that the House of Lords has determined, in a case concerning sado-masochistic sex but with a high degree of relevance for contact sports, that it is not legally possible to consent to actual bodily harm. Lord Mustill in *R* v. *Brown* noted:

> The boxers display skill, strength and courage, but nobody pretends that they do well to
> themselves or others. The onlookers derive entertainment, but none of the physical and

moral benefits which have been seen as the fruits of engagement in manly sports. I intend no disrespect to the valuable judgment of McInerney J in Pallante v Stadiums Pty Ltd (No 1) [1976] VR 331 when I say that the heroic efforts of that learned judge to arrive at an intellectually satisfying account of the apparent immunity of professional boxing from criminal process have convinced me that the task is impossible. It is in my judgment best to regard this as another special situation which for the time being stands outside the ordinary law of violence because society chooses to tolerate it.

R v. Brown [1993] 2 WLR 556, at 592

This judgement creates more questions than it answers as it identifies boxing as a 'special situation' with its relationship to the criminal law and defers any final question as to lawfulness to Parliament. However, there is an increasing range of other sports and activities such as the martial arts disciplines that require the infliction of force and Mustill's dictum doesn't address their legality. Historically the line was drawn between prize fighting (essentially the contemporary bare knuckle variety of boxing) and sparring (which might be seen as exhibitions of pugilistic skill) and a number of cases attempted to establish where the distinction should lie (see for example R v. Orton (1878) 14 Cox CC 226). The problem of violent play extends beyond boxing to any physical contact sport where tackles or contact that amounts to a physical assault takes place. It is assumed that players consent to all contact that is within the rules of the game but deliberate foul play goes beyond the rules and consequently beyond consent. Consequently there have been a number of examples of criminal prosecutions for on-field assaults, many of which have centred upon rugby; see for example the case of R v. Billinghurst [1978] Crim LR 533. The accused was charged under s20 of the Offences against the Person Act 1861 with inflicting grievous bodily harm after breaking an opponent's jaw in an off-the-ball incident. Outside of the criminal law, the internal mechanisms of sport might be thought to be a possible way of dealing with on-field violence. Indeed, in R v. Barnes [2005] 2 All ER 113 it was suggested that, where adequate internal provisions exist, recourse should not be sought to the criminal law:

> Post-Barnes and Blissett, it is extremely unlikely that any injury caused by a challenge even remotely connected with the playing of the game will be considered to be a criminal assault. Only where the injuries were caused by a fight or were in some other way 'off the ball' or 'behind the play' might prosecution be appropriate; in all other cases the Court of Appeal considered that these were matters best dealt with by the sport's governing body.
>
> James (2010, 117)

This raises questions about the extent of the role of law in sport and adds to the academic debate about the separation between the wider law and the internal laws of sport. What is clear is that physical harm inflicted outside of the laws of the game will amount to a breach of the criminal law; however, much will depend upon the willingness of the 'victim' to make a complaint and there are cultural norms that mitigate against this. Even highly publicized examples such as Welsh prop forward Graham Price leaving the field holding his jaw broken by a punch from his opposite number did not incur any prosecution. Similarly Roy Keane admitted in his autobiography to setting out to injure Alfie Haaland in revenge for a previous incident and faced internal discipline only (Keane and Dunphy, 2002). The difficulty in involving the law would be the sheer number of cases that could be generated if a strict approach was taken and the overall effect on sports such as rugby and football.

In addition to the criminal law, the civil law can have an important impact upon sport, more specifically liability in negligence. In terms of injuries to other players, the question is the extent of not only participant liability but also the vicarious liability of any employer (a club, for example) and possibly even liability of the relevant governing body. Vicarious liability is an attractive option if the person committing the injury does not have the means to settle a claim. To succeed in a claim for negligence the claimant must demonstrate that the defendant owes a duty of care, has breached it and caused harm. A number of issues have to be considered when applying these general principles to sport. These include a need to consider whether the rules of the game have been broken, showing again the tension that exists between the internal regulation of sport and the wider legal regulatory framework. In addition, the 'working culture' of the sport in question will need to be considered, along with a number of broader considerations centring upon the context within which the incident occurred. These might include the relative experience and skill of the players, whether it took place off the ball, etc. Each case will need to be treated on its own merits, taking into account not only the legal precedents but also the context of the particular situation and status of the participants. The distinction between amateur and professional players was considered in *Caldwell* v. *Maguire and Fitzgerald* [2001] EWCA Civ 1054. Two professional jockeys cut inside during the final straight of a race leading to a third rider tripping up a fourth rider, who suffered a serious injury and brought an action against the first and second riders. The Court of Appeal held that, first, following *Condon* v. *Basi* [1985] 1 WLR 866, a duty of care was owed by each contestant in a sporting contest to each, and all other, contestants. Second, that the extent of that duty is to do all that is *objectively reasonable in the prevailing circumstances* to prevent and avoid injury. The issue of prevailing circumstances was key here, and the Court detailed a number of issues that needed to be taken into account, including the objective of the sport being played, any inherent risks or dangers and the skills to be reasonably expected of a contestant. In this case the claim failed as it was held that the interference that led to the injury was a commonly occurring part of the sport, and an inherent risk that was part of the sport.

Aside from the direct participants, there are others that might potentially be liable for injuries to players. This could include referees (*Smoldon* v. *Whitworth & Nolan* [1997] ELR 249), coaches (*Van Oppen* v. *Bedford Charity Trustees* [1990] 1 WLR 235) and arguably even the groundsman (see Greenfield and Osborn, 1997), but also the governing bodies themselves. In *Vowles* v. *Evans & Welsh Rugby Union* [2003] EWCA Civ 318 a flanker was seriously injured whilst playing in an amateur 2nd XV local derby. One of the props was taken from the field after dislocating his shoulder and the referee offered the option of non-contested scrums. As this would have led to no league points being given for the game, Vowles played as a prop. He claimed that the referee was liable for his injury and, in addition, the Welsh Rugby Union was vicariously liable. Here the Court found that the referee was liable as he had not done all that was necessary in the circumstances (see the *Caldwell* considerations above) to minimize the dangers of what is a dangerous sport; in particular he had failed to apply law 3(12).

The issue of governing body liability came to the fore in *Watson* v. *British Boxing Board of Control* [2001] QB 1134 which concerned the fight between Chris Eubank and Michael Watson. The contest was stopped in the 12th round and Watson was observed, by his trainer, slipping into unconsciousness. However, there was a lack of suitable expert ringside medical equipment and personnel, and the correct treatment was not given to Watson for some 25 or 30 minutes, once he had been taken to hospital. Watson suffered permanent brain damage and paralysis and brought a successful action against the BBBC which effectively bankrupted the organization. The case demonstrated that governing bodies can be liable for negligence for contests where they exercise control or where the events are run under its authority. At the 2010 Vancouver Olympics problems arose with the luge and bobsleigh track after a competitor from Georgia died. The track itself came in for some stringent criticism, although it was unclear where liability might lie:

> As often happens during Olympic controversies, it is unclear who bears ultimate responsibility among numerous committees and federations. The IOC and Vanoc have both said they aren't responsible for the tracks because they essentially subcontract technical specifications out to the luge and bobsleigh federations. It's unclear whether anyone can be held legally liable. All athletes involved in the Games must sign a legal liability waiver with the IOC, which says that they participate at their own risk.
>
> Crawford *et al.* (2010)

Where the rules of governing bodies most closely resemble the law is in the charging of players with an infraction that has taken place either on or off the field of play. This may involve a charge, a disciplinary hearing, a conviction, an appeal and enforcement of some penalty, and one example of this can be seen in the case study involving the Harlequins Bloodgate scandal noted above. On-field violence has in fact been severely dealt with by the governing bodies of rugby union and the specific offence of gouging has attracted long-term bans. In January 2010 a disciplinary panel imposed a ban of 70 weeks on Stade Francais prop forward David Attoub for 'making contact with the eye/eye area' of Stephen Ferris during a Heineken Cup match against Ulster. In 1999 Richard Nones, the Colomiers prop forward, was given a two-year sentence for the same offence. Interestingly the ban is comparative to that handed down to Matt Stevens for his failed drug test in December 2008. The two-year sentence for drug test failure is mandatory, whilst the sanction for violent and other disciplinary offences is set out on a sliding scale according to whether the offence is deemed 'lower end' or 'top end'. As noted above, the internal procedures have been seen by the courts as the most appropriate arena for dealing with such acts. In terms of the process of juridification, this is an example of the internal procedures copying the law (creating their own case law, their own precedents) and increasingly becoming domesticated (Foster, 2006).

MANAGING SPECTATORS

The safety of spectators is a prime consideration for those involved in the management of sporting events and there is a long history of serious disasters at football grounds in the UK. This chapter does not deal with these events in any great detail; for more information see Greenfield and Osborn (2001), for example. Disasters have led to an increasing parliamentary intervention on the grounds of safety, for example the Safety at Sports Ground Act 1975, the Fire Safety and Safety at Places of Sport Act 1987 and the creation of the Football Licensing Authority. However, in the 1970s and 1980s, the focus shifted towards solving problems of crowd disorder as hooliganism was seen as a political problem. The two issues, of safe grounds and control of hooligans, often overlapped; for example, the terms of reference of the 1985 Popplewell Inquiry covered not only the tragic fire at Bradford but also the death of a fan at St Andrews and were further extended to cover the Heysel stadium disaster. Thus policy often had twin aims to ensure not only a safe or at least a safer physical environment but also to control the fans themselves and restrict the opportunities for hooliganism. So in addition to the statutes noted above, the Taylor Report (1989) led to a host of legislative measures including the creation of football-specific criminal offences including those found in the Football Offences Act 1991. The result was a dramatic change in physical environment with the requirement for all-seater stadia at specific levels, tighter controls on the supply of alcohol and bans for those committing football-related offences at or even away from grounds. Spectators became heavily policed with greater restrictions on travel and attendance. For example, at the Leeds v. Millwall Championship match in 2010, in addition to the 12.30 kick off the travelling Millwall fans were required to present a voucher at a designated service station on the M1 in order to obtain their match ticket. Much of the political debate notably in the 1980s revolved around whether hooliganism was an issue for football to solve or an issue for society more generally. Regardless of the policy dispute, the outcome was a plethora of legislation and far more proactive policing. More recently the role of the Football Licensing Authority has been reviewed, in line with the Hampton Implementation Review process. (See http://www.berr.gov.uk/assets/biscore/better-regulation/docs/10-689-football-licensing-authority-hampton-implementation-review.pdf.)

In terms of liability for injuries caused within the stadium, traditional principles of tort, largely those relating to negligence and the Occupiers Liability Act 1957, would apply. Even before the landmark negligence case of *Donoghue* v. *Stevenson* [1932] AC 502 there were examples of sports organizers being held liable for injuries suffered by spectators. In *Brown* v. *Lewis* (1896) 12 TLR 455 the directors of Blackburn Rovers Football Club were found liable for injuries suffered when a grandstand collapsed at Ewood Park; they were held responsible for failing to secure a competent contractor to do the work. Perhaps unsurprisingly, given the time of the incident, this did not lead immediately to better safety for spectators, but rather increased the trend towards clubs shifting future liability away from directors and on to the club (see James, 2010, 152). Outside of negligence, there is also a contractual dimension as paying spectators enter a contract that will have specific conditions of entry. These may be very broad ranging in nature. For example, there will be some typical, and basic, terms relating to ticket holder entitlement to enter the stadium and the contract will incorporate the specific ground rules or regulations, usually focused on spectator behaviour and conduct and often reinforcing criminal law provisions, such as those contained in the Football Offences Act 1991 concerning racist chanting, encroaching on the field of play and throwing missiles. Importantly, it will also specify what the ticket holder is able to do with their ticket. Crucially here, tickets will usually be non-transferable, so any transfer or resale of the ticket will amount to a breach of contract. For example, for rugby internationals at Twickenham in 2010, the following clause was incorporated:

Tickets are sold or otherwise issued by the RFU only to applicants who have agreed to observe the ticket distribution conditions ... If any ticket is acquired in breach of such ticket distribution conditions, the RFU may refuse to admit such ticket holder to the stadium and may eject such ticket holder from the stadium even after admission and, in addition, the distributor to whom the ticket is issued by the RFU may be liable for sanctions imposed by the RFU.

Outside of any criminal regulation for ticket touting, such as that which exists within football, under the contract there are remedies available that govern the right to enter the ground. One condition will be that the ticket holder agrees to be searched upon request and can be refused admission if he or she does not consent. However, in recent years commercial considerations have been incorporated into ticket conditions. These may prohibit the possession of named products that conflict with those of the sponsors of the event. Companies who are not official sponsors of worldwide mega events such as the Olympics or World Cup may try to link their own products to the event through indirect associations. This concept, referred to as ambush marketing, is often vigorously resisted to protect official sponsors.

At the 2010 World Cup in South Africa a group of 36 women wearing orange dresses were ejected from the Holland v. Denmark match and two organizers arrested. The orange dresses were associated with the Dutch brewers Bavaria, who had organized a previous campaign at the 2006 World Cup with orange overalls that had to be taken off to gain admittance. Charges against the women were later dropped. Undoubtedly the publicity concerning the ejection and the arrests overtook what might have been gained otherwise. Such draconian attempts to police clothing and consumption of non-authorized products raise civil liberty issues. Similarly, there have been attempts to regulate political gestures or acts, such as the 'Green and Gold' campaign at Manchester United, a fan movement designed to try and oust the Glazers and return the club to something more resembling the 'traditional' idea of the club. After the Football World Cup, many clubs have banned the use of vuvuzelas, concerned primarily that the noise might impact upon their commercial activities. This, along with the other commercial and political instances above, all illustrate new concerns with the regulation of spectators, outside of the public order and safety nexus, and shows that the issue of commercialization is likely to be of more concern to sports managers in the future.

THE COMMERCIAL DIMENSION

Areas of commercial law become intertwined with sport where there is the ability to exploit some element. Law will become involved when there is some type of dispute and there is something of economic worth. The four most obvious areas are:

1   The rights to broadcast popular events.
2   The transfer of sought-after players between clubs.
3   The exploitation of intellectual property rights, advertising and sponsorship.
4   The buying and selling of clubs themselves.

The buying and selling of the right to broadcast sporting events has become a contentious issue since the development of non-terrestrial broadcasters using satellite or cable as the means of delivery. Disputes over rights, however, go back to the 1970s and it was access to the rights to broadcast Australian Test Cricket that was at the heart of the dispute between Kerry Packer and the Australian Cricket Board. The refusal to allow Packer to bid for the rights for his Channel 9 Station led to the formation of World Series Cricket and some of the innovations that are seen in the game today. In the UK it has been the emergence of BSkyB that has altered the demand and consequent value of rights in popular sports. For example, the first contract between the Premier League and BSkyB was signed in 1992 and was worth £191m for the five-year period. By 1996 the value of the contract was £670m spread over four years and by 2000 Sky was paying £1.1bn for a three-year deal. In 2006 matches were split between Sky and Setanta with the former paying £1.31bn for 92 live games and the latter £392m for 46 matches. One of the initial legal issues has been whether it is permissible for collective selling of rights, i.e. for the Premier League to bundle up access to all the separate clubs and sell as a package. This approach does allow for a more even distribution of income than would otherwise occur if individual clubs were to sell their own rights freely, which occurs in Spain and Italy. Clearly there would be a marked difference in the value of the rights to broadcast the home matches of Manchester United or Chelsea and Bolton or Wigan.

One of the consequences of packaging rights is that a broadcaster can hold a monopoly which denies the public access unless a subscription is paid. The European Commission took the view in 2002 that the structure set up with one holder of rights was anti-competitive and it required that a number of packages be available to dilute ownership. This led to more players entering the marketplace; unfortunately for one of the winning bidders, Setanta, they were unable to develop their business model and went into administration in 2009. This mirrored the collapse of ITV digital in 2002 which had a serious effect on the finances of Football League clubs. It is the influx of television income into the Premiership that has made it an attractive proposition for players from around the world. This has led to a significant rise in player wages and the value of transfer fees. Players have become marketable commodities which have led to an increased role for player agents who seek to maximize earnings for their client from both football and outside sources. This led to concerns, and a *Panorama* programme was aired in 2006 about the integrity of some transfers. This led to the establishment of an inquiry undertaken by Lord Stevens who produced reports which raised questions in relation to a small number of transfers.

Agents are policed through a set of FIFA Regulations which are then delegated to enforcement at a national level. Agents and managers will owe a fiduciary duty to their clients and must act in the best interests of the player, above all not creating a situation where a conflict of interest can exist. This is a long-established principle, and courts will render contracts unenforceable where a breach of the fiduciary relationship occurs. This problem has arisen in professional boxing when the boxer's personal manager also acts as a fight promoter for his own boxer, thus having a separate financial interest in the contest. This has been an ongoing problem for the British Boxing Board of Control (BBBC) and was considered by the High Court in *Watson* v. *Prager*. Attempts to prohibit dual licensing have in the past fallen foul of legislation relating to anti-competitive practices (Greenfield and Osborn, 1995).

Intellectual property rights have become more valuable as the marketing of successful clubs has become globalized. New markets have emerged particularly for the leading Premier League clubs in the East. The 'brand' has increased in value, supported by constant global television exposure leading to increases in sponsorship value. There has also been the development of new income streams such as stadium naming, a common occurrence in the USA. This has generally happened with stadia that have been newly built, thus avoiding any clash with the history associated with the old ground. Thus Arsenal's move from Highbury to Ashburton Grove allowed it to find a sponsor, with Emirates Airline paying a reported £100m for a five-year deal; the stadium has quickly become known as 'The Emirates'. However, in 2009 Chelsea FC announced it would consider a naming rights deal for the existing ground, Stamford Bridge. This new commercial environment has encouraged legal action to enforce intellectual property rights. For example, Arsenal brought a trademark infringement action against a street seller of unofficial merchandise.

The buying and selling of clubs has provoked controversy as the models of corporate ownership have altered. Private limited companies were replaced in a number of examples by public limited companies as clubs like Tottenham and Manchester United were floated on the stock market. Public companies are required to have a certain level of transparency and the annual reports provided some interesting detail. However, any publicly quoted company is liable to a turnover and the result has been a switch back to private ownership. For Manchester United there was first the attempt by BSkyB to purchase the club; this move was rejected by the Monopolies and Mergers Commission as not being in the public interest. Malcolm Glazer was however able to buy the club through acquiring the shares and there remains a high level of fan discontent about his ownership and business model.

At the other end of the scale, supporters trusts have emerged as a model at clubs who are on the verge of liquidation. The major concern of takeovers with smaller clubs is the fear that asset stripping will take place and the ground sold for redevelopment. The football authorities have reacted rather belatedly by introducing the concept of a 'fit and proper person' test, but given the global nature of the business interests and the short timescales, it is difficult to see how a sufficiently detailed forensic analysis can be undertaken. This is an ongoing issue which represents a clash of cultural and commercial values, an idea than runs through much of the business of sport.

SUMMARY

There are many ways in which the law interacts with sport. Even in amateur games there are disciplinary and administrative processes that draw upon legal approaches. Fear of litigation has driven much of the protective agenda for sport where children are concerned, and there are concerns as to the level of resources that this welfarist agenda utilizes in relation to the perceived threat. The role of law as regards the management of both participants and spectators has become more pronounced, and it is likely this trend will continue. As we have argued above, however, the way in which the external law regulates this is more complex than purely a consideration of how the law encroaches into these areas, but any analysis of this process of juridification needs to appreciate its more subtle effects. That said, the chapter has identified a number of key areas where the civil and criminal law has impacted upon the management of sport, and introduced the increasingly important aspect of commercial impacts.

REVIEW QUESTIONS

1   Is the law the right vehicle to regulate sport?
2   Is physical contact on the sports field a criminal or civil matter?
3   What do you understand by the term juridification?
4   Should referees or other officials be potentially liable for their acts? How is public policy best served here?
5   If banning scrums in rugby would eliminate a significant proportion of serious injuries, should they be removed from the game? Does the level of participation matter?
6   How are spectators regulated and protected at sports grounds?
7   Should ticket touting be banned? Why?

FURTHER READING

Anderson, J. (2010) *Modern Sports Law*. Hart Publishing.
Gardiner, S., James, M., O'Leary J. and Welch R., with I. Blackshaw, S. Boyes and A. Caiger (2005) *Sports Law*. Cavendish Publishing.
Hamil, S. and Chadwick, S. (2010) *Managing Football: An International Perspective*. Elsevier.
James, M. (2010) *Sports Law*. Palgrave Macmillan.

WEBSITES

Entertainment and Sports Law Journal
  http://www2.warwick.ac.uk/fac/soc/law/elj/eslj
Sport and EU
  http://www.sportandeu.com
World Sports law blog
  http://e-comlaw.com/sportslawblog

REFERENCES

Anderson, J. (2006) 'An accident of history: Why the decisions of sports governing bodies are not amenable to judicial review', 35 *Comm L World Rev* 173.
Crawford, D., Albergotti, R. and Johnson, I. (2010) 'Speed and commerce skewed track's design', *Wall Street Journal*, 16 February.
Foster, K. (2003) 'Is there a global sports law?', *Entertainment and Sports Law Journal*, 2 (1), 1.
Foster, K. (2006) 'The juridification of sport', in Greenfield, S. and Osborn, G. *Readings in Law and Popular Culture*, Routledge.

Foster, K. and Osborn, G. (2010) 'Dancing on the edge of disciplines: Law and the interdisciplinary turn', 8 *Entertainment and Sports Law Journal*. http://www2.warwick.ac.uk/fac/soc/law/elj/eslj/issues/volume8/number1/foster_osborn

Greenfield, S. and Osborn, G. (1995) 'A gauntlet for the glove: The challenge to English boxing contracts', 6 *Marq. Sports L. J.* 153 (1995–1996).

Greenfield, S. and Osborn, G. (1997) 'Aesthetics, injury and liability in cricket', 13 *Professional Negligence* 9.

Greenfield, S. and Osborn, G. (2001) *Regulating Football*. Pluto Press.

Greenfield, S. and Osborn, G. (2010) 'Regulating sport: Finding a role for law', 13 *Sport in Society* 2, 367.

James, M. (2010) *Sports Law*. Palgrave Macmillan.

Keane, R. and Dunphy, E. (2002) *Keane: The Autobiography*. Michael Joseph.

Chapter 17

Managing high performance sport

Bill Gerrard, Leeds University Business School

TOPICS

High performance sport: defining the field of study • Effectiveness and efficiency in professional team sports • The valuation of playing talent • Coaching • Leadership

---

OBJECTIVES

At the end of this chapter you should be able to:

- Understand the key management issues in high performance sport;
- Distinguish between organisational effectiveness and efficiency;
- Use efficiency ratios to analyse performance;
- Recognise the alternative methods for valuing playing talent;
- Outline the key aspects of the coaching function in professional sports teams;
- Explain the different roles of the coach-leader.

KEY TERMS

Comparative valuation – the valuation of playing talent and productive assets through comparison with recent market valuations for similar entities using valuation ratios and/or multivariate valuation formulae.

Fundamental valuation – the valuation of playing talent and productive assets based on projections of their expected future impact on cash flows.

Organisational effectiveness – the extent to which an organisation achieves its targets.

Organisational efficiency – the relationship between organisational performance and the resources utilised; higher efficiency implies higher output per unit of input.

Statistical performance analysis – the use of statistical techniques to investigate the trends in team and player performance across games.

OVERVIEW

This chapter introduces high performance sport as an identifiably separate field of study in sport management. Focusing on professional team sports, a distinction is drawn between organisational effectiveness and organisational efficiency. The win–cost ratio is introduced as a measure of sporting efficiency. Organisational efficiency is decomposed into transactional and transformational efficiency and linked to the distinction between the resource-picking and capability-building functions of management. A key aspect of transactional efficiency in professional team sports is the valuation of playing talent. The different methods of comparative and fundamental valuation are described with examples from soccer transfer fees and baseball player wages. Transformational efficiency depends on the coaching function. The various aspects of coaching are considered – the recruitment function, the development function and the tactical function. The developing use of statistical performance analysis in professional team sports is examined. The chapter concludes with a short discussion of the task and relationship dimensions of leadership and the role of the coach as leader. Three case studies are provided to examine the different factors involved in achieving success in high performance team sports – John Wooden's emphasis on morals and values in the success of the UCLA basketball team, Billy Beane's use of statistical analysis to overcome resource constraints at the Oakland Athletics in Major League Baseball, and Sir Clive Woodward's adoption of business principles and a formal performance management system to produce the England Rugby Union World Cup 2003 winning team.

CASE STUDY: JOHN WOODEN AND THE PYRAMID OF SUCCESS

John Wooden ranks as one of the most successful coaches ever and indeed he was voted Coach of the Century by ESPN, but he is little known outside North America. Wooden coached the UCLA basketball team for 27 years from 1948 to 1975 when he retired. Between 1964 and 1975 his UCLA team won ten NCAA national championships including seven-in-a-row championships from 1967 to 1973. His record is unlikely ever to be surpassed. As with all successful coaches, Wooden had a great eye for a player and was able to scout and recruit very talented individuals. He was also a brilliant and innovative tactician who was able to formulate effective playing systems that suited his players and allowed them to use their talents to the full. But what sets Wooden apart most of all was his coaching philosophy, more a philosophy of life based on very strong ethical principles.

Wooden never used winning and losing as a measure of success. He recognised that match results are a transitory phenomenon determined by a range of factors, many of which are beyond the control of a coach and the players. Wooden focused on the controllables, believing that if players developed their technical skills, physical fitness and decision-making abilities combined with the right attitude, this constituted success and would increase the likelihood of winning on court. Wooden defined success as excellence in individual performance, not team wins. 'Success is peace of mind which is a direct result of self-satisfaction in knowing you did your best to become the best you are capable of becoming' (Wooden, 2004: 85).

Wooden's philosophy is summarised in his Pyramid of Success. The Pyramid consists of five tiers of attributes required for success, with each tier of attributes building on the lower tiers. The first tier consists of Industriousness, Friendship, Loyalty, Cooperation and

Enthusiasm. The next tier has Self-Control, Alertness, Initiative and Intentness. Importantly it is not until the third tier that the traditional attributes of successful players appear in Wooden's Pyramid – Condition, Skill and Team Spirit. This highlights the importance that Wooden puts on basic human values as a prerequisite for sporting success. Exceptional technical skill and outstanding physical and mental strength are necessary but not sufficient requirements for success in high performance sport. These sport-specific attributes must be grounded in a strong commitment to principles such as hard work and mutual respect. The second-top tier consists of Poise and Confidence, with the apex of the Pyramid comprising Competitive Greatness, which Wooden describes as 'Be at your best when your best is needed' (2004: 88–89).

Wooden's coaching philosophy demonstrates the importance of adopting a holistic approach to managing high performance sport. All four As are required for success – Ability, Athleticism, Awareness and Attitude. Identifying players with exceptional talent and then developing and deploying that talent effectively are fundamental tasks for the coach-leader. But without the right attitude, players and teams can never fully realise their potential. Wooden, above all else, shows that instilling the right attitude in a team can be the crucial function of the coach-leader.

HIGH PERFORMANCE SPORT: DEFINING THE FIELD OF STUDY

Sport management is the study of the organisations involved in the production of sport and sport-related products and services. The field of study draws on the various business disciplines such as economics, finance and marketing, and the various branches of management including organisational behaviour, organisational theory, strategic management and human resource management, in order to analyse the behaviour of organisations in the sports context. From the perspective of sport management, the sports context is often conceptualised in core–periphery terms with the core consisting of the production of sports activities surrounded by a sport business periphery producing sport-related products and services. The core production processes are often usefully categorised as either participation sports activities or spectator sports activities. Participation sport relates to the provision of opportunities to participate in sport as an activity whereas spectator sport relates to the provision of opportunities to either attend sports events at the host venue or receive broadcasts of these events via radio, TV or the internet. High performance sport encompasses all of the activities associated with the production of elite-level sporting performances by individual athletes/players and teams. High performance sport is at the core of spectator sports since ultimately spectators are attending or receiving broadcasts of elite sporting performances. But there has been relatively little attention in the sport management literature on the management of high performance sport *per se*. Rather the traditional focus in the sport management literature on spectator sports has tended to be the business aspects. Aspects of the management of high performance sport have been addressed in the sport science and coaching literatures. This chapter attempts to fill this gap in the sport management literature and outlines some of the key management issues involved in producing elite performances by individual athletes/players and teams.

Although high performance sport includes both individual and team sports, the focus of this chapter will be managing elite performance in professional team sports. A crucial difference in team sports is that between striking-and-fielding sports such as baseball and cricket, and invasion sports such as the various codes of football, field and ice hockey, and basketball. One fundamental structural difference between these two types of team sports is the degree of interdependency between players within the team and the separability of their individual contributions to team performance. Striking-and-fielding games are more atomistic in nature with relatively high separability of individual player contributions. Invasion sports are much more complex with a high degree of interdependency between players so that the whole (i.e. team performance) is much more than the sum of the parts (i.e. individual player contributions). Invasion team sports are much more tactical, requiring players to be more able to make decisions on actions and movements in and out of possession that co-ordinate effectively with the decisions of their teammates. The importance of the tactical dimension in invasion team sports has profound implications for the management of high performance in those sports compared to striking-and-fielding sports.

EFFECTIVENESS AND EFFICIENCY IN PROFESSIONAL TEAM SPORTS

The operation of a professional sports team can be summarised very powerfully using the Marxist characterisation of the capitalist mode of production: M – C ... C' – M. There are three components of the capitalist mode of production:

1   M – C represents the exchange process in which production input resources (C) are identified and acquired at a financial cost (M);
2   C ... C' represents the production process in which production input resources are transformed into production outputs (C'); and
3   C' – M represents the exchange process in which the produced goods and services are sold.

The first two components together, M – C ... C', represents the high performance sport process while the sport business process is concerned with the final component, C' – M, and the commercialisation of sporting performance into revenue streams such as gate receipts, media revenues, sponsorship income and merchandising sales. The management of performance sport in professional team sports is principally the management of the transformation of financial resources (M) into sporting performance (C'). In professional team sports the key production input resource is elite playing talent. Teams must identify players through the scouting process and calculate their financial value in order to determine the salary contracts to offer and willingness to incur other acquisition costs such as transfer fees. The production process involves developing individual players and producing player and team performance in competitive tournaments. This is the core of the coaching process. One specific area of interest in high performance sport is player development in those sports in which professional teams are heavily involved in youth development, as is the case in European football academies.

In evaluating the high performance sport process in different professional sports teams, it is useful to distinguish between effectiveness and efficiency. Effectiveness is defined as the degree to which an organisation and its sub-units achieve their performance targets. Effective organisations achieve their targets. Efficiency is defined as the performance of an organisation and its sub-units relative to the resources expended in generating the performance. Both effectiveness and efficiency can be measured as performance ratios. Effectiveness is measured as the ratio of actual performance to target performance while efficiency is measured as the ratio of performance to resource (i.e. output–input ratio).

Measuring effectiveness in professional sports teams is not clear-cut because of the possibility of multiple, conflicting organisational team objectives. It has been long recognised that professional sports teams cannot be assumed to operate in the same way as other business organisations pursuing financial objectives of profit and shareholder value. Sloane (1971) was one of the first to suggest that professional sports teams should be seen as utility maximisers not profit maximisers. Vrooman (1997) identified the sportsman-owner effect with owners concerned more with sporting objectives than financial objectives. Gerrard (2005) formalised the issue of team objectives as a performance trade-off with fully efficient teams eventually facing a choice between sporting and financial performance. As teams enhance the quality of their playing squads, there comes a point at which the increased revenues from the expected improvement in sporting performance will be insufficient to cover the increased wage costs incurred in recruiting more talented players. Team owners who put more weight on sporting performance will, therefore, tend to invest in playing talent beyond the level consistent with profit maximisation. Inefficient teams may avoid the performance trade-off and pursue improvements in sporting and financial performance simultaneously through efficiency gains. In his study of English Premiership football teams, Gerrard (2005) found evidence that those teams that were listed on the stock exchange achieved higher operating profit margins with no significant decrease in their league performance, suggesting that stock market listing led to improved efficiency.

Team objectives and the impact of ownership, governance and financial structures are key issues in understanding the allocation of financial resources in professional sports teams and their effectiveness as a sport business. However, the focus of the management of high performance sport is the efficiency with which the allocated financial resources are transformed into sporting performance. Sporting performance depends on both the quantity of financial resources available to teams as well as the efficiency with which these financial resources are utilised. The efficiency of high performance sport is under-researched in sport management. Traditionally the emphasis has been on the differences between teams in their economic and financial power and how leagues can use cross-subsidisation and player labour market interventions such as salary caps and player drafts to avoid financial determinism and maintain a high degree of uncertainty of outcome and competitive balance.

The efficiency of the high performance sport process in professional sports teams is defined as C'/M, that is, sporting performance (C') divided by financial resource (M). Sporting efficiency is usually expressed as the win–cost ratio, defined as the wage cost per win, calculated as the team's wage costs (i.e. financial resources) divided by wins (i.e. sporting performance). The win–cost ratio is the inverse of the output–input ratio. A team with a higher win–cost ratio is less efficient, having spent more on player wages per win than other teams.

The relationship between sporting performance and financial resource is illustrated in Table 17.1 which reports league points, wage costs and win–cost ratios for the FA Premier League in season 2007/08. Table 17.1 also reports the respective rankings. Given that football leagues allow drawn games and use a 3–1–0 points system (i.e. three points for a win, one point for a draw, and zero points for a loss) to determine league performance, it is more appropriate to define the win–cost ratio in this context as the wage cost per league point. As can be seen, there is a close association between sporting performance and financial resource. The correlation between league position (i.e. performance ranking) and wage costs (i.e. resource ranking) is +0.859, indicating a very strong positive relationship between what clubs spend on wages and their league performance. The so-called 'Big Four' (i.e. Arsenal, Chelsea, Liverpool and Manchester United) had the largest wage costs and finished in the top four places in the FA Premier League and so qualified for the lucrative UEFA Champions League the following season. The three clubs (Birmingham City, Derby County and Reading) with the lowest wage expenditures finished bottom of the league and were relegated to the Football League Championship. However, both Birmingham City and Reading, despite their resource constraints, almost avoided relegation – Reading finished level on points with Fulham and were only relegated on goal difference and Birmingham City finished only one point behind. Both Birmingham City and Reading achieved above-average levels of sporting efficiency, with Birmingham City ranked as the third most efficient team in the FA Premier League that season and Reading ranked sixth. The average wage cost per league point for the whole league in 2007/08 was £1.15m whereas Birmingham City spent only £761k per league point and Reading spent £920k. The two most efficient teams were Blackburn Rovers and Everton who both had win–cost ratios of £684k. Blackburn Rovers ranked 12th in wage costs but finished seventh in the league while Everton ranked 11th in wage costs but finished fifth. Chelsea had the second highest win–cost ratio finishing second behind Manchester United but spending £51.0m more on wages. The least efficient club was Derby County who finished bottom with 11 points despite spending on wages just less than Birmingham City who gained 35 points. The other highly inefficient team was Newcastle United who were the fifth highest spenders but finished mid-table in 12th position and only seven points above the final relegation place. Newcastle United's sporting inefficiency eventually resulted in relegation to the Football League Championship in the following season.

Efficiency in the high performance sport process in professional team sports can be decomposed into the two constituent components of the M – C ... C' process. The overall efficiency ratio, C'/M, can be decomposed into an efficiency ratio for the exchange process (C/M) and an efficiency ratio for the production process (C'/C). The efficiency of the exchange process by which playing talent is identified and recruited represents transactional efficiency. Teams that are highly efficient in transactional terms are able to maximise the quality of the playing talent acquired given the available financial budget. The efficiency of the sporting production process by which players are deployed to produce team performance represents transformational efficiency. The valuation of playing talent is a key factor in transactional efficiency and is discussed in the next section. Transformational efficiency depends on the coaching process and is discussed later in the chapter. The distinction between transactional and transformational efficiency links with the distinction that Makadok (2001) has drawn between the two functions of management – resource picking and capability building. Resource picking involves the identification and valuation of individual strategic resources to order to optimise the utilisation of the resource acquisition budget. Managers who excel as resource pickers spend well and achieve high levels of transactional efficiency. Capability building involves the enhancement and deployment of the stock of acquired resources to create synergy and deliver more than is attainable in rival contexts. Managers who excel as capability builders achieve high levels of transformational efficiency and get the most out of the work group both individually and collectively.

Table 17.1 *The relationship between sporting performance and financial resources, FA Premier League, 2007/08*

Club	League points	Wage costs £000s	Win–cost ratio £000s	Performance ranking	Resource ranking	Efficiency ranking
Manchester United	87	121,080	1,392	1	2	17
Chelsea	85	172,096	2,025	2	1	19
Arsenal	83	101,302	1,221	3	3	15
Liverpool	76	90,438	1,190	4	4	14
Everton	65	44,480	684	5	11	2
Aston Villa	60	50,447	841	6	10	5
Blackburn Rovers	58	39,661	684	7	12	1
Portsmouth	57	54,680	959	8	7	9
Manchester City	55	54,222	986	9	8	10
West Ham United	49	65,145	1,329	10	6	16
Tottenham Hotspur	46	53,281	1,158	11	9	13
Newcastle United	43	79,329	1,845	12	5	18
Middlesbrough	42	34,761	828	13	17	4
Wigan Athletic	40	38,351	959	14	15	8
Sunderland	39	37,091	951	15	16	7
Bolton Wanderers	37	39,033	1,055	16	14	11
Fulham	36	39,344	1,093	17	13	12
Reading	36	33,123	920	18	18	6
Birmingham C	35	26,624	761	19	19	3
Derby County	11	26,109	2,374	20	20	20

The distinction between transactional and transformational efficiency can also be related to the different functions of leadership as considered in the final part of the chapter. Leadership also involves a third type of efficiency relating to the ability of a group or organisation to respond to a changing environment over time. This dynamic efficiency is of crucial importance in the ultra-competitive context of professional team sports in which, just as in the Land of the Red Queen, you must keep running just to stay still.

THE VALUATION OF PLAYING TALENT

Achieving high levels of transactional efficiency in professional team sports requires an ability to identify what financiers call arbitrage opportunities when assets can be traded at a profit because of temporary market inefficiency in setting prices. In particular, arbitrage opportunities can occur when the current market value of an asset diverges from the expected productive value of the asset in generating future returns. In the case of professional team sports, arbitrage opportunities can occur when the current market value of a player diverges from the expected sporting and marketing contribution of the player. Hence teams can reduce their win–cost ratio by identifying players who are undervalued by the market and offer a high win contribution relative to their salary costs compared to other players. Thus the valuation of playing talent by teams is a crucial aspect of managing high performance sport.

There are two basic approaches to valuation – comparative valuation and fundamental valuation. Comparative (or benchmark) valuation involves valuing assets through comparison with similar assets that have been traded recently. Comparative valuation is an anchor-and-adjustment method in which the anchor is set by the observed market values of recently traded assets with similar characteristics, with adjustments for the specific characteristics of the asset being valued. By contrast, fundamental valuation involves projecting the incremental impact of the asset on expected future cash flows (and, if relevant, expected non-monetary returns).

There are two main methods of comparative valuation – valuation ratios and hedonic-pricing (or multivariate) methods. Valuation ratios are applicable when asset values are directly proportional to a single characteristic of the asset or a single performance outcome/driver. Valuation ratios are most widely used in corporate valuation, with the market value of a company's equity being measured relative to company performance as measured by profit after tax (i.e. the price-earnings ratio) or relative to a company size as measured by the book value of the company's equity as shown on the balance sheet (i.e. the market-to-book ratio). The market value of a company's equity can be estimated by multiplying its profit after tax or book value by the respective ratio derived from similar companies. The problem with applying valuation ratios to playing talent is that there is no single characteristic of the player that acts as a good predictor of future performance. Rather there are multiple characteristics of a player that together provide a predictor of future performance. In this case comparative valuation requires hedonic-pricing methods in which statistical analysis of the observed market values of similar assets is used to decompose market values into a set of imputed (or hedonic) prices for each asset characteristic. This methodology has been applied in a number of studies of football transfer fees (Carmichael and Thomas, 1993; Reilly and Witt, 1995; Dobson and

Gerrard, 1999). Broadly speaking, these studies identified four sets of factors linked statistically to observed transfer valuations of players in English professional football:

1   Player characteristics such as age, career experience, squad status (i.e. regular starter or substitute), goal-scoring record and international recognition;
2   Selling-club characteristics such as size, divisional status and league performance;
3   Buying-club characteristics such as size, divisional status and league performance; and
4   General market conditions both between and within seasons including the effects of transfer deadlines.

Published studies showed that around 70–80 per cent of the variation in individual transfer fees could be explained statistically by these four sets of factors. Importantly it should be noted that the published studies referenced above used data prior to the introduction of Bosman free agency in European football in the mid-1990s. Bosman free agency introduced another crucial driver of transfer fees, namely the length of time until the player's contract expires, since players become free to move to another club at the end of their contract with no transfer fee payable (with the exception of players aged under 23 for whom compensation for training costs is payable).

The effectiveness of comparative valuation turns on two crucial assumptions. First, the asset characteristics are assumed to be good, stable predictors of the asset's future performance. Second, the market values of the whole class of similar assets are assumed to have been anchored appropriately. Comparative valuation creates a bootstraps property where the market value of any individual asset is justified by the market values of all other similar assets. If the market becomes more confident about the future, all asset values will be pulled upwards. This implies an inherent precariousness in market values, with asset values subject to bubbles and crashes whenever there is a major shift in market confidence. Witness for example the sharp drop in football transfer fees in 2002/03 following the collapse of ITV Digital which created uncertainty and loss of confidence about future TV revenues. As the *Moneyball* case study illustrates, market traders may be susceptible to relying too heavily on conventional wisdom as to the appropriate predictors of a future performance, creating a potential arbitrage opportunity for those innovators who use new and better predictors.

Determining the fundamental valuation of a player requires estimating the expected incremental cash flow that a professional sports team can derive from the player's expected win contribution (i.e. sporting performance) and expected image value (i.e. marketing contribution). In addition, the player's fundamental valuation would need to include the value to team owners of any non-financial benefits from sporting and marketing contributions such as glory and prestige effects. The methodology for determining the fundamental (financial) value of playing talent is well established in the academic literature and dates back to Scully's estimation of the marginal revenue product (MRP) (i.e. incremental revenue effect) of Major League Baseball (MLB) players published in the *American Economic Review* in 1974. Scully developed a two-stage statistical procedure for estimating the MRPs of baseball players. The first stage is to estimate a team-performance function that relates the aggregate performance of players to the team's win percentage. The second stage is to estimate a team-revenue function that relates the team's win percentage to revenues.

Scully's estimated team-performance function using data for MLB in 1968 and 1969 is reported below:

PCTWIN = 37.24 + 0.92TSA + 0.90TSW + controls, R^2 = 88%
where
PCTWIN = team regular-season win percentage
TSA = team slugging average
TSW = team strikeout-to-walk ratio

Scully used the TSA to measure the performance of hitters and the TSW to measure the performance of pitchers. TSA can be decomposed into the slugging averages of each individual hitter weighted by appearance rate as measured by the at-bat percentage. Scully's estimates imply that each hitter's contribution to the team's win percentage equals their slugging average multiplied by their appearance rate multiplied by the estimated impact coefficient 0.92. TSW can be similarly decomposed into the strikeout-to-walk ratio of individual pitchers weighted by their appearance rate as measured by the percentage of innings pitched. The estimated impact coefficient for pitchers is 0.90. Scully also included a series of control variables in the team-performance ratio – league affiliation, and whether the team was in or out of contention to win their divisional pennant. Overall the estimated team-performance function explained 88 per cent of the variation in win percentages across teams.

Scully's estimated team-revenue function using data for MLB teams in 1968 and 1969 is reported below:

REVENUE = 1,735,890 + 10,330PCTWIN + controls, R^2 = 75%
where
REVENUE = team ticket receipts and broadcasting income
PCTWIN = team regular-season win percentage

Scully also included a series of control variables – league affiliation, population size of the team's metropolitan area, the sensitivity of the team's gate attendances to winning, whether or not the team had an old stadium with limited parking, and the racial diversity of the team. Overall the estimated equation explained three-quarters of the variation in revenues across teams. Scully's estimated team-revenue function implied that each base point contribution to a team's win percentage was worth an additional $10,330. So, for example, on Scully's estimates, a hitter with a slugging average of 350 and 8 per cent of a team's at-bats would contribute additional revenues of $266,000. A pitcher with a strikeout-to-walk ratio of 2.0 who pitched 14 per cent of the team's innings would contribute $260,300 of additional revenues.

Scully's principal interest was to show that the restrictive MLB reserve clause that gave teams exclusive rights to retain out-of-contract players led to players earning only a fraction of their MRP. Subsequent studies such as Zimbalist (1992) have refined Scully's two-stage procedure and assessed the impact of the introduction of free agency in the MLB players' market. But essentially the statistical techniques exist to estimate the financial value of elite playing talent at least in respect to the incremental revenue effects of their sporting performance. And as the *Moneyball* case study demonstrates, MLB teams are utilising valuation techniques to help determine their optimal player trading strategy. However, it is no surprise that both academic research on player valuation and the practical application of valuation techniques by professional sports teams should be pioneered in baseball given that it is a simple atomistic striking-and-fielding game in which individual player performance is highly separable and measurable by a small number of key metrics. The question arises as to whether or not the *Moneyball* approach is transferable to more complex invasion team sports such as basketball, and the various codes of football, rugby and hockey (Gerrard, 2007).

There are a number of dimensions to the complexity of invasion team sports compared to striking-and-fielding team sports including the range of different types of player actions, the interdependency and jointness of player actions, the importance of position, movement and team shape, the differences between offensive and defensive phases of play and the specialisation of playing roles. In order to measure player performance and hence determine player valuations in invasion team sports, it is necessary to resolve three problems:

1   Tracking problem: the identification, categorisation and enumeration of different types of player actions;
2   Attribution problem: the allocation of individual contributions to joint and interdependent actions; and
3   Weighting problem: the significance of different actions in determining match outcomes.

The atomistic structure of cricket and baseball with clearly separable plays means that a comprehensive record of player performance can be recorded by paper-and-pencil methods with the data publicly available through the press and other media outlets. In contrast, the complexity and continuity of play in invasion sports has meant that historically performance statistics have been limited to very basic data on appearances, scoring and discipline. However, the development of video analysis and image recognition software has largely resolved the tracking problem so that player performance data is now readily available to teams able to afford the necessary technology. Using this data to value players in invasion team sports is still in its infancy and depends largely on the development of performance analysis to resolve the attribution and weighting problems (see next section).

CASE STUDY: THE OAKLAND AS AND THE *MONEYBALL* STORY

The Oakland As are a small-market team in Major League Baseball with one of the lowest player salary budgets and spending only around one-third of that of the biggest teams such as the New York Yankees. *Moneyball: The Art of Winning an Unfair Game*, the best-selling book by Michael Lewis (2003), tells the story of how the As have attempted to remain competitive despite their limited economic resources. The book focuses on the 2001 and 2002 seasons when the As had the second best regular-season win percentage in both seasons yet ranked in the bottom three in terms of salary expenditure. The As succeeded by operating with exceptional levels of efficiency. A study by Gerrard (2007) showed that Oakland achieved an efficiency gain of 59.3 per cent over the period 1998–2006 compared to the league average.

Under the leadership of the General Manager, Billy Beane, Oakland developed a 'David strategy', creating a knowledge-based advantage with which to challenge their resource-rich competitors. At the heart of the As' innovative approach was the systematic utilisation of player performance data to inform decisions on recruitment, remuneration and field tactics. Beane recognised that sabermetrics, the statistical study of baseball, offered valuable insights on the limitations of conventional player performance statistics. In particular Beane exploited market inefficiencies in the valuation of player performance by using statistically better predictors of performance. So, for example, instead of relying on only batting and slugging averages, Beane also used on-base percentage (OBP) which statistical analysis had shown to be the most reliable predictor of game outcomes. Hakes and Sauer (2006) have shown that, despite OBP being the best predictor of team-win percentages over the period 1999–2003, it had no statistically significant impact on hitter salaries. Following the publication of *Moneyball*, OBP became a highly significant driver of hitter salaries in 2004. The arbitrage opportunity had gone as the market corrected the inefficiency in the valuation process. Even without the publication of *Moneyball*, rivals had begun to realise that the As were putting more emphasis on OBP in evaluating hitters. The book probably only accelerated the rate of adoption of OBP as a league-wide KPI (i.e. key performance indicator).

Another strategic change by the As was to shift the focus away from recruiting high school graduates in the annual player draft and instead to recruit a much higher proportion of college players with exceptional records. There were a number of reasons favouring this change in recruitment strategy. The market for college draft picks tends to be less inflated than that for high school draft picks, with fewer teams competing actively and bidding up salaries for these players. Many teams deemed college players as 'rejects' who had failed to be recruited out of high school. But Beane realised that college players could offer real value for money. The performance data for college players were more readily available and the greater competitiveness of college baseball meant that the statistics were more reliable as a predictor of performance at the elite level. College players are also older and more mature physically and psychologically, which gives greater confidence that they will succeed if drafted. Again the success enjoyed by the As from the change in player recruitment strategy was observed and imitated by other teams, so that the arbitrage opportunity was again only temporary.

Moneyball has clearly influenced the behaviour of other MLB teams and led to more widespread use of statistical analysis in their day-to-day operations. But the book has also had a profound and potentially long-term impact on other professional team sports, with Billy Beane seen as a success-champion for the application of statistical performance analysis in elite sport. The long-term impact of *Moneyball* may be ultimately most significant in the invasion team sports to the extent that it is changing the perception of the value of quantitative data. The complexity of player interdependency in invasion team sports has led to a more subjective, qualitative approach with a deep-rooted scepticism towards a more quantitative approach. But with technological advances allowing easier and more comprehensive data collection in these sports, *Moneyball* is encouraging teams to put more effort into finding competitive advantage from better use of their performance data.

COACHING

Managing high performance sport with a professional sports team is the responsibility of the coaching staff. Coaching represents the human resource management (HRM) process in a professional sports team. Coaching can be broken down into three principal functions that are generic to HRM across all organisations: recruitment, development and deployment. The coaching staff must identify and recruit the best potential talent that is available and afford-able, and then develop and deploy that talent to get the best performance. Player recruitment represents the resource-picking function of management (Makadok, 2001). As discussed in the previous section, teams that achieve high levels of transactional efficiency are able to recruit and retain players who provide high productive value relative to their salary and acquisition costs. Player development and deployment can be seen as the capability-building function of management (Makadok, 2001) and the drivers of transformational efficiency.

The player development function of coaching can be summarised as developing the four As – Ability, Athleticism, Attitude and Awareness. The Football Association, the governing body for association football in England, uses a similar categorisation of the different aspects of long-term player development, designated as the Four-Corner Model, that has been derived from a multi-sport framework for long-term athlete development (FA Learning, 2006). The Four-Corner Model identifies the Technical, Physical, Psychological and Social corners and is advocated as a general framework for guiding the development pathway of all players regardless of age or ability. The coaching staff in a professional sports team usually comprises skills coaches often specialised in certain phases of play (e.g. defensive, offen-sive and special-team coaches in gridiron football; backs and forwards coaches in rugby), and strength and conditioning coaches concerned with the physical preparation of players. Increasingly teams are also bringing in sports psychologists to work on the mental prepara-tion of players. In addition, European teams with their own in-house academy set-ups for developing young players have coaches that specialise in youth development. The coaching staff also includes support staff such as physiotherapists, sports scientists and performance analysts. The use of cutting-edge sport science has been seen by some teams as a potential source of competitive advantage. For example, the resource-constrained English Premiership football team Bolton Wanderers, under the management of Sam Allardyce, made extensive use of sport science as a means of emulating the *Moneyball* strategy of the Oakland As, and over the period 2001–2007 achieved exceptional levels of sporting efficiency (Gilmore and Gilson, 2007; Gilmore, 2009; Gerrard, 2010).

The tactical function of coaching is most significant in the invasion sports characterised by a high degree of player interdependency and the need to co-ordinate the decisions and actions of individual players in order to maximise the effectiveness of the team. A common solution to the co-ordination problem across organisations and work groups is to develop a specific way or style of doing things that becomes embedded in the culture of the group or organisa-tion and provides guidelines on how individuals should behave in particular situations. In this way individual behaviour becomes predictable and facilitates better co-ordination. Of course, the downside of predictability is that it helps facilitate the development of more effec-tive counter-strategies by competitors. In the case of a professional sports team, the coaches establish a particular style of play for the team, and practise on the training field what players should do in commonly occurring game situations. Berman *et al.* (2002) conceptualised this process as the creation of tacit knowledge through learning-by-doing. They found strong evidence in basketball that the more successful teams in the NBA exhibited higher levels of shared experience, giving more game time to players who had been with the team for longer periods. Gerrard and Lockett (2008) found a similar phenomenon in English Premiership

311

football but conceptualised the process as the accumulation of team-specific human capital involving both formal and tacit knowledge. They also recognised that the process involved two-way causation since successful teams tend to remain together and so accumulate more shared experience, whereas unsuccessful teams tend to be broken up and replaced by new players with a consequent decrease in shared experience.

Across the invasion sports particularly in the various codes of football, there are commonalities in different styles of play. For example, in soccer some teams put an emphasis on attacking play, adopting a combination style of play with quick short passing between players. A similar attacking style in rugby union has been variously described as '15-man rugby' or 'total rugby' (Greenwood, 2003). An alternative approach is to concentrate on gaining good field position deep in the opposition half by playing the ball long and following up quickly to put opponents under pressure so that they are unable to clear the ball effectively. In association football this style of play has been called 'direct play' or 'the long-ball game' and is particularly associated with Charles Hughes, a former FA Director of Coaching, who based his advocacy of direct play on the statistical evidence that the majority of goals scored in soccer involved less than three passes (Hughes, 1996). Direct play was a feature of Bolton Wanderers' success under Allardyce (Gerrard, 2010). In rugby union this emphasis on establishing field position is often associated with the adoption of a 'kicking game' or what Greenwood (2003) calls 'play-safe rugby'. There is no single tactical approach that dominates all others along the style spectrum encompassing combination play at one end through to more direct play at the other end. What seems clear, however, is that successful teams establish a way of doing things that best suits their players and provides an effective way of co-ordinating the contributions of individual players.

A developing feature of the management of high performance sport is the adoption of formal performance management systems similar to those used in corporate organisations. The case study of the England national team that won the Rugby Union World Cup in 2003 managed by Sir Clive Woodward provides a very successful example of how performance management techniques taken from the business world were adopted and customised for an elite sports team.

Another recent innovation in professional team sports is the use of statistical performance analysis (SPA). SPA is the tactically informed cross-match forensic investigation of team and performance data to identify trends and patterns, and identify the possible explanations. SPA involves both ratio analysis as well as statistical modelling of match performance. It represents an evidence-based approach to coaching decisions that allows coaches to pre-test their beliefs about players, teams and tactics. SPA provides a complement to traditional coaching decision systems that rely on critical incident analysis of match video. By analysing across matches, SPA provides a wider perspective that facilitates the setting of priorities for further, more qualitative investigation of individual teams, players and events. The *Moneyball* story of how the Oakland As have used SPA to achieve high levels of transactional efficiency has proved a crucial exemplar of success that has facilitated the adoption of SPA in other sports. Nothing persuades better than success.

LEADERSHIP

In all organisations in all spheres of activity, success requires effective leadership. In each of the three case studies in this chapter the coach-leader played a central role in the success of the team. John Wooden, the most successful coach ever in college basketball, built team success at UCLA not just on tactical acumen but crucially on a set of core principles and ethical values, summarised in his Pyramid of Success. Billy Beane, the General Manager of the Oakland As, developed a successful and innovative David strategy using SPA to overcome his team's economic disadvantages. Sir Clive Woodward, the manager of the England national rugby union team that won the World Cup in 2003, developed a team culture heavily influenced by lessons of success drawn from the business world. Each of these coach-leaders adopted very different paths to success for their teams but each exemplifies effectiveness in the two core dimensions of leadership – the task dimension and the relationship dimension. Theories of leadership abound, but ultimately leadership comes down to the ability to formulate a vision of a successful outcome for a group of people with a strategy of how to get there (i.e. the task dimension), and then persuading the group to implement the strategy to get there (i.e. the relationship dimension).

Different leadership theorists have formulated the task and relationship dimensions in different ways. For example, Adair (2002) has developed the Action Centred-Leadership model in which he identifies three needs of leadership – task, team and individual. The team and individual needs in Adair's ACL model can be seen as twin aspects of the relationship dimension that determine the transformational efficiency of an organisation. More recently, Yukl (2008) has proposed a synthesis of leadership theories in his model of flexible leadership, distinguishing three fundamental dimensions of leadership: task-oriented, relationship-oriented and change-oriented. The change-oriented dimension can be seen as the dynamic component of the task dimension of leadership in situations in which the external environment is changing and requires innovation and refinement of the vision of how to be successful. Successful change-oriented leadership will lead to high levels of dynamic efficiency in an organisation. Wooden, Beane and Woodward all succeeded in the task dimension by creating a vision of how the team could succeed and refining that vision as circumstances changed, and then succeeded in the task dimension by getting their players and coaches both as individuals and as a team to buy-in to the vision and implement it successfully.

CASE STUDY: ENGLAND RUGBY UNION WORLD CUP WINNERS 2003

Sir Clive Woodward was appointed as head coach of the England national rugby union team in September 1997. He immediately set the target of winning the Rugby Union World Cup in 1999. He failed to achieve this target, with England being eliminated by South Africa in the quarter-finals of the tournament. But four years on, his England team triumphed, beating the host nation, Australia, 20–17 in the final after extra time. Although England is the historic home of rugby union and the biggest of all the rugby-playing nations, its playing record is one of underperformance, ranking only fourth behind New Zealand, South Africa and France in international win percentages. Woodward's achievement was to overcome this chronic inefficiency and effectively exploit the available resources.

Woodward was a 'shirt-suit' who combined his experience as an elite player and coach (i.e. a 'shirt') with his experience as a successful businessman (i.e. a 'suit') to produce what he called the 'Winning!' formula (Woodward, 2004). Woodward defined Winning! as the combination of playing flawlessly as individuals, fluidly as a team and winning convincingly. A Winning! performance is a performance at the highest level that is deeply meaningful and satisfying. It is about being the best and being the most prepared, getting more from the body and achieving more synergy than anyone else. According to Woodward, Winning! is only possible if everyone in the organisation is working well as a team, with leaders giving strong guidance and inspiration through example, and fully supported by the management, sponsors and fans. The Winning! formula incorporated various management insights that Woodward had gained from the business world. For example, he stressed the T-CUP principle – Think Correctly Under Pressure – and cites Johnny Wilkinson's World Cup winning drop goal as an example *par excellence* of T-CUP, with the effective implementation by the team under extreme pressure of a pre-rehearsed move to create the drop-goal opportunity for Wilkinson who then executed his kick expertly.

At the core of Woodward's approach was a formal and very detailed performance management system. He identified nine high performance behaviours – defence, basics, contact principles, pressure, kicking game, attack, self-control, tactics and leadership. These high performance behaviours were broken down into 34 separate sub-behaviours. Performance in each of these sub-behaviours was monitored using measurable key performance indicators (KPIs). In total 135 KPIs were used in Woodward's Winning! performance management system. Woodward's performance management system demonstrates more than anything his keen attention to detail.

Two key lessons can be drawn from Woodward's World Cup winning team. First, it takes time to build success and the process is far from linear. The first period of Woodward's tenure as England coach was, at least in terms of results, disappointing. His win percentage in the period 1997–1999 was 53.6 per cent which was below England's all-time win percentage of 57.4 per cent for the period 1871–2007. Crucially also, Woodward's record against the Southern Hemisphere teams (i.e. Australia, New Zealand and South Africa) in 1997–1999 was only 15.4 per cent compared to the all-time win percentage of 36.5 per cent. However, in the four-year period 2000–2003, Woodward's win percentage in full internationals was 89.4 per cent, losing only five games out of 47 full international games. And against the Southern Hemisphere teams his record in those four years was an incredible 12 wins from 13 matches, a win percentage of 92.3 per cent. When England won the World Cup in 2003 it was on the basis of sustained success over the previous four years when they had become established as the number one team in world rugby.

The second lesson to be drawn from Woodward's experience is that success is difficult to maintain and not easily transferable to other contexts. England have struggled since 2003. In part this has been due to the natural life cycle in teams as experienced players retire and are replaced by new players with limited international experience. Woodward himself stepped down as England coach in 2004 but continuity was preserved initially through the appointment of his assistant, Andy Robinson, as head coach. The current team manager is Martin Johnson, the captain of the 2003 World Cup winning team. The difficulties of transferring his approach to different contexts are evidenced by Woodward's post-2003 career. Woodward coached the British and Irish Lions team on the New Zealand tour in 2005 and, despite including many of the players and coaches from the England World Cup winning team, the Lions lost all three test matches. Woodward subsequently moved to association football and became Performance Director and then Director of Football at Southampton. Media coverage of his time at Southampton suggests that he faced enormous difficulties in establishing his credibility in a different sport in which he had never played or coached at the elite level. He is now Director of Elite Performance at the British Olympic Association and applying his performance management approach in a number of individual and team sports.

SUMMARY

This chapter has provided an introduction to the different aspects of the management of high performance sport particularly in professional team sports. Effective management such that teams achieve their sporting targets requires sufficient resources and the efficient utilisation of those resources. Small-market teams can compensate at least partially for their lack of financial resources by developing knowledge-based advantages (i.e. a David strategy) to achieve a low win–cost ratio indicating high levels of sporting efficiency. Sporting efficiency can be broken down into transactional and transformational efficiency. Transactional efficiency relates to the resource-picking function of management and measures the team's ability to identify and recruit playing talent at lower cost than rival teams. Crucial to transactional efficiency is the valuation of playing talent using comparative and fundamental valuation methods and searching for arbitrage opportunities where the productive value of a player exceeds the current market valuation. The success of Billy Beane as GM of the Oakland As exemplifies the possibilities for using statistical performance analysis to achieve high levels of transactional efficiency. Transformational efficiency is about getting the best out of your players through the coaching function. John Wooden's success with the UCLA basketball team demonstrates the importance of instilling the right values in players so that their exceptional potential can be realised collectively in the team. Sir Clive Woodward's success in winning the Rugby Union World Cup with the England national team shows the transferability of performance management techniques from the business world to the world of high performance sport. And common to all successful business, public-service and high-performance sport organisations is effective leadership in both the task dimension of creating a vision of how to succeed and the relationship dimension in getting individuals to work together as a team to achieve the vision. Beane, Wooden and Woodward in their own unique ways show the importance of the coach-leader in managing successfully in high performance sport.

REVIEW QUESTIONS

1 Explain the difference between effectiveness and efficiency in assessing the performance of a professional sports team.
2 In what ways can a professional sports team improve its win–cost ratio?
3 What is the significance of the distinction between transactional and transformational efficiency?
4 What are the two different methods of comparative valuation? Which method is likely to be most useful for valuing playing talent? Why?
5 What are the two stages in Scully's method for estimating the fundamental value of playing talent?
6 What are the four corners in the Four-Corner Model of long-term player development?
7 What are the different management functions of the coaching staff in a professional sports team?

8 Briefly outline the task and relationship dimensions of leadership. Which of the two dimensions of leadership do you consider to have been critical to the success of John Wooden? Billy Beane? Sir Clive Woodward? Why?

FURTHER READING

Berri, D. J., Schmidt, M. B. and Brook, S. L. (2006) *The Wages of Wins: Taking Measure of the Many Myths in Modern Sport*, Stanford University Press, Stanford.

Gray, S. (2006) *The Mind of Bill James: How a Complete Outsider Changed Baseball*, Doubleday, New York.

Jackson, P. and Delehanty, H. (1995) *Sacred Hoops: Spiritual Lessons of a Hardwood Warrior*, Hyperion, New York.

Kerwin, A. (2005) *Clive Woodward: A Biography*, Orion Books, London.

Lewis, M. (2003) *Moneyball: The Art of Winning an Unfair Game*, Norton, New York.

Marturano, A. and Gosling, J. (2008) *Leadership: The Key Concepts*, Routledge, London.

Wooden, J. and Jamison, S. (2005) *Wooden on Leadership*, McGraw-Hill, New York.

REFERENCES

Adair, J. (2002) *Effective Strategic Management*, Macmillan, London.

Berman, S. L., Down, J. and Hill, C. W. (2002) 'Tacit knowledge as a source of competitive advantage in the National Basketball Association', *Academy of Management Journal*, vol. 45, pp. 13–31.

Carmichael, F. and Thomas, D. (1993) 'Bargaining in the transfer market: theory and evidence', *Applied Economics*, vol. 25, pp. 1467–1476.

Dobson, S. and Gerrard, B. (1999) 'The determination of player transfer fees in English professional soccer', *Journal of Sport Management*, vol. 13, pp. 259–279.

FA Learning (2006) *The FA Level 1 Club Coach Handbook (2nd edition)*, Coachwise, Leeds.

Gerrard, B. (2005) 'A resource-utilisation model of organisational efficiency in professional team sports', *Journal of Sport Management*, vol. 19, pp. 143–169.

Gerrard, B. (2007) 'Is the *Moneyball* approach transferable to complex invasion team sports?', *International Journal of Sport Finance*, vol. 2, pp. 214–230.

Gerrard, B. (2010) 'Analysing sporting efficiency using standardised wage cost: evidence from the FA Premier League', *International Journal of Sports Science and Coaching*, vol. 5, pp. 13–35.

Gerrard, B. and Lockett, A. (2008) 'A dynamic model of human capital and team performance', unpublished mimeo.

Gilmore, S. (2009) 'The importance of asset maximisation in football: towards the long-term gestation and maintenance of sustained high performance', *International Journal of Sport Science and Coaching*, vol. 4, pp. 465–478.

Gilmore, S. E. and Gilson, C. H. J. (2007) 'Finding form: elite sports and the business of change', *Journal of Organizational Change Management*, vol. 20, pp. 409–428.

Greenwood, J. (2003) *Total Rugby (5th edition)*, A&C Black, London.

Hakes, J. K. and Sauer, R. D. (2006) 'An economic evaluation of the *Moneyball* hypothesis', *Journal of Economic Perspectives*, vol. 20, pp. 173–185.

Hughes, C. (1996) *Soccer Skills: Tactics and Teamwork*, Parragon Books, Bristol.

Lewis, M. (2003) *Moneyball: The Art of Winning an Unfair Game*, Norton, New York.

Makadok, R. (2001) 'Toward a synthesis of the resource-based and dynamic-capability views of rent creation', *Strategic Management Journal*, vol. 22, pp. 387–401.

Reilly, B. and Witt, R. (1995) 'English league transfer prices: is there a racial dimension?', *Applied Economic Letters*, vol. 2, pp. 220–222.

Scully, G. W. (1974) 'Pay and performance in Major League Baseball', *American Economic Review*, vol. 64, pp. 915–930.

Sloane, P. J. (1971) 'The economics of professional football: the football club as a utility maximiser', *Scottish Journal of Political Economy*, vol. 18, pp. 121–146.

Vrooman, J. (1997) 'A unified theory of capital and labour markets in Major League Baseball', *Southern Economic Journal*, vol. 63, pp. 594–619.

Wooden, J. (2004) *They Call Me Coach*, McGraw-Hill, New York.

Woodward, C. (2004) *Winning! The Story of England's Rise to Rugby World Cup Glory*, Hodder & Stoughton, London.

Yukl, G. (2008) 'How leaders influence organisational effectiveness', *The Leadership Quarterly*, vol. 19, pp. 708–722.

Zimbalist, A. (1992) 'Salaries and performance: beyond the Scully model', in P. M. Sommers (ed.), *Diamonds are Forever: The Business of Baseball*, The Brookings Institution, Washington DC.

Chapter 18

Sport, the media and strategic communications management

Raymond Boyle, University of Glasgow
Richard Haynes, University of Stirling

TOPICS

Sport and digital media • Sport, celebrity and reputation management • Image management, endorsements and image rights

---

OBJECTIVES

At the end of this chapter you should be able to:

■ Provide a brief context to the changes that have taken place in the sports industry and its link with the media;

■ Identify some of the key areas that media managers need to be conscious of when examining the sports industry's relationship with the media;

■ Understand the growing importance of 'reputation management' within the sport industry;

■ Identify the opportunities and challenges offered by digital media platforms within sport;

■ Appreciate the potential conflicts of interest between the fields of sports journalism and public relations (PR);

■ Understand the growing importance of PR for sports stakeholders given the growth of financial and political stakeholders in the field, with a particular emphasis on association football.

KEY TERMS

Image rights – are the contractual rights to prevent unauthorised use of an individual's name, likeness or other personal attributes, such as physical or style characteristics, signatures, nicknames or slogans associated with them.

Journalism – the investigation and reporting of events, issues and trends to a wide audience.

New media – the incorporation of traditional media such as film, images, music and the spoken and written word, with the interactive power of computer and communications technology, computer-enabled consumer devices and the Internet.

PR – is the practice of presenting the public face of an organization or individual, which encompasses longer-term strategic aims, such as brand building and working with local communities as well as managing reputation.

OVERVIEW

This chapter focuses on the sports industry and its relationship with media industries. The first part of the chapter highlights a number of issues around the engagement of the sports industry with the emerging digital media environment and the opportunities and challenges that digital platforms, such as the Internet, offer media managers. This section also offers a case study regarding the British Broadcasting Corporation's (BBC) digital sports strategy as it relates to the London 2012 Olympics.

The second part of the chapter focuses on issues for media managers relating to the developing relationship between digital media, journalism and public relations. Specifically we focus on the theme of reputation management for sports stars and offer case studies around two high-profile cases that emerged in 2010 involving golfer Tiger Woods and England and Chelsea footballer John Terry.

CASE STUDY: THE BBC – THE DIGITAL OLYMPIC BROADCASTER[1]

The year 2012 promises to be a big one as Britain goes digital and London stages the 2012 games. It will also be a big year for the BBC – the Olympic broadcaster. The BBC, whose budget for sport has struggled to match the inflated prices being negotiated by others for 'live' sport (in particular football), has found their sports portfolio shrinking year-on-year. However, since the announcement in July 2005 that the Olympic Games would take place in London in 2012, the economic, political and cultural position of sport in the UK was transformed. Big sporting events are important for media organisations to prove their worth, whether it be to advertisers, subscribers or, in the BBC's case, their credentials as a public service broadcaster.

When the Olympic Games were last held in London in 1948 the 'age of austerity' did not prevent the BBC from spending £250,000 on hosting the world's broadcasters, showcasing the new technology of television and wholeheartedly immersing itself in the ideology that hosting the Olympics was important for British prestige. Fast forward to the Beijing Games of 2008 and the BBC's role in championing Olympianism was as strong as ever and its technological innovation in the delivery of the Games was an undoubted opportunity to showcase its position in the digital media landscape. The Beijing Games in 2008 were available in

HDTV for the first time, the BBC's iPlayer, launched in 2007, was used to enable multiple live and on-demand video streams, and its coverage encouraged interactive participation by its audience.

Given the huge investment of resources in the coverage of major sporting events like the Olympics, broadcasters are always eager to release positive figures reflecting high ratings and audience share. Roger Mosey, the BBC's then Director of Sport, was in an ebullient mood as audience figures for the Games exceeded expectations: 'We predicted 30 million and privately hoped for about 35 million, so to get to 40 million even before the closing ceremony is terrific' (Conlan, 2008). In an age of diminishing audiences for individual channels the figures were truly remarkable.

But the significance of equating the performance of the broadcaster to the athletes themselves makes all too apparent the pressure felt by the BBC to maintain its prestige in the coverage of the Games. The remarks hint at some of the wider pressures connected with the performance of the BBC in its coverage of sport. As a public service broadcaster it must transmit a range of programming to suit various audiences, as well as showcase those events, like the Olympics, that have broad national appeal. The problem for the BBC, noted above, is that budgets for sport are limited, so when it covers sport there is considerable pressure to both draw a 'national' audience and maintain its historic position as 'the home of sport'. Arguably the former is increasingly difficult in a diverse multichannel environment and the latter mantle of a leader in sports coverage has been significantly undermined by the growth and power of Sky Sports in particular.

The BBC's television coverage of the Beijing Games had peaked at 7 million viewers on the second Thursday of the event, and on the final Saturday it also took a very respectable 42 per cent share of the UK audience. When equated with audiences for sport in the 1970s and 1980s the Beijing Games do not compare favourably. But in the new media age the mainstream television coverage is only the partial story of its overall coverage. The BBC has attempted to respond to the challenges of multichannel competition and dominant niche sports channels through its development of new web-based, interactive, High Definition (HD) and on-demand services that provide far more depth to the coverage of individual events than ever before. The BBC introduced six live feeds via its website and a range of 'catch up' opportunities via its iPlayer with 400,000 users downloading the 100 metres final in one day alone. The different modes of delivery do have some interesting consequences for the viewing experience.

The standard television format of linking to events from an anchor and panellists in the studio get short-circuited when coverage is delivered online, on-demand. In the online viewing experience the events stand alone and editorialising is by design of the web developer not the television producer. Although certain events are prioritised – invariably around British achievements and medallists – there is no framing of the event by the studio. It is almost a pure outside broadcast, in an old-fashioned sense of television being there to capture the moment.

The BBC's HD coverage was mesmerising in its depth and colour, but remained experimental in 2008. While the BBC broadcast more than 300 hours of the Olympics on its dedicated HD channel, the number of households watching the service remained relatively small. Although more than 40 per cent of British households had HD-Ready television sets in 2008, only an approximate 10 per cent could actually watch HDTV services. This fracturing and bifurcation of audiences is an increasingly familiar pattern of sports viewing in the twenty-first century. Even where viewers are watching the same sporting event, their experiences of how they watch, where they watch and the technologies used may be incredibly varied.

The ideological battle the BBC faces in continuing to innovate its television coverage of sport is a reflection of its wider institutional problems of justifying its existence and public funding during an economic recession in a highly liberalised, market-driven media environment. Many of the BBC's competitors in television, but especially in the online world, point to the relatively low level of commercial risk the BBC takes as it innovates in its coverage. Such subsidy is viewed as anti-competitive and represents an unfair advantage over new enterprise. The BBC's brand ensures it commands a prominent place in the minds of audiences and web users in the UK and, increasingly, globally. However, without such a commitment to innovation in sports coverage, the availability of quality sports programming, news and myriad services may be diminished, leaving certain social groups excluded from premium televised sport. Sport as a national shared experience would also suffer. This is not an argument that suggests things should stay the same, rather a sentiment that comes through strongly in the following statement from Mosey:

> Given this richness of our history – and we're enormously proud of it – there's an easy trap of thinking that the BBC is what the marketers call a 'heritage brand' ... The point about the people who launched all these wonderful new services is that they were pioneers not traditionalists.
>
> (Mosey, 2007)

The pioneering spirit of the BBC Sports Department is perhaps one of its most enduring features.

The BBC's new media coverage of the 2008 Games enabled multiple and novel ways in which the Games and its cast of characters could be communicated. Television coverage was supplemented by blogs from producers and BBC journalists. There was more exposure and time given over to the variety of sports on show, enabling the varied stories of the Games to be revealed. There were behind-the-scenes views of the Games itself, including some of the more contentious moments of the event. For instance, the arrest of the ITN journalist John Ray who went to cover one of the several protests against Chinese rule in Tibet was captured by a BBC crew and promptly put online as evidence of the overbearing surveillance that surrounded the Games in Beijing. In these ways and more, the mediation of the Olympic Games by the BBC opened up new vistas from which to experience the Games and to identify with athletes and nations.

Roger Mosey is now BBC Director of London 2012, managing the Corporation's engagement with the Games across the genres of news, sport and current affairs and its media platforms. For Mosey the London Games are crucial for the BBC. He argues:

> What we have in 2012 is the biggest event in our lifetimes at the very point when the UK goes fully digital, and therefore we believe that what we would like to show both the viability of some conventional broadcast models and the viability of the BBC in terms of digital media. Ultimately we would argue that you need public service broadcasting as much if not more in the digital age as you did in the analogue age.
>
> (Interview with author, 16 September 2009)

At the core of this is the BBC's web presence. The 2008 Olympic Games saw more video streaming on the first day of Beijing than during the whole of the Athens Games in 2004. It went from 2.6 million video streams in 2004 to 38 million video streams in Beijing four years later. This will grow in London 2012, as will HD 'take up' in advance of the Games. The BBC will also have every Olympic event available 'live' through its interactive web-based service for the first time.

However, Mosey is clear that the BBC's coverage is also about continuity as well as embracing new possibilities. Regarding the role of social networking, for example, he notes:

> I think it is probably fair to say in the Olympics that our messages boards and our blogs and our interactivity will be as they are now. I don't see them massively impacting on the prime BBC1 coverage because at the moment it appears the audience demand really is to see the athletics and hear from commentators such as Michael Johnson. They don't particularly want endless people reading out emails and Twitter messages.
>
> (Interview with author, 16 September 2009)

So the BBC's strategy sees television remaining the prime Olympic channel, with online services offering content to particular fans to engage with coverage and also follow niche sports. The BBC is also keen to capture some of the 2012 Games in 3D, for while they understand that people may not have this technology at home, in the future it may become an increasingly mass technology. This is not to say that social networking will not be an important part of the BBC's media planning. Indeed, social networking sites have been crucial in building community involvement in the run up to the Games and have helped in connecting volunteers and young people across London and beyond in feeling part of the broader event. Rather that a more complex media landscape requires a more sophisticated strategic approach that clearly recognises what differing media platforms can offer differing publics and stakeholders in any sporting context, from spectators to sponsors.

SPORT AND DIGITAL MEDIA

Issues and opportunities for media managers

The Internet has undoubtedly had a dramatic impact on the global media environment in which the sports media industry now operates.[2] The degree of engagement with new media clearly varies, but there is general consensus among sporting organisations that the Internet presents a range of new possibilities for communicating with various publics and, with that, the opportunity to increase revenue streams.

It is becoming clear that sports clubs require a multimedia capacity to be in a position to exploit the online and image rights that will become more important over the next decade, although exactly how important remains unclear, as this chapter will reveal. It also raises a key question for the sports manager involved in the development of any new media strategy, albeit one that is surprisingly often overlooked: *What exactly do sports clubs want to achieve through interacting with digital media?*

Internet strategy

For the elite football clubs their strategy is one that seeks to use the various digital platforms to develop long-term revenue streams. For the majority of clubs whose fan base isn't global, however, revenue from new media sources will remain small for the foreseeable future, and as a result any investment must be planned with clear, achievable goals.

The major change in the last few years has been the growth of social media through networks such as Facebook and sharing content through sites like YouTube. This area raises a number of issues for media managers. These include how to utilise these media to build and connect with fan bases; the need to manage one's digital rights across this fast-moving arena;

and to develop the need to protect one's reputation in an age of interconnectedness, which allows fact and fiction to be disseminated across the globe within seconds. A number of these issues are addressed in the case studies in the early part of this chapter and discussed further when the relationship between journalism and PR is unpacked later.

Thus a challenge for the sports manager is that every major club is keen to develop their media capacity for fear of being left behind when the projected revenues begin to material-ise. A clear communicative strategy of how new media can benefit the differing aspects of sport needs to be considered. One of the major challenges for managers is sorting through the rhetoric that surrounds digital media and its impact from the reality. Too often the focus has been on driving additional revenues from the Internet, rather than using it to nurture, develop and extend the relationship between sports and their fan bases. Of course this com-municative element is not mutually exclusive with driving revenue, but in the absence of a clear understanding of the role of the Internet and social networking sites, a concern with revenue streams has often emerged at the expense of long-term relationship building.

For example, most football clubs have developed dedicated club websites. Initially these were used simply to give information about forthcoming matches and to sell club mer-chandise. However, it was envisaged that new income would be generated from streaming audio-visual material, which fans would pay an additional premium to view.

For elite clubs with a large national and international fan base, such as Liverpool FC (LFC), this initially saw them charge £39.99 for its e-season ticket in 2002. What is significant, after examining the situation in 2010, is how this model has failed to generate the revenues origi-nally envisaged. A LFC TV online season ticket eight years on can be bought for £44.99, a marginal increase given the rise in the cost of season tickets and BSkyB television subscriptions over this period. Even Manchester United note that a £45 season ticket for online MUTV is all the market will bear. Other clubs such as Celtic FC charge £40 a season for access to the Channel67 site available online. Of course all these channels are available on a range of digital television platforms through Sky and Virgin Media, but the key point is that people watching football content online remains marginal; the preference is for television access, and as long as this market remains strong and clubs get healthy revenues from it, then online sports con-tent remains a mere add-on. Thus while clubs with a large local and global fan base may be able to extract financial value from their web presence, a range of problems exist which make it unlikely that club websites will provide substantial revenue streams for more than a handful of clubs. What it does is allow other forms of digital content to be sold through the website, including phone ringtones and other downloadable content, most of which is increasingly aimed at mobile phones and PDAs. The website also acts as a platform for club sponsors, and so long as reasonable levels of traffic can be retained to a given site, then advertising revenue is also an ongoing consideration.

However, what is striking is *how important digital television remains to sports media manag-ers*. Digital technology is viewed as central to the economic well-being of any country in the twenty-first century. It is possible to watch television on one's personal computer or latest mobile phone and send emails through one's television or download music across the web. At the core of digitisation is the notion of the extension of choice, as the technology allows vastly increased amounts of information to be sent and received.

323

Not only is 2012 the year of the London Olympic Games but it is also the year the UK goes digital and the existing analogue signal will be turned off. This is the means by which currently 40 per cent of homes in Britain receive their television pictures. This will therefore be the year of the first truly digital Olympic Games, yet television will remain an important element in this changing environment. Public service broadcasters such as the BBC have embraced the digital age as a way of ensuring that it remains viable and relevant in an era of increased competition and a fragmenting audience.

Despite this, it appears that it is the commercial imperative that remains one of the key drivers of the digital television age. Media content (what used to be simply referred to as television programmes) increasingly must have a cross-media dimension to allow revenues to be maximised. Programmes such as ITV's *X Factor* and the BBC's *Strictly Come Dancing* all utilise the ability of the audience to interact through either their digital television or by texting on their mobile phones. These are what are called 'event' television programmes – those 'must see' broadcasts that are rarely time shifted. 'Live' sport also falls into this category; it has become one of the few content areas of the digital landscape that doesn't work if time shifted. That is why 'live' football remains such compelling television content and has retained and enhanced its commercial value over the last decade.

Whilst the impact of interactivity on coverage of reality-type TV programmes and sports coverage is widely understood (the BBC's coverage of Wimbledon, which allows viewers to choose which match they wish to follow, being a good example), predictions abound about the impact of interactive technology on other areas of television output, such as popular drama.

In 2010 the Japanese manufacturer Fujitsu launched a computer/TV hybrid piece of hardware, which can store almost 500 hours of television on its hard disc. What we think television is for and how we use it is dramatically changing as the commercial drive to make money from the digital age intensifies. Yet against this backdrop of huge technological change the range of technological hardware on display should not blind us. It's the social role and usage of technology that remains crucial in determining its impact. Who controls it, and for what purpose, will shape the role that television continues to play politically, culturally and economically in the time ahead.

Although more than 85 per cent of British households have digital television, the Office of National Statistics estimate that 9 million adults have never accessed the Internet (ONS, 2010). These figures suggest a form of digital divide, of those who have access to this landscape and those who financially or culturally may be cut adrift. The importance of being addressed as digital citizens (with rights and entitlements) and not simply as consumers is a major challenge for public service broadcasters in the twenty-first century. Digitalisation opens up a range of possibilities for how we might want to use the ability to communicate, build and strengthen communities, and television, with its unique power to move and mobilise people, remains a key element of that aspiration.

Future thinking: the age of screens and content

Sports, as well as other facets of our daily lives, are set to be dramatically affected by the growing importance of the Internet, video gaming and other multimedia applications, placing more control in the hands of the consumer who may choose from a vast array of services through 'many-to-many' communication. However, the rampant optimism that drives the promotional strategies of large computer-based corporations is only heard and acted upon by a small technological élite.

In analysing the rapidly expanding 'online' services for the sports fan, we must guard critically against any oversimplified linear approach to technological change in media sport and its promise to empower its audience. While the interactive possibilities of the World Wide Web of sport are exciting, it is also true that any deeper understanding of media technologies of sport requires a concern for social, economic, political and cultural processes in order to appreciate the complex ways in which power is structured and manipulated. We would argue that a key conceptual shift needed by media managers in the digital age is to think of screens and content. These screens may be in the home, and we would strongly argue that the television in the living room is a fixture for some time to come. They may equally be on a mobile, a computer or in one's car. The issue will be what sort of content is on that screen, how it gets onto that screen and how people are willing to pay for that content.

A clear strategic vision of what the various new media platforms will be used for is necessary. Are they being developed for revenue generation, communication and feedback from supporters, the promotion of the club, the countering of negative media coverage, or some/all of these? For smaller clubs, the Internet in particular may be an important part of its wider community networking as it builds long-term relationships with supporters.

An understanding of the media marketplace is essential. Given the changes discussed earlier, some analysts argue that, if the money on offer from traditional broadcasters ultimately fails to satisfy the market leaders, then clubs across Europe will be tempted to go it alone, or set up their own channels. It has even been mooted that clubs will deliver exclusive subscription matches via the web across broadband networks and ostensibly cut out traditional broadcast networks by migrating the sport from television to the web. We still remain highly sceptical of this, not least because this is not how fans typically watch the sport, while the building of robust and reliable broadband networks remains some way off. The pace of technology change also means that a broad strategy is required that is not wedded to any one dominant market player. Twitter may not be what everyone is talking about in two years' time, but some other social media may have usurped it, as YouTube did with MySpace, or Facebook achieved with Bebo.

Issues of journalism and public relations

There has always been a symbiotic relationship between the journalism and sports industries (Boyle, 2006). This has been particularly true in terms of print media. Here, sports news, gossip and speculation has sold newspapers, while in turn this type of coverage has raised the profile of particular sports and helped to create and sustain a sporting star system.

However, the changes in the sports industry described in the opening part of this chapter have helped to change this relationship. The commercialisation of the sport and the growing financial underpinning of key sports, such as football, through money from television have made access to exclusive material more important. This process has been dramatically

heightened with the growth in media outlets covering the sport, which have grown expo-
nentially in the last decade. Football and footballing issues are now covered across a media
landscape which includes the broadsheet and tabloid press; the growing print football
magazine market; commercial and PSB radio outlets; terrestrial and satellite 24/7 news programming; social media; and dedicated free to air and pay TV channels. Add to this the more
general Internet coverage, which can reach a potential global audience, and the media's fixa-
tion with all things celebrity, and sport and sports stars have never had the media exposure
they are currently exposed to.

The issue of access and control of information has become more important for sports
media managers in recent years. First, with the new range of financial stakeholders across
sport, speculation about possible transfers, the future of the next manager or sponsorship
deal and such like can have potentially serious financial implications for sports clubs and
organisations. This highlights the growing importance of club PR in communicating with all
its various publics including fans, sponsors, shareholders and the media.

Second, in the football industry post-Bosman, the growth in player power, and with this
the attendant rise of the football agent, has meant that the media have become an important
arena in which stories, advantageous to a particular player and his agent, may be placed and
speculation about a player's future raised. While this has always been a feature of the game,
the growth of 'player power' requires particular management skills to deal with potential
clashes between club and player sponsors.

Third, as many sports clubs increase their own in-house media capacity to provide exclusive information to their own media platforms, for example the club television channel or
website, which has led to tensions between traditional media outlets and the clubs with regard
to access to information.

Fourth, the rise of social networking sites, blogs and Internet traffic more generally means
that these networks are important in terms of setting news agendas and spreading information (however truthful) about particular sports, players or fans. Indeed, a recent report from
the US indicated that the majority of journalists used social networking sites when researching stories (Cision, 2010), indicating the broader issue of the shifting nature of journalistic
sources and the importance of understanding the social networking world.

All these issues are set against a relationship between journalists and sports organisations
which appears to increasingly be based on mutual mistrust as the pressure in both sectors has
intensified in an increasingly 'always on' news environment. This process has intensified as
the boundaries between PR and journalism have blurred in the last decade, and the print sector has seen its access to sporting elites diminish as television's financial control of large areas
of sport, and the immediacy of the Internet, changes the rules of engagement (Boyle, 2006;
Steen, 2008; Boyle, Rowe and Whannel, 2010).

In addition the use of micro-blogging sites such as Twitter have made managing media
reputation a lot more difficult, as information gets 'out' onto the Internet and is then often
uncritically reproduced very quickly, even if untrue. There have been a number of occasions
when stories have been broken by players posting a Tweet that has been then picked up on by
mainstream journalists and carried, often to the embarrassment of the club or the player in
question. In 2009 Sunderland's Darren Bent voiced his displeasure with transfer negotiations

with Tottenham Hotspur via Twitter. More recently Manchester United have taken the step to inform the media that its players do not belong to any online networks, and that 'extreme scepticism' should be attached to any Tweets claiming to come from players. While not banning players from using social media, it was significant that Wayne Rooney, Ryan Giggs and Darren Fletcher, three Manchester United players with genuine Twitter accounts, all closed them in 2010.

As the money involved in a sport such as football has escalated, clubs have developed more formal relations with the media. The 'beat' journalist still exists and may have an inside track on developments in a club, but because of the increasing media focus on football, clubs realise that they have to communicate to various publics through a range of formal PR activities. In addition, there are now more media outlets to service, which are covering football, including a new online media community. Press releases and press conferences are now commonplace. New signings will be paraded in front of the media with structured events, including media briefings, Q&A sessions, photo calls and press packs.

A key issue for football media managers over the next few years will be balancing the needs of the club with that of individual players and the range of stakeholders in the sport (including the media). The demarcation lines will continue to be re-drawn as clubs seek to extract commercial value from all their assets, while media institutions (in particular those not holding specific coverage rights) will argue for the importance of continuing to journalistically report on all aspects of the football industry.

For sports managers in the football industry, the media matters. The range of media outlets is now extensive. They all have differing needs and characteristics. They provide income, exposure for a club and a means of communicating with a range of stakeholders in the game. What is beyond doubt is that an ability to manage a club's media strategy is an increasingly important part of the contemporary sports industry scene. The next part of this chapter develops this point further and examines a number of recent high-profile cases that has placed centre stage an issue that has become increasingly complex in the digital age: that of reputation management.

SPORT, CELEBRITY AND REPUTATION MANAGEMENT

In this section we will discuss the increasing media focus on sports stars, in particular the image and commercial tensions caused by public crisis, often forged on private impropriety. We analyse some of the ways in which reputation or crisis management in sport has emerged to combat or constrain such media scandals around sports stars and celebrity culture. At the same time, we connect this media phenomenon to some wider structural issues pervading contemporary elite sport, namely the connections between sport, the media, brands and the commercial management of sporting celebrity, commonly associated with rights in publicity or image rights (Haynes, 2007).

In the age of the celebrity sports star, audiences have been conditioned to expect a media scandal virtually on a daily basis. As each news story unfolds, with layer upon layer of reconstituted information, constantly updated and replenished on 24-hour news stations and websites, it also becomes harder for audiences to avoid such media scandals around famous sports celebrities as information is exchanged across media platforms. Whannel (2001) has attributed this process to what he calls 'vortextuality', whereby the entire news agenda gets pulled in to a singular event or media narrative focused on sport stardom and celebrity. Another aspect of this process, of the panoply of information across different media outlets, is that audiences find it increasingly difficult to assimilate what is happening – to make sense of the volume of 'media noise'.

In the contemporary media environment, it is the volume, speed and accessibility of information flows that create such an overwhelming inability to make sense of this information – what Manual Castells (2009: 425) has recently called 'information turbulence'. In media scandals, the amount of dis-information, hearsay, rumour and conjecture often overpower information that is anchored in more substantive forms of reportage. Psychologists have for many years labelled the tension between what people know and what they believe 'cognitive dissonance', which suggests people usually fall back on what they know to understand information. If we expand that concept to media audiences, a tension emerges between what the audience knows and how they make sense of the various media narratives in circulation at any given time.

This is none more so than in the revelations that surround sports stars, to which celebrity is now an adjunct of their fame, wealth and media attention. In this context, gossip and speculation supersede hard news stories. It is the soft news stories that pervade the dominant news media outlets, often driven by media narratives that provide commentary on the commentary of observers and onlookers rather than the actual people on whom these news events reside.

Contrary to popular media perceptions of declining ethical standards in sport, recent research in the UK suggests spectator perceptions of professional sports stars remain positive, particularly around individual sports like tennis and golf (McNamee *et al.*, 2007). Nevertheless, a prevalent media discourse focusing on the crimes and misdemeanours in and around sport remains a powerful cultural force in wider narratives of professional sport that arguably gain wider purchase in the formation of public opinion about particular sports stars. We now turn to some specific examples of how media sports stars are subject to complex media narratives that at times serve to bolster the public image of athletes while, at others, undermine and vilify them. How sports stars manage these media relations is also considered as part of this section.

CASE STUDY: TIGER WOODS AND THE NEW ERA OF MEDIATED CONTRITION

Within the world of golf, and indeed global sport, Tiger Woods creates a centrifugal force that has the power to suck in and render redundant all other 'newsworthy' items from other players, tournaments and competitions. This power is not only premised on his preeminent achievements in sport, but also, more prosaically, through the confluence of his golfing prowess and his commercial influence on sport and the media. Woods, the global superstar, is a construct of public relations, advertising and television, increasingly carried over into multiple forms of convergent digital media that pervade a multitude of both public and private spaces. He is the celebrity athlete *par excellence*: a symbol of commercialised and commoditised sport.

His status in the corporate marketing culture of sport, therefore, makes the implosion of his personal and public life in November 2009, after revelations regarding a series of infidelities while on the PGA Tour, both shocking and something of a morality tale. Woods' media crisis led to some profound soul-searching and introspective analysis on the part played by himself, the media and the commercial institutions that had made him the richest and most famous sports celebrity in the world. In many ways Woods' circumstances were unique, given his status and life history, almost exclusively dedicated to spectacular success in golf. But the episode did raise wider questions regarding the place of sports stars in our culture and society, and also the interrelationships sport and its principal performers have with the media and promotional culture. An example of the profound impact the Woods scandal had on US media can be seen in the following commentary by Thomas Boswell, sports columnist for the *Washington Post*:

We spend our lives drawing and re-drawing the portraits of everybody we know – our family, friends, and colleagues and, of course, those public figures that interest us most. We even redraw our own self-portraits. For better or worse, Tiger will redraw his public picture, probably more than once, over the rest of his life. No, not just his marketing image. Long careers, especially in golf, work against keeping secrets indefinitely. I wish him luck with the project. But like millions, I'm also disappointed in him, even though it's not my business to be disappointed in anybody else's private life.

(Boswell, 2009)

The article captures a contradictory fascination with the narrative trajectories of media sports stars. As Whannel (2009: 78) has argued, the media-driven stories of stars like Woods 'serve to illustrate that public image is a complex and unpredictable form that is always uncertain and can never be completely controlled'. Boswell's response to the Woods story also alludes to the implosion of the public and private, an urge to look and not look, to empathise and scrutinise, and to engage or disengage with the squalid spectacle of someone losing their public reputation.

The Woods news scandal raised an interesting volume of discussion regarding the role of public relations in sport, and whether or not his communications strategy was appropriate, well managed or effective. The anatomy of the news scandal reveals something of how source-news relations and reputation management of Woods' public image exposed a great deal about the contemporary media-centric world of elite sport.

In November 2009 the US tabloid *The National Enquirer* ran a story claiming Woods had had an affair with a New York nightclub hostess, Rachel Uchitel. Shortly after, US television news networks reported an incident involving Woods who had crashed his car into a fire hydrant outside his home. Although initial reports focused on the fact Woods had not been seriously injured, attention soon focused on a rumour that his wife Elin Nordegren had used a golf club to smash the rear window of the car to release her husband. Florida Highway patrol released a statement to the effect that they had not spoken to the sports star regarding the accident and damage to the hydrant. The police statement, and Woods' public silence on the accident, fuelled further media speculation that there were some suspicious circumstances to the events. Media supposition, effectively filling a void left by a lack of communication from Woods and his advisers, led to stories that the accident was due to a domestic dispute regarding the reported infidelity; moreover, that Nordegren had pursued Woods with the golf club as a weapon, rather than using it to assist Woods' escape. With speculation in the US and global media rising, and further revelations of affairs with other women starting to emerge, Woods made a brief statement of apology via his website and made a plea for privacy:

Although I am a well-known person and have made my career as a professional athlete, I have been dismayed to realize the full extent of what tabloid scrutiny really means. For the last week, my family and I have been hounded to expose intimate details of our personal lives. The stories in particular that physical violence played any role in the car accident were utterly false and malicious. Elin has always done more to support our family and shown more grace than anyone could possibly expect.

(http://web.tigerwoods.com/news/article/
200912027740572/news, accessed 24 February 2010)

From this point on, through December 2009 and January 2010, Woods' private life and public image appeared to go into a tailspin of increasingly desperate proportions. Further revelations of affairs emerged, his mother-in-law collapsed and was hospitalised, his wife left for a vacation in Sweden before filing for divorce, and Woods announced an 'indefinite break' from golf and checked himself in to a clinic to deal with what was termed a 'sex addiction'.

Aside from the private trauma caused by the revelations, this series of events did serious damage to the golfer's public reputation, and in February 2010 Woods made a much-awaited televised statement to a select group of family, friends and business associates at the PGA headquarters in Sawgrass, Florida. Amid intense media spotlight from the US and other global media outlets, Woods made a 14-minute announcement that was measured, apologetic, addressed to both personal and public audiences, and revealed the difficulty in managing the real and symbolic damage caused to his identity in both private and public domains. While the apologetic tone of his statement was clearly targeted at his wife and family to atone for transgressing some very private values, in the nature of its very 'publicness' it was also a point of mediated contrition, designed to appease the prying eyes of the world's celebrity-hungry media that 'he's sorry, and something is being done about it'. Unfortunately for Woods, criticism among many media commentators persisted, as did acerbic comments from fellow golf professionals confused and annoyed at Woods' behaviour and timing of his televised pronouncement.

British journalist Peter Preston went as far as to suggest that Tiger's 'contrition extravaganza helps slot apology into a universal format' (Preston, 2010). Preston's point, that televised apologies had virtually become another saleable format, may have been overtly cynical, but does correctly discern an emergent trend in celebrity culture for a new form of reputation management that attempts to short-circuit tabloid rumour and misinformation through a highly visible performance of contrition. For some, such as the Golf Writers Association of America, Woods' 'closed-circuit' approach to media relations, addressing a handpicked audience and casting the remainder of the media to watch with the rest of the nation via television, was an affront to the traditional gate-keeping role of sports journalists. It revealed a lack of trust and, quite possibly, a deliberate snub to those journalists who had traced his rise to success and fame over the preceding two decades. The fact that Woods did not take any questions, even from those he had invited, provided further credence to this argument.

But in an era of celebrity-obsessed media gossip and public scandal, the response from Woods and his advisers was not without exception. Politicians confronted with sex scandal, from Bill Clinton in the US to John Major in the UK, have had to wage symbolic battles in the media in order to restore reputation and trust (Thompson, 2000).

In a sporting context, Woods' own public humiliation had also been preceded by former Major League Baseball star Mark McGwire. In 2009 McGwire admitted to using performance-enhancing drugs during the 1993–94 season in order to overcome injury – this prior to his record-breaking years of hitting multiple home runs in the mid-to-late 1990s. McGwire had previously refused to answer claims of steroid use during a Congressional hearing in 2005, which effectively damaged his reputation and standing in the sport and acted as a barrier to his entry to the MLB Hall-of-Fame. Putting aside McGwire's inconsistencies in justifying his reasons for taking steroids, the more intriguing aspect of his confession was how it was managed. His moment of contrition was televised on the MLB's very own channel, MLB Network, in an interview with leading sports presenter Bob Costas. In a moment not unlike the famous David Frost interview with former President Richard Nixon in 1973, McGwire let down his guard and wept as he explained why he took steroids and how sorry he felt for doing so. However, the integrity of the interview came in to question when it became public knowledge that managing the 'news event' was Ari Fleischer, former White House press secretary during the George Bush presidency. After leaving the White House Fleischer joined forces with global sports marketing company IMG to form Ari Fleischer Sports Communications to assist American sports franchises and stars in their media training and 'crisis management'.

In 2009 McGwire had been named the new batting coach of the St. Louis Cardinals, one of Fleischer's clients. From then on, McGwire's sullied reputation became the focus of intense public relations management, culminating in the one-to-one television interview in January 2010. In the context of American sports, the move to micro-manage such a momentous confessional interview on the MLB's own television outlet broke new ground in strategic communications and news management. The tactic to cleanse McGwire's closet before re-entering professional baseball as a coach was an essential part of the strategy, as was the move to release the interview on a Monday in January, a day of minimal sports news, ensuring maximum exposure on other news networks. This final news management device was designed to play to a new context of agenda setting where the consumption of news is more diffuse than ever before. Where interviews of this kind would have previously been conducted through existing television chat shows or news programmes on one of the major networks, the McGwire–Costas confrontation was scrupulously stage-managed on a niche network to 'clean the closet' of the defamed sports star. It is also significant that media corporation Comcast, part-owner of the MLB Network, also owns a number of MLB teams.

The media strategies of both Woods and McGwire provide examples of direct personal interventions from the individuals concerned in media-source relations in order to emotionally engage with a wider audience. Niche television outlets and their ease of access via Internet-based communications like YouTube mean that sports stars have multiple sources for airing their views through self-communication (Castells, 2009). At the same time, further rumour and conjecture also proliferates online in virally circulated communication, increasing the 'media noise' created around sports scandal, at the expense of mainstream news journalists, who find their role as gatekeepers of information undermined (McNair, 2006). The media management of stars in this way is not particularly new. The power of publicists, agents and sponsors to position sports stars in the media spotlight is now a well-known industrial process. Celebrity-style interviews with sports stars not only cost money but are yoked to the promotion of new products and services associated with sponsors and commercial partners (Boyle, 2006).

CASE STUDY: JOHN TERRY AND THE BATTLE TO SET THE MEDIA AGENDA

Although we have focused here on American sport scandal, the desire for media scandal is a global phenomenon. Like all global processes, there are localised variances to its impact and influence. The economic and political structures of newspapers and broadcast news play their part in differentiating the ways in which sport scandal is sourced, editorial framed, distributed and ultimately consumed. Cutting across this process are social and cultural differences, predominantly focused around national differences in news reporting. There are, for example, significant differences to news cultures across Europe and, within sports journalism, quite different styles of writing about sport. The reception of sports news may also vary. In the UK, a media scandal arose involving the Chelsea footballer and England captain John Terry based on his alleged affair with the former girlfriend of fellow player and friend Wayne Bridge. The scandal, which caused much media hype and commentary, specifically centred on the impact it might have on the England national team in which both players were involved. In response, the England manager Fabio Capello decided to strip Terry of the England captaincy in a public show of retribution for his private infidelity. The decision by the Italian-born manager was in keeping with the 'stiff-upper-lip' moral code of the Football Association. Other cultures may have viewed Terry's behaviour differently.

For example, FIFA President Sepp Blatter suggested that the scandal surrounding John Terry was a particular feature of what he termed 'Anglo-Saxon countries'. In a news conference before the 2010 Winter Olympics in Vancouver he suggested: 'Listen, this is a special approach in the Anglo-Saxon countries,' he said. 'If this had happened in let's say Latin countries then I think he would have been applauded' (Press Association, 2010).

Blatter, hardly averse to media scandal himself, may have raised a point of dispute, not least in terms of gender politics and national stereotyping, but his comments do at least hint at an understanding that scandal around sport plays out differently to different national cultures and audiences. This clearly has an impact on how such news is handled by strategic communication managers in the sports industry. In the British marketplace, where tabloid scrutiny is intense, Terry had turned to the former editor of the *News of the World*, Phil Hall, as his press adviser. The other party in the affair, Vanessa Perroncel, had hired leading celebrity publicist Max Clifford, presumably to help manage the advances from tabloid newspapers wanting a 'kiss-and-tell' story. Terry had paid an undisclosed sum to Perroncel in an agreement that prevented her from selling the story to the press, but the failure of Terry's legal 'gagging order' meant any privacy sought from the affair was effectively blown to pieces, and his control of the situation undermined. Knowing the various publics for different forms of news then, for stakeholders in national sporting cultures, is arguably the most important contextual factor in strategic crisis management. In the Terry affair the story crossed both sport and celebrity gossip, not least because the front-page headlines caused by the affair derailed Terry's England captaincy and also led Wayne Bridge to retire from international football. Undoubtedly both players would have lost income from commercial deals because of this scandal.

With this last point in mind, it is all the more salient that the mediated and symbolic gestures of contrition on the part of Woods and McGwire also reveal attempts to manage the fears and concerns of broader stakeholders in their sports celebrity, in their status as media sport brands. The issues of media sports scandal and the commercial promotional culture that surrounds sport are intricately intertwined.

IMAGE MANAGEMENT, ENDORSEMENTS AND IMAGE RIGHTS

A key characteristic of modern, corporate sports culture is the bond between global sport stars and global super-brands. Through advertising endorsements and licensing agreements with sponsors, the elite sports stars of the world have generated incredible personal wealth. Athlete endorsements are a central element of the sports marketing industry, but media scandals or any form of damage to the image and reputation of a sports star can have detrimental consequences for the individual and sponsors concerned.

In the wake of the Woods furore, one of the most often-asked questions was, 'How would this affect his sponsorship income?'. There were some immediate answers to this question as blue-chip endorsements with Accenture, AT&T and Gillette were withdrawn and other endorsements with Gatorade (owned by PepsiCo) and Tag Heuer saw both companies scaling back their ties with the golfer. In the US, and globally, television and print advertising involving Woods was pulled, causing massive disruption to both the brands concerned and the income of commercial media. Woods had become a prominent face for many of these brands, associated for both his sporting prowess and also his personal, moral and character traits. The Woods episode began industry speculation about the risks associated with single-athlete endorsements, with no guarantee that their behaviour will consistently hold up to media scrutiny outside the sports arena. Such fears have led sports organisations and sponsors to insist on insurance policies against media scandal and impropriety, building morality clauses into commercial contracts.

In regard to Woods and Terry the media were quick, in both cases, to frame what had happened in well-rehearsed narratives of 'cheating husbands' in combination with a failure to meet a broader discourse of media sport role models. But as Whannel (2000: 52) has persuasively argued, 'Expectations of sports stars should be scaled down: we should not expect them to be role models.' However, it is because of media and public discourses on sports stars, with an associated weight of importance in our culture, that the pressures of carrying this burden appear innumerably worse when scandal strikes. Damage caused on this symbolic level, of the value drawn from sporting success and the cache of media exposure, is also damage caused to the ability of athletes to attract financial capital.

Sports stars have much to lose from poor media exposure, a reason why many have turned to litigation to resolve media disputes. Sports stars are likely to use defamation laws to protect their public name, claim financial damages or stave off media scandal. Increasingly, the fear among journalists is that media regulation over privacy is being enacted through the British courts protecting celebrities through recourse to human rights legislation. Terry, in attempting to block news stories of his alleged affair with Vanessa Perroncel, had applied for a 'super-injunction' against the *News of the World*. However, on this occasion the High Court judge ruled against the injunction, announcing that the legal action seemed more designed to protect the footballer's lucrative endorsement deals than it did his privacy and marriage, which he was not prepared to accept.

In Britain, the contractual complexities caused by the cultural capital of sports stars and their economic value have become particularly acute in the cash-rich, television-driven world of the English Premier League. The influx of huge sums of money from television rights has underwritten an inflationary spiral in player wages. Salaries account for 50 to 80 per cent of the annual turnover of a Premier League football club, something that has undermined the sustainability of some clubs, such as Leeds United, Southampton and Portsmouth, who at different times overstretched their finances in failed attempts to maintain success in the top flight. With the explosive growth of the football industry throughout the 1990s and the intense media focus on players and clubs, there has been an extensive development in commercial, legal and public relations activities in and around the sport. The desire to manage news and information about the game has led to the employment of PR and communications managers at many football clubs and to new media practices to shore up commercial partnerships and reward (Boyle and Haynes, 2004).

The cost of retaining star talent has given leading European clubs the motivation to pursue new policies to control and reduce the wage burden they currently face. One solution has been to distinguish between the two main roles in a player's professional activities: performance (training and playing the game) and promotion (including merchandising and sponsorship). Significantly, clubs have begun to negotiate payment for players' 'image rights' to enable them to use a player's value as a celebrity to develop new commercial opportunities through a range of licensed products and services. The control and management of image rights not only provides a stream of income for clubs, but also provides a way of lessening the wage burden through various tax incentives. Players are also encouraged to set up offshore companies to house income from image rights and gain beneficial tax incentives (something that the Inland Revenue has been keeping a close eye on).

Unlike the right of publicity in the US, which enables every person to control the commercial use of his or her identity, or similar personality rights in other European states, image rights are not protected under British law (Haynes, 2007). Image rights in the UK context have become a contractual agreement above and beyond the 'standard form agreement' set out in accordance with the Professional Footballers Association. Image rights can be made up of indices of a player's personality, including their photographic image, their voice, name and even their association with a particular shirt number. These individual agreements extend the ability of clubs to exploit a player's image in a group context – such as squad photographs or promotion of club sponsors – to licensing such rights for various commercial purposes exploiting the player's distinctive 'brand'.

From this brief review of the commercial management of players' image rights and brands it is important to understand what is at stake for many young athletes as they build careers in the sports industry. Most careers in sport are relatively short, so the pressure to maximise income during that period has intensified. Under the media spotlight, elite athletes now rely on a team of advisers – legal, communications, marketing – to ensure these interconnected aspects of their playing and non-playing lives are managed effectively for maximum economic reward. Does this mean the imperatives of athletes are misplaced or adversely affect their sport? Arguably sometimes they are. Does it alter the nature of sport? At the elite level, most certainly, due to the economic imperatives of commercialisation. Does it adversely affect the spectacle of sport? For many sports fans the answer would be 'no', as they are more willing than ever to invest both their emotions and income on their sporting heroes. But managing these often conflicting elements of sport has become increasingly complex.

SUMMARY: EMERGING TRENDS AND ISSUES

The next decade will see the web and television convergence go mainstream. The ability to 'pull down' material from the Internet onto your living room television (or screen) with ease will change the nature of how we search for screen content. Sports content will remain a compelling part of that mix. The year 2010 saw 20 per cent of televisions sold in Europe being Internet enabled, and the joint venture platforms such as Project Canvas saw catch-up services for the BBC, ITV and Channel 4 become mainstream in the way that Freeview has taken off in the UK. As we write in 2010, the BBC is launching apps for the iPhone that will allow both catch-up and live sports content to be viewed on the iPhone.

There are also more radical innovations in the coverage of sport that compete with the main players in the economic and political success of sport on the Internet. Fan websites have evolved with the nature and character of the web itself. Fans are now the authors of their own websites, blogs, discussion forums, online commentaries, social networking sites, podcasts and digital video productions distributed via YouTube. All these developments serve to reveal the passions that surround sport in new and creative ways.

This process means that there is wider coverage of different sports from increasingly different perspectives. Where football dominates mainstream media, particularly press coverage of sport, online media sport provides a communicative space for sports that struggle to get exposure on television or by sports journalists. One particular dimension of this explosion is the use of YouTube by governing bodies of sport, sports clubs and sports fans to distribute audio-visual coverage of sporting events. In 2006 the National Hockey League in the US was one of the first governing bodies of sport to launch its own YouTube channel. The channel enabled the NHL to bypass traditional television outlets, giving more direct editorial control of how the sport is produced and analysed as well as opening up other revenue streams through advertising and subscription.

One problem of these 'official' channels is the lack of critical comment or investigative journalism. When editorial control goes in-house this is always likely to be the outcome. However, YouTube offers an antidote to the official views from sport. The proliferation of digital cameras and mobile phones with video capturing has led to a new phenomenon of 'home-made' videos being posted on the web along with the rise of Twitter comment from fans and players alike. The ease of use, malleability and global distribution of material means that biographical accounts of 'going to the match' populate the web via YouTube. Such viewings from the stadium may not offer any real insight into the action on the field of play, but they do reveal the social experience of many who watch live sport.

Governing bodies of sport are conscious of these developments and in some cases have banned the use of mobile phones and cameras at sporting venues in an attempt to control the images that emerge from sport. Again, digital rights management of sports media and the policing of official, licensed coverage of sport has become big business. Company's like Net Result or Soccer Dataco, who are contracted by governing bodies of sport and sports broadcasters like BSkyB, scrutinise the web to trace any copyright infringement of televised sports images. Unsuspecting fans who copy copyrighted material – such as fixture lists – and distribute the images or information via the web receive curt and rapid legal writs if they do not desist. However, as the music industry has discovered, keeping a lid on the mass disobedience of copyright is no easy undertaking. Live feeds of BSkyB's coverage of the Premier League frequently appear on the Internet.

Other emerging areas see the growing importance of digitising archive material and in some cases deriving value from it; sport on mobile phones will not go away, although making money from it remains a challenge. Companies such as Eurosport are keen to use developments such as the Apple iPhone App to drive users to their content; building a long-term business model for paid content in an age when the digital natives are used to 'free' online content is another challenge.

However, for media managers, understanding the changing media landscape remains key, as does recognising that media consumption patterns are characterised by strong elements of continuity and change. While convergence is happening and offering new opportunities, in 2010 90 per cent of all viewing of screen content still took place through television, rather than via the web. Thus change often takes place not at the expense of other consumption patterns but often in complex and contradictory ways. Being alert to that complexity is part of the challenge for those working in sports content in the digital age.

NOTES

1 This updates some material given in the inaugural lecture of the 2009 Chair in Olympism, *Why Sport Matters: New Challenges in the Digital Age*, Centre d'Estudis Olimpics (UAB), Barcelona, October 2009.
2 While accepting the argument that in many ways the definition of new and old media may be a false dichotomy (in other words, rather than there being old and new media, there is in fact only media), for the sake of this chapter we will talk specifically about some of the challenges offered by new media platforms, and here we include the Internet, digital television and a range of telephony services which telecom companies are keen to develop, to sports managers.

REVIEW QUESTIONS

1 How has television transformed the football industry in the last decade or so?
2 Why should the issue of players' image rights be an area of concern for media managers?
3 What are the key cornerstones of any digital media strategy for sports clubs?
4 How has the growth of public relations impacted on the role of the media manager in the sports industry?

FURTHER READING

Boyle, R. (2006) *Sports Journalism: Context and Issues*. London: Sage.
Boyle, R. and Haynes, R. (2009) *Power Play: Sport, the Media and Popular Culture*, 2nd edition. Edinburgh: EUP.
Fuller, L. (2009) *Sportscasters/Sportscasting: Principles and Practices*. New York: Howarth Press.
Hobsbawn, J. (2010) *Where the Truth Lies: Trust and Morality in the Business of PR, Journalism and Communications*. London: Atlantic Books.
Hopwood, M., Skinner, J. and Kitchen, P. (2010) *Sport Public Relations and Communication*. London: Butterworth-Heineman.
Kennedy, E. and Hills, L. (2009) *Sport, Media and Society*. London: Berg.

WEBSITES

http://www.guardian.co.uk/media

http://www.sportbusiness.com

http://www.sportsjournalists.co.uk

Many sports stars and sports journalists now keep up-to-date information on news, views and gossip on the world of sport on Twitter. It is used as a wire service, as a promotional platform and as a means to interact with readers/fans. For managers, being connected through social media is important as it plays an important part in the process of reputation management.

REFERENCES

Boswell, T. (2009) 'Looking at Tiger Woods with Fresh Eyes', *Washington Post*, 4 December 2009. http://www.washingtonpost.com/wp-dyn/content/article/2009/12/03/AR2009120304282.html

Boyle, R. (2006) *Sports Journalism: Context and Issues*. London: Sage.

Boyle, R. and Haynes, R. (2004) *Football in the New Media Age*. London: Routledge.

Boyle, R., Rowe, D. and Whannel, G. (2010) '"A Crass Lack of Seriousness"? Questions for Sports Journalism', in S. Allan (ed.) *The Routledge Companion to News and Journalism Studies*. London: Routledge.

Castells, M. (2009) *Communication Power*. Oxford: OUP.

Cision (2010) *2009 Social Media and Online Usage Study*. George Washington University and Cision.

Conlan, T. (2008) 'Olympics: BBC's Games audience hits 40 million', *The Guardian*, 22 August.

Haynes, R. (2007) 'Footballers' Image Rights in the New Media Age', *European Sports Management Quarterly*, Vol. 7, No. 4, pp. 361–374.

McNair, B. (2006) *Cultural Chaos: Journalism, News and Power in a Globalised World*. London: Routledge.

McNamee, M., Jones, C., Cooper, S. M., Bingham, J., North, J. and Finlay, V. (2007) 'British Spectators' Perceptions of the Values and Norms in Selected Professional Sports: A Comparative Ethical Survey', *Leisure Studies*, Vol. 26, No. 1, pp. 23–45.

Mosey, R. (2007) Speech given to Broadcast Sports Forum, Hilton Waldorf Hotel, London, 29 November.

ONS (2010) *Office of National Statistics Opinions Survey*, 27 August 2010. http://www.statistics.gov.uk/cci/nugget.asp?id=8

Press Association (2010), guardian.co.uk, Thursday 11 February 2010.

Preston, P. (2010) 'The Sorry Business', guardian.co.uk, 21 February 2010. http://www.guardian.co.uk/commentisfree/2010/feb/21/tiger-woods-apology-cash-sponsors

Steen, R. (2008) *Sports Journalism: A Multimedia Primer*. London: Routledge.

Thompson, J. (2000) *Political Scandal: Power and Visibility in the Media Age*. Cambridge: Polity Press.

Whannel, G. (2000) 'Stars in Whose Eyes?', *Index on Censorship*, Vol. 29, No. 4, pp. 48–54.

Whannel, G. (2001) *Media Sport Stars: Masculinities and Moralities*. London: Routledge.

Whannel, G. (2009) 'Between Culture and Economy: Understanding the Politics of Media Sport', in B. Carrington and I. McDonald (eds) *Marxism, Cultural Studies and Sport*. London: Routledge.

Chapter 19

Information and communications technology and its use in sport business

Cameron O'Beirne, Curtin University, Margaret River Education Campus

OBJECTIVES

At the end of this chapter you should be able to:
- Identify a variety of information technology applications that are used by sports businesses;
- Consider how the development of information technology impacts upon sports businesses;
- Understand the convergence of sports media through the use of information technology;
- Explore how changing Internet technology will continue to impact upon the sports eBusiness.

KEY TERMS

Broadband – technology that allows a high rate of data transmission.
Disintermediation – the process of doing away with middlemen from business transactions.

HTML – hyper text mark-up language is a page description computer language that forms the basis and composition of most web pages on the Internet.

Internet – a global system of inter-connected networks providing links to millions of computers that allow access to billions of web pages on a huge number of topics. It relies on a system of computer protocols to allow information to be exchanged between networks.

IT – information technology.

Virtual communities – groups of people with similar interests who communicate and interact in an online environment.

WWW – World Wide Web is the graphical user interface supported by HTML that displays web pages on the Internet and is accessed using computer software called a browser.

OVERVIEW

The advent of the World Wide Web in the early 1990s, coupled with the continually evolving sophistication of computer hardware and software, has led to many changes to the way that sport businesses can maximise growth of their business goals. This continual innovation of information and communications technology (ICT) and the predominance of the World Wide Web and the other Internet resources in our media, social and work landscapes has led to the creation of what is termed 'sport eBusiness'. There is a wide variety of sport organisations, such as sports information services and retail sports merchandisers, as well as various international leagues and teams, and national, state and local sport associations, that are using the Internet and associated technologies to help develop a presence for consumers and members alike in order to grow the business of sport.

It is inevitable that a level of uncertainty exists within sport organisations as to how the Internet can best be utilised to drive sport outcomes. The Internet has transformed markets and industries within a short span of time; the World Wide Web began in 1993, and since then these changes continue to occur at a rapid rate and, becoming more integral to our daily lives, challenges will remain. With increasing speed and bandwidth to transfer large multimedia files around the world, the Internet is now ubiquitous. The challenges to taking advantage of the Internet can include a lack of knowledge of Internet technologies, including the application of technology, the resources required to develop and implement websites, specific business objectives, website features and the value of such website features to the organisation in delivering business outcomes.

The concept of the global village is now a reality; the Internet is widely accepted as the most significant business instrument in the post-industrial age (Joshi, 2007; Raney and Bryant, 2006). This chapter focuses on providing an understanding of the role of management information systems, information technology and the use of the Internet by sport organisations. The role of information technology processes, convergence social network media and key components of information systems for the successful sport eBusiness are also discussed.

CASE STUDY: NIKE PLUS – FITNESS NETWORKING

In 2008, thousands of runners lined up for a 10K race in Taipei. They also lined up in Melbourne, Istanbul, Paris, Munich and 20 other cities around the globe. They were all taking part in Nike's 'The Human Race', with a focus on collective data and information sharing using the Internet. Even if you weren't in one of the 25 cities you could still participate: by running 10 kilometres and then uploading your results via your Nike-enabled wireless shoes to Nike Plus. That day, over half a million people participated both at the race sites and virtually, together running more than 8 million kilometres!

Nike describes its Nike Plus system as an innovative running experience combining music, personal coaching and fitness networking. The Nike Plus system is an iPod nano that can 'talk' to Nike Plus-enabled running shoes through a wireless Nike+iPod Sport Kit. As you run or walk, data on time, distance, calories burned and pace is stored on the iPod nano and then uploaded to the nikeplus.com website. Nikeplus.com provides a virtual community by allowing users to interact with one another. They can track their own data and also challenge others and participate on online forums. People can also create goals with the software, and advise friends about training goals with the system, with Nike sending an email to your listed friends informing them of your progress, good or otherwise.

Nike Plus was created in 2007, and according to Nike:

> in its first year, Nikeplus runners logged over 22 million miles on nikeplus.com, the equivalent of completing more than 800,000 New York City marathons and burning off the calories of more than 5 million slices of pizza ... It started as a simple idea and has quickly become the world's largest networking place for runners. Whether their goal is fitness, fun or a cause, runners of all levels are embracing nikeplus.com to become part of a global running community.
>
> (Nike, 2007)

Personalisation of the software provides additional functionality for users. This includes a challenge feature that provides users with the ability to choose their own challenge theme, set their own rules, and select participant numbers and team names. They can also upload their own pictures to highlight their challenges on the nikeplus.com homepage. Other features include the Nike Plus Distance Club where if runners achieve 100, 500 or 1,000 miles they are initiated into this select club.

Another aspect of personalisation is the use of music. According to Nike:

> the Nikeplus community is fuelled (sic) fuelled through Nike Sport Music ... inspiring runners by creating a growing collection of original ultimate running soundtracks. This new music content category is delivering unique mixes and expert coaching from the world's best artists and athletes. Nike Sport Music offerings are sold via the iTunes Store in 22 countries. As Nike+ usage continues to grow globally, more Nike Sport Music products are planned to keep the community running to new and inspirational beats.
>
> (Nike, 2007)

Visit Nike Running for more information: http://nikerunning.nike.com/nikeos/p/nikeplus/en_US.

INTRODUCTION

Advances in the use of information and communications technology (ICT) and in particular the use of the Internet has changed the way that sport services can be delivered to consumers and clients.

Today's sport business has access to a wide range of technologies that can assist in developing and delivering business efficiency. These include highly efficient networked computers, digital television services, mobile telephony, personal digital assistants and intelligent appliances in the home and office that allow a level of connectiveness that is unparalleled throughout history.

Although this chapter discusses traditional uses of information technology such as the use of computers and associated networks to provide desktop applications including word processing, spreadsheet analysis and database management, it focuses specifically on business that is conducted over networks that use non-proprietary protocols (open to everyone) such as the Internet. The reason for this is the increasing dependence on the use of the Internet to facilitate the functions of management information systems and eBusiness which is in part driven by the ability of everyone to access the Internet's vast global network at a relatively low cost using existing telecommunications infrastructure.

Some of the reasons that the Internet has proven so popular and transformed markets so quickly are due to the following:

- Cost of access is low compared with other proprietary networks. Most people can afford access at home or have Internet access through their employment.
- The ease with which connection to the Internet by the average person can be obtained.
- Enabling new technologies that allow one-to-many and many-to-many communications and the transfer of information across a variety of devices using the Internet as the medium for access.

DEFINING EBUSINESS

The concept of eBusiness or eCommerce can be defined in many different ways; however, it can be broadly understood as 'every type of business transaction or interaction in which the participants prepare or conduct business electronically' (Talha and Subramaniam, 2003).

This may be as simple as sending an email to a colleague requesting information about an upcoming event, to purchasing tickets for a sports event online or watching live sporting events 'streamed' directly into your home via a broadband connection. The basic components to operate such a system include:

Selling	Buying
• Content production (word processing, video and still cameras) • Digitisation of content (editing software) • Storage of digitised content (either online on remote servers or locally in hard drives and portable storage devices such as CDs) • Link to an electronic network (usually the Internet) • Link to an electronic payment system (usually through the Internet utilising a PC with a web browser) • Link to physical distribution systems (when there is an exchange of goods)	• Link to an electronic network (usually the Internet) • Search and locate content (goods and services) through search engines, directories or specific websites • Retrieve and display information from network • Place order through web browser interface • Link to an electronic payment system (usually through the Internet utilising a PC with a web browser)

Some people distinguish between eBusiness and eCommerce as two separate functions. The former focuses mainly on business activities that include communicating with clients and partners, and utilising technology to enable business processes. The latter can include all forms of financial and commercial transactions such as electronic data interchange (EDI), electronic funds transfer (EFT) and debit and credit card activities.

There are four main types of eBusiness based upon the type of transaction that occurs (Table 19.1).

Table 19.1 *Types of eBusiness*

eBusiness classification	Description
Business to Consumer B2C	Online store or shopping sites providing an additional sales channel for existing companies or for new 'pure play' Internet companies to have direct access 24/7 to consumers. Examples include amazon.com and liverpoolfc.tv. Other examples include online banking facilities and informational sites for niche markets such as sporting events, team information and fan sites.
Business to Business B2B	B2B websites act to create 'virtual supply chains' in linking suppliers, distributors, resellers, consultants and contractors electronically to facilitate the flow of information. The main reason to use B2B practices in dealing with other companies is to streamline business processes, thereby creating efficiencies in the business and reducing costs. Sport examples include manufacturers' directories (gymnasticsequipments.com) and industry networks (sportsvenue-technology.com).
Consumer to Consumer C2C	C2C websites provide a means by which consumers can directly interact with one another to exchange information, services and products. Examples include online classified advertisement sites, auction sites such as ebay.com and memorabilia sites for sports fans.

eBusiness classification	Description
Consumer to Business C2B	C2B websites are characterised by individuals offering professional services to others, such as lawyers, accountants and consultants. As well, C2B allows the consumer to control transactions through processes such as a reverse auction, whereby the bidder sets the price for services or goods, and requesting quotations for goods and services. Other examples include paying government charges and taxes online.

THE RISE OF THE INTERNET

The Internet is a worldwide connection of many thousands of computer networks. The networks are connected to one another through communications channels, many of which remain permanently open. The standardised organisation and structure of the networks that form the Internet enables the instantaneous transmission and reception of digital data in many forms between computer systems across the globe. The Internet is a cooperative community of networks. No particular body owns the Internet. It is made up of many small parts in many different countries. Within each country, there is an organisation that supports the Internet and provides the main communications channels. People often comment that the Internet belongs to everyone and yet to no one. The Internet is structured in an hierarchical form. At the top, each country has at least one major backbone network that carries Internet data between its main cities and centres. These networks consist of high-speed communication channels that carry the digital data. There are then many smaller networks that connect homes, schools, universities and commercial users to the backbone networks. Networks of channels are then used for connections between countries and continents.

Part of this network is a graphical user interface called the World Wide Web (WWW). The Web supports interactive multimedia, including photographs, images, video and sound clips. Whilst the Web and its accompanying browser interface through a personal computer is the predominant platform for accessing the Internet at present, changes in technology such as computer speeds, and most importantly bandwidth (the size, speed and ability of the network to carry information), will continue to alter the way that information is accessed through the Internet in the future.

Categorisation of information communication systems in sport business

Aside from the predominance of the Internet, there are a number of traditional forms of IT that the sport business uses in its day-to-day operations. This includes the technology that drives core business functions such as personal computers for word processing, database management, software for event scheduling and other operational activities, and facsimile, printers and other peripheral devices that store and manage data. Needless to say, the increasing reliance of the Internet by sport business has led to a wide range of sport organisations that use the Internet to leverage their business. Whether they are professional sport businesses

343

with large financial capital and concomitant member and supporter bases, or the small local sport team that has a website, each organisation can benefit as a result of utilising eBusiness processes.

Typically, the Internet is utilised by sport businesses to offer a wide range of experiences for the fan, member or consumer. From the post-match results or fixture times, they offer the whole experience – from buying team merchandise in the online shop, to watching the events through the site itself. To sports goods manufacturers, retailers and marketers, the Internet is another part of their global brand strategy and, for advertisers, sports websites represent a proposition with definite future potential.

Sport websites can be classified into various categories which may be dependent upon the sport business they deliver.

Various commentators have suggested a number of uses of the Internet by sport organisations or associated groups that can be categorised (Brown, 2003; Kahle and Meeske, 1999; Lange, Nicholson and Hess, 2007).

For our purposes, we can identify three major categories of sport eBusiness:

- Content delivery of commercial sport and eMarketing of sport by organisations with a specific profit focus;
- Educational, coaching and training applications within sport organisations, including tools for managing team performance; and
- Delivery of services and content to members and stakeholders in non-profit sport organisations.

By far the most widely used and accepted use of the Internet by sport organisations are the sites that provide content and services to a wide market with a global reach. These sites are usually in the format of a portal, which means the sites act as a gateway for supporters or other users to access information and services. Typically, the goal of the portal is to provide a resource on an ongoing basis for the sports fan or club member, whereby they visit the site at regular intervals.

Portals typically offer free or subscription services such as a search engine; local, national and worldwide sporting news, plus general news; email and chat rooms; fan and member information; and, of course, up-to-date sporting results. Many portals can be personalised so that the fan only receives information about his or her favourite sports or teams. An example of a specialised portal is surf.transworld.net, which is a one-stop place for anyone interested in surfing activities. Portal sites have proven very popular in deriving revenue through advertising, subscriptions and merchandising.

Governments are now investing heavily in sporting portals and gateways. For example, Sport England (sportengland.org) is a British government initiative with a mission to develop sport by providing 'funding in organisations and projects that will grow and sustain participation in grassroots sport and create opportunities for people to excel at their chosen sport' (Sport England, 2010). The different sport portal types are outlined in Table 19.2.

Table 19.2 *The different sport portal types*

Sport portal type	Function	Example
Commercial sport sites	Content delivery Entertainment alternative to other media Profit focus with various revenue models such as advertising, ticket sales and merchandise sales Information source, with a focus on aggregating services around a portal	swimnews.com Olympics.com Nike.com afl.com.au
Education sport sites	Education, training and coaching applications Alternative to traditional delivery methods	Australian Sports Commission: ausport.gov.au Personalised training: sportstrainingonline.com.au
Service focus sport sites	Provides services to members and other stakeholders Content delivery Timetabling and results Information focus Community focus Virtual communities	*Government sport services* Sport England: sportengland.org *Non-profit sport organisation sites* Surfing Australia: surfingaustralia.com British Stand Up Paddle Association: bsupa.org.uk standupzone.com

It is accurate to suggest that there is not a professional sports team in the United States that does not have its own dedicated website, and most are linked together through networks of websites coordinated through the various league offices that teams compete in. These relationships and linkages between competitor teams are driven in part by agreements between the league teams on activities such as revenue sharing for media broadcasting and merchandise sales. Portals have also emerged through a common interest and have been driven in part by advances in communications technology. This is exemplified by the site at http://icc-cricket.yahoo.net, the home of the International Cricket Council (ICC), that brings together all major international cricket events, news and information, rules and regulations, and various links to member bodies.

Sport information

Other uses of the Internet such as online teaching and training are engaged with by researchers in sport science (Abt and Barry, 2007) and those teaching sport coaching (Taylor, 1999) as well as distance education (Rushall, 1999) and web-based learning (Chappelet, 2001; Danylchuk, Doherty, Nicholson and Stewart, 2008).

Sport coaches use the Internet for a variety of reasons, including information searches on trends and new topics, communication with colleagues and athletes, background on competitors' teams, players and coaches and competition locations, weather, transport and accommodation. The Internet makes it possible for coaches and athletes to analyse and integrate information and resources in order to improve training, decision making and development.

An example of the use of technology to manage team performance is DSV Capture. This is a digital video capture and playback system used by international cricket teams in which stored data can be analysed in real time as the game is being played. Data is accessible to both coaches and players anywhere on the ground. Reports can be produced instantly and data can be archived for retrieval later. An example of a report shows many different features in graphic format for easy reading.

Technology can impact broad-based participation in sport and promote social inclusion. Data management tools and systems are extremely useful for the sports administrator, especially in the area of event management, as exemplified in Table 19.3.

Table 19.3 *Data management tools*

Sport function	Database content
Teams and individual athletes	Demographic information: name, age, sex, contact information, medical details, performance history
Coaching	Training and conditioning, timetabling
Administration	Rosters of volunteers, officials, timekeepers, equipment and inventory lists, facility maintenance software packages, marketing information such as ticket sales, accounting and business records, employee directories
Marketing	Donors or potential donors whether this be for money or in-kind services, source of their motivation or affiliation, frequency of participation

Other applications include the use of flexible teaching models within tertiary institutions to assist learning in the sport management and science field that allow students to utilise online bulletin boards, upload assignments and download course notes and other resources.

Other applications, such as that considered by Holcomb (1997), used virtual reality modelling language (VRML) to illustrate a virtual athletic training room as an adjunct to the training of athletic trainers. Trainers are educated on appropriate modalities of treatment for the real world. The model has been found to be a beneficial educational tool for teaching training room design, function and application of rehabilitative tools to athletic trainers. Other specific uses in sport coaching can include game analysis, electronic training diaries and various hand-held devices for recording athletic performance.

CHANGING TECHNOLOGY AND THE SPORTS EBUSINESS

As technology advances, its impact on the business of sport continues to grow daily. For technology to be truly useful it needs to be ubiquitous, and this is true for both business and sport. The following are a few of the issues that are now impacting on sport and will further advance the way in which sport is pervading everyday life.

Geo targeting

Geo targeting is location-based marketing that works by using Global Positioning System (GPS) technology to deliver targeted content or ads to consumers, based on their physical location. Almost all 3G phones nowadays (iPhone, Blackberry, Nokia) come with built-in GPS capability and the new Apple iPad ships with similar capability. Geo targeting will be a key marketing focus for the sport event and tourism industries going forward. Spectators and fans can be targeted specifically by their team, based on where they are, and the facilities nearby.

M-commerce

Mobile commerce (or M-commerce) is the ability to use one's credit card to purchase something online through one's mobile phone, or to use a mobile phone to gain access to something, or complete a transaction by showing a bar code or authenticated redemption icon on the phone. Customers can store tickets on their mobile phone for later use at an event, or point of travel, to gain venue access, or at the cinema. The purchase of the ticket can be completed on the mobile phone, or online at an eCommerce website, via a telephone call centre or alternatively at a physical ticket outlet or kiosk.

Interactive TV

The advent of interactive television is going to have many interesting benefits for both sports businesses and sports fans. For example, Cadability, a company that develops innovative interactive sports data-casting content for the Internet, interactive TV and emerging multi-media technologies, has produced CD-ROMs for training cricket umpires. By using existing materials and videos, they have put together a product called 'interactive umpiring'. By using the Internet in conjunction with the CD or video, they can access an online agent in the form of a genie which asks questions and talks to the user, making the CD engaging and interesting to use. The CDs contain self-assessment methods, the results get posted to the sports association and an online certificate is issued.

ePublishing

Although not something that is readily associated with sports business, ePublishing has the potential to add value to the dissemination of results, as well as being of enormous benefit to sports fans. ePublishing comes in many forms, one of which is e-ink. This is an electronic ink technology aimed at mobile applications such as Personal Digital Assistants, mobile communication devices and electronic readers, such as the iPad and Amazon Kindle. Electronic ink allows highly portable devices to offer a paper-like look with exceptionally low power consumption, and an extremely thin, light form. E-ink devices are purportedly six times brighter than normal LCDs and are more easily read because of high contrast and good visibility in even low ambient light. The image is retained on the screen after the power source is terminated, meaning that users can read articles, scores and data analysis without using battery power.

Another contributor to the growing demand for ePublishing is electronic paper. E-paper is essentially a very thin, flexible electronic display, similar to a computer monitor, but one which can be rolled up and carried around in a brief case. One major commercial application has been the development of electronic signs connected via a wireless link. This is an application that has now been expanded from retail stores to the sporting arena, allowing more information to be displayed around the grounds, and providing sponsors with comprehensive exposure at venues. It is also possible that each spectator has their own piece of electronic paper, to which is sent statistics, scores, advertising material, and anything else the sports promoters feel appropriate. The text remains on the e-paper until the next update, meaning that the need to print documents such as programs may be eliminated.

SUMMARY

This chapter has emphasised the importance of the Internet as a vital communications tool for the sport business and sport organisation at every level of sophistication. The use of the Internet and incorporation of technology into the sport business brings many challenges that include types of eBusiness models that work for sport business, the use of technology, and the application of resources to gain efficiencies from the use of the Internet.

As media sources continue to collide and ultimately converge, the abundance of technology and associated tools that enable business via the Internet will become more and more entrenched. Already traditional media and business are scrambling to develop new models for revenue and creating value using the Internet.

We will continue to see a wide range of platforms that will enable us to engage with customers, members, sports fans and the like to drive the business of sport.

REVIEW QUESTIONS

1 How would the more effective use of information and communications technology improve managing a sport organisation?
2 What sort of services could be provided utilising information and communications technology that could benefit customers of sport?
3 What issues are impacting on sport that will advance the way sport pervades everyday life?
4 Take a sporting activity and discuss how technology could enhance the business of that sport.

FURTHER READING

Beech, J., Chadwick, S. and Tapp, A. (2000a) 'Towards a schema of for football clubs seeking an effective presence on the internet', *European Journal of Sport Management*, special issue, p. 31–51.

Beech, J., Chadwick, S. and Tapp, A. (2000b) 'Emerging trends in the use of the internet – Lessons from the football sector', *Qualitative Market Research: An International Journal*, 3 (1), 38–46.

Galla, P. (1999) *How the Internet Works*, Indianapolis, IN: Que Publishing.
Nordström, K. and Ridderstrale, J. (2000) *Funky Business*, Stockholm: Bookhouse Publishing.

WEBSITES

The IBM website at http://www.ibm.com highlights case studies and the company's involvement with sport organisations.

REFERENCES

Abt, G. and Barry, T. (2007) 'The quantitative effect of students using podcasts in a first year undergraduate exercise physiology module', *Bioscience Education Journal*. Available: http://www.bioscience.heacademy.ac.uk/journal/vol10/beej-10-8.pdf [2011, 3 June].

Brown, M.T. (2003) 'An analysis of online marketing in the sport industry', *Sports Marketing Quarterly*, 12 (1), 48–55.

Chappelet, J. (2001) 'Web-based learning for sport administrators: The example of the SOMIT Project', *Proceedings of the 11th IASI World Congress: Sports Information in the Third Millennium*. Available: http://www.museum.olympic.org/e/studies_center/iasi_e.html [2001, 6 July].

Danylchuk, K., Doherty, A., Nicholson, M. and Stewart, B. (2008) 'International sport management: Creating an international learning and teaching community', *International Journal of Sport Management and Marketing*, 4 (2–3), 125–145.

Holcomb, B.E. (1997) 'The virtual athletic training room', unpublished MA thesis, San Jose University.

Joshi, S. (2007) 'Virtually there: Cricket, community, and commerce on the internet', *International Journal of the History of the Sport*, 24 (9), 1226–1241.

Kahle, L.R. and Meeske, L. (1999) 'Sport marketing and the internet: It's a whole new ball game', *Sport Marketing Quarterly*, 8 (2), 9–12.

Lange, K., Nicholson, M. and Hess, R. (2007) 'A new breed apart? Work practices of Australian internet sport journalists', *Sport in Society*, 10 (4), 662–679.

Nike (2007) '22 million miles and counting: Nikeplus.com becomes the world's largest online running destination'. Available: http://www.nikebiz.com/media/pr/2007/07/26_nikePlus.html [2010, 12 August].

Raney, A. and Bryant, J. (2006) *Handbook of Sports and Media*, USA: Lawrence Erlbaum Associates.

Rushall, B. (1999) 'The internet and coaching education', *International Coach Education Conference Proceedings*, Canberra.

Sport England (2010) 'Funding guidelines'. Available: http://www.sportengland.org/funding.aspx [2010, 12 August].

Talha, M. and Subramaniam M. (2003) 'Role of e-Commerce in economic growth', *Journal of Internet Marketing*, 4 (1), 1–7.

Taylor, J. (1999) 'Coach education in the 21st century: Challenges and opportunities', *International Coach Education Conference Proceedings*, Canberra.

Chapter 20

Planning and managing the stadium experience

Paul Kitchin, University of Ulster

TOPICS

From windy terraces to iconic designs: Stadium developments • Case study: Arsenal Football Club – Managing the 'Emirates' experience through design and operations

---

OBJECTIVES

At the end of this chapter you should be able to:

- Understand external and internal drivers for stadium developments;
- Review the importance of managing the customer experience within the stadium;
- Discuss how managing design and operations can influence the customer's experience within the facility.

KEY TERMS

Accessibility – the combination of stadium design and space management procedures to ensure that all customers have equal access to any area of a facility.

Aesthetics – the ability of the built environment to invoke pleasurable and positive customer reactions.

Customer experience management – a term coined by Schmitt (1999) to conceptualise the management actions to plan, organise, lead and control customer experiences within the service environment.

Fourth generation stadium – the latest generation of stadium developments that mix high quality sporting and customer service environments with the latest technology.

Servicescape – a term coined by Bitner (1992) to refer to the built environment for service-based firms. Wakefield and others applied the theory to spectator sports to create the sportscape.

Space management – the skill of maximising the value of existing space and minimising the need for new space (Langston and Lauge-Kristensen, 2002).

OVERVIEW

This chapter will provide an overview of how the planning and management of the stadium can impact on the customer experience. The task of ensuring that the customer's experience within the 'sportscape' (Wakefield, Blodgett and Sloan, 1996) is memorable is one strategy for increasing stadium attendance and customer satisfaction. In the business of stadium management, many experiential aspects are influenced by aesthetics, space and accessibility within the built environment. The increasing professionalisation of sport has seen stadium developments begin to reflect the requirements of the sport business. Modern stadia are more than just sporting facilities and their services; sporting and non-sporting organisations now have to cater for more than one type of customer. These stadia can also assist in the acquisition of major events to cities and regions. For instance, the staging of the Olympic Games has led to many host cities building or redeveloping their stadium in order to meet event requirements. These requirements are one of a number of factors that have led to a proliferation of stadium development in many countries. This chapter will examine strategic management considerations for providing optimal customer experiences to ensure long-term benefit to the sport business. First, this chapter will review the key drivers of stadium developments. Designing stadia to be accessible, spacious and aesthetically pleasing is important in order to provide the setting for enhanced customer experiences (Bitner, 1992; Bodet, 2009; Wakefield *et al.*, 1996). These designs provide the link to allow operations to support memorable experience creation and will be the focus of the second part of the chapter. The final part of this chapter will review how Arsenal Football Club designed the Emirates Stadium to cater for their purple members (supporters with disabilities). This case forms a practical example of the issues discussed.

CASE STUDY: ICONIC DESIGN – WHY DOES IT MATTER?

The importance of an iconic facility should not be underplayed. Already the budget required for the staging of the London 2012 Games has been hit by the economic recession of 2008–2010. This has led to cost-control measures being undertaken by the Olympic Delivery Authority, the organisation in charge of constructing the platform for the games. The Olympic Stadium in Stratford has been designed and constructed with cost savings in mind. The facility has been labelled the 'Bowl of Bore' by local residents and media commentators, as prudence has limited its design features. In a contrast example, the following quote highlights how the arch in the design of Wembley Stadium (see Figure 20.1) provides it with an iconic image.

Figure 20.1 *The raising of the Wembley arch*

Industry insight – Sir Norman Foster: Wembley Stadium and iconic design

In July 1999 the [original] model [for Wembley Stadium] proposed four support masts on one side of the stadium, the expression with those four masts could have been like many other stadia around the world... later [in the design process] we saw the arch for the first time. So it's doing all the things it has to do in terms of holding up the roof and cables more efficiently, more elegantly; but vitally giving an image that is unique and special to Wembley.

BBC Online (2006)

FROM WINDY TERRACES TO ICONIC DESIGNS: STADIUM DEVELOPMENTS

New stadium developments are significant projects and should not be undertaken without due consideration. Langston and Lauge-Kristensen (2002) state that facilities such as stadia should support business goals and objectives and that a strategic approach to development is therefore required. They suggest this process (the strategic facility plan) should follow a series of steps that cover short-range (2–3 years) and long-range (3–10 years) periods. These steps focus on the following areas:

■ Forecasting the need for organisational facilities.
■ Comparing this forecast with current facility provision.

Only once this process is complete can management take the next step:

■ If a gap exists in the first two criteria, a range of facility options are considered.

Part of the forecasting process is an understanding of trends impacting upon facility provision within the industry. Sheard (2001) highlighted the Industrial Revolution as the starting point for the development of the modern stadium, conceptualising four generations of stadia (see Table 20.1).

Table 20.1 *Stadium evolution and catalysts for change*

Generation	Focus	Catalyst for development
1st Late 19th century to the early 20th century	Designed within urban areas for mass attendance to ensure maximum gate receipts	Increased need for safety and comfort of customers Increasing needs of radio and television broadcasting companies
2nd Early 1920s to the 1970s	Designed in suburban areas for better customer parking and sight lines Desire for stadia to be more aesthetically pleasing and also to ensure dual purpose use (sports teams shared the facility)	The increased need for multi-purpose design to cater for a wider range of sports but inadvertently the lack of 'atmosphere' limited customer experience Increasing rise of 'franchise free agency' (Beauchamp et al., 2009, p.276)
3rd 1970s to the late 1980s	Designed for customer service needs and enhancing the stadium experience to compete with the televised broadcast A strong focus on multi-purpose use of sport and non-sport bookings	Issues regarding stadium safety Convergence of digital media technology through satellite platforms Advances in broadcast technology
4th 1990s–present	Designed for myriad customer service needs for B2B markets as well as B2C markets Facilities incorporated increased integration with technology (closable roofs) to satisfy the needs of media broadcast	Future developments?

Adapted from Beauchamp, Newman, Graney and Barrett, 2009; Paramio, Buraimo and Campos, 2008; Sheard, 2001.

Among the myriad of drivers for stadium redevelopment, three forces have consistently provided the catalysts for these generational shifts: technology, competition and customer needs.

Technology, competition and customer needs

The materials required to design, construct and provide services at facilities have been advanced by technology allowing for greater flexibility in design. Additionally, as the range of stakeholders that support sport has increased from owners and fans to include broadcasters,

353

corporate partners and increasingly lucrative fan segments, so too have the demands put on stadia to meet expectations. Many facilities were located in urban, inner-city areas (Sheard, 2001). However, post-World War Two the availability of land in out-of-town areas and automobiles providing greater consumer mobility permitted stadium development in suburban areas. In Britain, association football facilities dominate the stadium market. Traditionally these stadia have been owned by the sporting clubs themselves. Many of these facilities were developed in piecemeal stages, with one spectator stand being built at a time and new stands being added over a period of years. Arguably these stadia developed differently to the generation-based model. With their bookings provided by the club's matches, infrastructure developments were geared around club priorities and not customer needs. In the latter part of the twentieth century, a combination of poor licensing systems, fan behaviour and poor investment created dilapidated and dangerous stadia (Paramio *et al.*, 2008; University of Leicester, 2002).

A major catalyst for dramatic change in the UK was the Hillsborough tragedy on 15 April 1989 where 96 Liverpool supporters were crushed and killed at the FA Cup semi-final at Hillsborough in Sheffield. The subsequent Hillsborough report into this event led to wide-reaching changes to the design and operational procedures of stadia. One example of this change could be seen in the role of the usher, which can be seen in the quote below:

> *Industry insight – Sharon Circo, Operations Manager, Arsenal Football Club*
>
> Stewarding used to be a glorified usher role: showing people to their seats and really not doing much else. If anything, the Hillsborough disaster taught us that trained people are needed to deal with match day safety of the fans that we get through our doors.

Stadium developments increased in the 1990s with projects being undertaken across Europe, with the Hillsborough tragedy being the major catalyst for this development in Britain, North America and in many other countries with professional sporting leagues. In North America the development drivers were public bodies in cities and regions competing against each other for the right to host professional sporting teams. This created a system of 'franchise free agency' (Beauchamp *et al.*, 2009, p.276). By offering new facilities to professional sport teams, it was hoped that team relocation would lead to other important economic benefits for the region. In Australia the economics of running professional sport leagues in a small market led to a 'facility rationalisation strategy' being adopted by the Australian Football League (Westerbeek, Smith, Turner, Emery, Green and van Leeuwen, 2006, p.7). This led to the move from traditional suburban stadia to more modern centrally located facilities offering higher quality standards.

These developments coincided with the growing international trend of marketing cities as destinations (Hankinson, 2001). The significant regeneration of Barcelona along with the success of the 1992 Summer Olympic Games led to a repositioning of the city's image (Gratton, Shibli and Coleman, 2005). The transformation from former industrial port to a key European tourist city provided an example for others to follow. The regeneration benefits and international profile gained from bidding for and securing international sporting (Winter and Summer Olympics, FIFA World Cup) and cultural events (World Expo, Cities of Culture) led also to an increase in competition for the right to host these events. In the post-industrial economic era of the new millennium, the quest for major events and facility developments allowed regions that lacked established professional sport leagues to construct sport cities in order to position themselves as event destinations. This competition also has led to the development of iconic facilities, such as the Yas Marina race circuit in Abu Dhabi and the National 'Bird's Nest' Stadium in Beijing, amongst many others.

Fourth generation design and operational aspects must be considered in the planning phase in order to increase the potential for managers to attract these events. Once construction starts on the facility, it is difficult, time consuming and expensive to adjust plans or even add on facilities once complete. The planning phase needs to ensure that facilities are well equipped, not just for sport but also to attract non-match day events and bookings. This year-round business model is a common feature of modern stadium design and provides a more diversified base for generating revenue (Paramio et al., 2008; Westerbeek et al., 2006). However, a commercial business model of this type relies on more than just good physical design. It also relies on effective operational procedures controlled by management actions to create a high level of service quality.

The operational management of the 'servicescape' is important for meeting customer expectations. The term servicescape was coined by Bitner (1992) and refers to the physical or built environment of a service-based organisation, such as a sports stadium. Bitner stated that, 'through careful and creative management of the servicescape, firms may be able to contribute to the achievement of both external marketing goals and internal organizational goals' (p.67). This concept was developed by the work of Wakefield and Blodgett (1994, 1996) and Wakefield, Blodgett and Sloan (1996) through empirical testing on customer experience in sport and leisure facilities. They tested the concepts of servicescape or 'sportscape' (Wakefield et al., 1996) on sport spectators. Throughout their studies, two key aspects of facilities were deemed important: aesthetics and space/functionality. Shilbury, Westerbeek and Quick (2003) suggested that if these considerations are met this could lead to greater customer satisfaction, encourage the fan to stay longer and increase the likelihood that they will return again. Service quality is a significant body of research in facility management. One burgeoning aspect of service quality is the concept of the customer experience and how it can be effectively managed within the sportscape.

Customer experience is a concept of focusing on the individual's experience in the consumption process (Holbrook and Hirschman, 1982). The management of the customer experience is a growing area of practice and study and many sport organisations are beginning to see the importance of this process (Bodet, 2009; Kang and Chou, 2009). Schmitt (1999, p.26) provided the first definition for the concept: customer experience management is 'the process of strategically managing a customer's entire experience with a product or a company'. This philosophy seeks to investigate and exploit the relationship between the customer and his/her 'experience' with the product or service; this approach can lead to long-term relationships and increased customer loyalty. The goal is to create experiences that appeal to both the rational and emotional sides of the customer (Thompson and Kolsky, 2004) and involve all the senses

(Holbrook and Hirschman, 1982; Schmitt, 1999). Bodet (2009) examined French rugby club Stade Français Paris and their use of experiential marketing to create special customer experiences. The staging of spectacle at each home game played at the Stade Français (90,000 capacity) created consistent crowds over 70,000, peaking at one particular match at a world record club rugby attendance of 79,741 (Bodet, 2009). The premise of managing the customer experience is that, every time a company and a customer interact, the *customer* learns something about the *company*. Depending upon what is learned from each experience, customers may alter their behaviour in ways that affect their individual profitability. Thus, by managing these experiences, companies can orchestrate more profitable relationships (Thompson and Kolsky, 2004). Tickets for the men's and women's finals at Wimbledon are particularly difficult to obtain. However, the hill directly outside Centre Court is packed with tennis fans who watch the finals on the big screen (see Figure 20.2). This experience is managed by the event organisers, the All England Lawn Tennis and Croquet Club, and provides an alternative space to Centre Court. This provides the customer with space to get close to the action and even ensure that those playing hear their cheers and support. Considerations like these need to be addressed when forming the facility management plan.

Figure 20.2 *Providing experiences at Wimbledon*

Linking design and operations for memorable experiences

The management of space is an important factor in facility planning (Langston and Lauge-Kristensen, 2002). Space management attempts to provide an equitable use of space based on user needs. The multitude of customers that attend sporting events each requires different levels of space within the stadium. In some instances stadia have been built to meet public/community requirements, particularly those built with public funds, and hence managers must be aware of these needs and plan accordingly. Considering the needs of match day and non-match day customers can provide a useful starting point.

Match day

For the purposes of this chapter, match-day attendees are divided into two cohorts: those seated in premium sections and those who attend in general admission. Many sporting organisations break these into different membership categories and allow those paying higher fees access to a wider range of facilities (see Table 20.2 for the premium seating categories at Wembley Stadium). To entice these high-paying customers, modern stadia have included features such as dedicated entry, a range of premium food and beverage options, including bars and restaurants with silver service dining, premium seating areas with added space and comfort, and in certain cases reserved car parking spaces, amongst other aspects. These features are designed to make attending the sporting event more convenient for the customer while offering a more memorable experience through high levels of service.

Table 20.2 *Wembley Stadium premium seating options*

Seat type	Club	Silver	Gold	Corinthian Club
Licence fee	£3,900	£5,600	£8,400	£16,100
Annual ticket price	£1,350	£2,000	£2,800	£5,450
Seat position	Behind the goals	Wing position	On the half-way line	Unrestricted views from half-way line
Access	To Café East and West	To Café East and West and to the Atrium, Arc and Venue restaurants and bars	To Café East and West and to the Atrium, Arc and Venue restaurants and bars	Direct access to the Corinthian restaurant
Additional benefits			One car parking space per four seats	A three-course pre-match meal, half-time canapés, light buffet post match, beers and soft drinks throughout One car parking space per pair of seats

For general admission customers, modern stadia are designed to enhance the sporting event experience. Food and beverage concession stands are designed to be efficient. Designing beverage dispensers that can pour a vast number of drinks during breaks in the match allow the staff to keep up with these periods of intense demand. The availability of automatic bank-tellers allowing customers to withdraw cash for purchasing facility services or the design of the retail store to allow high match-day demand for sporting merchandise are elements of design that offer increasing levels of service to all customers. Areas for those with general admission are designed with broad concourses to allow for the smooth flow of customers around the venue. Wakefield *et al.* (1996) found that narrow walkways and busy concourses led customers to experience crowding, which in turn reduced the pleasure they experienced, and that being crowded would reduce their desire to return to the facility in the future.

Non-match day

The business model of sporting stadia relies on flexible design, which is the ability to incorporate multi-purpose areas such as event spaces that allow for business-to-business customers. During matches these can be used as dining areas, while on non-match days they can double up as conference and banqueting venues for a range of business customers. The Great Hall at Stamford Bridge, the home of Chelsea Football Club, is one such conference venue that can hold dinners for up to 800 guests or allows for conferences of up to 1,000 attendees. When it is not being used for this purpose it is part of the general concourse of the stadium. The use of hospitality suites that form executive boxes on match days can double up as meeting and seminar venues. Some of these boxes even double up as hotel rooms. The use of non-match day facilities for business-to-consumer markets is also possible. Paramio *et al.* (2008) highlighted that FC Barcelona's museum and stadium tours are not only the sport-industry leader but one of the city's top tourist attractions. In addition the design of retail spaces can act as non-match day attractions to the facility. The revenue that can be generated from these additional services can also assist in providing the sport business with maximum use of this asset.

Another important element that impacts on both match day and non-match day customers' experiences is aesthetics. Aesthetics attempts to ensure that the built environment is pleasing to the customer and reflects certain qualities. In sport and leisure settings, aesthetics was found to have a positive impact on perceived quality (Wakefield and Blodgett, 1996) and customer pleasure with the sport service (Wakefield *et al.*, 1996). Modern facility design makes the most of building materials such as steel and glass to ensure maximum use of available light. The Cowboys Stadium in Dallas (site of the XLV Super Bowl) uses mezzanine levels and large windows at the north-east and south-west ends of the venue to provide maximum natural lighting. In addition to this, the facility has a 'world-class collection of contemporary art' that aims to ensure that the facility offers more than just football and an 'experience more thrilling' than previously seen (Cheek, Daniels and Pagel, 2009, p.4).

The operational aspects of stadium management include a broad range of considerations. Many of the operational aspects are covered by Schwarz, Hall and Shibli (2009) in a text dedicated to the topic; however, given the broad remit of this textbook, the reader should be able to envisage how the human resource, financial, legal and event management principles covered in other chapters contribute to operations. Nevertheless, the goal of the operational procedures are to ensure that what has been constructed positively influences the customer experience and can provide equitable access for all. In the Wakefield *et al.* (1996) study aesthetics was associated with 'first impression' management. While it is unlikely that all sporting organisations may have the funds available to redevelop their facilities, aesthetic qualities can however be reinforced through maintenance operations. They suggested that painting and decorating the facility can achieve aesthetic benefits which could in turn have a positive impact on the customer experience. Restoring the aesthetics of the cricket ground once the concert has been held would not require redevelopment, but would involve a number of ground staff operations.

Stadium accessibility is influenced by legislation to ensure the equitable access for spectators with disabilities. Many countries now have legislation to ensure that individuals with disabilities are considered when designing new facilities. In the UK the relevant legislation is the Disability Discrimination Act 2005 (for other countries please see the recommended reading and Chapter 21). To ensure that the legislation is adhered to, the facility design team have options. They can consult with specialists on accessibility issues or they can consult with advocacy groups for individuals with disabilities and involve them in the planning phases (Walters and Kitchin, 2009). The range of impairments and disabilities are broad; however, they can be grouped under physical, sensory (hearing and vision) and learning (difficulties) disabilities. Although these groups contain many individual variations and combinations, managers can use these three categories as a starting point for considering accessibility issues.

The involvement of steering groups for stadium accessibility issues and/or the appointment of disability liaison officers can ensure that accessibility issues are reported and incorporated into the facility management plan. Paramio *et al.* (2008) highlighted the work of Phil Downs in establishing the Manchester United Disability Supporters Association (MUDSA) that not only improved the accessibility of the stadium at Old Trafford but was instrumental in establishing the National Association of Disabled Supporters (NADS) in English football (for a discussion of this and similar issues see Chapter 21). The role Downs fulfils involves both planning and operations and ensures that Manchester United attempt to go above and beyond on accessibility issues.

Increasing accessibility within the stadium also assists other areas of operations. Emergency services, catering, maintenance and security all benefit from facilities that are constructed whole. To highlight this, older stadia that have multiple stands may have premium seating away from the catering areas. When food is prepared for those in the premium seats, it needs to be fresh: food and drinks that should be hot or food and drinks that should be cold. Having premium seats too far from catering areas can lead to service issues, and considering the value of premium seating these customers may not accept anything less than excellent service. Therefore accessibility needs to consider the full range of operational management functions. The important point for aspiring managers is that by ensuring accessibility adheres to best practice principles they can simultaneously enhance the experience for all of their customers.

CASE STUDY: ARSENAL FOOTBALL CLUB – MANAGING THE 'EMIRATES' EXPERIENCE THROUGH DESIGN AND OPERATIONS

The purpose of this case study is to focus on how Arsenal Football Club (AFC) considered their purple members (supporters with disabilities) in the design and operations of the Emirates Stadium. The elements from the chapter will be applied through this case. The case will demonstrate how facility management planning ensured that design aspects assisted in the creation of high quality operations to generate memorable experiences.

Walters and Kitchin (2009) highlighted that the increasing commercial pressures of the late 1990s meant that many professional sporting clubs had to search for new revenue streams. Moving from their traditional home at Highbury in North London (as seen in Figure 20.3) presented AFC's management with a number of options. The most suitable of all the options presented was a move to Ashburton Grove, a site located close to the Highbury ground.

Figure 20.3 *Highbury Stadium*

During the planning phase the facility design focused on a yearly event schedule aiming to provide multiple opportunities for the creation of revenue. One of the key elements of offering this schedule was the contracting of a quality caterer. Delaware North Companies signed a £12.5 million deal to be the official catering provider within the stadium. The company's experience in providing these services in North American sport facilities meant that AFC knew this important aspect would be quality managed.

Purple members are a group of supporters of Arsenal that have a disability or impairment. Arsenal has a long history of providing services for supporters with disabilities – their services for the hearing and visually impaired date back to the 1950s. Importantly for the future operational management of purple member experiences, AFC instigated a steering group to involve the disability community in the planning and design of the new facility (Walters and Kitchin, 2009). While a wide variety of membership options were adapted from Highbury offering to entice a greater number of customers to the new stadium (see Table 20.3), the Disability Discrimination Act 2005 and the steering group ensured that supporters with disabilities would have equal access to the full range of seating options at the Emirates Stadium. Hence each of these seating options offers a guaranteed space within the new stadium.

Table 20.3 *Emirates Stadium premium and purple seating options*

Seat type	Purple membership	Gold membership: general admission	Club level	Executive boxes	Diamond club
License fee		Waiting list	Waiting list		£25,000
Annual ticket price	Base price £400 (rises for club level and above)	£925–1,825	£2,500–4,750	£65,000–£125,000	£25,000 per pair
Duration	1 season up to 4 seasons	1 season	1, 2, 3 or 4 seasons	1, 2, 3 or 4 seasons	4 seasons
Seat position	Various	Levels 1 and 4 various	Level 2 various	Level 3 various	Level 2 half-way line
Access	All areas based on ability to pay. Depending on seating level all memberships are available for purple members	Guaranteed seat for all 19 Premier League home fixtures and the first seven fixtures in the FA Cup/ Champions League. Priority is given to gold members on any further fixtures in the Carling Cup and cup finals.	Guaranteed seats for all Arsenal fixtures at Emirates Stadium. –Priority is given to these members for cup finals. Enhanced features such as free drinks and access to exclusive restaurants	150 executive boxes with host/ hostess	From its stunning art deco interiors to the balcony seats, the Diamond Club is the Rolls-Royce of football viewing (Versi, 2009b)
Additional benefits	Additional entry for carer. Possibility of accessible parking (granted on a per-match basis)	A range of customer facilities including hot and cold food and beverages	Dedicated entry, access to restaurants and bars. Free drink at half-time.	Dedicated entry, access to executive lounge bars. Within the suite a full dinner or buffet can be served, with complimentary beverages	Private entrance, car parking spaces. Buffet or four-course dinner, complimentary beverages

Sources: Alun Francis, personal communication, 19 June 2009; Kitchin (2009); Versi (2009b).

The Emirates Stadium has four tiers of seating offering five different levels of customer care and comfort (see Figure 20.4).

Figure 20.4 *The levels of the Emirates Stadium*

Of these levels, levels 1 and 4 create a variety of seating options for match-day ticket purchasers and season ticket holders (including many purple members). These areas offer: easier access to the stadium, with more entry points than were available at Highbury; a variety of food and beverage concessions available before, during and after the match; and also other important aspects like a greater number, and higher standard, of WC facilities, that offer adult changing spaces (Versi, 2009a).

The design of levels 2 (including the Diamond Club) and 3 in the Emirates Stadium caters for the more salubrious member or corporate guest. Level 2 is club level, which offers a variety of vantage points around the ground. They are designed for individual fans of AFC or smaller companies that might not be able to afford an executive box. These seats are priced between £2,500 and £4,750 (per annum for a four-year contract). This level allows patrons access to exclusive restaurants and bars, where not only is high quality service provided but each ticket-holder is entitled to a free drink at half-time. On level 3 are the executive boxes. According to Chris Lee, a director with architects HOK Sport, the 150 executive boxes on level 3 were designed to be 'unparalleled by any other [English Premier League] club'. They offer lobby areas outside the boxes to allow visitors to mingle with other guests, creating a 'hotel lobby' feel and enhancing networking opportunities (Versi, 2009a, p.48).

The Diamond Club offers exquisite levels of service but is only available to 84 members and their guests. The Diamond Club is a concierge-serviced, invitation-only area with a £25,000 licence fee and then £25,000 annual fee (per pair, per annum for four years), and for that fee no expense is spared (Versi, 2009b). The Diamond Club offers the very best of the services at the Emirates Stadium. Their private suite is accessed from an exclusive entrance from the car park or the stadium concourse. The stairs to the suite walk the guests right past the players' area and past the Club's trophy cabinet. The room is art-deco designed, with marble flooring and dark oak furniture; these features are designed to ensure the aesthetics are first class. On the level 2 stand outside the private suite, the 164 leather seats offer the best views in the stadium. They are located above the half-way line and behind the team areas, getting the members closer to the action. Central to each of these offers is the competence of the caterer, thus reinforcing the importance of the Delaware North Companies deal.

Arsenal's Disability Liaison Officer Alun Francis states that, while many design aspects (such as hearing loops and tactile pathways) are standard regulations for new facilities, Arsenal go above and beyond in many other areas. One example of this is the guide dog toilet, the first of its kind in British stadia (personal communication, 19 June 2009). The move to the Emirates Stadium has also offered purple members up to 100 blue-badge parking spaces which were not available at Highbury.

All of these design aspects are tested through the operations with customers. This operational phase is where issues regarding aesthetics, accessibility and space are revealed. Walters and Kitchin (2009) revealed that the Emirates Stadium was named 'Business Venue of the Year 2007' and 'Best Venue for Meetings and Events in England 2008'. These awards demonstrate the ability of design to provide memorable operations for business-to-business customers. In addition to these awards, the Emirates Stadium has provided AFC with a significant increase in turnover and has allowed them to rise up the Deloitte Money League since the facility opened in 2006 (Deloitte, 2009).

In many football stadia, supporters with disabilities who required mobility aids such as wheelchairs and are seated pitch-side had to concern themselves with excited supporters to their front standing at crucial moments in the match. One way many facilities avoided this was by placing these customers at the front of the stand. While the intention is good it has some drawbacks. In some cases the shape of many football pitches meant that they could only see the ball when it was on their side of the pitch; in others this prime seating location exposed these supporters to all the weather elements such as rain, and sometimes hail and snow. At the Emirates Stadium the design of the facility ensures that the club's level 1 purple members are seated on a raised platform at the rear of the seating concourse so they can see the entire match, no matter how bad the weather or how excited the supporters to their front might be (Walters and Kitchin, 2009).

Francis revealed that ensuring accessibility for spectators with disabilities can sometimes be operationally difficult. The lifts that are essential to some purple members are very busy just before and after the match, resulting in long delays for those unable to use the stairs. The original design for disabled toilets allowed access for all, once again meaning that purple members had to wait until other non-entitled members had finished with the facilities in order to gain access. In order to prevent these issues from continually recurring, Francis states that RADAR fobs are now used to control access to these facilities (personal communication, 19 June 2009). The flexible design of the stadium can also solve the lift issue. The number of lifts in the stadium can be doubled, as during construction twice as many lift shafts were designed into the facility. While installing new lifts may take some time, Francis is sure that this can alleviate this accessibility issue.

Nevertheless, some experiential aspects are more difficult to control. At Highbury all of the purple members were grouped together, creating a 'community feel'. However, while the Emirates Stadium provides best practice in equitable seating arrangements, Francis noted that it has reduced this 'community feel' of the supporters with disabilities (personal communication, 19 June 2009). This is very difficult to control, but Francis hopes to source space for a purple members' lounge like the one used by MUDSA at Old Trafford. It is his hope that this will reignite the community feel and create a more memorable experience for the customer.

SUMMARY

This chapter has provided an overview of how planning and management considerations can ensure the provision of memorable experiences. Ensuring that the customer's experience within the sportscape is memorable and long-lasting is one strategy to increasing organisational effectiveness. The link between design and operations in stadia is central to ensuring that these experiences can be exceptional. The case of Arsenal and the design of the Emirates Stadium highlighted the opportunity for high quality experiences for spectators with disabilities to be created by considering customer needs in the design phase.

REVIEW QUESTIONS

1   The technological environment has changed dramatically over the past 20 years. Considering stadia are built to last for many years, what technological changes would necessitate stadium developments in the future?

2   This chapter presents a brief introduction to experiential marketing and managing the customer experience. What does the literature say the difference is between managing customer service and managing the customer experience?

3   What are the emerging competitive forces that could pose a threat to the current fourth generation of stadia?

4   How important is an iconic design in the construction of modern sport stadia? Make a case for and against such a design being used to build a new national stadium in a country of your choice.

5   Under the Disability Discrimination Act 2005 disabled supporters who attend English football matches must have access to a range of seating options, not just seats that are located in one area of the stadium. In what ways would you seek to resolve the lack of 'community feel' that could be experienced by disabled supporters if they are seated in separate areas on match days?

6   What experiential marketing ideas or tactics can you devise to manage the customer experience of attendees aged under 18?

FURTHER READING

Schwarz, Hall and Shibli (2009) and Westerbeek *et al.* (2006) provide texts linking many features of managing the sport business into the management of sporting facilities. These texts review the management of operational issues concerning facility managers and are recommended for any reader wishing to advance their knowledge in the area. Many countries have disability discrimination legislation; in many countries these are combined or used in conjunction with other discrimination legislation. This chapter focused on Britain's Disability Discrimination Act 2005 due to the setting of the case; however, the following countries have relevant legislation in this area:

Australia: Disability Discrimination Act 1992
Germany: General Equal Treatment Act 2006
United States of America: Americans with Disabilities Act 1990

See also Paramio, Campos and Buraimo in Chapter 21 for a more complete discussion of the impact of legislation on sporting facilities.

WEBSITES

Many facilities have virtual tours that allow you to see inside the facility and witness how the aesthetics and layout provide spaces for customer experience creation. Some sites of note are the following:

Cowboys Stadium – promotional video/virtual tour

http://stadium.dallascowboys.com/tours/tourInfo.cfm

Emirates Stadium

http://www.arsenal.com/emirates-stadium/virtual-tour

The Melbourne Cricket Ground

http://www.mcg.org.au/Tours/Virtual%20Tour.aspx

REFERENCES

BBC Online. (2006). *Timeline: The New Wembley*. Accessed at http://news.bbc.co.uk/sport1/hi/football/4735072.stm on 21 November 2009.

Beauchamp, N., Newman, R., Graney, M.J. and Barrett, K. (2009). Facility management. In L.P. Masteralexis, C.A. Barr and M.A. Hums (eds). *Principles and Practice of Sport Management* (third edition), pp. 273–293. Sudbury, MA: Jones and Bartlett Publishers.

Bitner, M.J. (1992). Servicescapes: the impact of physical surroundings on customers and employees. *Journal of Marketing, 56*(April), 57–71.

Bodet, G. (2009). 'Give me a stadium and I will fill it': an analysis of the marketing management of Stade Français Paris rugby club. *International Journal of Sport Marketing and Sponsorship, 10*(3), 252–262.

Cheek, L.W., Daniels, B. and Pagel, P. (2009). *Art + Architecture*. Arlington, TX: Dallas Cowboys.

Deloitte. (2009). *Lost in Translation. Football Money League: Annual Review of Football Finances*. Accessed at http://www.deloitte.com/view/en_GB/uk/industries/sportsbusinessgroup/4fe984458 81fb110VgnVCM100000ba42f00aRCRD.htm on 21 July 2009.

Gratton, C., Shibli, S. and Coleman, R. (2005). Sport and economic regeneration in cities. *Urban Studies, 42*(5/6), 985–999.

Hankinson, G. (2001). Location branding: a study of the branding practices of 12 English cities. *Journal of Product and Brand Management, 9*, 127–142.

Holbrook, M.B. and Hirschman, E.C. (1982). The experiential aspects of consumption: consumer feelings, fantasies and fun. *Journal of Consumer Research, 9*, 132–140.

Kang, C.N. and Chou, Y.H. (2009). *An examination of the relationship between experiential marketing, participative motivation, customer satisfaction and customer loyalty: The National Taiwan University indoor swimming pool*. Paper presented at the European Association of Sport Management Conference, Amsterdam, 16–19 September 2009.

Kitchin, P.J. (ed.) (2009). *Arsenal Business Cases*. London: London Metropolitan University.

Langston, C. and Lauge-Kristensen, R. (2002). *Strategic Management of Built Facilities*. Oxford: Butterworth-Heinemann.

Paramio, J.L., Buraimo, B. and Campos, C. (2008). From modern to postmodern: the development of football stadia in Europe. *Sport in Society, 11*(5), 517–534.

Schmitt, B.H. (1999). *Experiential Marketing.* New York, NY: The Free Press.

Schwarz, E.C., Hall, S. and Shibli, S. (2009). *Sport Facility Operations Management.* Oxon: Butterworth-Heinemann.

Sheard, R. (2001). *Sports Architecture.* London: Spon Press.

Shilbury, D., Westerbeek H. and Quick, S. (2003). *Strategic Sports Marketing* (second edition). Sydney: Allen and Unwin.

Thompson, E. and Kolsky, E. (2004) How to approach customer experience management. *Gartner Reports: G00125606.* Stamford, CT: Gartner.

University of Leicester (2002). *Fact Sheet 2: Football Stadia After Taylor.* Accessed at http://www.le.ac.uk/sociology/css/resources/factsheets/fs2.html on 14 February 2010.

Versi, G. (2009a). Spoiling corporate guests. In P.J. Kitchin (ed.) *Arsenal Business Cases* (pp.46–49). London: London Metropolitan University.

Versi, G. (2009b). VIP guests. In P.J. Kitchin (ed.) *Arsenal Business Cases* (pp.50–52). London: London Metropolitan University.

Wakefield, K.L. and Blodgett, J.G. (1994). The importance of servicescapes in leisure service settings. *Journal of Services Marketing, 8*(3), 66–76.

Wakefield, K.L. and Blodgett, J.G. (1996). The effect of the servicescape on customer's behavioural intentions in leisure settings. *Journal of Services Marketing, 10*(6), 45–61.

Wakefield, K.L., Blodgett, J.G. and Sloan, H.J. (1996). Measurement and management of the sportscape. *Journal of Sport Management, 10,* 15–31.

Walters, G. and Kitchin, P.J. (2009). Stakeholder management and sport facilities: a case study of the Emirates Stadium. *Birkbeck Sport Business Centre Case Study, 1*(2). Accessed at http://www.sportbusinesscentre.com/research/casestudy/Walters%20and%20Kitchin on 14 February 2010.

Westerbeek, H., Smith, A., Turner, P., Emery, P., Green, C. and van Leeuwen, L. (2006). *Managing Sport Facilities and Major Events.* Oxon: Routledge.

Chapter 21

Promoting accessibility for fans with disabilities to European stadia and arenas

An holistic journey sequence approach

Juan Luis Paramio, Universidad Autónoma de Madrid, Spain

Carlos Campos, Universidad de Extremadura, Cáceres, Spain

Babatunde Buraimo, University of Central Lancashire, UK

TOPICS

The nature of accessibility for fans with disabilities at stadia • Accessibility to sport facilities • Recent legislative developments of accessibility provision at stadia and arenas in the USA and Europe • Design and operational principles as part of the holistic journey sequence approach to any stadium • Disability football policy and the disability liaison officer (DLO)

OBJECTIVES

At the end of this chapter you should be able to:

- Define and understand the core issues affecting fans with disabilities and their access to stadia;
- Understand the main legislation in different western countries relating to universal accessibility of stadia and the current accessibility standards for new stadia;
- Understand the main demands of fans with disabilities attending events at stadia as part of an 'holistic journey sequence approach' and how these demands affect operation within venues;
- Identify the best practices in promoting access by fans with disabilities at European football leagues;
- Describe the specific competencies, responsibilities and management skills of a disability liaison officer (DLO);

■ Identify the main challenges and actions that should be taken to promote accessibility within sports venues.

KEY TERMS

Accessibility – is a characteristic of urban design, buildings and transport that determines the ease with which various individuals and groups can experience the built environment.

Accessible stadia guide – is a technical guide on universal design and access to sporting stadiums throughout Europe.

Accessible stadium – is a stadium that complies with all regulations and caters for the needs of all types of fans with disabilities when in attendance at any event and/or at any venue. It ensures that all possible spectators have equitable access to the facility.

Fans with disabilities – are, according to the (English) National Association of Disabled Supporters, any persons who, because of their disability or impairment, are unable to use ordinary stand seating without contravening health and safety regulations, guidelines or policy or where the club has provided a 'reasonable adjustment or auxiliary service' to enable those supporters to attend the venue.

Holistic journey sequence approach to stadia – is an approach that comprises five major stages to systematically guide the entire sequence of events from the moment that fans with disabilities decide to plan a visit to any stadium, until they leave the venue.

Universal accessibility and design for all – is a paradigm that goes beyond the notion of accessibility and seeks to ensure equal opportunities for all people, including those with disabilities.

OVERVIEW

Sports organizations need to demonstrate that they are responsible to all customers, including those with disabilities (Zeigler 2007). Therefore, promoting as well as improving access by fans with disabilities to European stadia and arenas should be one of the main concerns for international and national football federations, not to mention individual clubs. As Phil Downs, Disability Liaison Officer at Manchester United FC, states:

> Those who choose to ignore providing good standards of accessibility for disabled fans to European stadia and wait for it to go away will be doing themselves a disservice as well as everyone else. Those who choose to see the benefits of dealing with the general accessibility issues are likely to be able to spread the cost over an extended period rather than have to squeeze an increased amount of spending into a shorter period in order to catch up.
>
> (Phil Downs, personal communication, 20 December 2009)

The incipient political, academic and managerial interests in this subject stem from at least five interrelated factors. First, promoting accessible environments to fans with disabilities to large venues should not be considered isolated, but instead should form part of the corporate social responsibility policies of governing bodies and individual football clubs (Breitbarth and Harris 2008; Walker and Kent 2009).

Second, now more than ever, social expectations coupled with increased pressure from people with disabilities have forced the issue of accessibility to services and facilities, including events at stadia and arenas, onto the mainstream political agenda as part of a wider agenda entitled 'universal accessibility and design for all'.

Third, this combined pressure emerges from a realization that large sections of the population have a variety of disabilities. Indeed, it is estimated that there are more than 100 million people with disabilities in Europe alone, which represents around 10 per cent of the continent's population (Horne and Howe 2009; CAFÉ 2010). Figures reach as high as 40 per cent of the total population when the criteria for disability are broadened to include, for example, diabetes, epilepsy or heart diseases. Attendance at sports stadia is becoming more popular than ever before, as recent data from three of the most profitable football leagues in Europe, the English Premier League, Primera Division and Bundesliga, confirms, and this increase in demand extends to spectators with disabilities.

Fourth, over the last two decades, we have witnessed the emergence of new stadium development across many European countries and these, in theory, are more accessible than their predecessors. A central conclusion emerging from a growing body of work concerning accessibility to European stadia, albeit mainly within the three aforementioned national leagues, and including work from the United States of America (Sanford and Rose 1998; Grady 2006), confirms the view that it is no longer acceptable that the needs of people with a range of disabilities are not taken into account (Cook 2009).

Fifth, during a period when customer loyalty may prove difficult to sustain, people with disabilities are amongst the most loyal supporters. They show great passion for their clubs and the game itself, and it is self-evident therefore that they should have the same opportunities to enjoy all aspects of the game on an equal footing with other followers.

Despite some notable exceptions (see Tables 21.4, 21.5 and 21.6 below), progress towards the development of agreed standards has not advanced far enough, as Joyce Cook, current president of the UK National Association of Disabled Supporters (NADS) (currently known as Level Playing Field since March 2011) and founding director of CAFÉ (Centre for Access to Football in Europe), notes. There are still many challenges that prevent a growing number of fans with disabilities attending matches in many countries. Football organizations and individual football clubs themselves are still failing to comply with the terms and conditions of the regulations and relevant legislation for universal accessibility at stadia. On the basis of those deficits, the field of sport management, as this Routledge collection acknowledges, should investigate and understand precisely the effects accessibility (or the lack of it) to all types of sports venues has on the lives of fans with disabilities and society as a whole. As in other sectors of the leisure industry where accessibility represents an emerging managerial issue (Waterman and Bell 2002), most football clubs should consider the advantages of providing accessible environments to fans with disabilities.

The primary aim of this chapter is therefore to raise awareness about the need to promote universal accessibility at all venues for all people. It is primarily intended for those students who are following courses in a diverse range of subjects. It can also be beneficial to sport governing body administrators, civil servants and industry practitioners. The planning, design, management and operation of stadia should not be the concern of architects and engineers alone as it has been in the past, and they should work closely with key stakeholders such as managers, professional experts like disability liaison officers (DLOs) at club level, groups of fans with disabilities and local officers from the early stages. All of them should be familiar with best practices across different countries. By doing this, more people with disabilities will be convinced that it is possible to attend football matches and other events at stadia in Europe just like everyone else.

The chapter proceeds as follows. In the first section, the main terms and concepts relating to people with disabilities and fans with disabilities and those that are central to understanding accessibility at large sports venues are explained. The following section offers a brief historical overview of the transition of provisions for fans with disabilities across different generations of stadia. Further consideration is given to the legislation, specific guidelines and minimum standards of access to stadia and arenas, and the types of policies promoted by different countries over the last half century. Then the chapter provides an analysis using a case study to highlight the level of provision for fans with disabilities in the top stadia of three of the main leagues in Europe. This analysis is based on research interviews with stadium architects, experts on accessibility and stadium managers from these leagues. Comments from an extensive interview with Phil Downs, MBE, based on over 20 years of experience at one of the world's largest football clubs, follow. Phil Downs is the founder of the Manchester United Disabled Supporters Association (MUDSA), the first of its kind within European club football. He is also a key figure at the National Association of Disabled Supporters (NADS), where he was the chairman between 1998 and 2006 (a full transcript of the interview can be read at www.managingsport.com). Additional information was gathered from 'live' experiences by the authors during stadium visits around Europe in the past years.

CASE STUDY: PHIL DOWNS, MBE, DISABILITY LIAISON OFFICER AT MANCHESTER UNITED

From a sport management perspective, the job of disability liaison officer at club level is a relatively new development that has not been examined systematically either from an academic or a practitioner perspective. Looking back to the origin and evolution of this position at Premier League clubs, the first recognized person in this position within Premier League and even European club football was Phil Downs, who was recruited to Manchester United in 1993 at a time when there were more obstacles for fans with disabilities to attend matches than there are today.

Phil Downs previously contributed in 1989 to the first official disabled supporters association at club level, the Manchester United Disabled Supporters Association (MUDSA), the first of its kind within European club football. Phil then replicated this organization years later at national level with the establishment of the National Association of Disabled Supporters (NADS), where he was the chairman between 1998 and 2006 (see more details in Downs 2006).

When he was asked how he became involved with Manchester United as a football fan and where his interest in promoting accessibility at his club came from, he mentioned that 'it was probably in late 1976 that I first wrote to the club asking to attend the matches as a wheelchair user and I continued writing for five years. One of our local "bobbies" called to see me one day and we chatted about going to see the games and he took it upon himself to write to the club on my behalf and, behold, I received three postcard-type passes for the last three matches in 1981 ... just before the following season started I received a pass for the entire season which was renewed for many years.'

At that time, disability and accessibility to stadiums for fans with different types of disabilities was, according to him, definitely at the bottom of the agenda for most businesses. Nevertheless, a club like Manchester United reacted positively to his demands and in the early 1990s an elevated viewing platform was constructed in the Old Trafford stadium. After that, different strategies have been implemented which have contributed to the improvement of the quality of services to disabled fans, estimated nowadays to be more than 2,000 with disabilities. Drawing on his long-time experience, he remarked that 'there are no "quick fix" solutions to the overall subject of disability. Each club or national association needs to consider advancements in this area as part of a strategy that is essentially "evolution not revolution"'.

As part of this process, the introduction of this emerging managerial position at any club is probably the starting point for putting disability on the agenda for every club and even football governing bodies.

The full transcript of the interview can be read at www.managingsport.com. Further reading on the role of the disability liaison officer at club level can be found in a later section of this chapter, 'Disability football policy and the disability liaison officer (DLO)'.

THE NATURE OF ACCESSIBILITY FOR FANS WITH DISABILITIES AT STADIA: KEY TERMS

An appropriate starting point is a review of the key terms relating to the central issues of this chapter. These include terms such as a person with disability, fans with disabilities, types of disabilities, universal accessibility and design for all at major sports facilities. In the field of disability, there is a relatively general consensus on some of the main terms but, across different countries, there is no general consensus on who should be classed as a person with disability. In general, it should be stressed that disability is diverse and ranges in severity. This may be visible or non-visible, or both. In this aspect, the main types of disability comprise those people with mobility, sensory mechanism, learning and communication difficulties, mental health disabilities and hidden disabilities such as diabetes, epilepsy, heart diseases or health problems. Many of these forms of disability are treatable or may be alleviated by broader changes in social perceptions. Unfortunately, the majority of sports managers of clubs and professional leagues are unfamiliar with the nature and types of disabilities.

Accessibility is a characteristic of urban design, buildings and transport. However, 'universal accessibility' goes beyond the notion of accessibility and is an integral part of universal design: design for all. As it is claimed in this work, dealing with accessibility goes beyond architectural aspects of any stadium, as we will address later, and it is a policy that seeks to ensure equal opportunities for all people, including those with disabilities. In terms of what is the best term to address accessibility, there is a diverse range of terminology. In fact, some people refer to it as universal accessibility, others as just accessibility and still others as universal accessibility and design for all. Despite these differences, what is clear is that promoting good accessibility from the early stages of any design is the one that exists but goes unnoticed by most users ('unnoticed accessibility' as Rovira-Beleta (2009) notes) and benefits the whole society. Providing accessible environments in stadia will enhance the experience of fans with disabilities and increase their quality of life. This concern from the initial design stages will not substantially increase the final costs of any venue, and as far as we know will reduce investment in the medium and long term.

Within the football industry, the Premier League was the first to establish guidelines, 'Guidance for Clubs on Disabled Fans and Customers', for dealing with fans with disabilities (Premier League Guidance for Clubs on Disabled Fans and Customers 2010). This guideline coincides largely with accessibility legislation in Britain and defines a person with disability as someone who 'has a physical or mental impairment which has a substantial and long-term adverse effect on their ability to carry out normal day-to-day activities or has had such impairment in the past'. For further information about the term disability and what defines it, see Chapter 20, 'Planning and Managing the Stadium Experience', of this collection. In reference to football disabilities policies, NADS's or Manchester United's policies for disabled fans consider that a fan with disability is

> any person who, because of their disability or impairment, is unable to use ordinary stand seating without contravening health and safety regulations, guidelines or policy or where the club has provided a 'reasonable adjustment' or 'auxiliary service' to enable that supporter to attend the venue.

Any such person will be considered for use of the 'designated areas' of the stadium.

ACCESSIBILITY TO SPORT FACILITIES

Prior to the 1960s, access to sports facilities and associated services did not have the same consideration as there is today. Over the years, most of the literature that has been written on promoting full access at sports venues has come from the work of architects rather than from academics. However, those architects involved did not have a holistic approach to this issue. One of the earliest writings on this field came from Selwyn Goldsmith's book *Designing for the Disabled* (Goldsmith 1963). Similarly, other texts examined in more detail how to remove physical barriers in a variety of sports facilities (e.g. Walter 1971; Cabezas 1978; Thomson, Dendy and de Deney 1984). At this point, it is appropriate to highlight that many of the architects mentioned before were also disabled.

More recently, there has been an increasing impetus in the literature in this field by established journals in the design, building and operation of stadia and arenas (e.g. *Stadia, SB Sport Facilities* or *PanStadia*), each of which has published special issues on accessibility at sports venues. These publications have motivated conferences like those promoted by the International Association for Sports and Leisure Facilities (IAKS). In their 21st Congress in 2009 incorporating the theme *Accessible Sports and Leisure Facilities*, Beijing 2008, Vancouver 2010 and London 2012 featured as examples. Studies like *The Accessible Stadium* project concerning the Spanish First Football Division or *The European Standards for the Design and Construction of Facilities* are evidence of this. In addition, the recent partnership between the IAKS and the International Paralympics Committee (IPC) has also contributed to raising the issue of accessibility by issuing an annual award to the best examples of accessible facilities around the world.

Still, some of the few dedicated books and documents which address accessibility issues at big venues come mainly from architects rather than from academics, with few exceptions (see for example Grady 2006). Architects like John, Sheard and Vickery (2007) have included in their book *Stadia* a specific chapter dealing with accessibility to those venues, or the work of architects such as Goldsmith (1997) and Rovira-Beleta (2003) are further markers. In addition to these, the best documents to guide anyone dealing with this issue at large venues come from the USA: for example, *Accessibility Guidelines for Stadia and Arenas* (2004) provides probably the highest standards in accessibility in the world. In Europe it is perhaps the *Accessible Stadia Guide* (2004) by the architect Jim Frogatt which is the most authoritative guide to the design of a new stand or accessible stadium to disabled people. This document is considered definitive in respect of facilities available for people with disabilities in stadia and provides detailed information for architects, managers and others on all aspects of making a stand or stadium accessible to people with disabilities. The *Accessible Stadia* in August 2009 inspired the publication of the European Technical Report CEN/TR 15913 – 'Spectator facilities: Layout criteria for spectators with special needs' – which aims to be adopted as a European standard for stadia.

RECENT LEGISLATIVE DEVELOPMENTS OF ACCESSIBILITY PROVISION AT STADIA AND ARENAS IN THE USA AND EUROPE

To place this relevant issue in an historical perspective, we will focus on legislation and best strategies promoted by sport governing and non-governing bodies in countries such as the USA, Australia, the UK, Germany and Spain from the 1960s to present times, as shown in Table 21.1. Looking back to the 1960s, the majority of stadia incorporated innovation in their design and operation, but in our analysis of the evolution of stadia in Europe throughout the last century to the present (Paramio, Buraimo and Campos 2008), we found that clubs and their stadia at that time offered basic facilities for fans with disabilities, usually located in uncovered spaces at pitch level with limited views of games. Some British clubs went further and started to offer additional services as audio commentary guides and offered free entry.

Table 21.1 *Landmarks in accessibility legislation for public and private buildings, including stadia and arenas, and the setting of organizations of fans with disabilities in different countries: 1989–2010*

USA	1990 Americans with Disabilities Act (ADA)
	1991 Americans with Disabilities Act Accessibility Guidelines for Buildings and Facilities (ADAAG) (updated in 2004)
	2004 Accessibility Guidelines for Stadia and Arenas
Australia	1992 Disability Discrimination Act (DDA)
European Community	2009 European Technical Report, CEN/TR 15913 – 'Spectator facilities: Layout criteria for spectators with special needs', European Committee for Standardisation (CEN)
	2009 Centre for Access to Football in Europe (CAFÉ)

Continued

Table 21.1 Continued

UK	1989	First Disabled Supporters Association at Manchester United (MUDSA)
	1990	Taylor Report
	1992	Designing for Spectators with Disabilities
	1995	Disability Discrimination Act (DDA)
	1998	Improving Facilities for Disabled Supporters (Assessment of Stadiums)
	1999	NADS (National Association of Disabled Supporters)
	2004	Accessible Stadia Guide
Germany	1999	German association of disabled football fans and disability officers within the clubs (BBAG) (Bundesbehindertenfanarbeitsgemeinschaft)
	2001	Behindertengleichstellungsgesetz (BGG) (Equal Opportunities for People with Disabilities Act)
	2001	First Guidelines for Accessibility at German Stadiums (BBAG)
	2009	New Accessibility Guidelines for Stadiums (DFL and BBAG)
Spain	2003	Equal Treatment, Non-Discrimination and Accessibility for All Law (LIONDAU)
	2004	I Plan Nacional de Accesibilidad 2004–2012 (First National Plan to Promote Access for All 2004–2012)

Source: Adapted by the authors

Also, building regulations described the requirements for universal accessibility in buildings in general, but did not address sport-specific issues such as match day attendance at stadia. Beyond Europe, it is worth mentioning the Astrodome, the first domed stadium in the world, built in 1965 in Texas, which raised the standards in a number of areas, including access for people with disabilities. Nearly four decades later, on 26 June 1990, the promulgation of probably the most influential piece of legislation, the Americans with Disabilities Act (ADA), marked a change of paradigm in North American disability law. Since then, people with disabilities have witnessed fundamental changes in public attitudes and experience greater access to sports stadia and arenas (Grady 2006). In fact, this progress became a reality more than a decade later with the approval of the *Accessibility Guidelines for Stadia and Arenas* (ADAAG) in 2004. Among other requirements, this influential piece of legislation demanded that at least 1 per cent of the total number of seats available to the public in stadia and arenas should be allocated to wheelchair users, with their companions seated next to each wheelchair seat. Whenever more than 300 seats are provided, wheelchair areas must be dispersed throughout all seating areas of the venue.

After the promulgation of the ADA, other countries followed suit and passed legislation to tackle the discrimination faced by disabled people in society – disability and accessibility has become part of the mainstream policy. Australia passed the Disability Discrimination Act (DDA) in 1992. In Europe, the UK passed its own Disability Discrimination Act (DDA) in 1995 and, in 2001, Germany approved the 'Behindertengleichstellungsgesetz' (BBG). Two years later, Spain approved the 'Ley Igualdad de Oportunidades, No Discriminación y Accesibilidad Universal' (LIONDAU) (Ministerio de Trabajo y Asuntos Sociales 2004) (see Table 21.1).

These legislations require that buildings (including stadia) and means of transportation, as well as public information systems have to be constructed in a way that people with disabilities will be able to use them without restriction.

Focusing on stadia, the most significant development in accessibility policy for these buildings took place during the 1990s. In the early 1990s, the *Taylor Report*, probably the most influential document on safety and on accessibility in stadia, was published and contributed to what we refer to as the 'emergence of postmodern stadia', which included among other features the provision of good standards of accessibility for all types of users (Paramio, Buraimo and Campos 2008). The *Taylor Report* recommended both to football governing bodies and clubs that 'facilities for disabled football supporters should be an integral part of stadium development, not an optional extra'. Although laws vary from country to country in Europe, only the UK and Germany have developed explicit guidelines to promote access by fans with disabilities to stadia, while the LFP in Spain has not issued any further recommendations on this matter yet. There are substantial differences in accessibility at European stadia: viewed as 'very poor or nonexistent' in countries like Spain while, on the other hand, there are good examples of accessible stadia, as noted in the case study below.

The *Accessible Stadia Guide* has proved successful as a technical document which forms part of the British Building Regulations (Part M) and has recently inspired the European Technical Report CEN/TR 15913 – 'Spectator facilities: Layout criteria for spectators with special needs' – issued by the European Committee for Standardisation (CEN). CEN is tasked with trying to harmonize good practice within the European Community. Although not legally binding for European stadia, it will be compulsory for those stadia that will host the European Football Championship in Poland and Ukraine in 2012 to obtain UEFA approval (Mandetta and Salerio 2009). Table 21.2 summarizes the minimum recommended provision of wheelchair spaces at a newly built spectator facility in stadia in Europe.

Table 21.2 *Minimum recommended provision of wheelchair spaces at a newly built spectator facility in stadia in Europe*

Under 10,000 spectators	Minimum 6 or 1 for every 100 (100) of seated (whichever is greater)
Between 10,000 and 20,000 spectators	100 plus 5 per 1,000 for those over 10,000 (150)
Between 20,000 and 40,000 spectators	150 plus 3 per 1,000 for those over 20,000 (210)
40,000 spectators or above	210 plus 2 per 1,000 for those over 40,000 (290)

Source: Football Stadia Improvement Fund (2004) and CEN (2009)

DESIGN AND OPERATION PRINCIPLES AS PART OF THE HOLISTIC JOURNEY SEQUENCE APPROACH TO ANY STADIUM

A fundamental principle of any contemporary organization should be to provide high standards of accessibility within their venue. First, cross-disciplinary work is required between architects, engineers, administrators, civil servants, managers, owners, disability liaison officers and organizations for supporters with disabilities, working together from the initial design and planning stages. By doing so, common mistakes that usually occur in the design of new stadia could be avoided. In this respect, John, Sheard and Vickery (2007:18) clearly recommend: 'do not start by planning a "new" stadium for "general users", and then check documents such as Accessible Stadia Guide at a later point to add special features for "disabled" users'. Those aforementioned architects offer a useful approach known as 'the journey sequence' to guide the entire sequence of events from the moment that fans with disabilities decide to plan a visit to a venue until leaving it. However, in our opinion, this model is missing other psychological and emotional benefits for people with disabilities. We include these and other aspects in what we have described under the term 'holistic journey sequence approach'.

Attending matches at stadia can, therefore, be defined as a multi-phase experience comprising of five major stages:

1 Anticipation, which comprises the motivation of travelling
2 Pre-travelling to the stadium
3 Attending the event at the stadium
4 Leaving the stadium
5 Recollection (Campos 2004)

Table 21.3 offers a useful summary of the assessment of this holistic journey sequence approach.

The experiences of match attendance by fans with disabilities are different from those of other fans. This justifies the necessary introduction of the first and fifth phases just mentioned. To illustrate examples of these benefits, we introduce a comment from a family of a young fan with disability:

> Thomas feels that this has given him fun in his life and something to look forward to. He loves the ritual of match days, the walk to the ground, the buying of his programme and sitting in his seat with a brilliant view of the match. It has given him confidence and something to talk about and discuss with his mates and fellow students at college.
>
> (NADS 2009)

The reader can understand that these sentiments are only the starting point to undertake a systematic study of the needs and experiences of different types of fans with disabilities when they plan on visiting venues. Unfortunately, most of the needs and demands of fans with disabilities are not standard in the offerings of sports venues. When we asked a key figure in the area, Phil Downs, about the approach proposed, he made the following comments:

I suppose its fair to say that the 1–5 sequence doesn't even exist for many non-disabled supporters but there should be every opportunity for the sequence to be applied to any new stadia and it should be applied in general to the 'thinking' when a club or a venue sit down to examine how best to make their venue accessible to disabled people. The only thing I would say in addition to that is that there is a general level of unawareness in the disabled community because disabled people are still seen as a 'problem' when it comes to managing a venue or facility … I ask this question, 'how often do you see any venue, whether it's a football stadium, cinema or running track, openly advertising and welcoming disabled people with a full explanation of what they have on offer in terms of facilities and how they have prepared in terms of training staff etc.' By and large this doesn't happen … part of it is to do with the fact that we are still building the awareness culture but we aren't quite there yet. It'll take a long time to totally develop a fully inclusive society simply because it will take hundreds of years for every building to change into an accessible form. However, this shouldn't be an excuse for not going through the 1–5 sequence in the thought processes to at least get some of it right at the very early stages of development.

(Phil Downs, personal communication, 26 February 2010)

Furthermore, an additional phase might be considered. On many occasions, fans with disabilities themselves think that they are not able to attend a football match. This we label the 'able phase'. Paraphrasing Adidas' logo, these people with different capabilities need to assume that 'impossible is nothing' is also applicable in this context. In this line of argument, it is worth mentioning the case of Manchester United, who decided to name its special suite for fans with disabilities at Old Trafford the Ability Suite instead of the Disability Suite. As Phil Downs stressed, 'The efforts of MUDSA [Manchester United disabled fans association for fans with disabilities] and the club over a number of years has resulted in a "can do" mentality which benefits everyone.' The conclusion is that any positive development around accessibility depends on club strategy.

In our experience, the overwhelmingly most common obstacle to promoting access to stadia comes from managers' and officials' perceptions and attitudes, and even ignorance. In the same line of enquiry, Sanford and Rose (1998), drawing on their study of North American stadia and arenas, pointed out that management awareness and sensitivity, as well as management policies and practices designed to accommodate people with disabilities and their companions, can compensate other deficits found. In fact, it is highly recommended that clubs should address all the recommendations outlined in Table 21.3 as part of a club disability policy.

Table 21.3 *Main phases and considerations from fans with different types of disabilities as part of the holistic journey approach to any stadium*

Phases	Main considerations
Anticipation (pre-experience)	Create the motivation for fans with disabilities to travel to the stadium
Pre-travelling to the stadium (second phase of the pre-experience)	Includes getting relevant information to plan the trip. Therefore, clubs should offer easily accessible official web pages in different formats, including Braille, disk and audio cassettes, or in different languages for those fans whose first language is not the same as the club's home base. Offering significant accessible information to current and potential home, but also away, fans with disabilities wishing to attend a live football match at the stadium. The information should, at least, include aspects such as: • Public and private transport means with their locations and stops • Number of parking spaces reserved for fans with disabilities and their location and distance to the main entrance to the stadium • How to contact the clubs and person responsible for this service • A stadium guide – virtual tour of the stadium with the location of seats for them and services outside and inside the ground • Ticketing policy for fans with disabilities and their companions for match days • Accessible tours to the stadium and club museum and club stores If the fan finally decides to travel to the stadium, this information will be useful to plan the journey and to arrive at the stadium easily.
Attending the game at stadium (the experience itself)	Once there, they will wish to park in a dedicated and safe reserved parking area, with the help of trained staff, providing main circulation routes which lead to dedicated gate entrances to the stadium. From this point, they will wish to go to their allocated seats through accessible entrances, ramps and wide corridors and comfortable and adapted social zones, which will allow them either independently or with companions to use complementary services (such as restaurants, food and catering points, shops, hospitality boxes, toilets, lifts, tours and museum) offered in the stadium. Once both the home and away fans are in their seats with/alongside their companion and their own supporters in different parts of the stadium, they will want to be seated comfortably without having to worry about the weather and, above all, to enjoy a good view of the pitch at all times like other spectators. From this position, fans with disabilities will expect to be entertained and informed of everything that happens during the event.
Leaving the stadium (travel back)	When the match is over, they will want to leave the stadium by an easy route without any great difficulty and to return to their homes.
Recollection (post-experience)	After the travel experience is over and fans have returned home, they are likely to reflect upon their experiences, which will include psychological and emotional benefits that remain for a while.

Source: Adapted by the authors from *Accessible Stadia Guide* (2004) and personal communication with Phil Downs

CASE STUDY: THE STATE OF ACCESSIBILITY AT PREMIER LEAGUE, BUNDESLIGA AND SPANISH PRIMERA DIVISION STADIA

Britain might be considered to be one of the first examples of how the growing power of the people with disabilities movement has brought policy change in their stadia. In quantitative terms, the 20 stadia of Premier League clubs offer 2,900 seats for fans with disabilities; there are approximately 30,000 people with different types of disabilities attending matches regularly, with around 60 organizations for supporters with disabilities at club level (NADS 2007, 2009). Furthermore, it is worth noting that NADS was set up in 1998 and full- or part-time disability liaison officers were appointed at most football clubs. As part of this concern, Britain has pioneered explicit guidelines to promote access to their stadia.

Despite these developments, there are some demands that need to be addressed as there is still a deficit of provision for fans with disabilities at UK stadia, with 71 per cent of clubs meeting the recommendations set up by the *Accessible Stadia* document. This situation got the attention of the national political agenda after 29 July 2008 when Don Foster (Member of Parliament), Liberal Democrat Spokesman for Culture, Media and Sport, sent a letter of concern to Andy Burnham (Member of Parliament), where the former stated that 'there is a shortfall of almost 1,500 wheelchair spaces in Premier League stadia and that only two clubs currently meet Green Guide recommendations.' NADS reduces this figure to 1,162 seats.

The Bundesliga has also incorporated the issue of accessibility to stadia as part of its culture (Bundesliga 2009a). As part of its commitment, the German Football Association (DFL) states that 'no one is excluded' from the game. Similarly to NADS, the German association of disabled football fans and disability officers within the clubs (Bundesbehindertenfanarbeitsgemeinschaft) (BBAG), created in 1999, developed explicit guidelines to promote access to their stadia in 2001. Seven years later, in 2008, the Bundesliga has published the policy directions for fans with disabilities in their stadia in a document known as the *Accessible Stadia – Barrierefreiheit im Stadion*. This guide can be seen as the first comprehensive step to improve the conditions and number of seats for disabled spectators in German stadia. Among other things, this policy includes aspects referring to the needs of wheelchair and blind and deaf spectators. In this process, the DFL collaborated with several German organizations for supporters with disabilities with the aim of raising the awareness of German clubs concerning the needs of fans with disabilities. Despite the fact that they had good provisions for fans with disabilities before the 2006 World Cup in Germany, the organization of this event contributed to improvements in the conditions for fans with disabilities in the new stadia built (for example, the Commerzbank-Arena in Frankfurt) and to further take into consideration the issue of accessibility of venues into the agenda. As was confirmed by the person responsible for this issue at the DFL, he estimates that 'out of 800,000 wheelchair users living in Germany, 30,400 are interested in football' (Ruehmann, personal communication, 18 December 2009). However, they still do not have accurate figures of the number of fans with disabilities that regularly attend matches at Bundesliga stadia.

As a member of the Bundesliga confirms, Bundesliga stadia provide 2,800 seats for wheelchairs, 410 seats for blind fans and 61 seats for other types of disabilities and additional seats for their companions. In particular, 25 of 36 venues supply an audio descriptive commentary service for those fans with vision impairment. In addition, it was reported that all Bundesliga clubs have a DLO. As an added value, since 2006 the DFL issued the Bundesliga-Reiseführer für Menschen mit Behinderung (Bundesliga travel guide) (updated in 2010) in conjunction with BBAG to improve the travelling conditions for fans with disabilities on match days. Among other issues, this document provides useful information about getting to the stadia as well as a list of contact persons in the venues. Despite these developments, 'the DFL is of the opinion that this approach will have more success in the long run, but we certainly know that we have to improve the situation and the work has not finished yet' (Ruehmann, personal communication, 18 December 2009).

Accessibility at Spanish stadia has, in many respects, been a marginal issue for Spanish football governing bodies and clubs themselves. There are no official statistics about the provision for any kind of fans with disabilities at Spanish stadia (INE 2008), though the research revealed that there are substantial differences between the accessibility standards at Premier and Bundesliga stadia and those of their Spanish counterparts. As can be seen from Tables 21.4 to 21.6, the Premier League and Bundesliga clubs' stadia offer so far the best standards for fans with disabilities in Europe, including historical stadia such as Manchester United's Old Trafford and new ones like Arsenal's Emirates, Bayern Munich's Allianz Arena and, above all, England's new Wembley. For further information about the operation of the Emirates Stadium for fans with disabilities, see Chapter 20.

Table 21.4 *Provision for fans with disabilities at seven stadia of the Premier League and the new Wembley, season 2009–2010*

Club name and web contact	Stadium, date of building, capacity	Seats for fans with disabilities	Capacity/seats for fans with disabilities (%)	Other accessible services
Manchester United FC www.mudsa.org	Old Trafford, 1910, 76,312	120 (wheelchairs) (108 home and 12 away) (+helpers' seating) 21 (severe mobility difficulties) (+helpers' seating) 13 (moderate mobility difficulties) (+helpers' seating) 40 (visually impaired) (+companion seating)	76,312/288 =0.37%	Tickets and membership services 249 parking spaces Hospitality areas (Ability Suite) and 9 toilets 8 suites and executive boxes with adjacent accessible toilets New food, beverages and concession stands Museum and tour centre and club store Radio headsets and away transport
Liverpool FC disability@ liverpoolfc.com	Anfield Road, 1906, 42,536	100 wheelchairs (92 home and 8 away fans) 36 (visually impaired) 12 (ambulant)	42,536/148 =0.34%	15 parking spaces 6 toilets Concession stands
Chelsea FC disability@ chelseafc.com	Stamford Bridge, 1910, 42,536	100 (wheelchairs) (+ companion seating)	42,536/100 =0.23%	5 parking spaces Toilets and concession stands Match commentary and induction loop system Away transport

Club name and web contact	Stadium, date of building, capacity	Seats for fans with disabilities	Capacity/seats for fans with disabilities (%)	Other accessible services
Arsenal FC disability@ arsenal.co.uk	Emirates Stadium, 2006, 60,000	241 (wheelchairs) (229 home and 12 away) 98 (ambulant and visually impaired)	60,000/339 =0.56%	Ticket offices 100 parking spaces Match commentary (visually impaired) Tactile pathway inside venue 40 toilets and 1 dog toilet Tour and museum and away transport
Everton FC www.evertonfc. com	Goodison Park, 1908, 40,565	96 (wheelchairs) (83 home and 13 away fans) 8 (visually impaired)	40,565/104 =0.25%	48 parking spaces 6 toilets Away transport
Tottenham Hotspur FC www. tottenhamhotspur. com	White Hart Lane, 1899, 36,240	56 (wheelchairs) (51 home and 5 away fans) 25 (ambulant) (23 home and 2 away fans)	36,240/81 =0.22%	6 toilets Headsets Facilities for dogs Away transport
Sunderland AFC www.safc.com	Stadium of Light, 1997, 49,000	200 (wheelchairs) (180 home and 20 away fans) 40 (visually impaired)	49,000/240 =0.48%	160 parking spaces 23 toilets Away transport
National Stadium FA www. wembleystadium. com	New Wembley, 2007, 90,000	310 (wheelchairs) (+310 companion seating) 90 additional seating 100 (ambulatory)	90,000/810 =0.90%	250 parking spaces 147 toilets and 2 toilets for dogs Audio commentary Lift access to all parts of stadium Dedicated turnstiles for wheelchairs Food, beverages and concession stands Induction loop in all facilities Away transport

Source: NADS (2009)

Table 21.5 *Provision for fans with disabilities at seven top stadia of the Bundesliga, season 2009–2010*

Club name and web page	Stadium, date of building (last upgrading), capacity	Seats for fans with disabilities	Capacity/ seats for fans with disabilities (%)	Other accessible services
Hamburger SV www.hsv.de	HSH Nordbank Arena, Hamburg, 2000, 57,250	95 (wheelchairs) (10% away fans) 30 (blind)	57,720/125 =0.22%	Headphones (visually impaired) 2 toilets
Hertha Berlin www.herthabsc. de	Olympiastadion, Berlin, 1936/2004, 74,244	174 (wheelchairs) 50 (blind)	74,244/224 =0.30%	77 parking spaces Concession stands and 6 toilets
FC Bayern Munich www.fcbayern. de	Allianz Arena, 2005, 69,901	200 (wheelchairs) (+200 companion seating) 16 (blind)	69,901/416 =0.59%	150 parking spaces Level 2 is considered barrier-less for fans with disabilities Headsets (match commentaries) Stadium tour
VFB Stuttgart www.vfb.de	Mercedes Benz Arena, 1933/2006, 42,344	115 (wheelchairs) 20 (blind)	42,344/135 =0.32%	150 parking spaces
FC Schalke 04 www.schalke04. de	Veltins Arena, 2001, 61,481	98 (wheelchairs) 20 (blind)	61,481/118 =0.19%	6 toilets with radar key Club magazine
Borussia Dortmund www.bvb.de	Signal Iduna Park, 1974/2003, 80,708	72 (wheelchairs) (10% away fans) 20 (blind) (10% for away fans)	80,708/92 =0.11%	45 parking spaces 2 toilets Special fan club for blind
Bayer Leverkusen www.bayer04. de	Bay Arena, 1923/2009, 30,000	70 (wheelchairs) (15 for away fans) 40 (blind)	30,000/110 =0.36%	2 parking spaces 3 toilets Headsets (match commentaries)

Sources: Bundesliga (2009b); Marco Ruehmann (personal communication, 18 December 2009)

Table 21.6 *Provision for fans with disabilities at six stadia of the Spanish Primera Division, season 2009–2010*

Club name and web page	Stadium, date of building, capacity	Seats for fans with disabilities	Capacity/ seats for fans with disabilities (%)	Other accessible services
FC Barcelona www.fcbarcelona.cat	Camp Nou, 1957, 98,787	24 (only for wheelchair fans)	98,787/24 =0.02%	Parking spaces 4 toilets Tour to museum and club store
Real Madrid FC www.realmadrid.com	Santiago Bernabéu, 1947, 80,000	92 (18 non-wheelchairs plus 74 wheelchairs)[1] (+15 companion seating)	80,000/107 =0.13%	Dedicated turnstile (wheelchairs) 1 toilet
Villarreal SAD www.villarrealcf.es	El Madrigal, 1923, 23,500	15 (wheelchairs) (+15 companion seating)	23,500/30 =0.12%	2 toilets
Atlético Madrid SAD www. clubatleticodemadrid. com	Vicente Calderón, 1966, 54,571	40 (wheelchairs) (30 season ticket holders and 10 for general public)	54,571/40 =0.07%	4 toilets Concession stands
Getafe SAD www.getafecf.com	Coliseo Alfonso Pérez, 1998, 14,400	None	14,400/0 =0%	6 toilets
Real Murcia SAD www.realmurcia.es	Nueva Condomina, 2006, 31,200	80 (wheelchairs) (+80 companion seating)	31,200/160 =0.51%	9 indoor parking spaces Lift access to the platform 2 toilets and club store

Source: Paramio *et al.* (2009a/2009b, 2010)

1   The current provision of the Bernabeu stadium has been modified and upgraded due to the pressure exerted by UEFA before hosting the 2010 UEFA Champions League Final on 22 May 2010. As part of the standards required by UEFA and among others, Real Madrid was forced to build a new platform in the East Stand to add an additional 42 wheelchair seats and to raise the existing South Stand fans with a disabilities platform (16 wheelchair spaces) to provide an unobstructed view of the pitch for Real Madrid fans.

Meanwhile, except for La Nueva Condomina (Real Murcia SAD), the Spanish stadia analysed are clearly behind the minimum requirements. To improve the situation, in March 2009, an executive summary report was presented to the Spanish LFP that summarized the existing facilities and services available to fans with disabilities in selected clubs' stadia. The report highlighted the areas of best practice, but also identified some of the main barriers that may discourage people with disabilities to attend a match. With respect to communication between fans with disabilities and clubs, it found that the majority of clubs in the top two divisions were failing to meet minimum accessibility standards on their websites. In addition, the majority did not provide any useful information either for their own fans with disabilities or those of the away team. When we look at the level of provision of seats at the stadia analysed, except La Nueva Condomina or Santiago Bernabeu, there was a poor supply of seats for fans with disabilities. Most of the facilities provided in Spanish stadia were only for wheelchair users; there was no provision for other types of fans with disabilities as happens at Bundesliga and Premier League stadia. Despite these conditions, it was estimated that more than 30 fans with disabilities plus their companions regularly attend matches. Most of them go on their own and only two organizations for supporters with disabilities were found. But it is still unknown how many more follow the games. After identifying major deficits in most stadia, the study provided some recommendations to Spanish governing bodies in order to establish good standards of accessibility in new and existing stadia as part of the Master Plan to Improve Accessibility at Spanish Stadia (2009–2014). On the basis of the evidence provided, the authors of the study had several meetings with LFP representatives to address these issues and to find effective solutions to improve the conditions for fans with disabilities within stadia. However, no positive action has yet been taken.

DISABILITY FOOTBALL POLICY AND THE DISABILITY LIAISON OFFICER (DLO)

Having a qualified disability liaison officer (DLO), as a full- or part-time member of staff, can make a substantial impact on the overall experience of fans with disabilities and is obviously critical to the management of any stadium. With some exceptions, the role of DLOs are new within the context of Premier League and Bundesliga teams, but one that does not exist in Spanish clubs. In general, as Phil Downs' extensive knowledge suggests, this position should cover all aspects of the club's operation, from the information given on websites to the accessibility of executive areas or even Directors' Lounges. Among other qualifications, skills and experience, any DLO must possess good knowledge and understanding of disability and of any related legislation, and how it relates to football spectators with disabilities. The job requires a detailed knowledge of accessible environments. A good DLO must have understanding of design and of baseline facilities for disabled fans. In addition, they must also possess good operational skills, including those relating to provision of season tickets or match day tickets for all types of people with disabilities and carers (if required), responsibility for parking areas for fans with disabilities and their companions, management of all match day staff who might provide care and assistance to people with disabilities, coordination of events run in tandem with the club's sponsors and so on. They will have a good anticipatory ability, with a strategic thought process capable of developing the best possible scenario from an existing or old stadium through to getting everything right in a new-build stadium.

SUMMARY

Moving forward, in promoting good standards of accessibility at stadia in Europe in this decade, fans with disabilities are clearly demanding that UEFA undertake specific and clear actions. After the introduction of those requirements for making stands or stadia accessible to people with disabilities at UK stadia, the recent approval of European requirements by CEN will force UEFA to introduce this policy into their Club Licensing Scheme and should demand that each club meet the 'minimum' recommended number and placement of seating places for people with disabilities. Instead of being reactive, there is no doubt, in our opinion, that both individual clubs and governing bodies should become more proactive in the promotion of accessible stadia in decades to come. Those clubs that are still reactive and do not explore the benefits of dealing with providing good standards of accessibility within their stadia will be considered, as Downs states, as part of the problem rather than the solution, especially when some top clubs in Europe are clearly moving forward on this issue.

From a management perspective, there is a need to share knowledge and experience across Europe on this matter, as we have included in our discussion. It is also necessary to have more studies that directly look at different issues explaining the experience of certain clubs when moving from their historical stadia to a new stadium or, in particular, those clubs that own an old stadium. As the Manchester United experience has shown, providing good standards of accessibility on match and non-match days will support the idea that there are clear relationships between the philanthropic strategy of any club and the clear economic and social benefits that providing good standards of accessibility for all fans can bring to clubs, as the well-known strategy expert Michael Porter (2009) suggests. This kind of approach can be seen nowadays and in the years to come as a competitive advantage for clubs linked to their corporate social responsibility.

REVIEW QUESTIONS

1 After examining some of the key documents related to accessibility at large venues in the text, explain the similarities and differences between North American and European standards on this issue.
2 You are charged with the design of a venue with a 30,000-seat capacity; explain the level of provision that should be considered in the project to meet the needs of different types of people with disabilities following the holistic journey sequence approach.

FURTHER READING

Goldsmith, S. (1997) *Designing for the Disabled: The New Paradigm,* Oxford: Architectural Press.

WEBSITES

Allianz Arena, Bayern Munich, Germany
   www.allianz-arena.de/en/service/barrierefreie-arena
Americans with Disabilities Act 1990
   http://www.ada.gov/index.html
Australia Disability Discrimination Act 1992
   www.hreoc.gov.au/disability_rights
Centre for Access to Football in Europe (CAFÉ)
   cafefootball.eu
Dogs for the Disabled
   www.dogsforthedisabled.org
English Football Association
   www.thefa.com
European Committee of Standardization
   www.cen.eu/cenorm/homepage.htm
Football Supporters Europe (FSE)
   www.footballsupporterseurope.org
German association of disabled football fans and disability officers within clubs (BBAG)
   www.bbag-online.de
German Association of Visually Impaired Football Fans
   www.fanclub-sehhunde.de
German Bundesliga
   www.bundesliga.de
International Paralympics Committee
   www.paralympic.org
Managing Sport (Spanish Sport Business web page)
   www.managingsport.com
Manchester United Disabled Supporters Association
   www.mudsa.org
Premier League
   www.premierleague.co.uk
Spanish Instituto Nacional de Estadística (Spanish Statistics Institute) (INE)
   www.ine.es
Spanish Liga de Fútbol Profesional (Spanish Professional League) (LFP)
   www.lfp.es
UK Disability Discrimination Act 1995
   www.disability.gov.uk
UK Disability Rights Commission (DRC)
   www.drc-gb.org
UK National Association of Disabled Supporters (NADS) (currently known as Level Playing Field since March 2011)
   http://www.levelplayingfield.org.uk

REFERENCES

Breitbarth, T. and Harris, P. (2008) 'The Role of Corporate Social Responsibility in the Football Business: Towards the Development of a Conceptual Model', *European Sport Management Quarterly*, 8: 179–206.

Bundesliga (2009a) *Annual Report 2009*, Frankfurt: DFL Deutsche Fußball Liga GmbH.

Bundesliga (2009b) *Bundesliga-Reiseführer für Menschen mit Behinderung, Season 2008–2009*, Frankfurt: DFL Deutsche Fußball Liga GmbH.

Cabezas, G. (1978) *Manual para proyectar sin barreras arquitectónicas. Arquitectura para Todos*, Madrid: COAM.

Campos, C. (2004) *Dirección y Marketing de Servicios Deportivos*, Barcelona: Gestió I Promoció.

Centre for Access to Football in Europe (CAFÉ) (2010) Retrieved 18 July 2010 from http://www.cafefootball.eu.

Cook, J. (2009) 'Raising Awareness on Disabled Fans' Rights', Proceedings of the Second European Football Fans Conference, Hamburg. Retrieved 4 January 2010 from www.footballsupportersinternational.com.

Downs, P. (2006) 'Joining Forces', *Gazetta*, 9: 3.

European Committee for Standardization (CEN) (2009) *European Technical Report CEN/TR 15913 'Spectators facilities: Layout Criteria for spectators with special needs*, Milan: CEN.

Football Stadia Improvement Fund (2004) *Accessible Stadia*, London: Football Stadia Improvement Fund and Football Licensing Authority.

Goldsmith, S. (1963) *Designing for the Disabled*, London: RIBA.

Goldsmith, S. (1997) *Designing for the Disabled: The New Paradigm*, Oxford: Architectural Press.

Grady, J.M. (2006) 'Toward an Understanding of the Needs of Sport Spectators with Disabilities', unpublished PhD thesis, The Florida State University.

Horne, J. and Howe, P.D. (2009) 'Guest Editorial', *Leisure Studies*, 28, 4: 371–373.

INE (2008) *Encuesta sobre Discapacidades, Autonomía Personal and Situaciones de Dependencia*. Retrieved 19 October 2009 from www.ine.es.

John, G., Sheard, R. and Vickery, B. (2007) *Stadia: A Design and Development Guide*, Oxford: Elsevier.

Mandetta, S. and Salerio, G.L. (2009) 'European Standards for the Design and Construction of Stadia', Proceedings of the 21st IAKS Congress, Cologne.

Ministerio de Trabajo y Asuntos Sociales (2004) *I Plan Nacional de Accesibilidad 2004–2012*, Madrid: Ministerio de Trabajo y Asuntos Sociales.

NADS (2007) *State of the Game Summary*. Retrieved 19 October 2008 from www.nads.org.uk.

NADS (2009) *Annual Report 2008/09*. Retrieved 27 January 2010 from www.nads.org.uk.

Paramio, J.L., Beotas, E., Campos, C. and Muñoz, G. (2010) *Manual de Equipamientos e Instalaciones Deportivas: Aproximación Arquitectónica y de Gestión (Handbook of Sport Facilities. Architectural and Managerial Implications)*, Madrid: Editorial Síntesis.

Paramio, J.L., Buraimo, B. and Campos, C. (2008) 'From the Modern to the Postmodern Stadia: The Development of Football Stadia in Europe', *Sport in Society*, 11, 5: 517–534.

Paramio, J.L., Campos, C., Downs, P., Beotas, E. and Muñoz, G. (2009a) 'Disability Provision in European stadia within a Corporate Social Responsibility Framework: The Case of Primera División-Spanish Football League', Proceedings of the XVII European Association Sport Management Conference, 2009, Amsterdam.

Paramio, J.L., Campos, C., Downs, P., Beotas, E. and Muñoz, G. (2009b) 'The Accessible Stadium Project in the First Spanish Football Division', Proceedings of the 21st IAKS Conference, 2009, Cologne.

Porter, M. (2009) *Ser Competitivo* (On Competition), Bilbao: Ed. Deusto.

387

Premier League Guidance for Clubs on Disabled Fans and Customers (2010) Retrieved 19 October 2009 from http://www.levelplayingfield.org.uk.

Rovira-Beleta, E. (2003) *Libro Blanco de la Accesibilidad,* Barcelona: Ediciones UPC.

Rovira-Beleta, E. (2009) *La Nueva Medida de la Arquitectura del siglo XXI.* Retrieved 11 January 2010 from www.managingsport.com.

Sanford, J.A. and Rose, B. (1998) 'Accessible Seating in Stadia and Arenas', *The Journal of Urban Technology,* 5, 1: 65–86.

Thomson, N., Dendy, E. and de Deney, D. (eds) (1984) *Sports and Recreation Provision for Disabled People,* London: The Architectural Press Limited.

Walker, M. and Kent, A. (2009) 'Do Fans Care? Assessing the Influence of Corporate Social Responsibility on Consumer Attitudes in the Sport Industry', *Journal of Sport Management,* 23: 743–769.

Walter, F. (1971) *Sports Centres and Swimming Pools,* Edinburgh: Disabled Living Foundation.

Waterman, I. and Bell, J. (2002) *Disabled Access to Facilities,* London: Butterworths Tolley LexisNexis.

Zeigler, E.F. (2007) 'Sport Management Must Show Social Concern as it Develops Tenable Theory', *Journal of Sport Management,* 21: 297–318.

Chapter 22

Sport event management

Sean O'Connor, University of Ulster

TOPICS

Sport event management • Reasons for hosting major sports events: Pre-event evaluations • The bidding process • Planning an event • Crisis management planning • Event implementation • Evaluating an event

---

OBJECTIVES

At the end of this chapter you should be able to:

■ Explain what a sports event is and describe its distinguishing features;

■ Explain what the determinants are of a successful bidding process;

■ Explain the reasons for hosting an event;

■ Discuss the life cycle of a sports event;

■ Recognise the theoretical and practical components of effective sports event planning.

KEY TERMS

A sports event and its distinguishing features – events can be classified by size, structure and who they cater to under the terms mega events, hallmark events and major events.

Sports reimaging – hosting cities and regions rely on their ability to project and sell a positive image of the city to an external audience of potential visitors and consumers, 'making it more attractive to economic enterprises, tourists and inhabitants' (Kearns and Philo, 1993:3).

The bidding process for major and mega events – the eight key success factors which are required for a successful bid: accountability, political support, relationship marketing, ability, infrastructure, bid team composition, communication and exposure, and existing facilities (Swart and Bob, 2004[1]).

> **The economic impact of hosting an event** – is defined as 'the net change in the local economy which can be directly attributable to the staging of a particular event' (Turco and Kelsey, 1992).
>
> **The event life cycle: its stages** – the life cycle of a sports event refers to the major stages which it progresses through: planning the event, running the event and post-event evaluation of the event.

OVERVIEW

Ceremonial, political, religious and sporting events have been recorded as part of the normal culture of ancient societies (Baum *et al.*, 2009:3), just as they are today perceived as being part of modern day life. The size and classifications of these events have expanded within the public, commercial and voluntary sectors, which has allowed event management to escalate in structure and stature as it adapts elements of project management and political science dimensions into its core. It can be described as 'one of the most exciting and fastest growing forms of leisure, business, and tourism-related phenomena ... frequently their celebratory and festive ambience elevates them above ordinary life experiences' (Getz, 1997:1).

The event industry has been categorised into numerous sectors by authors, who aid us 'in identifying the diversity of the event industry, its sectors and its markets' (Tum *et al.*, 2006). Getz (1997:4) categorises the event industry into three main sectors – private, public and voluntary – and proposes:

> A special event is a one-time or infrequently occurring event outside the normal program or activities of the sponsoring or organizing body. To the customer or guest, a special event is an opportunity for leisure, social or cultural experience outside the normal range of choices or beyond everyday experience.

The one component missing in this definition of an event is the concept of time. Walsh-Heron and Stevens (1990) addressed this discrepancy by referring to the tourism sector, where they suggest that visitor attractions are predominantly permanent features whereas events are of a temporary nature. Torkildsen (1999:471) additionally stresses the factor of time: 'an event is speeded up and delivered within a short space of time; this concentrates all the advanced planning and actions into specific hours and moments'.

Table 22.1 depicts the event characteristics and organisational criteria which impact on an event.

Table 22.1 *Event characteristics and organisation criteria*

Characteristics of an event	Event organisation criteria
A specified starting and finishing point.	Size and volume of output.
Fixed, absolute deadlines.	Complexity and variety of services/products offered to the consumer.
One-off organisation, normally superimposed on other work.	Uncertainty of numbers attending, cost, time, schedule and technical requirements.
Greater risks and greater opportunities.	Interaction with the consumers, and degree of consumer and customer contact.

Event examples: a local charity event; the UEFA Champions League; the Melbourne Festival.

Sources: Torkildsen, 1994, and Tum *et al.*, 2006

CASE STUDY: THE ABU DHABI GRAND PRIX 2009

The Etihad Airways Abu Dhabi Grand Prix set new standards in the hosting of Formula 1 races and in event management practice. With construction starting on the 191 hectare site in February 2007, the management team were under ongoing time pressure to deliver the first Formula 1 event in October 2009. The race itself was dependent upon a water-tight event life cycle plan, which had a stringent time schedule at its core, as illustrated in Table 22.2, and was organised by Abu Dhabi Motorsport Management (ADMM).

Several major challenges faced the organisers:

1 To ensure the construction of the 5.5 km track and surrounding infrastructure was finished on schedule.
2 To guarantee that the inaugural Grand Prix was run to the highest sporting and promotional standards.

Constant evaluation was required in order to ensure the Grand Prix was a success, and also interaction with key stakeholders, including sporting bodies, commercial rights holders, the Government and the construction contractor, as depicted in Figure 22.1.

Figure 22.2 depicts how CEO Richard Cregan managed a team of almost 200 employees split into the organisational sectors as highlighted in the chart.

Despite the time constraints, the inaugural Grand Prix was a success in terms of event management. It was also the first race to be run at twilight to enhance TV coverage and also won the prestigious FIA Promoters of the Year award. Richard Cregan[2] was quoted as saying: 'Having clear event objectives coupled with securing the services of the best possible managers for each key function of the event' are the key ingredients needed to host a successful event.

Table 22.2 The Abu Dhabi Grand Prix time schedule

Time	Group	Activity	Time	Group	Activity	Time	Group	Activity
09.45	Radio issue in village	ADMM	13.05	GP2 Asia	Cars released to F1 pits	16.30	Formula One	Pit lane open
10.30	All marshals leave village by coach	ADMM	13.10	GP2 Asia	Pit lane open	16.45	Formula One	Pit lane closed and grid formation
10.30–10.45	Formula One	Marshalling system track test	13.20	GP2 Asia	Pit lane closed	16.46	Formula One	National anthem
11.00–12.00	Formula One	Paddock club pit lane walk	13.30–14.20	GP2 Asia	Second race (22 laps or 45 mins)	16.48	Formula One	Etihad fly past TBC
11.15	BARC/ATCUAE	Marshals on post	TBA	GP2 Asia	Podium presentation	16.55	Formula One	Lead car leaves the grid
11.30	FIA	Medical inspection	14.00	Formula One	Drivers' meeting	17.00	Formula One	Grand Prix (55 laps or 120 mins)
11.45	FIA	Circuit inspection	TBA	Porsche Mobile 1 Supercup	Cars released to the grid	19.05	ATCUAE	Circuit opening lap
12.00	ADMM/commercial	Paddock club pit lane walk ends	14.45–15.20	Porsche Mobile 1 Supercup	Race (14 laps or 30 mins)	19.00	Entertainment	Event concert – Aerosmith
12.00	ATCUAE	Track inspection and close	TBA	Porsche Mobile 1 Supercup	Podium presentation	19.30	Security	Circuit close and full lockdown
TBA	Chevrolet Supercar Middle East	Cars released to the grid	15.30–16.20	Formula One	Paddock club pit lane walk	19.30	Marshals return to village	ADMM
12.15–12.45	Chevrolet Supercar Middle East	Race (12 laps or 25 mins)	15.25	Formula One	End of season drivers' photograph	20.00	Radio return in village	ADMM
TBA	Chevrolet Supercar Middle East	Podium presentation	15.30	Formula One	Drivers' track parade	20.30–23.00	Evening meal	700 PAX-village
12.45–13.30	Lunch on post	Marshal support team	15.30–16.00	Formula One	Starting grid presentation	21.00	Farewell	ATC
13.00	GP2 Asia	Support teams released to the F1 pits	16.00–16.20	Formula One	Track inspection	23.00	IBN Buttata RTA bus leaves	ATC

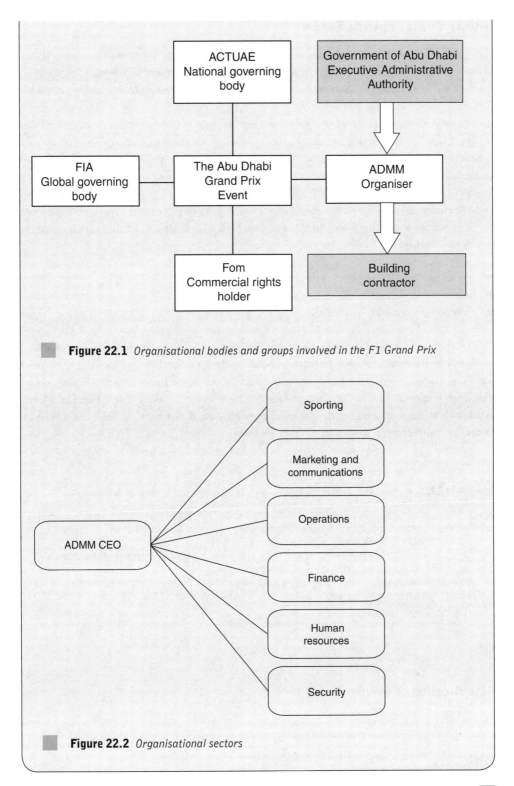

Figure 22.1 *Organisational bodies and groups involved in the F1 Grand Prix*

Figure 22.2 *Organisational sectors*

393

SPORT EVENT MANAGEMENT

Sport event management is viewed as a specific sector within event management. It is a diverse field which incorporates the four functions of management – planning, organising, leading and controlling – in conjunction with project management, marketing, communications, event bidding and lobbying. At its core is the brief for the sport management professional to plan and execute a successful event. As such, sport event management can be described 'as all functions relating to the planning, implementation and evaluation of a sports event' (Pike Masteralexis *et al.*, 2009:294). These three phases are normally referred to in the life cycle of an event and will be discussed in the subsequent sections. Each element is vital for hosting a successful event in conjunction with strong effective leadership and organisational skills. Events take on new criteria as they grow in size and transition from participation in a sporting event to a large-scale business seeking to quantify its objectives, which may consist of:

- Increasing financial profit of the event;
- Increased public and media exposure;
- Increased sponsorship potential.

The evolution of sport event management has led to it becoming a multimillion euro business, which benefits its hosting country's economy through tourism and social development schemes. The blurred border between business and sport can be found in the following examples from Formula One[3] (F1), where the author Henry (2003) asked 'Can F1 be considered as a business, since it is currently classified and recognised as a sport?'. Table 22.3 relays a sample of answers from the leaders in motorsports.

Table 22.3 *Motorsports leaders' views on the classification of sport as a business*

'F1 motor racing is certainly not a sport; it's a business with a sporting element' (Tony Purnell, CEO of Ford's Premier Performance Division)
'For six-and-a-half days a week, F1 is a business, then on Sunday afternoons it becomes a sport' (Frank Williams, Williams F1 Team Principal)
'It is clear to me that Grand Prix racing is no longer sport, but business. We are now talking about teams which employ over 100 people with a huge budget' (Flavio Briatore, Renault F1 team principal)

Sources: Henry, 2003:145, and Jenkins *et al.*, 2005:68

Classification of events

Events can be classed by size, structure and who they cater to under the terms mega events, hallmark events and major events. Many authors have written on this classification area and Table 22.4 contains sample, descriptive definitions of these terms.

Table 22.4 *Mega events, hallmark events and major events*

Mega event	Hallmark events	Major events
Mega by virtue of their size in terms of attendance, target markets, level of public functional involvement, political effects, extent of television coverage, construction of facilities, and impact on economic and social fabric of host communities. (Hall, 1997)	These are major one-time recurring events of limited duration, developed primarily to enhance the awareness, appeal and profitability of a tourism destination in the short term, the long term or both. They rely for their success on uniqueness, status or timely significance to create interest and attract attention. (Ritchie, 1984)	Major events are of a smaller scale to the mega and hallmark events; being large enough and prestigious enough to attract the attention of the national media, to attract large spectator numbers and provide economic benefit. (Torkildsen, 2005:469)
By virtue of their very large scale, the extent and intensity of their international public appeal and interest, the time-cycles in which they occur and their various impacts on their hosts ... they are a multi-dimensional phenomena – they are simultaneously urban events, touristic events, media events and international or global events. (Roche, 2002)	It takes place repeatedly in the same destination, to the extent that mention of the event automatically brings to mind the location where the event is held.	UK Sports defines a major event as having an international dimension to it: 'Attracts a number of nations, with significant public interest through attendances and media coverage, and features prominently on the UK international calendar.'
Examples: the Olympic Games, the FIFA World Cup, the Rugby World Cup, F1 Grand Prix.	Examples: the Oktoberfest, the Carnival (Rio de Janeiro), the Cannes Film Festival, the Edinburgh Festival, the Tour de France, the FA Cup Final.	Examples are the Glastonbury Music Festival and the Australian Open Tennis Championship in Melbourne.

Mega events, hallmark events and major events have substantial similarities; it is the scale and frequency of occurrences which generally identify how they differ, with economic impact, employment, image enhancement and political involvement also playing a role in signifying what type of event you are hosting.

Effective sport event management

Sport event management requires planning and precession timing in order to be effective. The theory behind event management theory has predominantly evolved from project management theory (which has developed from both organisational and management theory). Emery (2001) quotes Kerzner (1995:4), who suggests: 'Project management is the planning, organizing, directing, and controlling of company resources for a relatively short-term objective that has been established to complete specific goals and objectives.'

A project normally has a designated end point or completion date, for example with regards to a soccer match; the event is concluded once the match has ended and all post-evaluations are completed. According to Newton (2009:15), one of the key approaches in project management is not just to complete a task, but to predict in advance how long it will take, how much it will cost and what the outcome will be. The task of predicting time lines, costs and outcomes is connected to the concepts of planning which drives the life cycle of an event. Hence, 'planning is dependent on an understanding of the desired outcomes from a project. This is specified in the project objectives, scope and requirements' (Newton, 2009:160).

Consequently there is a strong connection between sport event management – 'all functions relating to the planning, implementation and evaluation of a sports event' (Pike Masteralexis *et al.*, 2009:294) – and project management as defined above. Project management is often evaluated using the project management triangle, which distinguishes the key factors required to successfully run a project (see Figure 22.3). The triangle is composed of time, cost and scope, commonly called the triple constraint. These form the vertices with quality as a central theme.

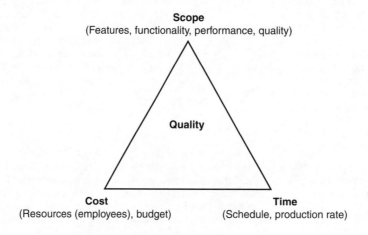

Figure 22.3 *The project management triangle*

The project management triangle is used to gain an understanding of the project objectives and priorities. Reflecting on Tum *et al.* (2006) and Torkildsen's earlier criteria, one can see that time is of immense importance when running an event, as you have a set timeline to complete the event in; thus pristine planning, scheduling, management and execution are required for a successful event.

REASONS FOR HOSTING MAJOR SPORTS EVENTS: PRE-EVENT EVALUATIONS

The main reasons for hosting a major sport event are:

- To generate an enhanced image of the host country to the viewing public. This is known as sports reimaging;
- To increase economic revenue to the area through increased tourism. This is commonly referred to as the economic impact.

The acquisition of event hosting rights can generate a substantial amount of infrastructure and facilities redevelopment, which is known as reimaging.

Sport reimaging

Sport reimaging allows hosting destinations to redefine global perceptions of what the city/country is famous for (tourism and image wise). This reimaging has been driven by globalisation, which has pushed the boundaries of tourist destination points by increasing access through reduced travel costs.

Hosting cities and regions rely on their ability to project and sell a positive image of the city to an external audience of potential visitors and consumers, 'making it more attractive to economic enterprises, tourists and inhabitants' (Kearns and Philo, 1993:3). This is commonly referred to as place marketing.

An example of place marketing can be found in Ireland's first staging of the World Rally Championships (WRC) in 2007.[4] It was organised as a cross-border all-Ireland event, which drew 250,000 live spectators and a global TV audience of 62 million (Hassan and O'Connor, 2009).

All sports events can be seen as an opportunity for a country to utilise media coverage and presents a global 'banner' of advertising which can be utilised as the basis of tourism campaigns. The result of the staging of the World Rally Championships in Ireland 'was the delivery of indirect tourism impact in the longer run' (Wilson, 2008:11).

Economic impact

Sports bodies use the positive economic impact of hosting an event to attain public and government party support for an event during the bidding proposal phase and 'to justify the initial expenditure of public funds in the bid process and the subsequent operational costs'(Chalip *et al.*, 2003). Economic impact is defined as 'the net change in the local economy which can be directly attributable to the staging of a particular event' (Turco and Kelsey, 1992). According to Shibli and Coleman (2005:14), it focuses on spending in the local economy of people from outside the local economy (visitors) such as players, the media, spectators and event organisers. Major events provide substantial benefits to the host nation as they entice 'significant numbers of visitors to the country during the event and act as an excellent shop window to showcase the country and develop a tourism campaign afterwards' (Wilson, 2008:5).

Governments and local authorities look at the long-term economic benefits of hosting a sporting event, in terms of positive media publicity generating tourism revenue, inward investment and new business during and after the event, as being the main incentive for bidding and hosting the events. Additionally any built sporting facilities can be employed by the local and national sporting communities as is envisioned with the Olympic Games facilities in East London. The initial economic impact of the London 2012 event is substantial, with the cost of building all the facilities estimated at £9.3bn in 2009, a quadruple of the 2005 bid estimate (London 2012 Olympic and Paralympic Games Annual Report, 2009).

THE BIDDING PROCESS

The bidding process is of crucial importance in securing the right to host a major sporting event. It involves a great deal of investment – financially, politically and time wise. No city, country or organisation can be guaranteed success in their bid and the actual process of mounting the bid campaign must be funded by the bidder. A feasibility study[5] is used to analyse the risks and viability of initiating a successful bid in advance of a bid.

The benefits of a successful bid are:

- Exposure to international marketing, especially in relation to tourism, enhanced image of the bidding nation and marketing of existing infrastructural and human resource capacity;
- The creation of short-term jobs and skills development;
- The development of public and private sector partnerships, both nationally and internationally, and the development of national pride and community participation.

Adapted from Swart and Bob (2004)

Swart and Bob (2004) described the eight key success factors which are required for a successful bid as: accountability, political support, relationship marketing, ability, infrastructure, bid team composition, communication and exposure, and existing facilities.

The Olympic Games

The Olympic Games is one of the most famous events to be decided by bidding. The actual decision on who will host the event takes place seven years in advance of the event, which means the 'bidding cities' commence planning for the bid a substantial amount of time before this deadline; 'the whole process of bidding for and staging an Olympic Games takes nearly a decade' (Toohey and Veal, 2007:66). The International Olympic Committee (IOC) oversees the bid process that contains a structured application process, which is examined in Table 22.5.

The first four items are relevant in all event bid types and not just in relation to the Olympic Games.

PLANNING AN EVENT

The planning stage of an event varies depending on the scale of the event. Table 22.6 can be used to confirm that all areas have been covered in the planning of the event.

The life cycle of the event fully expands on all of the planning components involved in an event.

Table 22.5 *Essential requirements for the Olympic Games event bid*

Item	Explanation
A feasibility study	This outlines a practical and rational proposal and determines the plausibility of meeting the bid requirements with the resources[1] available.
Item	Explanation
Candidature document	This outlines the essential schedule of deadlines and processes that must be followed for a bid submission to be eligible for consideration.
A bid questionnaire	This is a summary of the bid book and an outline of how the city plans to stage the event. For example, the Olympics bid is broken down into 18 topics, including venues, budgets, finance, accommodation, past experience and transportation.
A bid submission	Provides answers to the lists of questions posed by the bid questionnaire.
A bid tour	This involves hosting the members of a bid evaluation commission that will decide on the winning bid. A place is normally shortlisted if they are included in a bid tour.

Source: Adapted from Mallen and Adams, 2008

1 It assesses resources such as facilities and equipment, financial resources and staffing and technical resources.

Table 22.6 *Event plan checklist*

Pre-plan stage	Planning stage	Event stage
1. Establish the event: ➢ Aims ➢ Objectives ➢ Policy ➢ Strategy ➢ Vision. 2. Carry out a feasibility study for the event. 3. The outcome will influence the decision to proceed with the event or not.	4. Determine and communicate: ➢ The event plan ➢ The budget ➢ Personnel requirements ➢ Personnel duties ➢ The team structure ➢ The time scale. 5. Design the: ➢ Marketing and communications promotions ➢ The crisis communication plan ➢ The incident plan.	6. Execute the event plan ➢ All personnel should carry out their duties as per the schedule and plan for the event. 7. Monitor the event and make all required changes. 8. Close the event. 9. Hold a post-evaluation meeting. 10. Debrief all involved on how the event went and what changes had to be implemented during the event.

The life cycle of a sports event

A life cycle is not fully predictable, nor is the model deterministic. Stages in the life cycle are not always clear, but they do have a birth, they grow and mature and many die or require rejuvenation (Getz, 2007:111). Therefore, the life cycle of a sports event refers to the major stages which it progresses through: planning the event, running the event and post-event evaluation of the event. The scale of the event may change, which will decipher how we class the event, and possibly how much extra outside interest and staff are employed to complete the event, but essentially the cycle is always the same. Toffler (1990) referred to organisations that regularly expand and contract over their commercial life cycle as regular rhythm pulsating organisations. This description is relevant to sporting events as 'the number of personnel employed in the lead up to the event increase substantially, peaking during the event, and then falling after the event ... events are not perceived to be normal organisations, as these tend to have a relatively stable workforce in terms of staff headcount' (Hanlon and Jago, 2000:93). These peaks in size are what complicate the life cycle of an event.

Table 22.7 attempts to simplify and classify the stages and sub-stages through which most sports events progress, whilst at the same time linking the core management processes to these stages (Emery, 2001). The model is broken down into three identifiable stages: pre-event, event and post-event. Each stage then constitutes a self-evident boundary of time, and includes different sub-stages, from conception to completion.

Table 22.7 *Life cycle of the stages and core management processes of major sports events*

Stages	1) Pre-event			2) Event	3) Post-event	
Sub-stages	A) Idea & feasibility	B) Bidding process (if required)	C) Detailed planning & preparation	A) Implementation	A) Clear away	B) Feedback
Core management processes	←	Planning			→ - - - - - - - - - - -	
	- - - - - - - - - - - →					
	←	Organising			→ - - - - - - - - - -	
	- - - - - - - - - - →					
	←				Leading	
	→					
	←				(Formative)	
	Evaluation	(Summative) →				
Time line						

The pre-event stage

1 The initial planning phase of the project, which identifies the project's objectives.
2 A feasibility study is completed, where feasibility and justification questions are examined, as formal approval to proceed with the project is normally sought before continuing.
3 The bidding process stage involves all stakeholders in a campaign to exploit the unique selling points of the host.
4 The central management team is established and responsibilities are delegated to each team member.
5 The event strategy is formulated, which lists all of the team tasks which must be completed.
6 An event time schedule and financial budget are finalised.
7 The event plan is now complete and ready for implementation.

The event stage

8 The project manager is in charge of overseeing the smooth running of the event schedule and in informing staff members of their tasks.
9 Monitoring is crucial to ensure that the event time schedule plan is adhered to and that any required changes to the event are made and documented for later post-event evaluation.
10 The project team is required to remain focused on meeting the objectives developed and agreed upon at the outset of the project.

The post-event stage

11 The event is now being wound down.
12 It is assessed to see if it fulfilled its objectives.
13 A sample of volunteers, staff members, participants and the general public attendees may be asked to evaluate the event.
14 Any event discrepancies are analysed, recorded and adjusted for future projects.
15 The project closes.

CRISIS MANAGEMENT PLANNING

Every event requires crisis management planning as it is a fact of life that incidents can occur during the life cycle of an event, which means pre-event planning for such incidents is critical in running a successful event. Interpretations of what constitutes a crisis or incident varies; it can be defined as: 'a fatality; a serious injury; multiple casualties' (The World Rally Championships – Rally Ireland Crisis Communications Plan). According to Reid (2000), 'the goal of a crisis management plan is to reduce the potential adverse effects of a crisis by ensuring an organized response to them' through the planned provision of 'a blue print document which covers how to handle a crisis before one can occur' (Reid, 2000:35). This is known as proactive planning, as you have planned how you will control the damage to your brand and event by limiting the negative publicity generated in the media due to the incident. Figure 22.4 describes the process which takes place when an incident occurs.

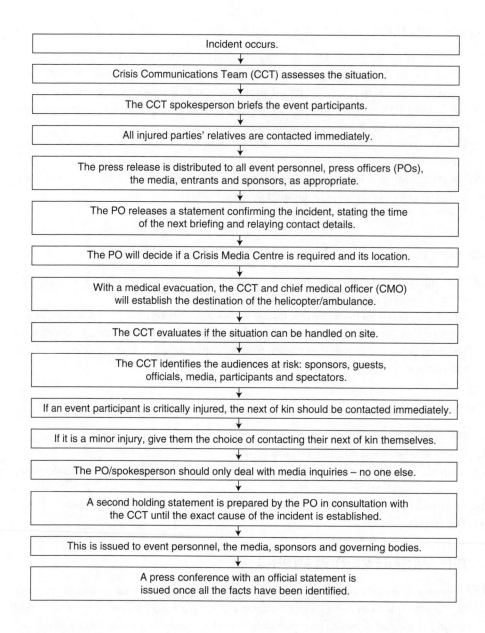

Incident occurs.

↓

Crisis Communications Team (CCT) assesses the situation.

↓

The CCT spokesperson briefs the event participants.

↓

All injured parties' relatives are contacted immediately.

↓

The press release is distributed to all event personnel, press officers (POs), the media, entrants and sponsors, as appropriate.

↓

The PO releases a statement confirming the incident, stating the time of the next briefing and relaying contact details.

↓

The PO will decide if a Crisis Media Centre is required and its location.

↓

With a medical evacuation, the CCT and chief medical officer (CMO) will establish the destination of the helicopter/ambulance.

↓

The CCT evaluates if the situation can be handled on site.

↓

The CCT identifies the audiences at risk: sponsors, guests, officials, media, participants and spectators.

↓

If an event participant is critically injured, the next of kin should be contacted immediately.

↓

If it is a minor injury, give them the choice of contacting their next of kin themselves.

↓

The PO/spokesperson should only deal with media inquiries – no one else.

↓

A second holding statement is prepared by the PO in consultation with the CCT until the exact cause of the incident is established.

↓

This is issued to event personnel, the media, sponsors and governing bodies.

↓

A press conference with an official statement is issued once all the facts have been identified.

Figure 22.4 *Incident process flow*

Media relations during a crisis

During a crisis the media are eager to ascertain what has happened. If you do not provide the information first, they will find sources such as staff, hospitals, officials, teams and spectators who will provide the story. This type of reporting leads to inaccurate, biased or unfairly critical information being reported. Therefore it is important to keep the media briefed through a delegated spokesperson whose role is to provide details of the crisis via statements and press briefings, and follow up feedback when requested by the media (see Figure 22.5).

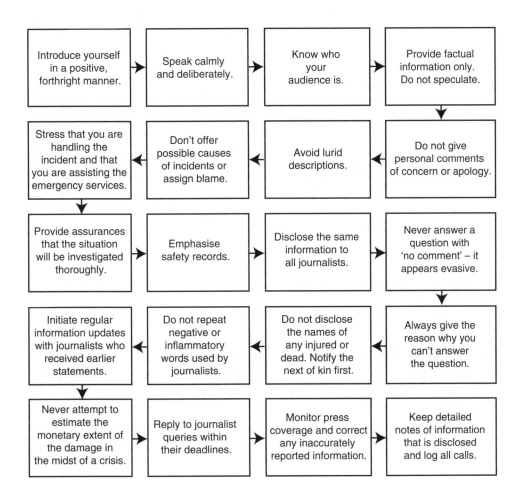

Figure 22.5 *Guidelines for handling the media during a crisis*

EVENT IMPLEMENTATION: THE RUNNING AND MANAGEMENT OF AN EVENT

As detailed in the event life cycle, the implementation involves putting into place and project managing the time schedule which was developed and updated during the planning phase. This is the point where everything can change suddenly; timing is of immense importance as schedules need to be followed to keep the event flowing and for it to be a success. Getz and Frisby's (1988) event management system highlights all of the factors which are impacting on an event, as it is implemented (see Figure 22.6).

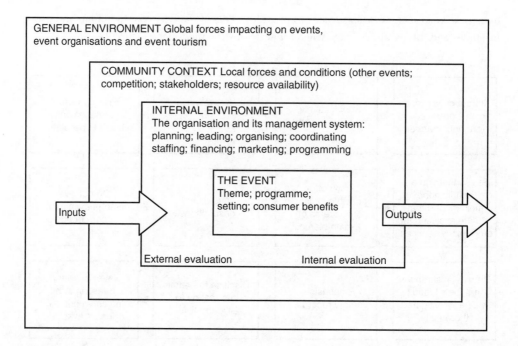

Figure 22.6 *The event management system*

In order to secure a successful event one must:

- Thoroughly pre-plan the event and monitor it during the event.

When running an event it is vital that you:

- Have an implementation plan.

Implementation

- Have a detailed schedule covering: time, activity, persons involved, contacts and the location. *Include everything*.
- Delegate responsibility to individuals.
- Make necessary timing changes during the event training sessions.
- Brief them on the crisis or incident plans.
- Train all staff members (including volunteers) on their roles and duties.
- Have a clear chain of communications in place.
- Monitor and evaluate the event from beginning to end.

EVALUATING AN EVENT

When running an event, the event evaluation, monitoring and feedback process is of central importance as it allows the event organisers to learn what did, and did not, work during the event and what improvements are required. The evaluation process will gauge the economic impact of the event and the overall fulfilment of the event objectives.

According to Watt (1998:204), event evaluation is characterised by the following criteria:

- Compulsory: It should be completed for every event, large or small.
- Constant: Appraise how you will evaluate the event's success or fulfilment of objectives, from the planning stages up to the post-event evaluation stages.
- Customised: Plan your evaluation criteria and questions. Use a checklist against the event objectives and adjust them throughout the event as the objectives change or develop.
- Concurrent: It should go on during the event as well as after it.
- Consult widely: Acquire the opinions of as many people involved in the event as possible, for example, participants, officials, media, VIPs, sponsors, customers and colleagues.
- Circulate and communicate the evaluations and the opinions gathered and the debriefing documents as widely as possible to help everyone involved build for the future.
- Copied: Repeat successful evaluation methods as this will allow you to emulate the event's success in the future.

CASE STUDY: THE LONDON BID FOR THE 2012 OLYMPIC GAMES

In event management the cost of putting together a bid for an event is dependable upon the scale of the event. The London 2012 Olympic Games bid has been estimated to cost £13 million, while the actual hosting of the event will result in a further cost of £5.2 billion. The bid for the 2012 Olympics started in 2003. The London 2012 Olympic Games bid timeline[6] in Table 22.8 indicates the amount of time and resources that went into securing the bid.

Table 22.8 The London 2012 Olympic Games bid timeline

Date	Details
2003	• Bid team formed, led by Barbara Cassani. The team put together the original 'Applicants Questionnaire', outlining details of how London would stage the Games.
16 January 2004	• Bid officially launched at Covent Garden. Applicants Questionnaire sent to the IOC. • Eight other cities send in Questionnaire – Havana, Leipzig, Madrid, Istanbul, Moscow, New York, Paris and Rio de Janeiro.
18 May 2004	• IOC shortlists London, Madrid, Moscow, New York and Paris. Event marked by firework display at the London Eye. • Sebastian Coe becomes Chair of the bid company; Keith Mills continues as Chief Executive.

Continued

Table 22.8 Continued

Date	Details
May to November 2004	• Candidate File is comprised, spelling out in detail how the London Games will be staged.
15 November 2004	• 15-year-old east London schoolgirl Amber Charles hands in Candidate File to IOC headquarters, Lausanne.
February 2005	• IOC's Evaluation Committee visits London to inspect the plans.
February to July 2005	• London 2012 team works on the final bid presentation. • Public support for the Games grows: 75 per cent 'back the bid', with four million signed-up supporters.
6 July 2005	• London 2012 delegation travels to Singapore to make its final presentation. The group includes 30 young people from east London. • Sebastian Coe presents London 2012's vision for an Olympic Games to inspire the youth of the world.[1] • Members of the IOC vote in secret electronically, until one city has more than 50 per cent of the total votes. After each round, the country with the lowest number of votes is knocked out. • Voting goes down to the final two cities – London and Paris. • 12.46pm: Jacques Rogge announces London as the 2012 Host City, winning by 54 votes to 50. • 12.46pm: London celebrates. And then the hard work begins.

1   The PDF presentation is available from the London 2012 website.

The London 2012 bid used substantial royal, political, celebrity and sporting support to provide a voice to the bid within the public sphere and to strengthen the bid within the IOC. The IOC 2012 Evaluation Commission report[7] stated that London's bid highlighted the 'significant' sporting and social legacy of London's plans for the East End of the city. It spoke about regeneration and development; of the sports legacy of the event; and how the London Games would have a positive impact on the city's environment. The other points from the bid were:

There is a strong emphasis on the integration of environmental considerations across all aspects of planning and operations, ensuring minimum impact and maximum sustainability and the integration of those plans and actions into wider regeneration and environmental strategies for London.

The budgeting process is very detailed and meticulous, and assumptions are well supported and documented.

When you evaluate these statements against the earlier important factors for event bids, you can see that the theory plays into the practice and both support each other. To conclude, Table 22.9 shows us the scale of the London Olympic Games bid in numbers and gives perspective about what is required in a bid of this magnitude and how then to run it.

Table 22.9 *The London Olympic bid in figures*

The London bid in numbers	The scale of the London Olympic Games
4 million supporters around the UK	26 Olympic sports in 34 venues
3 years of hard work	20 Paralympic sports in 21 venues
30 youth ambassadors from east London attended the presentation	10,500 Olympic athletes and 4,200 Paralympic athletes
London and Paris in the final vote	20,000 press and media
54 votes for London in the final round	More than 9 million tickets

SUMMARY

1 An event unlike a normal ongoing programme is speeded up and delivered within a short space of time; this concentrates all the advanced planning and actions into specific hours and moments.
2 Sports event management can be described as all functions relating to the planning, implementation and evaluation of a sports event.
3 Mega events and hallmark events are identified as being of a far greater scale – attendance, participation, media coverage, construction build and impact on the economic and social fabric of host communities – than that of major and local events.
4 A local event, as the name suggests, is local to the area that it is being hosted in. It is of a smaller scale both in attendance and media coverage and can be a one-off event or occurs annually.
5 The predominant reason for the Government to fund hosting a sports event is to increase economic revenue to the area through increased tourism (economic impact) and to generate a better image of the venue's country or venue to the viewing public (sports reimaging).
6 Economic impact is defined as 'the net change in the local economy which can be directly attributable to the staging of a particular event'.
7 Project management plays a key role in event management. It is the planning, organising, directing and controlling of company resources for a relatively short-term objective that has been established to complete specific goals and objectives.
8 The project management triangle distinguishes the key factors required to successfully run a project. It is composed of time, cost and scope, commonly called the triple constraint. These form the vertices, with quality as a central theme. Emery's project management environment extends this theory.
9 The life cycle of a sports event refers to the major stages which it progresses through: planning the event, running the event and post-event evaluation of the event. Emery's life cycle model is broken down into three identifiable stages: pre-event, event and post-event. Each stage then constitutes a self-evident boundary of time, and includes different sub-stages, from conception to completion.

10 The benefits of a successful bid are exposure to international marketing, especially in relation to tourism; enhanced image of the bidding nation; marketing of existing infrastructural and human resource capacity; the creation of jobs and skills development; and the development of public and private sector partnerships, both nationally and internationally.

11 'The goal of a crisis management plan is to reduce the potential adverse effects of a crisis by ensuring an organized response to them' through the planned provision of 'a blue print document which covers how to handle a crisis before one can occur' (Reid, 2000:35). This is known as proactive planning.

12 When running an event, the event evaluation, monitoring and feedback process is of central importance as it allows the event organisers to learn what did, and did not, work during the event and what improvements are required.

NOTES

1 Swart and Bob, in their evaluation of the Capetown 2004 bid, used Westerbeek *et al.*'s 2002 survey instrument and findings regarding criteria deemed important to the bidding process by seasoned bid campaigners.

2 CEO of Abu Dhabi Motor Sport Management and organiser of the inaugural Formula 1 Etihad Airways Abu Dhabi Grand Prix.

3 Formula 1 Grand Prix Racing – Motorsports.

4 The WRC represented the first sports mega event to be held in Ireland since the implementation of the Belfast Good Friday Agreement.

5 A feasibility study is an assessment that presents an expert opinion on the capability of a group to stage or host the particular event. It outlines a practical and reasonable initiative and determines the plausibility of meeting the bid requirements with the resources available. Resources such as HR, facilities and equipment, financial resources and technical resources are elements that are assessed.

6 The London 2012 Olympic Games bid timeline table is from the official London 2012 website.

7 This is the IOC 2012 Evaluation Commission report on Paris, New York, Moscow, London and Madrid's bid for the 2012 event: http://multimedia.olympic.org/pdf/en_report_952.pdf.

REVIEW QUESTIONS

1 What are the characteristics of an event?

2 What is sports event management?

3 Identify and describe the different classifications of an event.

4 Describe the project management triangle.

5 What are the reasons for hosting sports events?

6 What are the criteria for running a successful bid?

7 Identify the ten components of the event plan checklist.

8 Describe the life cycle process stages of an event.

9 Explain the media guidelines to follow during a crisis incident.

10 What is required for the successful implementation of an event?

11 What can we learn from evaluating an event? Explain the characteristics of event evaluations.

FURTHER READING

Ingerson, L. and Westerbeek, H. (2000) 'Determining Key Success Criteria for Attracting Hallmark Sporting Events', *Pacific Tourism Review*, Vol. 3, No. 3/4, pp. 239–253, Cognizant Communications Corporation, New York.

Lee, M. (2006) *The Race for the 2012 Olympics: The Inside Story of How London Won the Bid*, Virgin Books Ltd, London.

Mallen, C. and Adams, L. (2008) *Sports Recreation and Tourism Event Management: Theoretical and Practical*, Elsevier/Butterworth-Heinemann, London.

Tassiopoulos, D. and Damster, G. (eds) (2004) *Event Management: a Professional and Developmental Approach*, 2nd edn, Juta Academic, Lansdowne, SA.

WEBSITES

FIFA
 http://www.fifa.com
London 2012
 http://www.london2012.com
London 2012 Olympic and Paralympic Games Annual Report, 2009
 http://www.culture.gov.uk/images/publications/DCMS_GOE_Annual_ Report_2009.pdf
National Center for Spectator Sport Safety & Security
 http://www.sporteventsecurity.com
Sports and Business
 http://www.sportbusiness.com
The Federation Internationale de l'Automobile (FIA)
 http://www.fia.com/en-GB/Pages/HomePage.aspx
The International Olympic Committee
 http://www.olympic.org/uk/index_uk.asp
The IOC 2012 Evaluation Commission report
 http://multimedia.olympic.org/pdf/en_report_952.pdf
Tokyo Olympic Games bid site
 http://www.tokyo2016.or.jp/en

REFERENCES

Baum, T., Deery, M., Hanlon, C., Lockstone, L. and Smith, K. (2009) *People and Work in Events and Conventions: A Research Perspective*, Cab International, London.

Chalip, L., Green, B.C. and Hill, B. (2003) 'Effects of Sport Event Media on Destination Image and Intention to Visit', *Journal of Sport Management*, Vol. 17, No. 3, pp. 214–234.

Emery, P.R. (2001), 'Bidding to Host a Major Sports Event: Strategic Investment or Complete Lottery?', in C. Gratton and P. Henry (eds), *Sport in the City: The Role of Sport in Economic and Social Regeneration*. Routledge, London.

Getz, D. (1997) *Event Management and Event Tourism*, Cognizant Communications Corporation, New York.

Getz, D. (2007) *Event Studies: Theory, Research and Policy for Planned Events*, Butterworth-Heinemann, Amsterdam.

Getz, D. and Frisby, E. (1988) 'Evaluating Management Effectiveness in Community Run Festivals', *Journal of Travel Research*, Vol. 27, No. 1, pp. 22–27.

Hall, C. (1997) 'Mega-Events and their Legacies', in P. Murphy (ed.) *Quality Management in Urban Tourism*, Chicester, John Wiley and Sons, pp. 75–87.

Hanlon, C. and Jago, L. (2000) 'Pulsating Sporting Events: An Organizational Structure to Optimize Performance Profession', *Events Beyond 2000: Setting the Agenda. Proceedings of Conference on Event Evaluation, Research and Education*, Sydney, July 2000, Australian Centre for Event Management, Sydney.

Hassan, D. and O'Connor, S. (2009) 'The Socio-Economic Impact of the FIA WRC 2009', *Sport in Society*, Vol. 12, pp. 709–724, Routledge, London.

Henry, A. (2003) *The Power Brokers: The Inside Track on the Controllers of Formula 1*, Motorbooks International, USA.

Jenkins, M., Pasternak, K. and West, R. (2005) *Performance at the Limit: Business Lessons from Formula 1 Motor Racing*, Cambridge University Press, Cambridge.

Kearns, G. and Philo, C. (1993) 'Introduction', in G. Kearns and C. Philo (eds) *Selling Places: The City as Cultural Capital, Past and Present*, Pergamon Press, Oxford, pp. 3–8.

Kerzner, H. (1995) *Project Management: A Systems Approach to Planning, Scheduling and Controlling*, Hoboken, NJ, John Wiley and Sons.

Mallen, C. and Adams, L. (2008) *Sports Recreation and Tourism Event Management: Theoretical and Practical*, Elsevier/Butterworth-Heinemann, London.

Newton, R. (2009) *The Practice and Theory of Project Management: Creating Value through Change*, Palgrave Macmillan, Basingstoke.

Pike Masteralexis, L., Barr, C. and Hums, M. (2009) *Principles and Practice of Sport Management*, 3rd edn, Jones and Barlett Publishers International, London.

Reid, J. (2000) *Crisis Management: Planning and Media Relations for the Design and Construction Industry*, Wiley, New York.

Ritchie, J.R. (1984) 'Assessing the Impact of Hallmark Events: Conceptual and Research Issues', *Journal of Travel Research*, July, Vol. 23, No. 1, pp. 2–11, in G. Bowdin and J. Allen (2006) *Events Management*, 2nd edn, Elsevier, London.

Roche, M. (2002) 'Olympics and Sport Mega-Events: Reflections on the Globalization Paradigm', in K. Wamsley, R. Barney and S. Martyn (eds) *The Global Nexus Engaged: Past, Present, Future Interdisciplinary Olympic Studies*, University of Western Ontario, London, Ontario, pp. 1–12.

Shibli, S. and Coleman, R. (2005) 'Economic Impact and Place Marketing Evaluation: A Case Study of the World Snooker Championship', *International Journal of Event Management Research*, Vol. 1, No. 1, pp. 13–29.

Swart, K. and Bob, U. (2004) 'The Seductive Discourse of Development: The Cape Town 2004 Olympic Bid', in *Third World Quarterly*, Vol. 25, No. 7, pp. 1311–1324.

Toffler, A. (1990) *Future Shock*, Batam Books, New York.

Toohey, K. and Veal, A. (2007) *The Olympic Games: A Social Science Perspective. Sports and Recreation*, 2nd edn, CABI, Oxfordshire.

Torkildsen, G. (1994) *Leisure and Recreation Management*, 3rd edn, Routledge, London.

Torkildsen, G. (1999) *Leisure and Recreation Management*, 4th edn, Routledge, London.

Torkildsen, G. (2005) *Leisure and Recreation Management*, 5th edn, Routledge, London.

Tum, J., Norton, P. and Nevan Wright, J. (2006) *Management of Event Operations: Business and Economics*, Elsevier, Oxford.

Turco, D.M. and Kelsey, C.W. (1992) *Conducting Economic Impact Studies of Recreation and Parks Special Events*, National Recreation & Park Association, Arlington, VA.

Walsh-Heron, J. and Stevens, T. (1990) *The Management of Visitor Attractions and Events*, Prentice Hall, London.

Watt, D. (1998) *Sports Management and Administration*, 2nd edn, Routledge, London.

Westerbeek, H., Turner, P. and Ingerson, L. (2002) 'Key Success Factors in Bidding for Hallmark Sporting Events', *International Marketing Review*, Vol. 19, No. 2, pp. 303–322, Emerald, United Kingdom.

Wilson, J. (2008) *Potential Economic Impact of the Rugby World Cup on the Host Nation*, Deloitte and Touche, Manchester. Online. Available HTTP: http://www.deloitte.com/view/en_GB/uk/industries/sportsbusinessgroup/7d73942e84ffd110VgnVCM100000ba42f00aRCRD.htm (accessed 10 March 2010).

Chapter 23

Managing social responsibility in sport

Geoff Walters, Birkbeck, University of London

TOPICS

Corporate social responsibility • Corporate social responsibility and sport • Implementing corporate social responsibility in sport

---

OBJECTIVES

At the end of this chapter you should be able to:

- Understand the development of corporate social responsibility (CSR);
- Discuss key managerial issues in CSR;
- Identify unique features of sport CSR;
- Identify different types of sport organization that address the issue of CSR;
- Discuss the nature of the CSR initiatives in the sport industry.

KEY TERMS

Corporate social responsibility – the societal responsibilities that a business has beyond profit maximization.

CSR implementation – one of five key managerial areas of CSR research.

CSR implementation in sport – the implementation of CSR within the sport industry is multi-dimensional and relies on the development of relationships between stakeholders.

OVERVIEW

The aim of this chapter is to introduce the reader to the concept of corporate social responsibility (CSR) and how it is implemented within the sport industry. CSR is a key aspect of business ethics that has grown in popularity over the course of the last 30 years. Over this period, there have been many different definitions and intepretations; however, the broad conceptualization of CSR as the societal responsibilities that a business has beyond profit maximization (Carroll 1979) has remained relatively constant. In part, the rise to prominence of CSR has been prompted by failures in corporate governance and the increasing desire for corporate accountability and transparency (Clarke 2004), leading to increasing pressure on organizations to consider their role within society (Blowfield and Murray 2008). CSR is also becoming a more important issue within the sport industry, although many different sport organizations have implemented CSR-related initiatives for almost 30 years. This chapter begins by providing a background to the development of CSR and identifies five key managerial issues: communication; implementation; stakeholder engagement; measurement; and the business case. The chapter will then introduce CSR in sport before focusing on eight different ways in which CSR schemes are implemented in the sport industry, drawing on case study examples from the UK, Europe and the US. These include athlete foundations; professional sport teams; professional sport leagues; sport governing bodies; sport events; sport venues; sport manufacturers; and commercial organizations.

CASE STUDY: THE FC BARCELONA FOUNDATION

The FC Barcelona Foundation was created in 1994 as the charitable arm of the football club. Between 1994 and 2006 the Foundation relied on donations from FC Barcelona members, supporters and commercial organizations. From 2006 the board of the football club took the decision to expand community work beyond Catalonia and Spain and pledged to donate 0.7 per cent of income annually to the Foundation. The six objectives of the Foundation are:

1 To promote actions concerning the fight against extreme poverty and illnesses that affect mainly the most vulnerable children of the planet and to favour education for all and gender equality, as stipulated by the Millennium Development Goals.
2 To promote and offer tools to foster the values of sport among children, such as effort, respect, companionship and tolerance, both on a school level as well as on that of sports and leisure centres.
3 To favour and encourage actions aimed at the social normalization of people with disabilities, immigrants and other groups at risk of social exclusion.
4 To contribute to the development of culture and the defence of civilian values, freedom and democracy, which have always defined the club and the history of the country.
5 To promote youth sport and the academic training of the sportspeople forming part of the Barça institution.
6 To give support and assistance to veteran players that have formed and still form part of the history of the club.

The FC Barcelona Foundation is meeting these objectives in a variety of ways. They have developed an international network of solidarity centres that operate in many poor nations across the world, including India, Mali, Senegal and Malawi, and provide education, medical

413

and social support for children. The Foundation has also developed a CSR partnership with UNICEF in which the FC Barcelona shirt, one of the most recognized football shirts in the world, carries the UNICEF logo. The Foundation also donates 1.5m Euros to UNICEF annually, which contributes towards AIDS-related projects in Africa. Further partnerships have been developed with UNESCO (United Nations Educational, Scientific and Cultural Organisation), with the Foundation working on a 'Youth Voices Against Racism' project, and the United Nations High Commissioner for Refugees on the MES project, which is providing education and sports programmes in Nepal, Rwanda and Ecuador.

Source: http://www.fcbarcelona.cat/web/Fundacio/english/fundacio/missio.html

CORPORATE SOCIAL RESPONSIBILITY

Until the 1960s discourse on CSR was limited (Carroll and Shabana, 2010). It was in this decade in which there was an increase in awareness of the issue of CSR and what it meant for business and society, although in practice organizations engaged in philanthropic activities unmotivated by a return on their activity (Carroll and Shabana, 2010). During the 1970s, the literature on CSR expanded and there were the first attempts to define the concept, with Frederick (1978, in Carroll and Shabana, 2010) stating that CSR represented a company taking a socially responsible position. This differed from corporate social responsiveness, which referred to the implementation of measures to achieve a socially responsible position, and corporate social performance, which was an attempt to reconcile CSR and corporate social responsiveness in which the outcomes of socially responsible activities were considered (Carroll and Shabana, 2010). Carroll (1979) produced a broad definition of CSR as the societal responsibilities that a business has beyond profit maximization, and at the same time developed an influential framework for understanding CSR with the identification of four key elements. Organizations have an economic responsibility to produce goods and services; a legal responsibility to do this abiding by laws and regulations; an ethical responsibility to adhere to standards of moral behaviour expected within society; and can engage in discretionary activities that go beyond ethical responsibilities and which represent a commitment to philanthropic behaviour.

In the 1980s a range of themes associated with CSR emerged, including stakeholder theory, business ethics theory, corporate citizenship and cause-related marketing (Carroll, 1999). It is clear, then, that, despite no one agreed definition, the CSR concept 'served as the base-point, building block, or point-of-departure for other related concepts and themes, many of which embraced CSR-thinking and were quite compatible with it' (Carroll, 1999: 288). In the 1990s and 2000s CSR moved from ideology to reality (Lindgreen and Swaen, 2010). In part this was a result of high-profile failures in corporate governance and increasing public concerns over corporate excess and irresponsibility, which led to greater pressure on organizations to demonstrate a commitment to CSR. This has led to an increasing emphasis on linking CSR with corporate financial performance, with CSR seen as a way to add value to a business (Porter and Kramer, 2006). Lindgreen and Swaen (2010) argue that this demonstrates a shift from normative justifications for implementing CSR to more instrumental, performance-oriented motivations, and identify five key managerial issues related to CSR.

First, organizations need to communicate their CSR activities as a way to position their brand (Lindgreen and Swaen, 2010). While there is evidence to demonstrate that many organizations are undertaking and reporting CSR activities (Margolis and Walsh, 2003), with over 80 of the FTSE 100 listed companies in the UK producing a CSR report separate from the annual report (Owen, 2005), there are concerns that marketing CSR activities can be perceived as a form of public relations and lead to increased scepticism and cynicism (Mohr *et al.*, 2001).

The implementation of CSR into the activities of an organization is the second key issue that managers have to consider, although this is an area in which there is a lack of empirical and theoretical support (Lindgreen and Swaen, 2010). For many organizations, CSR implementation is reflected in the adherence to codes of conduct, for instance in relation to supply chains. However, Cramer *et al.* (2006: 381) argue that companies are increasingly encouraged to use CSR language yet do not completely understand what the concept means. The implementation of CSR activities is therefore a reflection of individual preferences, norms and values (Cramer *et al.*, 2006), and can relate to a wide variety of activities. Blowfield and Murray (2008) illustrate that CSR relates to many different types of organizational activity including leadership, workforce activities (e.g. fair remuneration, employee communication), supply-chain activities, community activities (e.g. sponsoring social causes, financial donations, employee volunteering) and environmental activities (e.g. resource/energy use, pollution and waste management). This demonstrates that there is no one overarching framework or series of guidelines but that CSR implementation within the business context requires a tailor-made approach (Cramer *et al.*, 2006). However, it is only by engaging in CSR-related activities that an organization will develop a better understanding of CSR (Cramer *et al.*, 2006).

The third issue with CSR is how to engage with stakeholders. Stakeholder theory is based on the understanding that a corporation should recognize the interests of a wide range of constituents that have a stake in the organization, for example customers, employees, suppliers and communities. Given that the central issue within CSR is the nature of the relationship between business and society and how this is defined and acted upon (Blowfield and Murray 2008: 36), many authors have argued that there is an explicit link between CSR and stakeholder engagement, particularly as 'the stakeholder nomenclature puts "names and faces" on the societal members or groups who are most urgent to business, and to whom it must be responsive' (Carroll, 1991: 43). Stakeholder engagement can also be considered as a way in which to implement CSR.

The fourth issue in relation to CSR is measurement of CSR activities. The key question here is, how should CSR be measured and what criteria should be used? The fact that CSR is related to many different organizational activities also means that measuring CSR is complex.

The final key managerial issue within CSR is presenting the business case for undertaking CSR activities. Since the 1990s there has been a shift in the perception of CSR as a charitable, philanthropic activity to a part of strategic management; as such, there is a need to demonstrate that CSR activity improves business performance. While CSR has been argued to benefit organizations in a number of ways including through improved corporate reputation, competitor differentiation, brand loyalty development and improved financial performance (Mullen, 1997; Dean, 2003; Porter and Kramer, 2006), there is still a lack of evidence to

415

support these claims, although it is clear that focusing on environmental efficiency and sustainable development can lead to cost savings (Blowfield and Murray, 2008). While considered as distinct issues, it is also clearly the case that the five issues are closely tied. For example, the measurement of CSR outcomes and the need to demonstrate a positive correlation between CSR and business performance is required to support the business case, which in turn will increase the likelihood that CSR initiatives will be implemented.

CORPORATE SOCIAL RESPONSIBILITY AND SPORT

Although literature on CSR has grown significantly over the last 30 years, it is only recently that the role of sport and CSR has been open to analysis (e.g. Babiak and Wolfe, 2006; Smith and Westerbeek, 2007; Bradish and Cronin, 2009; Godfrey, 2009; Walters, 2009; Walters and Tacon, 2010). This is due to the fact that the role of sport in society is becoming more prominent and sports organizations have become increasingly influential members of the global community; as such, the concerns of transparency and accountability that are evident within the corporate world have transcended into sport (Walker and Kent, 2009). This has led some to suggest that sport organizations cannot ignore CSR and that they have to implement it (Babiak and Wolfe, 2006). Nevertheless, it is clear that many sport organizations are aware of CSR, as over the last 30 years several different types of sport organization have entered into CSR initiatives, including philanthropy, community involvement, youth educational activities and youth health initiatives (Babiak and Wolfe, 2009; Walker and Kent, 2009).

It has been argued that sport organizations are unique social and economic institutions (Bradish and Cronin, 2009) and that, despite the fact that many sports organizations are multi-million-pound businesses, they also have a highly significant role that is reflected in the representation of notions of community and tradition. The unique social role of sport organizations underpins seven unique characteristics of sport CSR (Smith and Westerbeek, 2007). First, the popularity and global reach of sport can ensure that sport CSR has mass media distribution and communication power. It can be argued therefore that the prominence of sport within the media helps to promote and communicate CSR activities to a wide audience. Second, sport CSR has youth appeal; children are more likely to engage in a CSR programme if it is attached to a sport organisation or a sports personality. Third, sport CSR can be used to deliver positive health impacts through programmes and initiatives designed around physical exercise. Fourth, sport CSR will invariably involve group participation and therefore aid social interaction. Likewise, this can also lead to a fifth benefit, which is improved cultural understanding and integration. It is clear then that sport is often seen as a way to deliver a range of social benefits, although it has been argued that there is a need for better evidence and more understanding of the processes through which sport is presumed to lead to these benefits (Coalter, 2007). Sixth, particular sport activities may lead to enhanced environmental and sustainability awareness. Finally, participating in sport CSR activities can also provide immediate gratification benefits. These seven factors demonstrate that sports organizations are inherently different from conventional organizations and serve to illustrate a strong association between sport and CSR, leading some to state that CSR and sport are ideal partners (Babiak and Wolfe, 2006).

416

IMPLEMENTING CORPORATE SOCIAL RESPONSIBILITY IN SPORT

While there is a growing awareness of the issue of CSR in the sport industry, discourse on the implementation of CSR initiatives is at a relatively embryonic stage. It is true that many sports organizations are increasingly encouraged to engage in CSR activities; however, there is little guidance on how to do this or what constitutes CSR in the sport context. Moreover, it is further complicated by the fact that CSR does not refer to a single activity and instead can relate to many different types of organizational activity. Nevertheless, different types of sport organizations have been implementing CSR activities for almost 30 years. This section provides an overview of eight different ways in which CSR is implemented in the sport industry and the nature of the activities that are delivered. These include athlete foundations; professional sports teams; professional sports leagues; sport governing bodies; sport events; sport venues; sport manufacturers; and commercial organizations. Providing knowledge of the different ways and the nature of CSR activities is the first step towards a better understanding of the implementation of CSR in sport.

Athlete foundations

Over the past 15 years many elite athletes, particularly from the US, have created charitable foundations. The heightened popularity of many sports stars enables these athletes to raise awareness of a particular issue and draw on their status to generate revenues that are then redistributed to worthy causes. These foundations are an example of philanthropic CSR. However, the foundations offer the opportunity for commercial organizations to develop a partnership as part of a cause-related marketing strategy. This is particularly the case at the Lance Armstrong Foundation, Livestrong, which provides financial resources and support to people living with cancer. The foundation has grown to be the largest individual athlete foundation since it was created by Lance Armstrong in 1997 after he had suffered from cancer at the age of 25. Since it was created in 1997 the foundation has raised over $250m, of which a large part has come from commercial organizations that tie in with the foundation as part of their cause-related marketing. For example, in 2008 the annual report revealed that the foundation had revenues of $40.2m, of which 32 per cent came from cause-related marketing (Livestrong, 2008); while Nike has helped to raise over $80m for the foundation since 2004 and created the Livestrong wristband that has further helped to raise awareness. The revenues have been used to provide financial support to over 550 organizations that support cancer sufferers, and to provide grants for community schemes, cancer research and to fund survivorship centres (http://www.livestrong.org). The Andre Agassi Foundation for Education is also another leading athlete foundation. Created in 1994, the objective of the foundation is to work with state and national legislators to transform the public education system to better serve under-privileged communities (http://www.agassifoundation.org). In Europe and the UK, athlete foundations are not as prominent or advanced as in the US. However, there are still examples such as the Rio Ferdinand Live the Dream Foundation, which was created in 2009 with the aim to develop the skills and employment prospects for young people in marginalized communities (http://www.rioferdinandltdf.com).

Professional sports teams

While there has been a rise in commercial organizations reporting CSR activity, within the sport industry CSR reporting is still in the relatively early stages of development. However, there are examples, particularly from professional leagues, governing bodies and teams. For instance, in 2007 Chelsea Football Club produced their own CSR report separate from the annual accounts which revealed that the club had invested £4.39m (or 2.3 per cent of turnover) into community projects and charitable donations (Chelsea Football Club, 2007). However, football clubs in the UK have been implementing a variety of CSR-related schemes for well over 20 years through the Football in the Community (FITC) schemes. The schemes were set up as a way for the football clubs to engage with and develop closer links with community stakeholders, to encourage more people – in particular, children – to play and watch football, and to promote closer links between professional football clubs and the community. More recently there has been a trend for FITC departments to seek independence from football clubs and to set up community sports trusts (see case study below). A community sports trust is constituted as a charity and therefore has structural autonomy, responsibility for its own strategic and financial direction, greater access to a wider variety of funding streams, and more flexibility to deliver a wider range of CSR-related activities in areas such as health, education and social inclusion. Many of these projects are delivered in partnership with UK government schemes such as Positive Futures and Playing for Success, which provide financial support.

CASE STUDY: CHARLTON ATHLETIC COMMUNITY TRUST

Charlton Athletic Football Club created the Charlton Athletic Community Trust (CACT) in 2003 with the objective to bring together seven key aspects of community work under the responsibility of the trust. CACT is registered as a not-for-profit charitable organiza-tion with structural, strategic and financial independence from the football club. Structural independence means that the community trust is governed by its own board of trustees who are responsible for setting the strategic direction of the trust. Implementing strategy is the responsibility of the chief executive of CACT. In total, CACT employs over 20 full-time staff supported by an additional 250 part-time coaches. The Community Trust acts as the key delivery agent for a number of community initiatives focused on social inclusion, education and health that aim to use football coaching and sporting activities as a way to address issues such as crime; sport development; substance misuse; community integration; and community safety. The social inclusion work is funded through a variety of partnerships with the local authorities in Greenwich, Bexley and Kent, public sector organizations, and commercial organizations including British Airways and Axis Europe.

In the US the community trust approach is the model of CSR that many professional teams from the Major Leagues have adopted. During the course of the 1990s there was a rapid increase in the number of teams in the Major Leagues that created a charitable founda-tion. In 2009, 84 per cent of NFL teams had a charitable foundation. This compares with 100 per cent, 93 per cent and 77 per cent of MLB teams, NHL teams and NBA teams respec-tively (Babiak and Wolfe, 2009: 721). Many of the foundations associated with Major League teams receive funding from wealthy team owners. For example, the Atlanta Falcons Youth

Foundation is one of the largest foundations with a long history since its creation in 1985. Following the buy-out of the Atlanta Falcons by Arthur Blank in 2002, the Foundation has received increased funding that has been distributed to non-profit organizations, primarily focused on addressing the issue of obesity in children (http://www.atlantafalcons.com/community/falcons-youth-foundation).

Professional sports leagues

Professional sports leagues are increasingly implementing league-wide programmes to address social concerns. In 2007 the Premier League in English football launched Creating Chances, a central CSR brand. Underneath this brand sit a range of community initiatives that fall into five categories: social inclusion (Kickz; Prince's Trust Football Initiative); education (Premier League Enterprise Academy; Premier League Reading Stars); health (Premier League Health); equalities (Premier League 4 Sport); and international (Premier League, 2009: 7). The wide range of community initiatives are supported by funding from the Premier League and the Professional Footballers Association, with community departments at Premier League football clubs responsible for delivering the projects. In rugby union the Guinness Premiership is also involved in a number of projects, including the Hitz programme aimed at working with children from disadvantaged communities.

In the US, the PGA Tour launched the Drive to $1 Billion campaign in 2005 as part of the philanthropic strategy of the Tour. The PGA Tour is structured in such a way that all the net proceeds from the tournaments that it is responsible for organizing are donated to charitable causes. By 2010, almost $1.5 billion in charitable contributions has been provided by the PGA (http://together.pgatour.com/the-program.html). Moreover, the NFL, the NBA, the NHL, MLB and MLS have all put in place CSR schemes (Babiak and Wolfe, 2006). In part this has been sparked by controversial issues such as drug abuse that have received negative publicity (Giannoulakis and Drayer, 2009). In the NBA a series of events attracted negative publicity between 1997 and 2004, culminating in a mass brawl between the Indiana Pacers and the Detroit Pistons in 2004, in which nine players were suspended. In 2005, the NBA launched the NBA Cares Program to improve the reputation and credibility of its players (Giannoulakis and Drayer, 2009). Although a reactive or defensive strategy to the negative publicity that occurred following the brawl in 2004, the programme is responsible for a number of CSR initiatives in areas such as health, education, and youth and family development, supported by NBA teams and players, with over $115m raised for charity since 2005 (http://www.nba.com/nba_cares/mission/our_work.html). It is also a way for the NBA to engage with key stakeholders: 'The league coordinates a wide-reaching effort among NBA teams and players, community partners, non-profit organizations and business partners to benefit communities worldwide' (NBA, 2010: 14).

Sport governing bodies

CSR is firmly on the agenda of many sport governing bodies. In 2007 the executive committee of UEFA (Union des Associations Européennes de Football), the governing body for

European football, approved a Social Responsibility partnership portfolio for 2007–2011 and UEFA now works with a number of charity partners to address specific issues including racism, reconciliation and peace, football for all, violence, health and humanitarian aid. UEFA has also committed to allocating 0.7 per cent of annual revenue to social projects, while the fines received through the disciplinary authorities at UEFA are invested in social responsibility activities. The Football Association in England has also demonstrated a commitment to CSR through the development of the FA Charity Programme, which provided funding for five charities in 2009: The Bobby Moore Fund; The British Heart Foundation; Keep Your Eye on the Ball; Coaching for Hope; and the Geoff Thomas Foundation (http://www.thefa.com/TheFA/WhatWeDo/FACharities.aspx).

Sport events

Many sport event owners require that sport event hosts stage a range of events alongside the main sport event as part of a CSR commitment. For example, a range of projects were implemented throughout Detroit as part of the CSR commitment of the 2006 Super Bowl, including educational, cultural and environmental initiatives (Babiak and Wolfe, 2006). Whilst the Super Bowl is a one-off event, the aim of the CSR initiatives is to have a longer lasting impact, although this is an area where further research is needed. With many sport events owned and organized by governing bodies, this can be seen as an additional way in which they address the issue of CSR. For example, CSR is now an integral part of the Olympic Games, with the International Olympic Committee (IOC) requiring that the hosts of the Olympic Games also host cultural events such as community projects, exhibitions and arts festivals (Masterman, 2009). This was illustrated by the Olympic Arts Festival at the 2002 Winter Olympics in Salt Lake City where 50 community projects were held (Masterman, 2009). In the run up to the London 2012 Olympics, a Cultural Olympiad began in 2008, involving ceremonies, major arts, music and theatre projects, and local and regional projects, which aim to leave a positive legacy after the 2012 Games.

CASE STUDY: WIN IN AFRICA WITH AFRICA

In 2006, FIFA launched Win in Africa with Africa, a CSR initiative that has the overarching objective to promote African development. FIFA has set aside $70m in order to implement a range of initiatives that enable African nations to develop the necessary skills for progression. Three key aspects of the project include: Developing the Game, focusing on improving football infrastructure in African nations; Touch the World, which will draw on forthcoming FIFA international tournaments in Africa to promote unity; and Build a Better Future, that will promote football as a vehicle for broader development goals, including social integration, community development, peace promotion, health and education. The Win in Africa with Africa project is seen as a way to empower individuals and communities through sport to aid the development of African nations.

Source: http://www.fifa.com/aboutfifa/worldwideprograms/wininafrica/index.html

---

There is also increasing concern over the environmental impact of hosting sport events. The 1994 Winter Olympics in Lillehammer, Norway, was the first Olympics to incorporate environmental projects into the hosting of the games, while the Sydney Olympics in 2000 was the first Summer Olympic Games to be declared a 'green games'. The Sydney Games was supported by a number of environmental initiatives; for example, 90 per cent of the hard waste used in the building of solar-powered housing in the Olympic village was recycled on site. The Athens Olympics in 2004 also implemented environmental policies including building venues using environmentally friendly materials and improving standards of waste management (Masterman, 2009). The organizing committee for the 2014 Winter Olympics in Sochi has agreed a partnership with the United Nations Environment Programme to ensure the protection of the environment, with the bobsleigh and luge venues having been relocated in order to protect the Grushevy Ridge, an area of ecological importance (Stevens, 2008). Before the IOC short listed Chicago, Tokyo, Rio de Janeiro and Madrid, the seven applicant cities for the 2016 Olympic Games all stated the environmental credentials of their respective bids. These examples illustrate that event bids will increasingly have to consider the implications on the environment and include environmentally friendly policies in the hosting of an event. In the context of the UK, the BS8901 is a sustainable management standard that was published in November 2007 and offers a framework for events to improve environmental performance and reduce environmental impacts such as carbon emissions and waste.

Sport venues

The increasing concern over the environmental impact of hosting sport events has had an impact on sport venues, which are now more than ever required to demonstrate a commitment to CSR. This is particularly the case for new stadium developments that have to address the issue of environmental sustainability during development and post-development. The New Meadowlands Stadium in New Jersey is a case in point (see case study below) while, in Taiwan, the main stadium constructed for the World Games in 2009, an event featuring non-Olympic sports, includes almost 9,000 solar panels that provided all the electricity during the event and continues to generate electricity now even after the games have finished (http://www.worldgames2009. tw/wg2009/eng/Venues_connect2.php). In the UK, Lords Cricket Ground has been implementing a range of initiatives to improve sustainability. Since 2007 Lords has increased recycling after match days, improved energy efficiency through modern insulation and low energy light-bulbs, and reduced water needs by putting in place water storage tanks. The environmental initiatives have also had a clear business benefit as cost savings have been made.

CASE STUDY: THE NEW MEADOWLANDS STADIUM

The New Meadowlands Stadium in New Jersey will open in 2010 and host both the New York Giants and New York Jets. The development of the 82,500-seated stadium has been in partnership with the US Environmental Protection Agency and is set to become one of the greenest sports stadiums in the world. Throughout the construction of the new stadium many environmental initiatives have been implemented. Following completion, the stadium will also look to minimize energy use. The following six key areas are illustrative of the ways in which the issue of CSR has been addressed during development and will continue to be addressed post-development:

1 Wetlands and wildlife protection: the stadium has been developed on a brownfield site and a stormwater management initiative has been implemented to minimize the flow of storm water into the surrounding environmental area.

2 Construction green practices: throughout the development, green construction practices including the use of low sulfur fuel, recycling waste, using recycled and scrap materials, using local contractors and minimizing water usage have helped to minimize the environmental impact of the stadium build. When the stadium is complete, over half of the interior finish products will have green certification.

3 Water conservation: the new stadium has a target of reducing water usage by 25 per cent in relation to the old stadium by using synthetic turf instead of natural grass, waterless urinals and low-flush toilets, and a high efficiency irrigation system.

4 Energy management: the new stadium has a target of reducing energy usage by 30 per cent in relation to the old stadium by using energy-efficient lighting throughout the stadium. The stadium managers are also looking to build a solar power energy system on site to supply energy as well as purchase energy produced from environmentally sustainable sources.

5 Recycling, composting and solid waste programmes: the new stadium has a target of reducing waste production by 25 per cent by recycling and composting. For example, recycling bins will be installed throughout the stadium and outside, while all plates, cups and trays will be made from eco-friendly compostable material.

6 Fan and community initiatives: fans will be encouraged to use public transport to access the new stadium on matchdays including the bus and the new rail system.

Source: http://www.newmeadowlandsstadium.com

Sport manufacturers

Major sport manufacturers are also addressing the issue of CSR and increasingly producing CSR reports alongside their annual financial reports. The leading sports manufacturer Nike received a lot of adverse publicity over the use of sweatshops in the 1990s. Since then it can be argued that Nike is one of the leading sports organizations in the area of CSR. Over the past decade, the CSR strategy at Nike has mirrored that of other corporate organizations, with increasing focus now placed on incorporating CSR into long-term strategy and improving sustainability at the same time as delivering increased returns. Key to this is innovation and design; innovative CSR initiatives include increasing the use of organic cotton, designing products made from more sustainable materials, establishing codes of conduct and monitoring and auditing supply-chain factories, and the creation of the Nike Foundation (Nike, 2009). The Foundation is a charitable organization funded by Nike that invests in many communities in less-developed countries across the world to provide a range of educational and development programmes targeted at young girls (Nike, 2009).

Commercial organizations

It has been argued that the implementation of CSR initiatives by sport organizations can have a greater impact than commercial organizations and other industry sectors (Babiak and Wolfe, 2006). For this reason, many commercial organizations are developing CSR-related partnerships with different types of sport organization. The partnerships can take different forms. It can involve a charitable donation to develop facilities. For example, as part of their commitment to community investment, Barclays has invested £30 million into grassroots sport since 2004 through their Spaces for Sports initiative. Working in partnership with Groundwork, an environmental regeneration charity, and the Football Foundation, the largest sports charity in the UK, who have both contributed an additional £29 million in funding, more than 200 facilities have been opened in disadvantaged communities to allow better access to sport (Barclays, 2009). Over 50,000 people use the facilities every week and the project has won many community awards, while the success in the UK has prompted Barclays to expand the project into South Africa, Zambia and the US (Barclays, 2009).

There are other types of partnership in which commercial organizations develop a close association with a sports team, league or athlete as part of a cause-related marketing strategy. This enables the commercial organization to address the issue of CSR, which may lead to reputation benefits and to 'bask in the reflected glory' of having an association with a sports organization (Babiak and Wolfe, 2009). There are also benefits for the sport organization. For example, the sport organization receives much-needed funding from the commercial organization to deliver a range of CSR programmes. There are many examples of this – the community trust model in the UK and charitable foundations in the US operate many programmes on this basis. The earlier case study of the Charlton Athletic Community Trust outlined how some of the CSR schemes that the trust delivers receive funding from commercial organizations such as British Airways and Axis Europe. A key factor underpinning these partnerships is that the sport organizations have the expertise and trained staff to deliver educational or social inclusion-oriented programmes, in contrast to many commercial organizations.

SUMMARY

This chapter has introduced the concept of CSR and provided an overview of eight different ways in which CSR is implemented in the sport industry, including athlete foundations; professional sports teams; professional sports leagues; sport governing bodies; sport events; sport venues; sport manufacturers; and commercial organizations. Although considered in separation, it is clear that there are many overlaps and interdependencies. For example, CSR initiatives developed at a league level or by a governing body are more often than not implemented by individual sport teams. Moreover, sport governing bodies are the owners of sport events, so CSR initiatives implemented at sport events are often driven by the governing body. This chapter has also identified that the nature of the activities that are delivered by these different types of sports organizations is wide-ranging and can be classified into eight broad categories. These are: health; education; community; social inclusion; equality; youth development; cultural; and environmental. Again there are overlaps between these

423

categories. For instance, a project aimed at addressing social inclusion can be targeted at youth and might involve sports participation and therefore also have positive health impacts. It is clear that the implementation of CSR within the sport industry is multi-dimensional and relies on the development of relationships between stakeholders. However, what is also clear is that while many sports organizations are engaging in CSR activities there is little formal guidance on how to do this or what constitutes CSR in the sport context, hence the wide-ranging nature of the activities. This chapter has therefore provided a first step towards a better understanding of the implementation of CSR in sport. However, as outlined at the beginning, there are other key managerial issues including communication, stakeholder engagement, measurement of CSR schemes and the business case for CSR. Although some of these aspects have been touched upon in this chapter, they offer potential areas for further research in sport and CSR.

REVIEW QUESTIONS

1 Why is corporate social responsibility relevant for sport organizations?
2 What are the key managerial issues that sport organizations need to consider in relation to CSR?
3 Are any of the different CSR activities implemented by sports organizations more important than others?
4 Are there any other ways in which sport organizations address the issue of CSR?

FURTHER READING

Godfrey, P. (2009) Corporate Social Responsibility in Sport: An Overview and Key Issues, *Journal of Sport Management*, 23: 698–716.
Lindgreen, A. and Swaen, V. (2010) Corporate Social Responsibility, *International Journal of Management Reviews*, 12(1): 1–7.

WEBSITES

FIFA Win in Africa Project
    http://www.fifa.com/aboutfifa/worldwideprograms/wininafrica/index.html
NBA Cares
    http://www.nba.com/nba_cares/mission/our_work.html
The Andre Agassi Foundation
    http://www.agassifoundation.org
The Atlanta Falcons Community Youth Foundation
    http://www.atlantafalcons.com/community/falcons-youth-foundation
The FC Barcelona Foundation
    http://www.fcbarcelona.cat/web/Fundacio/english/fundacio/missio.html

The Football Association Charity Programme
    http://www.thefa.com/TheFA/WhatWeDo/FACharities.aspx
The Lance Armstrong Foundation
    http://www.livestrong.org
The New Meadowlands Stadium
    http://www.newmeadowlandsstadium.com
The PGA Tour
    http://together.pgatour.com/the-program.html
The Rio Ferdinand Live the Dream Foundation
    http://www.rioferdinandltdf.com
The World Games Stadium
    http://www.worldgames2009.tw/wg2009/eng/Venues_connect2.php

REFERENCES

Babiak, K. and Wolfe, R. (2006) More than Just a Game? Corporate Social Responsibility and Super Bowl XL, *Sport Marketing Quarterly*, 15(4): 214–222.

Babiak, K. and Wolfe, R. (2009) Determinants of Corporate Social Responsibility in Professional Sport: Internal and External Factors, *Journal of Sport Management*, 23: 717–742.

Barclays (2009) *Spaces for Sports: Developing People and Places through Sport*, Summary Report, Manchester Metropolitan University.

Blowfield, M. and Murray, A. (2008) *Corporate Responsibility: A Critical Introduction*, Oxford University Press, Oxford.

Bradish, C. and Cronin, J. (2009) Corporate Social Responsibility in Sport, *Journal of Sport Management*, 23: 691–697.

Carroll, A.B. (1979) A Three-Dimensional Conceptual Model of Corporate Performance, *Academy of Management Review*, 4(4): 497–505.

Carroll, A.B. (1991) The Pyramid of Corporate Social Responsibility: Toward the Moral Management of Organisational Stakeholders, *Business Horizons*, July–August: 39–48.

Carroll, A.B. (1999) Corporate Social Responsibility: Evolution of a Definitional Construct, *Business and Society*, 38(3): 268–295.

Carroll, A.B. and Shabana, K.M. (2010) The Business Case for Corporate Social Responsibility: A Review of Concepts, Research and Practice, *International Journal of Management Reviews*, 12(1): 85–105.

Chelsea Football Club (2007) *Corporate Social Responsibility Report for the 2006/07 Season*.

Clarke, T. (2004) Cycles of Crisis and Regulation: The Enduring Agency and Stewardship Problems of Corporate Governance, *Corporate Governance: An International Review*, 12(2): 153–161.

Coalter, F. (2007) *A Wider Social Role for Sport: Who's Keeping the Score?*, Routledge, London.

Cramer, J., Van der Heijden, A. and Jonker, J. (2006) Corporate Social Responsibility: Making Sense Through Thinking and Acting, *Business Ethics: A European Review*, 15(4): 380–389.

Dean, D.H. (2003) Associating the Cooperation with a Charitable Event Through Sponsorship: Measuring the Effects on Corporate–Community Relations, *Journal of Advertising*, 31(4): 77–88.

Frederick, W.C. (1978) From CSR1 to CSR2: The Maturing of Business and Society Thought, *Working Paper 279*, Graduate School of Business, University of Pittsburgh.

Giannoulakis, C. and Drayer, J. (2009) Thugs Versus 'Good Guys': The Impact of NBA Cares on Player Image, *European Sport Management Quarterly*, 9(4): 453–468.

425

Godfrey, P. (2009) Corporate Social Responsibility in Sport: An Overview and Key Issues, *Journal of Sport Management*, 23: 698–716.

Lindgreen, A. and Swaen, V. (2010) Corporate Social Responsibility, *International Journal of Management Reviews*, 12(1): 1–7.

Livestrong (2008) *Annual Report*.

Margolis, J. and Walsh, J.P. (2003) Misery Loves Companies: Rethinking Social Initiatives by Business, *Administrative Science Quarterly*, 48(2): 268–305.

Masterman, G. (2009) *Strategic Sports Event Management: Olympic Edition*, Elsevier/Butterworth-Heinemann, London.

Mohr, L.A., Webb, D.J. and Harris, K.E. (2001) Do Consumers Expect Companies to be Socially Responsible? The Impact of Corporate Social Responsibility on Buying Behavior, *Journal of Consumer Affairs*, 35: 45–72.

Mullen, J. (1997) Performance-Based Corporate Philanthropy: How 'Giving Smart' Can Further Corporate Goals, *Public Relations Quarterly*, 42(2): 42–49.

NBA (2010) *NBA Community Report*.

Nike (2009) *Corporate Responsibility Report*.

Owen, D. (2005) CSR after Enron: A Role for the Academic Accounting Profession, *Working Paper No. 33*, International Centre for Corporate Social Responsibility, University of Nottingham.

Porter, M.E. and Kramer, M.R. (2006) Strategy and Society: The Link between Competitive Advantage and Corporate Social Responsibility, *Harvard Business Review*, December: 78–92.

Premier League (2009) *Creating Chances Annual Report*.

Smith, A. and Westerbeek, H. (2007) Sport as a Vehicle for Deploying Corporate Social Responsibility, *Journal of Corporate Citizenship*, 25: 43–54.

Stevens, A. (2008) Ever Greener Games, *Sport Business International*, 137, August, 36–37.

Walker, M. and Kent, A. (2009) Do Fans Care? Assessing the Influence of Corporate Social Responsibility on Consumer Attitudes in the Sport Industry, *Journal of Sport Management*, 23: 743–769.

Walters, G. (2009) Corporate Social Responsibility through Sport: The Community Sports Trust Model as a CSR Delivery Agency, *Journal of Corporate Citizenship*, 35, December, 81–94.

Walters, G. and Tacon, R. (2010) Corporate Social Responsibility in Sport: Stakeholder Management in the UK Football Industry, *Journal of Management and Organization*, 16(4), September, 566–586.

Chapter 24

Researching sport management

James Skinner, Allan Edwards and Wayne Usher, Griffith University, Gold Coast, Australia

---

TOPICS

What is sport management research? • Types of sport management research • Ethical considerations • Approaches to sport management research • Types of sport management research methodologies • Research design • Writing the research report

---

OBJECTIVES

At the end of this chapter you should be able to:

■ Explain the evolution of sport management research;

■ Make a clear distinction between qualitative, quantitative, and mixed methods approaches to sport management;

■ Understand the difference between basic and applied research;

■ Explain the research process and how it can be applied to sport management research.

KEY TERMS

Applied research – a type of research that has direct value to practitioners but in which the researcher has limited control over the research setting.

Basic research – a type of research that may have limited direct application but in which the researcher has careful control of the conditions.

Paradigm – is a set of propositions that explain how the world is perceived; it contains a worldview, a way of breaking down the complexity of the real world, informing researchers and social scientists in general what is important, what is legitimate, and what is reasonable.

> **Qualitative research** – research that seeks to provide an understanding of the human condition and which utilizes an interpretive approach to data analysis.
>
> **Quantitative research** – the collection and analysis of data that can generally be expressed in a numeric format.

OVERVIEW

In this chapter we will discuss the importance of sport management research as well as the different research methods currently employed by sport management researchers. By looking at the current state of research in sport management, we can examine what the future of sport management research may look like – how new and innovative ways of conceptualizing and investigating issues of importance to sport management researchers and practitioners can offer potential solutions to emerging problems in the world of sport management research.

There is not just one way to do research. Some people do undertake research from this perspective whilst others are critical of the methods used by different researchers. Instead research should be disciplined inquiry, not a set of specific procedures.

The two main types of research are basic and applied. Basic research deals primarily with theoretical problems, and these results are not intended to have immediate application. Applied research, on the other hand, strives to answer questions that have direct value to the practitioner. Sport management research is not only important for the researcher. By undertaking relevant research that asks and seeks answers to important questions and issues that are of direct relevance to practitioners, we are developing not only proficient researchers but proficient and informed consumers of research.

CASE STUDY: USING A MIXED METHODS APPROACH

Estella (Terry) Engelberg completed a study entitled 'The Commitment of Volunteers in Junior Sport Organisations: A Mixed Methods Study'. The purpose of this study was to examine the dimensionality and targets of the commitment of volunteers in junior sport organizations, and the links between commitment and behavioural outcomes, specifically one's intention to stand down from a volunteer role, intention to cease volunteering for the club or centre, and self-assessed performance. Terry utilized a sequential explanatory mixed methods design consisting of both quantitative and qualitative phases. The quantitative phase studies assessment commitment to three organizational targets: the organization, the team of volunteers, and the volunteer role. The qualitative study explored and explained the findings of the quantitative phase in more depth and allowed the volunteers to 'use their own voice' in the discussion. The results of the studies indicated that commitment is a multidimensional construct that can be applied to various organizational targets, and that there are differences in commitment amongst volunteer subgroups, such as committee members and volunteers in other roles, volunteers with children, and volunteers without children.

Source: Edwards and Skinner, 2009, p. 7

WHAT IS SPORT MANAGEMENT RESEARCH?

At its basic level, research is a way of investigating problems with the aim of finding solutions to those problems, or at least raising questions and issues that future researchers will investigate. This is true of sport management research as well. The sport management researcher devises questions that relate to specific problems or issues in the field, and then devises methods by which these problems or issues can be answered or explained. Sport management research involves systematic exploration, guided by well-constructed questions, and producing new information or reassessing old information. Creswell (2008) defines research as 'a process of steps used to collect and analyse information to increase our understanding of a topic or issue' (p. 3). Sport management researchers spend a great deal of time evaluating other people's research, deciding what the strengths and weaknesses are in each case, and hoping to apply their conclusions to their own reading and to the procedures they follow in their research. In this chapter, the issue of a sport management researcher's own value systems is discussed as these value systems will inevitably come into play when a researcher uses qualitative research methods. Sport management researchers therefore need to look carefully at the claims of others, judging for themselves whether or not those claims are convincing. To do that, they need to understand the process by which other researchers have come to their conclusions, and this means understanding both their methodologies and the intellectual frameworks within which they have operated.

Origins of sport management research

Edwards and Skinner (2009) discuss the evolution of sport management as an independent discipline throughout the 1980s and 1990s. Costa (2005) suggests that the discipline of sport management was finally defined following the founding of the North American Society for Sport Management (NASSM) in 1985, and the subsequent formation of the European Association of Sport Management (EASM) in 1993 and, in turn, the Sport Management Association of Australia and New Zealand (SMAANZ) in 1995.

The mere recognition of sport management as an independent discipline, however, would be insufficient to sustain it in the academic world. Pitts (2001) suggests that 'a field of study cannot exist without a body of knowledge and literature' (p. 2) that has been formed through the process of research. Research in sport management has historically been dominated by positivistic, quantitative methodologies (Amis & Silk, 2005); however, more recently sport management researchers (e.g. Chalip, 2006; Edwards & Skinner, 2009; Frisby, 2005) have acknowledged the need to consider and embrace alternative worldviews and eclectic methodological approaches to examine questions about the social world (Quatman, 2006).

Quatman (2006) indicates that the 2005 special issue in the *Journal of Sport Management* reflected on the 'Constrained idea space (i.e., content and diversity of knowledge circulating) in the field and focused on "expanding the horizons" of sport management research through critical and innovative approaches' (p. 2). Quatman goes on to suggest that the core theme of the special edition clearly suggests that there is a need to move beyond current research practices and embrace socially inclusive approaches to understanding the lived experiences of sport managers in order to promote a more inclusive culture for the generation of knowledge in the field.

429

Why do sport management research?

Research and reflection are essential in any discipline if that discipline is to grow in a positive and beneficial way. Thomas, Nelson, and Silverman (2005) assert that one 'of the primary distinctions between a discipline or profession and trade is that the trade deals only with how to deal with something, whereas the discipline or profession concerns itself not only with how but also with why something should be done in a certain manner (and why it should even be done)' (p. 6). Thomas *et al.* further go on to discuss some of the problems associated with research and its applicability to practitioners and professionals in the field, and these can be directly related to sport management research and the sport management practitioner. In particular they discuss the language and jargon of research which can be at times too technical, too unfamiliar, and, dare we say, too 'academic'. Additionally, practitioners do not see the relevance of the work they are actually undertaking. These are all concerns that the sport management researcher should heed before embarking on their research project. They should ask some important questions of themselves – Is this topic relevant? Who will benefit from this research? Perhaps if the answers to these questions are that the topic is of relevance only to the researcher, and the researcher themselves is the primary beneficiary of the research outcome, then serious consideration should be given before proceeding down this particular path.

Sport management research can add important information to the discipline's knowledge base – and such information, where relevant, can be drawn on by other researchers, practitioners, policy makers, and even other stakeholders such as club members, athletes, fans, existing and potential sponsors, advertisers, marketers, and any other interested member of the general public. For the researcher, a particular research study may be on a topic or issue previously ignored, or perhaps on a 'new' topic which has never been considered before. The research may also build on previous research studies – providing results to confirm the previous study, or even to question these. This is true of any academic discipline, and sport management is no exception. A research report might provide a study that has not been conducted and thereby fill a void in existing knowledge. It can also provide additional results to confirm or disconfirm results of prior studies. It can help add to the literature about practices that work or advance better practices for the sport management professional.

Research can also suggest improvements for practice, giving sport management practitioners new ideas with which to develop new processes and procedures and ultimately to become better at what they do. It also offers sport management practitioners new ideas to consider in their profession. It also helps practitioners evaluate approaches that they hope will work in their own management settings. At a broader level, research helps the sport management practitioner build connections with other practitioners who may be trying out similar ideas in different locations.

Research also creates conversations about important issues when policy makers debate issues that directly impact on sport managers, for example sport policy relating to drugs in sport. Research can help the policy makers weigh various perspectives. When the policy makers read research on issues, they are informed about current debates and stances taken by other public officials. To be useful, the research needs to have clear results, be summarized concisely, and include data-based evidence.

430

TYPES OF SPORT MANAGEMENT RESEARCH

The two main types of research are basic research and applied research. These are, in effect, the 'extremes' of the research continuum – with basic research being at one end and applied research being at the other, as their methods and applicability to the sport management practitioner are so diverse. In the field of sport management, research is generally not only basic or applied, but often a combination of both.

Basic research is theoretical in nature, and deals with theoretical problems. It looks to try and make sense of the world and the way in which it operates. In general the research takes place in a controlled setting such as a laboratory, but for the sport manager this could be an interview room or any other venue where the researcher can control the conditions under which the research takes place. In this situation the results of research may have little direct application for the practitioner. The research may yield important data for the researcher; however, in the form in which the research is obtained and the types of data collected, it is unlikely to be of direct relevance to a sport management setting.

Applied research, on the other hand, takes place in the real world, or real-world settings such as the sporting organization, and therefore, if undertaken well, can produce results that are relevant to the sport management practitioner and can be implemented within the sporting organization to improve practice.

Most sport management research is neither purely applied nor purely basic but incorporates some aspects of both.

The sport management research process is outlined in Figure 24.1.

The research process

The first step to conducting sport management research is to identify the problem. Once the problem has been identified, reading and thinking about relevant theories and concepts, as well as a careful search of the literature for relevant findings, leads to the specification of hypotheses or questions. Operational definitions are needed in a research study so that the reader knows what the researcher means when they use certain terms. Operational definitions describe observable phenomena that enable the researcher to examine empirically whether the predictions can be supported. The study is designed, and the methods are made operational. The data are then collected and analysed, and the findings identified. Finally the results are related back to the original hypotheses or questions and discussed in relation to theories, concepts, and previous research findings.

The research topic

The researcher begins a study by identifying a topic to study – this may be an issue or problem in the sport management area that needs to be resolved. This may be a high-profile issue recently identified in the media, or an issue around which little or no research has previously been conducted but which is of concern to sport managers. Once an issue is identified, the researcher will develop a justification for studying it, and suggest the importance of the study.

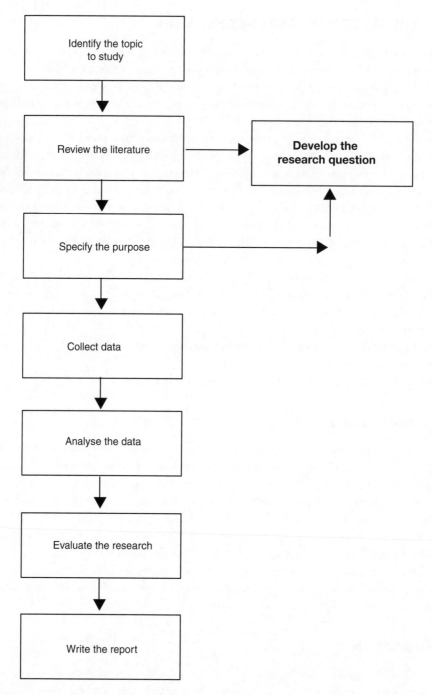

Figure 24.1 *The sport management research process*

Reviewing the literature

Once a topic or problem has been identified, the researcher needs to know who has already studied and reported in this area. This is important because your study should build on existing knowledge and add to the bank of findings on a topic – not merely replicate existing studies.

Reviewing the literature means locating summaries, books, journals, publications, websites etc. on a topic. The researcher then selects which literature to include and summarizes them in a written report.

Specifying a purpose for research

This is where the sport management researcher specifies the overall objective or intent of the research. This is an extremely important section in the research study as it not only introduces the whole study, but lets the reader know what procedures will be used to collect data, and indicates the types of results you hope to find.

Develop the research question

Having decided on a topic, reviewed the literature, and defined the purpose of the research, the sport management researcher will develop a specific set of research questions that the research to be conducted will seek to answer or explain. These research questions will build on the purpose statement developed in the previous section.

Collecting data

Having established the parameters of the research and the research questions, the next step in the research process is actually to collect data. It is important that the data collected is accurate so that the hypotheses and answers generated by the research are valid. There are various methods of collecting data dependent on the theoretical model followed by the researcher. The major differences in data collection between quantitative, qualitative, or mixed methods approaches are discussed in more detail later in this chapter.

Analysing the data

Analysing the data involves drawing conclusions about the information collected. The results are often depicted in tables or figures in the case of quantitative data, with a discussion in words that aims to provide answers to the research questions. These will be reported in sections of a research report usually entitled Results, Findings, or Discussions, depending on whether the researcher has approached the research from a quantitative or qualitative methodology.

Reporting and evaluating the research

After conducting the research, one must develop a written report. Reporting research means deciding on the audience for the research, structuring the report in a format acceptable to that audience, and then writing the report in a manner that is sensitive to all readers. The audience for a sport management research report will range from academics actively researching in the area, to practitioners such as club and team managers, through to stakeholders in the government and private sector, as well as members of the general public who are actively interested in issues that affect their favourite team or sport.

ETHICAL CONSIDERATIONS

In all steps of the research process the sport management researcher needs to engage in ethical practices. At its most basic level this can consist of respecting the rights of participants, the research site itself, through to reporting the research fully and honestly. The importance of research ethics extends beyond this moral imperative to operate legally and ethically. Compliance with ethical standards can be a condition on which a researcher receives funding as well as a condition of publication in many journals. Access to certain research sites – sport schools, for example – can also be restricted and require high levels of compliance with ethical standards. Of major importance to sport management researchers is the perception and confidence of potential research participants in the ethical integrity of the research, which can help to ensure that these potential research participants are more likely to take part in the research study.

Respecting the rights of participants

Professional associations generally have a set of ethical standards by which researchers should abide. Students of sport management research should review the ethical standard requirements of their tertiary institution as a guide prior to commencing any research.

The sport management researcher needs to adhere to a basic concept – that participants in any study have certain rights, the most fundamental of which is not to be harmed in any way, whether it is physically, mentally, or emotionally. Participants also have the right to know the purpose and aims of the study prior to agreeing to participate, as well as any possible or likely consequences of participation – otherwise known as 'informed consent' (or assent if the subjects are minors). At any stage participants can refuse to engage with the research and can withdraw from the study at any time. The concept of privacy and anonymity is also extremely important and must be adhered to. This involves not only the identity of participants but also of the information provided.

Respecting the integrity of the research site

Before commencing research at a site, be it a sports club or sporting venue etc., the researcher should gain permission and aim to disturb the site as little as possible. This ensures not only the validity of the data collected but also that the research site will be more likely to agree in the future to participate in research studies.

Reporting research fully and honestly

Information and data collected should be reported honestly, without changing or altering the findings to satisfy either the research questions or interest groups. There are times when the findings do not support the initial aims of the research question, and in some instances these can be viewed as exciting new research opportunities.

Ethical context

The sport management researcher should be reflecting on ethical considerations throughout the research process. There may be times when the sport management researcher faces difficult choices in relation to the conduct of the research and needs to weigh up the benefits of the research against any possible harm caused to participants in the study or the research site. Adhering to a system of research ethics will serve to guide the research in making those correct moral choices that will benefit both the participants in the study and the research study itself.

APPROACHES TO SPORT MANAGEMENT RESEARCH

The sport management researcher can approach their study in different ways or methods – through a quantitative study, a qualitative study, or a combination of the two. The approach or method chosen is often driven by the type of problem being researched.

Research paradigms

Edwards and Skinner (2009) believe that most sport management researchers have an intellectual framework that governs the way they perceive the world and their own place within it, even if they are unable to articulate just what that framework is. This paradigm or framework shapes research from the beginning to the end, because it provides the structure within which choices (including the initial choice of a research subject) are made. This framework comes partly from the institutional setting within which research takes place – the position taken by employers or those who commissioned the research, or by supervisors, by the department within which researchers work, and by the university/college which employs them. Part of it will come from the personal position of the sport management researcher, which may have been shaped by their biography of experiences as well as their previous education, political and religious beliefs, gender, sexual preference, and race and/or class affiliations.

Frisby (2005) argues that if researchers are to understand all aspects of sport management then research needs to be conducted from 'multiple paradigms' (p. 2). Further, she says that the paradigms a researcher operates from 'shape the questions we ask, the methods we use, and the degree to which our findings will have an impact on society' (p. 2).

There is no single paradigm, and/or methodology, that meets the needs of all sport management researchers and all research questions, because the field of sport management research is diverse, complex, and evolving. The sport management researcher will adopt the methodology most appropriate for the research being conducted.

TYPES OF SPORT MANAGEMENT RESEARCH METHODOLOGIES

There is no one best research approach. The sport management researcher will determine which approach will be most effective for the resolution of the research question, and is often determined by the nature of the question or topic being investigated. The research methodology chosen will generally be influenced by the philosophical beliefs of the researcher as well as the resources available to conduct the research – including available participants and the research site. Undertaking research from a quantitative or qualitative perspective affects the approach to the research process itself.

Quantitative research

Some researchers suggest (Amis & Silk, 2005; Cunningham & Mahoney, 2004; Cuskelly & Boag, 2001; Fink *et al.*, 2003; Murray & Howat, 2002; Quatman, 2006; Shilbury, 2001; Skinner & Edwards, 2005) that quantitative approaches to sport management research have historically dominated the discipline. Quantitative research is a type of research in which the researcher decides what to study, asks specific, narrow questions, collects quantifiable data from participants, analyses these numbers using statistics, and conducts the inquiry in an unbiased, objective manner. Creswell (2008, p. 48) sees three main features of quantitative research that are prevalent today:

- Collecting and analysing information in a numeric form;
- Collecting scores and then using them to measure the performance or attributes of individuals and organizations;
- Procedures and processes by which groups are compared or which factors common to individuals or groups are related through experiments, surveys, correlation studies, and other methods.

Identifying the research problem

The researcher will look at trends or variables whose relationship can be defined in a quantifiable manner. For example, variables such as gender or age, and attitudes towards a specific type of behaviour such as illicit drug use in sport or bad off-field behaviour, could be studied to determine whether there is a relationship between the two and whether one variable influences another.

Reviewing the literature

In quantitative research the literature justifies the need for the study and suggests potential purposes and research questions. Within the literature the researcher will identify key variables, relations, and trends, and use these to provide direction for the research questions or hypotheses. For example, a literature review on drug use in a particular sport may show little in the way of trends or reported incidences in that particular sport; however, the literature may reveal useful data in relation to increasing trends in related sports as well as changing trends in public perceptions and tolerances for such behaviours.

436

Specifying a purpose for research

In quantitative research, the purpose statement, research questions, and hypotheses tend to be specific and narrow and seek measurable, observable data on variables. The major statements and questions of direction in a study – the purpose statement, the research questions, and the hypotheses – are specific and narrow because one identifies only a few variables to study. From the study of these variables, one may obtain measures or assessments on an instrument or record scores on a scale from observations.

Collecting data

In quantitative research, the data collection tends to consist of collecting data using instruments with preset questions and responses, gathering quantifiable (numeric) data and collecting information from a large number of individuals. An instrument is a tool for measuring, observing, or documenting quantitative data. It contains specific questions and response possibilities that one establishes or develops in advance of the study. Examples of instruments are survey questionnaires, standardized tests, and checklists. The instruments are administered to participants and data is collected in the form of numbers. The intent of this process is to apply the results from a small number of people to a large number. The larger the number of individuals studied, the stronger the case for applying the results to a large number of people. For example, a survey sent to 500 parents of teenage football players from one club should provide a significant amount of data from which to extrapolate relevant information.

Analysing and interpreting data

In quantitative research the data analysis tends to consist of statistical analysis. Statistical analysis consists of breaking down the data into parts to answer the research questions. Statistical procedures such as comparing groups or relating scores for individuals provide information to address the research questions or hypotheses. These results are then interpreted in light of initial predictions or prior studies. Examples of data collected by the sport management researcher that could be analysed statistically include attendance figures at different sporting events (including a more detailed demographic analysis), club membership figures, and sporting participation rates.

Reporting and evaluating research

In quantitative research the researcher aims to take an objective and unbiased approach, ensuring that their own biases and values system do not influence the results. The format for a study follows a standard pattern of introduction, literature review, methods, results, and discussion. The research is also reported without reference to the researcher or their personal reaction to the results achieved.

Clearly there are many studies in which the sport management researcher will obtain useful and valuable data through the use of quantitative methods. Analysis of athlete performance across a number of events, a demographic analysis of attendance figures at sporting events, and even the analysis of sport merchandise consumption can provide valuable data to practitioners which can be used to shape and develop training regimes, develop marketing strategies, and address other specific areas of concern.

Qualitative methods

Qualitative research presents an alternative to the traditional form of quantitative research. Qualitative research has been constantly evolving since the late 1800s, with the development of naturalistic inquiry or constructivism to emphasize the importance of participants' views, to take into account the setting or context in which the participants expressed those views, and look at the meanings that people assign to different issues. During the 1980s and 1990s, types of qualitative research design emerged, including case studies, grounded theory research, and narrative inquiry, along with the emergence of qualitative computer software programs for data analysis.

In the 1990s and 2000s, researchers have seen the emergence of participatory and advocacy practices in qualitative research, themes which express concern for the needs of individuals in lower social classes, racial groups, and women. These themes called for researchers to report in their studies their own personal biases, values, and assumptions. It cast research into politics in which it considered the rights of women, gays, lesbians, racial groups, and different classes in our society, and honoured different viewpoints during both the writing and the reading of qualitative reports. It also spoke about qualitative data collection procedures in which inquirers were sensitive to participants, actively collaborated with them (rather than studying them), and respected the dignity of each individual who offered data for research.

Creswell (2008, p. 51) sees the current characteristics of qualitative research as:

- A recognition by researchers that they need to listen to the views of research participants;
- A recognition that researchers need to ask general, open questions and collect data in those places where people live and work;
- A recognition that research can advocate for change and better the lives of individuals.

Identifying the research problem

Qualitative research tends to address research problems where little is known about the problem and the researcher is looking to achieve a detailed understanding of a central or specific phenomenon. The literature may have provided little information about the area of study, and the researcher will seek to learn more from participants. The research problem may be an issue that has been presented in the media as being of concern to the public, such as (again) the use of illicit drugs in sport, and sport management research may seek to devise a study that will look at community attitudes towards this.

Reviewing the literature

In qualitative research the literature tends to play a minor role in suggesting a specific research question, but does justify the importance of studying the research problem. This is because qualitative research relies on the views of participants in the study and less upon the direction in the literature identified by the researcher. There are many issues that may be of interest to researchers and practitioners that may be far too current to have attracted much previous research.

Specifying a purpose for the research

In qualitative research the purpose statement and research questions tend to be general and broad and seek to understand the participants' experiences. The purpose will be more open ended than in quantitative research.

Collecting data

In qualitative research the data collection tends to consist of using forms with general, emerging questions to permit the participant to generate responses. Data collection may be in the form of text (words) or images (film, photos etc.), and will generally involve collecting this information from a small number of individuals and sites. The aim is to learn from the participants in the study, and to develop forms (protocols) for recoding data as the study proceeds. Often the questions used will change and emerge during data collection as the information is collected from participants. The researcher may also record their own observations of the participants, which may involve recording notes about their behaviour.

Analysing and interpreting data

In qualitative research the data analysis tends to consist of text analysis, involve developing a description and themes, and tends to consist of stating the larger meaning of the findings. When analysing text, the researcher may gather a text database so that an analysis of groups of sentences or words (text segments) can be made.

Reporting and evaluating research

In qualitative research the reports tend to use a flexible structure and evaluative criteria, and the researcher tends to take a subjective approach, or at least states any biases they may have.

Mixed methods approach to sport management research

Edwards and Skinner (2009) discuss how, for a true mixed methods approach, qualitative and quantitative methods have to be combined. If qualitative and quantitative methods are combined effectively to answer a specific research question then one of the following outcomes may arise:

1   Qualitative and quantitative results may 'converge'.
2   Qualitative and quantitative results may relate to different objects or phenomena, but may be 'complementary' to each other and thus can be used to 'supplement' each other.
3   Qualitative and quantitative results may be 'divergent' or 'contradictory'. (p. 6)

Further, Edwards and Skinner (2009) believe that using more than one method to study the same phenomenon in sport management research 'has the potential to strengthen the validity of the results' (p. 7). A typical mixed methods approach may be to start out with a qualitative segment such as an interview, which could then be followed by a quantitative structured interview to clarify some of the survey findings. A mixed methods approach may also lead sport management researchers to modify or expand the research design and/or the data collection methods.

RESEARCH DESIGN

Research designs are the specific procedures involved in the last three steps of the research process: data collection, data analysis, and report writing. These research designs will differ depending on whether quantitative, qualitative, or mixed methods of research are utilized.

Quantitative research designs

Creswell (2008) identifies three main types of quantitative research design: experimental, correlational, and survey.

Experimental designs – where the researcher determines whether an activity or materials make a difference in results for participants. This is done by giving one group a set of activities (the intervention) and withholding the set from another group.

Correlational designs – are procedures in which researchers 'measure the degree of association (or relation) between two or more variables using the statistical procedure of correlational analysis. The degree of association, expressed as a number, indicates whether the two variables are related or whether one can predict another' (p. 60). To accomplish this, the researcher 'studies a single group of individuals rather than two or more groups as in an experiment' (p. 60).

Survey designs – 'these seek to describe trends in a large population of individuals. In this case, a survey is a good procedure to use. Survey designs are procedures in which one administers a survey or questionnaire to a small group of people (called the sample group) to identify trends in attitudes, opinions, behaviours, or characteristics of a large group of people (the population)' (p. 61).

Qualitative research designs

There are a number of research designs in qualitative methods including ethnography, ethnomethodology, narrative inquiry, grounded theory, and a range of emerging ethnographies including netnography, ethnodrama, and phenomenography. We will now examine a few of the more commonly used designs briefly.

Ethnography – relates to social research in which the behaviours of participants are studied in their everyday context, rather than under experimental or laboratory conditions. Observation and interviews are the primary methods of data collection, and the data is collected in an 'unstructured' manner, meaning that it is collected in its raw form. In general, the researcher will focus on a single setting or group, and the data analysis will involve the interpretation of the meanings and functions of human actions and is primarily conducted in the form of verbal descriptions and explanations (Hammersley, 1990, p. 1).

Grounded theory – aids the researcher seeking to study social phenomena in their natural setting. For the sport management researcher, this could be a study of athletes at a competition, specific consumers attending a sporting event, or even the management team within a sporting organization. The researcher will engage in a data collection process of field observation, in-depth interviews, and document analysis (Glaser & Strauss, 1967). Following analysis of one set of data, the researcher then decides what data to collect next and where to find them from other participants, sites, and/or events or incidents. Therefore, the grounded theory researcher develops the theory as it emerges in this ongoing process – referred to by Glaser and Strauss (1967) as 'grounding' the theory in the data. Because of the continual 'grounding' process, the theory accurately reflects the data.

Mixed methods designs

With the mixed methods approach, the sport management researcher decides to collect both quantitative data (quantifiable data) as well as qualitative data (images, interviews, stories). This is not merely a process of collecting two distinct types of data – quantitative and qualitative. The researcher needs to merge, integrate, link, or embed both strands.

One form of mixed methods design that can be successfully utilized by the sport management researcher is triangulation mixed methods.

In a triangulation study the researcher gathers both quantitative and qualitative data, analyses both datasets separately, compares the results from the analysis of both datasets, and makes an interpretation as to whether the results support or contradict each other. The direct comparison of the two datasets by the researcher provides a 'triangulation' of data sources.

The strength of this design is that it combines the advantages of each form of data – that is, quantitative data provides for generalizability whereas the qualitative data offers information about the context or setting. This design enables a researcher to gather information that uses the best features of both quantitative and qualitative data collection. It can be difficult, however, to transform one form of data into the other form in order to integrate and compare data. Additionally, even if integration of the data is possible, inconsistent results may emerge, making it necessary to collect additional data or revisit the collected databases to reconcile the differences.

441

WRITING THE RESEARCH REPORT

Once one has completed one's research, the next step is to write up the research report. Different mediums will require different formats in a research report, so the steps that follow are a general guide. It is important, however, that the report be constructed in a systematic way and address all aspects of the work carried out and offer an appropriate selection from the findings. By adopting a systematic approach to constructing the research report, the sport management researcher will produce a cohesive and well-defined report.

Introduction

This is the first section of the research report and outlines the research project – why it was done and how it relates to other research in this same area.

Aims of the research

This is where the researcher outlines what the aims were, and what they hoped to have achieved. It also describes how the research is significant and whether it addresses an important problem. At the end of the report the researcher should be able to look back at the aims of the research project and reflect on whether or not these aims were achieved and whether they lead to future research.

Literature review

In this section the researcher will outline how they searched the literature for relevant and key research reports as well as providing details of relevant literature that relates to the current research question. A thorough review of the literature can aid in the development of the research question and the scope and direction of the current research by enabling the sport management researcher to find gaps in the current literature and research questions that need to be addressed.

Sample

If sampling has been used during data collection, the sport management researcher needs to let the reader know the size and type of sample used.

Questions guiding the investigation

How were the specific research purposes and aims adapted into the research questions? Good research questions are clear and concise, informed by a review of the literature, motivating and meaningful, significant, and probably most importantly they are questions that need to be answered.

442

Data collection methods

In this section the sport management researcher will discuss how they have approached the collection of data. If the researcher has used qualitative research methods then the specific data collection methodology related to the theoretical framework needs to be outlined here. The sport management researcher then needs to report on exactly what they did and how they went about doing it.

Data analysis methods

Here the sport management researcher will describe the data analysis methods used.

Findings or results

In a quantitative study this section will normally appear under the sub-heading 'results' and in a qualitative study it will usually be under 'findings'.

Discussion

In this section the sport management researcher will aim to present the findings in a factual way and then offer a discussion that stays within the parameters of the data.

Conclusions

Here the researcher both summarizes their findings and suggests applications of these findings. The researcher may choose to be critical of their findings or the process undertaken, and can look to further research possibilities as a result of this particular study.

References

All references used in the text need to be included in this section.

Appendices

Information that is not essential to explain the findings, but that supports the conclusions, should be placed in an appendix.

Abstract

Whilst this is the final part of the writing process, the abstract will actually appear at the front of the paper. A good abstract should include details of the background to the study, the aims, samples, data collection and analysis methods, and a summary of the findings.

SUMMARY

This chapter has provided an introduction to the sport management research process for the budding sport management researcher. The field of sport management research is diverse, complex, and constantly evolving. The last two decades have seen a dramatic change in the research landscape with diverse and emerging methodologies that challenge the existing and sometimes conservative approaches to conducting research. These emerging methodologies can provide sport management researchers with new and exciting ways to conduct, analyse, and report their research findings. However the sport management researcher chooses to approach their research study, the basic premise remains the same – which is that the sport management researcher is seeking to answer important questions and investigate issues of relevance to both the researcher and the sport management practitioner in order to provide potential solutions to emerging problems in the world of sport management research.

REVIEW QUESTIONS

1   Why is sport management research important? Justify your response with reference to the literature.
2   What are the key differences between qualitative, quantitative, and mixed methods approaches to sport management?
3   Outline the basic research process and apply it to a specific research problem such as community attitudes to the use of illicit drugs in sport.

FURTHER READING

Amis, J. & Silk, M. (2005). Rupture: promoting critical and innovative approaches to the study of sport management. *Journal of Sport Management, 19*, 355–366.
Edwards, A. & Skinner, J. (2009). *Qualitative Research Methods in Sport Management.* Oxford: Butterworth-Heinemann/Elsevier.
Edwards, A., Gilbert, K., & Skinner, J. (2002). *Extending the Boundaries: Theoretical Frameworks for Research in Sports Management.* Melbourne: Commonground.
Frisby, W. (2005). The good, the bad, and the ugly: critical sport management research. *Journal of Sport Management, 19*, 1–12.
Gratton, C. & Jones, I. (2004). *Research Methods for Sport Studies.* Oxon: Routledge.
Skinner, J. & Edwards, A. (2005). Inventive pathways: fresh visions of sport management research. *Journal of Sport Management, 19*, 404–421.

WEBSITES

European Association for Sport Management (EASM)
   http://www.easm.net

North American Society for Sport Management (NASSM)

  http://www.nassm.com

Sport Management Association of Australia & New Zealand (SMAANZ)

  http://www.smaanz.org

REFERENCES

Amis, J. & Silk, M. (2005). Rupture: promoting critical and innovative approaches to the study of sport management. *Journal of Sport Management, 19,* 355–366.

Chalip, L. (2006). Toward a distinctive sport management discipline. *Journal of Sport Management,* 20, 1–21.

Costa, C. A. (2005). The status and future of sport management: a Delphi study. *Journal of Sport Management, 19,* 117–142.

Creswell, J. W. (2008). *Educational Research* (3rd ed). Upper Saddle River, NJ: Pearson.

Cunningham, G. B. & Mahoney, K. (2004). Self-efficacy of part-time employees in university athletics: the influence of organizational commitment, valence of training, and training motivation. *Journal of Sport Management, 18,* 59–73.

Cuskelly, B. & Boag, A. (2001). Organisational commitment as a predictor of committee member turnover among volunteer sport administrators: results of a time-lagged study. *Journal of Sport Management, 4,* 65–88.

Edwards, A. & Skinner, J. (2009). *Qualitative Research in Sport Management.* Oxford: Elsevier.

Fink, J. S., Pastore, D. L., & Riemer, H. (2003). Managing employee diversity: perceived practices and organizational outcomes in NCAA division III athletic departments. *Sport Management Review, 6,* 147–168.

Frisby, W. (2005). The good, the bad, and the ugly: critical sport management research. *Journal of Sport Management, 19,* 1–12.

Glaser, B. & Strauss, A. (1967). *The Discovery of Grounded Theory: Strategies for Qualitative Research.* New York: Aldine.

Hammersley, M. (1990). *Reading Ethnographic Research.* London: Longman.

Murray, D. & Howat, G. (2002). The relationships among service quality, value, satisfaction, and future intentions of customers at an Australian sports and leisure centre. *Sport Management Review, 5,* 25–43.

Pitts, B. G. (2001). Sport management at the millennium: a defining moment. *Journal of Sport Management, 15,* 1–9.

Quatman, C. (2006). *The Social Construction of Knowledge in the Field of Sport Management: A Social Network Perspective.* Unpublished doctoral dissertation, The Ohio State University, Columbus.

Shilbury, D. (2001). Examining board member roles, functions and influence: a study of Victorian sporting organisations. *International Journal of Sport Management, 2,* 253–281.

Skinner, J. & Edwards, A. (2005). Inventive pathways: fresh visions of sport management research. *Journal of Sport Management, 19,* 404–421.

Thomas, J. R., Nelson, J. K., & Silverman, S. J. (2005). *Research Methods in Physical Activity* (5th ed). Champaign, IL: Human Kinetics.

Chapter 25

Managing the business of sport

Future trends and challenges

David Hassan, University of Ulster

TOPICS

The challenges presented by an increasingly globalised sport market • The emergence of wider responsibilities concerning the management of sport • The resourcing of sport now and in the future

---

OBJECTIVES

At the end of this chapter you should be able to:

- Identify the strengths and weaknesses of the globalisation thesis;
- Outline the multi-dimensional, interdependent nature of the sport management profession;
- Detail the particular challenges presented by an era of instant communication for those pursuing a career in the sport industry.

KEY TERMS

Challenges of resourcing sport in the future – against increasing calls for resource justification, the expectation of meeting consumers' rising demands with declining levels of available resources may constitute the single-biggest challenge facing sport managers in the future.

Critical interrogation of the globalisation thesis – the need for students of sport to appreciate that, whilst the processes of globalisation appear largely inevitable and exercise a formidable influence on the sport industry, this gives rise to both positive and negative consequences.

Sport e-business – in an age of instant communication this term is used to describe businesses that use the internet and other forms of telecommunication to engage with actual and potential customers in 'real time'.

Sport's wider social responsibility – this term relates to an emerging debate around the precise role of sport in any defined setting. Should it be organised solely for the purposes of a healthy and pleasurable pastime on the part of its participants ('sport for sport's sake') or rather does it have a broader role to play in helping to address societal problems ranging from teenage delinquency to community integration?

Transformational efficiency – a term used to define the capacity of any individual, in this case a sport coach, to redress the fortunes of an underperforming team without the need for significant investment in additional resources.

OVERVIEW

There are three key themes underpinning the concluding chapter of this collection. These are: the challenges faced by increased levels of globalisation and its effects upon the sport industry; the ongoing reduction in resourcing within the sector, which is beginning to exercise considerable influence upon the decisions being made by managers now and will do so in the time ahead; and, finally, the ever-changing ways in which service providers communicate with consumers. It seems the challenges faced by new sport managers have never been more apparent or immediate. Yet, strangely, the opportunities these processes offer have rarely been as plentiful as they are at present.

INTRODUCTION

As this collection of chapters draws to a close, it is appropriate to reflect upon the central themes that emerge from it and to consider the likely implications of these for the future management of the sport industry. The worldwide economic downturn, which began in September 2008 with the demise of some of the world's leading financial institutions, has cast a long shadow over many sovereign nations. It has also reminded us of the extent to which societies are interconnected with, and indeed interdependent upon, one another. Thus the issue of globalisation was one covered explicitly in several chapters of this book.

GLOBALISATION

The contribution of Gratton and Kokolakakis detailed the economic importance of sport, the rise of the sport industry generally and the implications of this for its management now and in the future. By drawing upon data dating back over a quarter of a century, they demonstrated the extent to which consumer spending in one country – in this case the UK – is impacted upon by global trends and prevailing circumstances elsewhere in the world economy. Thus the globalisation of sport markets, primarily in the apparel business but also in the mediatisation of elite sport in countries throughout the world, is likely to continue apace in future years (Hargreaves, 2002).

However, it behoves the diligent student of sport management to consider, in a critical manner, the full extent of these globalising influences (Bairner, 2001). As Lucie Thibault makes clear, there is a 'dark' side to the globalisation agenda, which impacts upon sport in a similar – if occasionally disproportionate – manner to any other industry. These outcomes include people trafficking, enforced player migration, the exploitation of labour (especially young labour) in emerging countries by transnational companies concerned with producing more for less and, increasingly, the full environmental impact of sport (Thibault, 2009). The latter introduces sport to a wider debate regarding the degree of social responsibility it should demonstrate as its influence grows ever more dominant in the modern age. Concern regarding the environmental damage caused by staging major sporting events in delicate ecosystems is one emerging point of interest and debate. Notwithstanding the importance of these arguments, there are also issues of both a political and economic nature surrounding the staging of mega sports events by certain nation-states. Increasingly countries have to absorb sizeable infrastructural and security costs, which need to be viewed against the realities of life for many living in what are often impoverished countries. Thus when considering the irrefutable evidence of globalising trends upon the sport industry, the reader is also required to reflect upon the social, economic and political costs that inevitably flow from society's insatiable desire for more, quicker and cheaper than has ever been the case heretofore.

As the sport industry grows and becomes an increasing aspect of people's daily lives, it will need to offer more robust responses to society's desire for managerial accountability, especially on behalf of publically funded bodies (Petroczi, 2009). It's a theme unpacked in the excellent work of Geoff Walters who considers the responsibilities that some sport businesses have beyond profit maximisation. Because sport is an increasingly accessible medium, the need for effective governance and transparency has, it seems, never been more relevant than it is at present. It has prompted a period of reflection on the part of many sport bodies throughout the world concerning the wider roles they perform and the need to provide reassurance to their stakeholders that they are engaged in wholly ethical business practices. Thus individual athletes are considering the personal leadership that is now expected of them – often by establishing charitable foundations designed to address issues of personal concern – whilst clubs and franchises are increasingly doing likewise. In addition it appears that national and international governing bodies are also becoming aware of the benefits that may be accrued by acting in more socially responsible ways. In the time ahead it seems likely that we will witness greater evidence of this practice in sport as the industry, in all its forms, accepts that it can no longer exist in splendid isolation from the environs in which it operates.

THE 'SPECIFICITY' OF SPORT

This discussion, around sport's wider responsibilities, feeds into a broader debate concerning its very management, specifically whether we should indeed regard sport as distinct and separate from other industries operating in the modern world. Such a focus has appeared to gather pace in recent times, especially in Europe with the publication of the European White Paper on Sport (European Commission White Paper on Sport, 2007). Several high-profile figures from the world of sport, amongst them UEFA President Michel Platini, have expressed their concerns at the apparent unrelenting nature of sport's commercialisation ('Platini plea for values', UEFA.com, 2008). Thus as part of this collection Hassan revisits sport's claim for specificity on account of its supposed social and cultural importance within society. What emerges is recognition of sport as presenting something of a broad vista – one that reflects the very positive social and cultural impact it exercises in most societies whilst also encompassing an elite component, which on occasions can give rise to some of society's worst excesses. It is clear that there can be no universal response to the suggestion that sport should be managed in the same way as any other industrial sector, and to argue that it is somehow more socially or culturally important is simply no longer credible. At its core these debates remind the student that sport management is a multilayered discipline, and collectively we must delineate the highly professionalised and indeed commercial prerogative of some codes from the overwhelming nature of sport, which is organised for mass participation and is in receipt of widespread support through its capacity to fulfil a range of socially beneficial objectives. Whether it will ever be possible to manage the full breadth of these competing perspectives in the context of one sport may prove increasingly unlikely, but Hassan does highlight the case of the GAA, Ireland's largest sporting body, as evidence that all is perhaps not lost. A not-for-profit organisation, which posted pre-tax profits of Euro 70 millions in 2009, an organisation whose players are amateurs and who receive no payment for their services (yet attract tens of thousands of people to view their games) and a governing body with a presence in every community throughout the island of Ireland presents a perfect antidote to those who claim that sport has lost touch with its grassroots (GAA, 2009; Hassan, 2010). Whether economic and societal changes will mean other governing bodies of sport elsewhere in the world pause to reflect upon their activities in the time to come will again be fascinating for students of sport management.

All of this points to a fundamental reappraisal of the relationship between sport and high finance on the part of many nation-states. This collection has highlighted these implications for sport at a number of levels, including its management and governance, and indeed the recruitment of volunteers to help stage its events. In their chapter entitled 'Managing Sport in the Nonprofit Sector', Chris Auld and Graham Cuskelly profile the many challenges faced by organisations with limited financial reserves but which serve their local communities in an unrivalled manner. However, it appears no field is immune from external pressures, and this chapter also points to the extent of governmental influence upon the 'third sector', meaning that heightened expectations are imposed upon voluntary bodies to, in many cases, meet the shortfall in service provision expected of national administrations. Beyond this, such voluntary agencies can expect increased compliance burdens concerning accountability and wider demands for professionalisation designed to move them towards a financially self-sustaining situation. It appears this sector is finding it problematic to deal with the level of expectation placed upon it 'from above' whilst responding to challenges 'from below' where individuals are experiencing difficulty in justifying previous levels of volunteerism and wider acts of altruism as a result of other pressures, which inevitably may have a detrimental impact on sport, particularly at the grassroots level.

VOLUNTEERS

The crucial role of volunteers – their recruitment, retention and training – is afforded further coverage later in the collection by Cuskelly and Auld and is reflective of the fundamental role such individuals play in sport now and will do so in the years to come. Most organisations are reasonably adept at recruiting at least some volunteers, but considerably fewer are able to retain them for any period of time, in part due to their failure to manage them properly or train them effectively (Hoye and Cuskelly, 2007). As Cuskelly and Auld make clear, the value of volunteers to a range of community organisations and the delivery of services has been recognised by a host of international organisations including the United Nations and the European Union. Many national administrations have devised their programmes for government around the need for volunteerism and recognise the range of positive benefits that can be achieved by encouraging people to give freely of their time for the good of others. Within sport, such volunteers underpin a large number of programmes, activities, services and events which benefit a host of end users. Understanding the needs of people who volunteer and creating a context in which they feel inclined to keep doing so is a task that is likely to fall upon the next generation of sport managers.

This challenge of persuading people to give freely of their time for sport's benefit is perhaps not made any easier when those operating at its elite end earn a reputation for ineffectual governance (Bower, 2003; Hoye and Cuskelly, 2007). The body of academic literature emerging from Birkbeck College in London in the field of sport governance is widely recognised beyond sport scholarship. In this collection Geoff Walters and Sean Hamil portray vividly the financial complexity of the economics of the professional team sport industry, primarily in Britain. Referring back to an earlier debate concerning the supposed specificity of sport management, the authors draw attention to the undoubted peculiarity of sport's economics, including the unique situation, it appears, in which clubs and leagues constitute a form of joint production, and competitive balance in a sports league is considered the optimum trading environment for its member clubs. Calling for the increased hand of regulation to protect the financial well-being of individual clubs and the teams that constitute their membership, Walters and Hamil draw the reader's attention to an undoubted future trend in sport management – the need for more robust regulation and external auditing of professional sport, especially in Europe. In 2012 UEFA intend to respond to this suggestion by introducing a programme of financial 'fair play' in which clubs wishing to play in European club competitions must demonstrate open, accountable and judicious use of football-related income in the running of their clubs. Not only will this make for fascinating viewing for students of sport management, if effectively implemented by UEFA and accepted by member clubs it must be considered likely that other governing bodies of sport will follow suit.

ORGANISATIONAL PERFORMANCE

Notwithstanding genuine concerns about the future resourcing of sport, it is reasonable to conclude that it will continue to be defined by individuals and teams seeking to achieve ever-greater levels of success and thus the management of high-performance sport, as Bill Gerrard has made clear, will always attract attention. The viewing public appears to retain a disproportionate fascination with elite level, professional sport but, at an organisational level, questions are increasingly being asked about what Gerrard refers to as 'sporting efficiency' or the win–cost ratio. Could it be that professional sport, especially in Europe where there are less solidarity arrangements in place, is about to enter a period of relative austerity in which owners and boards begin to consider return on investment in a much more meaningful way? On the face of it some professional clubs already accept that the financial outlay thought necessary to win the league in which they compete is simply unsustainable and thus abide by an operating model of more modest proportions. Yet there is clearly a role for the team coach in this analysis, particularly in what Gerrard refers to as their 'transformational efficiency', and it's apparent that even a cursory examination of some sports franchises reveals the remarkable capacity of certain managers and coaches to maximise the talents of those players under their instruction. As financial realities begin to take their toll on all parts of the sports industry, the future will undoubtedly be marked by demands for greater returns from reduced investment.

In all settings, therefore, the effective management and measurement of organisational performance perfectly captures the challenges that lie ahead for the next generation of sport personnel (Petroczi, 2009). Leigh Robinson, in her chapter addressing these issues, has examined this phenomenon, designed to achieve continual levels of performance improvement whilst remaining conscious of the expectations placed upon it by its stakeholders. The ability of sport managers to respond to a multitude of demands is not in itself new but it is clear that proper performance management – the unpacking of an organisation's strategy – places levels of expectation upon sport managers that are only likely to increase in the years to come. Of course all of this is dependent upon the organisation possessing a credible plan in the first place, as Parent *et al.* confirm. As the sport industry is a fast-paced and evolving sector, it requires a confident and committed management to abide by an established strategy or, still more, to react and respond to often unforeseen environmental impacts. Exactly how effective many sport bodies are in devising an appropriate strategy is a matter of debate but, in keeping with a theme already established in this concluding chapter, the challenge for managers ahead is to present a clear rationale for the organisation of which they are part, resource it as effectively and efficiently as possible and seek to maximise outcomes across agreed performance measures. It will be by no means a straightforward undertaking.

MANAGING AVAILABLE RESOURCES

To achieve this, however, they're likely to require both human and financial resources. This collection has provided comprehensive coverage of both these fields. Identifying and managing good people in any organisation are undoubtedly amongst the biggest challenges facing any sport manager. Individuals are acutely aware of their own worth, and identifying ways in which personnel can be rewarded for their endeavours without drawing upon dwindling levels of finance will be occupying the minds of most managers in this new age of financial constraint. The challenge in this regard will be to diversify revenue streams, retain control of costs, deploy business models that keep outgoings low without compromising increasing consumer expectations and, where appropriate, to prioritise profit maximisation. Such a challenge will prove considerable for all but the most talented and hard-working sport managers.

The answer may well lie in a more sophisticated use of sport marketing and, specifically, communication strategies designed to engage new consumers. Garland and Hautbois unpack this specific field and highlight, as Cousens and Bradish similarly do in their chapter, the crucial role of sport sponsorship regarding the financing of all levels of the industry. Here the authors draw specific attention to the need to interpret sponsorship as part of a strategic investment on the part of the funding body. Long gone are the days when benefactors, in an act of apparent irrational altruism, decided to donate money without any expectation of return. Sport for many sponsors now represents the site of untold opportunity but managers must work harder and smarter to avail of what remains a limited pot of money. Thus marrying the strategic objections of potential sponsors to those of the sporting body by whom they are employed appears to represent yet another challenge for sport managers over the early part of the twenty-first century.

A final task all managers will face in the future is that of responding to the increased speed of communication between producers and consumers of sport and leisure services. There is now an expectation on the part of sport consumers that they will receive information and updates instantaneously, and failure to meet these requirements may render certain businesses obsolete. Both Boyle and Haynes and O'Beirne discuss these issues, in the former case by examining the sport industry's relationship with the media and in the latter by focusing upon the emergence of so-called 'sport e-businesses'. In both cases, from relaying one's message to potential consumers to enacting increased sales, it is self-evident that the sport manager who can respond to the needs of a consumer base requiring regular and accurate information will be well placed in the years to come.

SUMMARY

In an industry sector defined by shifting tastes and variable consumer expectations, it is evident that there has never been a more challenging time to enter the field of sport management. Yet it could also be argued that never before have there been greater opportunities for talented, focused and inspirational leaders to emerge and meet the challenges of resourcing, managing, promoting and securing the future of sport. The managers that step forward in the next decade are likely to have a profound effect upon the future of the sport industry as the speed of change and the levels of possibility appear particularly pronounced.

REVIEW QUESTIONS

1 Outline three of the key challenges facing sport managers now and in the future.
2 Having identified these issues (Question 1 above), detail a strategic response to each, explaining how you would resource your agreed approach.
3 Detail the specific skills and attributes expected of sport managers in the future and explain how you intend to acquire, develop and refine these in the time ahead.

FURTHER READING

Gratton, C., Liu, D., Ramchandani, G. and Wilson, D. (2011) *The Global Economics of Sport* (London: Routledge).

Robinson, L., Bodet, G., Downward, P. and Chelladurai, P. (2011) *Routledge Handbook of Sport Management* (London: Routledge).

Wolsey, C., Abrams, J. and Minten, S. (2011) *Human Resource Management in the Sport and Leisure Industry* (London: Routledge).

WEBSITES

Institute for the Management of Sport and Physical Activity

www.imspa.co.uk

International Sports Management

www.sportism.net

Sport Management On-line Magazine

www.sportsmanagement.co.uk

REFERENCES

Bairner, A. (2001) *Sport Nationalism and Globalization* (New York: SUNY).

Bower, T. (2003) *Broken Dreams: Vanity, Greed and the Souring of British Football* (London: Simon and Schuster).

European Commission White Paper on Sport (2007) (Brussels: EU).

Gaelic Athletic Association (GAA) (2009) *Official Report 2009* (Dublin: GAA).

Hargreaves, J. (2002) Globalisation theory, global sport, and nations and nationalism. In J. Sugden and A. Tomlinson (eds) *Power Games: A Critical Sociology of Sport* (London: Routledge), pp. 25–43.

Hassan, D. (2010) Governance and the GAA: Time to move beyond the amateur ideal? In D. Hassan and S. Hamil (eds) *Who 'Owns' the Game?* (London: Routledge), pp. 72–85.

Hoye, R. and Cuskelly, G. (2007) *Sport Governance* (Oxford: Elsevier).

Petroczi, A. (2009) The dark side of sport: Challenges for managers in the twenty-first century, *European Sport Management Quarterly*, Vol. 9, No. 4, pp. 349–352.

'Platini plea for values', UEFA.com, accessed 24 January 2008.

Thibault, L. (2009) Globalization of sport: An inconvenient truth, *Journal of Sport Management*, Vol. 23, No. 1, pp. 1–20.

Index

454